D0505805

THE CHURCH OF SCOTLAND

GENERAL ASSEMBLY

2009

Published in 2009 by
THE CHURCH OF SCOTLAND ASSEMBLY ARRANGEMENTS COMMITTEE
121 George Street, Edinburgh EH2 4YN

© The Church of Scotland Assembly Arrangements Committee 2009

ISBN 978-0-86153-394-7

British Library Catalogue in Publication Data
A catalogue record for this book is available from the British Library

All copy keyed by the Church of Scotland
Designed and produced by APS Group,
7-9 North St David Street, Edinburgh EH2 1AW
Indexer Peter B Gunn

Embargoed until 21 April 2009

Authorised for official use
within the Church of Scotland only,
and not for publication until 21 April 2009

CONTENTS

COUNCIL OF ASSEMBLY
May 2009

PROPOSED DELIVERANCE

The General Assembly
1. Receive the Report.
2. Approve the proposals anent the role, selection criteria, remits and timescale for appointment of:
   (a) Principal Clerk to the General Assembly (Section 2.1.3 and Appendix I)
   (b) Secretary to the Council of Assembly (Section 2.1.4 and Appendix II)
   (c) Depute Clerk to the General Assembly (Section 2.1.3 and Appendix I).
3. Appoint the voting members of the Council of Assembly to act as the Charity Trustees for the Unincorporated Councils and Committees of the General Assembly (The Church of Scotland, Scottish Charity number SC011353) with effect from 1 June 2009. (Section 2.1.4)
4. Require that members of the various Councils and Committees of the General Assembly apply to their duties the same standards as are required of charity trustees. (Section 2.1.4.4)
5. Agree that the membership of the Council of Assembly be increased by two Assembly appointed members one of whom shall have appropriate knowledge and experience of Christian stewardship. (Section 2.2.1)
6. Approve the amendments of the Council's remit. (Section 2.2 and Appendix III)
7. Approve the amendments of the remit of the Ministries Council. (Section 2.4 and Appendix IV)
8. Agree that the Convener and Vice-Convener of the Assembly Arrangements Committee should cease to be members *ex officiis* of the Legal Questions Committee. (Section 2.5)
9. Commend the Council in the progress made in its commitment to Gaelic, welcome the development of resources and encourage the Council in its ongoing development and resources discussions. (Section 3.6)

REPORT

1. The work of the Council

1.1 Much of the Council's work is conducted through its committee structure and this is reported on under the various headings which follow. As is customary the main budget proposals for 2010 will be presented in a Supplementary Report.

1.2 The Council meets monthly except in January, May and July and each meeting's agenda includes reports from Councils and Committees which come within the monitoring, evaluating and co-ordinating remit of the Council. Through a rota system Councils make substantial presentations twice a year, though the opportunity is provided at every meeting for bringing matters before the Council. More detailed scrutiny of budgets and requests for replacement or additional staffing are first undertaken by the Budget or Staffing Group as appropriate.

1.3 Much of the Council's attention this session has been given to following up the remit of last year's General Assembly to bring recommendations for the establishment of a post of full time Secretary to the Council separate from the post of Principal Clerk to the General Assembly. This is reported on under the Governance section of the Report.

2. Governance

2.1 Posts of Principal Clerk and Secretary to the Council of Assembly

2.1.1 Last year's General Assembly, on the Report of the Special Commission on Structure and Change, approved the following deliverance:

"The General Assembly instruct the Council of Assembly to make the position of Secretary to the Council, upon the retirement of the present Principal Clerk, (i) a separate role from that of Principal Clerk, and (ii) a full time position. The General Assembly instruct the Council to report to the Assembly of 2009 as to the role, selection criteria, remits and timescale for appointment of: (a) a new Principal Clerk to the General Assembly and (b) a full-time Secretary to the Council of Assembly."

2.1.2 In taking this matter forward the Council has been guided by the following statements of the Special Commission regarding each post:

- *The Principal Clerk has a number of duties ex officio but the principal functions are to act as Clerk to the General Assembly and, both during the Assembly and throughout the year, to give advice and guidance on matters of procedure and church law to those who may require it. The Commission also refers to the Principal Clerk's role as that of an independent and authoritative legal adviser.*

- *We would see the Secretary of the Council's responsibility as one of leading change, motivating people and undertaking the task*

in accordance with the principles of good governance. It may be appropriate for an appointment to be made of someone with relevant experience gained in the private or public sector that experience including experience in the management of change.

2.1.3 Principal Clerk

2.1.3.1 The Council has consulted with the Assembly Arrangements and Legal Questions Committees and the job description for the Principal Clerk is brought to the General Assembly with the agreement of both Committees. The Council, again with the agreement of both Committees, recommends that the Principal Clerk should continue to be a minister of the Church of Scotland. This requirement was laid down by the General Assembly of 1939 and reflects the desirability of the Clerk having personal experience of the pastoral and presbyterial context in which many procedural and legal issues arise.

2.1.3.2 Under current arrangements the duties of Principal Clerk, Depute Clerk and Secretary to the Council of Assembly are carried out by two full time posts. With the change to a full time Principal Clerk and a full time Council Secretary it is proposed that the post of Depute Clerk revert to a part time, honorarium based appointment.

2.1.3.3 The Council envisages that the Principal Clerk should be a member ex officio of the Council of Assembly along with the General Treasurer and Solicitor of the Church.

2.1.3.4 The appointments of Principal Clerk and Depute Clerk should continue to be made by the General Assembly.

2.1.3.5 Proposed job descriptions for Principal and Depute Clerk are set out in Appendix I.

2.1.4 Council Secretary – Remit and Role of Council of Assembly

2.1.4.1 With regard to the Council Secretary post the Council considered it important to give prior consideration to the role of the Council of Assembly. This was to ensure complete clarity as to the nature of the post being created. In particular, the Council judged that, before any appointment was made, the opportunity should be taken to revisit the question of who are the charity trustees for the Unincorporated Councils and Committees of the General Assembly (SC011353).

2.1.4.2 Charity Trustees are required to exercise "general control and management of the charity". In 2007 the General Assembly, on the recommendation of the Council, agreed that the charity trustees for the Unincorporated Councils and Committees should be all the members of these Councils and Committees, a number totalling around 450. What this means is that every member of every Council or Committee is a charity trustee not only for their own area of work, but for **all** the Councils or Committees. The question therefore arises as to what extent, say, members of the Assembly Arrangements Committee can exercise "general control and management" of the Social Care Council, or members of the Church and Society Council can act as effective trustees in respect of the work of the World Mission Council.

2.1.4.3 Over recent years the Council of Assembly has developed an effective system under which all Councils and Committees report regularly to it. In addition the Budget Group gives detailed scrutiny to departmental budgets and the Staffing Group assesses all proposals for filling vacancies and creating new posts. By this means the Council fulfils its remit "to monitor, evaluate and co-ordinate the work of the Agencies of the General Assembly".

2.1.4.4 In light of these considerations the Council ventures to propose that with effect from 1 June the voting members of the Council of Assembly, which include Council Conveners, should assume the role of Charity Trustees for the Unincorporated Councils and Committees of the General Assembly (SC011353). At the same time the General Assembly is invited to make very clear that members of the various Councils and Committees are expected to apply to their duties the same standards as are required of charity trustees.

2.1.4.5 By this means individual members of Councils and Committees will be relieved of an unreasonable expectation that they act as charity trustees for areas of work of which they have absolutely no knowledge or experience. At the same time they are given their proper place and reminded of their very real responsibilities for specific areas of work.

2.1.4.6 Councils and Committees would continue to report to the General Assembly and receive instructions on matters of policy only from the Assembly.

2.1.4.7 Apart from the specific issue of charity trusteeship the Council considered it helpful, when preparing a job description for a full time Council Secretary, to take stock more generally of its remit and role.

2.1.4.8 The Council was established in 2004 and "given authority to take necessary administrative decisions between General Assemblies, to co-ordinate work done by the 'central administration' and make determinations with regard to resources, finances and staffing" *(Assembly Reports 2004, page 10/7).*

2.1.4.9 In its first Report the Council commented: *"The Council is keenly aware that a considerable degree of trust has been placed in it by the General Assembly. At the same time, it is very clear that its authority is limited and derives, not from any inherent power in itself, but entirely from the remit given to it by the General Assembly. The Council understands its role as standing in the place of the Assembly throughout the year, with a responsibility to defend the decisions of the Assembly and ask questions which the Assembly itself has neither the time nor the detailed background information to ask" (Assembly Reports, 2005, page 10/1).*

2.1.4.10 In short the role of the Council is to keep a check on the size and cost of the Church's central administration and to ensure the efficient and effective operation of that administration in the service of the wider Church. It was, therefore, a matter of great encouragement to see the positive terms in which the Special Commission spoke of the Council's role "as an instrument for more efficient administration" and a mechanism for "getting the agencies of the Church to work together in a co-ordinated fashion".

2.1.4.11 It is against such an understanding of the role of the Council that the proposed job description of the Council Secretary (see Appendix II) has been drawn up.

2.1.4.12 In particular the Council would highlight a number of points to which it has given detailed consideration:

- The Council was not attracted to the job-title "Chief Operating Officer" which was tentatively suggested by the Special Commission, preferring the simple and clear designation "Secretary to the Council of Assembly".
- However, the Council does welcome the Commission's suggestion that it may be appropriate for an appointment to be made of someone with relevant experience gained in the private or public sector (the Council would suggest adding a reference to the charitable sector), including experience in the management of change.
- The Council considers that this appointment should be clearly designated as one in which a commitment to the Christian faith should be a genuine occupational requirement. It may, indeed, be desirable that the post-holder be a member of the Church of Scotland. The only reason that this is not proposed as a requirement is a concern not to limit unnecessarily the pool of potential applicants for what is a crucial senior management role.
- The Council considers that the Council Secretary should have line management responsibility in relation to Council Secretaries and other designated senior posts. In the case of Council Secretaries this would, of course, be undertaken in full consultation with the relevant Convener who has operational oversight of the Secretary. This is in line with standard charity governance practice and appropriately reflects the Council's monitoring role. The Secretary's line management responsibilities would not extend to the Principal Clerk.
- The Council recommends that the Council Secretary act as Secretary to the Nomination Committee. This underlines that Committee's charity governance responsibility to ensure that the nomination process produces suitably qualified individuals to serve on the various Councils and Committees. The arrangement also preserves the independence of the Principal Clerk.
- While recognising the clear separation of function between the Council Secretary and the Principal Clerk, the Council does not consider it desirable to have two entirely separate departments of the Principal Clerk and the Council of Assembly. It therefore proposes the creation of a Department of the General Assembly in which both officials can interact, while at the same time exercising their respective responsibilities for administration and matters of church law, practice and procedure. This arrangement can also allow for some sharing of support staff which can be helpful in terms of absence cover.
- It is recommended that the post of Secretary to the Council of Assembly should be a General Assembly appointment as is the case with the Principal Clerk, Solicitor of the Church and General Treasurer of the Church.

2.1.5 Timetable

The Council was also instructed to report on the timescale for these appointments. The Principal Clerk is due to retire on 1 July 2010 and, in terms of the deliverance of last year's General Assembly, that is the point at which the move to two separate posts will become operative. It is therefore proposed that the recruitment process should begin early in 2010. This will allow for both names, along with a nomination for Depute Clerk, to be brought for formal appointment to the General Assembly in May of next year. In the interests of a smooth transition there may be merit in a period of overlap, though this is difficult to quantify at this point. The Council would be grateful for some flexibility to make appropriate arrangements when the time comes.

2.2 Proposed Changes to the Council's Membership and Remit

2.2.1 On the basis of the proposals (a) to designate the voting members of the Council as the Charity Trustees for the Unincorporated Councils and Committees and (b) to merge the work of the Stewardship and Finance Committee with that of the Council, it is recommended that the membership of the Council be increased by two Assembly appointed members. It is further recommended that one of these should be someone with particular knowledge and experience of Christian stewardship.

2.2.2 As indicated above, the Council has taken the opportunity of reviewing its remit in light of the need to prepare a job description for a new Council Secretary. The amendments proposed relate to the following areas:

- The updating of the original section 1 which was specific to the re-structuring instructed in 2004 (revised remit 1).
- Charity trusteeship, as already outlined (revised remit 3).
- A specific reference to the Co-ordinated Communication Strategy (revised remit 6).
- The incorporation of the remit of the Stewardship and Finance Committee into the work of the Council (revised remit 7, 12, 13, 14).
- Proposed arrangements for the setting of stipends by voting members of the Council on the advice of the Ministries Council (revised remit 8). [See section 2.3 immediately below.]
- The extension of the Council's responsibility to approve

property sales and leases over a particular value to include the entering into contracts (revised remit 17).

For ease of comparison the Council's current remit and the proposed revised remit are set out at Appendix III.

2.3 Setting of Stipends

A matter which has been of concern to the Council's Governance Group relates to the delegation originally granted to the Committee on the Maintenance of the Ministry and now exercised by the Ministries Council to set stipend scales. It is a cardinal principle of good governance that individuals should not be involved in setting their own remuneration because of the perceived conflict of interest which arises. Because of the specialised nature both of the Ministries Council's work and skills and experience necessary to undertake it, the majority of those serving on the Council are parish ministers. During discussions with representatives of the Council, the possibility of the Ministries Council setting up a Remuneration Committee was considered but not considered the best option. A more practical solution was felt to lie in the transferring of the delegation to those of the voting members of the Council of Assembly who are not in receipt of either a salary or stipend from the Parish Ministries Fund, the decision to be made, however, having regard to a prior recommendation made by the Ministries Council. As well as securing the governance objective, this proposal has the advantage of retaining the specialised knowledge and expertise of members of the Ministries Council, whilst also resulting in a more "joined up" approach to the Church's overall budgeting process. It has the approval of both Councils and, if approved, will be achieved through the addition of a new section 8 of the Council's remit.

2.4 Changes to the Remit of the Ministries Council

It became evident in the course of the above discussions that the Ministries Council remit, established at the time of the restructuring, did not clearly outline a number of areas of that Council's responsibility. The redrafted remit now reflects more appropriately both the detail and the priorities of that Council's responsibilities as developed in Assembly reports over the past four years. The Council is happy to commend the revised remit to the Assembly (Appendix IV).

2.5 Assembly Arrangements and Legal Questions Committees

Following consultation with both Committees it has been agreed that it is not necessary for the Convener and Vice-Convener of the Assembly Arrangements Committee to be members *ex officiis* of the Legal Questions Committee. This arrangement was put in place when the former Board of Practice and Procedure was replaced by these two Committees each reporting direct to the General Assembly. The Assembly is invited to approve this change to the membership of the Legal Questions Committee.

2.6 Representation of the Views of Presbyteries on all Church Councils

Last year's General Assembly instructed the Council of Assembly "to consider new ways of promoting the representation of the views of Presbyteries on all Church Councils and to report to the General Assembly of 2009 with proposals". During the year the Council sought information from each of the Councils about the way in which they engaged with Presbyteries and was encouraged to note that in different ways they were all engaged in processes that facilitated a two-way sharing of information. However, aware of the current work of the Panel on Review and Reform on an alternative Presbytery structure, the Council is of the view that it would be premature to bring any firm proposals to the General Assembly before the Panel reports next year. The Council will continue to monitor the matter as the Panel's work progresses.

3. Communication

3.1 Annual Review

The first Annual Review of the Church of Scotland was launched in May 2008 and was very well received. The Annual Review was distributed to Commissioners to the General Assembly, all congregations, staff, MEPs and MSPs, local authority executives, enquirers to the Church and many others. Points made in the feedback include that the Annual Review "offers a good insight into the activities and life of the congregations throughout the Church of Scotland" and is "an excellent summary of all that the church 'does'". The Council intends to replicate that in the second Annual Review which will be distributed during the General Assembly in May. Once again the Council is grateful to Newton Investment Management Ltd for a financial contribution towards the cost of this publication.

3.2 Visual Identity Policy

A new Visual Identity Policy was presented to the Council of Assembly in November 2008 as the beginning of a process to try and achieve consistency in the way the Church presents itself to internal and external audiences. The purpose is to use our visual identity to communicate who we are and to do this consistently so that opportunities are not lost to show the full range of worshipping, witnessing, nurturing and serving activities that come under the Church of Scotland. The Council intends that further work should be undertaken on this project over the coming year.

3.3 Events

3.3.1 A small group was set up to examine the Church of Scotland's representation at events and exhibitions. The group concluded that attendance at events needs to be more focused and materials used need to be more relevant for target audiences. It is planned that the Church of Scotland will take a stand at Frenzy, a Christian youth music event in June at Ingliston.

3.3.2 A new exhibition stand has been used at General Assembly, National Gathering, Cramond Church and RE-Energise 4 and is available for churches to borrow.

3.4 Internal Audit – Communication

An internal audit was carried out on implementation of the Church's Communication Strategy. The auditors' report concluded that the Church is developing an effective approach to its communication activities. Some areas were highlighted for improvement and these have been discussed with all the Councils of the Church.

3.5 Introductory leaflet and homecoming postcard

The introductory leaflet continues to be requested by churches and is proving very popular in connection with promotion around Homecoming. "You welcomed me as if I were an angel" has been adopted as the theme of the Church's approach to homecoming, emphasising welcome and spiritual homecoming to home and overseas visitors.

3.6 Development of Gaelic within the Church

3.6.1 The Council, through its Communication Committee, continues to move forward the encouragement of the use of Gaelic within the Church, following the instruction of the General Assembly of last year 'to continue to support the development of Gaelic within the Church, including discussions with appropriate funding bodies.'

3.6.2 In the area of development, some significant progress is being made:

- The inclusion, for the first time, of Gaelic within the Church of Scotland Year Book has been appreciated, not least the Moderator's Introduction, now included in both Gaelic and English.
- For the first time also, the General Assembly Gaelic service was available on-line as part of the General Assembly webcast. The General Assembly is indebted to the Rev Dr Roderick MacLeod, Mrs Phyliss Rioch and the Rev Dr Richard Fraser for the continuing work done to arrange the service annually.
- On the initiative of An Comunn Gaidhealach, a fruitful roundtable meeting was held amongst interested denominations, to discuss the ways in which An Comunn could encourage the development of the use of Gaelic within the churches. It is hoped that this might become a regular discussion, not just fruitful for Gaelic but for ecumenism.

3.6.3 In the area of resources, there is also some progress to report. The Council welcomes the availability now on-line of Dwelly's Gaelic Dictionary (www.cairnwater.co.uk/gaelicdictionary/index.aspx), the magnum opus of Edward Dwelly (1864-1939). Database technology now allows this resource to be used from English to Gaelic as well as vice versa, and is a very powerful tool in fostering the language for those who wish to extend their abilities in the use of Gaelic. The work was undertaken by two volunteers with no public funding and the Church, as well as others, is deeply in their debt. Furthermore, a member of the Committee is involved in the preparation of the first Gaelic Thesaurus. In course of preparation also is a resource booklet for ministers and others who have the occasional need or desire to use Gaelic in worship, wedding or funeral services *(see page 4/36 of the Report of the Mission and Discipleship Council)*.

3.6.4 In the area of discussions with appropriate funding bodies, including Broadcasting companies, these are at a crucial stage:

- The Gaelic Digital Channel, BBC Alba, is now live and being well received. The Council welcomes this. However, the Council is concerned about two matters. There is an apparent lack of dedicated religious programming. In addition, it is the case that in much of the area indigenous to the Gaelic language, the channel is not available on Freeview. We are pursuing this in conjunction with the Church and Society Council. The BBC Trust is undertaking a review of the channel this year.
- Bòrd na Gàidhlig is a crucial resource provider, and at the time of writing, discussions are in progress with them. The Church will be required to produce a competent funding proposal, and we hope to forward this in early course. It is hoped that the plans will

involve not only the Church but relevant constituent parts of the University of the Highlands and Islands.

3.7 Website

3.7.1 During the year, the Moderator started a weekly blog on the website which has proved successful and attracted a consistently high number of readers each week. Work has also been done with several groups within the Church to redevelop existing content or produce new material. All local congregations have been asked to provide some information about whether they have their own websites, and some of the issues they face in getting online or keeping their sites updated, with a view to looking at what help the Church might be able to provide.

3.7.2 Given the size of the site, there is concern about how users navigate around it and the difficulties they have in finding specific information. The Web Editor has been reviewing how the content might be reorganised into more general themes to help users find information more easily, and also looking at the role of the extranet in providing more internal information to members and church officers. These areas will be part of the design improvement and technical development of the site.

3.8 Strategic Communication

3.8.1 Last year's General Assembly instructed the Council "to develop further a strategic approach to directing external communication, including the possibility of establishing a post for a director of Strategic communication, and bring recommendations to the General Assembly of 2009".

3.8.2 The Council asks for a further year to give consideration to this remit. This is in light of a need identified by the Council to undertake a full review of present arrangements for delivering the Communication Strategy and the relationships between the various departments which contribute to this process. Once that review is complete the structure and staffing required for the future will become clearer.

4. Staffing

4.1 The Staffing Group has continued to meet regularly to ensure that there is strong and effective governance in relation to recruitment of staff employed by the various Councils and departments in the central administration.

4.2 The past year has seen a strengthening of the professional HR service, with the relationship between the HR Department and both the World Mission and Ministries Councils continuing to evolve. Both Councils have acknowledged the high standard of professional support and service that is provided in relation to human resource and wider management issues.

4.3 Last year's General Assembly instructed the Council "to consider creative ways to encourage vocational development and fresh opportunity for new challenges in respect of senior appointments". In response to this, and as part of the ongoing development of senior staff, Council Secretaries have recently participated in a pilot 360 degree appraisal process which will be followed by management development training in the summer. This will examine a number of skills areas before identifying personal learning and development strategies for the future. Both of the above programmes will be evaluated prior to identifying how they can effectively develop further in the future.

5. Budget

5.1 As is customary, due to the necessities of printing deadlines, the main budget proposals for 2010 will be presented in a Supplementary Report.

5.2 The Council's consistent policy of making additional resources available to congregations continues for 2009, with the total contributions required increasing by less than 1% (£400,000), following a freeze in 2007 and a reduction of £1 million in 2008. While early indications are that congregational income was marginally higher in 2008, the current global financial situation indicates clearly that many congregations are likely to find that their members' ability to maintain their offerings will be seriously tested in 2009 and possibly beyond. As a result, the budgets of Councils and Committees will continue to be regularly reviewed and challenged to ensure that work is being prioritised within a realistic and robust framework.

5.3 The Council's Budget Group now receives summarised monthly management accounts from all Councils and Committees and is therefore able to engage more timeously with their elected members and senior staff to review progress against budgets and to discuss current concerns and future requirements.

5.4 As indicated in the Council's 2008 Supplementary Report (Order of Proceedings, page 42, section 3.1.4), and starting with the 2010 Budget proposals, the principle of 'gross budgeting' will be introduced. This will indicate the total proposed level of expenditure for each Council, together with a breakdown of how this is to be financed. This will be an agreed combination of funding from some or all of the following sources:
• income from congregational contributions
• external income generated by the Council's own activities
• income from invested funds and reserves
• capital released from surplus reserves.

In this way, the total funds available to the Church will be more effectively managed to ensure that, if not all approved areas of work or projects can be funded, resources will be targeted at those judged to be the most worthwhile, in line with the General Assembly's strategic priorities of congregational resourcing and parish staffing.

5.5 While the Council is prepared to continue to utilise reserves for a limited period, Councils and Committees will require to demonstrate that they are acting to bring their total expenditure within their sustainable sources of income over a reasonable timescale, while retaining an

agreed and appropriate level of reserves. In the long term, the level of services provided by all Councils must be linked to the ability of congregations to provide financial support, and any decline in the pattern of that support will inevitably have to lead to reductions in staffing and other costs.

6.   Internal Audit

6.1   During 2008 the Internal Audit Committee, through Scott-Moncrieff (Chartered Accountants), continued to work through the three year programme agreed in 2007 to evaluate the effectiveness of the Church's internal systems and controls on the basis of the risk inherent in each area.

6.2   The following reviews were completed during the year:
• CrossReach (Social Care Council) income
• CrossReach non-payroll expenditure
• Communications strategy
• Council of Assembly governance arrangements.

6.3   While a number of recommendations were made which will improve the control environment, no major weaknesses were found. In addition, a follow up review was carried out to ensure that recommendations agreed from previous reports had been satisfactorily implemented. Almost all had been fully or partly completed and the few outstanding will continue to be monitored.

6.4   In his Annual Report to the Council, the partner in Scott-Moncrieff who acts as chief internal auditor stated that 'in my opinion the Church of Scotland has a sound framework of control which provides reasonable assurance regarding the effectiveness and efficient achievement of its objectives'.

6.5   During 2009 reviews are planned on budgeting and planning, HR management, strategic planning, risk management systems and the usual follow up of previous reports.

7. Panel on Review and Reform

7.1 When the Panel was set up by the General Assembly of 2004 it was agreed that it should "be reviewed by the Council of Assembly after not more than five years, and its effectiveness, necessity and reporting arrangements considered at that time, and reported to the General Assembly" (Reports 2004 p10/8).

7.2 However, last year's General Assembly gave to the Panel the substantial remit "to bring to the General Assembly of 2010 proposals for an alternative Presbytery structure, including size, devolved powers, staffing and appropriate budgets, along with the resources necessary to facilitate and sustain such changes".

7.3 In light of this, the Council has judged it not appropriate to undertake the five year review at this time and trusts that the General Assembly will agree that this is entirely reasonable.

8. Co-opted Members

The Council reports that Mr Martin Sinclair is a co-opted member of the Budget and Governance Groups; Mr Findlay Turner (representing the General Trustees) also serves on the Governance Group; and the Rev Peter Johnston is a co-opted member of the Communication Committee.

9. Society for the Benefit of Sons and Daughters of the Clergy

Last August the Trust Administrator for the Society for the Benefit of Sons and Daughters of the Clergy of the Church of Scotland sought General Assembly approval for the appointment of two new trustees to its Board of Management. The Council noted that the Rev Peter Graham and Ms Sheila Moyes had been approached and were happy to serve in this way. Acting under the powers granted to it by the General Assembly, the Council agreed these appointments.

In the name of the Council

ALAN GREIG, *Convener*
PETER BRAND, *Vice-Convener*
FINLAY MACDONALD, *Secretary*

APPENDIX I
JOB DESCRIPTIONS FOR PRINCIPAL CLERK AND DEPUTE CLERK

Church of Scotland
General Assembly

1. **Job Title:** Principal Clerk of the General Assembly.

2. **Responsible to:** The General Assembly and, when acting specifically as Secretary to one of the bodies serviced by the Principal Clerk, to the relevant Convener.

3. **Purpose of Post:** To make all necessary arrangements for the General Assembly, to advise the Assembly and the Moderator on matters of church law, practice and procedure, including interpretation of Acts, Regulations and Standing Orders, to oversee the preparation of Assembly minutes, the collating of Assembly deliverances and the promulgation of Assembly decisions, to support the Moderator in the exercise of his or her duties throughout the year and to provide training courses and offer advice on church law, practice and procedure to Kirk Sessions, Presbyteries, Ministers and other individuals and to Assembly Councils, Committees, Agencies and Partner Churches.

4. **Main Duties:**
4.1 To act as Clerk to the General Assembly.
4.2 To act as Clerk to the Commission of Assembly.
4.3 To act as Clerk to the Judicial Commission of the General Assembly.
4.4 To act as Clerk to the Ministries Appeal Panel.
4.5 To ensure that clerical and administrative support is provided for Special Commissions of the General Assembly.
4.6 To act as custodier and legal extractor of the records of the General Assembly.
4.7 To sign such deeds and documents as may be required in terms of Act I, 2003 anent Granting and Signing of Deeds.
4.8 To convene the Committee on Classifying Returns to Overtures.
4.9 To convene the Delegation of Assembly.
4.10 To convene the Committee on Overtures and Cases.
4.11 To prepare the Reports of the Committee on Classifying Returns to Overtures and the Committee on Overtures and Cases.
4.12 To be responsible for those aspects of the work of the Department of the General Assembly which relate to Church Law Practice and Procedure, General Assembly Arrangements and Moderatorial Support.
4.13 To act as Secretary to the Assembly Arrangements and the Legal Questions Committees, to attend meetings of both committees and ensure the implementation of their decisions.
4.14 To provide a drafting service to assist Councils and Committees in the revision and framing of legislation.
4.15 To manage the annual revision and promulgation of material (printed and electronic) containing the legislation of the General Assembly.
4.16 To act as Secretary to the Moderator of the General Assembly.
4.17 To act as Secretary to the Committee to Nominate the Moderator.
4.18 To teach Church Law to Ministries candidates and to offer seminars and courses to others within the Church.
4.19 To maintain *Fasti* records.
4.20 To undertake such trusteeship and other duties as relate to the office of Principal Clerk.
4.21 To serve as a non-voting member of the Council of Assembly.
4.22 To serve as a non-voting member of the Safeguarding Committee.
4.23 To serve as a non-voting member of the Support and Services Council.
4.24 To serve as a member of the Life and Work Editor's Advisory Committee.

4.25 To serve as a member of the Scottish Churches' Committee and of other ecumenical bodies as required from time to time.

4.26 To advise Kirk Sessions, Presbyteries, Congregations, Ministers and other individuals and Councils, Committees and Agencies of the General Assembly on church law, practice and procedure.

4.27 To act as the Church's principal liaison-contact with outside agencies for policy relating to the use and letting of the Assembly Hall.

4.28 To undertake such other duties as may be required from time to time by the General Assembly

5. Skills and Qualities Required:

5.1 Ordained Minister of Word and Sacrament of the Church of Scotland.

5.2 Specialist knowledge and understanding of the history and constitution of the Church of Scotland and of the Church's law, practice and procedure and the ability to facilitate the implementation of that law, practice and procedure.

5.3 An ability to represent the Church of Scotland effectively in ecumenical and inter-faith bodies.

5.4 An understanding and knowledge of the Church of Scotland's involvement in the World Church through its overseas partnerships.

5.5 Excellent organisational skills.

5.6 Excellent communication, presentational and inter-personal skills.

Church of Scotland
General Assembly

1. Job Title: Depute Clerk of the General Assembly.

2. Responsible to: The Principal Clerk and, when deputising for the Principal Clerk, to the General Assembly or relevant Convener.

3. Purpose of Post: To assist with arrangements for the General Assembly; to prepare Assembly minutes,

collate Assembly deliverances and promulgate the law of the Church.

4. Main Duties:

4.1 To act as Depute Clerk to the General Assembly.

4.2 To act as Depute Clerk to the Commission of Assembly and the Judicial Commission.

4.3 To deputise for the Principal Clerk whenever he/she is unavailable *eg* holiday cover.

4.4 To undertake such other duties as are directed by the Principal Clerk.

5. Skills and Qualities Required:

5.1 Preferably an ordained Minister of Word and Sacrament of the Church of Scotland, with some legal training or knowledge.

5.2 Specialist knowledge and understanding of the history and constitution of the Church of Scotland and of the Church's law, practice and procedure.

5.3 Excellent organisational skills and the ability to deliver work on time.

APPENDIX II
JOB DESCRIPTION FOR SECRETARY
TO THE COUNCIL OF ASSEMBLY

Church of Scotland
Council of Assembly

1. Job Title: Secretary to the Council of Assembly.

2. Responsible to: The Convener of the Council of Assembly.

3. Purpose of Post: To act as Secretary to the Council of Assembly which is the monitoring body on behalf of the General Assembly for the Unincorporated Councils and Committees of the General Assembly by exercising leadership within the Church's central administration and acting as a facilitator of change.

4. Main Duties:

4.1 To act as Secretary to the Council of Assembly.

4.2 To exercise leadership within the Church's central administration and to act as a facilitator of change.

4.3 To be responsible for the administration of the Council and the implementation of its policies and decisions including their financial implications.

4.4 To facilitate regular meetings of senior staff.

4.5 In consultation with the relevant conveners to line manage the Secretaries of the Church and Society, Ministries, Mission and Discipleship, Social Care and World Mission Councils and other senior managers, whilst ensuring the proper consideration of their professional independence.

4.6 To exercise line management responsibilities in relation to the Head of Media Relations and Communication and the Facilities Manager.

4.7 To act as Secretary of the Nomination Committee.

4.8 To be responsible for those aspects of the work of the Department of the General Assembly which relate to the remit of the Council of Assembly.

4.9 To serve as a member of the Central Services Committee and of that Committee's Executive.

4.10 To undertake such other duties as may be required from time to time by the Council of Assembly.

5. Skills and Qualities Required:

5.1 A personal commitment to the Christian faith expressed through active membership of a Christian denomination.

5.2 Significant experience in the public, private or charity sectors including the management of budgets and staff.

5.3 Understanding and experience of governance issues.

5.4 Proven leadership skills, a capacity to motivate people and the ability to manage change.

5.5 A capacity to encourage staff in the development of their skills.

5.6 Excellent organisational skills, the ability to deliver work on time and within budget.

5.7 Excellent communication, presentational and inter-personal skills.

APPENDIX III
REMIT OF THE COUNCIL OF ASSEMBLY

1. Current Remit

The Council of Assembly shall be a standing Committee of the General Assembly to which it shall be directly accountable and to which it shall report through its Convener. The General Assembly has conferred on the Council the powers as described in the following remit and in particular the powers of supervision of its Agencies (said Agencies being as defined in the Appendix) in the matters as detailed therein.

Membership

The Council shall comprise the following:

1. Convener, Vice-Convener and eight members appointed by the General Assembly on the Report of the Nomination Committee.

2. Until 31 May 2005, the Conveners of the Boards of Ministry, National Mission, Parish Education, Stewardship and Finance, Social Responsibility and World Mission, together with the Convener of the Church and Nation Committee **or** the Education Committee, as agreed between the two Committees.

3. From 1 June 2005, the Conveners of the Councils namely Church and Society, Ministries, Mission and Discipleship, Social Care, Services and Support and World Mission.

4. Until 31 May 2005, the General Secretaries of the Boards of Ministry, National Mission, Parish Education, Social Responsibility and World Mission, together with the Secretary of the Church and Nation Committee **or** the Education Committee, as agreed between the two Committees, all with a right to speak on matters affecting the interest of their Board or Committee, but not to vote or make a motion.

5. From 1 June 2005, the Secretaries of the following Councils namely Church and Society, Ministries, Mission and Discipleship, Social Care and World Mission, all with a right to speak on matters affecting the interest of their Council, but not to vote or make a motion.

6. The General Treasurer and the Solicitor of the Church without a right to vote or make a motion.

7. The Principal Clerk of the General Assembly, as Secretary to the Council, without a right to vote or make a motion.

8. Other officials, as required by the Council to be in attendance from time to time without a right to vote or make a motion.

Remit and Powers

1. To implement the plan of re-organisation and structural change of the Agencies of the General Assembly as formulated by the Assembly Council and approved by the General Assembly of 2004.

2. To monitor, evaluate and co-ordinate the work of the Agencies of the General Assembly, within the context of policy determined by the Assembly.

3. To advise the General Assembly on the relative importance of work being undertaken by its various Agencies.

4. To receive reports from, offer guidance and issue instructions to Agencies of the General Assembly as required from time to time on matters of management, organisation and administration.

5. To bring recommendations to the General Assembly concerning the total amount of the Church's Co-ordinated Budget for the following financial year and the disposition thereof amongst Local Mission, Parish Staffing and the Mission and Renewal Fund.

6. To determine the allocation of the total budgets for the following financial year for Parish Staffing and the Mission and Renewal Fund amongst the relevant Agencies of the General Assembly and Ecumenical Bodies.

7. To prepare and present to the General Assembly an indicative Rolling Budget for the following five financial years.

8. To receive and distribute unrestricted legacies and donations amongst the Agencies of the General Assembly with power to specify the use to which the same are to be applied.

9. To consider and decide on proposals from Agencies of the General Assembly to purchase heritable property or any other asset (except investments) valued in excess of £50,000 or lease any heritable property where the annual rental exceeds £10,000 per annum, declaring that no Agency save those referred to in section 17 hereof shall proceed to purchase or lease such property without prior approval from the Council.

10. To consider and decide on proposals from Agencies of the General Assembly, save those referred to in Section 17 hereof, to sell or lease for a period in excess of five years or otherwise dispose of any heritable property, or sell or otherwise dispose of any asset (except investments) valued in excess of £50,000, held by or on behalf of that Agency, with power to allocate all or part of the sale or lease proceeds to another Agency or Agencies in terms of section 11 hereof.

11. To reallocate following upon consultation with the Agency or Agencies affected unrestricted funds held by or on behalf of any of the Agencies of the General Assembly to another Agency or Agencies with power to specify the use to which the same are to be applied.

12. To determine staffing and resourcing requirements of Agencies of the General Assembly, including inter-Departmental sharing or transfer of staff, in accordance with policies drawn up by the Council of Assembly in line with priorities approved by the General Assembly, it being declared that the term "staffing" shall not include those appointed or employed to serve either in particular Parishes or overseas.

13. Consult with the relative Councils and Agencies in their appointment of Council Secretaries to the Church and Society, Ministries, Mission and Discipleship, Social Care and World Mission Councils, to appoint the Ecumenical Officer, the Director of Stewardship, the Head of Media Relations and the Personnel Manager and to nominate individuals to the General Assembly for appointment to the offices of Principal Clerk of the General Assembly, Depute Clerk of the General Assembly, General Treasurer of the Church and Solicitor of the Church.

14. To keep under review the central administration of the Church, with particular regard to resolving issues of duplication of resources.

15. To provide an Internal Audit function to the General Assembly Councils, Statutory Corporations and Committees (other than the Social Care Council).

16. To attend to the general interests of the Church in matters which are not covered by the remit of any other Agency.

17. To deal with urgent issues arising between meetings of the General Assembly, provided that (a) these do not fall within the jurisdiction of the Commission of Assembly or of any Presbytery or Kirk Session, (b) they are not of a legislative or judicial nature and (c) any action taken in terms of this clause shall be reported to the next General Assembly.

18. To encourage all Agencies of the General Assembly to work ecumenically wherever possible and to have regard to the international, evangelical and catholic nature of the Church.

19. For the avoidance of doubt, sections 9 and 10 shall not apply to the Church of Scotland General Trustees, the Church of Scotland Housing and Loan Fund for Retired Ministers and Widows and Widowers of Ministers and the New Charge Development Committee and its successor body all of which may deal with heritable property and other assets without the approval of the Council.

Appendix to Remit

For the purposes only of this remit, the term "Agencies" shall mean the following bodies being Standing Committees of the General Assembly as at May 2004, namely:

The Boards of: Communication, Ministry, National Mission, Parish Education, Practice and Procedure, Social Responsibility, Stewardship and Finance and World Mission, together with their constituent Committees.

The following Committees: Artistic Matters, Central Co-ordinating, Chaplains to Her Majesty's Forces, Church and Nation, Education, Ecumenical Relations Committee and the, Parish Development Fund.

The Panels on Doctrine and Worship and their successor bodies (if applicable) constituted with effect from 1 June 2005.

2. Proposed Revised Remit

The Council of Assembly shall be a standing Committee of the General Assembly to which it shall be directly accountable and to which it shall report through its Convener. The General Assembly has conferred on the Council the powers as described in the following remit and in particular the powers of supervision of its Agencies (said Agencies being as defined in the Appendix) in the matters as detailed therein.

Membership

The Council shall comprise the following:

1. Convener, Vice-Convener and ten members appointed by the General Assembly on the Report of the Nomination Committee.

2. The Conveners of the Councils namely Church and Society, Ministries, Mission and Discipleship, Social Care, Support and Services and World Mission together with the Convener of the Panel on Review and Reform.

3. The Secretaries of the following Councils namely Church and Society, Ministries, Mission and

Discipleship, Social Care and World Mission, all with a right to speak on matters affecting the interest of their Council, but not to vote or make a motion.

4. The Principal Clerk, the General Treasurer and the Solicitor of the Church without a right to vote or make a motion.

5. The Secretary to the Council of Assembly without a right to vote or make a motion.

6. Other officials, as required by the Council, to be in attendance from time to time without a right to vote or make a motion.

Remit and Powers

1. To advise the General Assembly on matters of reorganisation and structural change, including adjustments to the membership and remits of relevant Agencies of the General Assembly.

2. To keep under review the central administration of the Church, with particular regard to resolving issues of duplication of resources.

3. To monitor, evaluate and co-ordinate the work of the Agencies of the General Assembly, within the context of policy determined by the Assembly, with the voting members of the Council acting as the charity trustees for the unincorporated Councils and Committees of the General Assembly (the Church of Scotland, Scottish Charity No SC011353).

4. To advise the General Assembly on the relative importance of work being undertaken by its various Agencies.

5. To receive reports from, offer guidance and issue instructions to Agencies of the General Assembly as required from time to time on matters of management, organisation and administration.

6. To oversee the implementation and development of the Co-ordinated Communication Strategy across the Church.

7. To determine policy in relation to:
   a) the teaching and promotion of Christian stewardship throughout the Church;

   b) Ministries and Mission Contributions from congregations, subject to the approval of Regulations by the General Assembly.

8. To determine annually the stipend rate, having regard to the recommendation thereanent of the Ministries Council, said determination to be made by the voting members of the Council of Assembly with the exception of those members in receipt of either a salary or stipend from the Parish Ministries Fund.

9. To bring recommendations to the General Assembly concerning the total amount of the Church's Co-ordinated Budget for the Parish Ministries Fund and the Mission and Renewal Fund for the following financial year, and to determine the allocation of the budget for the Mission and Renewal Fund among the relevant Agencies of the General Assembly and Ecumenical Bodies.

10. To prepare and present to the General Assembly an indicative Rolling Budget for the following five financial years.

11. To receive and distribute unrestricted legacies and donations among the Agencies of the General Assembly with power to specify the use to which the same are to be applied.

12. To approve and submit annually to the General Assembly the audited Report and Financial Statements of the Unincorporated Councils and Committees of the General Assembly.

13. To determine the types and rates of expenses which may be claimed by members serving on Councils, Committees and Statutory Corporations.

14. Through its oversight of the Stewardship and Finance Department, to be responsible for:
   a) providing support to Presbyteries and congregations in the teaching and promotion of Christian stewardship;

   b) determining with Presbyteries the Ministries and Mission Contributions required annually from congregations;

   c) providing assistance to Presbyteries and

congregations in adhering to financial standards required by charity law and by Regulations of the General Assembly;

d) setting standards of financial management and providing financial services for the Councils and Committees, Statutory Corporations and other Agencies of the General Assembly.

15. To consider and decide on proposals from Agencies of the General Assembly to purchase heritable property or any other asset (except investments) valued in excess of £50,000 or lease any heritable property where the annual rental exceeds £10,000 per annum, declaring that no Agency save those referred to in section 24 hereof shall proceed to purchase or lease such property without prior approval from the Council.

16. To consider and decide on proposals from Agencies of the General Assembly, save those referred to in section 24 hereof, to sell or lease for a period in excess of five years or otherwise dispose of any heritable property, or sell or otherwise dispose of any asset (except investments) valued in excess of £50,000, held by or on behalf of that Agency, with power to allocate all or part of the sale or lease proceeds to another Agency or Agencies in terms of section 18 hereof.

17. To consider and decide on proposals from Agencies of the General Assembly to enter into an agreement or contract (with the exception of contracts of employment or those relating to property transactions) with a total actual or potential financial commitment in excess of £50,000, declaring that no Agency shall proceed to enter into such an agreement or contract without prior approval from the Council.

18. To reallocate following upon consultation with the Agency or Agencies affected unrestricted funds held by or on behalf of any of the Agencies of the General Assembly to another Agency or Agencies with power to specify the use to which the same are to be applied.

19. To determine staffing and resourcing requirements of Agencies of the General Assembly, including inter-Departmental sharing or transfer of staff, in accordance with policies drawn up by the Council of Assembly in line with priorities approved by the General Assembly, it being declared that the term "staffing" shall not include those appointed or employed to serve in particular Parishes or overseas or by the Social Care Council in service provision facilities around the country.

20. To consult with the relative Councils and Agencies in their appointment of Council Secretaries to the Church and Society, Ministries, Mission and Discipleship, Social Care and World Mission Councils, to appoint the Ecumenical Officer, the Head of Stewardship, the Head of Media Relations and Communication and the Head of Human Resources and to nominate individuals to the General Assembly for appointment to the offices of Principal Clerk of the General Assembly, Depute Clerk of the General Assembly, Secretary to the Council of Assembly, General Treasurer of the Church and Solicitor of the Church.

21. To attend to the general interests of the Church in matters which are not covered by the remit of any other Agency.

22. To deal with urgent issues arising between meetings of the General Assembly, provided that (a) these do not fall within the jurisdiction of the Commission of Assembly or of any Presbytery or Kirk Session, (b) they are not of a legislative or judicial nature and (c) any action taken in terms of this clause shall be reported to the next General Assembly.

23. To encourage all Agencies of the General Assembly to work ecumenically wherever possible and to have regard to the international, evangelical and catholic nature of the Church.

24. For the avoidance of doubt, sections 15 and 16 shall not apply to the Church of Scotland General Trustees, the Church of Scotland Housing and Loan Fund

for Retired Ministers and Widows and Widowers of Ministers and the Ministries Council Emerging Ministries Task Group all of which may deal with heritable property and other assets without the approval of the Council.

Appendix to Remit

For the purposes only of this remit, the term "Agencies" shall mean the following bodies being Standing Committees of the General Assembly, namely:

The following Councils: Church and Society, Ministries, Mission and Discipleship, Social Care, World Mission.

The following Committees: Assembly Arrangements, Central Services, Chaplains to Her Majesty's Forces, Church Without Walls, Ecumenical Relations, Legal Questions, Panel on Review and Reform, Parish Development Fund, Safeguarding.

APPENDIX IV
REMIT OF THE MINISTRIES COUNCIL

1. Current Remit

The remit of the Ministries Council is recruitment, training and support of recognised ministries for the mission of the Church, and assessment of patterns of national deployment of parish ministries. In pursuance of this remit the Council is charged with:

- Developing patterns of ministry which allow the Church of Scotland to be effective in its missionary calling and faithful to the one ministry of Jesus Christ;
- Recruiting individuals of the highest calibre collaboratively to lead the Church through its ordained ministries;
- Providing the Church with a range of ministries including the ministry of word and sacrament, the diaconate, readers and specialist workers;
- Developing assessment processes which ensure that those who serve the Church in its various ministries do so in response to God's call on their life;

- Providing education, initial training, in-service training and personal development appraisal of the highest quality to ensure that all those engaged in the various ministries of the Church are equipped to engage in Christ's mission and make the Gospel relevant in a rapidly changing society;
- Building good relationships with, and offering quality pastoral support and care to, all the ministries of the Church;
- Assisting the whole Church in its responsibility to meet the gospel imperative of giving priority to the poorest and most marginalized in our society;
- Undertaking all of its local planning and appraisal work in full cooperation with Presbyteries, local congregations and other denominations in order to ensure that emerging patterns of church life are effective at a local level and a viable use of the Church's resources;
- Evaluating all developments in ministry in order to ensure their effectiveness and relevance to the life of the church today;
- Working transparently and in collaboration with the other Councils in order to ensure the most effective use of the Church's finance, property and human resources;
- Conducting an annual review of progress made in discharging the remit and providing a written report to the Council of Assembly.

2. Proposed Revised Remit

The remit of the Ministries Council is the enabling of ministries in every part of Scotland, giving special priority to the poorest and most marginalized, through the recruitment, training and support of recognized ministries of the Church and the assessment and monitoring of patterns of deployment of those ministries.

In the fulfilment of this remit, the Council offers strategic leadership in the development of patterns of collaborative ministry which enable the Church of Scotland to be effective in its missionary calling and faithful in its participation in the one ministry of Jesus Christ, and operates within the following spheres of work:

Priority Areas – Following the Gospel imperative of priority to the poor

- Working directly in support of the poorest parishes in Scotland to enable and resource ministries and to build communities of hope;
- Assisting the whole Church in fulfilling its responsibility to the gospel imperative of giving priority to the poorest and most marginalized in society;
- Enabling and supporting work in partnership with ecumenical, inter-faith and statutory agencies to achieve the goal of alleviating poverty in Scotland.

Vocation & Training – Identifying and Providing the Human Resources for Ministries

- Developing and implementing patterns of enquiry and assessment and vocational guidance which enable the identification of appropriately called and gifted people to train for recognized ministries;
- Developing and implementing training patterns for those accepted into training for the recognized ministries of the Church;
- Enabling the transfer of people from other denominations into the ministries of the Church.

Support & Development – Offering pastoral support and enabling lifelong learning

- Delivering pastoral support to those involved in the recognized ministries of the Church through the development and resourcing of local pastoral networks, direct one-to-one engagement and the provision of occupational health support, counselling, mediation and conflict resolution services;
- Promoting and providing vocational guidance and life-long learning opportunities for ministries personnel through in-service events, self-appraisal processes and a study leave programme;
- Supporting those engaged in chaplaincy services both directly employed by the Council and employed by other agencies.

Planning & Deployment – Presbytery Planning, Emerging Ministries and Employment Issues

- Working with Presbyteries, for effective deployment of ministries to meet the needs of the parishes of Scotland and charges in the Presbytery of England, including consulting with congregations and other denominations where appropriate;
- Working in partnership with other agencies of the Church and ecumenical partners, to enable the emergence of ministries to meet the needs of the people of Scotland in every part;
- Ensuring best practice in the employment, care and support of staff, including setting appropriate terms and conditions, offering developmental training to staff and those responsible for their management.

Finance – Ensuring good management of funds and monitoring budgets

- Planning strategically for the future funding of the recognized ministries of the Church;
- Managing the funds and overseeing the budgeting processes of the Council to ensure that maximum benefit is derived for the Church's ministries through the use of income and capital;
- Preparing recommendations on the level of stipends and salaries and liaising with Pension Trustees on matters relating to the setting of the Standard Annuity and discretionary increases in pension, and negotiating and reaching agreement with Pension Trustees on funding rates.

CHURCH AND SOCIETY COUNCIL
May 2009

PROPOSED DELIVERANCE

The General Assembly
1. Receive the Report.

Engage with Congregational Life
Resources
2. Instruct the Church and Society Council to work with other partners to develop worship and discussion resources, where appropriate using real life experiences and reflections of the issues, to support congregations to engage in and act on the questions and challenges explored in its reports.

Engaging with Education and the needs of Young People
Growing up in Scotland
3. Instruct the Church and Society Council to work with other Councils to introduce a Child Friendly Church initiative based on the United Reform Church's model.
4. Urge Scottish and UK Governments to evidence as a matter of course how young people's voices are heard in the development of legislation and policy.
5. Instruct the Church and Society Council, together with Presbyteries and other Councils of the Church, to bring to the General Assembly of 2010 a report on the ways in which each is enabling the voices of young people to be heard in their decision-making processes.
6. Instruct the Church and Society Council to lobby Scottish and UK Governments to invest further in support for parenting and to work together to ensure a consistent policy approach to supporting families.
7. Encourage Church members and congregations to engage in and support those involved in fostering, adoption and befriending.
8. Instruct the Church and Society Council to work with representatives of the National Youth Assembly to develop awareness of models of support in congregations on the issues involved in mental illness among young people.
9. Instruct the Church and Society Council to work with other Councils to facilitate dialogue between young people and the media to develop a more positive portrayal of children and young people.
10. Urge Scottish and UK Governments to strengthen their commitment to end child poverty by 2020 and ensure that policies and adequate resources are in place to achieve that aim.
11. Urge the Scottish Government to ensure that resources, including partnerships with Churches and others, are in place to deliver the ambitions of the Early Years Framework.
12. Demand that HM Government uphold, respect and protect the rights of children who are asylum seekers or who are trafficked into our country.

Education

13. Commend the development of a major partnership delivering training for Religious Observance in schools and instruct the Church and Society Council to report to the General Assembly on progress toward implementation.
14. Commend to congregations the Action of Churches Together in Scotland publication "A Christian Vision of Education" and encourage them to discuss the implications for their own circumstances.
15. Commend the increased work in supporting school and Further Education chaplains.

Engaging with Technology, Science and the Environment
Climate Change

16. Instruct Presbyteries, in association with the Church and Society Council, to produce a plan for each congregation in their bounds, setting out how they will measure energy consumption in their church buildings, ascertain their carbon footprint and achieve a year-on-year reduction of 5% of their carbon footprint using the Eco-Congregation Scotland carbon footprint module; and instruct the Church and Society Council, in consultation with the General Trustees, to report to the General Assembly of 2010 on the implementation of this instruction.
17. Welcome the proposed incorporation of Eco-Congregation Scotland as a Charitable Company and continue to support the work of eco-congregations.
18. Affirm the current commitment of the Church and Society Council to the 'Responding to Climate Change Project' and instruct the Church and Society Council, in partnership with other Councils, to complete the review of this project with a view to its development.

Engaging with Issues of Peace and Justice
Ethics of Defence

19. Instruct the Church and Society Council to meet with HM Government ministers in the Foreign and Commonwealth Office and the Ministry of Defence to urge that they carry out a fundamental review of HM Government's foreign and defence policies with the view of taking the lead in better supporting the United Nations Organisation in its peacekeeping and peace making roles.
20. Continue to oppose the presence of nuclear weapons within the UK defence strategy, and urge HM Government to have the courage and leadership to repudiate them to help facilitate international nuclear disarmament.
21. Urge congregations to participate in campaign activities against the renewal of Trident and in particular, to meet with or write to their MP to urge them to vote against its renewal.
22. Remember before God the commitment of all members of the armed services and their families, especially all those who daily face danger in the course of their duty and those who continue to suffer or who have paid the ultimate sacrifice in the service of others.
23. Commend the re-examination of the Military Covenant in the recent Government initiative and urge HM Government to ensure that it is both fully implemented and appropriately resourced.

Sri Lanka

24. Strongly encourage HM Government urgently to seek a political settlement in Sri Lanka which would be fair to all communities within the island and which recognises the legitimate concerns of the Tamil people.
25. Recognising the difficulties and dangers facing Sri Lankan Christians in being a prophetic voice, urge Church members to remember them and their plight in their prayers.
26. Encourage the Church, at all levels, to support the work of agencies working with internally displaced people within Sri Lanka, in calling for their safe return to their homes.

Israel/ Palestine

27. Express deep regret at the loss of lives in Gaza and Israel following the recent incursion by Israel into Gaza.
28. Strongly urge HM Government to continue to engage fully in the peace process and the two state solution for Israel/Palestine.

Engaging with Health and Social Issues
Addictions

29. Whilst recognising that the responsible use of alcohol has a place within today's society, encourage all Church members to re-examine our attitudes to alcohol in the light of its potentially addictive nature and the damaging consequences of its use.
30. Commend those congregations which make premises available to groups and agencies which support those suffering from addiction and encourage other congregations to do the same as appropriate.
31. Encourage congregations and Presbyteries to support Crossreach and other care projects concerned with addictions in their local area.
32. Commend the Scottish Government on the recent Scottish Government reports on drugs and alcohol; "Changing Scotland's relationship with alcohol", and "The Road to Recovery", and welcome the emphasis on recovery within its approach to drugs.

End of Life Issues

33. In the light of changing cultural attitudes, instruct the Church and Society Council to prepare material to encourage debate in churches and Presbyteries on the issues raised in the 'End of Life Issues' report.
34. Commend the work undertaken by both the health care and voluntary sectors in providing care and comfort to all those approaching the end of their lives; encourage local congregations, the government and the wider community to affirm the intrinsic dignity and worth of all people and recognise the pastoral needs of families, friends and the professionals involved in end of life issues.
35. Commend the report "Living and Dying Well: A National Action Plan for Palliative and End of Life Care in Scotland", recognise the need for increased resources in many aspects of palliative care and instruct the Church and Society Council to raise this matter with the Scottish Government.
36. Instruct the Church and Society Council to examine further the issues surrounding suicide in Scotland, especially amongst young men.
37. Encourage Church members to join the Organ Donor register.

Justice and Markets

38. Instruct the Church and Society Council to prepare a remit for a Commission which would consult widely and reflect theologically and which would aim to contribute to changing perspectives on how values and ethics should inform the operation of economic systems at a global, local and personal level and report to the General Assembly of 2010.

39. Encourage the Church and Society Council to explore the issues involved in the provision of micro credit and find ways in which the Church may consider supporting or enabling the use of micro credits as a means of contributing to ending poverty in Scotland, and to consult with other Councils and bring proposals to the General Assembly of 2010.

40. Instruct the Church and Society Council to meet with business organisations to discuss the Cadbury Code of Conduct, asking how it might be updated so that the culture within the financial services sector reflects greater social responsibility and justice.

41. Urge congregations to assess local community needs in light of the credit crisis and identify areas where resources can be found to help meet those needs.

Justice System

42. Commend to congregations the Joint Faiths Advisory Board on Criminal Justice publication, "What Can I Do?" and encourage them to respond to the suggestions contained in the document.

Thanks and Distribution

43. Thank all those who assisted the Council in the preparation of the Report, and instruct the Council to send copies of the Report with the Deliverance to appropriate Scottish and UK Government Ministers, Members of the Scottish Parliament, Members of Parliament representing Scottish constituencies, Members of the European Parliament representing Scotland, and others involved in the issues addressed by the Report.

Executive Summary

This years report combines the Council's dual tasks of theological reflection on some significant issues and delivery of specific project work along with the resourcing of congregations to support their engagement with social and political issues.

Whilst the Council often has the task to represent the Church in the public square it very much understands that the real manifestation of the Church is in the presbyteries and congregations that are its foundations. The Council understands that it is as much through the work and witness of congregations as it is through the quality of theological reflection undertaken centrally that the Church gains the right to speak out on issues of public concern and debate. This report sets out to reflect that dual mandate.

Education

The report outlines the very exciting project to create a university accredited training package which would allow every school in Scotland to have someone with real professional training in the delivery of Religious Observance. This course will be available to school staff, clergy and laity. The report also outlines plans for chaplains' conferences for school and FE Chaplains and the support given to Presbytery Representatives on Education Committees.

Growing up in Scotland

This report reminds us that the experience of young people growing up today will shape our nation tomorrow. It looks at how young people learn and practice values and what the role of the adults is in that process. For the vast majority of young people in Scotland, growing up in Scotland is a relatively positive experience. This report concerns itself primarily with those for whom growing up in Scotland is not a good start in life. It challenges the church to get its house in order, suggests ways in which the church community might support opportunities such as fostering and calls on the Governments of both Holyrood and Westminster to keep to their commitments to young people in poverty.

Justice and Markets

This report offers a theological critique of economic thinking, arguing for a fundamental review of the values that underpin economic decision-making. It poses the question "what is economics for?" and argues that the human perspective needs to be rediscovered. The paper divides the issue into global, community and personal economics and proposes actions for the church and church members on all three. A series of conferences leading to a major commission is proposed to investigate the global crisis. Community audits and an exploration of the potential for the church to become involved in micro credit are the main proposals for the community section and steps to a personal ethic of economic decision-making are suggested in the final section.

Ethics of Defence

This report develops an ethics of defence that allows the church to both challenge political decisions that deal with defence issues and at the same time support service men and women through our chaplain services, a task that is full of tension. This report sits in that tension and offers proposals that reflect both tasks. Congregations are encouraged to lobby their MP for the cancellation of Trident and look to how they can offer support for service men and women from their community.

End of Life Issues

The report develops some of the excellent work that has previously been completed on End of Life issues offering clear and helpful thinking on what is a very pertinent subject. In particular it deals with what is meant by palliative care and challenges the view that "dying with dignity" is the sole prerogative of those who support assisted suicide or euthanasia. Proposals include working on issues around suicide especially amongst young men and supporting increased resourcing of palliative care, "old age pastors" in congregations, congregational Bereavement Care Teams, utilisation of church resources (Halls for *eg* friendship clubs), and advice on legal issues such as powers of attorney.

Addictions

The struggle with addiction is a very real experience for thousands of people from all walks of life. This report grapples with why this is the case and what congregations can do to support those who face this difficulty from offering space for groups to looking at their own attitudes to alcohol and drugs.

Sri Lanka

This report gives a brief outline of the 25 years of civil war and human rights violations in this island nation and in particular the struggles of the minority Christian Community to survive in what is a very hostile environment.

Climate Change

The work on responding to climate change through the significant development of the Eco-congregations movement and change within the church's own structures leads this report to call for a demanding challenge of a 5% reduction in congregational carbon footprints year on year. That is backed with real, easily accessible resources and support to help achieve this along with suggestions of financial resources to assist the changes and investments that will be required.

Other Reports

The report covers new developments in the Council's communications strategy, the work of the Scottish Churches Parliamentary Office, the Society Religion and Technology Project, ecumenical work, including the expansion of the Action of Churches in Scotland (ACTS) racial justice work which council staff have been heavily involved in and the Conference of European Churches. In addition details are given of work with Iranian Christians, support for opposition in Burma, new work being developed on China and the interfaith pilgrimage to Israel/Palestine undertaken in summer 2008.

Local Involvement, Worship and resources

The Council commits in this report to provide both discussion and worship resources to help congregations engage with the agenda it has set out. These will be primarily web based, free and backed by a commitment to help resource events held by congregations and presbyteries with speakers and other support. Information on these can be found on the website, Facebook site and by becoming a congregational contact by registering with Irene Crosthwaite, the Council's local involvement officer.

REPORT

1. Introduction

1.1 The voice of the church is heard in many distinctive ways. Most of them are local: the funeral visit, the Sunday School lesson, the Christian Aid envelope, the school assembly, community councils. Witness to God's love, care and justice is perhaps best demonstrated, and experienced, face to face with our neighbour. For the Church and Society Council this is foundational, and that is why local involvement is placed right at the beginning of our report this and every year. Resourcing and supporting that local voice is central to the Council's

thinking and activities, and it is a privilege to have that task. Without that focus, anything else we say and do is a hollow echo of what the church needs and deserves. With it, a great deal becomes possible in relating to the fields of politics, education, science and technology, moral and social matters and international issues. Membership of the Council is drawn from people with experience in all of these sectors, and the Council's staff also bring their expertise to bear on the Council's work throughout the year. In partnership with the local church, it is the Council's aim to offer wider society a distinctive Christian perspective in the public arena and to reflect on what is happening in Scotland's common life both with the church and with those outside it.

1.2 Some aspects of the life of our society are relevant year on year. The use and abuse of alcohol and drugs is not seasonal, for example, but ever present. The state of the markets, while always relevant, has taken on a new significance in recent months, just as new initiatives to influence end of life matters have given urgency to some aspects of the nation's thinking, though perhaps not the aspects the church might wish to focus on as a priority. Judgement from outside, in this case UNICEF, has made it necessary to reflect seriously on the experience of growing up in Scotland, while the engagement of our armed forces in, for example, Iraq and Afghanistan, along with the continued progress towards renewal of the Trident weapons system, encourages renewed thinking on the ethics of national defence policy. In reality these are but a few of many issues that the Council could bring to the General Assembly, and the need to prioritise is always before us. Because of this, the Council is developing a specific set of criteria to use when deciding how to allocate its scarce resources. Why *this* issue? Why this issue *now*? What real difference will be seen because we pursued this concern? What is the insight from the Gospel that the church can bring to bear on study and action in this area? The Council is also conscious of the need to develop outcomes to its work beyond the formation of deliverances to the General Assembly, critically important though these are. An example can be seen in the work being done to train people in Religious Observance in schools, where the desired result is the prospect of every school in Scotland having someone trained to deliver excellence in the provision of this aspect of the curriculum. Again, work that we trust is destined to end up bearing fruit in every parish. While not all that we do as a Council will have that distinction, nonetheless all of it is rooted in the desire to communicate the Gospel that is needed in every part of Scotland.

2. Engaging with Congregational Life

2.1 Visiting Presbyteries

2.1.1 The Local Involvement Officer, Irene Crosthwaite, has continued to visit presbyteries and their committees relating to the Church and Society Council. Just over half of all presbyteries have had a visit from Irene and she would be happy to be invited to the remaining ones.

2.2 Sharing Information

2.2.1 The Council's main methods of communication are through the website and newsletters. It is encouraging that our web pages are gradually attracting more users. News and new resources are added regularly. The biannual newsletter and shorter, more frequent, updates are put on to the news page as 'Word' documents so that they can easily be cut and pasted into congregational news magazines.

2.3 Congregational Contact

2.3.1 The Council would like to have a contact in each congregation who would receive this news by e-mail and pass information from it to their church members. If you could provide such a contact to be added to this database please send an email to: icrosthwaite@cofscotland.org.uk

2.4 Feedback

2.4.1 The Council would welcome more feedback from presbyteries and church members. Please pass on what you are doing in your locality. The newsletters will be used to share good ideas and keep you in touch with what is happening around the country. Please feed back information, evidence and suggestions about the reports which are produced by the Council. To facilitate discussion a Facebook Group called 'Church and Society' has been set up. Please let Facebook members from your congregation know about this and encourage them to join in the debates.

2.5 Presbytery Events

2.5.1 At the Council's annual conference in September reports were given by three presbytery Church and

Society representatives. They inspired the audience with news of events that their committees had held locally. The topics they had covered included drug awareness, climate change and a 'market place' highlighting various community initiatives. Speakers at these events included an MSP, Church and Society staff and various experts in the field of drugs. Other presbyteries have plans for day or evening conferences in 2009. Climate Change is one of the most popular choices of topics but others include transport in rural areas and homelessness. Presbyteries are encouraged to organise events which would inform, inspire and promote discussion and action by their local church members on themes which are relevant to their situation. The Church and Society staff would be happy to provide speakers and resources if a presbytery organises an event.

3. Media

3.1 Gaelic Media Service

3.1.1 Following the deliverance agreed in May 2008, meetings with the Gaelic Media Service will take place in spring of 2009, the outcome of which will be reported to the Assembly and can be found on the Council's web pages. We have also made representations to the BBC Trust concerning the possibilities for BBC Alba to be broadcast on freeview.

3.2 Communications

3.2.1 The task of communicating a gospel perspective on public issues is always a huge challenge in a world of instant opinion and rapidly changing news agendas. It is particularly challenging to offer a coherent and reflective sense of discernment about what the theological first principles are on a given issue when most sections of the media thrive on 20 second soundbites, celebrity opinion-makers and the voracious desire for controversy as a method of making profits out of the task of reporting the news.

3.2.2 The role of web or internet based media is becoming increasingly significant and will continue to do

so. The business plans of most mainstream print media and much of the broadcast media now assume that the role of these traditional forms of communication is already changing. They are rapidly becoming a method of developing brand awareness to guide readers toward their web-based content as that is where profits are to be made. Internet based media is portrayed as more "democratic" in that they are seen as much more accessible to the general populace. However, with some notable exceptions, a great deal of what purports to be factual reporting remains significantly less rigorous in the checking of facts and the thoroughness of its analysis. In spite of these concerns over accuracy, it remains the case that understanding the potential of the World Wide Web as a context for communicating our message and developing the capacity to make extensive use of it must be central in developing the Council's communication strategy.

3.2.3 The next step for the Council in achieving this is the appointment of Virginia Cano as Communications Officer who, working closely with the Media department, will develop and implement the Council's communications strategy. This strategy will have a strong focus on internet based media but will, of course, still include traditional print and broadcast media.

3.2.4 It is the view of the Council however, that the Church's voice is not simply to be heard amongst the headlines and the sound bites but crucially where the Church is most manifest, in the life of our congregations and amongst the communities we serve. The Communications strategy will therefore include a strong element of ensuring that parishes are kept informed of both current thinking on issues and also how they might choose to respond locally in word and in action. It will include ways in which we can create the networks of support that both allow this work to develop and inform the Church's thinking on particular issues. Where the Council and others are in the public arena expressing the "voice of the Church", if that voice is rooted in the lives and the experiences of the parish communities who are the church manifest then it will be a voice that carries a great deal more integrity and impact.

4. Engaging with Politics and Government

4.1 The Council continues to engage actively with Governments in Edinburgh and London (through the Scottish Churches Parliamentary Office) and with the European institutions (through the Conference of European Churches (CEC) Church and Society Office in Brussels).

4.1.1 This engagement includes:
- communicating Assembly deliverances;
- responding to consultations;
- Moderatorial visits to Holyrood and Westminster;
- annual Council visit to Westminster;
- participation in meetings initiated by Government or the churches;
- church leaders' annual meeting with the First Minister; and
- ongoing informal contacts.

4.1.2 The SCPO continues to provide monthly updates on what is happening in the Scottish and UK Parliaments, and regular briefings on issues of particular concern to the churches. This work receives some financial support from the Scottish Government (funding part of one staff member's salary). Anyone can sign up to receive these updates by emailing Alison@actsparl.org.

4.1.3 It is particularly welcome that the work of SCPO was recently described by one of our partner churches as one of the most effective examples of ecumenical co-operation in Scotland. Working together, even when not all churches wish to speak with one voice, is a real strength of our work in this area.

4.1.4 The Scottish Government also continues to work through its Faith Liaison Advisory Group (FLAG) as one channel of communication with churches and other faith communities; SCPO is represented on FLAG and on the parallel UK body (the Faith Communities Consultative Council).

4.2 Structures of Government

4.2.1 The Council has contributed both to the Scottish Government's National Conversation on Scotland's Future and to the discussions of the Calman Commission. Discussion cards were prepared for congregations, an event was held at the Church Without Walls Gathering at Ingliston, and both written and oral evidence submitted to the Calman Commission. In so doing, the Council has tried both to stimulate debate within the Church and to interpret previous Assembly decisions in the context of current debate and questions posed to us. The Church has not taken a stand for or against independence, nor do we urge it to do so; but we believe strongly that a significant contribution to this, as to any debate about Scotland's future, can and should still be made.

4.3 Criminal Justice

4.3.1 Through SCPO, the Council continues to provide support for the Joint Faiths Advisory Board on Criminal Justice. During 2008, the Board continued to look for ways of encouraging faith communities to engage with their local Community Justice Authorities, and also produced (with Scottish Government funding) a new edition of "What Can I Do?" – a booklet on volunteering within the criminal justice system, which has been widely distributed and can still be obtained through SCPO.

4.3.2 Kenny MacAskill MSP, Cabinet Secretary for Justice, wrote a foreword for this booklet; there has been continuing dialogue with the Government, and the Council is encouraged to note the increased emphasis on community-based sentencing and other measures called for by the General Assembly of 2008. The Council also participated in a public debate in the Scottish Parliament on knife crime in January 2009.

4.4 Debt, Poverty and Social Inclusion

4.4.1 As the "credit crunch" bit more deeply in the second half of 2008, the Council played an active part in the debate, particularly on the impact on the most vulnerable. The Scottish Parliament Cross Party Group on Tackling Debt has been an important vehicle for that debate, and the Parliamentary Officer acted as secretary of that Group until he left SCPO at the end of the year.

4.4.2 During 2008, the Scottish Government consulted on, and then published, its framework for tackling poverty[1]. The Council worked with partners in the Scottish Churches Social Inclusion Network (SCSIN) to contribute to that ongoing discussion. We had hoped for greater recognition within the Framework of the contribution of faith communities to community regeneration and tackling poverty, but were disappointed at the lack of mention of this.

4.4.3 More success was achieved by the Free School Meals campaign, which the Church has supported along with other members of SCSIN. We therefore welcomed the announcement that all school pupils in primaries one to three are to be entitled to free school meals following successful pilot schemes, and look forward to further, funded expansion of this.

4.4.4 The Council has also been actively involved in the Get Fair campaign, an initiative of Church Action on Poverty and many other charities. This aims primarily to keep a focus on tackling poverty as the next UK election approaches, seeking commitments from all political parties to bring forward to specific measures to ensure everyone in Britain has:

- An income that meets minimum living standards;
- Affordable housing and decent neighbourhoods; and
- Fair access to services, without discrimination.

---

[1] Achieving our Potential: A framework to tackle poverty and inequality in Scotland and was published November 20 2008. http://www.scotland. gov.uk/Publications/2008/11/20103815/0

The Scottish launch of the campaign took place at the Parliament in January 2009. Since this includes a commitment to a living wage, this has been the main way in which the Council has taken forward that commitment by the Assembly of 2008; however, we would hope to be able to report further action on this by the time of this year's Assembly.

4.5 Consultation Responses

4.5.1 In the past year consultation responses have been submitted on the following subjects:

- Agricultural Wages in Scotland (Holyrood)
- Scottish Fuel Poverty Forum (Holyrood)
- Sexual Offences (Scotland) Bill (Holyrood)
- Scottish Devolution (Calman Commission)
- The Next Generation of National Qualifications in Scotland (Holyrood)
- Changing Scotland's relationship with alcohol (Holyrood)
- Curriculum for Excellence RME Experiences and Outcomes (Learning and Teaching Scotland)
- Safeguarding our Rural Schools and improving School Consultation Procedures (Holyrood)
- Strengthening for the Future: A Consultation on the reform of the Children's Hearings System (Holyrood)
- Welfare Reform : "No One Written Off" (Westminster)
- Adapting our ways: Managing Scotland's Climate Risk. Consultation on Scotland's Climate Change Adaptation Framework (Holyrood)
- Sentencing Guidelines and a Scottish Sentencing Council (Holyrood)
- The Looked After Children (Scotland) Regulations 2008 (Holyrood)
- Forced Marriage: A Civil Remedy? (Holyrood)

4.5.2 There is no doubt that using the method of responses to Parliamentary and Government consultations allows us to influence political thinking in the wider sense. Our contribution to the Calman Commission was, for example, very well received, both the written and the oral evidence. Taking time to do responses means we can offer some of the thinking time about first principles that political decision-makers often don't get. Our responses are therefore always rooted in theological first principles and should be seen as both a challenge and a reminder to political decision-makers to take time to lift their eyes when creating legislation and not to spend all their time embroiled in the detail.

4.6 Graham Blount

4.6.1 The Assembly will wish to note that SCPO Parliamentary Officer the Rev Dr Graham Blount has been appointed to a post doctoral research post at the Centre for Theology and Public Issues. Whilst the Council and the Assembly would want to offer him wholehearted congratulations on this appointment, his departure from the post is a sad loss and will leave a big hole to fill in the work, not only of the Church of Scotland in its engagement with Scottish and British Political life but also the 11 other denominations who are part of the work of the Office. Graham has made a huge contribution to the capacity of the Christian community in Scotland to engage effectively and creatively with the Scottish Parliament and with Westminster. He has been with the SCPO since its inception and it is a significant tribute to his work that as well as effectiveness of the SCPO being praised by many, it is seen as a model of good practice for working ecumenically.

4.7 Parliamentary Officer

4.7.1 The Council has appointed Chloe Clemmons as the new SCPO Parliamentary Officer.

5. Engaging with Education and the needs of Young People

5.1 Religious Observance in Schools

5.1.1 The advent of the 2005 guidelines for Religious Observance was both a dramatic change to how Religious Observance was to be delivered in schools and a huge opportunity for the Christian Community and other faith communities to influence that delivery. The chance to do everything we can to make sure that there are high quality opportunities to experience stillness, to struggle with the deep questions of our living and to enjoy spiritual uplift through a variety of media in every school through the implementation of these guidelines is one we cannot afford to miss.

5.1.2 To that end a partnership has been created between the Church and Society Council, Scripture Union Scotland and the University of Glasgow to work with practitioners, school chaplains, other denominations, education trade unions and teacher associations, the General Teaching Council of Scotland, Her Majesty's Inspectorate for Education, Directors of Education, Convention of Scottish Local Authorities, Learning and Teaching Scotland, Head Teacher Associations and others. This group is in the process of devising a flexible, peer-led, experience based and university accredited training course open to teachers and others involved in RO. Our ambition is to ensure that every school in Scotland will have the opportunity to have the staff responsible for the delivery of RO qualified to University level in that task, as would normally be the case for all other areas in the curriculum.

5.1.3 This group has held initial seminars, created a first group of trainers and intends to offer a pilot course in June with a view to launching the course nationally from autumn 2009. Further reports will be presented to future Assemblies where issues such as long-term support for this work and the need to involve other faith communities will be explored.

5.2 Curriculum for Excellence

5.2.1 The Outcomes and Experiences for Religious and Moral Education were released in May 2008. The Council responded to the consultation and this is available. The Council were guided by their Standing Committee on Education, and broadly welcomed the proposals. The Associate Secretary was involved in a Quality Assurance Group of Learning Teaching Scotland and their review process following the consultation.

5.3 Stevenson Prizes

5.3.1 The Council established the Stevenson Prize to mark excellence in the fields of Religious Education and Religious Observance. The Prize is named after the Rev Dr John Stevenson, the General Secretary of the Education Committee from 1992 – 2000 and we are delighted that he agreed to be one of the judges. In 2008 the Prize was awarded for Religious Observance to reflect the implementation of Circular 1/2005. The Council was delighted to receive a healthy number of entries for a first awarding of the Prize. The Prize was awarded by the Moderator during the General Assembly. The Primary School Prize went to Mossneuk Primary from East Kilbride; the Secondary to Liberton High School, Edinburgh. We were delighted that pupils from both schools were able to attend the General Assembly to receive the prize as well as attending a lunchtime reception. The prize will be awarded on the same theme in 2009 and we welcome all entries: details are available on the website as well as from the office.

5.4 Religious Representatives on Local Authority Education Committees.

5.4.1 The Education Representatives on Local Authorities met twice during the year. First, in June, for a well-attended conference, organised jointly by the Council and the Scottish Catholic Education Commission, in Edinburgh. Gill Robinson from LTS gave an overview of the Curriculum for Excellence and encouraged the delegates to attend any seminars being run by their Local Authority which explained what was involved in CfE. Barbara Jarvie and Paul Hayes gave excellent presentations about what was involved in being a Church Representatives in their local authority. There was extensive discussion and it highlighted the fact that local authorities view their representatives differently. The legal position is that the representatives have the right to vote on all educational matters and the Council continues to hold the importance of that position.

5.4.2 The Conference for Education Representatives in September was held in Dundee and was appreciated by all who attended. The speakers, Colin Brown, Curriculum Review Programme Manager; Frank Crawford, HMIe; Jim Stephen, Cosla; Jim Collins Director of Education, Dundee Council and Jen Robertson Scripture Union/Church and school development worker, all gave excellent presentations. After the civic reception hosted by Dundee City Council Lord Provost John R Letford, Ewan Aitken gave the evening lecture which added to the overall theme of the conference. The feedback from the delegates was very positive.

5.5 ACTS – Scottish Churches Education Group

5.5.1 The ACTS Education Group met four times during 2008. The Council was represented at all meetings. The major task of the Group has been the production of the revised *Christian Vision for Education* document that the Group first produced in 2000. The revised version is now available and has been widely distributed. The Council would like to congratulate the group for the work on this document which will be sent to every director of education encouraging its wider circulation to schools. Electronic copies can be downloaded from the ACTS website, a link is also included on the Church of Scotland website. The official launch of the document was held in February 2009.

5.6 Meetings with Scottish Catholic Education Service

5.6.1 The Standing Committee on Education has been represented at several meetings with the Scottish Catholic Education Service (SCES) that covered matters of mutual concern in relation to work with local authorities and discussions are under way for the next joint conference in June 2009.

5.7 Growing Up in Scotland

5.7.1 The Council has had a Working Party studying this matter for two years. A version of the Report formed the basis of the Moderator's visit to the Scottish Parliament in January 2009. The full Report is attached as Paper 1 for the consideration of the General Assembly.

5.8 Visits to MSPs etc

5.8.1 The Standing Committee on Education has continued to push for meetings with the key players in the educational field, HMIe, Learning Teaching Scotland, General Teaching Council Scotland and Education Ministers. Meetings have been arranged with the Education Representatives of various parties and will focus on the Concordat between the Scottish Government and Local Authorities, the Role of Religious Representatives on Local Authority Education Committees, Religious Observance and Curriculum for Excellence.

5.9 Rural Schools, National Qualifications and Children's Hearings

5.9.1 The Council, working in partnership with the Mission and Discipleship Council, responded to the Scottish Government consultations *Safeguarding our rural schools and improving school consultation procedures: proposals for changes to legislation.* The Council also responded to the Scottish Government Consultations on *Strengthening for the Future: A Consultation on the reform of the Children's Hearings System* and *The Next Generation of National Qualifications in Scotland.*

5.10 National Sexual Health and HIV Advisory Committee

5.10.1 This Scottish Government Committee is chaired by the Minister for Health, Shona Robison. During 2009 the name of the Committee was changed and the membership reviewed. At that point the Rev Andrew Philip stood down and has been replaced by the Associate Secretary. The Committee has met several times with its new membership and approaches its task with vigour.

5.11 Chaplains Conferences
5.11.1 Further Education

5.11.1.1 It is the view of the Council as a whole, and the Education Committee in particular, that there is a need for the church to engage further with and offer more support to Further Education sector chaplains. A step towards this was a conference held on Thursday 11 November 2008

where the subject was mental health issues. Speakers included Rev John McMahon, Lead Chaplain, NHS Lothian and Dr Ben Baig, Lecturer in Psychiatry, The University of Edinburgh. Responses from 40 plus participants were very positive and it is intended to develop this into an annual event and use that as a platform for offering other support and resources. This work is being done in partnership with the Ministries Council.

5.11.2 Schools

5.11.2.1 There has been a feeling amongst the committee that further work is needed to try to build on some of the significant contribution made by John Stevenson and others in the support of schools chaplains in areas other than religious observance mentioned above. It is recognised that this needs to be done in partnership with colleagues in the Ministries Council. A conference is to be held in the spring of 2009, the primary purpose of which will be to identify the priorities for support for School chaplains.

6. Engaging with Technology, Science and the Environment
6.1 Climate Change

6.1.1 Climate change is an ethical issue. The project *Responding to Climate Change* began in November 2007. Its purpose is to help the church develop an effective response to climate change, both in its own actions and in its contribution to the wider debate. The project reflects the Church's ethical concern about climate change. This was summed up at the outset of the project by the Convener of the Church and Society Council:

> *The Church of Scotland is concerned that climate change poses a serious and immediate threat to people everywhere, particularly to the poor of the earth; and that climate change represents a failure in our stewardship of God's creation. We accept the need to reduce the emissions of greenhouse gases urgently to avoid dangerous and irreversible climate change; and to promote a more equitable and sustainable use of energy.*

This ethical concern has informed the development of the project and remains its main driving force.

6.1.2 Progress to date

6.1.2.1 The project has developed in three ways:

- It has worked with councils, presbyteries and committees of the Church to help them identify and address the impact of climate change. This has included both practical issues such as reducing the carbon footprint of the church's own estate; raising awareness though presentations to councils and information on the climate change pages of the Church of Scotland website.
- It has supported the Eco-Congregation Programme in Scotland and encouraged congregations to consider how they can react to climate change. The Eco-Congregation Scotland Programme now includes over 200 congregations, both Church of Scotland and other denominations and is the largest movement of community environmental groups in Scotland.
- It has helped the Church contribute to the wider debate in Scotland, for example through the *Stop Climate Chaos* coalition. The Church has been closely involved in the national debate around the Scottish Climate Change Bill, both in Parliament, with the Scottish Government and though the European Christian Environment Network. The Church strongly supports the Scottish Government's commitment to an 80% reduction in greenhouse gas emissions.

6.1.3 Key achievements

6.1.3.1 The work of the project is not confined to one council or committee. There has been progress across the Church. While it is not possible to cover all this work, the following paragraphs list some of the main achievement of the project to date.

6.1.4 Councils

6.1.4.1 Three councils of the Church have supported the project financially (Church and Society, Mission and Discipleship and World Mission). All have been involved in the project and have contributed to its development. The World Mission Council has identified climate change as one of the main drivers of poverty and has featured climate change in WM magazine and other publications. With Christian Aid and other partners they have encouraged congregations to become more actively involved in climate change campaigns.

6.1.4.2 The Mission and Discipleship Council has supported the project through the involvement of development officers around Scotland and though the active participation of young people. The Youth Assembly held in September 2008 made climate change one of its main themes and participants engaged in four days of lively and passionate debate on the subject. The deliverances of the Youth Assembly are reported to the General Assembly elsewhere and set out many challenges for the Church to consider.

6.1.4.3 The Church and Society Council has taken overall responsibility for the development of the project; playing a major role in shaping its direction and its Local Involvement Officer, Irene Crosthwaite has been tireless in promoting climate change issues to Presbyteries to help them put into effect the instruction of the General Assembly 2008. This has resulted in a growing number of Presbytery conferences on climate change.

6.1.4.4 Other councils have been equally committed to the project. The General Trustees have recognised the close links between climate change and energy management in church buildings. Congregations and property conveners faced with growing fuel bills have a powerful incentive to manage their energy use effectively, but good energy management is also good stewardship of creation. Work carried out by the Church's energy consultants Argyle Energy in the Presbytery of Stirling has identified how congregations can reduce their energy bills and reduce their carbon emissions. The lessons learned from this project are important for all congregations. Good energy management is essential for both good financial management and reducing the emission of greenhouse gases: the three are inextricably linked. In an age of high fuel prices and increasing concern about climate change effective energy management is not an option: it is a moral and financial obligation for all congregations.

6.2 Eco-Congregation Scotland

6.2.1 Central to the development of the project is the growth in the number of eco-congregations across Scotland. In November 2008 the 200th congregation in Scotland registered as an eco–congregation (Strathfillan in the Presbytery of Argyll). The movement also received warm congratulations from MSPs and government ministers in a debate held in the Scottish Parliament on 17 December 2008. Congregations across Scotland were encouraged by MSPs both to continue their work and to tackle climate change as a priority. The debate was a milestone and an affirmation of the importance of eco-congregations.

6.2.2 How big is your congregation's carbon footprint?

6.2.2.1 With a grant from the Scottish Environment Protection Agency (SEPA) a pilot project was carried out to develop and test a simple carbon footprint tool for congregations. By keeping a close check on fuel bills and using a simple calculator congregations can now easily work out their carbon footprint. The pilot was highly successful and has led to a larger and more ambitious application to the Scottish Government Climate Challenge fund which is described below.

6.2.3 Governance and finance

6.2.3.1 Eco–Congregation Scotland has developed as an informal association of congregations. This arrangement served the movement well in its early years but as the number of congregations has increased it has become clear that it is no longer adequate. For this reason the Eco-Congregation Scotland steering group, with the support of the Church and Society Council and the Church in Society Committee of the Scottish Episcopal

Church agreed that the time was now right to establish Eco-Congregation Scotland as an independent legally constituted voluntary organisation. This is a major step for any organisation and involves considerable challenges for all stakeholders. At the same time it offers the opportunity for Eco-Congregation Scotland to grow and develop to play a greater role in the life of congregations, the Church and in their local communities.

6.2.4 The future

6.2.4.1 It is now clear that climate change will be one of the defining global challenges of the twenty-first century. Climate change represents a massive failure in our stewardship of the earth and a major contribution to poverty and social dislocation. For these reasons the Church must contribute to national and international action. By demonstrating our commitment and by taking action the Church of Scotland can take a leading role across Scotland.

6.2.5 Climate Challenge Fund (CCF)

6.2.5.1 The Scottish Government's Climate Challenge Fund represents a great opportunity to help us take forward this work. This fund has been established to help communities reduce their carbon emissions. The SEPA funded pilot project has demonstrated that congregations can measure their carbon footprint and the debate on Eco-Congregation Scotland in the Scottish Parliament encouraged congregations to take a leading role. To take forward this work an application has been submitted to the CCF for funds to employ an Eco-Congregation Scotland project manager and a small support team to work with congregations to help them:
- understand the causes and consequences of climate change
- measure their carbon footprint
- take action to reduce their energy use, in church buildings, their homes and communities.

6.2.5.2 Participating congregations will be asked to make a commitment to reduce their carbon footprint by at least 5% a year. This is a challenging commitment, particularly for church properties that are old and difficult to heat but it is the minimum commitment that is necessary to make an effective contribution to climate change.

6.2.6 Involvement in the national and international debate

6.2.6.1 To support eco-congregations it is proposed that the Church of Scotland engages more fully in the national debate, particularly on the implementation of the Scottish Climate Change Bill and its implications for all aspects of life in Scotland. Ministers and MSPs have welcomed the growing role of the Church and we should not be shy to develop this.

6.2.6.2 The Church is a member of the Stop Climate Chaos coalition which also includes other faith groups and environmental NGOs. The Church brings another ethical perspective to the coalition that complements the environmental and scientific expertise of groups such as WWF Scotland or RSPB. Scientists and campaigners have welcomed the growing role of the Church and, in conjunction with the SRT project, there are great opportunities to engage further with both groups.

6.2.6.3 The Conference of European Churches and World Council of Churches have identified climate change as a priority. The Church of Scotland can make a significant contribution to this international debate. The practical steps under way in Scotland and the experience we are developing means we can offer practical help and support to others and support the growing role of churches worldwide.

6.2.7 Conclusion

6.2.7.1 The first year of the project Responding to Climate Change has demonstrated the commitment and the potential that exists in the Church. Among congregations there is a concern and commitment to tackle climate change. However this is only the beginning

of the work that will be needed if the Church is to fulfil its mission. It now has the opportunity to reassert its national role in leading change; in challenging and supporting congregations and communities to respond to climate change.

6.3 SRT

6.3.1 Science and technology have had enormous impacts on all aspects of human life, in many cases changing the way we think of ourselves and society. Most of these impacts have been positive; some have had unforeseen consequences. Many have raised ethical and moral questions as to how and where technology can and should be applied to benefit the largest number of people.

6.3.2 The SRT project was initiated by the Church of Scotland in the 1970s, to help the church to engage constructively with the scientific community in Scotland and beyond. For almost 40 years, the SRT has been involved in informed debate with many interested parties: government, regulators, industry, scientists, the church, the general public. The variety of publications which have resulted from the work of the SRT project stand as eloquent testimony to the dedicated work of many people over the years, and many individuals have been stimulated to think – and to act – through the work of the project.

6.3.3 The church has something to say…

6.3.3.1 Many might argue that the church should stick to what it knows, and not interfere with issues which lie outwith its remit. Yet the Church in Scotland includes many people with professional expertise relevant to all kinds of areas – including areas which may be considered controversial. The SRT seeks to assist the church in being faithful to Jesus' call to his followers to be "salt and light" in the world.

6.3.4 Honest disagreement

6.3.4.1 It is also true that, within the Church, there exists a variety of views on almost any subject; as the SRT project often looks at areas which are by definition controversial, this could be seen as a potential weakness. However, the ability to honestly engage in dialogue with those who don't necessarily agree is one of the strengths of scientific investigation. While this may not result in the "black and white" answers that many seek, faithful honesty before each other is healthy and useful; progress on breaking down prejudice and misinformation (the false "science versus faith" dichotomy, for example) is contingent upon informed debate and discussion. Dialogue with the scientific community demands that we maintain integrity and respect, while engaging in constructive debate.

6.3.5 Salt and Light
6.3.5.1 Many opportunities present themselves to the SRT project at this time: it is key to setting the right priorities which will be of long term benefit to the Church and to society – we must never forget that we do not produce reports just for the sake of it, but as part of our calling to be "salt and light" in the world. Our responsibility is to understand what matters to God and to people, and to determine how best to positively impact society.

6.3.6 Infosheets and mini- working groups
6.3.6.1 One of the valuable resources of the SRT is a series of brief introductions to issues in science: these are aimed at the non-specialist, and have been generally well received. However, these need to be periodically updated; some of the issues covered in the series may no longer be relevant, while new sheets on subjects not yet covered may also be valuable. In consultation with the SRT steering group and other interested parties, it was also felt that some issues, such as Sustainable Agriculture, would benefit from a more thorough review than would be possible in the two page format to which the infosheets are limited. To this end, mini-working groups will be formed on an "as needed" basis. It is intended that these will usually be steered by a Council member.

6.3.7 SRT Trust
6.3.7.1 A significant fund was built up over the past few years by the SRT Trust: this included donations from other interested parties as well as consultancy fees earned by SRT staff. It has been felt that, with the recent changes which have taken place in the administration of the SRT, the SRT Trust and its associated fund should be wound up. This was done in agreement with the Trustees of the fund; OSCR has been informed.

6.3.8 Forty years of SRT
6.3.8.1 The prescience of the Church of Scotland in establishing the SRT project has been widely applauded. While not wishing to rest on our laurels, it is sometimes good to look back and to celebrate the achievements of the past. Planning is under way for an event to mark 40 years of the SRT in 2010; further details will be published in due course.

6.3.9 Current and future interests
6.3.9.1 A number of other issues remain on the horizon, for future consideration. A degree of "futurology" may be required in identifying what will be important, but areas such as nanotechnology, risk, synthetic biology, sustainable development and genetic enhancement are likely to be among these. As the SRT project looks towards its 40th anniversary, it is clear that much work remains to be done.

6.4 Justice and Markets
6.4.1 To some, the relationship between Christianity and material wealth is an inherently thorny subject: how do we (whether as individuals, congregations or a denomination) ensure that God and money each receive the attention they are due? None of us can avoid using money in our daily lives; in addition, it has been pointed out that much of the language of salvation (debt, redemption, value, exchange) is used in common with economics. A Report on this is attached as Paper 2.

7. Engaging with Issues of Peace and Justice
7.1 Migration
7.1.1 ACTS held a conference on 'The Scottish Churches

and Contemporary Migration' at the Scottish Storytelling Centre on Wednesday 8 October 2008. The Moderator opened the day. The Council was involved in this valuable and well received conference by the Convener who gave both the Introductory and Closing remarks. The Council was also represented by a number of members and staff. A fuller account of the conference is given in the Scottish Churches Racial Justice Officer's report elsewhere in this report.

7.2 Ethics of Defence

7.2.1 This is scheduled to be the last report which the Church and Society Council is producing as part of its response to the World Council of Churches' "Decade to Overcome Violence". A significant amount of groundwork has previously been done in the whole area of conflict and defence. Nevertheless, the issues surrounding defence present a number of important ethical dilemmas: proportionality, just cause and due authority in our actions. A Report on this is attached as Paper 3.

7.3 Racial Justice

7.3.1 The main avenues of the Council's engagement with Racial Justice matters are the Scottish Churches Racial Justice Group (SCRJG) and through CTBI. We are currently represented on the SCRJG by Rob Whiteman, the Associate Secretary of the Council, one of the Group's Co-Conveners, and Sandy Horsburgh, the Council Vice-Convener. As part of the CTBI reorganisation the work at this level has now become the Racial Justice Network. This had a first meeting at the end of 2008 and we hope that this work will develop in the next few years. The SCRJG is served by the Racial Justice Officer, Dr Nelu Balaj. The SCRJG Annual Report for 2008 reads as follows:

"Scottish Churches Racial Justice Group – Office Bearers' report for 2008

During the year of 2008 the Scottish Churches' Racial Justice Group continued to work effectively with churches and other partners to further its agenda of supporting the churches in their work for Racial Justice in Scotland. This report is a succinct summary of some of the past year's achievements of the Group.

The Group has been supported by ACTS member churches and two other denominations (the Baptist Union of Scotland and the Free Church of Scotland), even though two of the denominations (the Roman Catholic Church and the Congregational Federation) are not directly represented on the Group. The Group met four times in 2008 for business and three other times for special meetings, with an average of 12 members attending each meeting.

The Group has sought to continue to hold its meetings, whenever possible, at the central offices or facilities of our church members. The Group held a day of reflection in March at St Mary's Monastery, Kinnoull, which was very well attended and led by Bishop David Chillingworth. This day offered the Group members a good opportunity to get to know each other better and to reflect together on their call to serve God, both in their personal life and as a Group, in seeking to address the issues of inclusion and discrimination.

The membership of the Group was strengthened by the addition of four co-opted members from minority ethnic backgrounds who have great experience of and links with minority ethnic churches and church groups. This has enabled the Group to gain valuable insight and input into its work from a minority ethnic Christian perspective and experience. The Group has heard from two of the co-opted members about issues faced by Asian Christians in Scotland and the experience and reality of Black Christians in Glasgow.

As the three year funding cycle is coming to an end in summer 2009, the Group decided to undertake a comprehensive external review of its past three years' work. The review was conducted by AW Trotman Associates. The report highlights the many achievements of the work and emphasises the need for this work to be strengthened and continued. A copy of the report can be obtained either from the Officer or ACTS' office and it will soon be available from ACTS' website. On the basis of the review, the Group has put together a new three year plan, supported by ACTS. The Group is now seeking support and funding from the Churches. Copies of the proposal and the bid can be obtained from the Racial Justice Officer or from ACTS.

Some tangible achievements:

The Group continues to work very well with ACTS in setting out priorities, the work plan and the management of the Officer's work.

- Racial Justice Update Scotland is a monthly electronic update, edited by the Officer, covering news, relevant issues, events, and resources, which has been going out to over 100 email addresses and which is available on ACTS' website. The Update has received a number of very positive feedbacks and is seen as a valuable resource by many.
- The Officer worked very closely with churches and church representatives in providing advice and resources. For example the Officer supported the Methodist Church in Scotland in their effort to set up a Ghanaian Methodist Fellowship in Scotland; the Officer has also supported the small Romanian Orthodox community in Scotland to set up formal Churches in Scotland, the first one expected to officially open on the 18 January 2009 in Glasgow.
- The Group worked with Church organisations and bodies to keep racial justice issues on their agendas. These bodies and organisations included: ACTS Church and Society and Mission Networks; Scottish Churches Social Inclusion Network; Scottish Churches' Parliamentary Office; Scottish Churches Rural Group;
- Racial Justice Sunday was promoted this year through the CTBI Racial Justice Network.
- The Group is working closely with CTBI in helping to reshape the work of its Racial Justice Network
- Conference on Migration: The Group supported the Officer and a task group in organising this conference. The conference explored the main issues and challenges of migration in Scotland. There were contributions from a wide range of bodies and organisations working in this area, at the policy level and also directly with migrants, and input from migrants and communities affected by migration. The conference was very well attended and received very good reviews from participants. Among the outcomes from the conference were: recognition of the need for the churches to work more closely with the local authorities on migration issues; and of the need to develop resources that could help local churches work with migrants. A report of the conference can be obtained from the Officer or from ACTS' office, and is also available on the website.
- Legacies of Slavery: The Group has agreed to support and oversee one of the proposals which came out of marking the Bicentenary of the Abolition of the Slave Trade Act, in seeking to tackle the disadvantages faced by minority ethnic people in Scotland.
- The Group has started to work closely with black and minority ethnic Christians and churches in Scotland. It has supported the Racial Justice Officer in the work to develop a formal network for minority ethnic churches in Scotland, which is now formed but still needs support to develop.
- Through the Racial Justice Officer the Group worked

with other organisations such as: Cross Party Parliamentary Groups on Asylum and Refugees, and on Race Relations; and with the Scottish Government: Equality Unit and Faith Liaison Advisory Group;
– The Group has also worked with a number of non-governmental organisations over the past year in our common goal in tackling discrimination and building a fearer Scotland. These have included: the Scottish Refugee Council, Oxfam, Positive Action in Housing and Central Scotland Racial Equality Council.
– The Officer was featured in Don't Be A Stranger campaign, which is an Evangelical Alliance initiative set up to highlight stories of migrants and to encourage churches to engage with this work.

The work that the Scottish Churches' Racial Justice Group is undertaking, with and on behalf of churches in Scotland, is one of the most successful ecumenical ventures. The Group greatly appreciates the practical help and the prayers with which the Churches and its other partners have supported it during the past year and hopes that these will continue throughout 2009. The need for this work in addressing one of the greatest blights on the social landscape in Scotland has not declined and we must continue and increase this work that God so clearly calls us to."

7.4 Gambling

7.4.1 The Gambling Act 2005 was fully implemented during 2008 and the Council has been involved in the ongoing monitoring of that. The Gambling Prevalence Study that gives a benchmark of gambling practice prior to the implementation of the Act was published in 2008 and the Council made comment on that as well as taking a Report to the General Assembly. The Associate Secretary has continued to be in contact with colleagues in other churches working on gambling as well as being involved with the research of the Gambling Commission, including the build up to the next Prevalence Study. This

study is due in 2010 so this is a long term piece of work but an ongoing engagement is essential. The problems that gambling is causing in our society are not going to go away.

7.5 End of Life Issues

7.5.1 Much media attention in the past few months has been focused on issues such as assisted death and the right to refuse medical treatment. In addition, the proposed Bill on assisted suicide being brought to the Scottish Parliament has given fresh impetus to the debate over whether the laws surrounding these issues should be changed. A report on this is attached as Paper 4.

7.6 Housing and Homelessness

7.6.1 The Council engages with this area of concern ecumenically through Scottish Churches Housing Action. A summary of their current work follows:

Summary of activity, 2008-09

Scottish Churches Housing Action brings together the main Christian denominations, including the Church of Scotland, under the slogan *no room for homelessness!* Its purpose is to stimulate and support the churches in volunteering work to help homeless people; to secure affordable housing from church-owned property; and to provide an awareness-raising and advocacy role with the churches.

In May 2008, Chief Executive Alastair Cameron addressed the General Assembly, seeking reaffirmation of support for the organisation's programme. This was agreed. In discussion, Dr Andrew McLellan drew attention to the situation of people who are homeless on leaving prison, and Churches Housing has since taken up this issue as one of the many on which it is active.

The Churches Homelessness Initiatives Programme, through which volunteering work is developed, was active in the Scottish Borders, East Ayrshire and Argyll during the year, with schemes established in

---

Selkirk, Kilmarnock, Oban, Dunoon and Helensburgh. These mobilise volunteers from a variety of church denominations to provide household necessities to people taking up a tenancy as they move out of homelessness, and providing wellbeing and children's activity packs to homeless people and their families. In Kilmarnock, a befriending scheme was developed, helping break down the loneliness and isolation that result from homelessness.

The Church Property & Housing Programme invites churches to make redundant or under-used property available for affordable housing. This is much-needed, in cities, towns and rural areas, to meet the needs of those who become homeless, and to avoid others becoming homeless. An agreement with the Roman Catholic Diocese of Galloway has led to three properties being made available for this purpose, with the potential to create 55 homes for an estimated 160 people. Similar arrangements are being sought with other church property administrators.

Work has also been undertaken to support the congregations of two churches in Edinburgh in creating opportunities for affordable housing alongside development of new worship spaces; and to assess the viability of a disused church on the Isle of Arran. Churches Housing made a presentation to the conference of the General Trustees in Dunkeld in September, and interest in this work was expressed.

Scottish Churches Housing Action is one of the three partners organising the UK-wide Poverty & Homelessness Action Week, which incorporates both Homelessness Sunday and Poverty Action Sunday. In 2009, the main event was a performance of the play *Voices from the Edge* at the Traverse Theatre in Edinburgh. Devised and performed by Actors for Human Rights, this was based on the words and stories of people with experience of homelessness and poverty. The Edinburgh event was one of twelve theatrical performances held across the UK in the course of the week.

At the opening of Poverty & Homelessness Action Week 2009, Scottish Churches Housing Action published a paper, *Statement on homelessness in a time of recession*. The statement was endorsed by 13 church leaders from a range of denominations, including the Moderator of the General Assembly, Rt Rev David Lunan. It called on governments at both Holyrood and Westminster to co-operate in promoting an increase in new affordable housing as a response to economic difficulty.

7.7 Alcohol, Drugs and Addiction
7.7.1 *Changing Scotland's relationship with alcohol*
7.7.1.1 The Council responded to this Scottish Government consultation. The response is available on the Church and Society website.

7.7.2 Addictions Report
7.7.2.1 A Working Party of the Council has prepared a report looking at the wider questions surrounding addiction, using the lenses of alcohol and drugs in particular. This is attached as Paper 5.

7.8 Peace
7.8.1 The Council participates in the Scottish Government Working Group: "Scotland Without Nuclear Weapons". The group, chaired by the Minister for Parliamentary Affairs, is drawn from across civic society and is examining issues relevant to Trident in Scotland within the current devolution settlement. The remit is:

- In the event of a decision to remove nuclear weapons from HM Naval Base Clyde, to examine the economic impact and to identify options for the development of alternative employment opportunities.
- Explore the various international opinions that exist on the legality of nuclear weapons so far as relevant

to matters within the devolved competence of the Scottish Government.

- Explore the implications of seeking observer status at the Non–Proliferation Treaty meetings and advise the Scottish Government on that process.
- Consider the adequacy of the current licensing and regulatory framework that exists in relation to HM Naval Base Clyde in relation to environmental planning and transport issues.
- Identify good practice elsewhere in the world in developing peace and reconciliation and consider how Scotland might contribute to this work.
- Report to Ministers with advice, within the context of their devolved responsibilities, on a regular basis.

Minutes of the Working Group may be viewed at www.scotland.gov.uk/Topics/People/swnw-working-group/remit

7.8.2 The Council also participates in Scotland's for Peace, and co-sponsored the People's Budget for Peace, which aims to explore the opportunity cost of Trident replacement by suggesting alternative uses for the cost of the investment in renewing our nuclear arsenal. A range of suggestions, including one offered by the Council, may be viewed at www.scotland4peace.org/Budget4Peace/responses.html

7.8.3 There has recently been renewed talk about disarmament, including by UK Parliamentarians. Also, in a letter to "The Times" published on 16 January 2009, Field Marshal Lord Bramall, General Lord Ramsbotham and General Sir Hugh Beach dismiss the UK's nuclear deterrent as "virtually irrelevant". However, the UK Government continues to move towards the renewal of the Trident weapons system in a manner destined to preserve our nuclear status well into the second half of this century.

7.8.4 At a conference held in Edinburgh on 3 February 2009, entitled "Trident and International Law", Judge Christopher Weeramantry, former vice president of the International Court of Justice, opined: *"True, foreign policy and defence are the prerogative of the national government. Yet the safety of the population of Scotland is the concern of Scotland. The health of the Scottish people is the concern of Scotland. The welfare of future generations of its population is the concern of Scotland. The protection of the environment is the concern of Scotland. The purity of the seas and the ocean life around Scotland are the concern of Scotland."* … *"Do the people of Scotland have a right to demonstrate their concern with their safety, their health, their environment, their food chains, their future generations and their cultural inheritance? Modern human rights learning and doctrine would indicate an affirmative answer to these questions."*

7.8.5 The Council, on behalf of the General Assembly, intends to continue to press the UK Government to abandon its policy of holding nuclear weapons.

7.9 Europe

7.9.1 The Church and Society Council continues to support the work of the Church and Society Commission (CSC) of the Conference of European Churches (CEC). The CSC's main office is located in Brussels (with a second, smaller office in Strasbourg) in close proximity to the European Parliament and European Commission. The Churches' Commission for Migrants in Europe (CCME) became part of CEC in 2008. CCME will continue to share the same office building in Brussels as the CSC.

7.9.2 The CSC monitors the European Union and other pan-European institutions. The "no" vote in the Irish referendum of 12 June 2008 on the Lisbon Treaty has created considerable uncertainty as to the future direction of the EU; a second referendum is likely to be held in the autumn of 2009. Coupled with the current economic crisis, the conflict between Russia and Georgia in 2008, disputes with Russia over the importation of gas and conflict in the Middle East, the EU is facing considerable obstacles. The next elections to the European Parliament will be held on 4 June 2009.

7.9.3 Since 2003, the Church of Scotland has supported the secondment of the Rev Matthew Ross as Executive Secretary of the CSC, based in Brussels. This post is also funded by the Presbyterian Church in Ireland, the Methodist Church in Great Britain and The Salvation Army. Matthew's contract will end in 2009 and he has indicated that he wishes to return to parish ministry in Scotland; the stakeholders will review the future of the post.

7.9.4 CEC marks its 50th anniversary in 2009 and will hold its 13th Assembly in Lyon, France, 15-21 July. (The previous assembly was held in Trondheim, Norway, in 2003). A new Church and Society Commission will be appointed following the Lyon Assembly. The former Council Secretary Rev Dr David Sinclair will remain a member of the CSC until the Lyon Assembly; he was also a key speaker at a conference on Churches and Socially Responsible Investment (jointly organised by CEC, Oikocredit and the Evangelical-Lutheran Church of Finland) held in Brussels in 2008. This two-day conference was held within the European Parliament and in Scotland House, the office of the Scottish Government in Brussels.

7.9.5 In October 2008 the Council Secretary Ewan Aitken attended a meeting of the CSC's annual European Church and Society Secretaries' meeting in Leuven, Belgium.

7.9.6 Full details of CEC's work (including the Church and Society Commission's monthly "Brussels Update") can be found on the website: www.cec-kek.org.

7.10   International Affairs
7.10.1   Sri Lanka
An extended report on Sri Lanka is included as Paper 6.

7.10.2   China
7.10.2.1 In view of the interest in and importance of China, the Council has begun work on a report which will be presented to the 2010 General Assembly. The Council is very conscious of the sensitivities about China and is working closely with the Scottish Churches China Group, the Church of Scotland's Council for World Mission and the China Desk of Churches Together in Britain and Ireland to ensure that their expertise informs the report and that the ongoing work of church bodies within China is supported. The Council has begun the process of gathering evidence and is seeking to speak with representatives of the Chinese government, Chinese churches and the Chinese community in Scotland. Given that China is a vast country with such a long history, the Council is focussing its attention on a theological critique of modern China in which concerns such as justice, human rights and stewardship of God's Creation will be given prominence.

7.10.3   Iran
7.10.3.1 The General Assembly received a report last year on Iran. The Deliverance approved by the Assembly encouraged "fellowship with Iranian congregations in Scotland." The Council has been in contact with Iranian Christians in Scotland and looks to develop those links further in the coming months. The Iranian Christian community is not a large one. It has developed largely in Scotland since the dispersal of asylum seekers in the late 1990's. Ministers may come in contact with individual Iranian Christians and the Council would be very happy to help, in any way, to put these Christians in touch with others. The Council recognises that hospitality is a vital part of the witness of the Church. One aspect of this is hospitality as demonstrated in the stewardship of buildings. Emerging Christian communities often need support in finding affordable and appropriate accommodation. Church of Scotland congregations should be mindful not only of the untapped resource that their buildings represent but also of the Christian witness that the sharing of these buildings with other Christians can represent. We look to congregations and presbyteries to develop the hospitality that they extend not only to Iranian Christians but also to all other minority Christian communities.

7.10.4 Ukraine

7.10.4.1 The Moderator met with Mr Bohdan Yaremenko, Consul General in Edinburgh for the Ukraine, during the summer. He was accompanied at this meeting by the Associate Secretary. As part of a wide ranging discussion the Consul was anxious that the world did not forget the killing of over eight million Ukranians in the early 1930s, known as the Holodomor.

7.10.5 Zimbabwe

7.10.5.1 The Council has worked with the World Mission Council and the Moderator throughout the year. A Report is included within the World Mission Report.

7.10.6 Burma/Mynamar

7.10.6.1 The Council continues to view with deep concern the plight of the people of Burma under the present dictatorship. Following the devastating cyclone in May 2008, it supported the call from the World Mission Council for congregations to support the Christian Aid appeal. The former convener, Morag Mylne, commentated that "The apparent inadequacy of the Burmese Government's response only reinforces the view that the regime does not govern in the best interests of its people." The Council notes with deep regret that the military junta continues to hold at least 2,100 political prisoners. In November 2008, more than 215 activists, National League for Democracy party members, Cyclone Nargis relief workers, journalists, monks, and even some of their lawyers were each given draconian sentences of up to 68-years in prison. The need for the UK government to discourage Western companies from investing and operating in Burma remains, as does the urgency of its use of all diplomatic means and resources at its disposal to bring a return of democratic government to Burma.

7.10.7 Israel/Palestine

7.10.7.1 Inter Faith Pilgrimage to Palestine and Israel. The Council was represented, along with the Moderator and the Principal Clerk, in an inter faith pilgrimage group from Scotland drawn from seven faiths which visited Israel and Palestine in July 2008. The aim of the visit, planned by a group including Christian, Jewish and Moslem members, was to reflect on faith in the context of conflict and to begin a process of thinking about how we might engage together more effectively in our own society as a result of this experience. Funding was provided by the Scottish Government and the Church of Scotland, and the group of more than 30 participants represented the Jewish, Moslem, Sikh, Hindu, Buddhist and Baha'i faiths along with Christians from the Church of Scotland, Roman Catholic, Episcopal and The Salvation Army traditions.

7.10.7.2 Staying in St Andrew's Jerusalem and the Scots Hotel in Tiberias, visits were made to sites of importance to the Christian, Jewish, Moslem and Baha'i faiths. Sunday worship in St Andrew's was attended by the entire pilgrimage group, and a significant moment was when prayers were shared across the bullet proof glass between the mosque and synagogue at the tomb of Abraham in Hebron. The Holocaust Memorial at Yad Vashem provided another poignant opportunity for reflection.

7.10.7.3 As well as meeting religious leaders from many communities, the group engaged with Israeli government ministers round the cabinet table in the Knesset, the Israeli parliament, and with a former minister of the Palestinian Authority in Ramallah. In Hebron the group met with representatives of the settler community and with local Palestinians who spoke of the harassment they experience at the settlers' hands.

7.10.7.4 There was also the opportunity to meet with groups engaged in peacemaking, including the Holy Land Trust in Bethlehem which promotes non violence training, and One Voice, which encourages interaction between young Israeli and Palestinian people. The Ecumenical Accompaniment Programme in Palestine and Israel (EAPPI) stands alongside people engaged in peacemaking on both sides, and provided escorts for the visit to Hebron, a place of high tension.

7.10.7.5 The group has met since returning to Scotland to reflect further on what we might do together to further the cause of peace and to consider how faith communities might find common ground here in Scotland, for example in combating poverty. A development of the pilgrimage programme is also under discussion.

7.10.7.6 Since returning from Israel/Palestine the Convener has continued to reflect on the work that can be done to further the cause of peace. To this end the Council has been involved in initial discussions with the World Mission Council and partners on proposals to establish a reconciliation centre, based in Tiberias, drawing on experience in Israel/ Palestine and in the wider world on this issue. These discussions are at a very early stage and further developments will be reported to future General Assemblies

7.10.7.7 One area the group was unable to visit was Gaza. The Council's report to the 2008 General Assembly detailed the deteriorating situation there, quoting a report from Ha'aretz of 19/12/07. "Gaza" it said "is surrounded and starved." It described the high unemployment rate of over 60% and how the number dependant on UN food aid (76%) was the highest proportion of any country in the world. Israel's iron grip on border crossings had drastically reduced the supplies of food and fuel into Gaza, and had a devastating effect on its economy and infrastructure. The article also commented on the tremendous despair, saying "Hatred wins out and the desire to avenge is the only hope." This vengeance took the form of rocket attacks on the southern towns and communities in Israel within range of Gaza, carried out by Hamas militants.

7.10.7.8 The Council has always supported the rights of both Palestinians and Israelis to live without fear or violence, and condemns both the blockade of Gaza and the rocket attacks. In December 2008, Israel launched Operation Cast Lead, citing the rocket attacks as justification for a military attack on Gaza. There was almost universal outrage from the international community at the disproportionate force being used, yet despite international pressure, the attack continued for three weeks, with fierce fighting in densely populated areas. A death toll of about 1,300 Palestinians[2] was reported; many of whom were children. More than 50% of agricultural land was destroyed, as were hundreds of homes; schools and hospitals were attacked and reconstruction costs for the area are estimated by the UN as $1.9bn[3]. The Palestinian death toll was 100 times higher than that of the Israelis. There are moves afoot to bring Israel to account for perpetrating a 'war crime' because of the disproportionality of the attack and the high number of civilian deaths.

7.10.7.9 At the time, the Moderator publicly expressed his sadness at the senseless waste of life, and we condemn the continuing spiral of violence which makes a peaceful and just solution in the Middle East seem ever more distant. We commend to your prayers the efforts of all (including Jews, Israelis and Palestinians) who are working for that just peace.

---

[2] http://news.bbc.co.uk/1/hi/world/middle_east/7849630.stm
[3] http://news.bbc.co.uk/1/hi/world/middle_east/7839075.stm

PAPER 1
GROWING UP IN SCOTLAND TODAY[1]

"The true measure of a nation's standing is how well it attends to its children – their health and safety, their material security, their education and socialization, and their sense of being loved, valued, and included in the families and societies into which they are born".

1.1 In 2007, UNICEF published a "Report Card" on the Wellbeing of Children in Rich Countries, which showed the UK bottom of a league table of "economically advanced nations" based on a range of criteria covering material well-being, health and safety, education, family and peer relationships, behaviour and risks, and subjective well-being. Only in health and safety was the UK outwith the bottom five countries.

1.2 That report – headed with the quotation above – was the trigger for the Church and Society Council to establish a working group to look at "Growing Up in Scotland". In addition to members of the Council, the Group has been able to draw on expertise from other denominations, from other parts of the Church's work, from children's charities, and from young people themselves. We have opened up discussions on what's good about growing up in Scotland today, and what's bad; and we have explored what the Church and Government (UK, Scottish and local) can do to help.

---

[1] A summarised version of this report was prepared and published to be launched on the occasion of the Moderator's visit to the Scottish Parliament. With the Council Secretary he met with all the party leaders including the First Minister and had a reception hosted by Karen Whitefield MSP, Convenor of the Parliament's Education and Lifelong Learning Committee. Five young people representing a spectrum of churches and experience spoke about their personal experiences of growing up in Scotland today. Adam Ingram MSP, Minister for Children and Early Years responded to the report and the young people's stories at this event.

2. Context

2.1 This section of the report sets out some key challenges and opportunities faced by children and young people growing up in Scotland. A description of some of the key issues is followed by an analysis of some of the underlying factors that affect children growing up in Scotland.

Over the past couple of years there have been a number of reports that provide useful background information and much of the content of this section is drawn from those reports, namely:

- United Nations Convention on the Rights of the Child: A Report on Implementation of the UN Convention on the Rights of the Child in Scotland 1999 – 2007 (Scottish Executive, 2007)
- The NGO Alternative Report (Scotland) to the United Nations Committee on the Rights of the Child (Scottish Alliance for Children's Rights, 2008)
- UK Children's Commissioners' Report to the UN Committee on the Rights of the Child (2008)
- Report Card 7, Child Poverty in Perspective: An Overview of Child Well-being in Rich Countries (UNICEF, 2007)
- Index of Wellbeing for Children in Scotland (Barnardo's, 2007)
- Factfile 2008-09 (Action for Children in Scotland, 2008)
- The Good Childhood Inquiry (The Children's Society, 2009)

2.2 Key issues
2.2.1 Demographics and key statistics
There are over one million children under the age of 18 living in Scotland, which accounts for approximately 20% of the total population.

2.2.2 By age, the population figures show that there are:
- 275,200 children under the age of 4
- 273,440 between the ages of 5-9
- 302,694 between the ages of 10-14
- 329, 573 between the ages of 15-19[2]

---

[2] General Register Office for Scotland (GROS), Mid-2007 population estimates Scotland, July 2008

2.2.3 Scotland's birth rate has been steadily rising over the past five years with 57,781 births recorded in 2007 (the highest since 1997). 49% of births in 2007 were to unmarried parents.[3]

2.2.4 It is estimated that 1 in 40 children may have a learning disability and that 1 in 250 children will have moderate to profound disabilities that require significant additional support. The number of children with severe and complex disabilities is increasing.[4]

2.2.5 The 2001 census found that 2.32% of the population in Scotland are from a minority (non-white) ethnic group[5]; official figures show that the number of people living in Scotland who were born abroad grew to 255,000 in 2007 from 204,000 in 2004. The most common overseas country of birth in 2007 was Poland followed by Germany, Republic of Ireland, India and the USA. In 2007, 4 out of 5 births in Scotland were to Scots-born mothers.[6]

2.3 Good things about growing up in Scotland

2.3.1 Many of the issues covered in this section are 'problems' that need to be addressed but it is important to recognise that there are many good things about growing up in Scotland. Throughout the country, there are many examples where young people make positive contributions to their communities in relation to social, cultural and environmental matters. The Young Scot awards are now in their 4th year, recognising and celebrating the outstanding achievements of Scotland's Young People through 13 awards, from sports to cultural diversity, democracy and citizenship and volunteering.

2.3.2 The UK Children's Commissioners' report to the UN Committee on the Rights of the Child highlights several other factors that are good about being a child in Scotland, including:

- a strong sense of national identity, openness to immigrants and tolerance of difference
- a cultural expectation of greater autonomy for children at key stages of their life
- a juvenile justice approach, through the children's hearings system, that is focused on the child's best interests rather than punishment
- communities that have embraced asylum seeking families in their midst.

These issues will be examined in more detail later in the report.

---

[3] GROS, Scotland's population 2007: The Registrar General's annual review of demographic trends, August 2008

[4] Scottish Executive, Changing childhoods? The same as you? National Implementation Group: Report of the Children's Sub-Group, April 2006

[5] Scottish Executive, Scotland's Census 2001, February 2003

[6] GROS, Scotland's Population 2007 – The Registrar General's Annual Review of Demographic Trend, August 2008

We conducted conversations with children (at the Children's Assembly), teenagers (via the Youth Assembly) and adults (at the C&S Council conference) around four questions: What's good about growing up in Scotland today? What's bad about growing up in Scotland today? What can the Church do to help? What can the Government do to help? Some of the most striking quotes from the conversations are scattered through the report.

What's good about growing up in Scotland today?

Children's responses included:

(a) Lots of opportunities

(b) Good education

(c) Lots of snow

(d) Wildlife, scenery and views

(e) Lots of good youth clubs and facilities for young people

(f) The people

(g) Health care

(h) Fun places

Young people's responses included:

(a) I've felt more involved in political processes since devolution

(b) Acceptance of difference

(c) School – a lot of encouragement

(d) Activism

(e) Young Scot cards

(f) Good projects with asylum seeker young people

Adult responses included:

(a) Space, trees, beaches

(b) Choices and wider opportunities

(c) Peace

(d) Awareness of other cultures, and global responsibility

(e) Technology and gadgets

(f) More openness between parents and children

(g) Children treated as individuals, with rights

(h) Range of available opportunities

2.4 Health and well-being

2.4.1 Just as the UK ranked last out of 21 industrialised countries in the UNICEF report; so Scotland was ranked next to last out of 24 OECD (Organisation for Economic Co-operation and Development) countries in the Barnardo's Index of Wellbeing for Children report.

2.4.2 Child Poverty:

2.4.2.1 Despite being part of the 5th richest economy in the world, there are extremely high levels of child poverty. The most recent official statistics show that there are 210,000 children in Scotland living in poverty. Save the Children estimates that 90,000 children in Scotland are living in severe poverty[7] with no indication that that figure as reduced in recent years[8].

2.4.2.2 The impact of growing up in poverty is extreme – not just on the experience of growing up but also for children and young people's future life chances.

2.4.2.3 Children growing up in poverty are twice as

---

[7] The definition of poverty used here is those with incomes 60% below the UK median.

[8] The Government do not have a definition for severe poverty. Save the Children defines severe poverty as children living in families surviving on an average of £7,000 a year after housing costs (for a couple with one child). www.savethechildren.org.uk/scotland

likely to die in childhood compared to children in the most affluent areas[9]. In the most deprived areas in 2006 the rate of teenage pregnancies in the under 16 age group was more than four times the rate in the least deprived areas (15.3 and 3.7 respectively).[10]

2.4.2.4 Five year olds in deprived areas are three times more likely to have severe tooth decay[11]. Dental disease in childhood is a significant marker for later poor health and is associated with deprivation and disadvantage.

2.4.2.5 Recent NHS Scotland figures show that a child born in Calton, Glasgow, one of the most deprived areas in Scotland, can only expect to live to 54; is three times as likely to suffer heart disease; and four times more likely to be hospitalised than a child in the city's prosperous western suburbs. A girl born in poverty in Scotland today can expect to die 11 years earlier than a girl born in a better off family. A boy can expect to die 17 years earlier.[12]

2.4.2.6 It is not just physical health that is affected: 30% of children growing up in poverty end up with some sort of emotional disorder compared to 5% from better off households.[13]

2.4.2.7 Children who go to school in a deprived area are four times more likely to leave school without any qualifications. 25% of 16-19 year olds from deprived areas are leaving school and not in any form of education, employment or training. That compares to 10% for the whole of Scotland.[14] Nearly a third of all homeless households in Scotland are households with children; lone parent households make up nearly a quarter of all homeless households.[15]

2.4.3 Sexual health:
2.4.3.1 Rates of teenage pregnancies in Scotland remained relatively stable between 1998 and 2006, but have shown a slight increase since 2001.[16] This is despite a number of Government initiatives including the Respect and Responsibility strategy. The SACR report to the UN Committee on the Rights of the Child raises a number of concerns about the quality and availability of sexual health education, with a particular concern about some of the most marginalised groups of children and young people; those with learning difficulties; looked-after young people; LGBT (lesbian, gay, bisexual, transgender) young people and those from minority ethnic backgrounds.[17]

2.4.4 Mental health:
2.4.4.1 It is estimated that 1 in 10 children aged 5 to 16 have a clinically recognised mental disorder. There have been a number of national initiatives, such as the 'See me…' campaign and Heads Up Scotland, that have sought to address mental health issues affecting young people. The UK Children's Commissioners' Report to the UN Committee on the Rights of the Child found that children and adolescent mental health services are still under resourced and many children and young people requiring specialist treatment such as those who self-harm or who have experienced abuse do not receive this.[18]

---

[9] Information Services Division, Childhood hospital admissions and mortality, March 2008

[10] Information Services Division, Teenage Pregnancy, http://www.isdscotland.org/isd/2071.html

[11] Scotland's National Dental Health Inspections Programme, NDIP Survey 2003, http://www.dundee.ac.uk/dhsru/publications/ndip/DIP2003_det_partb.htm

[12] NHS Scotland, Healthy Life Expectancy in Scotland, March 2004

[13] Office for National Statistics, *The Mental Health of Children and Young People 2004*, 2005. The definition of emotional disorder in this research covers emotional problems involving depression, anxiety and obsessions.

[14] National Statistics, *Annual Population Survey in Scotland 2007: A Compendium of Labour Market Statistics*, June 2008

[15] Scottish Government, Operation of the homeless persons legislation in Scotland: 2007-08, September 2008

[16] Information Services Division, *Teenage Pregnancy*, http://www.isdscotland.org/isd/2071.html

[17] Scottish Alliance for Children's Rights, *The NGO Alternative Report (Scotland) to the United Nations Committee on the Rights of the Child 2008*, 2008

[18] UK Children's Commissioners, *UK Children's Commissioners' Report to*

2.4.4.2 A recent study by the Suicidal Behaviour Research Group based at Stirling University indicated that almost 14% of 15 – 16 year olds in Central Scotland reported having self-harmed; with around 70% of these instances of self-harm taking place within a year of the study[19]. Research has suggested that there is an increase in the levels of self harming and that it tends to be more prevalent amongst girls. The Children's Commissioner has noted that access to treatment and support for children and young people who self harm is sporadic.[20] Suicide rates amongst young men in Scotland are twice that of England and Wales [21]

2.4.4.3 Many young people report experiences of bullying, which accounts for 27% of calls to Childline and was highlighted by many MSPs in a recent Scottish Parliament debate[22]. A report by Beatbullying, the UK's leading anti-bullying charity, found that 1 in 4 young people in the UK who practise a religion have been bullied due to their faith or wearing of religious symbols. In this research, many young people went on to explain that this led them to self harm, drink alcohol or take drugs as a consequence[23].

2.4.4.4 This is an area in which the Church's work could be developed further. The expertise developed by Crossreach through the Sunflower Garden Project represents a significant initiative on which we hope it will be possible to build.

2.4.4.5 We endorse the view of the National Youth Assembly which in 2008 agreed to

1. *Encourage the Church of Scotland to help combat stigma by raising awareness surrounding mental health problems in local congregations and encourage them to form informal support networks.*

2. *Urge the Church of Scotland to ensure that everyone, and in particular key figures in congregations, are aware of the issues surrounding and resources available to people with mental health difficulties and encourage these to be used.*

3. *Suggest that the Church of Scotland provide training and information on mental health issues for those who provide pastoral support, but recognise that there are boundaries and situations where reference to a medical professional is necessary.*

4. *Encourage pastoral support to be available to the families of those suffering from mental health problems, as well as the individuals themselves, while respecting the need for confidentiality.*

5. *Recognise that, although Ministers and others with a pastoral role should be trained and resourced in understanding mental health issues, it would worthwhile to note that they are not mental health experts and should not be expected to be.*

2.4.5 Substance misuse

2.4.5.1 It is estimated that 60,000 children in Scotland are affected by parental drug use and 100,000 affected by parental alcohol abuse,[24] although it is recognised that

---

UN Committee on the Rights of the Child, June 2008

[19] Rory C. O'Connor and Susan Rasmussen, *Self-harm in adolescents: self-report survey in schools in Scotland,* The British Journal of Psychiatry (2009) 194: 68-72

[20] Ibid

[21] Suicide rate in young men in Scotland is twice that in England and Wales, Christie *BMJ*.2001; 323: 888)

[22] Debate on UN Convention on Rights of the Child, Official Report, 6 November 2008.

[23] Beatbullying, *Interfaith Bullying,* November 2008

[24] Scottish Government, *Hidden Harm – Next Steps: Supporting Children?*

these are likely to be under-estimates.[25] Substance abuse impacts on children in a number of ways – physically, emotionally and materially. One of the major difficulties in providing support to children and young people affected this way is the hidden nature of this issue and that young people are not often known to services.

2.4.5.2 In relation to behaviour of young people themselves, research undertaken by the Scottish School Adolescent Lifestyle and Substance Abuse survey (2006) found that:

- 57% of 13 year olds had had an alcoholic drink. Over half of those who had a drink had been drunk at least once.
- 84% of 15 year olds had had an alcoholic drink. 71% of boys and 75% of girls who had a drink had been drunk at least once.[26]

2.4.5.3 The most common age to try drugs for the first time is 16 although 1 in 12 people were younger than 14 when they first did so. In a recent study, 35% of 16 – 19 year olds admitted to taking drugs within the year of the study. This figure compares to 28% of 20 – 24 year olds over the same period.[27]

2.5 Leisure & recreation

Teenage Girls Magazines Report Summary
A survey of five popular magazines for teenage girls, *Sugar, Bliss, Mizz, Shout* and *TeenVogue* was undertaken. The popular stereotype is that media aimed at young people has a negative influence, for example in exacerbating eating disorder problems by promoting models who are too thin. However, a variety of steps have been taken by the different magazines to combat the problem of negative body image. One magazine uses only teenage readers with a variety of body-shapes to model clothes and make-up, whilst another publishes a story of a model's battle with anorexia. The primary purpose of each magazine is entertainment, but these magazines also have an important information-giving role. The questions sent to the problem pages show that the magazines are a trusted source of advice and information on a wide range of topics that affect a teenager's life. Through problem pages, which always publish sources of further advice, information and support, and carefully chosen 'real-life' stories, the magazines enable young readers to explore issues which may affect their lives without preaching or overtly 'teaching'. Life-issues which repeatedly occur across the magazines include mental illness (especially self-harm, eating disorders and depression), family problems, drug and alcohol abuse, bullying and internet misuse.

2.5.1 The lack of things to do or places to go are two of the most common concerns expressed by children and young people. 82% of 7-14 year olds have said that they would rather play outside in gardens and parks than stay in the house and play computer games but the lack of opportunities and a risk-averse culture sees many children restricted to their homes[28]. Conversely, this culture has

---

Working with Parents, May 2006

[25] Susan McVie and Lucy Holmes, *Family Functioning and Substance Use at Ages 12 to 17*, Edinburgh Study of Youth Transitions and Crime no 9, 2005

[26] These figures are based on information disclosed by young people themselves in the Scottish School Adolescent Lifestyle and Substance Abuse survey (2006) survey

[27] Scottish Government, *Drugs Misuse in Scotland: Findings from the 2006 Crime and Victimisation Survey*, 2007

---

[28] British Market Research Bureau, *Playday survey*, 2006

contributed to children often being unable to assess risk and danger[29]. One third of children say that they never play outside. One of the big problems in this area is the reduction and restriction in the number of play areas as a result of land being sold to developers. It is not always the case that new developments give adequate consideration to children's play areas.

2.5.2 The recent Byron Review[30] considered the issues arising from children's use of new technologies. The report concluded that "while new technologies bring incredible opportunities to children and young people, parent's general lack of confidence and awareness is leaving children vulnerable to risks within their digital worlds".

2.5.3 Despite a number of local councils providing free access to leisure facilities to under 12s, many children's access to leisure facilities is often restricted by prohibitive costs and the lack of affordable transport to actually get to the leisure facilities. It is increasingly common to see leisure and retail facilities that have restrictions on young people using their facilities.

2.5.4 However, this is not to say that Scotland's children and young people are devoid of opportunities for participation in leisure activities. The Scout Association has released census figures showing the highest membership for over 20 years, with both girls and boys participating in membership. Over recent years, several new strands of sports have seen a rapid uptake, such as girls football, where there are nearly 50,000 girls participating in primary and secondary schools across Scotland.[31] Skateboarding and the resultant popularity of skateparks is another popular form of recreation, with Skateboard Scotland listing 53 purpose-built skateparks across Scotland,[32] encouraging activity outdoors whilst also encouraging the social aspect to sport.

A Plea from a Church Youth Worker
So often people are ostracised from leisure and recreation facilities and activities through a lack of money or childcare provision. Why can't the Church help out? Why can't the Church help provide good quality childcare so adults can enjoy some time together? Why can't the Church help provide leisure and recreation opportunities, either by helping fund those less fortunate or by providing the service itself? The Church has a wealth of structures, talents, ideas and most importantly people in its service. Imagine the witness to our communities round the country if we selflessly provided a service, in whatever form, that means they can enjoy more time together as families/ groups of friends. There are many good examples of this happening already around the country, and obviously each community has different needs. But this is an avenue of service and outreach the Church needs to invest more in.

2.6 Crime & antisocial behaviour

2.6.1 Most offenders under the age of 16 in Scotland are dealt with by the children's hearings system. In 2007/08 there were 14,506 referrals to the children's reporter on offence grounds. Evidence has shown that there is a core group of 1300 – 1400 young people who are responsible for a disproportionate level of crime and anti-social behaviour. At the same time, it is worth noting that 19,212 children were referred to the reporter in 2007/08 because they were victims of Schedule 1 offences (offences against children, including cruelty, sexual offences, bodily injury and indecent behaviour against children).[33]

---

[29] Play England, *Risk and play: A Literature Review*, July 2008

[30] Department for Children, Schools and families, *Safer Children in a Digital World*, March 2008

[31] Scottish Football Association Annual Review 2008, http://www.scottishfa.co.uk/scottish_football.cfm?curpageid=1014

[32] Skateboard Scotland, http://www.skateboardscotland.com

[33] Scottish Children's Reporter's Administration, *Annual Report 2007/08*, November 2008

2.6.2 There is much concern in society about levels of violence amongst young people. In some communities there is a prevalent gang culture that has a huge impact on children and young people, both as perpetrators of violence and as victims. This is a problem for both boys and girls; with one study reporting that 1 in 3 11- 15 year old girls had been involved in a physical fight in the previous year.[34]

2.6.3 In a UK survey on young people's views on gun and knife crime, 29% of the young people said they had been affected by gun and knife crime and 36% of respondents were worried about gangs in their area.[35] Although young offenders make up a small percentage of the whole population and of the prison population, figures suggest that amongst young offenders there is an increasing trend of knives and other offensive weapons being part of the culture.[36]

2.6.4 Concern and reporting about anti-social behaviour has resulted in a widely held fear of young people by many members of the community. Whilst it is undoubtedly the case that most anti-social behaviour is caused by over 18s[37] there tends to be a disproportionate response aimed at under 18s and a demonisation of young people in the media. A MORI newspaper analysis indicated that media portrayals of young people were disproportionately negative in tone; with 71% media accounts in this category compared to 14% of articles portraying young people in a positive light.[38]

---

[34] The Guardian, *British girls amongst most violent in the world*, 23 January 2006, http://www.guardian.co.uk/education/2006/jan/23/pupil behaviour.schools

[35] Action for Children, *'Step inside our shoes' Young people's views on gun and knife crime*, 2008.

[36] http://www.scottish.parliament.uk/Apps2/Business/PQA/default. aspx?pq=S3W-18700

[37] Fabian Zuleeg et al, *Use of Antisocial Behaviour Orders in Scotland*, Scottish Government, 2007

[38] Ipsos MORI, *Media Image of Young People*, 13 October 2004

What's bad about growing up in Scotland today?

Children's responses included:

(a) Increasing gang culture

(b) Bullying

(c) Global warming

(d) Bagpipes

(e) Fighting and battles

(f) Weather

(g) Gangs

(h) Less kids going to Church

Young people's responses included:

(a) Teaching to test, particularly serious in high performing schools

(b) Mental health difficulties – not much awareness

(c) Teenage drinking culture

(d) Drugs culture – can become a part of your life when you're at a formative stage

Adult responses included:

(a) Insecurity in families

(b) Uncertainty about values and boundaries

(c) Exam pressures

(d) Assumed necessity of alcohol

(e) Pressure to have sex at a young age

(f) Too materialistic

(g) Fear of violence

(h) Loss of social skills and interaction

2.7 Vulnerable and marginalised groups of children and young people

2.7.1 Children who are looked after:

2.7.1.1 The SACR report describes looked after and accommodated children (those who in some sense are in the care of a local authority rather than a parent or parents) and young people as one of the most marginalised and socially excluded groups in Scotland. In 2006 there were 1,638 children looked after in residential settings and 3,731 children looked after by foster carers. Looked after children consistently have lower educational outcomes and are more likely to be excluded from school than the rest of the population. The mental health problems of looked after children are significantly greater than those of the rest of the population, with 45% of children aged 5 – 17 looked after by local authorities found to have a mental disorder.[39] Other statistics show that looked after children are more likely to become offenders and be homeless in later life.[40]

2.7.1.2   A Scottish Executive review of provision in 2006 sought to address the situation in which "some people regard looked after children and young people as a group who both have, and cause, problems". That review also recognised that "the longstanding patterns of particular disadvantage experienced by looked after children require specific and targeted intervention".[41] Yet in 2008, the Minister for Early Years and Children has said that "the way in which we have treated children in public care is a national disgrace". Challenging public perceptions and challenging public services to do better are both, as the Minister has said, crucial to turning this disgraceful situation round.

2.7.1.3   Concerns about the age of leaving care have been raised by the Scottish Commissioner for Children and Young People. Young people often report pressure to leave care at the age of 16 despite legislative and policy provision that strongly advises that young people should be encouraged and supported to stay in care until 18

years of age when their welfare requires it.[42]

2.7.1.4   Grandparents or other extended family members may not always be the answer for families in difficulty. Recent controversies over adoption and fostering by unmarried and same-sex couples may have deflected attention in the Church from the urgent need for more, committed people to offer these specialized forms of support for children whose families are no longer able to give them what they need. We see a role for the Church in encouraging and supporting people to offer this help for children in real need and commend adoption, fostering and befriending to members and congregations.

2.7.2   Children with disabilities:
2.7.2.1   The UK Children's Commissioners' report states that, despite a number of measures in recent years, disabled children experience significant barriers to their rights and are disproportionately affected by other issues such as poverty and access to play. It is estimated that disabled children are three times more likely to be abused than other children. Evidence in 2007 found that 93% of children with learning disabilities in Scotland have been bullied.[43]

2.7.2.2   There is evidence that services for disabled children are often poorly funded and poorly co-ordinated. Particular problems are faced in the transition between child and adult services that result in a lack of continuity of support. Often access to specialist health care and support is based on where the child lives or the ability of the parent or carer to advocate effectively on their child's behalf.[44]

2.7.3   Refugee and asylum seeking children:
2.7.3.1   One of the biggest concerns raised in the recent reports to the UN Committee on the Rights of the

[39] Meltzer et al, *The mental health of young people looked after by local authorities in Scotland,* The Stationery Office, 2003
[40] SACR, *The NGO Alternative Report (Scotland) to the United Nations Committee on the Rights of the Child,* 2008
[41] Scottish Executive, *Extraordinary Lives: Creating A Positive Future For Looked After Children and Young People in Scotland,* September 2006

[42] Scottish Commissioner for Children and Young People, *Sweet 16? The Age of Leaving Care in Scotland,* March 2008
[43] Enable Scotland, *Speak Up, The Bullying of Children with Learning Disabilities,* 2007
[44] Kirsten Stalker, *Foundations: Young Disabled People moving into adulthood in Scotland,* Joseph Rowantree Foundation, November 2002

Child has been the situation facing refugee and asylum seeking children. It is estimated that there are 10,000 asylum seekers and refugees in Scotland, the majority of whom live in Glasgow. There has been widespread condemnation within Scottish society around some of the UK wide policies such as detention of children, dawn raids and removal processes. The churches have been a leading voice in this campaign. Support for children during the asylum processes is often seen as inadequate, particularly given that many are dealing with traumatic experiences.[45]

2.7.3.2 Families are denied access to basic services and benefits. Asylum seeker parents are not allowed to work and are only entitled to 70% of social security benefits. Many asylum seeking families face destitution. Unaccompanied children seeking asylum are particularly vulnerable and there are major concerns about the processing of their claims and the support that is available for them.[46]

2.7.3.3 A sign of the effectiveness of campaigning on this issue was seen when Jim Murphy announced a pilot aimed at ending the incarceration of young people at Dungavel detention centre. He said, "This is a trial based on concerns raised, in particular by the churches in Scotland."

2.7.3.4 We are proud to be part of a country where our young people have bravely spoken up for their school friends who are victims of dawn raids, and to be part of a Church whose pressure to end the detention of children and families seeking refuge here has prompted the Secretary of State to look for alternatives. We welcome, too, the commitment of the Scottish Government to ensuring that these vulnerable children have access to the public services (health, education, housing, etc) which they need.

2.7.4 Trafficked children:
2.7.4.1 There is limited official data that records the number of children who have been trafficked into Scotland but qualitative evidence shows that it does happen and that, even when identified, these children are not adequately supported and protected by local authorities.[47]

2.8 Child Protection
2.8.1 As at March 2008, 2,437 children in Scotland were on the child protection registers, a decrease of 6% on the previous year. There were a similar number of boys and girls and just over 80% of those children were under 11 years old. The number of registrations on to child protection registers as a result of emotional abuse were up by 12%, for sexual abuse were down by 30%, for physical neglect were down by 17%, and for physical injury were down by 8%. More than 80% of referrals to the children's reporter were on care and protection grounds.[48]

2.8.2 In 2006, Childline Scotland counselled more than 29,000 children and young people. 27% of the calls were about bullying, 11% were in relation to physical abuse, and 9% in relation to sexual abuse. Figures from Childline Scotland in February 2009 showed that calls to the service about sexual abuse have gone up by nearly 50% in three years, with ChildLine in Scotland counselling 2,849 youngsters about the issue last year, more than at any other time in the service's 18 year history.[49]

---

[45] P Hopkins and M Hill, *This is a good place to live and think about the future… The needs and experiences of unaccompanied asylum-seeking children in Scotland,* Scottish Refugee Council, March 2006
[46] Ibid

[47] Save the Children, *A Hidden Trade: Child trafficking research in Scotland 2005/6,* 2007
[48] Scottish Government. *Child Protection statistics 2007/08,* September 2008
[49] Press Association, February 2009.

3. Underlying factors

3.1 The picture outlined in the previous section sets out some of the main issues affecting children and young people. It is also important to consider some of the underlying social and cultural factors that provide the context for the situation facing children growing up in Scotland today. There is no doubt that the experience of growing up in Scotland in the 21st century is markedly different from previous generations. In order to consider the appropriate responses for the Church and for Government, some of these underlying factors will need to be addressed.

3.2 A review of any day's media in Scotland would demonstrate the extremes of how children are viewed in our society. Children are often portrayed as a 'problem' where they are the cause of antisocial behaviour and disruption to communities; a recent Barnardo's report found that 41% of adults thought children were increasingly dangerous both to each other and to others[50]. Yet Victim Support point out that less than 1.5% of young people commit crime.[51]

3.3 The UN Committee on the Rights of the Child has also expressed concern at "the general climate of intolerance and negative public attitudes towards children, especially adolescents, which appears to exist in the (UK), including in the media, and may be often the underlying cause of further infringements of their rights". Many of our young people feel that adults routinely treat them with a mixture of fear, suspicion and hostility, and it is not hard to see how such attitudes can become self-fulfilling. Churches have a role in countering this culture – we are aware of good examples where this is happening; and Governments must also resist a temptation to look for easy votes in reinforcing such stereotypes. For both, this goes well beyond "hug a hoodie", but it is a challenge we can respond to in partnership with young people.

3.4 A practical proposal that the Church and Society Council would like to take forward is bringing young people from the Church together with journalists and press officers to challenge stereotypes and break down barriers by introducing a human face and tell positive stories.

3.5 On the other hand, deeply disturbing stories of child neglect and abuse understandably prompt demands to ensure that this cannot happen. This can lead to pressure on social workers and others to remove children from parental homes where there seems to be a risk of abuse, yet good decision-making in such circumstances is unlikely to come from a knee-jerk response to media headlines; nor will it come without investment of skilled and caring time. This is a complex area that demands a case by case response, specific to the child's context and with the child's best interests firmly at the centre.

3.6 For too many children, family life is blighted by a drug problem affecting one or both parents. Here again, the best interests of the children can be a guiding principle but do not provide an easy answer. The recognition of the increasing role of grandparents and others through the Scottish Government's support for kinship care is certainly a significant step in the right direction; the Church may also have a role in supporting kinship carers through pastoral care and practical help.

3.7 There is also a perception that there are areas in which the state has taken over the role of the parent, often to the detriment of the child and his/her development. For example the debate that followed a mother of three pregnant daughters all under sixteen, who said that it was the school's responsibility to teach her children sex education[52]. It is these kinds of attitudes that mean for some, the cumulative effect of policies on healthy eating, child protection, physical punishment and sex education has been to diminish parental responsibilities through

---

[50] Barnardo's Scotland , *Scottish Crime and Victimisation Survey*, 2008.
[51] Victim Support Scotland, *Parents and Carers of Young Victims of Youth Crime*, http://www.crimeandyoungpeople.net/c_parentsandcarers.htm

[52] http://news.bbc.co.uk/1/hi/talking_point/4574991.stm

their replacement by Government action. Clearly, it is very difficult to achieve the correct balance between helping parents and taking over or diminishing their role.

3.8 Cultural attitudes towards children in Scotland often work against the realisation of a situation where children generally feel valued, respected and loved by society. Often, the best interests of children are not always paramount. An example from within the Christian community would be in some churches where the priorities of the property committee and the youth club are in conflict. In wider society an example would be the message sent out to all young people about how they are viewed by signs on shop doorways saying 'only two teenagers at a time'.

3.9 Family breakdown, changing workforce patterns and the resultant impact on childcare arrangements provide an extremely challenging set of pressures on parents. In many families grandparents and extended family members play an increasingly important role in the care of children. The Good Childhood Inquiry suggested that while grandparents do more to help develop a baby's vocabulary, they may struggle to provide the other educational and social experiences infants need. Many other families are geographically separated from this potential source of additional support and do not always find support from other people within their communities. It is estimated that 13,500 children in Scotland a year are affected by the imprisonment of a parent, but it is recognised that this is likely to be an underestimate. [53]

3.10 In addition to the changing nature of family arrangements, there is little doubt that children and young people are today facing pressures and challenges

that didn't exist for previous generations. The availability and prevalence of illegal drugs and permissive attitudes towards sexual behaviour are some examples of issues that didn't exist for many children growing up 60 years ago. New technologies offer up great opportunities but also pose new threats. The internet, the pervasiveness of media and modern 'celebrity' culture bring additional pressures on young people in relation to their looks, their actions, their social interactions and their aspirations. At the same time, children and young people have more access to information and knowledge than any other previous generation and there are a range of examples where modern media can act as a positive influence.

3.11 The Scottish education system still has a strong international reputation and it is one area where Scotland continues to rank highly in international comparisons. However, the most recent OECD Programme for International Student Assessment showed that Scotland's international ranking had dropped since 2003. A specially commissioned report from the OECD looking at performance of Scotland's schools highlighted serious challenges including closing the opportunity gap and reducing the number of young people leaving schools with minimal or no qualifications. There are other countries which are more successful in educating children from disadvantaged backgrounds it reported, saying, "Who you are in Scotland is far more important than what school you attend, and at present Scottish schools are not strong enough to ensure who you are does not count."[54]

3.12 The time spent in school has a huge potential to influence and shape children's lives. There has been a notable shift in the style and emphasis of the education system in recent years. Although bullying and school exclusions remain as areas of concern, there have been many positive developments. There are increasing examples of schools that give priority to listening to and

[53] Scotland's Commissioner for Children and Young People, *Not Seen. Not Heard. Not Guilty. The rights and status of the children of prisoners in Scotland*, (2008). An Action for Prisoners' Families Parliamentary Briefing December 2007 noted that more children in any one year were affected by imprisonment of a parent than were affected by parents divorcing.

[54] OECD, *Review of the Quality and Equity of Education Outcomes in Scotland*, December 2007.

respecting children's opinions about their lessons and the running of the school, particularly in primary schools.

3.13   Despite this increasing willingness to listen to children in school and other settings, questions remain as to how much children's views are acted upon. The meaningful involvement of children and young people in decisions that affect them is a key indicator of the willingness of any organisation to give proper recognition to children as key participants in activities rather than recipients of a service.

3.14   The challenge to society as a whole is how to ensure a change in attitudes towards children and young people that provides a context and environment that gives value and respect to the lives of every child. Each of the factors considered above applies to Church settings as much as it does to the rest of our communities. The challenge for the Church is to consider whether it should be practising and demonstrating an alternative approach to children and young people.

4.   The Response
4.1 Government response: Overview of Government policy.
4.1.1   Whilst the Scottish Government has responsibility for many of the issues affecting children and young people, the UK Government still has a key role in relation to issues such as child poverty and immigration. Local Government has a key role in the delivery of services for children and young people and, as a result of the concordat between local authorities and the Scottish Government, has an increasingly greater role in the development of national and local policy. This section considers the response by the UK Government, Scottish Government and local authorities.

4.1.2   Since the opening of the Scottish parliament in 1999, there has been a significant amount of policy and legislative activity in Scotland aimed at improving the lives of children and young people. However, as evidenced in

section 1, many challenges remain to improving children's experience of growing up in Scotland.

4.1.3   The Scottish Government have set out their ministerial vision for Scotland's Children as:
"In order to become successful learners, confident individuals, effective contributors and responsible citizens: all children and young people need to be safe, nurtured, active, healthy, achieving, included, respected and responsible[55]".

4.1.4   This vision provides the basis for all Scottish Government action and policy in relation to children and young people.

4.1.5   There have been efforts to address the lack of joint working in the delivery of public services for children and young people. The issues identified in the Scottish Executive's For Scotland's Children report (2003) have led to increased support for local authorities to join up children's services and this approach has been further developed through the Getting it Right for Every Child programme. The Child Protection system reform programme completed in 2006 has established a system based around a children's charter[56] and a framework of national standards[57]. There has been improved regulation and inspection of services and a commitment to developing professionals who work with children and young people. Legislation and policy has also been implemented across the country to ensure the suitability of anyone who may take on a childcare responsibility in either a paid or a voluntary capacity.

4.1.6   However, there have been concerns that the levels of bureaucracy, delay and some confusion as to

---

[55] Scottish Government, *Vision of Scotland's Ministers for all Scottish children*, March 2007
[56] Scottish Government, *Protecting Children and Young People: The Charter*, March 2004
[57] Scottish Government, *Protecting Children and Young People: Framework for Standards*, March 2004

what is required in this process (especially with regard to separate disclosure for people who have more than one role) may be disincentives to volunteering.

4.1.7 We welcome the recent recommendation based on data from the Scottish Household survey that "To overcome barriers people face to volunteering (the Scottish Government should) simplify the Disclosure Scotland process – for example, removing the need to apply for a separate disclosure check for every voluntary position applied for, but, rather, place a time limit on when a single disclosure check (that is valid for any voluntary position applied for) requires to be updated."[58]

4.1.8 A recent survey by the Mission and Discipleship council found 6,348 volunteers working with young people in Church of Scotland congregations, an average of 9.7 per congregation. The Church has made a significant investment in ensuring that we have a safeguarding structure which not only complies with the law but seeks to be an exemplar of good practice. Alongside that is the challenge of recruiting, training and supporting volunteers in working with children and young people, to ensure that there remains a range of activities in which young people can safely participate.

4.1.9 For the Government, too, there is the challenge of building a system which goes beyond ticking boxes to effective protection of children while not deterring genuine and able people from volunteering. As the Children's Commissioner has said "Fear among adults of contact with children and young people has created an unhealthy climate that limits opportunities for play and hampers healthy development".

4.1.10 Within education, there has been a programme of improving schools following the Standards in Scotland's Schools, *etc* Act 2000, including a major review of the

curriculum (Curriculum for Excellence). A new system to assist children with additional support needs has been introduced. In the early years, there is now a guarantee of half time nursery provision for every 3 and 4 year old. These developments have been monitored and broadly welcomed by the Council's Education Committee.

4.1.11 One initiative which has proved extremely successful is the development of nurture rooms in a pilot project in some Scottish primary schools. Nurture rooms offer pupils a secure base with input and support from two adults, focused, small group support for part of the week, and opportunities to develop the skills necessary for good learning. This child-focused support will usually last a maximum of four terms, and seeks to improve children's ability to engage in learning.

4.1.12 Children and young people have featured prominently in many of the Government's policies to improve health. The Health-Promoting Schools initiative and Hungry for Success have now been followed by the commitment to roll out free nutritious school meals to all primary one to three children. The Church has supported the "Free School Meals" campaign led by the Child Poverty Action Group and welcomes this as a significant step forward.

4.1.13 The sexual health strategy, the national programme for improving mental health and well-being, and the report of the ministerial task force on health inequalities all include action and recommendations relating to children and young people.

4.1.14 Other initiatives include reform of the adoption and fostering systems and provision for children who are looked after, including young people who are leaving care; the implementation of a national youth work strategy; and measures to address antisocial behaviour by children and young people.

4.1.15 Both the UK and Scottish Governments have

---

[58] Scottish Government, *Report analysing Scottish Household Survey Data from 2005 and 2006 with respect to volunteering*, January 2008

pledged to end child poverty by 2020 (and halve the numbers in child poverty by 2010). It is evident that the Governments are going to struggle to meet their interim target but the commitment was reinforced in autumn 2008 when the Prime Minister announced his intention to incorporate the 2020 target into legislation.

4.1.16 However, a major focus of the Government strategy has been to encourage and support parents into work and introduce new forms of welfare assistance such as tax credits. One of the implications of this approach is further welfare reform that will withdraw entitlement to some benefits for parents if they are not in employment when their child reaches a certain age. In responding to a recent consultation on welfare reform, the Church has resisted this, on the grounds that:

> *"Responsibility in parenting means making decisions and acting in the best interests of one's child or children; it cannot be automatically assumed that in all circumstances this means seeking paid work. There is increasing recognition of the importance and value of supporting families, and a commitment to family life should be rewarded, not penalised as an impediment to the apparent economic imperative of an 80% employment rate."[59]*

4.1.17 The post of Commissioner for Children and Young People has been created to promote and safeguard the rights of children and young people across Scotland. The first Commissioner, Kathleen Marshall, took office in 2004 and has responsibility to:
- generate widespread awareness and understanding of the rights of children and young people
- consider and review the adequacy and effectiveness of any law, policy and practice as it relates to the rights of children and young people

- promote best practice by service providers
- commission and undertake research on matters relating to the rights of children and young people

4.1.18 The creation of the Commissioner post was widely welcomed by children's charities as an indication of a growing commitment to children's rights by the Scottish Parliament. It is an institution that has already demonstrated its value in drawing attention to breaches of children's rights, ensuring children's voices are heard, and authoritatively challenging Government where it does not go far enough.

4.1.19 It is not possible in this paper to go into detail on all of the legislation and policy that has been introduced over the past 10 years, but it is clear from this overview that a lot of Government time, energy and money have been invested in children and young people. This does however raise a major question about why outcomes have not significantly improved; the challenge remains to ensure the policy frameworks deliver what they say they will. The need to do better is widely recognised across the political spectrum and evidenced by the name of reports such as, "Looked after children and young people: we can and must do better"[60], "Getting it right for every child.[61]"

---

[59] Church of Scotland response to *"No one written off: Reforming welfare to reward responsibility"*, October 2008

[60] Looked after children and young people: we can and must do better, Scottish Executive, January 2007

[61] Scottish Government, *Getting it right for every child*, September 2008

What can Government do to help?

Children's responses included:

(a) Help children to recycle, reduce and re-use

(b) Make Christian youth groups

Young people's responses included:

(a) Engage young people in politics; raise awareness of other ways to be involved beyond voting

Adult responses included:

(a) More resources for positive things

(b) Listen to young people

(c) Build an inclusive, fair Scotland

(d) Extend educational/social opportunity

(e) Improve education for all

(f) Common sense re protection

(g) Stop drugs among children

(h) Build self-esteem

4.2 Recommendations by the UN Committee on the Rights of the Child

4.2.1 In 2008, the UN Committee on the Rights of the Child considered the extent to which the UN Convention on the Rights of the Child is being implemented in the UK. The Committee's concluding observations highlight some of the areas where Governments could make improvements.[62]

4.2.2 At a structural level, the Committee has called on the Governments to bring all legislation in line with the Convention and co-ordinate its implementation, highlighting the need to co-ordinate with local authorities as well. There was a recommendation that the Government "should allocate the maximum extent of available resources for the implementation of child rights, with a special focus on eradicating poverty and reducing inequalities"[63]. One of the main barriers to implementation of the Convention is the lack of awareness about its provisions amongst adults and children.

4.2.3 The issue of negative public attitudes towards children was noted by the UN Committee and 'urgent measures' were recommended to address this concern. In addition, the Committee was concerned about the failure to promote and implement the principle of respect for the views of the child.

4.2.4 Some of the other specific issues where the Committee made recommendations were:

- to reconsider the use of ASBOs for children, and other antisocial behaviour measures such as the mosquito device (a high pitched noise inaudible to adults, used to deter children from congregating *eg* outside supermarkets)
- to prohibit all corporal punishment in the family and promote positive and non-violent forms of discipline
- provide greater assistance for parents and particularly those who face crisis due to poverty
- effective implementation of legislation and services designed to support children with disabilities and develop a national strategy for the inclusion of children with disabilities in society
- additional resources to meet the needs of children with mental health problems
- intensify efforts to ensure young people have access to appropriate sexual health services and sexual health education
- identify root causes of adolescent substance use and take preventative action
- tackle educational inequalities and ensure a truly inclusive education system
- tackle bullying and violence in schools

---

[62] United Nations, *Convention on the Rights of the Child*, October 2008, http://www2.ohchr.org/english/bodies/crc/docs/AdvanceVersions/CRC.C.GBR.CO.4.pdf

[63] Ibid

- guarantee the right of all children, including those with disabilities, to engage in appropriate play and recreational activities
- take action on a number of issues affecting asylum seeking children such as detention, training of staff, guardians for unaccompanied asylum seeking children, and adequate safeguards for children returning to their country of origin
- find out more about sexual exploitation and abuse of children in order to prepare adequate responses
- implement international obligations in respect of trafficked children
- raise the age of criminal responsibility (currently eight, the lowest in Europe)

4.2.5 It will be another five years before the UK faces up to international scrutiny on its performance in relation to children and there is clearly a lot of scope for improvement. The Scottish Government has committed to implementation of the Convention and has begun the process of assessing how best they respond to the Concluding Observations.

4.2.6 Whilst the commitments are welcomed, it is still not clear how additional resources are going to be allocated to children and young people's issues. Until the gap between the policy and practice is addressed it is unlikely that Scotland's children will see an improvement to their outcomes. Meanwhile we welcome the attention given by the Scottish Parliament and Government to these issues and the Scottish Government's response to the Concluding Observations (due to be finalised in March 2009).

4.3 Towards a Theology of Growing Up

4.3.1 What has been sketched above as a picture of growing up in Scotland today is not distinctive to the Church in its perspective, and would be shared by many other groups involved in working with children and families. Do we bring anything distinctive to this discussion as a Church?

4.3.2 Crucially, we bring considerable ongoing experience of working with children and young people. For all the emphasis (inside and outside the Church) on recent decline, the numbers and depth of engagement – in traditional and innovative ways – remain on a very large scale. Nor is it accurate to caricature the Church as engaging solely with middle class young people. Hopefully, the experience of the successes and failures of that work inform not only this report but also much more of our thinking. But we are not unique in that.

4.3.3 We come to this as people of faith – the faith that inspires and challenges our practice. So, in the context already sketched, we explore some pointers from our faith as a contribution to discussion within and beyond the Church.

4.3.4 The Child in the Midst

4.3.4.1 There is a dramatic moment in the gospels when Jesus interrupts a lively debate among the disciples along the lines of "who is the greatest?" Imagine the embarrassed silence when he asks what they've been talking about! Then Jesus puts a child in their midst, and makes them focus, not on themselves, but on the child; paradoxically, he is telling them to stop bickering and grow up.

4.3.4.2 This turning upside down should not have been a surprise to people raised on Old Testament stories like those of Samuel (who heard God's call as a young boy) and David (in whom, as a weak wee boy, God dramatically showed his power); nor to those to whom the promise was given: "a little child shall lead them".

4.3.4.3 Children are neither peripheral nor preliminary; they are central. From the time of the promise to Abraham, they are a sign of hope for the future, but they are also central now. In them, we are to recognise, and welcome, Christ.

4.3.4.4 In *Honouring Children*: the *Human Rights of the*

Child in Christian Perspective, Kathleen Marshall and Paul Parvis conclude a review of Biblical passages involving children:

> "We can see that the image of children in the Gospels is not a particularly sentimental one. It is not primarily a picture of innocence or simplicity or gentleness or even humility. What is stressed is, rather, powerlessness and vulnerability, but also insight, hope and promise."

4.3.4.5 The Kilbrandon report of 1967 emphasised that 'The Children's Panel' was to be about what was best for **that** child. The Children (Scotland) Act of 1995 said, "Every child has the right to be treated as an individual… Children have a right to express their views about any issues or decision affecting them or worrying them. " Still today, the primary concern of any hearing is 'what is best for this child?'[64]

4.3.5 The Child in the Family

4.3.5.1 Churches have traditionally stressed a particular form of family as the primary context for growing up. Christian tradition has put an emphasis, rooted in the Ten Commandments, on parental authority and obedience by children. But "Parental authority is not primary. It does not exist for itself. It exists in order to enable the obligation to nurture and to care"[65]. Indeed parents are cautioned in Ephesians 6:2 "Do not exasperate your children; instead, bring them up in the training and instruction of the Lord".

4.3.5.2 With pragmatic, as much as Biblical, justification, Churches have argued that it is in the care of adults committed to each other in marriage that children are most likely to thrive. Of course, patterns of family life, and of relationships within that, change through the Biblical period, between then and now,

and – most obviously to us – in recent years. Much of that we welcome, while recognising the pressures on family life today. Increasingly, Churches are exploring a variety of ways in which families can be supported, and we highlight what we believe are good examples of this elsewhere in this report.

4.3.5.3 While churches have idealised family life[66]; and while it may be the view of many in the Christian Community that the 'conventional family' is the 'best one'; this must not restrict the reality that there is a great deal of love and support in other forms of family life.

4.3.5.4 It cannot be ignored that 1 in 4 girls and 1 in 6 boys are subjected to some form of sexual abuse and that in more than 75% of cases the abuse is committed by an adult the child knows and trusts, often a family member.[67] Around 100,000 children in Scotland live with domestic violence.[68]

4.3.5.5 The story of God's dealings with his people clearly does not limit his care to those who live in what we might describe as "conventional families". God's love also works in what we would see as unconventional or dysfunctional families.

4.3.5.6 That too should guide our view of public policy. Our consistent support for "family friendly" policies cannot, for example, mean penalising children of single or unmarried parents. On the contrary, if we see them as disadvantaged thereby, they need more, not less, support. It is because of our commitment to supporting families that we seriously question policies that seek to force single parents into work at an early stage, or wider policies which devalue the importance of rearing children in favour of "economic activity".

---

[64] Scottish Government, *Scotland's Children's Panels: Annual Report 2007*, November 2007

[65] Marshall and Parvis, *Honouring Children*, St.Andrews Press, March 2004

[66] Ibid

[67] STV news, *Adult survivors of Child Abuse*, 29 January 2009, http://news.stv.tv/scotland/71030-adult-survivors-of-child-abuse/

[68] *For Scotland's Children*, Scottish Executive, 2001.

4.3.5.7 Sadly, the increasing prevalence of family break-up has tended to be met with a polarised debate between those who want law and policy to take us back to an idealised bygone age and those who argue for acceptance of a new reality while supporting those affected. A faith-based response must go deeper: asking why more and more families are breaking up and dealing not only with the victims of break-up but with its causes. Churches must also acknowledge and address a generation gap in attitudes towards marriage. The 2009 British Social Attitudes Survey found that 84% of those aged 65 and over agree that 'marriage is still the best kind of relationship', compared with 38% people aged 18-34.[69]

4.3.5.8 Support for parents and families is an area in which there is scope for Churches and Government to work together, in ways which might help to balance the respective roles of state and parents and enhance both. We are aware of examples of good practice among Churches around the country (the Star Project in Paisley (see case study box); 'New Opportunities' in Motherwell, the St Andrew's Family Support Service in Dundee, Richmond's Hope in Craigmillar; all funded by the Parish Development Fund) and would hope that more can be done to spread models for this kind of work. Although much of our Church's work is targeted at particular generations, there is scope for bringing people together across these boundaries. We note and support the call from the 2008 Youth Assembly which urged the Church in Scotland "to work towards bridging gaps between social groups, especially young and old, both within and outwith the Church … (believing) that we should celebrate the differences of each group as each has an equal role to play while recognising that different groups have different needs".

4.3.5.9 For Government, "family friendly policies" are not straightforward. We welcome initiatives to extend

flexible working, maternity and paternity leave; but these are accompanied by proposals, through the reform of the benefits system, to force single parents into work. As indicated above, we believe that economic objectives towards full employment should not undermine the value of parental – and other caring – roles. There is a role for the law and for Government policy in valuing and supporting parental roles, and in enhancing and sustaining stable families. While we understand the reluctance to endorse any one model of family life in ways that appear to write off other patterns, that should not prevent positive work, with parents, to support family life.

Supporting Young Families in Dundee

In January 2005, with vision and an enormous leap of faith, St Andrew's Church in Dundee opened its doors weekly for two hours to single parents under twenty-one and their children. In partnership with the Early Years and Childcare Team of Dundee City Council, we provided a free healthy lunch for all followed by an hour of activities which were designed to encourage the mums to interact positively with their children, and give them "time out" via activities such as cooking, crafts, aerobics *etc*.

- The work is very much led by what the mums ask for and includes parenting support, emotional and social support, assistance with housing and financial issues, addressing drug and alcohol misuse, 'back into education' programmes, training, and jobseeking.
- Peer education has been of tremendous value to the young girls, and they have written and produced a five-minute play about their lives from school until now – a fascinating and moving insight into the poverty and isolation the girls face.
- The project is now a registered charity and opens two days a week for four hours. A crèche is provided Monday and Tuesday afternoons to allow parents to attend literacy, numeracy, and IT classes. They are

---

[69] National Centre for Social Research, *British Social Attitudes Survey*, January 2009

> seeking funding to employ two crèche workers for Friday mornings, allowing Sue, the Team Leader, to address moral and spiritual issues now being raised by the girls, *eg* "Why do you believe in God?" or "What is this Easter thing all about?"
>
> This project is funded and supported by the Parish Development Fund. This information is taken from an article in the PDF newsletter, "PDF 01".

4.3.6 The Child in relationships: Sexuality

4.3.6.1 Such a response must also consider questions of relationships and sexuality. Again, debate has been polarised and sometimes detached from reality; neither the giving of biological and other health information nor the withholding of it will of itself overcome the pressures on young people to experiment sexually before they are "ready". If we value sexual activity as the expression of a committed loving relationship, we need to find ways of commending this to our children, talking with them and equipping them to realise this for themselves.

4.3.6.2 While recognising this as a difficult area, we would encourage the Church at local and national level to deepen its involvement in working with young people – as appropriate to their age – and parents on matters of relationships and sexuality. Some crucial characteristics of helpful material are that they are; (a) designed for a youth work context; (b) imaginative; (c) ethical and relationships-based; (d) facilitative of open discussion, by treating young people – and their diversity – with respect; (e) encouraging of parental involvement; (f) open to a spiritual dimension and; (g) strongly emphasising the need for training of leaders. This is an area that the Council intends to explore further.

4.3.6.3 Recent public debate has focussed on the Scottish Law Commission's proposal to decriminalise consensual sexual relationships between young teenagers of similar ages; a campaign presented this as an erosion of the principle of the age of consent (which was itself the outcome of campaigning by Christian organisations). The Government agreed, not only proposing to retain the law but – in the interests of equality – to apply it to the actions of both girls and boys (currently only the boy commits an offence). While having some sympathy with the view that decriminalising runs the risk of giving out the wrong signals, the Church and Society Council agreed with the Children's Commissioner and others that giving 15 year olds who have sex with each other a criminal record for a sexual offence (with all the implications that carries) is not the way to deal with this. Our response, as a society, must be based on a concern for the welfare of those involved, and that is not well served by criminal provisions which are likely to remain unenforced.

4.3.6.4 We would want to welcome the increasing recognition within the Scottish Government's sexual health strategy (under the title of "respect and responsibility") of the impact of wider social and cultural factors in influencing especially – but not exclusively – young people's behaviour. Because we see this area of promoting young people's sexual health and healthy relationships as not solely the concern of Government, we would also welcome the growing willingness of Government and Health Boards to engage with faith communities in developing policies in this field, while expressing some concern that this good practice is not yet universal across Scotland. We encourage churches to engage in this process.

4.3.6.5 We have also argued, and emphasised in the context of this recent debate on the role of the law in influencing the sexual behaviour of teenagers, that consultation on policies that affect young people must not be reserved for "adults only" but should include – in ways appropriate to their age – the young people who will be affected.

4.3.7   The Child in the wider community: Rights

4.3.7.1   Children are part of a wider community, and growing up is at least partly about learning to live in that community. Perhaps we are more conscious than ever today of the vulnerability of children – to drugs, to violence, to other pressures.

4.3.7.2   In their examination of how Christian tradition views children, Marshall and Parvis conclude that:

> "One strength, one resource of the tradition is its thorough-going commitment to care and nurture. But on the whole the tradition has been more interested in discussing authority and obedience than in discussing care and nurture. And that leaves a problem in need of attention."[70]

4.3.7.3   However, if Christian tradition does contain this "thorough-going commitment to care and nurture", it does not confine that obligation to parents. Marshall and Parvis recognise that, for some, Christian tradition and recognition of children's rights do not sit easily together, but argue for "seeing the obligation to nurture and to care as correlative with a right to be nurtured and cared for; and defining that would have to start with the child".

4.3.7.4   The Christian basis for children's rights lies in the recognition of human beings as bearing the image of God. That does not depend on age or understanding, on maturity or mental or physical capacity. Indeed,

> "It gives priority to the most vulnerable. It lets us take as our paradigm, not those best capable of functioning in society, but those most at risk."[71]

4.3.7.5   We agree with the conclusion of Honouring Children, that a recognition of children as bearers of human rights is helpful from a Christian perspective.

This need not "encourage an attitude of self-seeking confrontation between child and parent and so reflect or even encourage the fragmentation of the family and society". It certainly does not see children as isolated individuals removed from a context of family, community and relationships, but recognises an obligation on wider society to nurture and care for them.

4.3.7.6   We are therefore happy to share with the Children's Commissioner and many of the charities working with children in seeking to respect children's human rights. It has been a matter for concern that the UK Government has placed a reservation[72] on its commitment to the UN Convention on the Rights of the Child, excluding children subject to immigration controls in the UK from its scope. Children who have committed no crime, and are particularly vulnerable, are therefore seized in early morning raids and held in detention centres that are prisons in all but name. We warmly welcome the UK Government's commitment to remove that reservation, and look forward to its implementation.

4.3.7.7   As this report is being written there are proposals to merge the office of the Children's Commissioner with that of the Scottish Human Rights Commission. We endorse the call from the Commissioner, "the Children's Commissioner must remain as a separate and independent organisation if the voice of children and young people in Scotland is to be heard and their rights protected."

4.3.7.8   This focus on children and their rights is one way of expressing our broad concern for the wellbeing of children in all respects. Central to that concern is the scandal of child poverty. Not only is child poverty a scandal in and of itself, but it is tragically bound up with so many of the other social factors that blight children's lives – the impact of drugs, the health inequalities that

---

[70] Marshall and Parvis, *Honouring Children*, St. Andrews Press, March 2004.
[71] Ibid.

[72] The UK entered its reservation when it ratified the Convention in 1991, restricting the rights of children who are subject to immigration control.

mean dramatic differences in life expectancy at birth between children born in neighbouring communities, the higher vulnerability to crime of children in deprived areas, and more.

4.3.7.9 We welcome the cross-party, and indeed cross-Governmental, consensus on the target of eradicating child poverty by 2020, and will continue to work with others to maintain pressure to "keep the promise". The UK Government now plan to embody the target in a statutory obligation. We applaud that ambition, but we join with others in urging a continued focus on the policies needed to fulfil the ambition.

4.3.7.10 While it is good news to learn that "the child poverty rate in Scotland is now among the lowest in the UK at 25%" (a fall of 1/5 since the late 1990s)[73], the figure, and what it represents, remains a scandal. In an economic climate in which mind-boggling sums of money are found at short notice to bale out the failings of our financial institutions, there is a danger that targets such as this may be sidelined or treated – with unconscious irony – as luxuries we cannot afford. There are Biblical as well as humanitarian priorities which insist we cannot afford to ignore or accept the scandal of child poverty in an affluent country.

4.3.7.11 Through the work of the Priority Areas Committee, Faith in Community Scotland and many local congregations, the Church is actively engaging with families and communities living in poverty. In this, and other ways, we are seeking to fulfil the gospel commitment to prioritise our poorest parish communities in directing our resources. The challenge of how the Church effectively plays a part in tackling poverty – and its most scandalous impact on children – is a job for everyone.

---

[73] Peter Kenway, Tom MacInnes and Guy Palmer, *Monitoring Poverty and Social Exclusion in Scotland*, Joseph Rowntree Foundation, November 2008.

4.3.8 The Child in the community of faith: Baptism

4.3.8.1 A key moment in our practical theology of growing up is the baptismal service. Recent forms of the service have sought to make clear the starting point for baptism is the gift of God's grace ("for you, Jesus Christ came into the world …"). It is in response to that grace that we invite parents to make a commitment "to teach your child the truths and duties of the Christian faith and by prayer and example to bring her/him up in the life and worship of the Church". It may be seen as a strength of our tradition that, because these are important commitments for the growth of the child, they are made by the parents.

4.3.8.2 But – as followers of Jesus, who looked beyond his own parents to a community of faith in which he had to grow – we also immediately look beyond the parents, and as a congregation we make a commitment in the baptismal service, to welcome the child and to "live before all God's children in a kindly and Christian way, and to share with them the knowledge and love of Christ". This moment, in which we recognise that the crucial role of parents is not an exclusive one, is where our acceptance of children in the midst of the faith community, and our wider work with them, start.

4.3.8.3 In recent years many Churches have very successfully started having 'Services of Blessing' for parents who struggle with the vows of Baptism. We are aware of a variety of good practice within the Church in emphasising what is happening through both these rituals: a welcoming gift, follow up through the cradle roll, birthday cards, invitations to special services and events, and the involvement of elders and/or children in these services as a way of personalising the shared commitment. If we hope that parents will see baptism as more than a formality, we must as a community of faith ensure that we do so as well: "she/he will always be at home in the Christian community and there will always be a place for her/him".

4.3.8.4 While this (and Jesus' stern warning to those who "cause any of these little ones to stumble") clearly means much more than ensuring that children are not harmed within the life of the Church; it includes that as a basic duty. That is why our Churches must be exemplars of good practice in safeguarding children from abuse.

4.3.8.5 That is not to deny that there is a real debate about the impact of a risk-averse culture on children, which we touch on elsewhere in this report. The extra thought and effort required to work carefully with children cannot become an excuse for turning them away; or not doing the work in the first place.

4.3.9 The Child in the Community of Faith: Child Friendly Church

4.3.9.1 Our first aim in presenting this report is to stimulate debate within the Church, particularly when conversations can be held across the generations.

4.3.9.2 As a Church we should view the numbers of children active within the life of our congregations with humility and concern. Yet there remain substantial numbers of young people who are lively parts of the Church, or actively involved in activities rooted in the Church. Research conducted in 2008 identified 16,672 young people aged 12-16 involved in Church of Scotland congregations and 4,383 young adults aged 17-25. [74] They are engaged in activities from traditional Sunday Schools to youth cafes, from after school clubs to uniformed organisations. There are diverse examples of successful new ventures from a high tech Sunday School in rural Dumfriesshire to film-making in a Glasgow housing scheme; many hard-pressed congregations are finding resources to focus on the young people of their parish communities. Many of these activities are carried out in partnership with other organisations and so may not be

fully reflected in the church statistics meaning that in this area the work of the church is under reported.

4.3.9.3 As we have gathered material for his report, we have kept in touch with the Mission and Discipleship Council's staff who support this work. That has convinced us that there are success stories to be shared.

4.3.9.4 We have also listened ecumenically, and we have been impressed by the work carried out in the United Reformed Church in developing the "The Child Friendly Church Award". [75] The URC themselves developed it from its first incarnation in an Anglican diocese.

4.3.9.5 The URC summarise the scheme thus; "The process is a simple and helpful one which will encourage you to look at your work with children and young people and ensure that you are taking account of the needs of these important members of your community and also fulfilling your responsibilities to keep them safe while in your care. Areas covered include: Child Protection; Safe environment; Training & support for leaders; Nurture of children & young people; Child friendly worship; Under 5s; Hearing children's voices; Feedback & evaluation; Your vision for Youth & Children's Work".

4.3.9.6 It is our view that relatively little work would require to be done to make this scheme applicable to the Church of Scotland situation (and the URC are happy to allow us to do that) and we would recommend that the necessary work is carried out to incorporate this useful and encouraging award into our systems, with the potential to bring children and young people to the centre of our ways of being Church.

---

[74] Research conducted by the Mission and Discipleship Council of the Church of Scotland, September 2008.

[75] This model was originally conceived by the Anglican Diocese of Liverpool.

What can Churches do to help?

Children's responses included:

(a) Provide clubs and outings
(b) Encourage children to come to Church
(c) More fundraising projects for charity (like people in poverty)
(d) Summer Sunday School

Young people's responses included:

(a) Charity work
(b) Got to combat trend where one goes to Church as kid and then grows out of it.
(c) Fairtrade groups within schools
(d) Charity work – unique position with volunteers and fundraising
(e) Challenge dogged traditionalism which is very intolerant and dismissive of children

Adult responses included:

(a) Help create community
(b) Affirm people's real, honest experience
(c) Make sermons less boring
(d) Provide appropriate activities and improve quality of religious education
(e) Prophetic voice
(f) Enable young and old to listen to each other
(g) Listen, beyond paying lip service
(h) Make safe places for young people to hang out and ask questions

4.3.10   The Child in the image of God: Spirituality

4.3.10.1   Most, if not all, of the international documents which define the rights of children recognise in some form a right to spiritual development. This is clearly an area of particular concern to the Church. If we are arguing that children have rights because they bear the image of God, then the spiritual dimension of growing up – the dimension that describes their relationship with God – cannot be ignored. For children who grow up in families of faith, the spiritual dimension of life will be embedded into their life together. Those who do not have that kind of family back-ground may only have the opportunity to discover the spiritual dimension of life either through engagement in church based activities or through schools.

4.3.10.2   This case, within the context of education, has been well made in the recently revised ACTS document "A Christian View of Education"[76]:

"The Christian Vision of education is founded upon an understanding of the human person as a unique individual, created in the image of God, worthy of respect and deserving to be nurtured in all his/her God-given talents, for self and for others. Each person, as a unique part of God's creation, deserves to be treated with respect and dignity – in other words, to be loved – for who we are and for what we can become. The purpose of education is to develop the full potential of each person – for our own good and for the good of others. Education should develop all our human capacities – moral, spiritual, emotional, physical and intellectual. It should help us to make meaning out of life and to acquire a sense of purpose in and for life. It should enable us to choose our priorities for life, to develop values and to grow in virtue, and to develop loving relationships with God, with self and with other people."

4.3.10.3   The YMCA and others have also been arguing the case for recognition of the spiritual dimension of youth work within the Scottish Government's youth work strategy.

4.3.10.4   There are widespread pressures, in education and in Government policies, which would reduce growing up to a preparation for life as an economically active

---

[76] Action of Churches together in Scotland Education Group 'A Christian Vision' for Education in Scottish Schools, http://acts-scotland.org/news/news2009/003visoneducation.shtml

consumer. That, we believe, is a recipe for disaster; stunting children's potential. Growing up is about growing, in body, mind and spirit, into the fullness of Christ, about discovering life in all its fullness; anything which narrows that denies both the rights of children and the image of God in them.

4.3.10.5 We do, at the same time, welcome the Government initiative that states that every school must have at least six Religious Observance Assemblies, in addition to traditional celebrations central to the life of the school community.

4.3.10.6 As a Church, we bear witness to a holistic view of young people, resisting anything which reduces them. That includes asserting the crucial spiritual dimensions of education and of youth work.

4.3.11 Growing Up – God isn't finished with me yet

4.3.11.1 At first glance, the New Testament might be seen as equivocal about growing up. On one hand, we are all encouraged to keep growing, in faith, hope and love, into the fullness of Christ; we are to leave childish things behind. Yet, on the other, we are to accept the kingdom with childlike faith. Perhaps this is not so much a contradiction as a challenge: to resist the tendency to assume we have "arrived" as grown-ups in faith and life – God is not finished with us yet.

4.3.11.2 At the heart of that challenge would be valuing children not for what they might become but for who they are and whose image they bear. Then – both personally and together – we can nurture them as they grow.

4.3.11.3 When Oliver James, the psychologist whose book "Affluenza" is a prophetic critique of our consumer society, was recently asked where we can start in building a different world, he said "by attending to the needs of the under 5s"[77]. Or, as, in more Biblical terms, Keith White puts it:

"In leading us to be alongside children He entrusts us with the heart of His mission and kingdom. He warns us of the costs and dangers. But He promises that as we open our hearts to one child, we welcome Christ himself. At the dawn of a new millennium we have an awesome calling to be alongside children at risk, and in the process to reshape the processes, nature and structures of Church, mission and society. If we fail, it is not just children who continue to suffer but civilisation as God sees it. Not only will children fail to have their rightful place, but Jesus himself will be misunderstood and unrecognised. He will have knocked at the door of our souls and fellowships in vain. But when we welcome a child in His name, we have opened our hearts afresh to Him."[78]

PAPER 2
JUSTICE AND MARKETS

1. Introduction

1.1 This report is being prepared in an economic context which is almost unprecedented in the history of the post-union Church of Scotland. Any commentary on recent events has the potential to aim at some obvious targets, both individual and cultural. The culture of greed, the obsession with possessions, the constant juxtaposition of wealth and success, the assumption that all wealth creation is inherently good and, if not morally acceptable, certainly morally neutral, are all easy targets. The actions or inactions of political leaders in assessing the need for scrutiny and regulation and those of the people who

---

[77] Oliver James, *Affluenza*, Vermillion, 2007
[78] Keith White, *A Little Child Shall Lead Them. Rediscovering Children at the Heart of Mission.* Paper presented to the Cutting Edge Conference, De Bron, Holland, 2001

inhabit the board rooms of financial institutions, who apparently built an industry on debt to make money, using financial models they didn't fully understand, are all open to rigorous questioning.

1.2 Important as these issues are, that kind of scrutiny will not, in itself, find the kind of answers which bring about systemic change in the way we as a society understand and engage with our economic system. We need to create a space so that deep, fundamental questions can be asked of the system itself: questions about justice and fairness. Questions which place the needs of humanity at their heart.

- **1.2.1** To provide a meaningful analysis of the seismic changes which have taken place in the global economic situation, changes which are rooted in decisions made in the past 20 and more years, is a task which cannot be done in six months. This report will therefore set out the context for further and deeper reflection, leading to a process where the Church seeks to help create the space where such serious and fundamental discussions can take place over a longer timeframe.
- **1.2.2** There are people in communities up and down the country who are suffering here and now and who cannot wait for longer term reflections which might lead to deep change. They live in communities served by congregations. This report will therefore also lay out some ideas and opportunities, set in a theological framework, as to how congregations might consider their more immediate response to those suffering as a consequence of the global financial crisis.
- **1.2.3** Congregations are gatherings of individual Christians, all of whom are on their own spiritual journey and many of whom will also want to reflect on how they personally respond to the global financial crisis in the here and now. How do Christians apply the Biblical injunctions of justice and fairness to their everyday economic activity? Is it possible to formulate a personal Christian ethic of economics? This report will attempt to lay out how that task might be approached.

1.3 This report thus seeks to set out some guidance for individual Church members, for congregations within the Church, and for wider society, in an effort to identify some ethically desirable actions, and also to outline the form of social conventions which might support their widespread adoption. It seeks to raise questions which have contemporary resonance, systematically exploring related ethical concerns in sufficient depth that it might be a point for reference for future discussion within and beyond the Church.

2. Seeking the Gospel view of Economics

2.1 In recent months it has become commonplace for commentators to suggest that only by going back to the Great Depression of the 1920s and 30s could we find a series of events which were comparable in scale and severity to the market conditions currently being experienced across much of the international financial system.

2.2 The response of the church to the industrial struggles of the 1920s and the social and economic miseries of the Depression years could perhaps best be described as inadequate. This failure has been attributed in part to a lack of compassion for and identification with the poorest and hardest hit sections of Scottish society. However, they were also seen as reflecting a failure on the part of the Church to develop an informed, theological vision of economics which would enable its voice to sound out clearly. They were simply not equipped or prepared to offer a critical analysis, or to bring a prophetic word.

2.3 By the 1930s this nettle had been grasped in a process largely directed by the Scottish ecumenical pioneer and statesman J.H. Oldham, rooted in preparation for the major ecumenical conference of Oxford in 1937. Rev Professor John Baillie of New College was a key Church of Scotland figure in this process and it is notable that at the Oxford Conference, Baillie chose to work in the section considering questions of 'Economic Order' along with R.H. Tawney, V.A. Demant, John MacMurray, T.S. Eliot, Paul Tillich and Reinhold Niebuhr. – an extraordinary concentration of Christian intellects by the standards of any age.

2.4 In addition to the major achievement of the Oxford Conference itself, the processes of preparing for and participating in it were the indispensable foundations for the widely acclaimed work of the Church of Scotland's Baillie Commission during the Second World War[1]. The key statements on economic questions in the reports to General Assembly of 1942 and 1944 must be seen as the fruits of a decade of serious preparatory work and engagement on the part of key figures within the church – both academics such as Baillie and former parish ministers, including George MacLeod, who convened the Commission's Industrial Relations group.

2.5 There are lessons to be drawn from this backward look at the Church's social theology. In particular, that our capacity to speak into a profound economic crisis may need to be developed over time through study, debate, and discussion, and through listening to the voices of the poorest in our society and those who advocate for them. The Assembly should consider seriously what learning from that model and applying a 21st century version of it means in practice.

2.6 This could be helped greatly by the work of Duncan Forrester and the Edinburgh- based Centre for Theology and Public Issues (CTPI). It was the vision of Forrester and his collaborators for a new era of theological engagement with public life which led to a series of theological consultations on public issues from 1984 onwards. This process lay behind the *Just Sharing* report of the Church and Nation Committee. Produced by a working group

chaired by Forrester and presented to Margaret Thatcher in 1988 after her 'Sermon on the Mound' address to the General Assembly, the report became a powerful symbol of the Church's critique of government policy in the 1980s.

2.7 Each of these previous eras called out a profound and hard won theological response from the Church of Scotland as it struggled to move beyond ethical generalities and pious sentiments and to produce a genuinely theological reflection on the economic principles and practice of the day.

2.8 The political and economic situation of 2008-9 demands a similarly serious and detailed response. Over a period of a few months, the international financial system has been shaken to its core by a series of economic crises which have raised profound questions about the structure and character of financial markets, about the effectiveness and seriousness of government regulation of the banking and financial services industries and about the assumed values of 'the market' and 'private enterprise' which had accompanied the so-called triumph of capitalism in the post 1989 world.

3. Capitalism – Roots and Ends

3.1 We believe that a theological understanding of these events is not a peripheral or eccentric reading of them, but is essential to penetrating to the heart of their significance. It is interesting that the language used by economic commentators to describe what is missing in the present system are words such as **trust, faith** and **confidence** – words with deep theological resonances. Theology is not only or even primarily concerned with questions of individual greed and the personal morality of key actors, although it is also concerned with these. In their 2007 study of theology, ethics and economics, Long and Fox remind us that a theological understanding insists on asking fundamental questions about the purpose of our human economies in relation to God's:

---

[1] Please see A. Hastings, et al (1994): *God's will in a time of crisis: A colloquium celebrating the 50th anniversary of the Baillie Commission.* Centre for Theology and Public Issues, University of Edinburgh. http://www.div.ed.ac.uk/fullpublicat_1.html

Theology and social analysis are always already linked. When we are doing theology we are already doing political and economic analysis. When economists are doing economics they are also doing theology. The question is which theology is being done, not if it is being done. Everything is theological.

To use God for political or economic ends is to take God's name in vain. That everything is theological then means something different from this; it means that everything which is creature, by virtue of being creature, bears some sign, some mark, some relation to the Creator and theologians must narrate all those creatures within the divine economy[2].

3.2 The year 2009 has been designated Scotland's Year of Homecoming. This year also brings together several major conferences on Adam Smith linked to the homecoming year[3], and others marking the 500th anniversary of the birth of the Swiss Reformer Jean Calvin.

3.3 Famously, both the sociologist Max Weber and the economic historian R.H. Tawney[4] have explored the connections between religion/ Protestantism and capitalism. Some 100 years after Weber, and 80 years after Tawney, we find ourselves once again at a critical historical moment when the foundations and 'spirit' of capitalism are being weighed and found wanting. In our time, we believe we too must ask searching questions about the role of theology in analysing and evaluating the structure and nature of capitalism. We are conscious that even twelve months ago, a sentence like the previous one which referred directly to 'Capitalism' might have sounded unusual in a way that it does not now. This

change has happened around us in recent months, as public discourse on mainstream media has begun to regularly and openly use the 'C' word in its reporting and debating of 'the credit crunch'. This in itself is significant: a word which by the millennium had largely retreated into the ritual vocabulary of a small minority of the Far Left has suddenly become a serious and even essential term in mass media discourse on the economy. It is a sign of the need for radical analysis, in the sense of analysis which means to get to the 'root' of things; and as Long and Fox remind us, the roots of economics are theological.

3.4 As well as tracing the roots of economic questions, asking questions of fundamental principle about how economics is related to the Creator, we need to also ask about the proper 'end' and goal of economic activity – to ask, that is, what our economies are made for. In his 2008 book *Being Consumed: economics and Christian desire*, William Cavanaugh draws on the Augustinian-Thomist tradition to assert that:

The key question in every transaction is whether or not the transaction contributes to the flourishing of each person involved and this question can only be judged, from a theological point of view, according to the end of human life, which is participation in the life of God[5].

3.5 This focus on ends, and upon the true end of human life, resonates with one of the central concerns of John Baillie from an earlier era of Church of Scotland reports. Baillie frequently invoked the first question in the Shorter Catechism,

What is the chief end of man?[6],

not just as a piece of pious rhetoric, but to insist, as Cavanaugh does, upon the key importance of a

[2] Long, D.S. and N. R. Fox (2007): *Calculated Futures*, Waco, Baylor University Press, p6-7; see also D. S. Long's previous volume *Divine Economy*. Routledge (2000)

[3] 2009 sees the 250th anniversary of the publication of his first book, *The Theory of Moral Sentiments,* in which he first uses the phrase "the invisible hand of the market".

[4] Weber, M. (2008): *The Protestant Ethic and the Spirit of the Capitalism.* IAP; Tawney, R.H. (2008): *Religion And The Rise Of Capitalism*. Hesperides Press.

[5] Cavanaugh (2008): *Being Consumed: economics and Christian desire.* Eerdmans Publishing

[6] Question 1 in *The Shorter Catechism*. Banner of Truth Books (1998) (*The prescribed answer to the question is:* "To glorify God and to enjoy Him forever").

teleological understanding of economics. In this globally historic moment, when both basic and ultimate questions are being asked about economics with renewed urgency, one of the key contributions the Church is called to make is to insist with renewed conviction that there is an end, a goal, a *telos* to all of our economic activity.

4. Confidence Games and Making (Un)Real Money

4.1 Developing a theological understanding of the economic convulsions and market failures which began in 2008 must also involve us in analysis of exchanges and the assumptions which lie behind the day to day workings of postmodern market capitalism. Here, we should remember that Christian theology has a rich tradition of experience in reflecting upon relationships between symbol and reality. Commenting on the current crisis in relation to his recently reissued study of money and markets, *Confidence Games*, theologian Mark Taylor argues that:

> What makes today's crisis of confidence unique is its unprecedented scale, and the threat it poses to the current form of capitalism. In previous forms, industrial and consumer capitalism, people made money by buying and selling labor and material objects. In the modern era of finance capitalism, wealth is created by circulating paper with marks, backed by other symbols and still more symbols behind them, in a regression that is limitless as long as confidence in symbols endures.

> This crisis of confidence goes beyond economics. The financial meltdown is a symptom of a profound crisis in our sense of reality, which is endemic to contemporary society and culture.[7]

---

[7] Taylor, M. C. (2008): *Confidence Games: Money and Markets in a World without Redemption*. University Of Chicago Press. Also http://pressblog. uchicago.edu/2008/11/12/the_economy_is_a_confidence_ga.html

4.2 At an everyday level, many of us will in the past have joked about taking our paper money to the banks and asking them to *"pay the bearer on demand"*. What Taylor reminds us of is the way in which that quaint, archaic inscription on our banknotes marks their function as indeed promissory notes. These 'promises' circulate within a symbolic economy whose "reality" is hugely dependent upon confidence in the stability of what those symbols mean. However, there has been no loss of trust in money in the capitalist system – the classic symptom of loss of trust in money is hyper-inflation, in which case people start bartering. Instead, the current crisis is a crisis of faith. Collateralised debt obligations (CDOs) and other financial instruments held out the promise of certain future returns that have been found wanting. The sub-prime mortgage market held out the promise of home ownership to people that did not have the resources to achieve it.

4.3 The events of 2008 have demonstrated all too clearly what happens to liquidity when this confidence collapses the science of economics is positioned within a broader set of assumptions and stories about 'how things are' and so we need the insights of philosophy and theology in order to get our bearings. Here economics itself, in Long and Fox's terms, needs to be narrated in terms of some larger economy.

4.4 As testimony to this, in times like these the vocabulary of our financial system becomes transparent to us in ways which reveal its profound dependence upon religious and theological concepts: we see through to the *credo* of credit; to the trust factor in trust funds and unit trusts; to the spiritual dimensions of values, worth and securities.

4.5 Taylor highlights three specific developments since the 1970s which have created the conditions in which the current crisis has occurred:
- *The computerisation of financial transactions and the real time instantaneous globalisation of trading networks through the internet has accelerated the speed and*

frequency of trading in ways which have introduced unprecedented potential for volatility and risk.

- *The valorisation or even idolisation of "the market" as a god-like collective intelligence which would always lead to appropriate self-corrections of pricing.*
- *A corresponding retreat from governance, fuelled by a Reaganite insistence that "government is the problem", by a loss of confidence within nation-states about their power to influence globalised flows of capital and by demands from large corporations for "light-touch" regulation.*[7]

4.6 To quote Taylor again:

The current crisis of confidence is part of a broader crisis of values rooted in how we have come to understand reality itself. Time-tested truths are unraveling, and foundations that long seemed firm are crumbling. In contemporary philosophical terms, money has become virtual, unmoored from the "real" economy. Reality, however, doesn't simply disappear. It is repressed only temporarily, eventually returning to disrupt what seemed to replace it.

The challenge is to turn this current threat into a long-term opportunity by fashioning new values and new regulations for a world in which realities are constantly changing and securities will never again be secure.[7]

4.7 It is the calling of the Church in the Public Square to bring light and direction to places of crisis, to aid the search for meaningfulness in the human condition and to offer guidance to a different view of human living. Human relationships and self understandings have become more and more shaped by economic transactions and ideas of wealth and status. In that change, there is a deep sense that the human element has been lost to the transaction part. If our economic system can evolve to a place where there are transactions so complex that no-one, not even those most closely involved, can truly understand them, then it is no surprise that the human consequences of the

risks involved in their failure were either ignored or not considered – or simply not comprehended.

4.8 In classical capitalist terms, trust between banks has now been lost because the vital system of assessing risk and uncertainty was turned on its head. That lack of trust has come because the stage was reached where bundles of unsecured debt were being sold as collateral, against which more debt could be obtained in financial instruments of such complexity that neither borrowers nor lenders knew who owed what to whom. Far from being the way in which human need can be met, the market place has become a house of cards whose collapsing was inevitable because of its own unwillingness to face its excesses – the very excesses which were seen as signs of its success. This collapse came at a huge cost for many people far removed from the decisions which took our financial institutions on that journey. All of us are involved in this process including churches who expected to gain from investments.

5. Economics and Ethics

5.1 This report works within a framework of virtue ethics. This is quite different from the utilitarian analysis typical of economics, in which outcomes are appraised according to some efficiency criterion. Economic analysis does not easily concern itself with the processes by which outcomes are achieved, or the relationships between actors: in order to justify action leading to greater equality of incomes, economic analysis might determine whether this results in an increase in some measure of total utility across society. Whether the outcome is achieved through charitable gifts, recognition of kinship relations (as in the story of Ruth[8]), theft, redistribution of wealth through the tax system or the mediation of the church as the representatives of the poor in Christ is less important, except insofar as the mechanism affects the utility of each of the parties.

---

[8] Ruth 4: 1

5.2 Within a virtue ethical framework, both the justice of the action and the outcome can be analysed. Justice in exchange represents the concept of commutative justice, (giving and receiving equally), while justice in outcomes represents the concept of distributive justice – giving to each their due. The demands of charity and justice often seem to be in opposition to each other.

5.3 Similarly, there may seem to be a tension between the practice of the virtue of temperance or moderation of tastes (in which resources are husbanded carefully to avoid risk), and the practice of the virtue of courage, which in an economic context is epitomised by entrepreneurial business activity intended to create wealth through the exploitation of innovation, on which risk necessarily attends. Such tension can be resolved by allowing for the practice of prudence or practical wisdom: the knowledge, in this case, of how to undertake a business venture so that risk is managed effectively. It is noteworthy that the institutions which seem to have survived the financial crisis better than others are those which resisted the transformation into a "savings bank bolted onto a casino"[9]. By concentrating on the core activities of banking and managing these effectively, they did not share fully in the large profits during the housing boom, but nor have they ended up with their businesses mortgaged, sold off, or closed down. In this sense, they are now seen to have acted virtuously, balancing prudence, courage and temperance.

5.4 The idea of value-free economics always masks beliefs and judgments, but, more importantly, prevents economists from being aware of the importance of the pursuit of virtue. Many economists understand that the belief that economics can be constructed without reference to values fails since some values are necessarily embedded in the account of human behaviour which reduces it to the simple pursuit of self-interest, unaffected by social norms or moral principles.

6.   A response

6.1 All of the foregoing demands a response which challenges all those who are involved – Governments and financiers, policy makers and the public – to change how they see the act of economic exchange in meeting human need. The response needs to explore what can be achieved through regulation and legislation along with the reworking of the voluntary commitments such as the financial sector's Cadbury Code[10]. It must deal with the issues of corporate social responsibility encompassing not simply charitable giving by companies, but by taking account of the consequences of their actions. The ethics of risk and the concept of improving the "social capital" of a business should be measured alongside its carbon footprint and its "bottom line" profit or loss[11]. The response needs to name injustice and recognise the power of forgiveness; it must help the nation review and re-articulate what it wants as the ethical drivers of economic decision-making and the place of wealth creation in our political and social priorities.

6.2 It is a significant task of the Church to be one of the spaces and places where that response is shaped. Not in order that the response is the Church's, but that the Church, in speaking prophetically and calling for justice, is engaging with those who have the power to make those words a reality. Our prophetic role to the nation is to name the kind of mistakes, including our own, which have taken us to where we now are. Our call for justice will be lost to the wind if it is not backed by action and witness. That is why this report recommends that the General Assembly uses this coming year to prepare a proposal and remit for a significant and broad based commission on a new perspective on the role of economics and society, to be presented to the 2010 Assembly. This might take the form

---

[9] Dr R Mochrie 2008 Personal Communication

[10] Report of the Committee on the Financial Aspects of Corporate Governance: The Code of Best Practice (Cadbury Code) – 1 December 1992.

[11] See, for example, http://www.transformingbusiness.net/

of preliminary conferences, drawing on expertise from within and outwith the Christian community, including leaders from business and industry, government, the Trades Unions, the financial sector, Churches and other interested parties in Scotland.

6.3 It is important that this be seen at the outset as dialogue leading to action. If the 2010 Assembly agrees to this commission, it would aim to give an interim report in 2011 and full report in 2012.

7.   Witnessing the Gospel view of Economics

7.1 From earliest times the story of God's people has called us over and over again to live responsibly with compassion. This applies as equally to our economics as it does to every other part of our lives. Throughout the Hebrew Bible the people were instructed to care for the widow, orphan and stranger, which means everyone in need. When they forgot they were called to account by the prophets. Justice pervades the entire Hebrew Bible, justice for all in every part of life, it is a central tenet to the law as well as the prophets. No one left out, all of us called to common action that builds a caring, responsible, just community. In the face of their failure the people were reminded of the call to love neighbour and stranger.

7.2 When Jesus talked of loving your neighbour and the stranger he was reminding us that there are not any no go areas for God. Even economics matters to God. When he touched the sores of those affected by leprosy he was reminding us that no-one should be left out, no matter how much we might struggle to see what it is we can do to help. When he healed the man lowered through the roof he reminded us that common action to help those who are struggling brings results far greater than we might otherwise have anticipated.[12]

---

[12] Mark 12: 31; Mark 1: 41; Mark 2: 1- 12

8.   Virtue and efficiency

8.1 Throughout its history, the church has tended to have an uneasy relationship with commercial activity. Augustine argued that, as the fall was absolute, and so man was inherently selfish, it was impossible for a Christian to be a merchant. The church sought to regulate commercial behaviour very severely, most famously by treating the charging of interest as the sin of usury for many centuries.

8.2 It is central to Calvinist theology that the signs of grace include a desire to do good works, which might be interpreted here as seeking to develop a virtuous disposition, not merely across spiritual practices but also in managing and using material resources. In common with other theological traditions, it emphasises the contingent nature of property rights – especially through use, the need for charity, and the strength of the ties of obligation which bind societies together.

8.3 Given his role in church leadership, it is easy to overlook the extent to which Thomas Chalmers, first as Professor of Theology at St Andrews, and then of Moral Philosophy at Edinburgh, developed a political economy in which can be discerned the influences of both the Scottish Reformation and the Scottish Enlightenment. Chalmers adopted much of the apparatus of Adam Smith, but presumed the necessity of religious institutions as mediators of social interactions at a local, as well as a national level. He believed that the guarantee of a modest stipend enabled the minister of a parish to be financially independent of his listeners, while the conditions under which the stipend was made available were sufficiently strict to ensure diligent performance of duties. For Smith, as for Chalmers, a Church minister was an important member of every community: the role of the minister was primarily relational, addressing the needs of both individuals and the community of the parish to whose charge he had been admitted.

8.4 The ideas of this period continue to shape thinking about economics. In particular, Adam Smith's conception of the social order has largely been carried forward to the present day: the self-interested actions of individuals create a spontaneous order through operation of markets in which free exchange occurs. The discipline of the market tends to cause free exchange also to be fair, and to ensure that society as a whole enjoys benefits. But Smith recognised that self-interest was constrained by social convention and by moral sentiments, and that there were tendencies in market behaviour that could prevent the outcome of social order, specifically the natural efforts by producers to limit competition (what would now be called economic power).

8.5 The Scottish Enlightenment tradition placed much emphasis on processes (how work is organised, how social relations are organised, etc) as being as important as, if not more important than, some end state defined in monetary terms. It would be wrong to increase wealth by processes which undermine the moral fabric of society, even if the wealth might be used to enhance the moral fabric of society. Smith's vision of the role of the state encompassed the provision of education to reduce alienation in the work force.

8.6 Chalmers developed these concepts extensively. Indeed, for Chalmers, there was no useful distinction between economic means and ethical ends. His solution to poverty lay in moral education, designed to prompt both greater charitable giving, and self-help among the poor. Rather than taking human goals as given, Chalmers argued that moral education could transform goals in support of social welfare. For Chalmers, the small community of the religious parish was the primary organisational unit of society. At the centre of the parish, the minister worked to encourage attention to the religious life, actively visiting parishioners, and managing a kind of social work within the parish. He argued in favour of private mechanisms, prompted by charitable impulses, but overseen by the Kirk Session, as a more effective mechanism for poor relief.

8.7 In addition, there are numerous examples of the social involvement of associates of Chalmers; for example:
- **Thomas Guthrie**, with his 'ragged schools,' which brought elementary education to many slum areas of Edinburgh
- **James Begg**, who founded the Edinburgh Cooperative Housing Company, to provide affordable housing for the working classes in many areas of the city
- **Henry Duncan** of Ruthwell, who established the first savings bank
- **Norman MacLeod** of the Barony, who undertook extensive social work schemes in central Glasgow

8.8 These and many others demonstrated the capacity of the Church to initiate social action. By the end of the nineteenth century, Archibald Charteris, through his efforts as Convenor of the Committee on Life and Work, had revived the diaconate, partly to enable women to realize their sense of vocation, but creating a primitive form of social work department. In the twentieth century, we see another attempt to revitalise the work of the Church through its parochial system in George McLeod's ministry in Govan, which developed into the community based theology of the Iona Community.

9. Today's church
9.1 While there were substantial theological developments across the 19th century, a common feature of this work has been a concentration on the Church as a local agent of change, with ministers interpreting their charge to a parish as the basis for engagement with the whole community, recognising that pastoral care cannot simply be restricted to the spiritual, but must also engage with the secular.

9.2 As the national Church, the Church of Scotland remains committed to a local ministry across the whole country. We believe that such a ministry has many strengths, not only in the capacity to represent the interests of all sections of society, but also in grounding ministry in locality so as to maximise its role. The community of practice which we hope will emerge from discussions around this paper should be able to relate to practical problems of everyday life, grounded in the Church's tradition of prudence – in the sense of wise management of resources – to address the needs of individuals, communities and organisations, providing a distinctive, anti-utilitarian voice in public discourse, reinforced by practical action embedded in parish life.

9.3 Amongst a wide range of practical responses to need, local Church of Scotland congregations – frequently in partnership with others – have developed a huge range of highly focused work throughout its history. In the most recent times this has included:

- **9.3.1 Orbiston Neighbourhood Centre** (Bellshill) where the local church building has served as a community centre since 1995, catering for more than 1,000 people every week through a wide range of community-led programmes.
- **9.3.2 Richmond's Hope** (Craigmillar) where a nationally recognised facility for children who have suffered traumatic losses in their families has grown out of the local congregation's response to the death of a young baby in the local community.
- **9.3.3 The Village Storytelling Centre** (Pollok) which uses the ancient skill of storytelling to enable people of all generations to recognize shared values and to celebrate creativity and diversity.
- **9.3.4 Bridging the Gap** (Gorbals) which was asked by the local community to coordinate its response to the increased numbers of asylum seekers and refugees who came to live in the Gorbals and is now responsible for a range of highly effective mentoring and integration programmes.

9.4 The Church of Scotland's Presbyterian roots have created a church built on collective interdependence. In living out our commitment to being a national Church with every inch of the nation in a parish, we have what might described as a "branch office" in every community – achieved by those with more subsidising those with less so that all might have the same opportunities[13]. Many congregations are at the heart of areas of particular concern and fragility, such as Priority Areas (PAs), transition towns or rural areas; the kirk has a skilled workforce, a motivated volunteer base, and a clear call to be salt and light in a needy world. It has buildings in strategic places, a voice which still carries considerable authority, and a compassion for those in need. Add in the congregations of all the other denominations in Scotland and it becomes understandable why Faith in Community Scotland should estimate that faith communities are already contributing £60m a year into their local economies.

9.5 At the time of the greatest financial and economic uncertainty in decades, the perspective and contribution of the Church at local level has taken on a new relevance. Churches can and do, must and will, give a lead in helping people to respond to the economic crisis. There will be opportunities for a congregation to embark on a new journey, with real potential for the Christian community to play a significant role in both supporting the victims of the global economic crisis and to be a witness to another way of using the resources God has given us all.

10. Holding out the word of life

10.1 While holding in focus the spiritual aspects of their mission, the first practical step for many churches will be to offer shelter from the economic fall-out. The lives of individuals and of whole communities will need to be rebuilt and healed.

10.2 For those Churches who want to take this route as a way of serving their community there are a huge number of examples of good practice from parishes across Britain. Preparation for action needs to begin with theological reflections and a practical audit.

---

[13] 2 Cor. 8: 13

10.3 Congregations need to look at the resources they have, the issues facing their communities, and the reasons why they must act. Faith in Community Scotland offers an auditing tool that can be shared by a number of neighbouring congregations, which can be a particularly effective way of richer congregations helping their less well-off neighbours, thus forming the basis of a real partnership between congregations in different socio-economic settings. Church Action on Poverty's (CAP) 'Just Church' series of materials is also a helpful tool in this regard. They include 'Just Money', offering an interactive journey through financial decision-making. Other churches around Scotland are affiliating to Christians Against Poverty, a campaign group and debt counseling charity which runs a three-week 'Money Management' course.

- **10.3.1** It was thinking such as this which led a number of congregations, including Irvine Fullerton and Holy Trinity Wester Hailes to develop more active work with Christians Against Poverty.
- **10.3.2** Further afield, the Church of England (C of E) has promoted 'credit crunch evenings', and in early 2008 it launched a 'Matter of Life and Debt' initiative, encouraging churches in poor areas to sponsor professional debt advice sessions on their premises.
- **10.3.3** Welsh churches have already adopted a programme called 'The Money Revolution', based on a book written by the C of E's John Preston. This encompasses advice on ethical spending, credit, debt, insurance, wills, and giving, and recognises clergy concerns that "social pressures in affluent neighbourhoods have encouraged people to borrow more than they can afford".
- **10.3.4** A United Free Church in Devon has housed and funded a free debt advice service, staffed by volunteers, which within months had helped 42 individuals or couples who owed between them some £500,000. Its staff teach budgeting skills and techniques, and act as intermediaries, negotiating with creditors.

- **10.3.5** In direct help of another kind in a Middlesbrough church, a 'Convoy of Hope' project gave away 500 bags of shopping to families struggling to cope with the 'credit crunch'.

11. Local Financial action

11.1 The General Assembly of 1997, noting the problem of personal debt in Scotland, encouraged congregations to become involved in credit unions, expressed alarm at the exploitation of the vulnerable in the credit market, and called for an effective means of providing cheap, accessible credit to those who need it.

11.2 Harder economic times, and the crisis in the banking system, have underlined the potential of community-based banking, an idea which is not new. Rev Henry Duncan, the so-called 'father of savings banks', set up the institution which would eventually become the Trustee Savings Bank (TSB),

a measure which claimed at his hands nearly 10 years of devoted work and pecuniary sacrifice[14]

11.3 He wanted financial independence for everyday people, feeling that government handouts were degrading and crushed the spirit. Within five years, banks based on his concept were found all over the UK.

11.4 Whilst the creation of a new bank might not be within the grasp of a congregation, Credit Unions have long been valued as alternative banks which encourage responsible saving and fair-rate borrowing. Many local congregations have taken the lead in the creation of credit unions in several places across Scotland[15].

---

[14] Inscription on memorial plaque on Ruthwell Savings Bank Museum
[15] In Dundee, the Church took the lead in setting up the now thriving Dundee West credit union. In Leith, the Council of Churches did the same in creating Persevere Credit union, now part of Capital Credit Union. In addition, for many years local churches have played pivotal roles in the establishment and support of Credit Unions in many parts of Glasgow, including Garthamlock, Cranhill and Ruchazie.

11.5 The structure of Credit Unions mean that the deposits to fund borrowings allow the better off in the community effectively to capitalise a bank which can help the less well-off. The Scottish government has recently announced additional support for Credit Unions and new rules mean that those requiring instant help with loans can now get it, as opposed to having to use companies such as Provident Financial with their outrageous rates of interest of around 180%.

11.6 Churches have not only often been in the forefront of setting up new credit unions, but active in leading the development of community enterprises and trading schemes.

11.7 Scotland is now home to more than 40 different barter schemes, ranging from Timebanks, where members donate an hour of their time and skill in exchange for an hour of someone else's, to Local Exchange Trading Systems. LETS allow people to exchange goods and services without using money. Each order or service provided earns points or currency which can be used to buy different offers from other members.

11.8 LETS currencies are usually valued in terms of sterling, which allows part-cash, part-currency pricing. The use of the currency in discount schemes can encourage participation by local businesses such as corner shops, cafes, and stalls at farmers' markets.

- **11.8.1** Glasgow's Healthland gym has launched its own community currency, essentially a timebank, inviting members to offer their skills in exchange for full or part membership of the club. There is good evidence that the motivation for joining is often social as much as economic, as the main attraction is the feeling of belonging to a community.
- **11.8.2** Castlemilk Timebank in Glasgow, established in 2002, won the Queens Award for Voluntary Service in June 2008. It works on the basis that "one hour of your time is worth the same as one hour of someone else's time, no matter what your skill involved".

11.9 These are all models congregations could use with their own resources.

11.10 Internet-based 'free' networks also play a part in alternative trading. Schemes such as Freecycle, Freeshare and Gumtree provide forums for the recycling and obtaining of unwanted things, on a local basis, at minimal cost. With the right kind of creativity, congregations can harness the power of the internet to make best use of their own resources.

11.11 The banking crisis, with small firms being starved of finance, has intensified efforts to develop alternative financial structures. Scotcash, a social enterprise backed by Glasgow City Council together with the city's housing association and the Royal Bank of Scotland, offers the financially excluded access to bank accounts, financial advice and affordable loans. Winner of the Guardian public services awards 2008, Scotcash said it saved clients £300,000 in interest payments, rescheduled £2m of debts and prevented around 80 evictions. Unlike money advice centre experience, where debts can be huge, the average debt of Scotcash customers is only £500.

11.12 Created without such banking and local authority support is Glasgow bank DSL, originally set up with cash from the Body Shop and now financed by credit unions, the Unity Trust Bank, a little DTI funding and the ongoing returns from its borrowers. DSL has loaned out more than £7m to over 600 businesses turned down by the High Street banks, and many of the projects financed by DSL have become cornerstones of their communities. Whilst individual parishes would be unlikely to have that kind of capital, a project which combined the local knowledge of parishes and the financial resources of the national Church could make a similar difference.

11.13 As has been seen, for many years parishes have used the social enterprise model to create economic opportunities in local communities. If there was ever a time that the Church needed to gather together that experience so others might draw on it, it is now.

12. Generating local Economic activity

12.1   Unemployment is rising fast, just as it did 30 years ago. Before the last election, Church Action on Poverty (CAP) published a report calling on the future government to confront the problem of joblessness. CAP also initiated an 'Unemployment Sunday' for congregations, to help congregations take time to reflect on what they might do and why they might do it in these tough times. As a starting point for congregations who might otherwise not be sure where to begin looking at the issue, it is to be recommended.

12.2   In each parish there will be unique opportunities. For example, Luss, which has no youth group of its own, brings youngsters from deprived central Glasgow to the shores of Loch Lomond for weekends of social learning, but only with community help. They discovered local businesses who want to help the church do exciting things, if they are done properly for a good reason. Luss Parish has also taken up an invitation from Scottish Enterprise to say yes, rather than no, to even more weddings at the much sought-after church, after the economic agency explained that each ceremony was injecting £20,000 to £40,000 (overseas weddings) directly into the local economy. The installation of in-church cameras which enable the ceremonies to be viewed over the internet have now led to Luss's regular church services being viewed by more than 10,000 people, after the idea was first put forward by local service personnel who said it would be much valued by soldiers in Iraq and Afghanistan. A journey into economic activity has led into another type of mission involving people from all over the world.

12.3   In rural communities churches are often the only communal buildings. Around 300 post offices in Scotland (one in every six) are due to close, with even more under threat as sub-postmasters die or retire without being replaced. Parishes can offer to house post offices in halls and other church buildings, to be rented out to local sub-postmasters or even run by congregation members. Post offices are such a vital part of community life, so why shouldn't the Church be helping to ensure that people have as much access to services as people in other parts of Scotland? There are opportunities for ministers and Church members to serve the community in new, exciting and relevant ways. A post office is already being run from the local kirk in Twatt, Orkney. Congregations participating in the scheme would need to find further information.

12.4   In each case the chosen action begins with a strategic look at the community the congregation serves and a reflection on the resources available to the congregation and from the Presbytery and the national Church. Lives can be turned around and the kingdom of God can be made real even, or perhaps especially at a time of economic crisis when people are asking what really matters.

12.5   At times like this it is helpful to look to other places for inspiration and creative reponses to financially challenging circumstances. One such place is Bangladesh and in particular the work of the Nobel Prize winner Dr Muhammad Yunus[16] who has used micro credit lending to revolutionise the financial circumstances and economic stability of thousands of individuals and local communities. This model uses small loans to fund start up costs of locally based businesses to provide employment and a significant sense of local communities being able to take much more control of their own economic destiny. There are already a number of organisations in Scotland looking at this work as a method of changing the way economic stability is provided.

12.6   It is therefore proposed that the Church consider

---

[16] http://muhammadyunus.org/

setting aside a substantial amount of money in order to help establish a fund which could be used in micro-lending projects. It would be envisaged that these funds would be utilized by congregations or groups of churches, within wider local partnerships to set up local schemes to benefit their local communities.

Some useful websites:

www.faithincommunityscotland.org
Faith in Community Scotland

www.church-poverty.org.uk
Church Action on Poverty

www.cas.org.uk
Citizens Advice Scotland

www.abcul.org
Assoc of British Credit Unions

www.capuk.org.uk
Christians against Poverty

www.traidcraft.co.uk
Traidcraft

www.themoneyrevolution.net

www.timebanking.org

www.letslinkuk.org

www.carplus.org.uk

www.lussonline.net

13. Living the Gospel view of Economics

13.1 A great deal of economic exchange is not simply about obtaining goods for basic human needs but involves the consumer in expressing their understanding of the nature of human relationships, including relationships with those they will never meet. Any entrepreneur will tell you that, despite the economist's ideal of humans acting in their own economic interest, *ie* based on price, those with some economic resources rebel and often make economic decisions based on how they feel as well. That is the basis of "brand loyalty" and a great deal of advertising, not to mention many luxury goods. One only needs to read of companies being sold for amounts significantly beyond their actual assets or even past income levels to see the power that some people see in a brand to persuade consumers that their consumption is not simply to meet a need but to change a life.

13.2 In a capitalist economic system there is a great irony that the desires of the consumer are seen as the driver of commercial decision-making, yet the individual may feel that their personal decisions can have no influence on bringing about change to that system. The evidence would suggest otherwise: the concept in economic thinking of the "green" or the "pink" pounds suggest that interest groups can significantly shape business decisions. The recent trend of larger corporations to make claims about their green credentials, or include carbon reductions in their annual report, back up this suggestion (although there may be questions about the veracity of some of these corporate claims).

13.3 The huge growth in demand for fairly traded goods and ethical investments are different examples of the same principle. Consumers act not in their own economic interest alone, but in the interests of others largely unknown. These actions are not driven solely by short term economic self interest, but by how the consumer feels about the purchase or investment. One might argue that it is a clear example of Smith's "invisible hand" at work. Business is aware of this significant motivating force and their marketing plays to that emotional response. Fair trade goods and ethical investments are just two examples of how consumer demand, created by a series of individual decisions can shift production decisions in such a way that ethics become integral to the process.

13.4 A number of authors have sought to ground this ethical decision-making in a way which is accessible and applicable to people of faith[17]. Questions are often asked such as:

- Which ethical decisions should I be prioritising?
- Who should I try to help with the influence I have as a consumer?
- If I use ethical criteria in one area of life but not another, does that undermine the integrity of the ethical decisions?
- What does it mean to invest ethically?
- Should I 'buy local' for green purposes or buy 'fair-trade' to help alleviate poverty?

13.5　Organic agriculture is seen as costly, but less spent on pesticides can also mean more employment on farms. Workers in the pesticide industry may see this as a threat, in the same way that opposition to military spending is often countered with arguments about the effect on jobs in that sector. In embarking on a journey towards a personal ethical consumerism, the Church needs to balance the prophetic words it is called to speak with the pastoral care of those whose employment such words might appear to threaten. There also need to be ways in which those struggling to make ethical consumerist choices can feel that those choices will make a difference.

13.6　This is thrown into stark relief in the context of the global financial crisis which can seem so overwhelming that the actions of an individual can appear meaningless in making a difference. In addition, with falling buying power, the ability and/or willingness to add ethics to domestic economic decision-making and thus not simply choose the cheapest product is significantly reduced. It also emphasises the point often made by the poorest communities that ethical consumerism, based as it is on an assumption that the consumer will pay a little more to make that "ethical decision", excludes those who do not have the resources to participate in the market other than for those goods which meet their basic needs. Fair-Trade would be one example: it is sometimes considered to be little more than "middle class angst", yet solidarity between workers in different parts of the world has a well documented history. Christians have been at the forefront of the Fair Trade movement – a good example of putting our money where our mouths are. It is also an excellent example of how, if people, families, households do make small everyday but sustainable lifestyle changes in favour of all the people and the whole of the planet, change does happen – even for those who, at present, do not have the choice of fair trade consumerism.

13.7　One of the many effects of the "credit crunch" has been to highlight the foolishness of "easy" credit and the effect of both individual and corporate greed. It has however created an opportunity to relearn that individuals need to control our use of money rather than letting money control us. Discovering how to achieve appropriate lending and borrowing is a key part of business and personal money management. There are excellent examples of how this can work; micro credit schemes are a good example. Triodos Bank also offers a responsible model, as do the Co-op Bank, Oikocredit and Shared Interest. Choosing to use Mutual Building Societies and Credit Unions should be encouraged. Local Exchange Trading Systems (LETS) offer an alternative to the use of money which, given the long track record of the sharing of volunteer expertise in the Christian community should be very adaptable to use in churches and the communities they serve.

14. Auditing ourselves

14.1　There are a wide variety of Biblical texts which can be used to begin a journey towards building an ethical framework for Christian economics. This report would not claim to be anything like exhaustive in offering guidelines

---

[17] See, for example: Smith, K.R. (2006): *God's Economic Mandate: A Perspective on Stewardship Economics.* Thankful Books; Dayton, H.L. (1999): *Your money counts*. Crown Financial Ministries; Sider, R.J. (2005): *Rich Christians in an Age of Hunger: Moving from Affluence to Generosity*. Thomas Nelson; Swinson, A. (2004): *Root of all Evil? How to Make Spiritual Values Count*. Saint Andrew Press.

for that process. Rather, what it hopes to lay out would be a methodology for beginning a personal theological audit of consumer engagement, and to offer a number of places were further advice and study could be achieved. The development of additional Biblical and reflective resources on the Church website will help this process.

14.2 This process recognises that each person's starting point on this journey is unique. Just as the interpretations of what it means to love an enemy will depend on who is seen as an enemy, so a judgement of whether making a choice about buying fair-trade is ethically more significant than buying locally will be shaped by individual experiences and understandings of the effect of each action. As this journey begins for each individual and for the groups who choose to work together and support each other in the journey, what will be significant is that ethical criteria are being applied to consumer decisions. That is always the significant first change. Reflection on that experience will then shape future decisions but the idea of holding an ethical light to consumer decisions should become embedded in the lifestyles of those involved.

14.3 It is hoped that individuals and groups within and among congregations will choose to sign up to the Church and Society Facebook Group[18], which has been

---

[18] Search for Church & Society Group on Facebook. http://www.facebook.com/

set up to support this process and through that sharing both offer support to others on a similar journey and also provide real experiences of taking this journey. A report to the 2010 General Assembly will be compiled using some of these inputs.

14.4 Many Christians already act in this way but it is hoped that these steps will still be of use to them whatever stage they are at in their journey to an ethical consumerism. These steps are deliberately couched in positive language rather than being a list of "thou shalt not's". This is too complex an issue to couch in proscriptive terms and such language will perhaps not help in endearing this perspective to those outside the Christian community.

15. Steps to a new Personal Christian economics

15.1 The Biblical references given are merely examples of the possible basis for reflection and should not be seen as in any way prescriptive. On the contrary, they should inspire challenge and reflection, debate and even disagreement as the journey to Christian ethical consumerism is taken.

15.2 It is hoped that a fuller description of each of these steps including some biblical references and real life stories of change and challenge will be gathered and placed on the Church and Society website.

Topic	Suggested Bible references	Notes
1. Begin with and return to reflection and prayer	Begin with the Bible	Using the stories of those whose economic power is limited or who face injustice or oppression, interrogate the texts that reflect the role of consumption and economic exchange. For example: Jubilee; Jeremiah; Consider the lilies; Rich young man; Parable of the talents; Give unto Caesar; Widow's mite. And pray. The kinds of changes in lifestyle involved here will take real and deep energy and that will need replenishment.
2. Start small	Thanksgiving: Deut 26:1-15 Small steps Matthew 10: 42	Be realistic and gentle with yourself. Start from the premise that every decision matters and can make a difference but that we will not make every decision as we might want to every time.
3. Trust God	Who am I?: Psalm 139 Consider the Lilies: Luke 12: 22-28	Trust God to provide for your basic needs. Understand that our consumerism is an emotional experience and so change will take time. (See "The Story of Stuff" – **http://www.storyofstuff.com/**) Start simply. Make one change in your consumerism at a time, reflecting on its effect and what it felt like before moving to the next one. A journey of a lifetime begins with a first step.
4. See the woods of change, not the trees that hinder	Choose this day: Joshua 24:14-18 Rich young man: Luke 18: 18-30 Workers in the Vineyard: Matt 20: 1-16	Choose what you want to achieve with every decision by choosing a few priorities, *eg* fair trade, or support for environment or commitment to animals or boycotting a particular regime or product *eg* arms trade use. Use these as the basis of economic decision-making. Remember that different things can be achieved with different actions.

5. Don't walk alone	**Ruth and Naomi:** **Ruth 1:11-18** **Sharing:** **Acts 4: 32-36**	Find a method of reviewing these decisions; for example, setting up a small group in your congregation to reflect on what we each can achieve individually and as a group. The strength of accounting to each other will help each individual as they make their choices.
6. Rediscover make do and mend	**Negotiating wells:** **Genesis 26:18-31** **Feeding of the 5000:** **John 6: 1-14**	Ethical consumerism can be a choice not to consume but instead to share and/or to reduce waste. An ethical lifestyle does not have to mean hair shirts. It may mean making the same shirt last longer. It might mean using the bus more and the car less rather than assuming that it's all or nothing.
7. Luxury is allowed but in moderation	**Restore my soul:** **Psalm 23** **Anointing of Jesus:** **Matt 26: 6-13**	It is important to recognise the different pressures on people and the need at times to relax. Stopping taking luxuries for granted does not mean we completely forsake such luxuries.
8. Walk the walk	**David and Goliath:** **I Sam 17** **Good Samaritan:** **Luke 10: 25-37**	Reflect on how actions can be a witness to others. The choices we make will affect others; the power of peers is the basis of capitalism but it can also be the basis of change.
9. Choose to give away	**Be generous:** **Leviticus 19:9** **Zaccheus:** **Luke 19: 1-9**	Make a decision about how to use what money you can give away in support of others. If money is short then use your time instead.
10. Learn from other people's stories	**Faithfully obey:** **Deut 6** **Life amongst the believers:** **Acts 2: 43-47**	Use websites such as: www.generous.org.uk, www.letslinkuk.org, www.ethicalconsumer.org, www.fairtrade.org.uk to help your thinking and for other sources of support.

16. Conclusions

16.1 While it must be acknowledged that this report is not comprehensive, it is also recognised that every journey begins with a single step. The challenges being faced at all levels of society are undoubtedly daunting, and many of the issues complex and technical. However, the outworking of these issues will be seen in the personal lives of real people, families and communities- in Scotland and throughout the world.

16.2 The Church of Scotland has the privilege of serving in communities throughout the land. Its members, as followers of Christ, have the responsibility to be faithful to their calling to be salt and light in the world. Unpacking and living out the implications of that call confronts us with many questions and challenges; this report has sought to engage these challenges, and to see how we (the church as a whole, as congregations, and as individual Christians) must act.

16.3 Criticisms will be encountered, and honest mistakes will be made. But our Lord requires that we: *act justly... love mercy, and walk humbly with our God* [19]

Acknowledgements

In addition to members of the Church and Society Council, we would gratefully acknowledge the following who were involved in the preparation of this report:

Mr Simon Bain   Business Writer with The Herald
Rev Dr Doug Gay   Lecturer in Practical Theology, University of Glasgow
Dr Robert Mochrie   Senior Lecturer in Economics, Heriot-Watt University, Edinburgh.

Proposed practical outcomes:

See deliverances.

[19] Micah 6: 8

PAPER 3
ETHICS OF DEFENCE

1. Introduction

1.1 Defence of the realm is an area of public policy which should concern everyone. The main focus is the development of tactical and strategic military responses which will offer security and protection to the sovereignty of the United Kingdom (UK) in the face of all external threats. The ethics of defence are central to all such considerations and to the subsequent implementation and execution of this policy, taking into account the international duties and responsibilities of a nation state.

1.2 In the modern world, four important factors influence and determine the overall defence posture of the United Kingdom:

- **1.2.1** The central pillar of UK defence policy is the exercise of political power in determining the final choices to be made over the potential use, deployment and re-equipping of the armed services. Her Majesty's (HM) Government, through the office of the Secretary of State for Defence, is able to bring proposals to the UK Parliament governing the future use of financial and human resources, working in close co-operation with the Foreign Secretary and other Ministers in charge of central departments. Defence is a reserved subject under the Scotland Act 1998 and the Scottish Parliament is therefore limited in its capacity to offer advice, to shape or determine the outcomes of UK defence policy. All mainstream political parties associate these decisions directly with particular electoral advantage and jealously guard this element of political power whenever possible. The process of progressive and significant change to the UK defence posture is consequently severely inhibited by historical precedent.

- **1.2.2** As a permanent member of the United Nations (UN) Security Council, the UK is in a powerful position to influence and assist in deliberations within the international community on all matters relating to global peace and security. However, the UN as a forum for international negotiation and peaceful reconciliation has itself been considerably weakened by the power of veto which permanent member states of the Security Council can exercise in their own national interest, especially regarding the right to self-defence under the terms of the UN Charter. The presentation of inaccurate and misleading information obtained from undeclared sources by the United States of America (USA) substantially undermined the role of the Security Council prior to the military invasion of Iraq in March 2003. Detailed reports of UN weapons inspectors were laid to one side, demonstrating that urgent reform of UN institutions is needed to allow more careful, open and constructive negotiation between member states in order to avoid the onset of war.

- **1.2.3**   In a world of increasing globalisation, the issue of ethical and moral leadership lies at the heart of any national defence policy. The apparent ending of the many long years of Cold War between the dominant super-powers of the 20th century, the USA and the USSR, brought much talk of a "peace dividend" into the debate about defence policy in the UK and elsewhere, notably across the widening European Union. The transition to a new age in which nuclear weapons would be substantially abandoned and removed from potential flash-points of international conflict under the terms of the UN Nuclear Non-Proliferation Treaty has, however, failed to materialise. While the Warsaw Pact disintegrated the NATO alliance persists, and grows, enabling new friendships but at the same time helping to perpetuate some of the old divisions. In place of the Cold War, the growing threat from international terrorism has entered the public consciousness. In these circumstances, the possibility exists that a nuclear weapons state such as the UK could adopt a different position, morally and ethically, by deciding not to advance the concept of a further generation of intercontinental ballistic missiles.

Instead, HM Government could in future choose to do much more to concentrate its military resources on peace-keeping and peace-making on behalf of the international community, protecting human life rather than sacrificing it.

- **1.2.4**   A key underlying reason – rarely mentioned openly in government papers – concerns the status and prestige in holding 'impressive' weapons, especially nuclear weapons. Too often the need to hold these weapons is discussed in terms of deterrence and providing the UK with a place at the top table in decision making. So often in reality it is really about status and prestige. 'We' have them, 'we' will hold on to them, 'we' would be crazy to give them up, 'we' will never give them up as long as the French or whoever has them. It is noteworthy that when India tested its nuclear bomb, people apparently danced in the street shouting 'now we are a developed nation'. Any reasons given about the importance of having nuclear weapons must have this aspect of status and prestige high on its list.

1.3   This paper on the 'Ethics of Defence' provides the background to possible important and unprecedented policy shifts, drawing on the long tradition of the Church of Scotland in advocating the continuing renewal of efforts for peace and reconciliation across the world.

2.   A Biblical Perspective

Therefore take up the whole armour of God, so that you may be able to withstand on that evil day, and having done everything, to stand firm. Stand therefore, and fasten the belt of truth around your waist, and put on the breastplate of righteousness. As shoes for your feet put on whatever will make you ready to proclaim the gospel of peace. With all these, take the shield of faith, with which you will be able to quench all the flaming arrows of the evil one. Take the helmet of salvation, and the sword of the Spirit, which is the word of God. Pray in the

Spirit all times in every prayer and supplication. To that end keep alert.[1]

2.1 Whenever a Scripture text, however apparently apposite, is used in a report to the General Assembly, questions arise as to why that particular text. To some, the use of these verses in a report on Ethics of Defence may be obvious, as they feature some words with a military connection – *belt of truth, breastplate of righteousness, gospel of peace, shield of faith, helmet of salvation, sword of the Spirit*. It is often said that these words have a primarily 'defensive' tone, the armour donned by a soldier to protect from attack. They also of course have an 'attack' tone, for they are worn with a view to soldiers winning a battle and conquering. Similarly, it could be argued whether any weapon is primarily a weapon of defence or attack as, like the armour, they can be used for both.

2.2 Texts can be used to justify all sorts of conclusions and it is crucial to ground the understanding of these words in Jesus Christ. All of us think we know what *truth* or *righteousness* or *peace* means, but we need only ask an Israeli or a Palestinian, a Georgian or a Russian, and very different answers would be given. Paul, as we see in Ephesians and elsewhere, grounded his letters and message in the life of Jesus Christ. This means that Jesus' life *in all its wholeness* is the key interpretative factor for the above text. His words and life interpret one another, each one illumining the other.

2.3 The meaning of *truth* (also translatable as *reality*) emerges as we see Jesus embodying in himself the reality of obedience and faithfulness to God in our human life, often with immense struggle and tears. He also embodied an open welcome to every person with the challenge for integrity and faithful living, and embodied in himself, especially on the cross, the human condition before the reality of God. Jesus refused power as the world understands it, and used only weapons of truth,

being who he is. Here in Jesus then we see the truth of what our human life may seek to aspire to, but also the truth of what human life has so often become in all its alienation and distortion. We find ourselves inspired to live as faithfully as we can, but are also aware that we fail and falter constantly. We cannot invite others to live in integrity and veracity, if we forget that we first and foremost are challenged to live this way ourselves.

2.4 The meaning of *righteousness* becomes clear when we see Jesus embodying in himself the God who seeks to grow and expand his way of living among all humanity. God himself is inherently righteous but our only way of understanding what this means is to follow through what he has done, which is to make people righteous in Jesus Christ, as Luther saw so powerfully. *Righteousness* is not primarily a *moral* word, but refers to God active in our world putting it right in himself, and as he puts us in the right we discover we were in the wrong even if we did not know it. He calls us and others to live within the sphere where his embrace is always that of welcome to all, rather than of any blanket condemnation or prejudice.

2.5 The meaning of other words in the text emerges similarly when we seek to place them first and foremost within Jesus' life, letting his life and words interpret them. *Peace* cannot then be detached from *gospel of peace*, and none of the words can be detached from *praying in the Spirit at all times*. There is recognition in the verses prior to the ones quoted above of vested interests, of powerful institutions, of the reality of evil, hence Paul's encouragement to prayer at all times. He recognises that the only ultimate way to defeat evil is not by evil or using evil means, but by the truth of the gospel.

2.6 For Paul, Jesus is the most potent attack the world has ever seen, simply by his being the *truth* of God. The truth of *love* and *righteousness* is the mightiest force in the universe, and as a Church we are called to understand and believe this. We find it incredibly hard to trust this gospel, for too often not only would we rather put our

---

[1] Eph. 6:13-18 (NRSV)

trust elsewhere – for example, in weapons – but we also want the trappings of worldly power and influence. That however is not the way that Jesus took. God's truth, which is inherently outgoing and creative, becomes truth in us when his word takes flesh in us so that we echo his truth in the way in which we live and act.

2.7 In the context of the ethics of defence then, the Church itself is called to live out of the heart of God having put us in the right with himself, and to seek to work out the very difficult issues in defence out of this perspective. This is not to say that we cannot defend ourselves from an attack, but use of defensive weapons must be thought through very carefully. There may well be considerable disagreement among Christians as to what defence means. Some would argue, for example, that nuclear weapons have in fact been an effective deterrent and have kept peace for decades; others disagree profoundly, holding that any deterrence gained is vastly outweighed by the evil of threatening to kill millions of people indiscriminately, and also of diverting colossal resources into arms which could be better used elsewhere.

2.8 In the past, the Church of Scotland has persistently viewed nuclear weapons as an evil, and we see no reason to change that perspective. So far as we can understand the life of Jesus, the great sweep of his life is about putting trust in God, in reaching out in love and welcome to others no matter their idiosyncrasies or failings, and in refusing to leave people in a state of fear or with a sense of condemnation.

2.9 While then there are references in the gospels to, for example,

I have come not to bring peace, but a sword[2]

or in the Garden of Gethsemane to a disciple carrying a sword which Jesus would presumably have known about[3], the primary focus of Jesus' life is standing before evil, absorbing its attack, healing the effects of the sword, and continuing to trust in God as the way forward.

2.10 As those who have been put in the right with God, knowing that all have also been put in the right with God:

God was in Christ reconciling the world to himself[4],

so the Church is summoned to put its trust in God, to invite all into that reconciliation, and to live the life of reconciliation with all. This includes refusing to place anyone in a position of fear or threat, but rather reaching out always to others, seeking to gather all together into the reality of the human family reconciled in Christ, and seeking to discover together what that reconciliation means.

2.11 The implicit evil of nuclear weapons, among other things, can be persistently and rigorously proclaimed. Only that which enables people to live within reconciliation, love and welcome reflect God's *truth, righteousness, gospel of peace, faith, salvation, sword*.

3. Pacifism

3.1 Throughout the history of Christianity, there has always been a minority of believers who have adopted a pacifist stance to conflict. The Oxford Reference Dictionary defines pacifism as "the belief that war and violence are morally unjustified and that all disputes should be settled by peaceful means." War is horrific and tends to develop its own dynamic where actions become more horrific in response. The pacifist response to this is that it must be avoided at all costs.

3.2 There are a number of understandings of pacifism, but generally it opposes war and participation in war. The reasons for adopting a pacifist stance vary. For some it is a pragmatic approach, where adopting pacifism

---

[2] Matt. 10: 34 (NRSV)

[3] Luke. 22: 49, 50

[4] 2 Cor. 5: 18

as policy will produce the most positive results for individuals, groups and/or nations. If the cycle of violence can be broken, long-term peace has a chance of being established. Non-violent opposition has often been a very useful (if painful) tactic in bringing about change in systems.

3.3 For others, pacifism opposes war on principle, based on Biblical teaching and understanding. War requires violation of the commandment not to kill; Jesus' instructions were to love our enemies, to turn the other cheek, to love our neighbours as ourselves; the Beatitudes bless the peacemakers[5]; Paul reminds the Corinthians that:

> we do not wage war according to human standards[6],

but are engaged in spiritual warfare – just as Jesus pointed out to Pilate that his followers were not fighting to save him as his kingdom was not of this world[7]. One of the most famous passages in Isaiah sums up our hopes:

> He shall judge between the nations,
> and shall arbitrate for many peoples;
> they shall beat their swords into ploughshares,
> and their spears into pruning-hooks;
> nation shall not lift up sword against nation,
> neither shall they learn war any more.[8]

3.4 Pacifism states that any use of lethal violence goes against not only the teachings of Jesus on non-retaliation and the love of enemies, but also the practice of Jesus, who suffered willingly at the hands of his enemies and did not strike back. In light of the Biblical understanding of peace, this stops the vicious circle of violence and counter-violence. As Moltmann has pointed out,

> Non-resistance to evil shows up the absurdity of evil. Evil's strength is violence. Evil's weakness is its wrongness. Counter-violence supplies evil with its supposed justification, and often enough stabilizes it. It is only the non-violent reaction which robs evil of every legitimation and puts the perpetrator of violence in the wrong.[9]

3.5 If, within pacifism, war is not available even as a last resort, does a nation simply allow injustice to be done in the world? There are many different approaches to peace-making (and many definitions of both "peace" and what "making" it might involve.) The Isaiah passage quoted above[8] already raises the idea of arbitration. Some would read Christ's instructions to turn the other cheek and go the extra mile as examples of non-violent resistance, opposing oppression and causing political and personal discomfort to the oppressor. The fact that Jesus suffered torture then a violent death at the hands of an occupying power offers the hope that He is alongside all those who suffer violence, and that we are called to do the same. Certainly modern pacifism is not an acceptance and capitulation to violence, but often finds creative solutions or challenges to war and its technology.

3.6 Historically, Christian pacifism went alongside a withdrawal from the world and earthly matters, to be concerned wholly with the spiritual. Pearse[10] argues that once Christianity was associated with states and governments, it had to legitimise war as, he claims, there can be no such thing as a pacifist state. All states either have forces or rely on other countries which have forces which could defend them. Pearse[10] also argues that pacifism does not work – that in a world where people will use violence,

> a refusal to use violence hands the world over to the person who will.

---

[5] Ex. 20: 13; Matt. 5: 44; Matt. 5: 39; Matt. 22: 39; Matt. 5: 9
[6] 2 Cor. 10: 3 (NRSV)
[7] John 18: 36
[8] Isa. 2: 4 (NRSV)
[9] Moltmann, J (1990): *The Way of Jesus Christ*, SCM Press
[10] Pearse, M. (2007): *The Gods of War*, InterVarsity Press

3.7 In order to protect the weak and oppose evil, it is argued that violence may be needed. However, Pearse also makes the distinction that Christians should never fight for their faith – that we are only asked to die for Jesus, not to kill for him.

4. An historical perspective

4.1 The tradition of the Just War approach as an ethical and sensible approach to logically assessing and restricting war has a long history in Christianity. As far back as the fifth century, Augustine reconciled the passivity of Jesus for Rome (political) by developing a first Just War definition[11]. Although this approach had been overtaken by aspects of International Law in modern times, there has a been resurgence since the Second World War as International Law is sometimes perceived to have failed to take action re Nuclear War, Terrorism, *etc.*

4.2 Early modern political thinkers such as Machiavelli and Hobbes deliberately replaced the concept of trust or faith in divine providence and a justly ordered universe with alternative doctrines. Machiavelli resorted to the explicitly atheistic concept of fate to replace the Christian God[12]. It was then the task of the Prince to be eternally vigilant in the face of external enemies, confirming that the safety of the state, in his judgment, could require him to disregard personal morality in the face of external enemies. Hobbes constructed much the same atheistic belief that all security had to come from an absolutely constructed Leviathan who had to be free of moral constraints to be able to defend the state from

external enemies[13]. Both figures combined a withdrawal from faith in a divinely ordered universe with a belief that international society was not governed by any moral norms. An exchange between two other thinkers illustrates a practical outcome: Alberto Gentili (Professor of Civil Law at Oxford) argued that a sovereign had a right of preemptive attack against any other state it feared as a threat, with little restriction on grounds. Subjective fear was enough. The famous Dutchman Hugo Grotius (The Law of War and Peace, 1625) responded that there was only a right of self defence against an actual danger, an imminent attack. Beyond that one had to put one's trust in Providence.[13]

4.3 On International Law and Pacifism, The League Covenant and the UN Charter are based upon the pacifist idea that war as an instrument of national policy is dysfunctional. The world wars of the 20th century show that war is too clumsy an instrument to achieve definite and limited goals: it becomes total and consumes the protagonists. Therefore war and the use of armed force except in self defence are forbidden (article 2/4 of the UN Charter); what the Security Council may authorize is collectively permitted police action on behalf of the world community to restore peace and order.

5. Defence based on right authority: the role of the United Nations

5.1 In the 2004 report from the UN Secretary-General's High-level Panel on 'Threats, Challenges and Change' – *'A more secure world: Our shared responsibility'* – there is a key statement on Collective Security:

> Any event or process that leads to large-scale death or lessening of life chances and undermines States as the basic unit of the international system is a threat to international security. So defined,

---

[11] Gonzalez, J. L. (1984). *The Story of Christianity*. HarperSanFrancisco; Ramsey, P. (1983): *The Just War*, University of America Press; Russell, F. (1975): *The Just War in the Middle Ages,* Cambridge; O'Donovan, O. (2003): *The Just War Revisited,* Cambridge.

[12] Panizza, D. (2005): *Political Theory and Jurisprudence in Gentili's De Jure Belli: The Great Debate between "theological" and "humanist" perspectives from Vitoria to Grotius.* IILJ Working Paper 2005/15 (History and Theory of International Law Series) www.iilj.org

[13] Carty, A. (2007): *Philosophy of International Law,* Edinburgh University Press; also Carty A. (2009): *Vattel's Natural Liberty of Conscience of Nations in a New Age of Belief and Faith,* forthcoming in Chetail and Haggenmacher, Emir de Vattel for the 21st Century , Presse Universitaire de Genève

there are six clusters of threats with which the world must be concerned now and in the decades ahead:

*Economic and social threats, including poverty, infectious disease and environmental degradation
Inter-State conflict
Internal conflict, including civil war, genocide and other large scale atrocities
Nuclear, radiological, chemical and biological weapons
Terrorism
Transnational organised crime*

The primary challenge for the United Nations and its members is to ensure that, of all the threats in the categories listed, those that are distant do not become imminent and those that are imminent do not actually become destructive. This ... will require leadership at the domestic and international levels to act clearly, decisively and collectively against all these threats ..... before they have their most devastating effect.[14]

5.2 This kind of approach as advocated and subsequently adopted by the UN should become central to any consideration of the ethics of defence in the UK. As a nation, we cannot stand apart and simply assert our right as an independent sovereign country to arm ourselves with overwhelming force in the face of an apparently unknown enemy. As a permanent member of the UN Security Council, the UK has a responsibility to show leadership.

5.3 Unfortunately our current defence posture, as set out in recent Government statements and Defence White Papers[15], is a reflection of the stagnant thinking and lack of creativity when presented with this form of UN assessment. Politicians argue that the UN has been progressively weakened and undermined by the failed diplomacy and sequence of events which led to wars in Afghanistan and Iraq. Latent and more overt forms of aggression as expressed by other states, particularly Iran and North Korea, fuels this concern.

5.4 Other recent UN documents underline the nature of these difficulties. In his 2005 report entitled *'In larger freedom – Towards Development, Security and Human Rights for All'* – the former UN Secretary General Kofi Annan made it clear that progress in both disarmament and non-proliferation of nuclear materials is essential and that neither should be held hostage to the other.

The unique status of nuclear-weapon States also entails a unique responsibility, and they must do more, including but not limited to further reductions in their arsenals of non-strategic nuclear weapons and pursuing arms control agreements that entail not just dismantlement but irreversibility.[16]

5.5 However, the UN can do little more than place such an appeal at the door of its member States, especially those which are capable of exercising immense military and economic power on a global scale. In effect, the UN itself is obliged to demonstrate both moral and ethical leadership in the absence of any willingness by a powerful nuclear-weapon state such as Britain to set a new agenda for the international community.

5.6 The current political context
5.6.1 No-one placed in the position of writing a political manifesto for the next General Election is likely to stray far in this direction. Indeed it can be argued that an electorate pre-occupied with events closer to home, including the downturn in the economy and wildly fluctuating food and fuel prices, is obliged

---

[14] http://www.un.org/secureworld/
[15] House of Commons Defence Committee, (2007): *The Future of the UK's Strategic Nuclear Deterrent: the White Paper.* Ninth Report of the Session 2006-7, Volume 1, HC 225-1, Feb 27th

[16] http://www.un.org/largerfreedom/

to focus inward and, for the time being at least, to concentrate on matters affecting hard-pressed people. Wider strategic visions and opportunities, it is claimed, must be set aside. The role of the UN and its agencies will be commended but largely discounted in the public debate over the political and economic future of Britain in the world of today.

5.6.2 This is a fundamental error of significant proportions. It is time for the ethics of defence to be brought much higher up the political agenda. The role of the churches, and in particular, the Church of Scotland through debate on the floor of the General Assembly, should be to initiate a different kind of investigation, namely, a probing examination of all these issues with lasting effect. The Church should encourage the UK Government to carry out a fundamental review of both its foreign and defence policies with the view of taking an international lead in urging all nations to better support the United Nations ability to maintain peacemaking and peacekeeping roles.

5.6.3 There is also an urgent need for the UK Government to refocus its defence expenditure to better support the stated aim of the Ministry of Defence (MoD) to increase the role of the armed forces in "strengthening international peace and stability"[17].

5.6.4 The Government of the day, whatever its ideological position, is unlikely to welcome or encourage this approach, but it should be noted that several leader writers and political journalists are turning their attention in this direction[18], as are very senior former military officers, retired diplomats and formerly senior politicians[19].

After all, what is the point in pursuing unnecessary public investment in weapons systems which can never conceivably be used to defend anybody?

6. Doctrine of Nuclear Deterrence

6.1 Throughout history, the capacity to defend and protect the citizens of a country has been a matter of basic political necessity. The need to deter the threat of an incoming invading force was elevated up the political agenda: with advancing technology, this included access to nuclear weapons and their delivery.

6.2 Regrettably, within Britain, an original nuclear weapons state and a permanent member of the UN Security Council, the doctrine of nuclear deterrence continues to prevail. The Ministry of Defence planners are not about to sacrifice their so-called trump card, the Trident missile system carried by Royal Navy and US Navy nuclear-powered submarines operating out of Faslane. However, the existing Trident fleet is rapidly ageing and MoD statements have indicated that Britain is only able to maintain a single nuclear submarine on global patrol, with its missiles no longer specifically targeted. Further to this, the Secretary of State for Defence has openly admitted that at present the UK is not facing a significant nuclear threat from any other nation.[20]

6.3 In the era of the Cold War, there were many scenarios played out by UK and US military strategists in response to potentially increasing threats from the Soviet Union. One of these was identified as *'no first strike'* and this for many years was cited as a central pillar of the doctrine of deterrence. The intention behind the Trident system has always been to deploy a fleet of nuclear submarines somewhere beneath the world's oceans with a capacity to respond to direct political command. Deterrence depends on the continuing capacity to use equally devastating force to counteract any 'first strike' against British cities

[17] http://www.mod.uk/DefenceInternet/AboutDefence/Organisation/DefenceVision/
[18] Hastings, M. (2009): *If defence is to be strategic rather than politically expedient, dump Trident.* The Guardian, Jan 19th
[19] Evans, M. (2009): *Three retired military commanders call for Trident to be scrapped.* The Times, Jan 16th
[20] Editorial, (2008): *Time to Outlaw the Use of Nuclear Weapons.* Disarmament Diplomacy, 87, Spring

from an incoming wave of nuclear missiles launched by an aggressive foreign power.

6.4 This doctrine remains in place despite the acknowledged absence of such a threat by the Secretary of State for Defence, and the inability to properly deploy the "deterrent". The time has come to draw a line under this theoretical defence posture. A political decision to abandon both the potential upgrading and the eventual replacement of the Trident nuclear missile system is now long overdue. If Britain was to take this unilateral action, then it could start to lay claim to a position of moral and ethical leadership which the rest of the international community would understand.

6.5 In addition, recent developments on both sides of the Atlantic have seen senior statesmen such as Kissinger and Shultz make statements such as:

> [nuclear] deterrence is decreasingly effective and increasingly hazardous.[21]

6.6 Mikhail Gorbachev wrote in January 2007 that, as someone who signed the first treaties on real reductions in nuclear weapons, he thought:

> it is becoming clearer that nuclear weapons are no longer a means of achieving security; in fact, with every passing year they make our security more precarious.

6.7 In a letter to The Times entitled: "Start worrying and learn to ditch the bomb", Douglas Hurd, Malcolm Rifkind, David Owen and George Robertson stated that:

> Substantial progress towards a dramatic reduction in the world's nuclear weapons is possible. The ultimate aspiration should be to have a world free of nuclear weapons. It will take time, but with political will and improvements in monitoring, the goal is achievable.[22]

6.8 To maintain the status quo and stagger forward into the future with a new Trident missile system which no political leader could ever realistically contemplate using is surely no longer to be tolerated, especially when the threat of international terrorism is manifestly not deterred by the existence of such a weapons system. The argument is stark enough to satisfy most reasonable men and women, but it continues to fall mainly on deaf ears amongst Government Ministers and members of the UK Parliament.

6.9 There are voices to be heard, both inside and outside of the Parliamentary chambers at Westminster and Holyrood, who have long advocated the need to stand apart from any kind of dependence on nuclear weapons for defence of the realm. The Church of Scotland has been consistent over the years in maintaining this position alongside many other churches, and indeed the World Council of Churches has also been strong in its condemnation of the existence and potential use of such weapons of mass destruction.

6.10 It also needs to be acknowledged openly that one of the key reasons for the UK or other countries having such weapons is in fact to do with kudos and prestige. If this is really what having these weapons is about, that needs to be right out in the open and challenged strongly. It is little wonder that some non-nuclear nations may wish such weapons in order to achieve its 'developed nation' status!

6.11 In these early years of the 21st century, when we are starting to give precedence to threats posed by global warming, climate change and the diminishing baseline of natural resources, especially energy and fresh water, it would be as well to focus attention once again on the reasons why a country such as Britain should seek to retain its capacity to exercise overwhelming force against any other nation. It simply does not make sense and is in direct breach of every civilised code of behaviour.

---

[21] Wall St Journal, Jan 15th 2008. http://www.acronym.org.uk/docs/0801/doc14.htm

[22] The Times, June 30th 2008, http://www.acronym.org.uk/docs/0806/doc08.htm

6.12   We reaffirm the historic position of the Church of Scotland of the need to remove the doctrine of nuclear deterrence from our national defence strategy. The time is now ripe for HM Government to move in this direction.

7.   Proportionate cause and last resort

7.1   War always causes harm. As Holmes observes, war often brings out the worst in nations, as it can create

…callous disregard for life and property, a cruel and vengeful spirit, utter disregard for the dignity of persons created in God's image and an almost idolatrous pride in nationality and might[23].

7.2   It must be understood that violence and retaliation can very quickly spiral out of control, affecting more and more people. With this downward spiral, any chance of resolving the situation becomes more difficult and it is easy to lose sight of the objectives of reconciling the original disagreement(s). Wounds become deep and much more difficult to heal.

7.3   However, it should be recognised that conflict situations can be useful to many parties who gain economically, politically or materially. For these, war is not the least preferred option, either at its start or once it is in progress. Keen[24] argues this is why many conflict situations seem intractable (*eg* Sierra Leone) and peace settlements do not always work. For peace to take hold the underlying problems must be solved and the gains of peace must outweigh the gains of conflict. This applies whether peace is being made through use of arms or other routes.

7.4   Within the just war tradition, proportionate cause asks whether what is perceived to be gained by going to war is worth the damage that will be done. A comparison should be made between the future if we

take up arms and the future if we don't take up arms. To make that judgement requires best-guesses of possible outcomes. This is very difficult to do, but must be done honestly.

- **7.4.1**   Other legal, economic and diplomatic measures must have been considered. Sometimes going to war will seem simpler, as a highly visible action in face of a perceived threat.
- **7.4.2**   Within political leadership, strong leadership in times of tension and conflict can be seen as a political strength, and potentially a distraction from domestic matters.
- **7.4.3**   The arms trade is politically very influential, partly due to the frequent exchange of roles between senior defence industry employees and senior civil servants.[25]
- **7.4.4**   Time is not always neutral in volatile situations – practical and humanitarian conditions can deteriorate.
- **7.4.5**   Costs to everyone should be considered – in the countries involved and their neighbours; for civilians as well as military; in damage to the environment and human rights; financial costs for war and reconstruction.
- **7.4.6**   While human rights abuses are often seen as a cause for engagement, in conflict situations human rights across the spectrum of civil, political, economic and social rights are likely to be threatened.
- **7.4.7**   Realistic judgements must be made; with probable outcomes compared like-for-like; with intelligence sources as transparent and neutral as possible.
- **7.4.8**   Adequate planning and finance must be in place for reconstruction and reconciliation after initial conflict has passed. Overall since the invasion of Iraq,

[23]   Holmes, A. F. (1984): *'A Just War: defining some key issues'*, in Oliver R. Barclay ed. *Pacifism and War*. Inter-Varsity Press.
[24]   Keen, D. (2008): *Complex Emergencies*. Polity.

[25]   Campaign Against The Arms Trade (2005): "Who Calls the Shots" February report. See http://www.caat.org.uk/publications/government/who-calls-the-shots-4pp-0205.pdf.

only around 8% of the total budget has been spent on reconstruction, mostly on oil infrastructure.[26]

- **7.4.9** In terms of use of nuclear, biological and chemical weapons, the horrendous consequences of their use (to people and planet, in short and long term) mean that their use cannot ever be justified as proportionate. In the case of biological and chemical weapons this has been recognised by outlawing them.

7.5 In contrast to "defence", the development and use of alternatives to arms tend to be underfunded. The European Union (EU) has recently established a Peace-building Partnership, designed to fund partners within civil society who are working to resolve conflicts, provide information about potential crises and deal with the consequences of conflict. The funding for this in 2007/8 was €15 million. This contrasts with the military spending in 2007 of UK of €46 billion (France €41 billion; Germany €28 billion; Italy €25 billion).[27] The comparison is instructive – a tiny fraction of the resources given to the military is allocated to avoiding the use of military conflict.

8.   The economics of defence

8.1 From earliest times, as evidenced for example by the reference to "trained men" in Gen 14: 14, humans have felt the need to provide for the defence of themselves, their families, territory or possessions. While this may have been achieved in the past by recruiting able-bodied non-professionals at a time of crisis, most countries now maintain a standing army. (There are a small number of countries, such as Iceland and Costa Rica, which are exceptions to this general rule). This obviously involves costs, both in financial and other terms; for example, personnel, buildings and land, which might otherwise have been used for other purposes, must be allocated,

and these must be maintained and serviced, incurring further resource costs, in terms of electricity, food, fuel, *etc.*

8.2 All governments need to make choices as to where to allocate the resources available to them. Military spending, along with spending on areas such as health and education, makes up a large part of the budget of many countries. However, it is often difficult to accurately assess how much a government actually spends on defence, as information relating to this may be classified for reasons of national security. In addition, much spending on defence may be indirect: for example, the UK MoD (Ministry of Defence) supports a significant amount of scientific research in Universities[28]. Estimating such "hidden" military spending can be problematic.

8.3 Many in the developed West have been rightly critical of developing countries which spend significantly larger portions of their budgets on military hardware than they do on more benign expenditure such as health and education: for example, the governments of Ethiopia, Yemen and Sri Lanka all allocate more than 15% of their budgets to military expenditure[29]. However, it is also recognised that, due to the skewed priorities of developed countries "millions of lives could be saved through basic health interventions that would cost a fraction of what the world spends on military forces every year"[30]. The world's total spending on defence is estimated to be US $1.47 trillion ($1,470,000,000,000). A number of comparisons can be drawn between the expenditure on weapons of war with areas such as health and international aid. These range from simple comparisons of how much a particular item of military hardware costs next to humanitarian aid,

[26] Figure derived from material published by the Federation of American Scientists. See http://www.fas.org/sgp/crs/natsec/RL33110.pdf and http://www.fas.org/sgp/crs/mideast/RL31833.pdf.

[27] Stockholm International Peace Research Institute 2008 Yearbook. http://yearbook2008.sipri.org/files/SIPRIYB08summary.pdf

[28] Scientists for Global Responsibility (2007): *More soldiers in the laboratory.* http://www.sgr.org.uk/pubdescs/MSITL.html.

[29] Ward, M. (2006): *International comparison of military expenditures.* SIPRI Yearbook. http://yearbook2006.sipri.org/chap8/app8e

[30] Stålenheim, P. (2007): *Military expenditure.* SIPRI Yearbook. http://yearbook2007.sipri.org/chap8

to comparing the entire budgets for defence and health for a particular country. Such comparisons indicate that not only is a disproportionate amount of money being spent on defence, but the disparity between this and spending on health and education continues to grow.

8.4 As has previously been noted, there are a number of "drivers" which affect the decision to go to war – for example, practical and political considerations. The political and economic power of the "military – industrial complex" in many developing countries has long been recognised. Thus the manufacturing and selling of weapons of war is often seen to be tightly bound up with the economic well-being of a nation or region. An example of this was seen in the recent allocation of the contracts for building the aircraft carriers for the Royal Navy, which were hailed as throwing a lifeline to shipbuilding on the Clyde.

9.   International arms trade

9.1 The UK has long been a "market leader" in military hardware and technology; this fact has significant political and economic implications. For example, any attempts to cut military research and development (R&D) spending are immediately protested as potentially affecting an industry which is integral to many communities, and which is also claimed to add significantly to the overall economy. Anything which detrimentally affects such a leading industry will diminish the UKs standing in the world, it is posited.

9.2 On coming to office in 1997, the Labour Secretary of State for Defence, Robin Cook, declared that under the new government's ethical defence policy,

> We will not permit the sale of arms to regimes that might use them for internal repression or international aggression.[31]

9.3 History has gone on to shown that such noble intent soon collides with commercial priorities- and that,

sadly, economic gain often trumps ethical concerns. The ongoing legal dispute over the investigation into the alleged bribery involved in the huge sale of BAE military equipment to the Saudi Arabian regime (whose human rights record, not least towards Christians, has been widely condemned, but which the "ethical" Labour government saw fit to continue to sell arms to) bears testimony to the kind of issues which need to be addressed. The significant level of lobbying required to persuade the UK government to support treaties limiting the use of certain munitions (land mines and, more recently, cluster bombs), and US government opposition to such treaties, are further examples of where ethical, economic and defence concerns conflict.

9.4 One of the many disconcerting aspects of military research is the extent to which it seeks to "dehumanise" conflict and combatants. Thus disturbing parallels have been drawn between footage of targeted "surgical strike" bombing raids in the first Gulf war and video games. Such "shock and awe" footage may make for good television, but gives an impression of unreality and little sense of the level of human suffering brought about by such actions. While it is recognised that part of the aim of developing high altitude bombing techniques may be to maintain the safety of the pilot and other aircrew, the fact that the aggressors do not actually see the targets being bombed makes it easier for them to dissociate themselves from the fact that the ultimate aim of their actions is to kill other humans. The development of pilotless "drones", aircraft controlled electronically from thousands of miles away, further extends this alienation. Thinking in terms of "just another target" may make the feeling of empathy which may lead to acts of restraint, forgiveness and reconciliation more difficult.

9.5 The precipitation of a conflict situation is good for suppliers of military hardware, as it means that ammunition must be replenished, and other hardware which has been damaged or lost needs to be replaced. The UK is one of the

---

[31] The Guardian (1997): *Cook gives ethics priority.* May 13th

largest and most successful manufacturers and exporters of military equipment in the world – yet, as a developed Western democracy, it surely has a moral responsibility to act in a manner which does not engender unnecessary conflict.

9.6 As both Chancellor and Prime Minister, Gordon Brown has been rightly lauded for the concern and leadership he has shown to increase the UKs international aid and development spending, to bring it closer to UN recommended levels, and to encourage other developed countries to do likewise. We as a Church have a responsibility to encourage those who lead us to show similar courage and determination in developing a responsible approach to reducing conflict and all of the costs associated with it – whether financial, environmental or human costs.

9.7 There is a need not only for a sober re-assessment of the allocation of our nation's resources to the pursuit of military might, but also a conscious decision must be made to disengage large sectors of the economy from this pursuit. Only then will the Biblical vision of swords becoming ploughshares[8] begin to become reality.

10. Military Covenant

10.1 The term Covenant has come to categorize the two phases of religious life and experience reflected in the pages of the Old and New Testaments. The Old Covenant refers to the religious order instituted by God through Moses with the people of Israel[32]. The New Covenant describes the renewal and extension of this through the death and resurrection of Jesus of Nazareth, celebrated in the Eucharist[33]. In Reformed theology, 'Covenant' usually refers to God's gracious promise to Abraham and his spiritual descendants that God will be a God and father to them and that they, enabled by God's grace, will live before God in faith and loving obedience.

10.2 In his book *"The Politics of Hope"* the Chief Rabbi Jonathan Sacks discusses covenantal rather than contractual institutions:

…where relationships are sustained, not by monetary exchange (market), nor by coercive use of power (the state), but instead by loyalty, faithfulness, mutuality and trust[34],

and goes on to argue that in covenant relationships,

…those bound by a covenant are obligated to respond to one another beyond the letter of the law rather than to limit their obligations to the narrowest contractual requirements.[35]

10.3 Sacks further suggests that

…covenants have a moral component that renders them more binding and open-ended than could be accounted for in terms of interest.[36]

10.4 According to the 2005 Army Doctrine Publication "Land Operations"[37] 'The Military Covenant' is described as follows:

Soldiers are bound by service. The nature of service is inherently unequal; soldiers may have to put in more than they receive. Ultimately, they may be called upon to make personal sacrifices – including death – in the service of the Nation. In putting the needs of the Nation, the Army and others before their own, they forgo some of the rights enjoyed by those outside the Armed Forces. So, at very least, British soldiers should always be able to expect the Nation, and their commanders, to treat them fairly, to value and respect them as individuals, and to sustain and reward them and their families with

---

[32] Ex. 19: 5, 6

[33] Luke 22: 20; 1 Cor. 11: 23-25; Richardson, A. and Bowden J. (ed) (1983): *A New Dictionary of Christian Theology*, SCM

[34] Sacks, J. (2000): *The Politics of Hope*, Vintage p. XVI.

[35] Ibid; p. 63.

[36] Op Cit.

[37] MoD Publication (2005): *ADP Land Operations*, May.

appropriate terms and conditions of service. This mutual obligation forms the Military Covenant between the Nation, the Army and each individual soldier. To a greater or lesser extent such a common bond of identity, loyalty and responsibility has sustained the Army and its soldiers throughout its history. It is a covenant, not a contract, and it is binding, in every circumstance... [38]

10.5 The concept of the Military Covenant lies at the heart of British Army doctrine. It describes the unwritten psychological contract between the soldier and the nation and implies that all parties have mutual obligations and responsibilities. It has perhaps its greatest manifestation in the annual Poppy Appeal and the national commemoration of Armistice Day, when

the nation keeps covenant with those who have made the ultimate sacrifice, giving their lives in action. [39]

10.6 In March 2007, following a series of stories on the medical neglect of British soldiers injured in Iraq and Afghanistan, the national press published an open letter to the Prime Minister stating that, while the Military Covenant is a cornerstone of our democracy, this Covenant appears to have been broken. Later in 2007 the British Legion complained that:

the British government was not honouring the Military Covenant and that troops were not being supported after returning from conflict. [40]

10.7 In response to demands for better casualty care, better accommodation and better resources for hard pressed troops, the Chief of the General Staff (CGS) and Professional Head of the Army General Sir Richard Dannatt stated that his firm aim was to restore the balance of the Military Covenant which he described as *clearly out of kilter at the moment.* [41]

10.8 Further to the comments of the CGS on the fractured state of the Military Covenant, Lord Guthrie and five other former defence chiefs also joined their voices to others who believed that relations between the military and the government were at an all time low.

10.9 In July 2008 the CGS commended the publication of a Government Strategy initiated by the Prime Minister to improve the level of support given to serving personnel, their families and veterans. This initiative not only sets out the nation's commitment to the Armed Forces but in certain cases also unashamedly promotes special treatment for all members of the armed services and their families who have sacrificed most, suffering death or major physical and/or mental injury, in the course of their duty. General Dannatt:

...[welcomed] this paper as an important step in the right direction for cross-Government support for what we in the Army call the Military Covenant. [42]

10.10 It remains to be seen whether and to what extent this will be resourced and implemented.

11. Christians in the Armed Services

11.1 It often seems to come as a surprise to some Christians that there are many serving with the armed forces and working in the Defence Industries who consider themselves Christians, and a significant number who are members of the Church of Scotland. While many Christians might struggle with the theoretical and academic aspects of the ethics of defence, many of

---

[38] *Land Operations*; p. 146.

[39] MoD Publication, *Army Doctrine Publication 5 – Soldiering – The Military Covenant.*

[40] http://www.bbc.co.uk/ethics/war; *Military Covenant;* Oct. 3rd 2008

[41] Rayment, S (2007): *"Our forces can't carry on like this, says General Sir Richard Dannatt".* Sunday Telegraph, 18th Nov. http://www.telegraph. co.uk/news/uknews/1569703/Our-forces-can't-carry-on-like-this,-says-General-Sir-Richard-Dannatt.html

[42] MoD Army Briefing Note 24/08: *Service Personnel Command Paper New Measures to Support Service Personnel, Their Families and Veterans.*

the issues that arise are a constant reality for Christians involved directly in our defence.

11.2 For many (though not all) Christians in the armed services, their career path can be considered as a calling, a desire to serve not only their country but also God, to make a difference and be a force for good. It goes without saying that these Christians find it difficult to share the perspective of Christians whose interpretation of the Gospel of our Lord Jesus Christ calls them to follow the path of pacifism. Nevertheless, there is a need to ensure that both these perspectives are held in balance to enable a sense of mutual understanding and respect to be developed between them.

11.3 For Christians in the armed services, resorting to violence would almost always be considered as a last resort and only called upon when all other options have been fully considered and exhausted. Nevertheless, on entering the armed services Christians realise they may be called on to take up arms and potentially take life in the course of their duties. Part of the motivation for most Christians entering the armed services is a belief that evil and violence is a reality. This is embodied in human nature's drive to exercise power over others, through nuclear and other weapons. Christian conscience calls us to resist evil, to preserve freedom, justice and peace. For some this may be interpreted as justification for applying appropriate and proportional violence to resist and turn back evil forces. They also feel that those in a position to conduct these actions should have a strong sense of what is right and wrong. Christians seek to imbue this in themselves and in others.

11.4 Arguably, the sense of respect which soldiers develop for their potential enemy is often far sharper and more sincere than most people would consider possible. Soldiers can often relate to other combatants in a way that civilians cannot as they see themselves being in similar situations. In traditional symmetric warfare, codes of honour and chivalry developed which servicemen

came to rely on. Unfortunately, these codes hardly exist in many of the current conflicts, where the principal motivation is not to defend but to attack indiscriminately to create terror. Supposed civilised forces are not innocent in this respect and in recent conflicts have descended to the level of terrorist themselves. In these circumstances, people with a strong sense of moral and ethical values are even more important to have within the armed forces.

11.5 Away from direct involvement in combat there are a myriad of ethical issues surrounding the research, development, procurement, deployment and planning for the use of weapon systems. Many decisions in respect of these have lead times in tens of years, and defence staff are faced with difficult judgements on the applicability and effectiveness of proposed new weapons systems and rarely linger long on ethical issues. Yet it is in this area where key decisions which shape the armed services, their effectiveness and applicability are taken which ultimately pose ethical problems. Once in service there are a wide range of other decisions on how systems are used and tactical scenarios derived that determine how training for the potential use of weapons is implemented and carried through. Again it could be argued that it is important that Christians engage in these decisions.

11.6 Few Christians would dispute that the ideal world would be one where justice and peace reigned supreme. This can be argued to be the main purpose of the armed services, who are a resource to help deter aggression and violence against society in general. Some consider defence forces as an insurance policy. Where this insurance fails these forces must be able to be used to mitigate and deter further escalation; to provide humanitarian aid; to help make and keep the peace; to resist insurgency and terrorism; and *in extremis*, where open unprovoked evil aggression and violence need to be resisted, to go to war.

11.7 At all levels within both the command structure and in direct combat situations there is a moral as well as a political imperative to ensure that decisions that are taken are justified and ethically supportable. However, beyond the training provided to all the armed forces there is little support given to ensure that the consciences and moral fibre are robust and stand up to the stress and pressures of combat. For those who turn to them the Chaplaincy service is vital. However, at critical times there is not often direct access to chaplains and they are rarely around when the most difficult decisions have to be made. God calls some Christians to be there when they are needed to help make the right decisions, resist evil and if required make the ultimate sacrifice.

11.8 As well as needing our prayers, serving personnel and chaplains also need our practical support and understanding as Christians in trying to be a force for good in what are inherently evil situations.

12. Conclusion

12.1 From ancient times, making preparation to defend one's territory has been seen as wise – indeed, divinely directed: see, for example, David building up the defences of the city of Jerusalem (2 Samuel 5: 9, 10), or Ahab receiving prophetic instruction to *"strengthen his position"* in anticipation of further raids by Aramean forces (1 Kings 20: 22). However, the dividing line between legitimate defence and a more aggressive, threatening posture has often been difficult to draw the more so as weaponry and warfare have become more "advanced" and technological.

12.2 Many of the issues raised in this report remain controversial: significant strands of Christian thought are to be found on both sides of the debate on pacifism and war[43]. The concept of the "just war"[44] (or indeed a "just peace") is one which continues to exercise much thought. Christ came as the servant king: assuredly, to *"lead justice*

to victory"* (Matt. 12: 20) – but to do so without violence, as the preceding verses (indeed, Christ's whole ministry) make plain. However, it is evident that justice is all too often emphatically not victorious in the world around us. How are we, as followers of Christ, to respond?

12.3 The General Assembly of the Church of Scotland has long held nuclear weapons to be immoral and wasteful; the UK has a moral responsibility to show leadership in abandoning the historic concept of nuclear deterrence.

12.4 Separating personal opinion and national interest from "doing the right thing" has often been problematic: perhaps, with Abraham Lincoln, we should remind ourselves that our concern

> …*is not whether God is on our side; [our] greatest concern is to be on God's side, for God is always right.*[45]

Acknowledgements:

In addition to members of the Church and Society Council, we would gratefully acknowledge the following who were involved in the preparation of this report:

Professor Anthony Carty Professor of Public Law, University of Aberdeen

Dr Anthony Lang Senior Lecturer, School of International Relations, University of St. Andrews

Professor William Walker School of International Relations, University of St Andrews

Suggested Practical outcomes:

The Church and Society Council would offer the following as some examples of practical responses local churches or Presbyteries could develop:

• Worship/study resources to make clear the issues

---

[43] Barclay, O.R. (Ed) (1984): *Pacifism and War (When Christians Disagree)* (Inter-Varsity Press)

[44] Guthrie, C. and M. Quinlan (2007): *Just War: The Just War Tradition: Ethics in Modern Warfare.* Walker & Company

[45] http://thinkexist.com/quotation/sir-my_concern_is_not_whether_god_is_on_our_side/164075.html

- Encourage a different budgeting priority within the MOD that focuses on mobile forces for humanitarian missions and policing missions.
- Meetings with Defence Secretary
- Internet petition against Trident
- Postcard campaign against Trident
  - Send stack of postcards to all congregations
  - Other lobbying of MPs/MSPs – pro forma letter
- Praying for all affected by military conflict (including "enemies")
- Support for local so ldiers: many members of congregations may know somebody serving with the military. Support could be offered in a variety of practical ways
  - Prayer
  - Letters/e-mails
- Support for military Chaplains
  - Prayer
  - Letters/e-mails
  - food parcels
- Support by congregations for local military personnel and families
- Evangelism: *eg* SASRA: Soldiers and Airmen's Scripture Readers Association (http://www.sasra.org.uk)

PAPER 4
END OF LIFE ISSUES

1. Introduction

1.1 The aim of this report is to consider many of the issues surrounding the end of life. Some of the areas considered are sensitive and emotive. A significant amount of media coverage in the past year has surrounded decisions by individuals to seek assisted death, or to refuse medical treatment. However, one of the great joys which the Christian church has is the responsibility to proclaim the message that there is more to life than simply this life: as Paul says,

If for this life only we have hoped in Christ, we are of all people most to be pitied [1]

1.2 It is also recognised that the church has the opportunity not only to offer spiritual comfort to those coming towards the end of their lives, but also to ensure that their last days are as fulfilled as possible.

1.3 There is a tendency in much of the public debate on issues surrounding death to infer some ill-defined excellence or worthiness, to refer to "dying with dignity", when the reality for the carer or onlooker may appear to be the converse. In general by 'death' we mean physical death and not spiritual death; in the Old Testament the ideal may be thought of as the death of Abraham, who:

breathed his last and died at a good old age, an old man and full of years [2],

in contradistinction to the many murders and massacres which are recorded.

1.4 It must be remembered that ethical decision – making near the end of life:
- **1.4.1** is not done in a vacuum. Wrestling with ethical issues around a time of death is done by patients, clinicians, carers and relatives who all bring their own life experience, values, beliefs and feelings to the decision-making process, which itself takes place in a specific context involving a unique patient with a disease or injury presenting itself in a particular way.
- **1.4.2** is an art not a science, no matter how many Biblical principles and ethical guidelines are followed.
- **1.4.3** has pastoral implications – spiritual (including an impact on beliefs and values, as well as raising 'why' questions) and psychological – for patient, relatives and staff. The death itself, the manner of the death, or the continuing survival of a patient and their subsequent

---

[1] I Cor. 15: 19 (NRSV)
[2] Gen. 25: 8

quality of life are significant, as is the decision-making process, and by whom decisions are made.

1.5 The whole focus of "end of life" should not just be on the moment of physical death, but on the period (days, weeks or months) leading up to that event, with the emphasis on achieving the best quality of life possible. The focus should follow the palliative care model of holistic care – physical, psychological, spiritual, social – with positive objectives which will enhance the remaining days of the patient, and of relatives and carers. This is true "dignity in death".

2. Definition of terms
2.1 Palliative Care:
2.1.1 Palliative care is an approach which improves the quality of life of patients and their families facing the problems associated with life-threatening illness, through the prevention and relief of suffering by means of early identification and impeccable assessment and treatment of pain and other problems (physical, psychological, social and spiritual). Palliative care:
- provides relief from pain and other distressing symptoms;
- affirms life and regards dying as a normal process;
- intends neither to hasten or postpone death;
- integrates the psychological and spiritual aspects of patient care;
- offers a support system to help patients live as actively as possible until death;
- offers a support system to help the family cope during the patient's illness and in their own bereavement;
- uses a team approach to address the needs of patients and their families, including bereavement counselling, if indicated;
- will enhance quality of life, and may also positively influence the course of illness;
- is applicable early in the course of illness, in conjunction with other therapies which are intended to prolong life, such as chemotherapy or radiation therapy, and includes

those investigations needed to better understand and manage distressing clinical complications.

For further information see www.who.int/cancer/palliative/definition/en

2.2 The Liverpool Care Pathway (LCP)
2.2.1 The LCP represents a continuous quality improvement programme for care of the dying. It allows for the transfer of best practice care of the dying in the hospice environment into other care settings. A key feature of the LCP is that it empowers generic healthcare workers to deliver optimum care to dying patients, irrespective of diagnosis.

For further information see www.mcpcil.org.uk/liverpool_care_pathway

2.3 The Gold Standards Framework (GSF)
2.3.1 The GSF is a systematic evidence based approach to optimising the care for patients nearing the end of life in the community. It aims to develop a locally-based system to improve and optimise the organisation and quality of care for patients and their carers, and to help people to live well until the end of life.

For further information see www.goldstandardsframework.nhs.uk

3. Spirituality and Religion
3.1 Spirituality is a well used and recognised term, yet one which lacks a clear definition. However, that lack of definition is a strength since it requires us to engage with people and to discuss spiritual needs rather than assess spirituality against set criteria. End of life care issues regularly lead to the concept of suffering, and a key element of suffering is pain. Spiritual suffering can contribute to physical pain but more often presents as distress rather than as pain. Common areas of distress include fear of dying, and questions such as "why me?", and "how and when will I die?". As the end of life draws

closer, these concerns for self often change to become focused on others and include concern for family, friends, social and financial needs, and religion[3].

3.2 Spirituality is also regularly confused with religion. Religion may be a part of a person's spirituality but not always. While all family carers and professional carers have the potential to provide spiritual care, in hospitals and hospices there are chaplains who have experience and expertise in spiritual and religious care. Chaplains are appointed to provide spiritual care to all patients, their visitors, and staff.

3.3 In recent years the provision of spiritual and religious care has benefited greatly from multi-faith and multicultural approaches to healthcare and also the move towards professionalisation of healthcare chaplaincy. Religious care, and Christianity in particular, was in danger of being sidelined. However, along with the other world faiths, the spiritual and religious needs of Christians are taken seriously by the Scottish Government and NHS Scotland. NHS Education for Scotland, in partnership with the Scottish Interfaith Council, produced the report: *'Religion and Belief Matter'*[4], which clearly states that spiritual and religious care are essential elements of healthcare.

3.4 The Church and Society Council acknowledges and endorses the Scottish Government definitions of Spiritual and Religious Care published in the Chief Executive Letter (2008) 49 which sets their relationship in context:

> *The NHS in Scotland recognises that the health care challenges faced by the people it cares for may raise their need for spiritual or religious care and is committed to addressing these needs.*

Spiritual care is usually given in a one to one relationship, is completely person centred and makes no assumptions about personal conviction or life orientation.

Religious care is given in the context of shared religious beliefs, values, liturgies and lifestyle of a faith community.

Spiritual care is not necessarily religious. Religious care should always be spiritual. Spiritual care might be said to be the umbrella term of which religious care is a part. It is the intention of religious care to meet spiritual need.[5]

3.5 Much of the contemporary discourse around end of life issues focuses primarily on physical illness, particularly when a terminal condition is diagnosed. The debate around mental ill-health and end of life choice is an equally complex area and, whilst not the subject of this report, the Church and Society Council recognise the importance of mental illness and acknowledge the need for appropriate study in this area.

4. Advance Decisions

4.1 An advance decision (AD), known as an 'advance directive' (commonly referred to as a 'living will'), is a document which expresses the wishes of an individual as to their treatment should they become mentally incapacitated in the future and unable to make decisions. Under the *Adults with Incapacity (Scotland) Act* 2000 there are two specific Powers of Attorney. The legislation provides for

(1) A "continuing attorney" who has authority to manage financial and property matters, and
(2) A "welfare attorney" who has authority to manage matters relating to personal welfare.

---

[3] Mitchell, D. (2008): *Spiritual and cultural issues at the end of life*. Medicine 36: 109-110.

[4] SCF, NHS Scotland, *et al.* (2007). *Religion and Belief Matter: A resource for all healthcare staff*. Glasgow, The Scottish Interfaith Council.

[5] The Scottish Government (2008). Chief Executive Letter 49 *Spiritual Care*. Edinburgh, The Scottish Government Healthcare Policy and Strategy Directorate.

These are registered with the Public Guardian in Scotland. The "welfare attorney" would (or should) be aware of any advance directives the patient has made, and has legal authority to be involved in any discussions/decisions relating to the patients medical/nursing care.

4.2 Why have advance decisions?

4.2.1 It is a growing concern that many people will end up in hospital or in a long stay institution and lose their competence, and thus autonomy, in decision-making. An AD gives them the same right to refuse treatment as a competent patient. The demand for advance decisions is partly driven by fear – of prolonged pain (and suffering), of indignity, and of dependence on others and/or on machines.

4.3 It has been long recognised that an individual has the right to self determination, and that every person has the right to have his bodily integrity protected against invasion by others:

> ...the right of the competent individual to refuse treatment is ingrained in both common law and human rights law – and this right persists even though it may result in the patient's death.[6]

4.3.1 It is argued that an adult should be similarly allowed to make decisions about their future treatment should that person lose competence.

4.4 An AD enables the doctor in charge of a patient with impaired decision-making abilities to take into account the individual's wishes. It can transfer some responsibility for difficult decisions from family onto medical professionals. Indeed, it can comfort families to have some 'steer' from the patient. In some cases, the wishes of relatives will not necessarily coincide with those of the patient, and may be biased by financial and other considerations.

4.5 What are some of the problems with advance decisions?

4.5.1 ADs assume that prognosis is a precise art when this is far from being the case. In the real world medical prognosis is frequently right, but often wrong. It is also difficult to draw up a document which clearly defines all possible circumstances and can unambiguously define what is a 'severe' disability or illness.

4.6 ADs indicate the patient's past, rather than their present, attitude to terminal care. Individuals often change their minds on this matter over time. The healthy do not choose in the same way as the sick. In other words, an AD is less conclusive than the current statement of a competent, fully informed person.

4.7 ADs may specify that no fluid or food should be provided by artificial means; however, some doctors do not regard nutrition and hydration, by whatever means provided, as medical treatment. There is concern that food and fluids could be prohibited in cases when it would be clinically appropriate. Changing circumstances may render the AD inappropriate or even obstructive to the best care indicated for new circumstances. If such a decision were to be binding, the best management may be precluded. It is also claimed that ADs are a 'Trojan horse' aimed at the legalisation of euthanasia.[7] Although they cannot demand that active steps should be taken to end life, ADs have been vigorously supported by pro-euthanasia organisations, such as Dignity in Dying.

4.8 The current position

4.8.1 ADs are legally valid for refusing treatment, but not for expressing treatment preferences, and will in all likelihood remain in use. We appreciate there are some benefits for their use but we are concerned that while the theory driving them may be simple, the practice is not. It is difficult to draw up a document which will be definitive in all potential circumstances leaving little room for change

---

[6] Mason, J.K. and Laurie, G.T. (2006): *Mason & McCall Smith's Law and Medical Ethics* 7th ed. Oxford: Oxford University Press, p630.

[7] Care not Killing: www.carenotkilling.org.uk

of mind during the critical time. We do not support any legal extension of their use or scope. However, the use of a welfare attorney, who has the authority to manage matters relating to personal welfare, who would be closely involved in discussions with health professionals and would be fully aware of the patients' wishes would be an alternative, whether or not the person has an AD.

4.9 A good relationship in which clear communication takes place between trained and experienced healthcare professionals and patient – as is usually the case with palliative care in hospices – is consistently better than an AD.

Previous deliverances by the General Assembly

The subject of Euthanasia has been discussed by the General Assembly of the Church of Scotland on four occasions, with Deliverances as follows :-

Deliverance in **1977:**

" …[while] *we are aware of no theological difficulty in allowing a patient* in extremis *to die naturally, [we] disapprove of the deliberate termination of life…"*

Deliverance in **1981:**

"The General Assembly re-affirms the view consistently held, that the Christian recognises no right to dispose of his own life…"

Deliverance in **1994:**

(following the submission of a Study Group report on "Euthanasia – AChristian Perspective"[8]). *".the General Assembly opposes the introduction of legislation on Euthanasia, abhors its practice, and rejects the principles on which it is proposed…."*

Supplement of **2008:**

A review was requested by the General Assembly in 2007 and this was based on the

---

House of Lords Select Committee on Medical Ethics report in 1994 which begins:

There should be no change in the law to permit euthanasia.

This Report contained 21 conclusions and recommendations. The 2008 Supplement reviewed the developments and medical advances over the last decade and was approved by the General Assembly of 2008.

---

5. Assisted dying

5.1 "Assisted dying" is a relatively new phrase which frequently replaces "physician assisted suicide" (PAS) or euthanasia in literature. Euthanasia has particularly unacceptable connotations, and the move to a less evocative terminology perhaps reflects a changing attitude in society to those who elect to take this route at life's end. In common with many Christians, the Church of Scotland through the General Assembly has long opposed euthanasia. However, for those with different, or indeed no religious beliefs, many would claim the right to exercise autonomy in taking this final decision.

5.2 Several factors have influenced this perceived change in attitude. The Kirk's 1995 Report on Euthanasia pointed out that

suicide is still recognised by most people as a tragedy, but no longer as a sin.[8]

Legislation now exists in several other countries permitting PAS within certain guidelines. The unsuccessful Bill introduced in 2006 by Lord Joffe sought to achieve this in the UK Parliament, and MSP Margo Macdonald's proposed End of Life Choices (Scotland) Bill to the

---

[8] Board of Social Responsibility, Church of Scotland (1997): *Euthanasia, a Christian perspective;* Church and Society Council, Church of Scotland (2008): *Supplement to Euthanasia, a Christian perspective.*

Scottish Parliament has the same aim. Facilities now exist in Switzerland (Dignitas) enabling other nationals to avail themselves of assisted suicide, and there has been widespread reporting in the media of patients travelling there from the UK. Such reporting has generally been of a sympathetic nature. Concern has also been expressed that, despite great advances in palliative care, resources for end of life care in the UK are less than satisfactory.

5.3 There is some support for permissive legislation, as was demonstrated by patients backing the actions of the Glasgow GP, Dr Kerr, who had to face GMC censure for providing a lethal prescription for a terminally ill patient. For the medical profession, the proposal to allow PAS represents a move away from one of its basic tenets – to preserve life. Despite this, a small on-line survey of 92 doctors in September 2008 showed 35% in favour of legalising PAS[9].

5.4 It is still difficult to assess whether the legalisation of PAS elsewhere has given rise to increasing numbers choosing to avail themselves of it. There is concern that some might feel themselves under pressure to accept PAS to avoid placing burdens of care on their loved ones. Data from Oregon suggest that in 10 years of legalised assisted dying there has been no rise in the number seeking the option[10]- although this conclusion is disputed in other studies[11]. There is also concern, however, that legalisation there has undermined, rather than enhanced, other aspects of end of life care. In the Netherlands a fall in assisted dying reporting in fact resulted from an increase in the use of terminal deep sedation (Deep sedation, defined as: "the use of pharmacological intervention intended to induce or maintain sedation (deep sleep) to

reduce the palliative patient's awareness of distressing and refractory symptoms", is NOT equivalent to euthanasia when the intention is not to induce death)[12].

5.5 Assisted dying is usually presented as a "dignified" death. This is not always the case, indeed relatives are frequently discouraged from being present at the point of death. NHS Scotland has produced a plan for improvements in palliative care, "Living and Dying Well"[13] to address the issue of current deficiencies. Clearly it would be a disgrace if vulnerable patients opted for assisted dying because of a lack of resources to give them an acceptable quality of life in their last months.

6.   End of life issues in children
6.1 This subject was dealt with extensively in the 1997 Report on Euthanasia[8] from the Church of Scotland Board of Social Responsibility, to which readers are referred. The authors of that report included a specialist neonatal paediatrician; the current study group contained no such expertise, and it was felt that no change to the previously established position was required. Some of the main points from the 1997 report are reproduced below:

6.2 Paediatric terminal illness: The conscious child
6.2.1   Most conscious children requiring terminal care are cancer patients; there has been significant recent expansion in the specialised hospice provision for children.

6.3 The emotional aspects of caring for a dying child are difficult for parents and staff to handle, irrespective of the symptoms of the condition. Carers must consider the autonomy of children, as well as considering them as people who have a right and a need to know what is happening to them in terms that they can understand.

[9] Foster, K. (2008): *One in three medics back mercy killing*. Scotsman, 8th Sept.

[10] Quill, T.E. (2008): *Physician assisted death in the United States: Essay – Are the Existing "Last Resorts" Enough?* Hastings Centre Report 38: 17-22.

[11] Hiscox, W.E. (2007): *Physician-assisted suicide in Oregon: the 'Death with Dignity' data*. Medical Law International 8: 197-220.

[12] Rietjens, J. et al (2008): *Continuous deep sedation for patients nearing death in the Netherlands: descriptive study*. BMJ 336: 810-3.

[13] The Scottish Government (2008): *Living and Dying Well: A National Action Plan for Palliative and End of Life Care in Scotland*. CEL 40.

A child, like an adult, has the right to express wishes, feelings and preferences; this must include the opportunity to accept or refuse treatment: *eg* further chemotherapy where there may be doubt as to the likelihood of response. It is responsible and necessary to give factual information to a child as much as to an adult, and experience has shown that children may handle the terminal care situation better than many adults.

6.4 Adequate symptom relief, sometimes self-administered and controlled by the child, and support for the family through the time of trauma are essential.

6.5 Involving family (including siblings) in decisions results in easier relationships and management of difficult situations. Counselling of the whole family is often necessary, and involvement of other children in family grief has a healing effect. Long family silence about a dead child, although common, generally has a destructive effect.

6.6 Paediatric terminal illness: The unconscious child
6.6.1 These are usually sufferers from trauma, head injury, and brain lesions of various kinds. The most frequent problem encountered is head injury related to traffic accidents. The criteria and debates for brain death are the same as in adults. 'Switch-off' decisions are generally made on the same grounds of negative expectation of recovery; parents usually have the veto and often wish to continue life support initially, but may reach a point of acceptance of the futility of this after an opportunity to come to terms with the realities of the situation. Where the life-support requires to be switched off, this is usually done with the parents present, one of them often holding the child in the period after switch-off.

6.7 The Christian response
6.7.1 The Christian response will involve
• Palliative care with appropriate responses and resources.
• Better communication in respect of the child, taking account of the need for counselling and a recognition and respect for the child, equally, as a person formed in the image of God.
• Valid motivation: the phrase 'compassion mingled with respect', attributed to Mother Teresa, perhaps sums up the most constructive attitude. The irreducible minimum of care could be defined as: fluid and nutrition, analgesia and tender loving care (TLC).

7. Definition of Cessation of Life
7.1 While it must be recognised that, in many cases, death is a process rather than simply a point in time, "brain death" as a legal definition of the cessation of life emerged in the 1960s as a response to the ability to resuscitate individuals and to mechanically keep the heart and lungs working. In simple terms, brain death is the irreversible end of all brain activity (including involuntary activity necessary to sustain life) following loss of blood flow and oxygenation.

7.2 Traditionally, both the legal and medical communities determined death through the end of certain bodily functions, especially breathing and heart beat. With the increasing ability to resuscitate people with no heart beat, respiration or other signs of life, the need for a better definition of death became obvious. This need gained greater urgency with the widespread use of life support equipment (which can maintain body functions indefinitely), as well as rising capabilities and demand for organ transplantation.

7.3 Today, both the legal and medical communities use brain death as a legal definition of death. Using brain-death criteria, the medical community can declare a person legally dead even if life support equipment keeps the body's metabolic processes working. A brain-dead individual has no clinical evidence of brain function upon physical examination. This includes no response to pain, no cranial nerve reflexes, and no spontaneous respirations. It is important to distinguish between brain death and states which may mimic brain death (eg barbiturate intoxication, hypoglycemia, coma or chronic vegetative states). Some comatose patients can recover, and some patients with severe irreversible neurological dysfunction will nonetheless retain some lower brain functions such as spontaneous respiration, despite the losses of both cortex and brainstem functionality.

7.4 The diagnosis of brain death needs to be rigorous to determine whether the condition is irreversible. Legal criteria vary, but it generally requires neurological examinations by two independent physicians; these must show complete absence of brain function, and may include two flat-line electro-encephalograms (EEGs) 24 hours apart.

7.5 Despite the adoption of such criteria in the United Kingdom, brain death has been questioned from the beginning. For example, brain dead pregnant women have lived up to 200+ days and given birth to healthy children[14]. Others have argued that there is insufficient evidence that the entire brain is dead in a brain dead individual. Some brain dead individuals have continuing EEG activity and others maintain normal or near-normal body temperature, implying continuing hypothalamic function. While it is unlikely that the medical profession will revert to the "heart death" definition of the cessation of life, it should be noted that this area remains controversial.

8. Sedation

8.1 Symptom control should be based on the needs of each individual patient. While deep sedation may not often be used deliberately, sedation can be a side effect of other treatments and must be assessed continuously. Symptoms such as pain, restlessness, obstruction with vomiting, breathlessness, swallowing problems and spiritual pain, can be very distressing not only for the patient but also for their carers and loved ones.

[14] Shewmon, D. A. (1998): *Chronic 'brain death': Meta-analysis and conceptual consequences.* Neurology 51: 1538–1545

8.2 Pain relief is usually given orally, following the World Health Organisation 'analgesic ladder'. If the patient cannot tolerate it, or if nausea is the main problem, medication can be given by a syringe pump until symptoms are under control, and patients often manage to revert to oral medication. Assessment should be done in a multi-disciplinary setting, and it is often the nursing staff who will alert the doctors and initiate change in symptom control as they are closest to the patient.

8.3 It is difficult to say at which point it could be argued that some of the drugs used might "hasten death", as the progression of disease is often relentless and symptoms need to be controlled. Sometimes patients require sedation to allow them to have a good night's sleep, as they are so anxious and exhausted. After this they can often cope better and are able to face things calmly.

8.4 The wishes of the patient should always be paramount. They may have preconceived fears, which when explained can be resolved. While relatives are closely involved, it is the patient who should decide. Many patients ask not to be allowed to suffer. The 2003 WHO declaration on palliative care states that suffering should be prevented or relieved (See Definition of Terms).

8.5 Many aspects of the physiology of dying are well established, such as withdrawal from the world, declining food, and sleeping. Alleviation of dehydration can be part of the palliative symptom control, such as by intravenous or subcutaneous fluids. Relatives often get alarmed when these things happen, and it is important that staff give adequate explanations. Many Scottish health boards now follow the Liverpool Care Pathway, training medical staff in spiritual aspects of palliative care, such as the concept of spiritual pain and suffering.

8.6 Most patients know they are dying. Many do not fear death itself but are afraid as to how they are going to die. Relatives can either help or hinder a 'good death' as they may refuse to accept the reality, even though the patient has done so. This can prevent the patient from fully opening up as they feel they have to be brave and pretend they are fine. Careful exploration of issues by medical and nursing staff can help.

9. Non- malignant conditions

9.1 More resources are often available to those with a diagnosis of malignancy (cancer) than to those with other, but no less life-threatening, conditions of a non-cancerous nature: a cancer diagnosis often attracts more sympathy and concern in a community, frequently stimulating major fund raising initiatives of great and lasting value. Financial aid, hospice facilities, and nursing support can be harder to access for sufferers from some of these "Cinderella" conditions. Much support for the terminally ill depends on charitable funding rather than the NHS. The hospice movement is one example of this, and support organisations such as Marie Curie Cancer Care, Macmillan Cancer Support, and the Maggie's Centres[15] also rely upon charitable giving. Unfortunately, some of these facilities are provided for cancer sufferers only[16].

9.2 The *"Living and Dying Well"*[13] action plan for palliative and end of life care in Scotland, produced in 2008 by NHS Scotland, recognises the need to address this problem, and gives a useful classification system for non-cancerous illnesses with poor prognosis.
- **9.2.1** The first category is those with Organ Failure. This includes heart disease (mainly heart failure), chronic lung disease, end-stage kidney failure, and neurological conditions. The three most significant illnesses in the last group are Motor Neurone Disease,

Multiple Sclerosis, and Parkinson's disease.
- **9.2.2** The second category comprises patients with frailty (multiple conditions leading to increasing impairment of function), Dementia, and Stroke.

9.3 None of these conditions can be described as curable, and thus sufferers are approaching the end of life, though that point may be months or even years away. The impact of any one of these diagnoses on a patient and their families can be devastating.

9.4 Many cancerous conditions are now treatable and some curable. People with organ failure or dementia can only look forward to their health deteriorating at an unpredictable rate. A good example of the problems surrounding this issue is the situation of people with dementia. In addition to living with an incurable condition, those with dementia must live with the knowledge that they will eventually lose control of their lives and actions. Patients with many of these conditions spend considerable periods of time at home with a partner, who is often also in their later years and with physical disabilities, and who may become increasingly worn down and frustrated. People often describe seeing a partner's decline into dementia and ultimate death as a "double bereavement".

9.5 From a subjective point of view, being helpless and in need of care because of dementia might well seem like a great indignity, especially in a society such as ours which puts a premium on autonomy and independence. But this does not mean that persons with dementia have lost their intrinsic human dignity. Philosophers have argued that people with dementia:

> …*should be retained within a circle of protection, because we remember what they have achieved and we honour their biographical past…Rightly so, for surely (all) those who are ill, dependent and dying remain our fellow humans. As such they never lose their dignity.*[17]

---

[15] Maggie's Centres have been developed with the express purpose of providing a wide range of care and assitance for cancer patients and their relatives. This includes help with information, benefits advice, psychological support both individually and in groups, courses and stress reducing strategies. See http://www.maggiescentres.org

[16] Shipman, C. *et al.* (2008): *Improving generalist end of life care: national consultation with practitioners, commissioners, academics, and service user groups.* British Medical Journal 337:a1720

[17] Sutton, A. (2008): *Christian Bioethics: A Guide for the Perplexed*, T&T Clark, p54

9.6 To be cared for by others requires trust in the carer. It requires recognition of the carer as caring and of the importance of human community. Decisions should not be influenced by perceived quality of life criteria because every patient, with or without dementia, should be equally valued and provided with the love and support of others.

9.7 Most patients in these categories require frequent hospital admission as time progresses. They cannot enjoy holidays as they may be uninsurable for travel, they are unemployable, and they cannot plan for an uncertain future. In addition, people with chronic lung disease and their families may be locked in legal struggles for compensation over a perceived cause of their illness, with settlements often outstanding at the time of death.

9.8 The main needs are for day-time support, and in the later stages night-time also; for good continuity of nursing and medical care; for adequate respite care; and, ultimately for many, a residential placement which allows partners to visit on a regular basis. Sadly, in much of rural Scotland this last need cannot be met, and many life partners are separated during their final months together. The *Living and Dying Well* plan is to be welcomed, addressing as it does the need to recognise the special requirements of families affected by these conditions. It also sets out to apply good models of practice such as the Gold Standards Framework and the Liverpool Care Pathway to non-cancer patients, ensuring a truly holistic approach. Palliative care practitioners are well aware of these needs and are striving to improve access to hospice beds[18]. The recent initiative by Marie Curie Cancer Care and the British Heart Foundation to set up a pilot centre in Glasgow for heart failure patients and their families is also a very welcome development indeed[19].

10. Nutrition and hydration

10.1 This subject is a much wider debate than simply "End of life issues". Within the euthanasia debate it usually focuses on the withdrawal of artificial feeding, as in the case of Tony Bland who was in a Persistent Vegetative State (see Airedale NHS Trust v. Bland, 1993[20]). In the Bland case Lord Lowry expressed his view as:

> *I do not believe that there is a valid distinction between omission to treat a patient and the abandonment of treatment which has been commenced, since to recognise such a distinction could quite illogically confer on a doctor who had refrained from treatment an immunity which did not benefit a doctor who had embarked on treatment in order to see whether it might help the patient and had abandoned the treatment when it was not seen to do so.*

10.2 If 'end of life' is strictly defined as the last hours or days, then thirst may be appropriately managed by good mouth care and soothing by whatever the patient finds helpful (*eg* sucking ice or pineapple).

10.3 Artificial nutrition and hydration have been considered as medical treatments by the British Medical Association (BMA) since 1992. Subsequently the BMA ethics committee in 1999 proposed that the withdrawal of artificial nutrition or hydration from incapacitated patients should not only be possible for patients in Persistent Vegetative State but should also be an option for patients who have suffered a "serious stroke or have severe dementia", states in which patients may continue for months or years. Guidelines have been given by the BMA Ethics Committee.[21]

---

[18] Sugden, C, Consultant Palliative Care Physician, St Andrew's Hospice, Airdrie: Personal communication

[19] Puttick, H. (2008). *Charities team up to give palliative care to patients with heart disease*: The Herald. Dec. 17th

[20] http://www.swarb.co.uk/c/hl/1993airedale_bland.html

[21] British Medical Association Ethics Committee report (1999): *Withholding or Withdrawing Life-Prolonging Medical Treatment – Guidance for Decision Making*: Section 21.4

10.4 Some health professionals regard the provision of artificial nutrition and hydration as basic care which should always be provided unless the patient's death is inevitable, in which case the benefits may no longer be proportional to the burdens. There has been considerable debate over the last decade on the subject of hydration. The ethical, legal and medical dangers of a regime of sedation without hydration in the dying has been reviewed in a 2005 publication *"No water – No life: Hydration in the Dying".*[22]

10.5 A serious issue arises in the general care of frail elderly patients where adequate fluid intake may be limited by difficulty in holding a cup or pouring a drink, and where adequate nutrition may be inhibited by inappropriate food or food presented in such a way that the patient cannot feed themselves. If adequate and appropriate nutrition and hydration is medical treatment then it must be supervised by a health care professional. If it is general care, there is a risk that it regarded as the responsibility of the patient and their 'human rights' to take or refuse what is provided.

11. Allocation of resources for end of life care

11.1 Palliative Care: In 2006/2007 in Scotland, £59 million was spent on specialist palliative care, half of which came from the voluntary sector. It is not possible to say how much is spent on non- specialist (generalist) palliative care. Part of the difficulty is in deciding when the end of life period starts. The Scottish Government launched an action plan for palliative care in Scotland in October 2008[13]. It is not clear how much money is pledged to implement this plan. Key elements of this strategy are two systems: the Liverpool Care Pathway and the Gold Standards Framework.

11.2 In terms of place of death, 58% of deaths occur in hospitals, 18% occur at home, 17% in care homes, 3% in hospices, and 3% other[23].

11.2.1 **Hospices:** Most specialist palliative care is focussed in hospices, where the majority of patients have cancer. Hospices care particularly for those who have complex problems such as hard-to-control pain.

11.2.1.1 The majority of people who are dying are therefore cared for by staff who are not specialists in palliative care, either in hospitals, care homes or in their own homes. Not everyone who is dying has complex needs which require a specialist. However, a recent report on palliative care services in Scotland identified that good palliative care is not always available to everyone who needs it. This is particularly true for those dying from non-malignant diseases such as dementia, heart disease and respiratory disease[24].

11.2.2 **Care Homes**: Scotland has an ageing population, and the number of people dying in care homes is increasing. There is evidence to suggest that there is suffering among those dying in care homes for various reasons, including:
- lack of access to palliative care education
- high turnover of staff
- low staffing levels
- an emphasis on rehabilitation which makes dying peripheral, despite the fact that those living in care homes are increasingly frail with complex needs on admission.

11.2.2.1 The majority of care home residents die within two years of admission[25]. Although care home staff training is largely co-ordinated by the Scottish Commission for the Regulation of Care, maintenance of levels of trained, competent and motivated staff is largely

[22] Craig, G.M. (2005): *No water – No life: Hydration in the Dying.* Fairway Folio

[23] Department of Health (2008): *End of Life Care Strategy – promoting high quality care for all adults at the end of life,* London

[24] Audit Scotland (2008): *Review of Palliative Care Services in Scotland.* Edinburgh, August

[25] Hockley, J., B. Dewar and J. Watson (2004): *Developing quality end of life care in eight independent nursing homes through the implementation of an integrated care pathway for the last days of life. Phase 3 of Bridges Initiative.* Copies are available from jwatson@stcolumbashospice.org.uk

the responsibility of individual care homes. Emphasis in training is usually given to nutrition, hydration and pain control; spiritual care is often considered less important.

11.2.2.2 Changing practice in care homes takes time as it involves a change in the culture of care. This requires adequate resources in terms of practice development projects which are long enough to allow changes to be embedded and sustained. A key recommendation of a recent feasibility study on the use of the Gold Standards Framework in Care Homes was the need for greater availability of palliative care support and more formal links between care homes and providers of specialist palliative care[26].

11.2.3 Hospitals: Hospital specialist palliative care teams are now well established in larger hospitals. These teams are usually small and have an advisory/educational role. However, most patients are only in hospital for a relatively short period of time (2-3 weeks in most cases).

11.2.3.1 More than half (54%) of all complaints made about the NHS are about deaths in hospitals. Many of these complaints relate to poor communication about death and dying[27]; with increasing awareness of these issues among hospital staff, it would be hoped that this would improve.

11.2.4 Home: Although many people with progressive illness say they would like to die at home, the majority of people continue to die in hospital. The factors which influence where people die are complex but include:

- Factors related to illness– clinical changes which occur because of illness
- Individual factors– patients' beliefs, wishes and inner

resources to cope with illness, and also carers at home who face increasing burdens with the advancing condition of the patient
- Environmental factors– healthcare input available and social support networks, in addition to layout of the house (for example, when the bathroom is on a different floor to the bedroom), and wheelchair access to and within the house[28]

11.2.4.1 In practice, some of the reasons why patients often require admission are symptoms which are difficult to manage at home, fear and anxiety of the patient and/or their family, and carer fatigue.

11.3 There is an opportunity for individual congregations or presbyteries to have a significant role in palliative care, in conjunction with Social Services. With a good organisation, staffed by volunteers alongside professionally trained people, a valuable Christian service can be made available. An example of what can be achieved is provided by the Evergreen Trust[29].

11.4 The challenge is to improve the quality of end of life care, wherever people die and whatever their condition or financial circumstances[30]. Good end of life care depends on appropriate levels of

---

[26] Hockley, J., J. Watson and S. Murray (2008): *The Midlothian 'Gold Standards Framework in Care Homes' project.* Copies can be downloaded from the Palliative Care Research Group website at the University of Edinburgh

[27] Lowson, S. (2007): *Why families complain about end of life care in the NHS.* End of Life Care 1, No 2

[28] Gomes, B. and I. Higginson (2006): *Factors influencing death at home in terminally ill patients with cancer: systematic review.* BMJ **332**, 515-518.

[29] The Evergreen Trust, based in Stamford, Lincolnshire, aims to promote holistic health in individuals and healthy attitudes towards ageing, challenging age discrimination and negative social expectations, and has grown to 26 paid staff and 110 registered volunteers in just 3 years. The Trust is supported by churches and agencies all working together in the community. It seeks the promotion of healthy ageing, working to build self-esteem and to restore social status, improving the circumstances of ageing and vulnerable people. It achieves this through home support services (helping with domestic, shopping and laundry needs) and volunteer services – including a befriending scheme, meal provision, a clean team and a hospital to home support team. See http://www.evergreencare.org.uk/ for further details.

[30] Barclay, S. (2008): *Place of death- how much does it matter?* British Journal of General Practice. Editorials, April

trained and motivated staff, access to palliative care education, access to specialist advice and support in more complex cases, adequate levels of support for staff to avoid burnout and, equally importantly, more intangible resources such as compassion. It is hoped that the national action plan, *Living and Dying Well*, will ensure that adequate and appropriate resources are made available to enable good end of life care to be delivered in all settings.

12. Education of Healthcare Professionals

12.1 Since its inception, palliative care education has used the model of multidisciplinary education. Palliative care is synonymous with holistic care which includes the body, mind, social and spiritual and so healthcare professionals from the disciplines which support these areas of care study and work together. The Scottish Government in its standards for palliative care identified chaplains, doctors, nurses, occupational therapists, pharmacists, physiotherapists and social workers as the key professions of the multidisciplinary team with additional access to identified specialists in psychological and other services[31].

12.2 A key and central element in palliative care education is training in communication skills: how to break bad news, dealing with difficult questions, coping with strong emotions, etc. These skills are now recognised and developed in the training of healthcare professionals, and of doctors in particular. The GP training programme offers doctors an opportunity to use these skills in real life situations and is a good example of how community healthcare services can also benefit from this approach.

12.3 Through enhanced communication skills and studying together, healthcare professionals gain an in-depth understanding of each others roles and expertise and therefore have a more informed and holistic approach to care. It is particularly helpful in ethical dilemmas such as assisted dying where the concept of suffering may be central but is rarely about pain alone, where informed decisions require a broader approach than simply understanding the physical needs of the patient.

12.4 The principle of multidisciplinary education is incorporated in the decision of NHS Education for Scotland in their recent commissioning of professional education for Healthcare Chaplaincy; a condition of the contract is that it should be set in the context of a multidisciplinary healthcare education programme.

13. Care for the Carers

13.1 When making an ethical decision in distressing circumstances a key question which must be asked by all those involved in the process is: **whose needs are being met?** Distress, including feelings of helplessness and lack of control, may be felt by the patient, relatives and staff involved. For example, a patient may become agitated and restless near the end of a terminal illness and the relatives may ask the staff involved to increase the amount of sedation the patient is being given. At times such distress may have to be lived with and through in order for the patient's and relative's spiritual and emotional needs to be assessed (is there unfinished business the patient and/ or relatives want to deal with?) and, where possible, met. However, staff can only make the offer to help patient, relatives and friends address these issues. Ultimately, it is their choice whether to address such issues or not.

13.2 At times it may be appropriate to sedate a patient heavily to meet the needs of relatives as well as the patient. Often near death, patients become increasingly more concerned about the needs of their loved ones rather than their own and do not wish to additionally burden their family with their own personal distress as well as the anticipatory grief relatives are already experiencing.

---

[31] NHS Quality Improvement Scotland (Formerly the Clinical Standards Board for Scotland) (2002). *Clinical Standards Specialist Palliative Care.* Edinburgh

13.3 *'Perhaps patients die as they live.'*[32] – some die in quiet acceptance, others restless and still wanting more, and others still raging against the world and the incomprehensible way God allows injustice and suffering. Relatives and staff often find it difficult when others die in a manner they would not want for themselves.

13.4 It is also hard when the collaborative decision made in any given circumstance is not the one certain persons involved would personally have come to. For example, for staff to continue to treat a patient whose best interests they feel would be served by ceasing all active treatment and be allowed to die when the consultant they work with insists treatment is still beneficial. Staff's emotional and spiritual needs also have to be recognised and attended to, where appropriate, during the process of dying (or not), and also following death(s).

13.5 Rituals, for patients, relatives and staff during the dying process, at death and afterwards, may provide a context, and permission, for the expression of or acting out of feelings and wrestling with issues of understanding and meaning. Other denominations, in Scotland and beyond, historically ritualise dying and bereavement more comprehensively than the Church of Scotland. However, for example, increasingly parish churches as well as healthcare chaplaincies hold regular memorial services or times of remembrance for the bereaved in the months following their bereavement. In our post-modern world, society has become bereft of a common language, symbols and stories to engage with the pain and mysteries of life and death – the majority of people are no longer familiar with the Judeo-Christian narrative. Therefore, utilising gestures and actions within ritual moments may provide a shared means of expressing grief and marking, with dignity, the importance of lives lived and lost: for example, the lighting of candles, the placing of flowers or objects relating to the dead, the planting of shrubs and trees or the sponsoring of lights on a community Christmas tree. Church representatives, as resident ritual 'experts', have much to offer in facilitating such rituals for individuals, families and communities in healthcare, parish and national settings.

14. Christianity and euthanasia

14.1 All faiths offer meaning and explanations for death and dying; all faiths try to find a place for death and dying within human experience. Religions regard understanding death and dying as vital to finding meaning in human life. Dying is a natural process, and is often seen as an occasion for getting powerful spiritual insights, as well as for preparing for the afterlife to come.

14.2 In common with virtually all religions, Christianity would recognise that those who become vulnerable through illness or disability deserve special care and protection, and that proper end of life care is much better than euthanasia. Euthanasia has been opposed for a number of reasons: for example

14.2.1 God has forbidden it
The command from God which says 'you must not kill' is usually interpreted as meaning 'you must not murder'. However, a broader interpretation is that you must not take human life. This rules out euthanasia (and assisted suicide), as carrying these out would be against God's commandments, and would be an attack on the sovereignty of God.

14.2.2 Human life is special
Human beings are made in God's image, therefore they have a special value and dignity. This value doesn't depend on the quality of a particular life, and taking a life violates that special value and dignity, even if that life is full of pain and suffering.

14.2.3 Human life is sacred
The sanctity of human lives derives from the fact that God created them; therefore human life should be protected

---

[32] Jeffrey, D. (2000): *Care versus Cure*. In *Ethical Issues in Palliative Care*, ed. P. Webb, 14-42. Manchester: Hochland and Hochland.

and preserved, whatever happens, and we shouldn't interfere with God's plans by shortening human lives.

14.3 One of the issues which repeatedly comes up in discussions around this issue is the area of personal autonomy: "it's my life, and I can chose how and when to end it". This may be particularly true in the individualistic West, where personal choice pervades all areas of life – including religion. While it must be recognised that personal autonomy is indeed an important issue, as has been argued elsewhere in this document, interpersonal relationships are also important. Life is lived and death experienced as part of community.

14.4 The worth of every human life needs to be emphasised and celebrated; in particular, the deliberate ending of life would be a matter to be deplored if it were to be seen as a means of saving (financial) resources, or that any person was perceived as merely a burden.

15. Pastoral care and end of life care

15.1 Whilst certain aspects of end of life care belong to the multidisciplinary team within the hospital and hospice services, the church remains a powerful source of healing for people as they near death, and for their families. This pastoral task takes on a number of forms. At one level, the church as a community is available as a form of support, encouragement and friendship. By offering important forms of relational and spiritual support, the church community provides an anchor which can help people to cope with the reality of their impending death and to die well. In terms of the issues highlighted in this report, this is no small point. There is evidence to suggest that if a person has their spiritual needs met, if they can find meaning and purpose in the midst of their dying, they are less likely to ask for physician assisted suicide[33]. In other words, if palliative care includes good spiritual care then

some of the ethical issues surrounding euthanasia and physician assisted suicide may not arise in the first place. It is when such needs are not met that people may feel the need to hasten their deaths. However, the pastoral role of the church has other important and often unnoticed dimensions. Earlier we stated that *"perhaps patients die as they live."* This is an important point that we need to return to here. When we discuss the issues surrounding end of life care we tend to think in terms of people's experiences during the last days and months of their lives: when they are dying. However, on reflection, end of life care begins much earlier in a person's life.

15.2   Living with hope, dying with dignity.
15.2.1 There is a good deal of research evidence which indicates that people's spirituality, and in particular their religious spirituality, can be of great help when approaching death[34]. The Christian tradition provides us with structures of hope, meaning and new possibilities even in the midst of pain and suffering. In a death-denying culture such as our own, Christianity enables us to look at death quite differently from the culture around us, offering us rituals, prayers, scriptures and communities that embody and live out the belief in the resurrection. This in turn provides both life and death with new meaning. This is important. Our beliefs and understandings of the world help us to die well. But our beliefs about life and death don't miraculously appear at the end of our lives. We die in precisely the way that we live. Dying well requires that we live well, not just at the end of our lives but throughout the whole of our lives. In other words, the time to begin to develop the types of beliefs and practices that will be so helpful to us as we face death is not when we are struck by illness, but rather in the practices of everyday life during seasons of illness and health.

---

[33] Breitbart, W. (2002): *Spirituality and meaning in supportive care: Spirituality- and meaning-centered group psychotherapy interventions in advanced cancer.* Supportive Care in Cancer 10: 272- 280.

[34] Sinclair, S., J. Pereira and S. Raffin (2006): *A Thematic Review of the Spirituality Literature within Palliative Care.* Journal of Palliative Medicine 9: 464- 479.

15.3 End of life care begins in the day to day life of the Christian community and not simply within the hustle, bustle and technical expertise of the medical ward at the end of a person's life. Our preaching, teaching, and community-building from cradle to the grave changes the meaning of death and dying in important ways, and forms the foundation for effective end of life care. End of life care therefore begins where we are right now. As Christians concentrate on their spiritual formation in the present time, so they begin to prepare themselves for that time when suffering and pain will form the tragic garland that decorates their experience, at least for a while. The church then provides a vital if often overlooked aspect of end of life care which relates both to pastoral care and to the types of ethical dilemmas that have been highlighted in this report.

16. Conclusion

16.1 The Church proclaims that Jesus came to bring *"life in all its fullness"*[35]. This report seeks to affirm this view, and to encourage all concerned to seek to help those approaching the end of their lives to experience as fulfilled a life as possible. It is recognised that many difficult decisions must be made as the end of life approaches – not least as those most profoundly affected may not be able to fully express their needs or desires. Although a natural process, the finality of death and the "letting go" which that involves for all parties means that the end of life can be a very stressful and emotional period – especially when, as is increasingly the case, this "end of life" period can extend over weeks or months.

16.2 Many areas where improvements can be made could be identified – from a wider understanding of palliative care beyond simply the alleviation of pain, to the need for the provision of appropriate pastoral and spiritual care – including for health care staff and carers. Making such improvements will in many cases require an increase

---

[35] John 10: 10

in resources – sometimes financial resources, although it must also be recognised that non-monetary resources (such as compassion) are important parts of the equation. The Church stands resolutely against the idea that human life is made less dignified or worthy by limitations in capacity, and affirms again opposition to legislation which seeks to bring about the deliberate ending of life.

16.3 Despite the inevitable sadness involved in saying farewell to a loved one, the church has a responsibility – and in some ways the privilege – to ensure that all participants in the process experience as fulfilled and comfortable a final journey as possible.

Acknowledgements:
In addition to members of the Church and Society Council, we would gratefully acknowledge the following who were involved in the preparation of this report:

Rev Dr Ewan Kelly Chaplain, St Columba's Hospice, Edinburgh

Ms Rosemary Lang Senior Nursing Officer, Lady Home Hospital, Douglas

Rev David Mitchell Parish Minister, West Cowal, and lecturer in Healthcare Chaplaincy, University of Glasgow Professor in Practical Theology and Pastoral Care, University of Aberdeen

Ms Philippa Taylor Senior Researcher, Bioethics and Family, Christian Action Research and Education (CARE), London

Ms. Helen Thomson Head of Dementia Services, Crossreach, Glasgow

Mrs Julie Watson Specialist Hospice Nurse, Edinburgh

Proposed practical outcomes
The Church and Society Council would offer the following as some examples of practical responses local churches or

Presbyteries could develop:
- "Old age pastors" in congregations
  - Pastoral care
  - Care of carers
  - Practical support for carers
- Utilisation of church resources:
  - Halls for *eg* friendship clubs
  - "Taxis" to get people to church/ doctor/ hospital visiting
- Legal issues- *eg* powers of attorney
- Bereavement care
  - Continuation and creative development of use of ritual to mark lives and deaths of deceased in local communities *eg* memorial services, times of remembrance
- Congregational Bereavement Care Teams (Trained and Supervised)
  - Liaising with local healthcare professions. Thus able to support and cross refer those bereaved identified as most isolated and vulnerable in communities by healthcare professionals and/or church.

Resources for End of Life Report

While not an exhaustive list the following are offered as examples of resources which are available for individuals and church groups to draw on.

Bereavement

Cancer Link Aberdeen & North (CLAN)
http://clanhouse.org/cms/

Cruse Bereavement Care
http://www.crusebereavementcare.org.uk/

Royal College of Psychiatrists
http://www.rcpsych.ac.uk/mentalhealthinformation/mentalhealthproblems/bereavement.aspx

Children and Bereavement

Child Bereavement Trust
http://www.childbereavement.org

Children's Hospice Association Scotland
http://www.chas.org.uk/

Notre Dame Centre
http://www.notredamecentre.org.uk/

(for children and families with complex needs)

Richmond's Hope
http://www.richmondshope.org.uk/index.htm

Winston's Wish
http://www.winstonswish.org.uk/

Useful websites

Alzheimer Scotland – Action on Dementia
http://www.alzscot.org/

CancerBacup
http://www.cancerbacup.org.uk/Home

Macmillan Cancer Support
http://www.macmillan.org.uk

Maggie's Centres
http://www.maggiescentres.org

Marie Curie Cancer Care
http://www.mariecurie.org.uk/

Motor Neurone Disease Association
http://www.mndassociation.org/

Multiple Sclerosis Society Scotland
http://www.mssocietyscotland.org.uk/scotland/

Patient UK
http://www.patient.co.uk

Scottish Motor Neurone Disease Association
http://www.scotmnd.org.uk/

Scottish Partnership for Palliative Care
http://www.palliativecarescotland.org.uk/

Widowed and Young Foundation
http://www.wayfoundation.org.uk

For Advice

All hospices offer 24 hour advice service for healthcare professionals. Hospice staff will be aware of what help is available locally.

PAPER 5
ADDICTIONS

1. Introduction

1.1 The General Assembly has received a number of reports on Drugs and Alcohol over the years. Many of the reports on alcohol have considered it in conjunction with another subject; most of these were produced by the Board of Social Responsibility. See Appendix 1.

1.2 Other Churches have produced reports on these matters over the years. Many other denominations, notably The Salvation Army and Methodist Church, have been instrumental in initiating projects, similar to Crossreach projects, to tackle addiction. It should be noted that different Churches hold differing views on these subjects.[1]

1.3 There are other forms of addiction that affect people within society including smoking, gambling, food, physical exercise, perhaps even sex[2]. This report will focus on drugs and alcohol as examples of the wider issue of addiction. However, the questions that the report raises should be seen as pointers to the wider questions around addiction.

1.4 The approach of this report is to explore the Church's attitude to these issues.[3] While it may be appropriate to make judgements on addictions, including the abuse of alcohol and drugs, is it right to be judgemental in our approach to those involved? A culture of blame is not a Christian response; rather the Church needs to look at solutions so that it can offer a better place of support for those whose lives are blighted by the effects of addiction. This is not to suggest that those who take drugs and alcohol to the detriment of themselves and others are innocent victims; such actions are the result of their own decisions. However, our response should be one of compassion and support rather than condemnation.

1.5 Drugs and alcohol are part of our society, for large numbers of people the controlled use of alcohol is a non damaging, often pleasurable and positive, reality of life.

The abuse of drugs and alcohol can, however, have huge effects on those who abuse them, their friends, families

---

[1] Eg Methodist Church http://www.methodist.org.uk/index.cfm?fuseaction=opentogod.content&cmid=1541
http://www.methodist.org.uk/index.cfm?fuseaction=opentogod.content&cmid=1554
Church of England
http://www.cofe.anglican.org/info/socialpublic/homeaffairs/alcohol/
Salvation Army
http://www2.salvationarmy.org.uk/uki/www_uki.nsf/vw-dynamic-arrays/35B4681D66E5CE6580256F960049B9A5?openDocument
These differing views include the classification of various drugs and whether abstinence is the best approach.
[2] There is disagreement as to whether sex addiction is genuine. The American Psychiatric Association does not recognise the condition as a mental illness in its official diagnostic handbook. Dr Marty Klein comments "Feeling out of control isn't the same as being out of control, and an unwillingness to exert self-discipline isn't the same thing as being addicted. People who masturbate too much, look at too much porn, or cheat on their partners are not 'addicts'. They just don't like the consequences of their decisions. They may be impulsive, or angry or lonely, but we [psychotherapists] know how to help them." However, some see sex addiction as very real. Sex Addicts Anonymous (www.saa-recovery.org) offers a diagnostic screening test and a 12 step programme for recovery. Over 16M in the US label themselves as sex addicts.
See *The Times* 20 December 2008 Body and Soul 18 http://women.timesonline.co.uk/tol/life_and_style/women/relationships/article5369623.ece
[3] This approach has been seen in earlier reports (e.g 1997 2.2, 6.1.1, 7) but has not been fully integrated into the life of congregations and thus merits repetition.

and wider society. The case of Leah Betts and others who have died or been damaged by often minimal yet catastrophic exposure highlight the dangers of illegal drugs. Innumerable people, particularly in Scotland have suffered lasting damage and death from the over consumption of alcohol.[4]

2.   What is addiction?

2.1 This report seeks to look behind the problems that drug and alcohol abuse cause in our society, to their root causes, and then suggest positive ways in which individual Christians, as well as the church both locally and nationally can respond. In order to do this it is necessary to understand what addiction is.

2.2 Defining addiction is not a simple task though we all have a sense of what it is. The clinical definition, commonly used, is based on the International Classification of Disease (ICD-10) (World Health Organisation, 1992). This pertains to alcohol, but is also appropriate for other substances that induce physical or psychological dependence. A diagnosis of dependence (*ie* addiction) requires the presence of three or more of the following:

1. a strong desire or sense of compulsion to take alcohol
2. impaired capacity to control alcohol taking behaviour
3. a physiological withdrawal state (*eg* tremor, nausea, rapid pulse rate when alcohol intake is abruptly stopped)
4. evidence of tolerance to the effects of alcohol (*ie* the need to increase the amount consumed to gain the same effects)
5. preoccupation with alcohol use (to the detriment of alternative pleasures or interests)
6. persistent alcohol use despite clear evidence of harmful consequences

2.3 Those who are addicted often speak of it being hell, like a prison but paradoxically also like a love affair. Addicts are sufferers but only seek treatment when they realise the nightmare that they have been in. When asked why they took drugs addicts often spoke of the enjoyment frequently describing heroin as "magic". For some in a life where there appears to be no hope, no future; the offer of something that will bring great pleasure has a predictable, though not inevitable, outcome. The same applies to the question of relapse. For addicts it will only be tolerable to come off if one retains the idea that one can go back. Addicts will always love it, and feel that if they want they can go back to it.[5]

2.4 The reasons that addicts get into the positions that they do are complex but it is clear that often the substance that leads to addiction provides a relief from pain or deep seated need of one sort or another. To use a parallel example: research with those who survive serious attempts at suicide has shown that they do not wish to die but they do want the pain to go away. They know that their death will be hurtful to those around but see that pain as less than the pain or distress with which they are faced. Addiction often provides a route out of pain or satisfies a deep seated need.

2.5 How should we respond to drug and alcohol addiction? There are three accepted general models: legal, medical and social.

---

[4] "The rate of alcohol-related deaths in Scotland is rising – and is more than double the rate for the UK as a whole, figures out yesterday showed.

Figures from the Office for National Statistics (ONS) revealed that in 2006, there were 13.4 deaths per 100,000 people linked to alcohol in the UK – up from 12.9 the previous year. The General Register Office for Scotland revealed that the equivalent rate north of the border was 27.3 deaths, up from 26.7 the previous year." The Scotsman 26 January 2008 http://thescotsman.scotsman.com/health/Scots-alcohol-death-rate-twice.3714009.jp

[5] This paragraph is based on the evidence that we received from a number of witnesses and contains direct, though unattributable, quotations.

2.6 The legal model is based on trying to prevent addiction and the damage it can cause by a combination of legislation, education, control, deterrence and the use of the criminal justice system. Some substances such as alcohol and prescription drugs are controlled; others are illegal. While this model disrupts the production and supply of drugs to addicts it has proved ineffective in preventing access to drugs or their continued misuse. Criminalising the use of these drugs has natural consequences which may, or may not, help in dealing with those who are addicted.

2.7 The medical model assumes that the addict has a clinical problem that can be addressed by the application of appropriate treatment and medication. This assumes that addicts first recognise their problem and want to be cured. While this can be effective, in most cases what results is seldom a cure but more often a regime that allows the addict to cope with their addiction through alternative medication or other coping mechanisms such as avoidance (*eg* avoidance "once an alcoholic always an alcoholic.").

2.8 The social model treats the addiction in the contextual environment of the addict. Here the addiction is treated alongside addressing those wider circumstances *eg* housing, mental illness, criminality and family relationships rather than simply the addictive behaviour. The various problems in an addict's life often have multiple causes and effects and can only be properly addressed holistically. Addicts often need considerable support if they are to be helped to change their environment to one where the temptation to turn back to their addiction is minimised.

2.9 All three models have their part to play in overcoming addiction. For many the move to seek help comes first from the individual addict recognising their problem; others require the intervention of another agency, most often, the justice system.

All people are individuals and thus require different approaches. Thus whatever strategies, policies, initiatives and interventions are used must be person centred and provide holistic care for the individual. We recognise that poverty makes a considerable contribution to the difficulties in overcoming addiction. In the end, however, we remain in no doubt that positive and supportive relationships are what carry people through and enable the most effective recovery.

3. Alcohol
3.1 What is the reality?

3.1.1 The Scottish Government consultation *Changing Scotland's relationship with alcohol: a discussion paper on our strategic approach* (2008)[6] has a good compendium of headline figures on the problems that alcohol causes in Scotland.[7] It notes that alcohol consumption in Scotland has grown dramatically in recent years and that the health effects of that have been dramatic.[8] One statistic is particularly striking: "alcohol industry sales data shows that enough alcohol was sold in Scotland in 2007 to enable every man and woman over the age of 16 to exceed the sensible drinking limits for men (the recommended limit is 21 units per week) every week of the year."[9] The causes

---

[6] *Changing Scotland's relationship with alcohol: a discussion paper on our strategic approach*, Scottish Government, 2008 http://www.scotland.gov.uk/Topics/Health/health/Alcohol/strategy

[7] Op cit 6-7.

[8] The Annual Report of the Chief Medical Officer shows that liver disease is rising rapidly in Scotland at a time when it is falling in Western Europe. Alcohol consumption is a major feature in this as 85% of chronic liver disease deaths are alcohol related. http://www.scotland.gov.uk/Publications/2008/11/26155748/4

[9] Op cit 8. The Nielsen data of sales shows that that average consumption of pure alcohol per person over 16 in Scotland is 11.9 litres per year, of this 3.4 litres is spirits. (http://www.scotland.gov.uk/Topics/Health/health/Alcohol/resources/nielson-data). This is significant because "The amount of alcohol consumed by a population is an important indicator because we know it is directly related to the burden of harm a population experiences. A major European study suggested that a one litre increase in average consumption was associated with up to a 30% increase in alcohol-related liver cirrhosis mortality.

for this increase in consumption are varied but can be identified in at least three contributory factors: availability, price and social acceptability. Alcohol is now, in relative terms, cheaper and more available in Scotland than ever before.[10]

3.2 Increased alcohol consumption affects Scottish society at all levels, but not equally. One measure of this can be seen in hospital admissions:

Figure 7.6

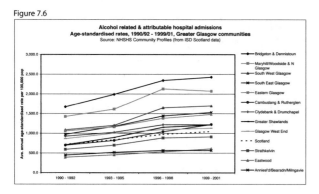

(Graph taken from the Glasgow Centre for Population Health website)

3.3 Alcohol related hospital admissions occur for three main reasons – accidents, violence and long term disease (*eg* cirrhosis). The graph above illustrates that numbers of

admissions have risen over recent years and that they vary markedly from one community to another. The figures given are detailed and are not available in such detail for more recent years. The total number of admissions in Scotland[11] has continued to grow at a similar rate since these figures. This graph is included to demonstrate that the problems caused by alcohol are serious, growing and disproportionately affect the most disadvantaged communities in Scotland.[12] One witness suggested that in the near future it will be necessary to set up residential units solely for those suffering from Korsakoff's Syndrome, and the increasingly early onset thereof.[13] One conclusion is inescapable – alcohol is causing problems within Scotland and those problems are getting worse.

4. Drugs
4.1 What is the reality?
4.1.1 The Scottish Government strategy *The Road to Recovery*[14] has a good compendium of headline figures on the problems that drug use causes in Scotland.[15] That Report notes:

"Scotland has a long-standing and serious drug problem".[16]

[Norstrom, T.(ed) (2002) *Alcohol in postwar Europe: Consumption, drinking patterns, consequences and policy responses in 15 European countries.*] The fact that Scots are drinking more than adults in England and Wales – almost 8 million litres more in 2007 – may help explain why the country's health record is so much worse than its neighbours'. In Scotland, rates of chronic liver disease are double those of England and Wales. Men in Scotland are twice as likely to die and alcohol-related death than men in England. And although harmful alcohol users are predominantly men, women in Scotland have a higher alcohol-related death rate than men in England. [Trends and geographical variations in alcohol-related deaths in the UK, 1991-2004, ONS, Spring 2007]" Scottish Health Action on Alcohol Problems press release (http://www.work-interactive-test.co.uk/ UserFiles/File/Sept%2008%20-%20Scots%20drinking%20more.doc)
[10] Op cit 8-12.

[11] "In 2006/07, there were 41,651 discharges from acute general hospitals with an alcohol-related diagnosis, a rate of 762 per 100,000 population. Over the last five years, the discharge rate has increased by 7 per cent from 710 per 100,000 population in 2002/03." NHS Scotland, Information Services Division
http://www.isdscotland.org/isd/5335.html
[12] The number of young offenders in Scotland blaming alcohol for their crimes has grown from 29.5% in 1979 to 56.8% in 2007; while the numbers for drugs have decreased with prescription medicines rather than heroin being cited. Incredibly 43% of young inmates had been drinking Buckfast immediately before their offence. Study cited in The Herald 6 October 2008 (http://www.theherald.co.uk/news/other/display. var.2457410.0.Alcohol_is_a_major_problem_in_our_society.php)
[13] Korsakoff's syndrome is a brain disorder caused by the lack of thiamine (vitamin B_1) in the brain and is the result of prolonged alcohol use or malnutrition caused by alcohol use.
[14] *The Road to Recovery*, Scottish Government, 2008
http://www.scotland.gov.uk/Publications/2008/05/22161610/0
[15] Op cit 1-4.
[16] "An estimated 52,000 people are problem drug users. [Hay, G., Gannon,

"The scale of the drug problem in Scotland today is unacceptably high. It is a significant driver of economic underperformance, crime, risk to children and health inequalities."[17]

4.2 The impact of the misuse of drugs is not merely on the user. It has a huge impact on family life, particularly on children,[18] and on the wider community of the drug user through both anti-social behaviour and criminality.[19]

M., McKeganey, N.P., Hutchinson, S. & Goldberg, D. (2005) *Estimating the National and Local Prevalence of Problem Drug Misuse in Scotland.* Edinburgh: Scottish Executive.] Put another way, almost 1 in 50 of our population aged between 15 and 54 are experiencing or causing medical, social, psychological, physical or legal problems because of their use of opiates, such as heroin and benzodiazepines. Although this represents a decline in the number of problem users since 2000 (when the comparable figure was 56,000), it is still notably higher than that for England. Although the use of different methodologies and definitions makes exact comparisons difficult, Scotland's rate of problem drug use also seems to be much higher than other similar European countries such as Ireland, Finland or Denmark." Op cit 1

It should be noted that this is problem drug use. Total drug use is far higher:

"The most commonly used illegal drug in Scotland remains cannabis: 1 in 3 adults in Scotland have taken cannabis at some point in their lives, 1 in 10 in the past year. Cocaine is now the next most commonly used, with a significant increase in its use over the last 10 years: 4% of adults in Scotland reported having used cocaine in the past year in 2006, compared with only 1% in 1996. The third most commonly used drug is ecstasy, with 3% of adults reporting they had used it in the past year in 2006, compared with 2% in 1996."; "Encouragingly, there appears to have been a significant drop in the reported use of drugs by both 15 and 13 year olds in the last 8 years. Between 2004 and 2006 prevalence of drug use among 15 year old boys declined from 21% to 14%, and among 15 year old girls declined from 20% to 12%. Prevalence among 13 year olds also halved. However, there is no room for complacency, given that the same survey also reports that a quarter of all 15 year olds had used drugs in the last year." Op cit 2

[17] Op cit 1.

[18] *eg* http://news.bbc.co.uk/1/hi/scotland/2933365.stm This reports that 50,000 children in Scotland and living in a home where at least 1 parent uses drugs and highlights the pressure that that brings to grandparents and the wider community.

[19] *The Road to Recovery*, Scottish Government, 2008 http://www.scotland.gov.uk/Publications/2008/05/22161610/0 3

4.3 Having recognised the size of the problem and the relative ineffectiveness of the various approaches to the problem tried thus far, the Scottish Government has outlined what it sees as a new approach. "Central to the strategy is a new approach to tackling drug use based on the concept of recovery. Recovery is a process through which an individual is enabled to move on from their problem drug use towards a drug-free life and become an active and contributing member of society."[20] The separation between the two conflicting approaches of abstinence and harm reduction is dismissed as a false dichotomy with the true goal being recovery. That requires the whole of people's lives to be addressed and not merely their drug use in isolation: "The strength of the recovery principle is that it can bring about a shift in thinking – a change in attitude both by service providers and by the individual with the drug problem. There is no right or wrong way to recover. Recovery is about helping an individual achieve their full potential – with the ultimate goal being what is important to the individual, rather than the means by which it is achieved."[21]

4.4 To achieve this goal, efforts are to be made to increase the effectiveness of education about drugs as well as to restrict the supply of drugs in Scotland through law enforcement. Most of all, the strategy looks to a redirection of all services towards recovery. The Report is not explicit and draws on a number of other publications to give more detail but it does set a framework and outlines an overarching philosophy.

4.5 There has been an ongoing debate about the legal position of some drugs and calls for discussion of and possible revision of the criteria used.[22] Our report does

---

[20] Op cit vi.

[21] Op cit 23

[22] The 1997 Board of Social Responsibility *Report of the Study Group on the Decriminalisation of Drugs* led to deliverance 9 which included a call for a Royal Commission "to consider and make recommendations on the issues involved in the legalisation of cannabis." The 2007 report of the

not enter into that debate as it concentrates on the social aspects of the issue.

5. How do we respond?

5.1 As Christians we recognise that all of us are made in God's image and are part of God's creation. Thus every individual has inherent, intrinsic value and all have equal value in the eyes of God. This must inform our approach to addiction. We are of value by dint of our existence and not through contributions that we may or not make to our wider world and society. Every individual is of worth and it should be our hope that all are able to fulfil their God given potential. Indeed we have a duty, as Christians, to be witnesses to the incredible love and grace of God towards each individual in society, an unconditional love that is the source of real hope.

5.2 The Scottish Government's policy is driven by its own aims: "we have set ourselves 15 national objectives to achieve our overarching purpose – to increase sustainable economic growth. Tackling problem drug use more effectively, with an estimated £2.6bn cost to the country every year, will make a significant contribution to achieving this. Reducing problem drug use will get more people back to work; revitalise some of our most deprived communities; and allow significant public investment to be redirected."[23] In this field our aim should be to seek to help and be alongside those with addiction problems because they have inherent value in themselves and not because they can potentially make a greater economic contribution when they have recovered from or are no longer controlled by their addiction. Economics may be the predominant driver for governments; it should not be for churches. While the recovery model chimes with both aims, the Church's focus should be on the person and their relationships. We have seen that for many, substance misuse is an escape from pain, from reality. The resulting problems have an impact on and relate to not just the user but often also their family, close friends and other relationships and any recovery model must take this into account.

5.3 This report seeks to concentrate the mind of the Church on what we can do individually, locally and nationally. The research evidence for the benefits of consuming low levels of alcohol is divided[24] but all agree that significant levels of alcohol consumption have serious health effects and that these increase dramatically as consumption increases.[25] We may not stand against all drinking; those who drink alcohol must seek to be role models of moderate and sensible consumption. Witness is always the most powerful advocacy. What is required if Scotland is to bring the damaging impacts of alcohol under control is not solely legislation but behavioural and attitudinal change so that drunkenness is seen as culturally unacceptable, rather than the desirable outcome of an evening. This is not a simple or short term process but it is one that we must not shirk. Individuals are responsible for their own health and thus we would call on all to take a realistic look at their own lifestyle. Attitudinal change must start from the individual if it is to be credible.

5.4 There is scope for individuals to involve themselves in Community Councils, Area Planning Committees etc. There is a particular opportunity for individuals to involve themselves on local licensing forums.[26] These forums look

---

RSA Commission on Illegal Drugs, Communities and Public Policy called for a complete reclassification of substances based on the harm which they cause.

[23] *The Road to Recovery* iv.
The approach to alcohol is similar: "We want to create a more successful country, with opportunities for all Scotland to flourish, through increasing sustainable economic growth…..- the reality is that Scotland's current relationship with alcohol is undermining our potential as individuals, families, communities and as a country. If we are to fulfil our ambitions, we must rebalance our relationship with alcohol." *Changing Scotland's relationship with alcohol: a discussion paper on our strategic approach* 1

[24] The balance appears to be that some alcohol is beneficial.
[25] See f9.
[26] Licensing Scotland Act (2005) § 10 – 12 and Schedule 2.

particularly at over provision of licenses in an area and may offer a significant opportunity for individuals to affect what goes on in their neighbourhood.

5.5 As local church communities Christians should consider what messages they are giving out on addictions. Are they showing a realistic and responsible approach to alcohol? Whilst a universal ban on the serving of alcohol may not be in touch with the realities of the modern world, particularly when it is probable that consuming some alcohol has health benefits, the provision of alcohol should be done with both care and respect. It is vital that alternatives are offered. It is important to remember those within their area who are troubled with addictions? This should be on a variety of levels. Church buildings are vital community spaces that can host groups for those with addictions and those affected.[27] Churches should consider making these available at an appropriate fee and time and ensuring that the facilities are sufficient for the task. As a worshipping community Churches could consider whether they truly welcome all. Churches should consider the welcome that people received when they appear under the influence of drugs or alcohol.

5.6 As a national church we need to consider what our contribution can be. This is not a blank sheet. Crossreach has been involved in the provision of quality services in these fields for many years. As part of our research members of the group met with a number of people in Crossreach and saw a number of projects. The practical response to those in need should remain our principal concern. The Church and Society Council also responded to the Scottish Government Consultation on Alcohol and that response is attached to this report. While the Council questioned some of the specific measures proposed, it fully supported the broad objectives of this consultation:
• "Reduced alcohol consumption
• Supporting families and communities

---

[27] These include Alcoholics Anonymous, Narcotics Anonymous, Gamblers' Anonymous and a large number of family and other groups.

• Positive public attitudes towards public health and individuals better placed to make positive choices about the role of alcohol in their lives; and
• Improved support and treatment for those who require it"

5.7 This report would endorse such an approach to any addiction, not just addiction to alcohol. It has to be recognised that alcohol is a major problem within Scotland, far bigger than drugs, and that it is only through a dramatic change in the way that it is viewed that the problem can be addressed. What is needed is personal and societal change. The example of the attitudinal and behavioural changes around smoking in Scotland in the last few years are grounds for optimism that other damaging addictive behaviour can be tackled. Much has been achieved in a relatively short timescale but work remains to be done. This report concludes that such change is only achievable if the hope in and benefits of other lifestyles are greater than and address the pain that many seek to avoid through their current addictive behaviour. The Church, if it is to be true to God's desire, must be part of a society that offers hope to all, a healthy society where everyone is reminded that they are valued and accepted for who they are in an unconditional manner.

We would like to thank the following who helped us in our research:

Alan Staff, Director, Crossreach
Gerry Robson, Head of Substance Misuse Services, Crossreach
Glen Liddell, Manager, Simpson House, Crossreach
Vic Walker, Manager, Rainbow House, Crossreach
Margot Ferguson, West Lothian Drugs and Alcohol Service
Dr Jonathan Chick, Consultant Psychiatrist, Royal Edinburgh Hospital, NHS Lothian
Dr Malcolm Bruce, Consultant Psychiatrist in Addictions, NHS Lothian

APPENDIX 1
PREVIOUS REPORTS ON DRUGS AND ALCOHOL

1980 Report of Joint Working Party on Alcohol, Crime and Violence and Further Report on Effects of 1976 Licensing Act (Scotland). The Deliverances link alcohol abuse with offences under the Road Traffic Acts and with crimes of violence and child abuse and neglect. They ask HM Government to strengthen the law on drink driving, to monitor the consequences of increasing alcohol consumption, to examine the part played by proliferation of retail outlets and the relatively low cost of alcoholic beverages, and ask the Secretary of State for Scotland to increase public awareness of the adverse effect of alcohol abuse. Deliverance 10 notes that the Licensing (Scotland) Act did not bring with it more civilised drinking habits and calls on the Government to combat alcohol abuse and eliminate, as far as possible, the mass advertising of alcohol.

1981 Deliverances 16, 17 and 18 note the problems of alcohol and drug abuse, urge The Secretary of State to increase awareness of the adverse effect of alcohol abuse and repeat the other 1980 concerns. The Report discusses increased drinking problems among women and the effect of alcohol on unborn children, and discusses the misuse of drugs, particularly cannabis use and glue sniffing.

1982 Deliverances 19 to 24 deal with the spread of alcohol abuse and the measures needed to control the availability of alcohol. The need for an employer's policy amongst the employing organisations of the Church is stated. Concern is expressed on the increased availability of heroin and other opiates.

1983 Deliverances 14, 15 and 16 continue the concerns previously expressed, note the conviction that social deprivation, family breakdown and unemployment have increased drug abuse, and comment on the role of local Church members and the role of congregations in the community and in assisting groups involved with these problems.

1984 Deliverances 19 to 25 are based on a report that concentrates on illicit drugs, abuse of prescribed drugs and alcohol abuse. Again the ready availability of cheap alcohol is a concern and HM Government and Licensing Authorities are urged to raise prices, reduce the number of outlets, and exercise firm control of licensing hours. The increased use of illicit drugs, particularly in areas of multiple deprivation, is noted.

1985 Deliverance 18 continues to recognise the problems associated with the abuse of alcohol and drugs, urging HM Government to provide resources for employment, education and leisure activity for young people.

1986 Deliverance 9 endorses the report of the Study Group on Alcohol and Drugs and encourages its discussion.

1987 The report of the Study Group on Alcohol and Drugs is endorsed in Deliverance 10, its discussion encouraged, and the grave damage caused by the current level of alcohol consumption noted.

1988 Deliverances 12 to 15 note growth in sports sponsorship by the alcohol industry, note the Boards monitoring report, instruct all Courts and Boards of the Church to ensure that all public areas are non-smoking, and recommend that HM Government increases in the price of alcohol and tobacco.

1989 The Study Group's Report covering drinking and driving, alcohol and sports sponsorship and licensing was considered, a blood alcohol level limit of 20mg/100ml was urged, and concern regarding Sunday sales of alcohol expressed in Deliverance 10.

1990 Deliverances 7 and 8 deal with the continuing work of the study Group.

1991 The Study Group's report notes the changes in Sunday drinking and other changes allowed by the Law Reform (Miscellaneous Provision) (Scotland) Act and the effects of increased consumption of alcohol and drinking and driving. These are recognised in Deliverances 7 and 8 which call on HM Government to introduce Random Breath Testing and a driving test for returning disqualified drivers.

1992 The final Report of the Study Group was received by Deliverance 13 which urges HM Government action on the levels of taxation on alcohol and welcomes the publication of a leaflet on addiction to prescribed drugs.

1997 Deliverance 9 welcomes the Report of the Study on the Decriminalisation of Drugs, and commends it to the Church and,

9.1 Whilst not advocating a change in the present law relating to the use of cannabis, calls upon the Secretary of State for Scotland and the appropriate legal authorities to ensure that resources are in place for greater and more consistent use to be made of diversion schemes in dealing with cannabis users.

9.2 Urges that a Royal Commission be appointed to consider and make recommendations on the issues involved in the legalisation of cannabis.

9.3 Calls for the Department of Health to initiate a review of the medical use of cannabis.

9.4 Urges the Board to continue to monitor, research and challenge the reasons for the misuse of drugs as they relate to the full range of social conditions (for example, family security, physical and sexual abuse, and pre-existing mental health problems).

2001 A brief situation update is given in the report.

CHURCH OF SCOTLAND
CHURCH AND SOCIETY COUNCIL
EAGLAIS NA H-ALBA

121 George Street, Edinburgh, EH2 4YN. Tel: 0131 225 5722 Fax: 0131 240 2239
Email: churchandsociety@cofscotland.org.uk Web: www.churchofscotland.org.uk

Charity Number: SCO11353
Official Response

SUBJECT	**Changing Scotland's relationship with alcohol**
REQUESTED BY	**Scottish Government**
AUTHOR	
REFERENCE	**OR – 006**
DATE:	**September 08**

The Church of Scotland is currently preparing a Report on Drugs, Alcohol and Addictions for the General Assembly. Thus we are unable to comment in detail at this time but would hope to contribute fully to the ongoing debate once the General Assembly has reached an agreed position.

Based on previous deliberations of the General Assembly the Church and Society Council has recognised that these are issues of great concern to the people of Scotland and welcome the Scottish Government's efforts to address the concerns about the place of alcohol within Scottish society and the great damage that it is doing. We recognise that alcohol is currently misplaced within Scottish society and that public attitudes and approaches to alcohol do not align with the appalling health and social impact that alcohol is having. That imbalance needs to be addressed urgently if Scotland is to be regarded as an attractive, responsible and civilised place to live.

The Church and Society Council supports the broad targets outlined in §3:

- "Reduced alcohol consumption
- Supporting families and communities
- Positive public attitudes towards public health and individuals better placed to make positive choices about the role of alcohol in their lives; and
- Improved support and treatment for those who require it"

We support proposals that can be demonstrated to achieve these aims. We recognise that alcohol is currently too cheap when viewed on an historic basis and have no doubt that both reduced cost and increased availability have contributed to the problems that are currently being experienced and are increasing.

We welcome the Consultation Document and the valuable digest of the problem that it contains. We look forward to seeing the legislation resulting from this consultation and hope that it will be rigorously enforced. It is essential that the impact of that legislation on the problems of alcohol abuse will be fully monitored and evaluated. Legislation can only be one tool in tackling the problem but it can set an important marker to change attitudes to alcohol within Scotland so that the harm that it causes can be reduced.

September 08

PAPER 6
SRI LANKA

1.1 Amongst the many conflicts going on in our world today, it is easy to overlook one of the longest running, the civil war which has been raging in Sri Lanka for twenty five years. The bitter struggle between the Liberation Tigers of Tamil Eelam ('Tamil Tigers') and the Government forces of Sri Lanka surfaces in our news occasionally, with reports of a suicide bombing, assassination or a major offensive. This is a war which since its inception in 1983 has claimed upwards of 70,000 lives and damaged those of hundreds of thousands more, through destruction of homes, livelihoods and the internal displacement of communities. The overall cost of the war can be measured not only in numbers of dead or refugees, but in terms of human rights abuses, damage to the economy and deterioration of relations between different ethnic communities and religions.

1.2 The report brought to the General Assembly in 2001 by the Church and Nation Committee raised awareness of the ongoing conflict in Sri Lanka and its devastating effect on civilians in that country. It acknowledged the intransigence of both sides engaged in the civil war, but pointed at that time to the possibility of an independent Norwegian mediation. It also expressed grave concern at the global trade in small arms (including those manufactured in the UK) which was supplying weapons to both sides and exacerbating the situation. Finally, it asked the Church to be aware of the needs of Sri Lankan asylum seekers here in the UK and the danger they faced if they were forced to return.

1.3 The World Mission report to the General Assembly of 2006 included the results of consultations regarding 'the presence or otherwise of religious discrimination against members of minority faith communities'. It also raised awareness of the potential implication for minority groups if the Prohibition of Forced Conversions Bill, which was at that time going through Parliament, was to become law. The progress of this Bill is still a pressing issue for Sri Lankan Christians.

1.4 Since 2006, the situation in Sri Lanka has deteriorated significantly, with an escalation of the civil war and an alarming increase in human rights violations.

2. Background

2.1 There have always been both Sinhalese and Tamils living in Sri Lanka. Located mainly in the north and east of the country, the minority Tamil community numbers three million and they are mainly Hindu in religion. Claiming that this minority has been discriminated against since independence (1948) by the majority Buddhist Sinhalese population, the LTTE is a paramilitary organisation fighting for an independent homeland.

2.2 It is generally acknowledged by independent historians that under British rule, the Tamil community enjoyed disproportionate power and positions; after independence, Sinhalese nationalism began to assert itself, and the pendulum swung until it was soon the Tamils who found themselves having their rights threatened. Peaceful protests were repressed and anti-Tamil riots ensued; ethnic divisions widened and failure to achieve political settlement led to armed militant movements; civil war broke out in the 1980s between the Tamils and the Government, with the LTTE establishing itself as the dominant military force fighting for independence.

2.3 Sri Lanka is a parliamentary democracy, and the Tamils do have political representation in Parliament. In the 2004 election, the Tamil National Alliance (made up of a number of Tamil nationalist parties) won 6.9% of the popular vote, giving it 22 seats out of a total of 225. The Tamil struggle is also supported by the large diaspora of Sri Lankan Tamils, estimated at 800,000. The greatest numbers of these are to be found in Canada and the UK, with most of the remainder in other Western European countries and the USA.

2.4 Tamil Nationalists want to merge the North and East Provinces into a single, Tamil-majority North East province. Sinhalese Nationalists oppose this, fearing that it would lead to separatism and loss of sovereignty. There is also a sense amongst some Sinhalese, that despite being in the majority in Sri Lanka itself, in the wider geographical area they are actually in a minority and under threat of being at the mercy of the 70 million Tamils in Tamil Nadu in neighbouring India. Sinhalese political parties are very reluctant to accept that the Tamils have any legitimate grievances and neither of the two major Sinhalese political parties supports the Tamil call for autonomy.

3.   The Civil War

3.1   The north of Sri Lanka has seen the bulk of the fighting, but the whole country has been affected by the suicide bombings in the capital Colombo and other towns and cities, along with assassinations of government ministers and officials. The Tamil Tigers were responsible for the assassination in 1991 of the Indian Prime Minister, Rajiv Ghandi and in 1993 of the Sri Lankan President Ranasinghe Premadasa; both were killed by suicide bombers.

3.2   A ceasefire was successfully brokered by Norway in 2002 and for a while the future looked more positive, with the promise of substantially increased funding for Sri Lanka from overseas if the war ceased altogether. However, the lack of any desire on either side to compromise saw this prospect evaporate, with Sinhalese governments maintaining a steadfast opposition to anything which smacked of federalism and the LTTE determined to achieve their own homeland.

3.3   During the years between 2003 and 2005, the LTTE effectively created their own state in the north, with their own banks, schools and courts. Their political base was in Kilinochchi, with their military base further east in Mullaitivu. This part of the country was effectively a 'no-go area', with Sri Lanka's second city, Jaffna, only

able to receive its supplies by sea or air. When the devastating Tsunami struck in 2004, killing an estimated 30,000 people, relief operations were hugely hampered by disagreements about where international agencies could or could not go.

3.4   There were many breaches of the truce during these years, and a growing unease within the Sinhalese nationalist community at the apparent autonomy which the LTTE were creating in the north. In 2006, President Mahinda Rajapaksa was elected on a strong nationalist platform and by the beginning of 2008, the six year truce was formally scrapped, amid claims that the LTTE had been using it to regroup and rearm.

3.5   Since 2006, the Government has been committed to a strong military campaign to defeat the rebels. During the whole of last year, there was fierce fighting in the north, with the land held by the Tamils gradually being reclaimed by government forces; in early January 2009, they captured Kilinochchi, and by the end of that month the strategic Elephant Pass and the town of Mullaitivu, the LTTE's important military base. By the middle of February 2009, the Sri Lankan Government was hailing the defeat of the Tigers; the territory under LTTE control had shrunk from 15,000 to 200 square kilometres, with the rebels being confined to a small area of jungle.

3.6   With no international or independent reporters being allowed into the LTTE controlled area, it was difficult to know the true scale of the crisis, but it was known that several hundred thousand civilians were trapped in an increasingly dangerous conflict zone. International aid agencies estimate that 250,000 have been made homeless by the war, moving from place to place, without adequate food or shelter and there were heavy civilian casualties as the fighting intensified. Particularly shocking was the bombing of a hospital in a Government-declared safe zone in which at least 50 people were killed. (Both sides denied responsibility.) The LTTE were accused of using civilians as human shields, while the Government was reluctant to allow safe corridors for civilians to leave the war zone.

3.7 Despite the claims of the Sri Lankan Government, a military victory by their troops is unlikely to see the end of the conflict. The LTTE are highly familiar with living in the jungle; it is widely assumed that they will resort to guerrilla methods again and the terror faced by ordinary civilians throughout Sri Lanka is likely to remain.[1]

3.8 The main arms suppliers to the Sri Lankan Government are China, India, Pakistan and Israel, while the LTTE buy their arms on the open market in SE Asia. The UK still issues export licences for arms; it is by no means the biggest supplier, and insists that the licences are only given for the sale of weapons for defensive purposes. However, UK Tamils are unhappy with the continuation of these arms sales, and have called for a total international arms embargo to Sri Lanka, while the Westminster Foreign Affairs Committee has called for continued careful monitoring of all arms sales.

4. Human Rights

4.1 The methods of the LTTE have been both ruthless and bloody; these have led many countries to proscribe them as a terrorist organisation, as has the European Union. While many moderate Tamils share the desire for some sort of autonomy within Sri Lanka, they do not support the Tiger's methods. It has often been observed that those who suffer most from the Tamil Tigers are the Tamil civilians and human rights abuses are well documented.

4.2 In a report from Human Rights Watch 'Trapped and Mistreated',[2] it was recorded that, within the Tamil controlled area, ordinary Tamils were being forcibly

recruited as fighters and forced to engage in dangerous labour near the front lines, often unpaid. The movements of the civilian population were severely restricted, with passes needed to leave the Vanni, as the area ruled by the LTTE was known; very few such passes were issued. Families of those who refused to fight or who escaped from the area were punished and the threat of such punishment was used to intimidate others, while child soldiers were 'recruited' at schools at the age of 16 or 17. The LTTE ruled through fear, and basic freedoms of assembly, association, expression, and movement were denied.

4.3 Human Rights Watch (HRW) have been equally critical of the Sinhalese Government and their conduct in the war zone. Tamil civilians have been encouraged by the Government to flee the area and take refuge in so-called 'welfare camps'. According to HRW's report "Besieged, displaced and detained", these are really detention camps, where paid informers identify LTTE sympathisers. As the war intensified at the beginning of 2009, there was international condemnation of the disregard shown by either side for the civilians trapped in the area where the fighting was happening. As in so many other areas of the world, the victims of this conflict are the civilians who are powerless to protect themselves and their families.

4.4 While civilians have great difficulty in leaving the area, others, particularly humanitarian workers, had the same difficulty in gaining access to bring much needed help. The Sinhalese Government was responsible for the order which, since September 2008, forbade any international aid workers to enter the Vanni. The International Committee of the Red Cross (ICRC) has been permitted to go in on occasion, but only a handful of food convoys were allowed in.[3] As the fighting intensified at the beginning of this year, international pressure was put on the Sri Lankan government to allow humanitarian aid to reach those trapped by the fighting.

---

[1] Within hours of the declaration of the fall of Killinochchi, a Tamil Tiger suicide bomber in Colombo killed two people and injured many others.
[2] November 2008, thus written before the latest fighting at the beginning of 2009.

---

[3] The area was hit by Cyclone Nisha on November 25 2008, and an estimated 60,000 lost their homes.

4.5 The resurgence of fighting over the past couple of years has also seen a worrying repression throughout Sri Lanka on the part of the Sinhalese government. When Sri Lanka reapplied in 2008 for a place on the UN Human Rights Council, (which it had first joined in 2006) a strong letter was sent to the UN from 20 international and national NGOs, urging that Sri Lanka did not deserve such a place because of its own human rights record. It claimed that in the previous two years, government forces had been engaged in a wide range of serious abuses, hundreds of extra-judicial killings (which included humanitarian workers), enforced disappearances, widespread torture and arbitrary detention. They had returned displaced people to unsafe areas and restricted and intimidated the media through harassment, threats and murder. They also pointed out that the government continued to obstruct the work of the UN Human Rights Council, ignoring its recommendations, publicly attacking UN officials who spoke out on human rights issues and being unwilling to engage in serious discussions about the monitoring of human rights. Sri Lanka was unsuccessful in its attempt at reselection to the Council.

4.6 When prominent newspaper editor and government critic Lasantha Wickrematunga was murdered by gunmen on 8 January 2009, human rights groups said that his death was 'a hammer blow for press freedom in the country.' He was just one more member of the media to be murdered; many other journalists have either died or been attacked, while many have left the country under threat of intimidation. Even the BBC has been accused of misreporting and they in turn stopped supplying news reports which they claimed were being warped and distorted by the Sinhalese authorities. In a remarkable article written just days before his death and published posthumously, Wickrematunga foresaw his own assassination as inevitable because of his commitment to speak out against corruption, oppression,

and the erosion of human rights in his country.[4] In a radio interview with the BBC World Service following the death of Wickrematunga, the Defence Minister Gotabaya Rajapaksa chillingly admitted that 'dissent at a time of war is treason.'[5] The lack of any action on the part of the Sri Lankan Government to arrest and punish those who carry out such attacks on any who dare to criticise the Government has engendered a dangerous culture of impunity.

5. The Church in Sri Lanka

5.1 A further casualty of the situation in Sri Lanka is the state of the other minorities in a country which at one time was seen to be a multi-ethnic home for several communities: Buddhist, Muslim, Hindu and Christian. With the rise of an aggressive Buddhist nationalism, non-Buddhists are understandably apprehensive. The Christian church in Sri Lanka shares that concern.

5.2 The Constitution of Sri Lanka gives Buddhism 'a foremost position' but it also provides for the right of members of other faiths to freely practice their religions. There are 1.5 million Christians in Sri Lanka, comprising less than 7.5% of the population.[6] The Church is not identified with any one racial group and includes both Sinhalese and Tamils; Christians serve in all areas of public life, including politics and the media. However, the Church is perceived by some as 'western' and of foreign origin, an impression confirmed for them by the influx of more modern, Americanised denominations. Since 2003, the country has witnessed a spate of attacks on Christian churches and congregations.[7] While some of these attacks have been clearly religiously motivated (and carried out by Buddhist extremists), there have been other cases where clergy may have been abducted or killed, not

---

[4] He also prophesied that no-one would be brought to account for his murder.

[5] BBC World Service, interview with Chris Morris 2 Feb 2009.

[6] 7% are Roman Catholic and 0.5% are Protestant.

[7] See Christian Solidarity Worldwide – Sri Lanka Briefing 2006.

because of their religion but because they have bravely spoken out against human rights abuses.

5.3 An Anti-Conversion Bill (against 'forced' or 'unethical' conversions) first introduced to Parliament in May 2004, was re-presented to Parliament in January 2009. The draft Bill advocates fines and jail sentences for anyone convicted of, or assisting in, 'unethical conversion', with heavier penalties for converting women and children. Both the convert and the person responsible for his or her conversion would suffer penalties if found guilty. The Bill's second reading was due in February, with the Christian community fearing intensified persecution and discrimination if the law is passed. In this beleaguered situation, it cannot be easy for the Church in Sri Lanka to speak out to challenge the human rights abuses perpetrated by both sides in the conflict, nor to speak out against the erosion of public freedoms instigated in the name of 'national security'.

5.4 The World Council of Churches gave a special focus to Sri Lanka during its UN Advocacy Week in 2008. Expressing solidarity with all the people affected by the 'forgotten war' in Sri Lanka, it called for global Church advocacy for a negotiated solution to the crisis facing the country. Recognising that the Christian Church is the only religious community to bridge the ethnic divide, it also stressed the need for the various denominations to speak with one voice in advocating for peace. Globally, the Church needs to be prepared to report human rights violations in Sri Lanka to UN bodies and to governments.

6. Conclusion

6.1 The outlook for Sri Lanka remains bleak. An increasingly fundamentalist Buddhist nationalism is supporting the present Government's commitment that a military victory over the LTTE is the only answer; the LTTE are equally committed to the armed struggle and despite the heavy defeats suffered in this year's fighting, they will inevitably resort to guerrilla tactics to continue their struggle for their own homeland. Many more innocent lives will be lost. It is generally agreed by international observers that a military victory will not bring about peace; the underlying causes of the conflict need to be addressed and a political solution found which must include a recognition of the legitimate claims of the Tamil community to more autonomy in the north.

6.2 The ferocity of the fighting in the north and the disregard for the safety of the civilians in the war zone, the triumphalism of the Sinhalese Government and their unwillingness to acknowledge the needs of the Tamil community have only exacerbated the tensions between the two communities. As Andrew Love MP said in a House of Commons debate on Sri Lanka on 5 February 2009 "there is a climate of bitterness and enmity, even greater than before…inevitably this has polarised opinion… that is not fertile soil on which we can build a peace process."[8] The increasing repression of the current Sri Lankan government has raised fears among the Tamils that they will be even more discriminated against. There is little sign that anything is being done to tackle human rights abuses against the wider community, including journalists, human rights campaigners and Christian congregations and pastors.

6.3 In the light of all this, it is therefore essential that the international community through the intervention of the UN Security Council keep up its pressure on the Sri Lankan government to work towards a political rather than a military settlement for the question of a Tamil homeland. Given the predominantly Buddhist culture of the island, a path to peaceful co-existence should be assisted by defining the basis for a long term settlement without further bloodshed. The Christian church, both within Sri Lanka and beyond, has its role to play too in working for peace and justice. In time, the model of the Truth and Reconciliation Commission, which worked so

---

[8] Hansard

successfully in South Africa, could be used to address the bitterness and enmity caused by the long civil war. Finally, the international community has its part to play in condemning and challenging the climate of fear which currently appears to prevail within Sri Lanka; we must continue to call for positive action so that an environment is created in which people from all communities in Sri Lanka may live without fear.

IAN GALLOWAY, *Convener*
EWAN AITKEN, *Council Secretary*

PROPOSED DELIVERANCE

1. Receive the Report
2. Note the work undertaken to this point in respect of the review of tenure, instruct the Ministries Council to continue to consult Presbyteries, the Legal Questions Committee and other appropriate bodies and instruct Presbyteries to respond to the Council by 1 Dec 2009. *(Section 1.1)*
3. Note the need for new enhanced disclosures to be completed by all Ministers and serving Deacons in 2009, and instruct Ministers and Deacons to cooperate with the Ministries Council and the Safeguarding Office in the timeous completion of this process *(Section 1.5)*
4. Note the work already undertaken on a major review of training processes within the remit of the Council and instruct the Council to bring a further update on progress to the General Assembly 2010. *(Section 1.7)*
5. Note the arrangements in respect of deploying an Auxiliary Minister in a Continued Vacancy, and instruct the Council to continue its work in seeking new and more flexible ways of deploying ministries, including a further report to the General Assembly 2010 on the operational possibilities of an Ordained Local Ministry *(Section 1.8)*
6. Note with concern the pressures being faced by the Church in Presbyteries facing numerous, lengthy vacancies, commend ministers, deacons, Auxiliary ministers, readers and elders who are enabling the Church in these presbyteries to evolve new patterns of life, and welcome in particular the possibilities that video technology, secondment and transition ministry offer. *(Section 1.9)*
7. Pass an Act anent Ministers from non-EEA Countries excluding Switzerland, amending Acts VIII 2003 anent Vacancy Procedure (as amended) and IX 2002 anent Admission and Re-admission of Ministers (as amended), as set out in Section 1.10. *(Section 1.10)*
8. Affirm the principles and priorities identified in the report *Celebrating the Past – Glimpsing the Future* and instruct the Council to bring forward to the General Assembly 2010 a detailed programme of activity for the next phase of Priority Areas work. *(Section 2.18)*
9. Pass an Act amending Act X 2004 anent Selection and Training for the Full-Time Ministry and Eligibility for Ordination (as amended), as set out in Section 3.2.1. *(Section 3.2.1)*
10. Instruct the Council to continue its review and updating of training for those engaged in supervision of candidates and probationers with a view to ensuring best practice in this vital area of work, and report to the General Assembly 2010 *(Section 3.6)*
11. Pass an Act amending Act IX 2002 anent Admission and Readmission of Ministers (as amended), as set out in Section 3.9. *(Section 3.9)*
12. Affirm the commitment of the Council to investment in the implementation of the Action Plan on Congregational Conflict, submitted to the General Assembly 2008, and commend to the wider Church the conference on The Church and Conflict, to be held from 15 – 18 Nov 2009 in Aviemore. *(Section 4.3)*

13. Instruct Presbyteries to liaise with the Ministries Council on the provision of training for Interim Moderators and members of Vacancy Advisory Committees and Nomination Committees. *(Section 4.9)*

14. Affirm the view of the Council that no retirement age be imposed for Readers and, in the light of this, remind Presbyteries of the importance of maintaining accurate and up-to-date records of active Readers within their bounds. *(Section 4.21)*

15. Remind Presbyteries that an annual review of the Presbytery Plan is required and that a major review involving consultation with the Ministries Council is required every 5 years under Act VII 2003. *(Section 5.6)*

16. Instruct Presbyteries which have not yet submitted their determination of buildings as required under Act VII 2003 to do so by December 2009. *(Section 5.6)*

17. Welcome the level of interest in Emerging Ministries and encourage all Presbyteries to consider whether an application to the Emerging Ministries Fund might be appropriate in exploring new forms of ministry. *(Section 5.12)*

18. Instruct the Ministries Council, in partnership with the Church & Society Council, to bring forward to the General Assembly of 2010 a template for use by all Parish Ministers and employees in creating a 'Green Travel Plan', and to set up a Reference Group to assist in this task. *(Section 5.17)*

19. Instruct the Council to ensure that an ongoing programme of support and training for those responsible for line management of Presbytery / Parish Workers (PPWs) continues to be developed and delivered, and remind line managers of the need for regular participation in such training. *(Section 5.18)*

20. Instruct Presbyteries to ensure that arrangements are in place from 1 Jan 2010 to cover costs relating to employment of PPWs in those charges within their bounds which are unable themselves to meet costs for approved expenses and equipment. *(Section 5.19)*

21. Note with concern the issue of affordability in respect of the ministries of the church and instruct the Council to bring forward a report with recommendations on future policy with regard to stipends, salaries and numbers to the General Assembly 2010. *(Section 6.2)*

REPORT

1. Introduction

The Ministries Council presents its report this year in a new format. This draws on the model of the Operational Plan through which the Council ensures diligence in undertaking its work and fulfilling its ongoing remit throughout the year. The Council hopes that this style of reporting will allow the Church at large to gain a good insight into the multifaceted work of the Council, while keeping the size of the report as tight as possible. The following guidelines seek to enable easy reading of this report:

(a) The report follows the main section headings of the Council's work, as follows:

Section 1 – Overall remit of Council;
Section 2 – Priority Areas;
Section 3 – Vocation and Training;
Section 4 – Support and Development;
Section 5 – Planning and Deployment;
Section 6 – Finance

(b) In all cases, the work described in the column headed

Task is followed by a brief note on work undertaken in the past year in the column headed *Progress/Update*. Where there is substantial *Additional Material*, this is indicated in the column so headed. In some cases this will be in the form of a short paper included immediately following the grid containing updates relating to this section of the work. In some instances, there is reference to supplementary materials which can be accessed on the Church's website. These are not essential for the debate at the Assembly, but give further information which commissioners may wish to consult in advance of the debate. The final column indicates if there is a section of the *Deliverance (Del)* which corresponds to the task described, and notes the number of the relevant section.

Finally, for the sake of clarity, the number in the extreme left column is the equivalent of a paragraph number. If there is *additional* material following immediately on the section of the grid, it will be numbered in cross-reference to the number in the extreme left column. So, for example, 1.1 in the left column is matched by material numbered *1.1 Consultation with Presbyteries on Tenure* following the first portion of the grid. The next block of material is then numbered *1.9 Facing Today's Challenges and Opportunities,* as this is the number allocated to that issue in the reporting grid.

	Task	Progress/Update	Additional Material	Del
1	**OVERALL COUNCIL WORK**			
1.1	In partnership with the Legal Questions Committee, the Worship and Doctrine Task Group, the Ecumenical Relations Committee and such other Councils, Committees and Agencies of the Church as may be necessary, prepare a detailed initial report on the options for tenure.	Work is progressing on a major report on the future of tenure, which will be brought to the General Assembly in 2010. The 2008 report offered a number of options for consideration, but no questions were asked and no discussion took place on the subject during the Council's report. As a result, the Council held a 24-hour consultation with representatives of Presbyteries in Oct 2008, at which the options were discussed in detail. A summary of the outcome of that discussion is appended below. The Council is now entering a wider process of discussion with the bodies listed with a view to conducting a formal consultation with Presbyteries in autumn 2009.	*Further details at Tenure Consultation below, Section 1.1*	2

	Task	Progress/Update	Additional Material	Del
1.2	Congregational Conflict Report: in the light of the report, urgently review practices to determine where these need immediate adjustment in order to (a) avoid destructive conflict and (b) deal more effectively with and resolve conflict situations when and where these arise, and report on any such adjustments to the Ministries Council by 31 March 2009. Implement the Action Plan on dealing with Congregational Conflict and the recommendations contained therein.	The Council's report on Congregational Conflict has been a catalyst in opening up new areas of cooperative work on this important issue. We await responses by the due date and an update on these will be given in a Supplementary Report. The Council sponsored a 2-day ecumenical planning event in Jan 2009 which laid the foundations for a major conference on conflict resolution, peacemaking and mediation, to be held from 15 – 18 Nov 2009. This will seek to take forward work on both the resolution of conflict in congregations and the development of a centre for peacemaking and conflict resolution amongst the churches in Scotland.	*Further details under Support & Development* *(Section 4.3)*	**12**
1.3	Continue research into the reasons that a disproportionately lower number of women than men present for training, and report to the General Assembly 2009.	The Vocation and Training Committee has continued the work begun in 2007-2008 investigating the reasons that fewer women than men are presently entering training. The importance of the issue has led the Council to delay making a final report this year to allow for more in depth study. The Council is grateful to those who have been assisting in this work, in particular Rev Dr Anne Logan, whose doctoral research work has provided key insights. A full report will be brought to the General Assembly 2010.		
1.4	Update the roll of Readers to indicate those who are currently recognized and regularly active in the service of the Church.	Presbyteries were instructed to update their rolls of Readers and transmit these to the Council by Sept 2009. At the time of writing, 30 Presbyteries had completed this task. Further reminders have been issued and the Council hopes to have a more accurate picture of the number and spread of serving Readers by the time Assembly meets in May 2009.		

	Task	Progress/Update	Additional Material	Del
1.5	Proceed with the next phase of obtaining enhanced disclosure certificates for all ministers of the Church.	During the past year, all processing of disclosures has transferred into the remit of the Safeguarding Office. This has necessitated some changes in procedures, but the task of obtaining enhanced disclosures from all ministers is now underway. The Council is covering the cost of this exercise, which will amount to more than £25K.		3
1.6	Implement the setting up of an Emerging Ministries Fund.	The Emerging Ministries Fund has now been established in its work, with grants totaling around £100K having been disbursed in the latter part of 2008. It is anticipated that the allocation of £300K for 2009 will be fully utilized.	*Further details under Planning & Deployment (Section 5.12)*	
1.7	Bring forward to the General Assembly of 2011 a coherent and integrated model of selection and training which allows for flexible engagement in ministry (in consultation with other appropriate partners).	The Council has begun the process of reviewing all its patterns of training at both pre- and post-ordination levels. In this first of three stages to be completed over the period to May 2011, work has been undertaken on establishing theological principles which will inform the future shape of training. A paper entitled *Enabling Ministries* is being shaped through discussion within the Council and in consultation with other Councils, academic and ecumenical partners. The full working document is available for study online at: www.churchofscotland.org.uk/generalassembly/gareports.htm.#ministries In the next two years, the Council plans to continue the review in partnership with those already involved and with others. In stage two, work will be undertaken on potential *models* for training, including looking widely at patterns established by others furth of Scotland. This will be followed in stage three by the detailed outlining of *training programs* relating to each of the recognised ministries of the Church.	*See further the working document entitled* Enabling Ministries, *to be found on the Church of Scotland website.*	4

	Task	Progress/Update	Additional Material	Del
1.8	Recognising the desir-ability of a more flexible approach to the exercise of the ministry of Word and Sacrament and acknowledging the existing difficulty in many parts of Scotland in meeting the needs of ministry using existing resources, bring forward proposals which seek to meet these urgent needs both through offering an increased flexibility in the deployment of existing forms of ministry and through the development of a pilot form of Ordained Local Ministry.	Some work has been undertaken on enabling more flexible patterns of ministry of Word and Sacrament. Although the General Assembly invited all Presbyteries to enter into dialogue with the Council about future flexibility, in reality, only a few of those Presbyteries most acutely affected by a shortage of ministers made approaches to the Council. In the past year, however, the Council has developed with one Presbytery a new pattern for using an Auxiliary Minister in a more flexible deployment, without need to alter any existing Acts. In this instance, the Presbytery of Shetland has declared a charge a Continued Vacancy and appointed the Auxiliary Minister as Interim Moderator and full-time Locum minister. The Auxiliary functions directly under the supervision of Presbytery and is paid as a Locum, in line with the provision of Act XIII 2003, section 18. Although that particular situation warrants a full-time Locum appointment, this procedure could also be applied in places where a full-time appointment may not be necessary. Council Staff are ready to work with Presbyteries in exploring any situation where such an approach might be of benefit. The Council has begun to look further at the question of an Ordained Local Ministry (OLM), but sees this within the wider task of considering training patterns, out of which will grow a clearer picture of the possibilities which OLM might bring. It is clear that a 'pilot' of an ordained ministry is not a realistic option, as ordination cannot be exercised in relation to an office which might not be developed beyond an experimental stage. The Council will bring a further report to the General Assembly 2010.		5

	Task	Progress/Update	Additional Material	Del
1.9	Ensure a good communication flow with Presbyteries, including a review of the annual meeting structure for consultation	The Council has sought to consult Presbyteries in a number of ways over the past year. A major conference was held on tenure in Oct 2008 *(see above 1.1)* to which all Presbyteries were invited. 38 Presbyteries sent representatives. Two joint consultations were held by the Ministries and Mission & Discipleship Councils: one in Lerwick with outer Island Presbyteries; a second in Fort William with mainland Presbyteries in the northwest. These consultations produced initiatives in four areas as detailed below: Video Technology; Transition Ministry; Secondment; Probationers' Roadshow.	*Facing Today's Challenges and Opportunities (1.9)*	**6**
1.9.1	Video Technology	The Council was encouraged to explore the use of video technology in worship. Two pilots are under way. (a) In Orkney the possibility of live video links is being explored so that a number of congregations in different islands may share in the one act of worship. The intention is that this will allow the minister to be physically present in a different island each week, and virtually present in the other ones every week. (b) In Caithness a library of filmed resources which can be incorporated into weekly worship is being developed. This is receiving support from the Council's newly established *Emerging Ministries Fund*.		
1.9.2	Secondment	The possibility of making arrangements for Ministers to be seconded temporarily from one charge to another experiencing a long term vacancy is being piloted. The scheme will run using existing legislation under Act V 2001. Ministers serving in other parts of Scotland, while unable to accept a call to remoter Presbyteries, might still be willing to relieve some of the pressure and would welcome the opportunity of a secondment for up to three months. Details of proposed implementation are outlined below.	*Secondment (1.9.2)*	

	Task	Progress/Update	Additional Material	Del
1.9.3	Transition Ministry	The Council was encouraged to explore a new form of ministry, akin to Interim Ministry but specifically for helping with issues of adjustment and restructuring in areas experiencing a number of long term vacancies. At the time of writing, one area had been identified for a possible pilot scheme.	*Transition Ministry (1.9.3)*	
1.9.4	Probationers' Roadshow	The Council was encouraged to develop one of the regular Probationers' Conferences away from the central belt, with a focus on the needs of rural ministry. For organisational reasons that will not be possible in 2009, but the Council will offer an opportunity for interested Probationers to meet representatives of vacant congregations in the North of Scotland at a Roadshow event.		
1.10	Ensure the continued possibility of admitting to ministry in Scotland those who come from outside the European Economic Area (EEA) and Switzerland	New government legislation on economic immigration took effect from 1 Nov 2008. This requires that any employer wishing to engage someone from outside the EEA and Switzerland must first obtain a Sponsor's Licence, under which the employer takes responsibility for those engaged in paid work. At the time of writing, the Church of Scotland has applied for such a licence, to enable the continued flow of ministers and others from outwith the EEA and Switzerland to work within the ministries of the Church. As a condition of issuing a licence, the employer must demonstrate that the post cannot be filled by a resident of the UK or the EEA and Switzerland. To satisfy this condition, an Act has been prepared offering a means by which a list of such posts, previously suitably advertised and remaining unfilled, can be drawn up and receive applications from those coming from outside the EEA and Switzerland.	*Text of Act anent Ministers from non-EEA Countries (1.10)*	**7**

Task	Progress/Update	Additional Material	Del
	Until a Licence is granted, no Certificates of Eligibility can be granted to Admissions applicants who fall within the above category. The Council regrets the delay which this inevitably creates for some seeking appointment and for charges awaiting applications. This lies, however, beyond our control. The new process will undoubtedly require a much greater degree of consistency in the way that posts are advertised and vacancy procedures are conducted. The Council will bring details of proposals in a Supplementary Report.		

1.1 Consultation with Presbyteries on Tenure

The consultation took place in Cumbernauld, 8 – 9 October 2008. Around 55 people attended, with most Presbyteries sending representatives. Of those present from Presbyteries, 3 were Elders and the remainder Ministers.

1.1.1 Description of the Process

The different options which had been presented by the Council in its report to the General Assembly 2008 were considered in detail. A plenary discussion invited people to offer examples from their Presbyteries about ways in which the current tenure position posed difficulties. This did not initially bring out a great deal, most of discussion being quite defensive of present system. At the end of this discussion, each participant was given 8 adhesive stars and was invited to stick these onto the option(s) they favoured, using whatever number of stars represented the relative weight they wished to give to any option. The resulting figures for this were:

Status Quo	**134**	Reviewable Tenure	**49**	Adjustable Tenure	**61**	Contracts (Regional)	**23**
Revision of Acts	**27**	Presbytery Tenure	**55**	Contracts (Central)	**11**		

Small Groups considered the benefits and drawbacks of these options and then were asked to come and 'sell' a particular model to the plenary group. This produced some imaginative and compelling presentations! Plenary discussion took place following the presentations and this continued informally into the evening in a variety of ways. On the following morning, the groups were asked to prepare a presentation outlining the drawbacks of their presentation option. This again produced some passionate and perceptive presentations. After further plenary discussion, participants were again issued with adhesive stars and asked to repeat the opening exercise. The resulting figures were (with variation from first exercise noted):

Status Quo	**122** **-12**	Reviewable Tenure	**79** **+30**	Adjustable Tenure	**28** **-33**	Contracts (Regional)	**8** **-15**
Revision of Acts	**46** **+19**	Presbytery Tenure	**52** **-3**	Contracts (Central)	**10** **-1**		

In the final session, participants were asked the question: *"If tenure is not the problem, what are the 'real' issues?"* This question intended to highlight some of the connected areas which had been either hinted at during the process, or had been raised on other occasions when tenure had been discussed. The following issues were noted:
- The number of vacancies
- The impression that appraisal is a negative thing

- Failure to implement the quinquennial visitation system effectively
- Presbyteries that refuse to 'bite the bullet' on issues such as competence
- People are asked to work in team ministries without sufficient training
- 'Square pegs in round holes'
- The culture of the Church
- Buildings
- Blurred boundaries between superintendence and appraisal
- Geographical and cultural differences in rural / remote and island ministries
- Effectiveness of pastoral care networks in Presbyteries

1.1.2 Outcome and Proposed Way Forward

Some shift was evident in opinions by the end of the process. While the largest number of stars still went on the status quo, it was clear that more stars in total went elsewhere. It was agreed that this pointed to the need for some change. Overall it was concluded that it would be good to explore three areas further:

- Combining the status quo with a careful scrutiny of existing acts to establish (a) what powers Presbytery currently has and is not using; and (b) to look at how existing acts might be revised to allow Presbytery to deal with occasions on which tenure is an obstacle to dealing with issues of discipline, intransigence or incompetence.
- To take the Reviewable Tenure option together with Adjustable Tenure, and to continue to explore how these might be developed, taking into account the model that Glasgow Presbytery has followed in relation to reviewable tenure.
- To develop further the notion of a Presbytery tenure, learning from the reasons for the failure of a not dissimilar model of flexible tenure put forward before.

It was clear from the process also that the question of moving to an employment model had no significant support and would not be worthwhile pursuing further.

In the final discussion session, it was noted that the timescale for any significant ongoing consultation with Presbyteries was much too short if a fully shaped report was to go to the General Assembly in May 2009. It was agreed that a better strategy would be simply to continue the process begun at this consultation by sending out a summary to Presbytery Clerks and to participants in the conference to enable those who had been involved to engage with their Presbyteries. Feedback would be welcomed by the Ministries Council as it undertakes to develop the three points above. A consultation paper would be prepared to be forwarded to Presbyteries around April, asking for discussion and response in the following months.

1.9 Facing Today's Challenges and Opportunities
1.9.1 Introduction

Some Presbyteries, particularly those distant from the main centres of population, are finding it difficult to attract ministers. They are experiencing numerous, lengthy vacancies. Recently some of these Presbyteries have had more vacancies than ministers. At one point in the autumn not only was there no Church of Scotland minister in Wick, there was no minister of any denomination living in the town. The pattern of church life we are accustomed to assumes that most charges will have ministers. Not surprisingly, sustaining both congregational and Presbytery life becomes very challenging when more than half of the charges in a Presbytery are vacant.

In autumn 2008, jointly with the Mission and Discipleship Council, the Ministries Council held two consultations in order better to understand the issues faced by the Church in the more remote Presbyteries. The first was held in Lerwick for the outer island Presbyteries of Lewis, Orkney, Shetland and Uist; the second in Fort William for Argyll, Caithness, Lochaber, Lochcarron & Skye and Sutherland.

Four initiatives found favour and are being taken forward:

(a) the use of video technology to assist in worship; (b) Secondment; (c) Transition Ministry; (d) Probationers' Roadshow.

Further details of (b) and (c) are given below.

1.9.2   Secondment

Act V 2001 enables the appointment of Assessor Ministers where a Presbytery has too few ministers available to fulfil all its functions. Classifying ministers coming under secondment as Assessor Ministers allows this scheme to operate without further legislation.

1.9.2.1   Vacant Charge and receiving Presbytery

- The vacant charge must have had permission to call a minister for more than a year. It must provide furnished accommodation for the minister during the period of the secondment.
- The vacant charge is free to continue its search for a minister but no induction can take place until the end of the secondment.
- The Presbytery of the vacant charge is responsible for deciding whether it is appropriate for the charge to receive a secondment and for approving the choice by the congregation of a minister to serve in that secondment.
- The secondment will be for a minimum of one month and a maximum of three.
- Once the details of a secondment have been agreed by the Presbyteries, the vacant charge and the minister concerned, the receiving Presbytery shall write to the secretary of the Legal Questions Committee stating that a particular minister is to be seconded under this scheme, and seeking approval in terms of Act V 2001 to appoint him/her to the Presbytery in order to moderate the Kirk Session.
- The seconded minister will be given membership of the Presbytery, allowing him/her to act as Moderator of the Kirk Session as well as locum. Those seconded will retain membership of the Presbytery in which their regular charge is situated; accountability for life and doctrine will rest with that Presbytery.

1.9.2.2   Minister and sending Presbytery

- The seconded minister must have served a minimum of five years in his/her current charge.
- Before agreeing to the secondment the Presbytery will seek the views of the Kirk Session(s). The Kirk Session(s) would not have the right to veto the secondment. Its views would help the Presbytery, however, in deciding whether to agree to the request. *(This is comparable to the way in which Presbyteries are consulted when ministers submit study leave requests)*
- For the duration of the secondment the Presbytery will suspend the ministry in the same way that it does for lengthy periods of study leave.
- The Minister would continue to receive his/her normal stipend and to have the use of his/her own manse.
- For the period of secondment his/her inducted charge will have an interim moderator and be entitled to the services of a locum two days a week, approved by the Presbytery in the usual fashion.

1.9.2.3   The Ministries Council

- The Ministries Council will be responsible for publicising those charges that are looking for a secondment.
- The Ministries Council will continue to pay the seconded minister his/her usual stipend and pay for a locum two days a week in their regular charge.

1.9.3.   Transition Ministry

Interim Ministry has shown the value of ministers with a specific skill set who come for a defined period of time in order to allow a congregation to move forward. Transition Ministry applies this principle in a slightly different way. While the Council will be delighted to be proved wrong, it suspects that the Presbyteries currently facing numerous lengthy vacancies will continue to face them in the short to medium term. This means that a pattern of church life will need to evolve which is less minister-dependent. Unfortunately the very leadership that would assist in this evolution is already stretched to the limit because the remaining ministers and experienced elders are serving as interim moderators. The appointment of a Transition Minister as detailed below could prove very valuable.

1.9.3.1 Objectives

Transition Ministers will be deployed with the aim of:

- Providing ministry to congregations experiencing long term vacancies and which are often therefore missing the very leadership they need to adjust to a radically different future.
- Working with the Kirk Sessions to develop patterns of ministry that depend less on the presence of full-time ministers of word and sacrament.
- Training worship leaders, interim moderators and pastoral visitors to undertake aspects of ministry locally.
- Introducing video technology which enables one minister of word and sacrament to conduct worship and meetings in different locations simultaneously.

1.9.3.2 Deployment

- The Transition Minister will be deployed to two or more charges. The charges will be linked for the duration of the appointment, with the minister being inducted to them.
- The deployment will normally be for a period of between three and five years.
- The Transition Minister will be an employee, under contract to the Ministries Council. At the end of one period of Transition Ministry he/she may be moved to another placement to undertake another assignment.
- A monitoring group, comprising representatives appointed by the Ministries Council and the Presbytery will support the Transition Minister.
- A manse will be supplied. The charges the Transition Minister serves will share the costs of housing and expenses.
- At the end of the period of deployment the Transition Minister will be free to apply to any vacant charge in the Presbytery, including those in which he/she has served.

1.9.3.3 Outcome

- At the end of the deployment, if the Presbytery plan allows, the link can be broken with each charge free to call a minister.
- If the Presbytery and congregations are in agreement, the larger linked unit may continue and be free to call a minister.
- In either case a further lengthy vacancy might ensue, but the congregations will, because of the Transition Ministry, be better able to face the challenges and seize the opportunities this will bring.

1.9.3.4 Support and Oversight

- The Interim Ministries Task Group will oversee Transition Ministry on behalf of the Ministries Council.
- The Ministries Council will provide training to enable the Transition Minister to fulfil this role.
- The Transition Minister will be part of the Peer Group of Interim Ministers, which meets regularly to reflect on and discuss team issues.
- A residential training event will be held annually and a detailed programme of learning and induction developed.
- Support will be offered by a Ministries Support Officer designated by the Council Secretary.

1.10 Act Anent Ministers from Non-EEA Countries Excluding Switzerland, Amending Acts VIII 2003 Anent Vacancy Procedure (as amended) and IX 2002 Anent Admission and Re-Admission of Ministers (as amended)
Edinburgh, XX May 2009 Sess. YY

The General Assembly hereby enact and ordain as follows:

1. Act VIII 2003 anent Vacancy Procedure (as amended) is hereby further amended by the addition of a new

paragraph 12(2)(d), with consequent renumbering, reading: "with the Kirk Session(s) as soon as an application is made for permission to proceed in terms of section 25A of this Act, to ensure that the requirements of that section are fulfilled"

2.   Act VIII 2003 is further amended by the addition of a new sentence at the end of sub-section 17(6) reading: "The holder of a Certificate of Eligibility who is a national of a country outside the European Economic Area and Switzerland shall be eligible to apply for charges only in terms of section 25A of this Act."

3.   Act VIII 2003 is further amended by the insertion of a new section 25A, immediately before section 26 (with no consequential deletions or renumbering) and reading:

(1)   "Six months after the vacancy has first appeared in a monthly vacancy list, and provided there are no applications currently under the consideration of the Nominating Committee, the Kirk Session (or in the case of a linkage the Kirk Sessions in agreement) may apply to the Presbytery to have the charge listed for the purposes of this section.

(2)   Such applications shall be considered by the whole Presbytery, and shall not form part of the remit of the Vacancy Procedure Committee.

(3)   The Presbytery must be satisfied that there are no outstanding issues of superintendence, or other factors that would make such listing inappropriate, and must consult with the Ministries Council before deciding whether to permit the listing. The Presbytery Clerk shall within seven days send an extract minute of the decision to the Ministries Council.

(4)   Upon receiving notification of the listing from the Presbytery, the Nominating Committee shall proceed again from section 16 of this Act, and holders of Certificates of Eligibility who are nationals of countries outwith the EEA and Switzerland shall now be eligible to apply.

(5)   For the avoidance of doubt, the Nominating Committee (a) must always dispose of any competent applications received in terms of section 17 of this Act before considering those made in terms of this section, but (b) shall not be obliged to make a nomination from any particular group of applicants.

(6)   When a Presbytery withdraws permission to call, or the permission lapses in terms of section 26 of this Act, the Presbytery shall decide whether permission to proceed in terms of this section remains in force during the ensuing process to make a nomination."

4.   Act IX 2002 anent Admission and Re-admission of Ministers (as amended) is hereby further amended by the addition, in paragraph 6(a), after the words 'Act XIII 2003 anent the Auxiliary Ministry (as amended)' of the words 'and Act VIII 2003 sections 17 and 25A'.

	Task	Progress/Update	Additional Material	Del
2	**PRIORITY AREAS WORK**			
2.1	Increase information and awareness of Priority Areas work through good communication.	The Priority Areas *eNews* is now circulated to almost 500 people per month. The publication of *Big Hearted Communities* (booklet, DVD & web resources) has helped to promote the work over the past year. The *Priority Areas* web pages are updated on a monthly basis. Information available at: www.churchofscotland.org.uk/priorityareas.htm *or e-mail :* priorityareas@cofscotland.org.uk	*See further on the Ministries Council, Priority Areas section of the Church of Scotland website*	
2.2	Effective delivery of the *Poverty Truth Commission.*	The *Poverty Truth Commission* is scheduled for 21st March 2009. The event will be hosted by the Rt Rev David Lunan in Glasgow and is seeking to bring up to 400 people together to hear – at first hand – people's experiences of poverty in Scotland and the steps which are necessary to overcome it.		
2.3	Establishment of new work in Drumchapel through *Together for a Change*	The work of *Together for a Change* – a global exchange of people with a direct experience of poverty – continues to attract a great deal of interest with ongoing work in Glasgow, Gambia and Malawi. New links are being established between Kenya and Drumchapel. Similar work planned for Carnwadric has not yet been possible to progress. The Council is also considering the possibility of a link between a priority area parish and Israel/Palestine.		
2.4	Establish and maintain Twinning partnerships	A number of new twinning partnerships have developed over the past year with 54 congregations currently involved. The Council has also been working with congregations in Glasgow Presbytery where a number of churches have been asked to undertake twinning partnerships as part of the approved Presbytery Plan. Details of how to go about twinning are available on the website: www.churchofscotland.org.uk/priorityareas.htm	*See further on the Ministries Council, Priority Areas section of the Church of Scotland website*	

3

	Task	Progress/Update	Additional Material	Del
2.5	Agreement on Capital Development projects for Church Extension charges (*Garthamlock & Easterhouse*)	Proposals for new church buildings in *Garthamlock & Craigend East* and *Easterhouse St George's & St Peter's* were approved in October 2008. This marks an important step for these two congregations. They will remain as Church Extension charges until this work is completed, but the Council intends that both will be able to move to full status at that point.		
2.6	Establish a strategy for Capital Building Development	Over the past year the Council has established good links with a number of key strategic public sector partners to consider how some of the critical building requirements in *priority areas* can be progressed collaboratively. The Council is also continuing to work closely with the General Trustees to see how this work can most effectively be taken forward.		
2.7	Deliver a second cohort of *Priority Areas Leadership Coaching* and establish ongoing sustainability for this work	A second group of 13 people involved in a range of paid ministries within *priority areas* has undertaken coaching for leadership. This has involved two residential conferences and ten one-to-one sessions. A small team of four coaches has been recruited from amongst previous participants in the course to support this work.		
2.8	Deliver the Priority Areas Ministries strategy (including communications, training & vocation)	As a result of the strategy a number of new areas of work have been developed including plans for a ten-week Summer Work Placement in priority areas for ministerial candidates. This will include time for weekly contextual theological reflection. The strategy is also helping to inform the Council's wider thinking about training and formation.		
2.9	Establish the *Transforming Lives* programme of localised coaching.	Funds for the next three years have been secured for this new area of work, which seeks to train local congregational members in coaching skills. Work will begin on its delivery through the aegis of a coaching organization in Spring 2009.		

	Task	Progress/Update	Additional Material	Del
2.10	Deliver a *Support & Training* programme for PA Ministries	Alongside opportunities for coaching and a range of activities designed for all those involved in priority area parishes, the Council has delivered a range of activities specifically focused on those involved in paid ministries, including theological reflection and development of spirituality. Three additional events are planned for 2009 in response to local requests, addressing traumatic death, Ignatian spirituality and Appreciative Inquiry.		
2.11	Deliver a *Worship Development* strategy (inc. *Soul Marks* & *Unlock Glasgow*)	The Council has continued to work closely with *Soul Marks* www.soulmarks.co.uk and *Unlock Glasgow* www.unlockglasgow.org.uk in the delivery of its strategy to support creative and participative worship in priority area parishes. In 2009 *Soul Marks* is supporting 5 congregations to develop *Sacred Space in Hard Places* – the development of Quiet/Prayer Rooms within their buildings or community spaces. *Unlock Glasgow* is continuing to work with a range of small groups, developing a range of downloadable resources.	*Further information on websites listed for* Soul Marks *and Unlock Glasgow*	
2.12	Develop a *Youth Work* strategy	The development of a *Priority Areas Youth Work Strategy* has been one of the core priorities over the last year. An independent consultant has carried out some initial work and there has also been close working with the Mission & Discipleship Council. The focus of the *strategy* is to ensure the development and delivery of new work in *priority areas* supporting some of Scotland's most vulnerable young people. In line with its operating model in other spheres of activity, the Council is seeking to develop a range of partnerships to take this work forward most effectively.		

3

	Task	Progress/Update	Additional Material	Del
2.13	Support of key strategic priorities within *Faith in Community (Scotland)* (including bereavement, Dundee, GIS, Storytelling & Participation Centre, Interfaith Trust, Prison Throughcare and Transformation Team)	This has been an exceptionally busy year within the work of *Faith in Community (Scotland)* – the multi-faith, anti-poverty organization of which the *Church of Scotland* is a member. A range of developments has been possible because of the appointment of an *Operations Director* in June 2008. The *Transformation Team* continues to provide high-quality support to a wide range of faith groups. In the last three years it has worked with 33 of the 38 *priority area parishes* in Glasgow. In the Spring of 2009, following a merger with the *Scottish Churches Community Trust*, a new grants programme (*FISCAF – Faiths in Scotland Community Action Fund*) was launched to support faith-based initiatives tackling poverty. Work is ongoing during 2009 to establish a support team in Dundee, a range of *Prison Throughcare Centres* across Scotland and an *Interfaith Storytelling & Participation Centre* based in Govanhill. For more information about this work, check out www.faithincommunityscotland.org	*Further information on the* Faith in Community Scotland *website*	
2.14	Develop and maintain *Priority Areas Women's Leadership Network*	A *Women's Leadership Network* has been established, providing support, leadership training and reflection space for a group of women from *priority areas* who are fulfilling a wide range of roles as community and congregational leaders.		
2.15	Deliver a *National Consultation* and establish *Regional Forums*	The *Priority Areas National Consultation* took place at Carberry Tower in November 2008. It was the best attended consultation of recent years (with over 100 participants). Entitled *Celebrating the Past – Glimpsing the Future*, the consultation was key to the development of thinking around the future work in *priority areas* over the next seven years.		

	Task	Progress/Update	Additional Material	Del
2.16	Deliver approved staffing levels within *Presbytery Plans*	The Council continued to work with a number of Presbyteries to seek to ensure that additional staffing for *priority areas* approved through the *Presbytery Planning* process are recruited and effectively supported. In the period to Feb 2009, nine new posts had been filled.		
2.17	Increase development and delivery of *Priority Areas Staffing Fund*	The Council continued to provide additional funding for staff in *priority area parishes* through the *Priority Areas Staffing Fund*. This work is undertaken in conjunction with the *Parish Development Fund* (PDF), which is responsible for its management and administration. The number of successful submissions for funding grew on the previous year, but continues to be below the maximum potential. Securing match funding also continues to be difficult for local congregations and over the next year the Council will be working closely with the *PDF* to consider ways in which these problems can be overcome.		
2.18	Write up the *Priority Areas* 'story' and 'theology' including the development of major report on the future of *priority areas work*	The Council has employed the services of Ann Morisy, a freelance theologian and well known speaker and author, to assist in the gathering of information about work within *priority areas*. During 2009 it is hoped that she will co-author a book with Martin Johnstone, the Council's Associate Secretary with responsibility for Priority Areas. As a first fruit of this work the Council brings to the General Assembly a report laying out the principles and priorities for its work in Scotland's poorest communities over the next seven years. A fuller version of this report can be found on the website at: www.churchofscotland.org.uk/generalassembly/gareports.htm.#ministries	*Celebrating the Past – Glimpsing the Future (2.18). A fuller version can be found on the Church of Scotland website.*	8

	Task	Progress/Update	Additional Material	Del
2.19	Develop a PA *Strategic Plan* (including *Monitoring and Evaluation Framework*)	The Council is committed to ensuring that the resources at its disposal in *priority areas* are used effectively and creatively. Over the last year, it has worked at developing an effective monitoring and evaluation framework and will take forward this work over the coming year. www.churchofscotland.org.uk/priorityareas.htm	*Details of Monitoring and Evaluation Framework available on the website*	

2.18 Celebrating the Past – Glimpsing the Future
2.18.1 Introduction

When the Priority Areas Committee was formed in 2003, a commitment was given to review the Committee's work no later than 2010 in order to discern what role such a body should have in the ongoing life of the Church of Scotland.

The Council brings a report this year in which it reviews some of the key elements of work in priority areas and lays out what it believes to be the core principles and priorities for the future. Over the next year the Council will continue to work on these priorities and will bring a more detailed programme of activity to the 2010 General Assembly.

This report is the product of an extensive consultation process which has actively involved over 100 people from priority area congregations in the process of shaping and writing it. Although the Council is delighted fully to support it, it is much more than a report from the Council – it is also the authentic voice of the Church in many of our poorest communities.

2.18.2 The Nature of Poverty and the Church's Response

Poverty remains a reality for a very significant percentage of Scotland's population. As the economic recession hits many over the coming year, it will be those who can least afford it who will suffer the most.

Poor people live in every part of Scotland. People struggling against poverty die younger than people who are better off. This is an affront to a country of Scotland's wealth and natural resources. It is also an affront to the Gospel and God's passion for the poor.

It was in response to the growing understanding of poverty in Scotland that the Church of Scotland established the Urban Priority Areas Committee in the early 1990s. That body did a great deal over a ten year period to raise awareness of the issues and to begin to effect change.

In 2009 many of the challenges which faced our poorest neighbourhoods then are sadly similar to those we face now: poor health, poor housing, poor schooling, low levels of income and high levels of unemployment. In other respects we now face new challenges. We are increasingly facing a time of enormous economic uncertainty locally, nationally and globally.

We have become increasingly aware of the huge impact which climate change is having on all of our lives. Once again, however, it is the poorest who will suffer most for the environmental irresponsibility of others.

2.18.3 Sharing the Pain – Holding the Hope

In 2002 the Board of National Mission brought the report *Sharing the Pain – Holding the Hope* to the General Assembly. It was the result of a three year process, investigating the needs and issues facing the very poorest parishes in Scotland and the Church of Scotland congregations which were serving them. The report stated:

Without action and a critical realignment of resources over the next five years many of the churches in Scotland's poorest parishes will die. If these congregations are allowed to perish through a lack of resources, the whole Church of Scotland will be critically, and perhaps irredeemably, damaged. If we cannot announce 'good news to the poor,' who can we announce good news to?

In response to this challenge the Church has committed to making priority area parishes a genuine priority. It has consistently over these years reaffirmed the statement of the 2002 General Assembly: 'Priority for the poorest and most marginalised is **the** gospel imperative facing the whole Church and not just the Church in our poorest communities.'

It is clear that the Church has come a long way over these last seven years. The very fact that the Church in priority areas is still here is testimony to that. The generosity and commitment of the whole Church has helped the Church in our poorest places to survive. At the same time, we are clear that we contribute an enormous amount to the wider Church, financially but also through the creativity and engagement which are foundational to the ways that we work.

Within many churches in priority areas there is a culture of increased resilience and togetherness which is complementing growing levels of commitment, the willingness to take risks and a spirit of generosity. We believe that these changes are significant not only for the Church in our neighbourhoods, but also for the Church as a whole. One person summed this up when he observed at our recent Priority Areas Consultation: 'A number of years ago we used to come to this event to share our problems and to have a good moan. Now we come to share possibilities and to celebrate together.'

2.18.4 What We Celebrate and Give Thanks to God for
The 2002 report highlighted crises in relation to buildings and staffing as the two most important challenges facing the Church in priority areas at that time. Whilst a great deal remains to be done – indeed in some cases the situation has become even more precarious – real progress has been made. It is critical looking forward that the additional posts agreed for priority areas in Presbytery Plans continue to be filled.

Alongside the increased staffing secured through the Presbytery Planning process, additional staff posts are also being created through the Priority Areas Staffing Fund, established by the Ministries Council in January 2007 and managed and administered on its behalf by the Parish Development Fund.

This long term commitment to increased staffing in the very poorest neighbourhoods has attracted interest from a wide range of other agencies and organisations across both Scotland and the rest of the UK. It is to the Church's credit that it has held its nerve and kept its commitment to these areas at a time of economic downturn and likely decreasing levels of public funding.

In terms of buildings there has been progress in a number of places, although there is also fear of impending crisis just around the corner for many and already here by the bucket load (quite literally) for others. The ongoing support and commitment of the General Trustees has been hugely important here. Significant grants have helped to lever in substantial external sources of funding in a number of instances. For example, in Ruchazie (Glasgow), a grant of £70,000 has helped to generate ten times that amount and has enabled the development of a significant community resource within the area.

Over the last seven years there are many other things to be celebrated. These include:
- *Twinning*: where almost 20 priority area parishes have developed deep relationships with congregations in more prosperous – and different – neighbourhoods.
- *Together for a Change*: our international exchange programme has enabled people who know about

poverty in their guts, rather than simply their heads, to share wisdom across the continents. One person, with a lifetime's experience in the Church and in international development, has described *Together for a Change* as 'the best thing the Church of Scotland has ever done.'

- *Coaching*: has enabled Church leaders to become more resilient and effective in their ministries, helping to produce, in turn, more effective and resilient congregations and communities. One highly effective minister, for example, has described the coaching programme as the most significant support he has received from the wider Church in over 20 years of ministry.

- *Unlock Glasgow* (www.unlockglasgow.org.uk) helps bring the Bible to life. It has worked with 19 congregations and communities, published 10 resources and supported 12 leaders to develop this work.

- *Soul Marks* (www.soulmarks.co.uk) harnesses the participatory arts, working with a small number of congregations (six over the last 2 years) for a period of up to a year. This work is helping to develop new models of worship which are inclusive, participatory and transformative.

- *Faith in Community Scotland* (www.faithincommunity scotland.org) initially began in Glasgow but is increasingly active in other parts of the country. It helps local faith communities to make the differences that they crave. In the last three years its team in Glasgow has supported work in thirty-three of the thirty-eight poorest neighbourhoods in the city.

In all of this we do not delude ourselves, or others, that everything we have tried has worked. Nor do we pretend that we are supporting anything other than a very small proportion of what needs to be done. Nevertheless, we sense that things are changing. We are seeing God at work in exciting and new ways in places that have always been special to God. This work is about more than staving off death. It is also about renewal and resurrection in places where the cross is a living reality for many people.

2.18.5 Looking to the Future

Over the past year the Committee, together with the wider priority areas constituency, has evaluated its work and tried to discern future principles and priorities. Key contributors have included representatives of other Councils and Committees, a number of our core partners and Ann Morisy, a well known theologian and writer. The most important contributors to this strategy, however, are correctly the people who work and live in the struggle and celebration of life in our very poorest communities. We acknowledge that these are the people who have the insights that really matter.

2.18.6 After Seven Years, Seven Marks

Over the past year, and particularly through our National Consultation, we have discerned a number of core principles which we hope will shape our future work. These sit alongside the four existing principles which have guided our work over the last number of years.

Our existing principles are:

- *Priority must mean priority*. When the Church talks about priority areas, this needs to mean that we choose to put a significant proportion of our energy, commitment and resources into our poorest neighbourhoods.

- *Accountability to the local*. It has been and remains an important privilege to be accountable to the Ministries Council and General Assembly for the effectiveness of the work in priority areas. Our first accountability, however, is to local churches comprising local people in struggling neighbourhoods. If they don't think we are doing a good job then we are not.

- *Partnership is the only way*. The days when the Church of Scotland could go it alone are, thankfully, past. Over the last seven years we have continually recognised how important it is to work with others who share our passion for things to be better. Of course, such partnerships are not always easy and partners will not always agree on everything, but it is clear that we achieve so much more by working together.

- *Priority Areas are good places to be*. The more we see how people in priority areas are prepared to support and care for each other, the more it becomes clear that there are significant positive features in our neighbourhoods. The real news story is not the people who fail but the extraordinary numbers of people who manage and flourish, apparently against all the odds.

Alongside these existing principles, we can begin to identify a number of emerging marks which we hope will help to guide and direct our work over the next period.

2.18.6.1 *God is in the real*. Our experience is that God is very present in the day to day realities of priority areas – in the pain and the struggle as well as in the laughter and the celebration. Our churches, our communities and our gatherings are places of tears intermingled with incredible humour. God's presence is palpable.

2.18.6.2 *The principle of "the cup half full."* We have been influenced by the principles of *Appreciative Inquiry*. Over and over again during the last seven years we have discovered that when people have been able to identify what is going right and why, they have been enabled to address some of the problems which have appeared insurmountable. Getting the good things in perspective is important.

2.18.6.3 *Valuing simplicity and the little things*. We are all inclined to shy away from brokenness and vulnerability. As a result we dismiss as failures many of the things which happen in churches. Our experience, however, is that it is in brokenness and vulnerability that we find the place where God becomes real and reliable for people. Through thousands of small acts of kindness people begin and continue to believe that their place is a good place to be and that God is present in their midst.

2.18.6.4 *Believing in the miraculous*. Virtually every person who was present at Carberry Tower at our National Consultation could point to times when God broke into their life, the life of someone close to them and into the life of their local community. It should not surprise us that these profound and transformative experiences of God appear to happen most regularly amongst people for whom life is hardest and where the pretence that we can manage on our own has been stripped away. We have a sense, backed up by a growing body of evidence, that many people are open to very deep spiritual experiences in which they sense that God is very close to them.

2.18.6.5 *Unity comes through shared commitment*. The network of people involved in priority areas draws from a wide range of theological perspectives and practices, but people have a deep sense of being part of a movement that demonstrates solidarity and energy. This solidarity is rooted in shared commitments – to Jesus, to the Church and to those who struggle against poverty. This is unity in diversity, a unity that comes through shared common tasks.

2.18.6.6 *Resourcing individuals to transform neighbourhoods*. Over the last number of years we have chosen to focus a considerable amount of energy on supporting individuals within priority areas. On many occasions these individuals have been involved in our paid ministries, but increasingly it is a far wider circle. Many folks in our churches are truly remarkable people, who have led astonishing lives and done incredible things often against all the odds. We have to find the ways to allow this group of people to take on new leadership roles and to be effectively supported, trained and resourced in these emerging ministries – and we are beginning to do so. This presents us with the opportunity of shifting from being a Church which supports the poor to becoming a Church which harnesses the exceptional gifts and capacities of the poorest and most marginalised in our society.

2.18.6.7 *Focused on the local*. Neighbourhoods are changing. The pace of change in priority areas can be overwhelming. The world has become local and in these increasingly 'glocal' neighbourhoods, where trust can often be in short supply, the local church has a critical role to play in extending the reach of neighbourliness. We have a strong sense that the Church has a unique role to play in the development of more cohesive, grounded and hopeful neighbourhoods.

These marks of the Church are the principles which we hope and believe should define our outlook as we face the future. We recognise that they are not unique to the Church in priority areas: of course not, but they are clearly evident within our particular context. Alongside these principles, however, action needs to be taken.

2.18.7   Seven Priorities for Seven Years

Looking back to the 2002 General Assembly report, it is clear there has been considerable progress in a number of areas, but some challenges have yet to be addressed adequately.

2.18.7.1   *We need to sort out the problem of buildings.* Church buildings are huge assets and enable a great deal of immensely important things to happen in local neighbourhoods. They have increasingly become key community resources as other local facilities have been forced to close or letting charges have made them inaccessible to local people and groups. At the same time, the struggle to look after our decaying buildings often places an intolerable burden on people who are already faced with difficult circumstances.

The 2002 Report advocated the establishment of a Property Unit serving priority area parishes. That was resisted because of concern to keep decision-making local. We need some creative solution(s), however, if the burden of that right to make decisions is not to be Pyrrhic in character. We are currently working with the General Trustees and others to try and discern visionary and achievable ways forward.

2.18.7.2   *Our structures and processes need to be simplified.* Developments such as the introduction of the Unitary Constitution, have reduced the need for local meetings, but our systems frequently remain unbearably cumbersome and demanding, particularly for small congregations with members unused to such bureaucratic processes and facing many other pressures. Additionally, when a decision is being made in relation to a priority area congregation, too many individuals and committees become involved in the process, often leaving the local congregation feeling excluded.

There is a commonly held view across many parts of the Church that much of the information which is requested by the Church's central administration is increasingly irrelevant, or that it is not properly used when supplied. Although numbers are important, we think that there is an increasing need to gather information through stories. Sharing our stories would help us to communicate something of what it means to be the Church today.

The Priority Areas Committee, as part of the central administrative structures of the Church of Scotland, is alert to the danger of becoming part of the problem rather than part of the solution. Notwithstanding, we issue a common plea that together we look at how things can be made simpler, so that local people in all churches, not just those serving our poorest neighbourhoods, can spend time dealing with the things that really matter.

Alongside these pieces of unfinished business are other priorities to which we seek to commit ourselves over the coming years.

2.18.7.3   *The time is right to extend our support.* The most important decision taken seven years ago was to shift from supporting 330 Urban Priority Areas to focus on just 54 of the most deprived Priority Area Parishes (extended to 58 in Nov 2007). This enabled the Priority Area Committee to identify more accurately the issues and to respond more effectively. It also helped the wider Church to focus time, energy and resources on the very poorest neighbourhoods. It is a strategy which has borne fruit.

We believe that the time is now right to extend our support to other parishes which are also striving to tackle the causes and symptoms of poverty in Scotland today. Some of that process is already underway with the funds available through the Priority Areas Staffing Fund, which is available to a group of parishes wider than those on the main Priority Areas List. We now want to look, however, at how we can go further in effectively supporting additional communities and congregations working with particularly poor and marginalised groups and individuals.

2.18.7.4 *We want to take our work right to the margins.* One of the things which Ann Morisy shared with us at our National Consultation was her sense that people in priority area congregations are losing fear. This confirms the sense that many of us have of increased confidence and willingness, relying on God's grace, to engage with some of the deepest and hardest problems facing our neighbourhoods. This will include working with children, young people and their parents, as well as with offenders, ex-offenders and people living with a range of addictions.

2.18.7.5 *We want to tackle causes not just symptoms.* Over the years many churches have done a phenomenal job in helping support people suffering the worst excesses of poverty. We celebrate this and we need to continue to develop and support that vital work. Alongside this, however, we want to invest increased time and energy in addressing the causes of poverty and not just its symptoms. This will require the whole Church, not just the Church in our poorest communities, to become more engaged and prophetic in our actions. This will also involve us in trusting people who have direct experience of poverty as the natural leaders of change.

2.18.7.6 *We need to be intentional about supporting leaders.* Our work over the last two years with faith leaders through our Coaching Programme is already beginning to pay dividends. Leadership, however, is wider than those in paid positions. It also includes, to quote some of the voices that we have heard, a growing number of people who are *'up for it'* and who are *'ready for something.'* A new group of ministries and leaders is starting to emerge. They are not like the sort of ministries with which the Church of Scotland has typically functioned in the past. These are individuals who are coming from the edge of marginalised communities and frequently with broken lives. This is a group of people who, if nurtured effectively, will help to give the Church a different shape and character in the future. It will also, importantly, be different in different places, as it is built around local leaders with local vision.

2.18.7.7 *Worship must be at the heart of what we do.* At our core the church is a worshipping community of faith. We draw our strength from God and our calling is to follow Jesus and to encourage others to do the same. It is clear that one of the things that is bubbling up in some priority area parishes is forms of worship that have become increasingly participative, multi-sensory and multi-dimensional. It is not just words. It is not just music. It is not just art. It is not just activity. It seems as if contextually appropriate models of worship are emerging. These new shapes of worship must be nurtured and enabled.

2.18.8 Towards an Emerging Theology
In these marks and new priorities, looking back and looking forward we begin to sense that a new theology is taking shape in our poorest communities. Of course it is still embryonic, but it also appears to function across priority areas and to be relatively cohesive and coherent.

Brokenness is holy ground.
It is a blessing to have a new day.
This new day will bring new challenges that may add to our brokenness, because vulnerability is inescapable.

It is in this place that we discover mysterious blessings that provide
Deep reassurance of God's presence.
We know this from past experience and we have no reason to doubt God's alongsideness and faithfulness into the future.

3

	Task	Progress/Update	Additional Material	Del
3	**VOCATION AND TRAINING WORK**			
3.1	Enquiry and Assessment	The Council remains heartened by the numbers of people who seek to discern the call of God on their lives, through attendance at an Enquirers' Conference and through engagement in the various stages of selection.	*Table of Statistics for the Enquiry and Assessment Process (3.1)*	
		Four new trainee Church Assessors have been appointed:		
		Rev David Collins; Rev Alastair Duncan; Mr James McLellan; Rev David Scott.		
		The Ministries Council remains aware both of the issue of gender balance and of the need for more people to come forward as potential Church Assessors. Presbyteries are therefore encouraged to send names forward, when invited each year, of people who have suitable gifts to serve as Church Assessors, Local Assessors and Presbytery Representatives.		
		The selection process for Church Assessors continues to be regularly reviewed, further strengthened and improved. The Council remains indebted to all who serve as Assessors. The following Church Assessors retire this year:		
		Rev Dr Iain Barclay; Mrs Eileen Brown; Rev Peter Dickson; Dr Dorothy Ferguson; Rev Graham Finch; Mr Charles Shepherd; Rev Elizabeth Spence		
		The following *Directors* also retire this year:		
		Rev David Arnott (Senior Director); Mrs Helen McLeod		
		New Senior Director:		
		Rev Donald MacQuarrie		
		New Directors:		
		Dr Dorothy Ferguson (2009); Rev Colin Renwick (2009); Rev Peter Dickson (2010)		
		A review of the Assessment Criteria has been undertaken in line with the Conflict Action Plan *(Section 1.2).*		

	Task	Progress/Update	Additional Material	Del
3	**VOCATION AND TRAINING WORK**			
3.2	Ministries Training	A wide range of ongoing and developmental work has continued over the past year in the area of training for Candidates for Ministry of Word and Sacrament, Diaconal Ministry and Readers in Training. This includes a redesign of the programme for Probationers' Conferences and a full revision of the Readers-in-Training Handbook.	*Statistics on Candidates in Training (3.2)*	
3.2.1	Amendment to Act X 2004	Some small amendments are proposed to Act X 2004 with regard to the timing and number of Candidate Reviews. This will allow that a review may take place as necessary at any time during the year.	*Amendments to Act X 2004 (3.2.1)*	**9**
3.3	Congregational Conflict Report: Review of Conference Programme with reference to: • Personality Type • Conduct of Meetings • Team Training • Healthy Leadership Styles	Current provision offers quality training in a range of core areas, with around 15% of Candidate Conference time being assigned to the areas noted. Further time is allocated within the Probationers' programme, where Candidates are involved in the practice of ministry on a full-time basis. A wide range of topics is covered during the rolling programmes in which an overall balance needs to be maintained. A review of the Candidate Conference programme is planned for the coming year linking into the Council's major review of training.	*See further in Section 1.2*	
3.4	Summer work experience	The Summer Work Experience programme has been expanded from 8 to 16 posts. Although this is not a formal part of the training programme, it is a useful addition to the opportunities offered to Candidates. Some new joint work with Priority Areas will offer increased opportunity for experience to be gained in this vital area of the Council's work.	*See further under Planning & Deployment Report (5.20)*	
3.5	Implement and develop the Ministries Training Network	The Ministries Training Network (MTN) has been piloted this year. Although there is broad positive feedback, this has placed considerable demands upon Candidates. The MTN remains under review and this coming year its role will be considered within the context of the wider training review.		

	Task	Progress/Update	Additional Material	Del
3	**VOCATION AND TRAINING WORK**			
3.6	Develop training, support and appraisal for Supervisors	It is recognised that, in the light of the changing nature of ministries and changes to society, training of Supervisors must also change. Some steps have already been taken. Self-appraisal has been implemented and training needs identified as a result have been built into the training programme. An overnight training event, facilitated by Rev David Tilley yielded many useful insights. A tailored training event was held for those who supervise Probationers. Further developments are planned for this coming year with a complete revision in place by the end of 2009.		**10**
3.7	Develop a spiritual accompaniment programme for Probationers	In a joint development with the Support and Development section, Probationers this year have been offered the opportunity to work with an experienced spiritual accompaniment practitioner. This has been funded by the Council and has had an enthusiastic uptake. It is planned that this will link into the ongoing first years of ministry programme as Probationers complete their initial training.		
3.8	Admissions and Readmissions work	Certificates of Eligibility have been issued to the following: Rev Gordon B Armstrong, United Free Church of Scotland Rev Dr Fyfe Blair, Presbyterian Church of Aotearoa NZ Rev Benjamin D W Byun, Presbyterian Church in Korea Rev W John Carswell, Presbyterian Church USA Rev Robert Cleland, Baptist Union of Scotland Rev David Cooper, Methodist Church in Scotland Rev D Brian Dobby, Methodist Church of Great Britain Rev Dráusio P Gonçalves, Presbyterian Church of Brazil Rev Martin Grashoff, Protestant Church in the Netherlands Rev Dr André J Groenewald, Dutch Reformed Church of Africa (NKHA)		

	Task	Progress/Update	Additional Material	Del
3	**VOCATION AND TRAINING WORK**			
		Rev Dr Jonanda Groenewald, Dutch Reformed Church of Africa (NKHA)		
		Rev Miriam Gross, Evangelical Lutheran Church in Bavaria		
		Ms P Ruth Harvey, Licentiate		
		Rev Marc B Kenton, United Reformed Church		
		Rev Geoffrey D McKee, Baptist Union of Scotland		
		Rev Dr Alexander M Roger, United Reformed Church		
		Rev James K Wallace, Presbyterian Church USA		
3.9	Increased flexibility in Admissions procedure	The Council recognises that an alternative route is required to enable ministers from other denominations to live and work in Scotland for a restricted period of time, with the purpose of gaining experience in ministry, without the need for a full Certificate of Eligibility (which allows application to be made for any vacant charge). A proposal is brought forward to amend Act IX 2002 to provide for a restricted Certificate to be issued. This would allow application to be made for a post other than that of a Parish Minister within a Presbytery Plan which requires a Minister of Word and Sacrament (*eg* Associate Minister). The post would be for 3 years, with the possibility of an invitation for another 3 years. Thereafter, someone who wished to stay in Scotland could make application under the Act for a full Certificate of Eligibility. This new process would also enable the furthering of ecumenical partnerships.	*Amendments to Act IX 2002 (3.9)*	11

3.1 Enquiry and Assessment Scheme Statistics: 2004 – 2008

	2004			2005			2006			2007			2008		
	M	F	Total	M	F	Total	M	F	Total	M	F	Total	M	F	Total
Applicants for Ministry (all types)	39	36	75[1]	35	26	61	40	23	63	50	31	81	40	32	72[2]
Entered Local Assessment	37	35	72	34	24	58	39	23	62	49	31	80	39	27	66
Chose to Withdraw (locally)	6	7	13	4	2	6	5	1	6	11	6	17	15	6	21
Completed Local Assessment	31	28	59	30	22	52	34	22	56	38	25	63	24	21	45
Readership (Applicants)										4	3	7	8	8	16
Readership Accepted										4	3	7	7	7	14
Attended Assessment Conference	31	23	54	26	19	45	30	15	45	31	22	53	18	18	36
Full-time Ministry (Applicants)	27	20	47	24	12	36	27	8	35	26	15	41	13	13	26
Full-time Ministry Accepted	19	13	32	16	8	24	15	6	21	17	6	23	9	7	16
Auxiliary Ministry (Applicants)	4	3	7	2	5	7	3	7	10	5	7	12	5	3	8
Auxiliary Ministry Accepted	1	3	4	2	2	4	2	6	8	5	5	10	2	2	4
Deacons (Applicants)	0	0	0	0	2	2	0	0	0	0	0	0	0	2	2
Deacons Accepted	0	0	0	0	1	1	0	0	0	0	0	0	0	2	2
First Time Applicants	24	19	43	19	20	39	26	15	41	26	18	44	15	15	30
Accepted	16	12	28	13	10	23	16	11	27	17	10	27	9	10	19
Returning Applicants	7	4	11	6	1	7	2	2	4	5	4	9	3	3	6
Accepted	4	4	8	5	1	6	1	1	2	5	1	6	2	1	3

M = male   F = female

[1] Includes three applicants for admission under Act IX 2002

[2] Includes one applicant for admission under Act IX 2002

3.2 Statistics on Candidates in Training	2006 – 2007	2007 – 2008	2008 – 2009
Full-time Candidates studying theology at University (across all years of study):			
Glasgow	28	20	14
Edinburgh	23	28	32
Aberdeen	11	8	7
St Andrews	4	4	3
HTC, Dingwall	1	3	6
Number of Auxiliary Candidates in Training	14	20	21
Number of Readers in Training	77	47	39

3.2 Statistics on Candidates in Training	2006 – 2007				2007 – 2008				2008 – 2009			
Number of Readers set apart	n/a				14				17			
Candidates beginning their formation process												
Full-time	18				26				15			
Auxiliary	7				11				4			
Diaconate	0				0				2			
Courses being followed by new full-time Candidates												
Studying for undergraduate theology degree	15				17				10			
Studying for 2 years on a post-graduate programme	4				7				2			
Tailored academic requirements	0				2				1			
Number of Probationers completing training												
Full-time	23				29				30			
Auxiliary	5				4				1			
Diaconate	0				0				0			
Gender of Candidates in Training	M	F	Aux M	Aux F	M	F	Aux M	Aux F	M	F	Aux M	Aux F
First Year	16	5	2	5	20	6	5	6	7	10	2	2
Second Year	16	11	1	1	16	5	2	5	20	6	5	6
Third Year	10	7	1	2	9	7	1	1	10	5	1	4

3.2.1 Act Amending Act X 2004 Anent Selection and Training for the Full-Time Ministry and Eligibility for Ordination (as amended)

Edinburgh, XX May 2009, Sess. YY

The General Assembly hereby enact and ordain that Act X 2004 (as amended) shall be further amended as follows:

1. Paragraph 21(5)(c) shall be amended by the deletion of the words "in respect of any candidate" and the substitution of "in any academic year".

2. Sub-section 22(2) shall be amended by the deletion of the words "An Annual Review meeting shall be held after twelve months, at which…" and the substitution of the words "A Review shall be held in the 12th month. This notwithstanding, a Review with full powers may be held at any time at the discretion of the Candidate Task Group. The Review shall follow the procedure described in s.21; and in addition to the conclusion reached in terms of sub-section 21(5)…"

3. The last sentence of paragraph 23(c) shall be amended to read: "Any such claim or complaint shall be intimated by lodging with the Leader of the Candidate Task Group a written statement providing specific details thereof. The Leader of the Candidate Task Group shall intimate the statement to all parties to the document or covenant, and the statement shall be retained by the Ministries Council for a period of one year."

4. Sub-section 24(1) shall be amended by the deletion of the words "Concern Slip" and the substitution of the phrase "statement referred to in section 23".

3.9 Act Amending Act IX 2002 Anent Admission and Readmission of Ministers (as amended)
Edinburgh, XX May 2009, Sess. YY

The General Assembly hereby enact and ordain that Act IX 2002 as amended shall be further amended by the addition of a new sub-section 6(c) reading as follows:

In granting a Certificate of Eligibility to the minister of another denomination, the Committee shall be entitled to impose the condition that it may be used only for eligibility for appointments made in terms of s.19(4) of Act VIII 2003 (as amended).

	Task	Progress/Update	Additional Material	Del
4	**Support and Development Work**			
4.1	Provide conferences and other opportunities for continuing development in Ministries	The Council continues to provide in-service opportunities for those in the first five years of ministry. The value of these conferences belongs as much in the strong peer support groups that are forged as in the content of conferences themselves. There have also been conferences for Presbytery / Parish Workers, Readership In-Service events and a conference designed to engage those who still had at least 10 years of active service to complete. In addition there has been a series of one day workshops for those working through transition and change.		
4.2	Organise and deliver a Pre-Retirement Conference for those engaged in the ministries of the church	This continues to be one of the most widely appreciated events in the Council's calendar. The conference, to which spouses are also invited, allows those in ministry to prepare financially, emotionally and spiritually for the journey into a healthy and fulfilling retirement.		

		Task	Progress/Update	Additional Material	Del
4.3		Organise an Integrated Ministries conference in relation to the issues arising out of the report on Congregational Conflict	As a first step towards the organisation of a major ecumenical event in Nov 2009, a planning conference was held in January 2009. This pointed again to the importance of finding ways to enable the transformation of our congregations into communities committed to reconciliation and peacemaking.	*Further detail Section 4.3 below*	**12**
4.4		Administer and monitor the Study Leave Scheme for Ministers, Deacons and PPWs	Study Leave continues to benefit the continuing personal development of those involved in the ministries of the church. Over the past 5 years, including a period when no financial support was available, 1085 two week units of study leave have been taken. It is a continuing cause for concern that the level of financial support available through the Scheme has not increased since its inception in 1999. Had it followed the annual rate of inflation the allowance would now stand at £350. The Council is reviewing this situation and will address it as resources allow.		
4.5		Continue to oversee the regional delivery of Occupational Health provision	The adoption of regional Occupational Health providers has proved a valuable resource for all ministries requiring this service. A number of ministers have taken the opportunity to self-refer, but the majority of those who make use of this service are referred by the Pastoral Staff of the Council.		
4.6		Continue to oversee the provision of a regional Counselling Service	The recruitment of a counsellor in the Inverness area has strengthened the team of regional counsellors. There has been a growing use of the service and an indication from users of high standards in quality and integrity. The Annual Review and Briefing meeting took place in early Spring as part of ongoing monitoring of the effectiveness of the service.		

	Task	Progress/Update	Additional Material	Del
4.7	Publications: • Code of Professional Standards and Practice • Code of Conduct for Office Bearers; • Counselling Directory • Policy for Locum provision in cases of Pastoral need	The Code of Professional Standards and Practice has now been incorporated in the 2009 edition of the Ministries Handbook and is also available through the website. The Legal Questions Committee has taken the lead, along with the Mission and Discipleship Council, in bringing forward a Code of Conduct for Office Bearers. A new Counselling Directory, together with updated information on the Telephone Counselling service, has been produced and circulated to all those in the ministries of the Church. This gives details of a variety of support agencies available both within and outside of the Church. In response to needs expressed across many Presbyteries a policy is now in place for the provision of locum cover in situations of ministerial illness or graduated return to work.		
4.8	Continue to build Presbytery pastoral networks, provide network training days for those involved in pastoral care at local level and offer a model of good practice for use in Presbyteries that have no formal pastoral care scheme	This work is ongoing and the Council is pleased to report that the number of Presbyteries with formal arrangements in place has increased significantly over the last few years. At the time of writing the Pastoral and Spiritual Care Task Group is arranging a network training day. Arising out of this, the Council hopes to complete work on models of good practice which will be made available for consideration across presbyteries. One particular aspect of such models is the provision of Supportive Supervision for those involved in this type of work. It is the development of the role and place of such supervision which has delayed the Council in completing this work in time for this General Assembly.		

	Task	Progress/Update	Additional Material	Del
4.9	Organise and deliver opportunities for Elders to train as Interim Moderators	A one-day national training day open to all Presbyteries has been held. In one Presbytery a course was run over two evenings. The Council continues to seek the highest standards of practice in relation to the settlement of vacancies in the church and will be happy to provide further training at Presbytery level for all those who may be involved as Interim Moderators, members of Vacancy Advisory Committees or Nominating Committees.		**13**
4.10	Continue to develop and monitor interim ministry, both regional and itinerant	The Council is in the process of recruiting two new Interim Ministers to serve the growing needs of the church in this area of work. Some new patterns of Interim Ministry are emerging and Interim Ministers are beginning to be used in situations where early and short-term interventions can help ministers, congregations or office-bearers deal with local difficulties.		
4.11	**Chaplaincy Work** Continue to develop lines of communication between the Ministries Council and those working in chaplaincy and other ministries under other employment agencies.	The Council strives to cultivate and improve all lines of communication. In this regard the third in a series of Regional Network Days was held in Inverness in June 2008. It was attended by about forty chaplains, part time and full time, from across the various sectors. In November 2008, a joint conference was held with Further Education College Chaplains allowing a broader sharing of ideas and views. This is a good example of collaboration between councils within the Church Offices envisaged by the 2005 reorganisation. The second annual *retreat* for chaplains working in all sectors was held at The Bield in Perthshire in March 2009.		

	Task	Progress/Update	Additional Material	Del
4.11.1	*University Chaplaincy*	University Chaplaincy continues to be demanding as both students and staff find themselves striving to attain success in an ever more competitive environment. Chaplains form a vital part of the support services for both staff and students and this can be especially onerous when the pleas for help come from those "high achievers" who are not expected to fail. Since the 1990s the Church has hosted an annual conference for full-time chaplains in Scottish universities and the chaplains who attend value immensely this time spent in learning and recreation. Following the retirement in 2008 of the Rev Howard Taylor, Chaplain at Heriot-Watt University, the Council was pleased to learn of the appointment by the University of the Rev Dr Alistair Donald as his successor in February 2009.		
4.11.2	*Forces Chaplaincy*	This area of chaplaincy continues to be supported and administered by the Committee on Chaplains to Her Majesty's Forces which reports separately to the General Assembly. Through its close relationship with this Committee, the Ministries Council is acutely aware of the unique pressures under which many military chaplains currently serve "on operations." Recruitment has been difficult in recent years but the Council has been supportive of the Committee's position, which has maintained the principle that these exceptional circumstances required the continued appointment of only ministers of Word and Sacrament as chaplains in the armed forces.		

	Task	Progress/Update	Additional Material	Del
4.12	Devise liturgy for a Service of Introduction for Chaplains and adapt for various sectors in consultation with the Legal Questions Committee and the Worship & Doctrine Task Group	The Assembly of 2008 agreed to "affirm the importance of Services of Introduction for all full-time chaplains and instruct(ed) Presbyteries to ensure that all new full-time chaplains ordained in the Church of Scotland have Services of Introduction organised and conducted in partnership with the place where chaplaincy is undertaken." The Council indicated then that it would bring a more detailed report to the 2009 Assembly. Various factors have prevented this from happening. Amongst these, the need for conversations with other bodies, which have still to be completed, and the complex nature of the diversity of chaplaincies, which militates against a 'one size fits all' approach, have been contributory factors. The Council expects to report on this topic to the General Assembly of 2010.		
4.13	Review the structure of Work Place Chaplaincy (Scottish Churches Industrial Mission)	A number of factors have led the Council to seek a review of the structure and management of Workplace Chaplaincy in Scotland. The Council is working on this review in collaboration with the Scottish Churches Industrial Mission (SCIM) Council. It is hoped that a new shape may be given to the role of the National Organiser, leading to an expansion in the work in the future. The Council sees this as a high priority for the future.	*Further detail Section 4.13 below*	
4.14	Continue negotiations with Health Boards to ensure the best possible conditions of service for part-time Chaplains seeking transfer to Health Board employment	In its report to the 2008 Assembly the Task Group intimated its desire to progress the outstanding matter of the "transfer" of part-time and sessional chaplain appointments to direct employment by Health Boards. A preliminary meeting with Scottish Government representatives took place in December 2008. It has been decided that there should be no formal transfer of sessional Chaplains to Health Board employment, and the Task Group will now pursue this matter with the local Spiritual Care Committees of the various Health Board Trusts.		

	Task	Progress/Update	Additional Material	Del
4.14.1	*Guidance for Spiritual Care in the NHS*	During 2008 a Working Group was established by the Scottish Government to prepare revised guidance for Spiritual Care and Chaplaincy in NHS Scotland. The Council was represented on this group and participated fully in the formulation of the report and recommendations. The purpose of the revised guidance was to understand and recognise the developments that had occurred in the area of spiritual care and chaplaincy since the previous guidance issued in 2002. It also had to encompass the Equalities Act of 2006 which created a robust legal framework against discrimination. The report therefore reflects the greater variety of faith, culture and belief now found today in Scotland, whilst at the same time providing a setting in which Christian religious care and pastoral support can readily be provided.		
4.14.2	*Appointments*	In March 2009, Rev Chris Levison retired as Healthcare Chaplaincy Training Officer and Spiritual Care Co-ordinator. Since his appointment in 2001, Chris has achieved great success in the development of chaplaincy services in NHS Scotland. Training for chaplains has been established as a valuable addition to the skills in pastoral care which Church of Scotland ministers, deacons, readers and elders bring to chaplaincy. Additionally, spiritual care now has a much higher profile within the NHS and is respected as an integral part of the holistic care which the service strives to deliver. The Council offers its sincere thanks for the contribution which Chris has made to healthcare chaplaincy. Rev Dr Ewan Kelly was appointed as the new Training Officer and Coordinator. The Council offers him its support and best wishes as he takes up this ongoing challenge to take forward healthcare chaplaincy in the years ahead.		

	Task	Progress/Update	Additional Material	Del
4.15	Monitor the use and effectiveness of new legislation on harassment, discrimination, *etc*.	This remains a new area of work and it is not possible to offer anything more than anecdotal evidence as yet of the effectiveness of the legislation. The Council intends to keep this under review and report to a future General Assembly.		
4.16	Manse Adjudication: continue to deal with requests to live outside the manse, as required by special circumstances	While there have been several enquiries about the possibility of living in accommodation other than the manse, no formal requests have been before the Manse Adjudication Committee during the past year.		
4.17	Issue Manse Condition Schedules to vacant congregations and then to all congregations	The rolling programme to issue schedules to all congregations was completed in October 2008.		
4.18	Continue to provide advice to ministers and congregations on graduated return to work	A programme of graduated return has proved to be invaluable to those who have had long-term absence through illness. The Guidelines for Graduated Return to Work are included in the Ministers' Handbook on the Church of Scotland website.		
4.19	Review the implications of the research on Ministry to the Deaf Community in Scotland	The implications of this research have resulted in the recommendation that a Development Officer for Deaf Ministries should be appointed. The process for implementing this proposal is underway.	*Further detail Section 4.19 below*	

3

		Task	Progress/Update	Additional Material	Del
4.20		Administer, track and fund the provision of In-service support for Readers undertaking mandatory triennial in-service training	It has now been established that Readers' In-service training requirements should be met by the Ministries Council. In effect this means that once every three years the Council will either provide a place for Readers at one of its own approved courses or provide individual Readers with a grant of £150 towards the cost of in-service training sourced elsewhere. Readers who wish to access funds in order to pursue courses provided outwith the Ministries Council should apply to the Ministries Council *in advance* of undertaking the course for approval and the release of funds.		
4.21		Update the roll of Readers and consider their retirement age with a view to achieving consistency throughout the recognized ministries of the Church	At the time of writing a number of Presbytery returns were still awaited. However, to the best of its knowledge the Council believes there are around 290 active Readers serving the Church of Scotland. Of these, 29 are Attached Readers and 21 are serving as Locums in vacancies. Their ages range from 29 to 87 with the average age being 61. The annual cost to the Council to provide in-service training, so that Readers can attend training once every three years, will be in the order of £13,500. Given the important contribution that Readers are able to give to the Church, the Council does not believe that a retirement age should be imposed. If Readers remain on the active list and maintain their attendance at in-service events they will remain "certificated" in the same way that Ministers or Deacons can remain in forms of active service even after their due date of retirement.		14
4.22		Investigate models of team ministry appropriate for urban and rural ministry, recognising that differing models may be appropriate.	During the past year, with the human resources of the Council at full stretch, this piece of work has not yet been developed. However, the Support and Development Committee has recognized the importance of helping people to develop new models of team ministry and is actively pursuing ways in which Staff and Committee time can be devoted to this work in the coming year.		

	Task	Progress/Update	Additional Material	Del
4.23	Continue to widen the understanding of team ministry as *collaborative working* and support congregations in working more closely together.	A widening understanding of collaborative working is being developed and a proper process of application for funding for training and team support is now in place for those involved in Area Team Ministry and in Parish Groupings. Details of the application process are available from the Council. The Council's Conference and Development Task Group is happy to receive and consider requests for such training and support.		
4.24	Continue to introduce the process of Accompanied Review for all the recognized Ministries of the church	After a very successful Pilot Scheme it has taken longer than expected to generate further interest and uptake in the process of Accompanied Review. A major publicity drive is now underway and there are real signs of interest amongst many Presbyteries. The Council is happy to promote this important initiative around the Presbyteries and this year fully expects a significant uptake in the training opportunities to follow.		
4.25	Set up wider consultation on the ministry of healing	The Ministries Council is keen to establish a wider understanding and ownership of the ministry of healing within the church. It sees this work as closely related to its work on addressing the pain and hurt which has resulted from unhealthy levels of conflict within the lives of individuals, congregations and communities. A greater understanding of well-being and wholeness as well as a generous understanding of the healing power of Christ has been a theme of the Council's discussions on this matter. The Council is deeply grateful to the Rt Rev David Lunan, who in the midst of the busyness of the Moderatorial year has found time to help lead regional consultations on health and healing. At the time of writing two further consultations were still to take place, after which the Council will take stock and make proposals on how this work might be developed.		

4.3 Developments arising out of the Report on Congregational Conflict

4.3.0.1 Following on the Report on Congregational Conflict which was presented to last year's General Assembly the Ministries Council has actively been pursuing ways in which it might help those in ministries and those who are members of congregations to deal more creatively and positively with conflict. Early returns from Presbyteries indicate a high level of interest in this matter, with a number of Presbyteries arranging special conference sessions in order to examine in more detail how they might be more effective in helping congregations deal with conflict situations and even in helping themselves transact their own business in a spirit of consensus and cooperation.

4.3.0.2 As a result of this significant piece of work a major malaise has been uncovered, namely, that Christian communities often present themselves as places of dispute and anger rather than places of peacemaking and reconciliation. Last year the General Assembly noted that "the real victim of so much congregational conflict is the communication of the Gospel itself". In pursuit of a satisfactory way of addressing these issues the Assembly adopted a far reaching set of recommendations which was designed to bring about a sea-change in the way the church does its work locally, regionally and nationally. This amounts to nothing short of an attempt to bring about a change of culture in the church, which in turn would bring about a change in the behaviour of its members and those in its ministries.

4.3.0.3 There is continuing and growing concern about the language and metaphors of our theology and hymnology, discussions, debates, conversations and preaching. These are often borrowed from confrontational models of behaviour which reinforce our tendency towards dispute. Our impatience and intolerance of one another in the Christian family and our inability to live with difference is one thing, but our tendency to turn this into personal attack is a matter that has to be addressed at the deepest level of our spiritual life.

4.3.1 The Expanding Scale of the Task and the Vision of building "Peacemaking Communities"

4.3.1.1 What began as an exercise which sought to provide the church with the tools that would allow it to deal differently with its internal conflicts has begun to grow into a project that could affect the life and purpose of every congregation. It is still the intention of the Council to identify and train a pool of mediators who will become ever more active in working with individual congregations. It is still the intention of the Council to enable the church's candidates and those in ministries better to understand conflict and how to manage it. It is still also the intention of the Council to tackle the wide range of recommendations that were approved by the Assembly last year. However, a far wider vision has begun to emerge; that of helping every congregation become a place where women and men can address their own inner conflicts as well as those which affect their common life and the life of the communities in which they are set.

4.3.1.2 There is a growing belief that the time is right for the churches to take a lead in helping to consolidate the work of peacemaking and reconciliation which is developing within its own life and within the life of other significant elements of our Scottish public life. At the heart of the Christian gospel is the affirmation that, "God was in Christ restoring his relationship with humanity. He didn't hold people's faults against them, and he has given us this message of restored relationships to tell to others" (2 Cor 5:19). It follows therefore, that as part of its vocation the church, as a peacemaking community, has this great gift to give to the people of Scotland.

4.3.1.3 This truth was confirmed at a 48 hour conference event which the Council sponsored as part of its preparation for a major conference later this year which will promote a new approach to understanding and dealing with conflict in our church life. Representatives of Councils, together with representatives of ten different denominations and other interested organisations (including experienced representatives of the Presbyterian Church in Ireland and the Church of England), shared their commitment to a major initiative which would motivate women and men throughout the churches to become involved in the work of peacemaking and reconciliation. The Council has been assured of the support of some of the leading figures in Scottish mediation services, as well as that of the Violence Reduction Unit of Strathclyde Police. The synergy that has emerged has convinced the Council that it should embrace with enthusiasm this unprecedented opportunity to address the deep rooted failings that were identified in last year's report.

4.3.1.4 It is with a great deal of optimism that the Council looks forward to launching this initiative at a conference to be held at the MacDonald Highland Resort from November 15th – 18th 2009. Entitled, "The Church and Conflict", this conference will examine the origins of conflict with a particular emphasis on the peculiar ways in which the Christian Church and the Scottish context have contributed to the creation of a culture of conflict. It will help us to understand how to engage in difficult conversations and it will lead us, with the help of renowned keynote contributors, to strive for the healing of relationships and sustainable means of peacemaking. A variety of workshops will allow people of all levels of understanding and commitment to participate in this major event and it is hoped that upwards of 400 people will attend. The Council is committed to this project as one of its major priorities and seeks the enthusiastic support and response of the whole church.

4.3.1.5 It is evident that the workload involved for Council staff in relation to this important and expanding area will be considerable. To this end, the Council is committed to providing the human resources necessary for undertaking the task effectively, including the likelihood of drawing upon reserve funds to do so.

4.13 Review and Development of Workplace Chaplaincy

4.13.1 The past twelve months have been a particularly challenging period for the small team of employed chaplains and volunteers serving in Scotland's workplaces. Amidst these tribulations the requests for chaplaincy are ongoing and the chaplaincy team was able to provide a new service to one of Scotland's major companies. A planned venture with a local parish church in Edinburgh will also bring an exciting dimension to the work. The onset of very difficult economic conditions has brought increased demand from many workers seeking solace and support in an extremely harsh environment. Without wishing to diminish the important contributions of all those involved in many industries, it is in the retail sector that some of the greatest pain has been felt. The disappearance of several well known household names has been well documented in the media. The pressure, however, has been on shop managers and their staff for a considerable time to maintain sales levels and this has created much stress for this often poorly paid workforce, who have little security of employment. Chaplains working in shopping centres along with their colleagues in the other sectors of the economy offer an independent and confidential listening ear which more and more seek out for the support they crave.

4.13.2 The Ministries Council is acutely aware that these chaplains are touching many people in our society that are unlikely ever to enter the doors of our churches. It is unfortunate that at such a time the team of regional Chaplains has not been at full strength. However, the Ministries Council is fully committed to the expansion of this ministry and in order to ensure its future development the Council has initiated a review of the strategy, structure and staffing needs of this vital work. During this coming year, the Council will seek, together with ecumenical partners, first to consolidate and then to develop a structure for this ministry which can build on the foundations of past service and reach out anew to those in need in Scotland's workplaces. Good progress is now being made in relation to the possible future shape of the management and development of this work.

4.13.3 The Council is pleased to report the appointment of Rev Allan Webster as regional chaplain in Dundee and the team has been further strengthened by the appointment of the Very Rev Dr Alexander McDonald, who is covering as a Locum in the regional chaplaincy post in Glasgow. It is now a matter of priority to complete the strategic planning work in collaboration with the SCIM Council and the Industrial Mission Trust and move as quickly as possible to make permanent appointments that will consolidate this important work.

4.19 Ministries to the Deaf

4.19.1 The Ministries Council has continued its consideration of strategies for the development of ministries among hard of hearing and Deaf people. To progress this research the Council engaged the services of Mrs Mary McDevitt. As an experienced sign language interpreter and a committed Christian, Mary was ideally placed to establish on the one hand the needs of the Deaf Community and on the other hand the issues which the church has to address in order to meet those needs. The research was conducted by consulting: deaf people, members of the Deaf Community, ministers working in Deaf Ministry as well as ministers who periodically work in Deaf Ministry and a sample of other Church of Scotland ministers. The aim of the research was to identify the issues and challenges for those with hearing loss and to explore the available options for the future shape of a realistic and deliverable ministry.

4.19.2 For the purposes of this study and consultation, people with hearing loss were divided into two categories: Group A – deaf people who are hard of hearing or deafened; Group B – members of the Deaf Community. Those in the former group are undoubtedly in the majority. Most will have become deaf after having acquired speech and English is most likely to be their first or preferred language. Within this group the largest proportion will have lost their hearing

through age related deafness and this group is prevalent within our congregations today. Group B are members of the Deaf Community and are referred to as 'Deaf' with a capital "D" rather than 'deaf'. Members of this group use British Sign Language as their first or preferred language. People belonging to this community are proud of their identity, language and culture. In this culture there are: Deaf Arts, Deaf Theatre, Deaf Poetry, Deaf History, Deaf Sports, Deaf Olympics and Deaf Humour. These and other components contribute to what is often referred to as the 'Deaf World'. There may be a small number of people who can intermingle in both groups, but in the main these two groups remain distinct from each other. The most obvious difference between each group is language and communication methods; their access requirements are completely different.

4.19.3 Not surprisingly the research indicated that both deaf people and members of the Deaf Community could be better served by the Church of Scotland. Among the findings from those of both groups were the following:
- *Loop systems were not always available or switched on or in working order*
- *Ministers walk away or turn away from the microphone whilst still talking (this makes lip-reading very difficult)*
- *The church environment is generally too noisy making it difficult to carry on individual conversations*
- *There are poor speakers who do not know how to make proper use of the microphone (bend head, turn away etc)*
- *Hearing aids have improved hearing but a great deal depends on who is speaking*
- *Many people have simply stopped going to church because their level of participation is so hampered*
- *No effort is made to provide printed orders of service or printed copies of the sermon*
- *The loop system is good but not always in a good position to work alongside lip-reading*
- *Lighting is sometimes not good enough to enable lip-reading*
- *The use of overhead or data projection would increase levels of participation*

- *So few people are able to conduct worship in BSL*
- *There is a lamentable level of awareness of the needs of the deaf and the Deaf*
- *Hearing people do not understand the limitations of hearing aids*

4.19.3 In response to the research questions, ministers reflected a general lack of understanding of deaf and Deaf issues. For instance, statistics show that 41.7% of over 50-year-olds and 71.1% of over 70-year-olds have some degree of significant hearing loss. If we compare these figures with the approximate figures supplied by ministers in relation to their understanding of hearing loss within their own congregations, we immediately see that the ministers have massively underestimated the scale of the situation. Notwithstanding this misjudgement, the majority of ministers were keen to learn more and if offered the opportunity to participate in deaf awareness training would willingly take part. The Council is convinced that a programme of such training is required for all those whose work brings them into contact with women and men who suffer from hearing loss.

4.19.4 Of much greater concern, however, is the fact that within the next 10 years, without a period of significant planning, recruitment and training, the Church of Scotland will have no minister in active full-time service who is fluent in BSL. This is a matter which has to be addressed through a programme of raising awareness of deaf and Deaf issues at all stages of ministries training. Currently there is a handful of ministers who have at least a modest level of BSL skills, but to take this to a level of competence that would permit an all round ministry amongst the Deaf would take a period of intensive training and immersion in Deaf life and culture. The Council recognises that it is now necessary actively to encourage enquirers and candidates to consider the possibility of Deaf ministry as a particular vocation.

4.19.5 Furthermore, members of the Deaf churches have expressed concern at the lack of real mission and outreach amongst the younger generations of Deaf people in Scotland. This issue needs to be addressed through some special programme ministry which has hitherto never been tackled in Scotland. Taking all these matters together the Council has proposed the appointment of a person with the specialist role of meeting some of the needs expressed in this report. Such a person would be responsible for delivering Deaf Awareness training throughout the Presbyteries, encouraging women and men to consider Deaf ministry as a specialised vocation and would begin to develop a structure that would allow for both outreach amongst the Deaf and integration (where possible) of Deaf people into the hearing church community. The Council hopes to make such an appointment in the near future.

	Task	Progress / Update	Additional Material	Del
5	**PLANNING & DEPLOYMENT WORK**			
5.1	Affirm the concept of a 'mixed economy church' within the Church of Scotland, where both existing expressions and fresh expressions of church co-exist, not at the expense of each other, but for the benefit of the whole.	Work has continued on this deliverance from last year's Assembly. The Council is pleased to note the indications of a growing interest around the country in the need to explore increasingly diverse patterns of church life, ministerial responsibility, and engagement with the variety of cultural expression in Scottish society.	*See Emerging Church Joint Report (pp. 3.1/1 - 3.1/9)*	
5.2	Land Acquisition	The Ministries Council is engaged in a very lengthy and frustrating process of engagement with one local authority. This has highlighted difficulties that are becoming more apparent in the willingness or ability of Local Authorities and developers to assign sites for Church buildings. A major conference was called by ACTS in 2008 to discuss these issues, and further developments are anticipated. Early planning is necessary, and the Church is exploring opportunities and possibilities for strategic land acquisition. A site has been identified for a new church building for Dunfermline East and the Ministries Council is in ongoing discussion with Hamilton Presbytery over the potential for obtaining a site within the proposed development of the Ravenscraig site in Motherwell.		

5.3	Produce a vacancy procedure manual of the entire vacancy process, together with an information leaflet for congregations which outlines what should be expected during a period of vacancy.	Work is ongoing on the production of both a comprehensive manual and an information leaflet in relation to vacancy procedures.		
5.4	Produce a pro-forma for the compilation of a Parish Profile and make it available on the Council's webpage for use by congregations.	Work is also ongoing on the production of a suitable resource to enable the production of Parish Profile and thereby ensuring some consistency in standards of presentation.		
5.5	Make the list of charges seeking a minister more readily accessible to prospective applicants.	The vacant charges list is available on the Council's web pages for download. In addition, a list of new vacancies is published each month and distributed in the Ministers' mailing.		
5.6	**PRESBYTERY PLANNING TASK GROUP** Continue to process annual reviews of plans from all Presbyteries and respond to requests for modification of plans between annual reviews.	At the time of writing 20 Presbyteries are fully up to date with their plans. Of the remainder 19 have not submitted an annual update of their plan within the previous twelve months and 21 presbyteries have not yet completed their categorization of buildings,		**15** **16**
5.7	Ensure that the new system of Presbytery monthly returns is fully operational	The Council is grateful to Presbyteries who are making regular monthly returns, greatly facilitating the handling of relevant information and statistics.		

3

5.8	Five-year reviews of plans	The time approaches for the five year review of plans. The Council looks forward to engaging with Presbyteries in fuller discussion of the nature of the planning process at the half-way point of the first ten-year planning period, as required by Act VII 2003.		
5.9	Statistics for 2008	The tables listing adjustments completed over the past year can be found on the Church's website pages at: www.churchofscotland.org.uk/generalassembly/gareports.htm.#ministries	*Tables listing adjustments can be viewed on the Church of Scotland website*	
5.10	In cooperation with the Mission and Discipleship Council prepare for the 2011 Census and the next Scottish Churches Survey.	A joint Statistics for Mission group has been set up with the Mission and Discipleship Council to take on this task. Geographical Information Software (GIS) will be used to process the information that will be made available to Parishes and Presbyteries.		
5.11	**EMERGING MINISTRIES TASK GROUP** Support and develop NCD as delineated by Act XIII 2000	The Council currently supports 11 New Charge Developments (NCDs) at:- Edinburgh: Gilmerton, Perth: Riverside, Paisley: St Ninian's Ferguslie, Dundee: Whitfield, Greenock: East End, Aberdeen: Cove, Glasgow: Robroyston, East Kilbride: Stewartfield, Glasgow: Whiteinch, Aberdeen: New Stockethill, Dunfermline: St Paul's East. Legislative reviews took place during the year at: Greenock: East End, Perth: Riverside, Glasgow: Whiteinch, Aberdeen: New Stockethill, Dunfermline: St Paul's East. The Council is also establishing two further NCDs at Wallacewell in Glasgow and in Inverness, where St Columba High is being transported from the City Centre to a new location in the rapidly expanding belt of housing to the south of the city. A working group is reviewing Act XIII 2000 anent NCDs with a view to bringing proposals for its amendment to the 2010 General Assembly		

5.12	Ensure that the Emerging Ministries Fund operates efficiently and effectively	The new Emerging Ministries fund has been successfully launched and the first allocation of £100,000 for 2008 was disbursed. Five projects received funding and a number of applications were turned down or deferred for further consideration. The Task Group is pressing ahead with allocating a further sum of £300,000 for 2009. The Council intends to research the projects as they progress.	*Further details are outlined below of some of the projects supported (5.12)*	**17**
5.13	Evolve a strategy for the development of emerging ministries in cooperation with the Mission and Discipleship Council.	Rev David Currie continues in the role of Development Officer (New and Emerging Ministries), jointly employed by the Ministries Council and the Mission and Discipleship Council. A group from the two Councils oversees his work and a second group – the Emerging Church Joint Working party – develops the wider theological and ecclesiological implications of the emerging church movement around the world and its applicability to Scotland.	*See Emerging Church Joint Working Party Report (pp. 3.1/1 - 3.1/9)*	
5.14	Encourage continuing thinking and debate about emerging church; ensure an ecumenical dimension to this.	A day conference was held in November 2008 which was considerably oversubscribed with over 100 delegates squeezing into The Hub in Gilmerton. Delegates attended from all over mainland Scotland, and also from a number of other denominations. Indications are that this agenda is becoming increasingly important for the Church in Scotland. An important aspect of the Joint Working Party's activity during the year was a delegation sent to consult with the Fresh Expressions initiative of the Church of England/ Methodist Church. Links with this network continue.	*Invitation to Emerging Church event, evening of Mon 25 May in Assembly Hall. Bishop Graham Cray (of Fresh Expressions network) is the main speaker*	
5.15	**EMPLOYMENT ISSUES TASK GROUP** Continue to see people employed around the country as posts identified in Presbytery plans become available for appointment.	The interest expressed in Team Ministry by Presbyteries in the first round of Presbytery Planning has been supported by the Council, with the number of PPWs continuing to grow. At the time of writing there are 109 such staff employed, with plans indicating a further 23 appointments in the process of being made.		

5.16	Continue to evaluate the Council's existing employment policies and update these as necessary.	Considerable work has been done to ensure that procedures are compliant with employment legislation and represent best HR practice. Issues that have been addressed during the year include :- • Line Management Training Review • Increased number of New Team Training events • Appraisal Training • Expenses Policy for PPWs • Home Working uptake • Car Lump Sum Payments Review • Redundancy Policy • Study Leave authorisation arrangements for PPWs • Salary Sacrifice • Advertising of posts on an open basis • Employees' Handbook – updated version on-line • Capability Policy • Support for Congregations with Financial Difficulties	*See below 5.17* *See below 5.19*	
5.17	Travel Costs for Parish Ministers and PPWs	The Council regularly receives enquiries about the level of reimbursement for mileage covered in the course of work. In attempting to address this matter, the Council is conscious of the need for a coherent approach across the Church. Mindful of work being undertaken by the Church & Society Council on environmental responsibility, consultations have taken place on the best strategy for addressing travel costs in the future. The Council now brings forward a proposal that a template be prepared for use by all Parish Ministers and employees in creating a 'Green Travel Plan', which would take account of their local context. This plan would assess the realistic possibility of using public transport, the necessity for car travel (particularly where public transport is poor or sporadic), the costs of fuel, the type of vehicle used, the affordability of travel (in relation to Parish income), and such other variables as may be necessary to determine travel requirements. In addition, the Councils will together set		18

		up a Reference Group made up of people from different contexts in Scotland to contribute to the development of the template for the 'Green Travel Plan'. In the light of this approach, the Council proposes no change in the current mileage rates, which are in any case dependent on rates set by HM Revenue & Customs. Two changes have been made, however, in the lump sum payments for PPWs, where a differential existed between Parish Ministers (£960 per annum) and some PPWs (£720): (1) the lump sum is increased to £960 for all PPWs using a car; (2) the qualifying level of 2,000 miles has been removed to bring this in line with Parish Ministers. These changes have been backdated to 1 June 2008 in line with a commitment given at the General Assembly 2008.		
5.18	Continue to evaluate training needs for PPWs.	Two main strands of training have been addressed during the year. A system of Employee Appraisal is now in place and training has been given to almost all Line Managers and Employees. This will be ongoing as new appointments are made. The Council's policy is that no appraisal of an employee will take place unless that employee's line manager has been trained. The Council's internal budget for training has been substantially increased in 2009 with the aim of continuing to work towards better and more effective team ministry for the Church in the future.		**19**
5.19	Congregations with financial difficulties	During the year difficulties have arisen when some congregations or groupings who have been assigned PPWs under their Presbytery's plan have been unable to provide the backup support necessary to comply with legislation, for example in the provision of adequate office furniture. In response the Council has agreed to meet the costs in 2009. From 2010 onwards it will be the responsibility of Presbyteries to ensure these costs are met.		**20**

5.20	Summer Student Programme	During 2008 the Summer Student Programme supported 8 Candidates for the Ministry in placements lasting between 4 and 9 weeks, mostly in the West Coast mainland and Island Presbyteries. In 2009 the scheme is being modified to incorporate a new Priority Areas Summer Work Experience programme, and an increased number of places – 16 – will be made available. The new programme will incorporate opportunities for theological reflection.	*See also Vocation & Training Report (3.4)*	
5.21	Bring to completion work done on the supply of ministers and PPWs over the next ten years, and integrate this into the Council budget	The Presbytery planning process in its first round did not envisage a reduction in the number of serving ministers – rather a reduction in the number of vacancies and a redistribution of ministry more fairly around the country. Detailed work is underway to assess more carefully the demographics and financial implications, and while the Council does not intend in 2009 – 2010 to reduce the number of ministries that it is able to support, it seeks the sympathy, prayers, and concern of the Church as it further considers these issues.		
5.22	Number of Ministries 2009 – 2010	The number of posts currently indicated as eligible for funding on Presbytery Plans is 1,230. The Council intends to continue underwriting funding for this number over the coming year while further research into future numbers in relation to affordability is undertaken.		

5.12 Emerging Ministries Fund Report
5.12.1 Tulloch Net

Based in the Tulloch area of the parish of Perth: North, Tulloch Net is an ecumenical fresh expression of church involving the Church of Scotland, the Baptist Union of Scotland, the Scottish Episcopal Church, Tulloch Knox Free Church and Tulloch World Wide Church of God. It was initially established (summer, 2007) as a research project to explore new ways of being church to the community of Tulloch.

Over the period 2007/2008 a mission audit was carried out, and positive relationships were developed with local Christians, community groups, the primary school, Perth and Kinross Council, and the police. Tulloch Net has identified two key areas for its work:

- Providing spiritual and social support and advice to those in the local community.
- Providing positive learning opportunities for residents who request support in relational issues, specifically between adults and children.

Part of the vision of the project is to plant a 'Fresh Expression' of Church for the Tulloch area, as engagement with the community deepens through addressing these themes.

5.12.2 Sanctuary First

Based within Sanctus Media at St. Andrew's Parish Church, Bo'ness, Sanctuary First will be an interactive multimedia worship community, centred around the internet while encouraging community members to engage in local social interaction through monthly worship events in various venues. It aims to create alternative opportunities for service and discipleship around food, fellowship and meaningful acts of service.

Sanctuary First writes: "We will be setting up one of the first online worshipping communities of its kind in Scotland. We recognise that we will become for some people their church family and community. Sanctuary First for many will become the ultimate Church Without Walls, allowing those who, for whatever reason, would be unable to attend a traditional service due to shift patterns or infirmity. We aim to capture a wider community who don't attend traditional worship services, but who are looking for a faith community that will engage them in creative worship and lead them into deeper discipleship."

5.12.3 New Housing in Whitburn

A Community Profile gave an accurate picture of the needs of the community and its demographics. The local parish church, Brucefield Parish Church, West Lothian Presbytery, describes its desire to build "a church for disconnected people. We recognise it is time to begin a new work alongside the existing congregation. Whitburn, and our parish in particular, has grown rapidly in a short time and we have no connection with the new population. Planting a new kind of church alongside the existing is our ecclesial aim. Planting a youth congregation or a presence in East Whitburn or Redmill are possibilities. We seek to reconnect with young couples and the under 50's. The initiative will explore the range of possibilities that are before us in an attempt to re-engage with our community in ways that are culturally relevant to demographic groups that are not around 'church as we are' and who are unlikely to be around our congregation."

5.12.4 The Ark

Following a successful Holiday Club for children in September 2007, Newmains: Coltness Memorial and Bonkle Parish Church (Hamilton Presbytery) launched The ARK (Actively Reaching Kids). "Our aim in the last year has been to establish a core worshipping community on a Tuesday night. Currently we have between 40 and 50 young people from age 5 – 14 as well as 15 adult leaders worshipping together regularly. This is much more than simply another children's club. The thing that sets it apart is its intentionality. Right from the beginning it has been the intention to build an ecclesial community which would see the children being the catalysts for change in their community. During the last few months an Alpha Course for adults has been running at the same time as the ARK on a Tuesday so that parents could attend. Plans are underway to establish a regular gathering for parents on a Tuesday night. This is an exciting development for us as we are now seeing adults gather round the 'edges' of ARK. In many ways we are doing things back to front as compared with traditional church where children's work is provided if the children come with adults. We are having to look at providing adult work for the adults who are coming with their children! We have a team of around 15 volunteer leaders, amongst them several elders from both churches, who head up this project. We are also well supported by in excess of 20 'Prayer Buddies' from the two Sunday congregations who pray regularly for the work of the ARK. We are constantly evaluating and restructuring in order to continue to meet the needs of the emerging faith community which God is building here in Newmains."

5.12.5 Glasgow Harbour Initiative

The project leaders describe the initiative in this way:
"The Glasgow Harbour Initiative is a project aimed at connecting with the people who live in the Glasgow Harbour area. At present the area has no visible Christian community and therefore this project is attempting to meet those who live there so that a worshipping community might eventually be born that is relevant

to them. Several groups could benefit from this initial project. Firstly the churches involved in the Parish Grouping will benefit from the insights gained as to how to move forward in encouraging a new expression of faith in the area. Secondly, the Church of Scotland will hopefully benefit from this project as it seeks to discover more about the emerging kingdom communities that are bubbling up in Scotland. Through the initial phase, we hope to learn about the people who live in Glasgow Harbour, but also about the complexities, joys and excitement of being part of an emerging ministry."

	Task	Progress / Update	Additional Material	Del
6	**FINANCE**			
6.1	Stipends and Salaries	The Council considered carefully what an appropriate approach should be to annual increments in stipends and salaries, given the current economic situation. In the past, the April RPI (RPIx for stipends) figure has been used to calculate increments. By the time of setting the stipends (October 2008), the figure of 4% from April appeared out of proportion given a rapidly falling inflation rate and the forecast of zero inflation in 2009. The Council agreed to fix the increase at a standard £900 for all stipends and salaries, which represents an overall cost under 4%. This allowed for those at the lower end of the scale to have a higher percentage increase than those at the top of the scales. In the current climate, the Council believes this to be an equitable way to proceed.	*Table of scales and allowances (6.1)*	
6.2	Affordability of Ministries	The Council currently finances a substantial amount of expenditure from reserve funds. This is partly due to the Council of Assembly's policy of enabling congregations to retain a greater share of their income for use locally, which inevitably means that less money is available to the Councils of the Church. More recently, the dramatically reducing level of the Council's reserves because of the current economic climate has meant less income from investment. Clearly the policy of funding expenditure from reserves cannot continue indefinitely and some difficult decisions will need to be made.		21

		Another factor in this, however, has been the outworking of the Stipend Scheme, approved by the General Assembly in 2003. This was designed at a time when it was envisaged that the numbers of those available for ministries would be falling considerably. This has not proved to be the case, with recruitment remaining relatively high and more people remaining in ministry beyond the age of 65. The base working number for calculation of the scheme in 2003 was a notional figure of 800 ministers by about 2007. This means that the scheme is now struggling to support the 964 ministers in parishes at the time of writing this report. Given that it costs approximately £1M for every 30 ministers, the Council faces an annual overspend of around £5.5M against the operating model assumed in the setting up of the Stipend Scheme in 2003.		
		An economic model constructed to take account of a variety of possible scenarios suggests that, should the Council continue on its present path, reserves would be exhausted by 2018. The two most obvious solutions would be either for the Church to reduce stipends and salary payments or for it to reduce proportionately the number of Parish Ministers and PPWs. Neither of these options is easy to contemplate, but the Council intends to review the situation carefully over the coming year and report further to the General Assembly in 2010.		
6.3	Reserve Funds	The Council's reserve funds have been adversely affected by the current economic climate. Funds held at the start of 2008 were valued at £74.5m. At December the value had fallen to £59m.		

6.1 Allowances and Expenses Rates for 2009

Stipend Scale 2009

Year 1	£23,139	Year 6	£27,187
Year 2	£23,948	Year 7	£27,997
Year 3	£24,758	Year 8	£28,807
Year 4	£25.567	Year 9	£29,617
Year 5	£26,377	Year 10	£30,426

PPW Scale 2009

Year 1	£22,220	Year 6	£24,657
Year 2	£22,707	Year 7	£25,143
Year 3	£23,195	Year 8	£25,631
Year 4	£23,682	Year 9	£26,119
Year 5	£24,170	Year 10	£26,605

Island Allowance

The inner and outer island allowances are held at 2008 levels:

Outer Island Allowance   £1,566
Inner Island Allowance   £616

Travel Expenses 2009

Rates are held at 2008 levels for those providing their own car, with the exception of adjustments to PPW rates reported in Section 5.17:

a) **reimbursed to ministers and PPWs providing their own car for pastoral duties**
40p per mile for the first 10,000 miles
25p per mile for all additional mileage

Ministers and PPWs also receive capital reimbursement of £80 per month

b) **reimbursement of travel expenses for students, probationers, auxiliary ministers and locums:**
40p per mile for the first 10,000 miles
25p per mile for all additional mileage

c) **reimbursement to ministers and PPWs providing their own motor bike for pastoral duties**
24p per mile travelled per annum

d) **reimbursement to ministers and PPWs providing their own pedal bike for pastoral duties**
20p per mile travelled per annum

Recommended Pulpit Supply Fee and Expenses

The Council agreed the continuance of 2008 rates from 1 April 2009

One diet of worship on a Sunday at £50 and for any additional diets of worship on a Sunday £10. Travel expenses at 25p per mile.

Disturbance Allowance 2009

The Council agreed that the level of disturbance allowance should be held at the 2008 level of £1,740.

Removal and Disturbance Allowance

The Council agreed that the removal and disturbance costs of all charges which have an average income base below £30,000 will be met from Council finances, and assistance given depending on assessment to charges which have an income base between £30,000 and £60,000, by way of a loan in the first instance. A grant may be available to such charges on application to the Finance Committee of the Ministries Council.

Vacancy Allowance 2009

The Council agreed the continuance of the 2008 rates. The vacancy allowance should be £580 per month during the vacancy, £630 for linked charges. Vacancy Allowance is deducted directly from each charge's Ministries and Mission Allocation.

Rev Barry Dunsmore

Rev Barry Dunsmore accepted a call to the charge of Christ Church, Warwick, Bermuda at the beginning of 2009. He had served as a Vice-Convener of the Council since the General Assembly 2007 and offered good leadership in relation to the Support & Development remit of the Council. Although his period of service on this occasion was relatively short, Barry brought to the work of the Council a wealth of experience from his previous involvement with the work, including membership of the Pastoral & Spiritual Care Task Group. The Council is grateful for his contribution over the past year and wishes him well in his new charge.

In the name of the Ministries Council:

GRAHAM FINCH *Convener*
NEIL DOUGALL *Vice-Convener*
LEZLEY KENNEDY *Vice-Convener*
MURIEL PEARSON *Vice-Convener*
J H A DICK *Acting Vice-Convener*
MARTIN SCOTT *Secretary*

JOINT REPORT OF THE MINISTRIES AND MISSION AND DISCIPLESHIP COUNCILS ON THE EMERGING CHURCH

Deliverance

1. Receive the report.
2. Welcome the many initiatives within the Church of Scotland that are part of the emerging church conversation.
3. Instruct the Joint Working Party to prepare study materials for use by Councils, Presbyteries and Kirk Sessions, to encourage reflection on how the emerging church conversation might enable them to develop new ways of engaging in God's mission in Scotland and beyond.
4. Instruct both Councils to continue to offer support, encouragement and critique to those involved in the emerging church conversation.
5. Instruct both Councils to continue reflecting theologically on issues raised by the emerging church conversation and to report further to the General Assembly 2010.
6. Instruct both Councils to identify the theological, practical and legal issues raised for a Presbyterian polity by the emerging church conversation and report to a future General Assembly.

REPORT

1. Introduction

This joint report seeks to offer a brief insight into the work that the Ministries and Mission and Discipleship Councils have been undertaking together in relation to the emerging church movement. The first section plots the outline story to this point, noting some of the resources and networks that are developing. The main section is an initial report from the Joint Working Party, established by the two Councils to engage on a regular basis with the theological issues arising out of emerging church.

A complete version of the paper that lies behind this joint report is available to download on the Church of Scotland website (www.churchofscotland.org.uk/generalassembly/gareports.htm.#ministries)

2. Roots and Shoots

In one sense emerging church is not new. Groups that might be described as emerging church arise wherever people take seriously gospel, tradition and culture.[1] Ministers and congregations have done this in every generation. Innovative patterns of church life have emerged in every decade. Some have flowered briefly, while others have been absorbed into the mainstream of the Church becoming part of the rich mix that engages people and nourishes faith.

In the Church of Scotland, a forerunner of emerging church is New Charge Development (NCD), which grew out of post-war Church Extension. During the last decade NCD's main focus has been planting congregations. Some of these have grown and become clearly rooted within the Church of Scotland, yet they retain a distinctive flavour and character reflecting the culture in which they have grown.

---

[1] John Drane, 'What does maturity in the emerging Church look like?' in *Mission Shaped Questions*, Stephen Croft (ed), London, Church House Publishing, 2008, p 90.

In another sense emerging church is new. The emerging church phenomenon that is expressed in different ways across the developed world, is a response to societal change and growing cultural dislocation. Increasing numbers of people find that in order to hold faithfully to gospel, tradition and culture, a way of being the church is needed that is significantly different from what has gone before.

In the Church of Scotland the pivotal role of the 2001 *Church Without Walls* report cannot be underestimated. This report began by affirming that the shape of the local church needs to be determined by four factors: the gospel; the locality; friendship; and the gifts of God's people. These four factors have helped thousands to see the Church not simply as an institution but as an organism. This report gave the Church permission and encouragement to think in different ways. *Church Without Walls* created a space within the Church of Scotland for emerging church through its insistence on taking gospel, tradition and culture seriously.

Church Without Walls has inspired many initiatives. Of particular importance for emerging church is the Parish Development Fund (PDF). Grants from this fund have enabled congregations across Scotland to try out new ways of engaging with local communities. Seven years on, some of the groups that began through PDF funding have developed significantly. Some that began as an initiative of the local church are now wondering if they might in fact *be* church? This prompts discussion about what the essential features of a church are. The Ministries Council report to the General Assembly in 2008 – *Building for the Future – From the Grassroots* – discussed a phrase from the Nicene Creed: '**One Holy**, **Catholic** and **Apostolic** Church'. It suggested that these four words are marks of the church and provide a framework for assessing which groups can actually be termed 'church'. The discussion is ongoing, but the positive impact of *Church Without Walls* on emerging church in Scotland is beyond doubt.

Since 2005, successive reports to the General Assembly have sought to describe, interpret and critique the stream of church life commonly called emerging church. A focus for the two Councils' engagement with emerging church is the work of the Rev David E. P. Currie *(New and Emerging Ministries Development Officer)*. Working across both Councils, he plays a coordinating role as Committees and Task Groups engage with the different aspects of the emerging church agenda. Four themes summarise the nature of this engagement: communication; reflection; networking and support; and training.

2.1 Communication: A primary goal in the first year has been to develop a better understanding of emerging church across the Church. This has involved:

- *The internet*. With the internet playing such a significant role within the emerging church conversation, finding a way of creating an effective interactive web presence within the Church of Scotland website is crucial. While progress has been made, considerable work remains. Conversations with the Web Development Team about new possibilities are ongoing.
- *Sharing in National, Regional and Local initiatives*. At a national level the Development Officer has been working with the Church Without Walls ReEnergise team, Hope Alba, Firestarters, Scripture Union, Youth for Christ and other agencies and denominations to look at ways of working together to develop new models of church.
- *Contact with Presbyteries*. The Development Officer has spoken at various Presbyteries on emerging church and the possibilities it brings, particularly for the planning process. Working with local leadership thinking anew about church planting or exploring emerging church, his role has been both to encourage and to challenge.

2.2 Reflection: Critique based on reflection has been a key focus for the Joint Working Party, and the Planning & Deployment Committee of the Ministries Council has begun reflecting on some of the issues around governance and the emerging church.

The emerging church is both an ecumenical and international phenomenon, so there is a great deal to be learnt from others. Representatives of both Councils visited London at the beginning of September 2008 to hear the story of *Fresh Expressions,* an initiative of the Church of England and the Methodist Church. They reflected on lessons that might be relevant to the Church of Scotland's engagement at this moment. The group met with a variety of strategists and practitioners at all levels, including a full day meeting at Lambeth Palace with key leaders of *Fresh Expressions* from both partner churches.

The Councils are delighted that Bishop Graham Cray, Chairman of the Working Party that produced the *Mission-Shaped Church* report in 2004 and from 1 May 2009 the Archbishops' Missioner and Team Leader of *Fresh Expressions*, has agreed to speak at a special evening session of the General Assembly on Monday 25 May. All commissioners are invited to take the opportunity of participating in a conversation that evening.

2.3 Networking and Support: The Councils are endeavouring to offer support to those involved in, and interested in, emerging church initiatives. An emerging church 'practitioners conference' was scheduled for early May 2009 and a Learning Network is being developed to enable conversations to continue with those who are most involved.

Funding has been made available through the Emerging Ministries Fund. Despite only becoming operational in September 2008, there has already been considerable interest, with applications for funding exceeding the amount available for distribution. Details of some of the projects that have received grants can be found in the Ministries Council report *(Section 5.12)*.

In November 2008, a day conference was held in Edinburgh with the intention of facilitating a conversation between the centre and the fringe, that is, between emerging church practitioners and those who shape policy within the Church. The event was oversubscribed. 110 attended, from Carlisle to Caithness. Some delegates were already involved in initiatives; others were looking to start them. The majority were from the Church of Scotland, but ecumenical partners were also represented. Rev Dr Doug Gay (lecturer in Practical Theology in Glasgow University and a member of the Joint Working Party) offered theological reflection. Representatives from four different initiatives described the work they were involved in. Hopes and fears were aired, as were the difficulties of working within a denomination. Hard questions were raised about training for ministry, funding for initiatives and what it means to be presbyterian. The conference offered clear evidence that the emerging church conversation is challenging, widespread and relevant. While some are actively engaged in it, others are looking to join, sensing that this might help them respond faithfully to the Spirit in their context.

2.4 Training: The Joint Working Party has identified two separate but related training needs within the Church of Scotland: (1) to add a 'pioneering' dimension to training for ministries; (2) to enable parish ministers and leaders from their congregations to train in new patterns of ministry with a view to developing mission within their own community. Two courses already offer potential:

2.4.1 Invest is "a leadership training and mentoring programme for those who sense that God might be leading them into creating new expressions of church". It has been developed by Whiteinch NCD in Glasgow and is a year-long, part-time course that promotes bi-vocational ministry in the leadership of new and contemporary church-planting initiatives. As reported previously to the General Assembly, "…it is *not* part of the Church of Scotland's ministerial selection and training processes, but it is a positive development in response to changing patterns of church in contemporary society."

2.4.2 Mission Shaped Ministry is a course developed by the *Fresh Expressions* team in England. This operates by distance learning and modules include: mission; building a team; auditing a community; and planting a church. Meetings have been held with ecumenical partners (Scottish Baptist Union, Scottish Episcopal Church and Methodist Church) who have expressed an interest in developing this course for Scotland.

3. Interim Report of the Joint Working Party on Emerging Church

3.1 Introduction

The Joint Working Party was conscious from the start of the need to exercise discernment in engaging with a theme which has generated a range of conflicting responses, from bafflement and frustration, through critique and opposition, to enthusiasm and excitement. Whenever a new emphasis or critique appears within the life of the church, it is right that there is debate and discussion about what value it might have for understanding mission and discipleship. This is at its best when it involves a well-rounded process of listening to both critics and advocates. The Working Party has been concerned neither to 'believe the hype' around this at times heavily promoted term, nor to 'refuse the hope' which might be drawn from serious engagement with it. The focus is on trying to discern the substantive elements within the emerging church conversation and to consider where they might, under God, inspire and enrich our own understanding and practice as a church.

3.2 Definition

A common source of frustration is the difficulty of defining *emerging church*. When a term becomes widely used, it is vulnerable to being claimed by or attached to a wide range of groups and contexts. This can cause two problems. First, the term can come to seem incoherent, since it is applied to very different examples of practice. Secondly, critics can seize on the examples of which they disapprove and use them to discredit all examples to which the term is applied. The Joint Working Party has been aware of this problem and encourages others also to be aware of rushing to judgment.

Canadian theologian James K. A. Smith describes emerging church as not so much a movement as a 'sensibility'.[2] In line with this, it is suggested that a helpful way to understand the term is to see it as describing an international, ecumenical conversation about the future of the church, primarily within Western societies, which has developed in dialogue with wider debates about 'gospel and culture' and postmodernity and postmodernism[3]. In describing it as a conversation, the Joint Working Party is accepting that it has a fluid and open-ended quality, but notes too that particular themes have been prominent in its development. This approach to definition moves us away from the question of whether particular groups are or are not 'emerging churches'. We are wary of applying additional adjectives to the terms church, congregation or ministry in ways which create unnecessary division or distinction. There is one Church *catholic* and there is one body constituted as the Church of Scotland within the *reformed* tradition.

The Joint Working Party does not regard the term 'emerging' as a descriptor on the same level of theological significance as these other two. Rather, it points to a conversation about *how* to be the church catholic and reformed within the contemporary world. If we can deploy the term carefully and provisionally, it may help us reflect on the continuing re-formation of the church, under the guidance and direction of the Holy Spirit. It can also serve for now as a helpful term to guide some of our own support and funding activities in respect of mission, discipleship and ministry.

3.3 The Church Emerging – Learning to be the Church in Five Moves

We are a pilgrim church, always reforming, always believing that there is yet more light and truth to inform our faith and

---

[2] "The Emerging Church: A Guide for the Perplexed", James K.A. Smith in: *Reformed Worship,* Issue 77.

[3] Postmodernism is an intellectual movement, postmodernity a constellation of cultural phenomena resulting from it. James K. A. Smith, *Who's Afraid of Postmodernism?*, Grand Rapids: Baker Academic, 2006, p20 n8.

life. We are always responding to the call of Jesus: *"Follow me"*. We are always learning how to be the church. Within the emerging church conversation it is possible to identify five moves that may help us to understand how that learning journey moves us towards being faithful to the call of God in our own time and place.

Firstly, the church should always be involved in **auditing** its own practice. This involves a reflective and critical enquiry into: (a) our history and traditions as they bear upon our mission and discipleship now; (b) the gifts and limitations of the reformed tradition as shaped by the history of the Kirk; and (c) what, in the light of scripture, remains vital for our own witness and practice, as well as what needs to be reformed.

Secondly, the emerging church conversation highlights the importance of **retrieval**. The whole of Christian history is a potential resource to reflect on: (a) belief and practice of the contemporary church; (b) forgotten or discarded emphases, which viewed from today may appear meaningful and valuable.

A third move uses the metaphor of **unbundling,** derived from computer technology where manufacturers sometimes 'bundle' software programmes inside their operating system. Emerging church conversations may enable the preservation of 'babies without bathwater', through: (a) selective recovery of practices and dimensions from earlier eras minus the theological package in which they were originally 'bundled'; (b) adapting, for example, some liturgical practices for contemporary use without compromising a reformed theology.

A fourth move in the emerging church conversation is **supplementing**. The church is always called to be open to what the Spirit is saying here and now. The creative presence of God has continually opened up the possibility of supplement tradition as we previously understood it. Historical examples would be: (a) technology: the printing press or the pipe organ; (b) theology: the ordination of women or the emergence of environmental theology; .(c) the arts: the introduction of hymns or floral art in churches.

The fifth move is **remixing**, drawing on a metaphor from contemporary music and video production. This offers an ecumenical dimension to the emerging church conversation, whereby there is: (a) transformation of existing congregations and planting and resourcing new ones; (b) engagement in a common mission-focused ecumenism from the grassroots up, alongside more established institutional forms of ecumenism. This final move brings together all the others in the journey of learning together.

3.4 Four Sources

The emerging conversation significantly draws on four very different influences: the evangelical tradition; charismatic renewal; the liturgical movement[4]; the ecumenical movement. The majority of those involved in projects, church plants or networks identified with the emerging church came from a low-church Protestant background. Most were formed in *evangelical* churches influenced by *charismatic renewal*. From this background, they brought a history of activism, confidence about church growth, church renewal and church planting and an emphasis on mission and evangelism. They also brought a critique of the tradition that formed them, of their worship practice and spirituality and, in various degrees, their theology.

For many people, these two traditions (*evangelical* and *charismatic renewal*) have intersected with the liturgical and ecumenical movements through direct or indirect contact with the work and worship of the Iona and Taizé communities. These two internationally influential communities have acted as a portal into catholic tradition for low-church Protestants. Both communities already represented a remixing of liturgical and ecumenical

---

[4] The liturgical movement' is the term commonly used to describe a movement dating from the early 19th century which sought to renew and reform worship.

traditions within their own practice. They have also inspired Anglicans and Lutherans to a new engagement with the high-church elements of their own communion. The quasi-monastic character of both Taizé and Iona has also been significant, with an interest in 'new monasticism' increasingly forming another important sub-theme in the emerging conversation in recent years. It was also significant that both of these communities had specific concerns for reconciliation and for the ecumenical themes of justice, peace and the integrity of creation.

It is from the encounter between these four different movements that we begin to see the characteristic themes of the emerging church conversation developing, bringing together a set of emphases that the different movements had largely held apart in their own historical development.

3.5 Two Dynamics – Mission and Authenticity

Two distinct dynamics that can lend a very different character to Christian communities run through the emerging church conversation. Some groups are particularly concerned for *mission* and they value the conversation, because it has helped them to think about how to reform church in ways which will increase their capacity to see churches grow as they reach out to others in a post-Christendom society.

Other groups have found in the emerging conversation resources to enable them to reinvent church when they were on the verge of leaving. For them, the key concern has been with *authenticity*, with creating a space in which they could express their spirituality honestly and practice faith with integrity. They are open to others and believe their own approach may well attract others, but they are less focused on 'reaching' those beyond their own groups.

These are subjective judgments, but the Joint Working Party thinks they capture something of the diverse dynamics that can give groups who identify with emerging church noticeably different 'personalities'.

3.6 Emerging Kirk?

Emerging church can be understood as a conversation about the future of church, a conversation that performs five moves, which connects four movements and which reflects two dynamics. One of the primary concerns has been to reflect on what this conversation means for the Church of Scotland. The Joint Working Party has asked itself: *what can we learn from it? How might we share in it?*

The answers to those questions are still forming, but we are agreed that we in the Kirk have things to learn and things to share. The Joint Working Party has no desire to see the Kirk simply follow a fad and we stress the enduring importance of the language of church, ministry, mission and discipleship. On the other hand, we appreciate the excitement and inspiration which this conversation has provoked internationally over the past decade or so.

The act of joining this conversation involves the church in a renewed reflection on the identity and practices of our own tradition. How do we describe what we value about our tradition to others within this conversation? How do we receive the insights and challenges to our own tradition from others who are curious, critical or sceptical about its worth and viability?

Describing our own tradition will first involve affirming how we share in broad 'catholic' understandings of the church. In common with other Christian traditions we recognise the scriptures as authoritative, we uphold the Apostles and Nicene Creeds, we believe there is one, holy, catholic and apostolic church and we are committed to the practice of Baptism and the Lord's Supper.

We also have to describe how those common understandings have been developed in distinctive ways to produce a Presbyterian Kirk which: (a) is governed by elders; (b) subscribes to the Westminster Confession of Faith; (c) is accountable to church courts; (d) recognises lawful ordination.

Reflecting on these characteristics of the Presbyterian Kirk, it becomes evident that these distinctives express fundamental principles that ecumenical partners also subscribe to and express in different ways. It seems natural that emerging churches in some way would also incorporate these, namely: (a) recognised local leadership within congregations; (b) a statement confessing the Church's faith; (c) a recognition of authority and commitment to accountability; (d) a concern for good order and effective ministry.

In conversation with those who are seeking fresh expressions of church, we need to be clear about the extent to which they will be invited to embody and reflect *our* tradition if they are to be welcomed and supported as Church of Scotland congregations. Should this forever involve an exact replication of the existing formats, titles and structures? For example, must all new 'emerging' congregations have Elders and Kirk Sessions which are called *Elders* and *Kirk Sessions?* Is there scope to consider how we might affirm the key theological issues at stake, but find ways to express them in new forms and structures? We need to consider carefully the cultural and institutional 'loading' we place on new church communities in Scotland that may be crossing significant cultural boundaries. This is necessary both because we want these new churches to be appropriately empowered, but also because we need the insights into our own practice which can flow from cross-cultural mission. In reflecting on this, we may uncover some profound and surprising insights into how better to enable the mission of the whole church.

Our concern to explore these questions does not mean that we are committed to recognising any initiative, anyhow, anywhere. We recognise that there will be many initiatives outwith the Kirk. Our dialogue with some groups may lead to our praying God's blessing on their work but concluding that their journey cannot fit within our polity and structures as a church.

3.7 Challenging Institutions

The emerging church conversation has not been directed or managed from any denominational head office. It has networked freely across denominational boundaries and has combined a new interest in church tradition with a well-developed suspicion of church hierarchies and authorities. It has largely been led by lay people, has been collaborative and participative, and has emphasised creativity and engagement with culture and the arts.[5]

The shape of this conversation, and of the communities and congregations associated with it, poses challenges for mainstream, institutional churches and their strategies for mission and discipleship. In particular it raises questions about how churches develop top-down strategies to resource and support like-minded initiatives within their own denominational structures. There is a markedly congregationalist feel to many of these groups and an independence of spirit which may not sit easily within a Presbyterian polity. Lay people have been enfranchised within them in ways which may chafe against existing patterns of ordination and ministry. There is also a can-do, entrepreneurial approach to church planting which may seem shocking to structures which are more used to guarding against intrusion and whose wheels grind slowly and cautiously when authorising new charges.

These are all questions which we in the Church of Scotland must ask ourselves if we are to be sharers in this conversation. The Church of England has found a way to 'hug it close' through their *Fresh Expressions* initiative and has evolved new programmes of ordination training for *Pioneer Ministry*. Underpinning their actions has been the widely discussed and influential report *Mission-Shaped Church* and Archbishop Rowan Williams' much-discussed

---

[5] For a detailed study of "Emerging Churches" and their characteristics in the USA and UK see Gibbs and Bolger *Emerging Churches*, London, SPCK, 2006

phrase, 'mixed economy church'. There is talk of this as a 'permission giving moment', and these developments are being accompanied by a stream of commentaries, discussions and publications, some of them highly critical. Like the Church of Scotland, faced with acute problems of decline and dilemmas about how to reach out in mission to a post-Christendom society, these institutions have created fresh channels in which new energies and approaches can flow. They have chosen to take the risk of experimenting with new ways of being church and committed themselves to bless, support and supervise them within their own polities.

4.   Conclusion

The General Assembly 2008 affirmed the concept of 'a mixed economy church' within the Church of Scotland, where both existing and fresh expressions of church co-exist, not at the expense of each other, but for the benefit of the whole. The emerging church conversation is part of this mixed economy.

The emerging church conversation is not commended to the Kirk as any kind of panacea for the challenges we face in our mission and discipleship within contemporary Scotland. However, we encourage the church to consider whether the energy and creativity carried within this conversation may offer a prophetic word to our own tradition, and whether sharing in this conversation may enrich our own life and work here in Scotland and wherever our churches are based. In particular the Joint Working Party asks the church to recognise that this emerging church conversation is not alien to our traditions and concerns, but that it crystallises a range of concerns for the future witness of the church which already exist within the body of the Kirk. This conversation mixes the accents of, amongst others, the Church Service Society, Summer Mission, the charismatic movement, the Iona Community and the Evangelical Alliance, and it accepts the challenge of

the Articles Declaratory to live as a church that is both catholic and reformed.

In doing so it takes the risk of pleasing none of the above, because it risks a synthesis which some may find incoherent and others unpalatable. If the Church of Scotland does not warm to it, however, it should not be because this is not our own conversation. Those who worked to produce this report believe it is. Moreover, it is keenly recognised that parts of the one body should always be wary of saying that they do not need other parts that are not like them.

In offering this interim report, while we hope for the development of many new types of congregations, we do not look for the establishment of a new brand or type, to be labelled 'emerging churches'. Descriptors and metaphors like evangelical revival, Scoto-Catholic, charismatic renewal, fresh expressions and Church Without Walls will come and go as ways of helping us to be renewed in faithfulness. Some will outlast others, but our basic vocabulary of church, congregation, ministry, mission and discipleship will remain primary. What matters is whether the whole church can allow that the visions and concerns of emerging church have a part to play for at least some sections of the Kirk in seeking to bear faithful witness to the gospel. Both Councils involved in nurturing emerging ministries accept that this is the case and we encourage the church to bless, support and oversee those who feel called participate in the conversation.

On behalf of the Ministries and Mission
& Discipleship Councils

GRAHAM FINCH, *Convener (Ministries)*
MARTIN SCOTT, *Secretary (Ministries)*
ANGUS MORRISON, *Convener (Mission & Discipleship)*
DOUGLAS NICOL, *Secretary (Mission & Discipleship)*

APPENDIX
MEMBERS OF THE EMERGING CHURCH JOINT WORKING PARTY

From October 2008
Rev Neil Dougall (Convener)
Rev Prof John Drane
Mrs Linda Dunnett
Rev Dr Jim Francis
Rev Dr Doug Gay
Rev Dr David Graham
Rev Dr Jared Hay
Rev Bryan Kerr

From December 2008
Mr Bill Greenock
Rev Hilary McDougall

Staff
Rev David E. P. Currie (Development Worker)
Mr John Jackson (Associate Secretary, Ministries Council)
Rev Alex Millar (Associate Secretary, Mission and Discipleship Council)

MISSION AND DISCIPLESHIP COUNCIL
May 2009

The Mission and Discipleship Council
resources Christ's mission through the whole Church
for witness, worship and discipleship

Tha Comhairle na Teachdaireachd agus na Deisciobalachd
a' cur air adhart teachdaireachd Chrìosd, tron Eaglais air fad
airson fianais, adhradh agus deisciobalachd

4

CONTENTS PAGE

PROPOSED DELIVERANCE

The General Assembly

1. Receive the Report and thank the Council, Task Groups and Committees and members retiring at the General Assembly.
2. Thank all Council staff and volunteers, especially those who have left the service of the Council in 2008, and welcome all new members of staff.
3. Encourage congregations to pray for the Council and its staff as they seek to fulfil the remit of congregational resourcing.

Mission and Evangelism

4. Note the Reflection on the Nature and Practice of Evangelism in Contemporary Scotland; recognise its changing patterns and trends; and affirm the importance of sharing faith positively and confidently in word and action (Section 2.2).
5. Acknowledge the 75th Anniversary in 2009 of Summer Mission in Scotland and welcome the plans in this anniversary year to consult on how best to develop iMPACT as a mission resource to local churches (Section 2.8).

Worship and Doctrine

6. Encourage congregations and Presbyteries to make use of the resource 'Seeing the World as other See it' in their reflections on the report to the General Assembly of 2007 (Section 3.1)
7. Commend the ACTS resource on the Language of the Trinity to the Church as a whole and acknowledge that this fulfils the remit given to the Council in 2005 (Section 3.2).
8. Receive the report 'Holy Communion and the Renewal of the Church' and commend it for widespread study in Presbyteries, Kirk Sessions and congregations (Section 3.6 and Appendix I).
9. Commend to the Church the forthcoming production of the Commentary on Holy Communion and resources for the celebration of Holy Communion (Section 3.6).
10. Affirm the importance of holding Word and Sacrament together in the life of the Church, and encourage joyful care in the celebration of Holy Communion so that there may be rich experiences of participation (Section 3.6).
11. Receive the Report 'Being Single in Church and Society' and in view of its significant conclusions, instruct the Mission and Discipleship Council to explore ways of disseminating it widely for study and engagement (Section 3.7 and Appendix II).

Education and Nurture

12. Welcome the ongoing developments in the area of Education and Nurture, including the National Children's Assembly and the development of new resources for congregations (Section 4).
13. Urge congregations to take seriously their ministry to and with children by participating in children's forums and the child friendly Church programme and ensuring that there are opportunities for children to participate in worship which nurtures their spirituality (Section 4.2.1.2).
14. Instruct the Council to support the Advisory Group on the future of Youth Work and to bring forward proposals on the key areas it has identified to next year's General Assembly (Section 4.2.10).

15. Urge congregations to explore ways to include people with learning disabilities in the life, work and worship of the Church (Section 4.3.5).

Publishing

16. Welcome the ongoing positive developments in the publishing area of the Council's work and encourage congregations to avail themselves of the resources of Saint Andrew Press and *Life and Work*. (Section 5).

Church Art and Architecture

17. Encourage early consultation with the Committee, preferably in electronic form, by congregations seeking to adapt and change their buildings so that the best advice and guidance and objective opinions will be available (Section 6.21).

18. Remind congregations of the requirement of the General Assembly to contact the Committee regarding any proposal to dispose of sacramental vessels, to ensure that the appropriate procedures are undertaken (Section 6.23).

Mission Forum

19. Welcome the identification by the Mission Forum of key themes for the mission of the Church; and instruct the Council to continue the development of the Forum in future years (Section 7).

Regional Development Team

20. Recognise the significant contribution made to resourcing congregations by the Development Team and encourage congregations to avail themselves of the support available through team members (Section 8).

Future Focus: a way forward for congregations

21. Thank all who are developing the use of *Future Focus: a way forward for congregations*; and encourage congregations to make use of the materials through their Regional Development Officer (Section 9).

Rural Scotland

22. Note the enlargement of the ecumenical and inter-Council partnership planning and representing the church's presence at the Royal Highland Show; welcome the expanding programme of events and seminars; and encourage those from parishes around Scotland attending the Show to visit the Church Stand (Section 10.2.1).

23. Encourage ministers serving in rural parishes and eligible for study leave to take full advantage of the proposed course in rural ministry to take place at Balmoral in November 2009 (Section 10.2.4).

Netherbow Scottish Storytelling Centre

24. Welcome the Christian contribution given by the Scottish Storytelling Centre to the cultural, political and artistic life of Scotland and encourage the wider use of the Centre and its resources by congregations (Section 11).

Strategic Use of Gaelic

25. Welcome the production of a Gaelic Worship Aid and other resources, and instruct the Council, in collaboration with the Council of Assembly Gaelic Group, to continue the development of resources to support the use of Gaelic throughout the Church (Section 12).

Church Visitor and Tourism Strategy

26. Commend the Year of Homecoming as an opportunity to welcome visitors from home and overseas into the life of the Church (Section 13).

'Why Believe?'
27. Encourage congregations to place accessible Christian apologetic literature in local libraries (Section 14).
Scottish Churches Community Trust (now *FiSCAF – Faiths in Scotland Community Action Fund*)
28. Welcome the establishment of the Faiths in Scotland Community Action Fund (FiSCAF) and encourage congregations to make applications to it (Section 15).

REPORT
Theme: 'Building the Future'

1. Introduction

Unless the Lord builds the house, those who build it labour in vain. (Psalm 127:1 NRSV)

1.1 As people of the church in Scotland, we live in interesting times. We approach, in 2010, the 450th anniversary of the Scottish Reformation, and the centenary of the Edinburgh World Missionary Conference. The last hundred years have witnessed a dramatic expansion of global Christianity, sadly not reflected in the Western World. Not since the sixteenth century has the church in Scotland, and the Church of Scotland, faced so many challenges and been so disconnected from the majority of the Scottish people.

1.2 It is within this broad context that the Kirk's Mission and Discipleship Council was established four years ago to enable and ensure a truly national mission. The purpose of the Council since its inception is encapsulated in its Mission Statement: 'The Mission and Discipleship Council resources Christ's mission through the whole church for witness, worship and discipleship.'

1.3 Our conviction, clearly shared by past General Assemblies, is that there has never been more need of the Christian gospel, with its truth and values, than today in the early twenty first century. The widespread hunger for community, for companionship, for love and for spiritual identity is abundantly clear. The need for justice and for fairness is as great as ever, while the scourges of family breakdown, child neglect, substance abuse and environmental degradation call out for a radical Christian response.

1.4 The so-called Credit Crunch has crystallised the vacuity and poverty of a worldly vision based only on material values. In turn, the Credit Crunch may be seen to pose us all in the church, and particularly in the Kirk, with a something of a 'faith crunch'. Are we to be still a national movement, committed to transformative change in all our communities? Is there a danger that under various pressures we settle rather for the managing of decline? It is the case that many congregations in these times struggle for survival. At the same time, there are in many places indications of new life and of growth, and of new commitment to the mission mandate given to us by our Lord whose abiding promise grounds all our work: 'I will build my church (Matthew 16:18 NRSV)'.

1.5 The Mission and Discipleship Council exists for the support and resourcing of local congregations in giving proper emphasis to these two mutually dependent sides of our corporate life in the Church. Since inheriting in 2005 much of the work of the former Boards of National Mission, of Parish Education and of Communication, along with that of the Panels of Worship and Doctrine and the Committee of Church Art and Architecture, the Council has sustained all its services to congregations, maintained and developed distinctive national engagements, and harmoniously incorporated the complementary emphases of the previous bodies. The Council has been asked to extend its responsibilities to include Church Without Walls and the Parish Development Fund. Furthermore, the Council believes that new strategic initiatives are required to enable the Kirk to continue to fulfil its vital role as a truly national institution.

1.6 The Council has committed itself to a root and branch review of all its wide-ranging work. In particular, consideration will be given to which areas of its remit most properly belong at regional, Presbytery or congregational level and which are primarily a national responsibility. The Council is deeply concerned that no vital new missionary endeavour will be neglected at a time of real challenge to the ongoing life and purpose of the Church of Scotland.

1.7 Throughout this first – four year – phase of its life, the Mission and Discipleship Council has sought to be true to its Mission Statement and to the many responsibilities with which it has been entrusted by the General Assembly. Much of lasting value for the mission of the Kirk has been accomplished. This Report provides clear evidence of the vigour and commitment with which our priority work continues to be addressed. All of us who are involved in the life of the Council count this a great privilege. We are grateful for all the prayerful and practical support which makes it possible for the Council to respond to many current challenges and opportunities. We trust that this support will in no way diminish at a time in our national history when the need for the Christian gospel has never been more pressing, and when mission, as 'that dimension of our faith that refuses to accept reality as it

is and aims to change it' (David Bosch), must remain our number one priority. It is in this way that together we shall build the future.

2.   Mission and Evangelism
2.1   Remit
The Mission and Evangelism Task Group (METAG) operates with a remit that, in summary, seeks to encourage local initiatives; offers, by way of support, expertise, research, development and training; highlights the importance of mission and outreach; reviews changing patterns in contemporary Scotland; and reflects theologically on the opportunities for the future that these changes represent.

2.2 A Reflection on the Nature and Practice of Evangelism in Contemporary Scotland
2.2.1   Introduction
Opinions about evangelism vary considerably from those who view it as an absolute imperative, to those who find it embarrassing, invasive or counter-productive. Negative connotations associated with it have contributed to a widespread avoidance of its use and practice, and in many cases the term 'mission'[1] has been substituted as a more acceptable synonym. The terms, although related, are not interchangeable, and before continuing it is important to clarify the terminology used here.

2.2.1.1   Mission is concerned with God's redemptive purposes for his whole creation,[2] whereas evangelism involves witness and testimony to people of what 'God has done, is doing, and will do'[3]. Evangelism is therefore a part – an essential part – of God's mission *(missio Dei)*,

---

[1] Bosch, D J, *Transforming Mission: Paradigm Shifts in Theology of Mission*, (Maryknoll, NY: Orbis Books, 1991), p 409. The section entitled 'Mission as Evangelism' provides a useful introduction to the shifting usage of the term 'evangelism' and a helpful attempt at understanding the term in a manner relevant to current cultural conditions pp 409-420.

[2] One example from scripture is in Gen 8:21-22, 9:9-12 following the flood. God makes his covenant not just with Noah, or even with humankind, but with all of creation.

[3] Bosch, Transforming, p 412.

but not the whole of it. Many agencies and individuals are active in social justice, caring for others, or environmental concerns – all of which fall within the bounds of holistic mission – but it is the message of the gospel that God and human kind can be reconciled through Jesus Christ which makes the Church's mission distinct. It is the aim of evangelism to communicate that distinctive Christian message.

2.2.1.2 Although there is a general consensus that evangelism involves the communication of the gospel, its content and methodology remain the subject of debate. Nor is there agreement about the evangelist's role. Does it end with the proclamation of the gospel, or is there a responsibility to see the process through to conversion, or discipleship? William Abraham states that,

> No rule exists for setting or limiting the boundaries of action that the responsible evangelist may have to perform in order to carry out fitting and appropriate acts of evangelism.[4]

2.2.1.3 He cautions, however, against expanding the definition of evangelism so much that evangelism does not actually take place. Unless acts

> are intimately related to a process that intentionally brings people into the kingdom of God, they are something other than or something less than evangelism.[5]

2.2.2 Evangelism in the New Testament

Many Christians cite the Great Commission[6] as the primary scriptural mandate for mission and evangelism, but it is only since William Carey used this text to convince others of that in 1792[7] that it has been commonly used in

Protestant mission.[8] The scriptural concept of evangelism is a little more complex. David Barrett noted that in English 'over 300 different definitions of the concept 'evangelize' have been proposed in print... employing over 700 different terms.'[9] Also, the word evangelise (euangelizo) is missing from both Greek and English accounts of Matt 28:19-20.[10] However, several other passages record Jesus' various commands to his followers after the resurrection.[11] Seven imperatives emerge from these instructions.

MANDATE	GREEK WORD USED	AMPLIFIED MEANING
Receive!	Labete	Receive the Holy Spirit
Go!	Poreuthentes	Go into all the world
Witness!	Martyres	Be witnesses to me
Proclaim!	Keruxate	Proclaim the good news
Disciple!	Matheteusate	Make disciples of all nations
Baptise!	Baptizontes	Baptise them into my fellowship
Train!	Didaskontes	Teach them to observe my commandments

Table 1: Mandates of Jesus' Great Commission[12]

2.2.2.1 Barrett found that although 'evangelise' is absent from the Great Commission texts and the records of the 40 day post-resurrection period, the noun euangelion ('good news', or 'gospel') is present (in Mk 16:15). Also, many synonyms and related words appear, so although 'evangelise' does not occur as an imperative, the seven mandates in Table 1 do, and 'may be regarded as aspects of the imperative Evangelize!'[13]

---

[4] Abraham, W, *The Logic of Evangelism*, (Sevenoaks: Hodder and Stoughton, 1989), p 104.

[5] Abraham, *The Logic*, p 105.

[6] Matt 28:19-20.

[7] Carey, W, A*n Enquiry into the Obligation of Christians to Use Means for the Conversion of the Heathens*, 1792.

[8] Bosch, *Transforming*, p 340.

[9] Barrett, D B, *Evangelize! A Historical Survey of the Concept*, (Birmingham, AL: New Hope, 1987), p.77. Barret's work provides a comprehensive examination of the concept of evangelism both in scripture and the church.

[10] Barrett, *Evangelize!*, p 20.

[11] Mk 16:15-18, Lk 24:45-49, Jn 20:21-23, Acts: 1:4-8, and as a parable in Jn 21.

[12] Barrett, *Evangelize!*, p 20.

[13] Barrett, *Evangelize!*, pp 20-21.

2.2.2.2 While recognising that a much more comprehensive study could be conducted on this, there are three Greek words used in the New Testament which describe different approaches to evangelism; kerygma, euangelion and mysterion.[14]

2.2.2.3 Kerygma has as its root a herald (keryx) whose primary function 'is to transmit the soteriological content of the Christ-event.'[15] The NIV translates kerygma variously as 'preaching'[16], 'message'[17], 'proclamation'[18] or 'what was preached'.[19] The emphasis is on communicating the informational content of the gospel. Kerygmatic forms of evangelism often have a strong educational content[20] and so lend themselves to methods which focus on transmission of information, *eg* Sunday School, Alpha Courses, etc. The information has two main elements: who Jesus is – Christology, and what he did – soteriology. In order to communicate this effectively the evangelist must be familiar with both. One of the main recommendations of the Church Without Walls report encouraged congregations to spend a year in one of the gospels, rediscovering the narratives of Jesus.

> *the primary purpose of the Church is to follow Jesus Christ... travelling where he leads us... A church which hears this call will be shaped by the gospel – a rediscovery of the grace of God as we commit to living one of the gospel narratives.*[21]

2.2.2.4 This provides not only information about the gospel message but also a scriptural and historical framework in which to interpret one's own spiritual encounter with God.

2.2.2.5 If kerygma is the content of the gospel, then euangelion is the method of communication. The words euangelizo and euangelion are found in scripture,[22] but are seldom translated as evangelise (or its derivatives) in English Bible translations.[23] Instead, euangelizo is usually translated as 'preach' or 'preached',[24] 'preaching' the gospel,[25] or other terms which describe the spread of the gospel message, and euangelion as 'gospel',[26] although euangelistes is translated as evangelist (or evangelists) three times in the NIV.[27]

2.2.2.6 The most common English words used for translating these verbs related to euangelizo are; preach, bring, tell, proclaim, announce and declare.[28] For many years 'preach' has been the favoured translation[29] (which is demonstrated in the wide-spread use of the evangelistic sermon as the primary means of communicating the gospel either in the local church or in a festival evangelism context), but 'tell' is increasingly taking its place.[30] 'Bring' stands out as the only one which does not describe verbal communication, but rather implies invitation and accompaniment and is the second most common translation after 'preach'.

2.2.2.7 Both kerygma and euangelion depend on communication, particularly in words. There is however a third element of the evangelistic process – mysterion. Mysterion is used 27 times in the New Testament and in

---

[14] Finney, J, *Emerging Evangelism*, (London: Darton, Longman and Todd Ltd, 2004), p 23.

[15] McGrath, A E, *Christian Theology: An Introduction*, 4th edn (Oxford: Blackwell Publishing, 2007), p 294.

[16] For example, Matt 12:41, 1 Cor 2:4.

[17] 2 Tim 4:17.

[18] Rom 16:25.

[19] 1 Cor 1:21.

[20] Finney, *Emerging Evangelism*, p 23.

[21] 'Church Without Walls', http://www.churchofscotland.org.uk/church withoutwalls/cwwreports.htm#2001, accessed 20 March 2008.

[22] 54 and 76 occurrences respectively in the New Testament.

[23] Bosch, *Transforming*, p 409.

[24] For example in Lk 3:18, 4:18.

[25] For example in Acts 8:25, 1 Cor 9:18, in the NIV translation.

[26] 60 times in the NIV, including Mt 24:14, Mk 13:10, Acts 15:7 and Rom 1:1.

[27] Acts 21:8, Eph 4:11, 2 Tim 4:5.

[28] Barrett, *Evangelize!*, p 36.

[29] As in the NIV.

[30] Barrett, *Evangelize!*, p 36.

the NIV is most often translated as 'mystery' or 'mysteries',[31] but also as 'secret'[32] or 'deep truths'.[33] It speaks of God's role in communicating with people and the Holy Spirit's activity in revelation, for example in Eph 3:4-5, and its 'revelation in history has the character of a veiled announcement of a promise of the future, and of anticipation.'[34]

2.2.2.8 While the evangelist can do much to contextualise the message, there are many points of the Christian story that rational means cannot explain, for example the meeting in Jesus of divinity and humanity, his miracles, his resurrection, and the personal testimony of an individual's own spiritual encounters. An evangelist may communicate the information to others but it is the Spirit who reveals that it is truth.

2.2.3 The Evangelist

Evangelism requires an evangelist. In his own earthly ministry Jesus shared news of the kingdom and called others to leave behind their old lives and join him in a new one. The most striking examples of this are the calling of the disciples[35] and Jesus' frequent invitation to 'follow me'.[36] He trained those who followed him and finally commissioned them to continue in his pattern – that they should in turn call others to leave their lives and follow him.

2.2.3.1 The Christian does not face the task unaided. At the birth of the church, believers received the Holy Spirit to empower the church's witness for Jesus – 'you will receive power when the Holy Spirit comes on you; and you will be my witnesses in Jerusalem, and in all Judea and Samaria, and to the ends of the earth.'[37] The

church must share the Christian message, inviting others to follow Jesus into a new life. In other words, Christians must evangelise. This does not mean that there are not those who are particularly gifted and called to the ministry of evangelism, but the task of communicating the gospel should be shared by the whole church.

2.2.3.2 As God's witnesses, Christians testify to what they know of Jesus' story and share their own. Perhaps most significantly, the Christian 'brings' people to Jesus. It is an act full of intention and involves inviting others to embark on a journey and accompanying them as they set out.

2.2.4 Evangelism Today

There is a feeling that evangelism is harder today than in previous generations. Certainly the church seems to struggle to engage effectively in evangelism. It is not that people are necessarily less interested in God, but that their questions have changed, the way information is received and communicated has changed, and the institutional church has an undeniable image problem. This means that the church has to take the challenge of evangelism seriously, and take steps to understand and address the cultural changes which have rendered traditional forms of evangelism less relevant and less effective.

2.2.5 The postmodern context

With regard to culture, it is inaccurate to claim that British society is wholly postmodern; there are areas where the influence of modernity remains strong (in churches, for example). Nevertheless, society is changing rapidly and the prevailing trend is towards postmodernity. While the following is not an examination of postmodernity, there are some points to note.[38]

2.2.5.1 Postmodernism appears often to be defined by what it rejects rather than what it embraces. However, it

---

[31] For example, Rom 16:25, Eph 3:3.

[32] For Example, 1 Cor 2:7.

[33] For Example, 1 Tim 3:9.

[34] Motmann, J *The Church in the Power of the Spirit,* (London: SCM, 1977), p 167.

[35] Matt 4:18-22, Mk 2:14.

[36] For example, Mk 8:34, Jn 1:43.

[37] Acts 1:8.

[38] For a useful overview of postmodernity, see Grenz, S, *A Primer on Postmodernism,* (Cambridge: William B. Eerdmans Publishing, 1996.

accepts a more holistic, less rational definition of truth.[39] It does not reject, as is often claimed, the notion of absolute truth, but rather 'any one individual's ability and right to determine absolute truth for another person.'[40] The argument runs that if one lives within the world, one cannot have an objective view of it. There is also a distrust of institutions, including the government and the church, and even the family in this age of divorce and abandonment, so there is a longing for something which can transform lives and communities, but which it is safe to invest in emotionally and spiritually. Postmoderns therefore do not verify truth only by empirical means but also by non-rational means (*eg* feelings and emotions) and in the context of relationships and community.

2.2.5.2 Postmoderns also perceive life as a drama, so 'their major concerns revolve around the process of fabricating stories that define personal identity and give purpose and shape to social existence.'[41] Narrative is extremely important in postmodernity – indeed in all human cultures – and is an effective way of communicating information and meaning.

2.2.5.3 Narratives can have tremendous power and are also essentially about people, and in a culture that is increasingly distrustful of institutions this is significant. Narratives convey the 'big picture' by how it affects those at the centre of the drama. This is not just about verbal storytelling, but includes drama, music, art, and perhaps most powerfully, the ongoing demonstration of how the Christian story unfolds in the lives of Christian individuals and communities.

2.2.6   Changing Trends in Evangelism
Much has been said recently about evangelism in postmodernity. This is not an attempt to summarise

current thinking, but rather to explore some of the changing trends in evangelism in an increasingly postmodern Scotland.

2.2.6.1   In the last century most evangelistic initiatives could be called 'attraction' evangelism.[42] Churches invited outsiders to services or events, for example in the Billy Graham missions, and often with notable success. By the end of the century however this no longer attracted outsiders in significant numbers and churches began to revise their strategies. There are several good reasons for this.

2.2.7   From attraction to projection
For many years, and partly due to the prominence of well known evangelists such as Billy Graham and Luis Palau, the Church has behaved as though the task of evangelism rests solely in the hands of a few specialists. A significant change in recent evangelistic thinking has been from attraction to projection evangelism,[43] requiring congregations to release their 'ordinary' members to reach those who would not come to a church building. This is not just church members physically encountering others, although this is obviously important; it is also about connecting conceptually and relationally. In this environment both personal evangelism and personal testimony – an individual's own faith story or narrative – becomes very important. In an environment where

> people no longer look to the institutional church for answers to their deep spiritual questions... the church will become increasingly dependent on its members to communicate its message outside the walls of the church.[44]

2.2.7.1 In other words, personal evangelism will become increasingly significant. Personal evangelism is most

---

[39] Grenz, *A Primer*), p 14.
[40] Lyon, D, *Postmodernity*, 2nd edn (Buckingham: Open University Press, 1999), p 119.
[41] Grenz, S, *A Primer*, p 46.

[42] McRaney, W, *The Art of Personal Evangelism*, (Nashville, TN: Broadman & Holman, 2003), pp 133-134.
[43] McRaney, *The Art*, pp 133-134.
[44] McRaney, *The Art*, p 7.

effective where a relationship already exists, and so has the potential to reach people who are increasingly alienated from the institutional church.

2.2.8　From proposition to conversation

Personal evangelism in the context of a relationship should be dialogical. It is a conversation, not just a series of propositional statements. Evangelism therefore is not just about telling stories; it is about listening to the stories of others. This helps to build and strengthen relationships, focuses prayer, and provides a community or relational context for people to evaluate information.

2.2.8.1　It is important to reiterate here that personal evangelism is not individual evangelism. It is not something undertaken by solitary believers in isolation from the body of the church, rather it should be supported by the leadership, forming an integral part of the church's evangelistic strategy. If personal evangelism is going to be a significant element of church evangelistic strategy as a whole, then the local church must recognise, train and release its members for service in this way.

2.2.9　From programme to relationship

Never before has there been so many excellent, ready to use resources for evangelism available 'off the shelf', including Alpha, Christianity Explored, the Essence course and many others. Despite this, many local churches fail to see any significant results. There are several reasons for this. Although often information is still communicated propositionally, the key to many of these resources is the opportunity for dialogue and the relationships that exist between those attending the course or event. People are far more likely to respond to a personal invitation from someone they know than to a poster campaign or leaflet drop, and are much more likely to keep coming where a personal relationship exists or develops. Personal engagement can be costly in time, emotionally and spiritually, and many congregations move from one resource to another, as though searching for the magic elixir which will bring people into the church without

the need to become involved in the lives of others. Many of these resources are excellent, but all are limited and all were created for a particular context. When they are employed with appropriate reflection, a robust invitation process and provision for appropriate follow-up they can be very successful. When they are used without proper understanding of the context that they were designed for, or adequate preparation either to invite people in at the beginning, or to assist in their further integration into the church community afterwards, they usually fail to reach expectations. This simply compounds feelings of discouragement about evangelism, and appears to confirm the apparent 'hostility' of the community to church and Christianity, strengthening the illusion that decline is inevitable.

2.2.10　From telling to living

Brad Kallenberg describes conversion as a change of social identity,[45] a change in allegiance from one community to another. Evangelism is, therefore, by definition, social, and occurs within a believing community. This new identity involves 'understanding one's place in the story line of the gospel... This story line ... continues in the telling and retelling of the gospel'.[46]

2.2.10.1　Where believers co-exist with authenticity and integrity, and in a manner distinctive from the way in which rest of the world lives together, evangelism occurs when this believing community invites someone to leave their old community behind and become part of a new one. The community of believers communicates the Christian story through their own narrative – individually and communally. This does not negate the need for an individual response to God's message, but it corrects a tendency in some areas toward an erroneous understanding of either discipleship or evangelism as an individual pursuit. The church community must

---

[45]　Kallenberg, B, *Live to Tell: Evangelism for a Postmodern Age*, (Grand Rapids, MI: Brazos Press, 2002), pp 32-38.

[46]　Kallenberg, *Live to Tell*, p 38.

corporately live out the gospel in their dealings with God, each other and the world. The sincere, authentic discipleship of people living a new life is a vital element of the evangelistic process. In allowing someone who does not yet believe to belong to that community before believing, the whole community becomes involved in evangelism. It is an invitation to cross the threshold into something new. By allowing him or her to enter into the life of the local congregation, he or she can become part of the narrative of that community. They have taken a step on what might become a transformative journey. Unfortunately not every congregation is a helpful hermeneutic of the gospel and this reinforces the need for discipleship to have a strong corporate component.

Classic Newbigin

2.2.11   Conclusion

The subject of evangelism is large and complex, and can only be lightly touched upon here, but there are several points worth particular emphasis.

2.2.11.1   Firstly, evangelism is a scriptural imperative – a commission given by Jesus to the whole church. It matters less that the word itself is used than that the practice is undertaken. The concept has been translated into many different terms such as 'tell' or 'bring to Jesus', but whatever term is used, the task must be undertaken.

2.2.11.2   It makes no sense to continue using evangelistic methods which have become increasingly ineffective throughout the life of almost everyone in church in Scotland today. It is the task of leadership to seek to understand the causes behind this and to face and address the challenges that this brings.

2.2.11.3   Evangelism is most effective when the local congregation is an attractive example of Christian community. The church in Scotland must rediscover at local level what an authentic Christian community looks like, and commit to working toward that end. In other words, successful evangelism will become increasingly dependent on a serious commitment to whole-life, corporate discipleship.

2.2.11.4   Finally, decline is not inevitable. The world-wide church is still growing, and even in Scotland there are congregations which are successfully taking the gospel into their communities. However, failure to review attitudes to and methods of evangelism will not reverse the trend of decline in Scotland's churches, nor will it even maintain the status quo. Without a commitment to 'grasp the nettle' of evangelism in this changing society, the culture of decline will only be reinforced.

2.3   Café Church

The Task Group contributed to a RUN (Reaching the Unchurched Network) conference in Glasgow in November 2008, exploring the culture of café church.

> *'This label is an attempt to group examples that seek to engage with café culture and whose external characteristic is a deliberate change of ambience and 'feel' when people meet corporately. In short, gatherings are around small tables rather than in pews. Drinks and often nibbles are routinely available at the start, rather than an option at the end. People characteristically sit and talk, rather than stand or defend their personal space. Interaction rather than spectating is encouraged. The venues are often secular: community centres, youth clubs, cafes and pub rooms…* '(Mission-Shaped Church *p 50, Church House Publishing*)

2.3.1   By way of follow up, a Café Church Network training day was held in January 2009, the first time the Network has presented an event of this type in Scotland.

2.4   The Church in a Changing Culture

Reflecting, too, the changing pattern of evangelism in a changing culture, the Task Group is participating at a Body and Soul Fair in February. The aim is to offer at an exhibition stand prayer, anointing and spiritual guidance through a variety of means, including the use of Jesus cards – which are neither Tarot cards nor fortune telling – but a resource that introduces the words of Jesus and encourages personal reflection. Body and Soul Fairs attract the spiritually curious and the issue of follow-up will be a particular challenge. The week-end in question, however, falls just before the start of Lent and some churches are planning special events during this time, making particular use of Gloria Deo and Christian Enquiry Agency resources, and highlighting occasions for participation in 'spiritual' events, such as the prayer labyrinth or, for example, courses in Ignation Spirituality.

2.5 Emerging Church

The Mission and Discipleship Council, in partnership with the Ministries Council, has a particular interest in the area of new models and fresh expressions of church. This is highlighted by the joint appointment from March 2008 of David Currie as the Development Officer (New and Emerging Ministries), with the aim of combining a 'grass roots' experience in new models and fresh expressions with reflection on the practical and strategic implications of these initiatives upon ministry, mission and deployment.

2.5.1 It is sufficient here to note that in 2009 the early reflections of the Development Officer are incorporated in the Joint Report of the Mission and Discipleship and the Ministries Councils (on page 3.1), the intention being that in 2010 the next stage of reporting to the General Assembly be through the Mission and Discipleship Council. In the meantime, co-ordination between the Councils is maintained by a joint Reference Group with the following remit:

1. To co-ordinate collaboration and joint initiative between the Ministries and Mission and Discipleship Councils in relation to New and Emerging Ministries and report regularly to both Councils.
2. To meet periodically to reflect on practical and policy implications, if any.
3. To offer advice to the Development Officer on priorities and future development.

4. To encourage reflection on 'emerging church/ ministries' by other Councils and agencies of the Church.

2.5.2 For similar reasons, the Emerging Church Joint Working Party, approved by the General Assembly last year as a parallel collaboration, will report in 2009. This will coincide with the evening event on Mission-Shaped Church on Monday 25 May 2009, with input from Bishop Graham Cray, the leader of Fresh Expressions in the Church of England.

2.5.3 The Council is pleased to be associated with the Ministries Council in these major joint initiatives and regards the 'Mission-Ministries' axis as of fundamental importance in responding with imagination to the challenges before the Church in the 21st Century.

2.6 The Well Asian Information and Advice Centre

2008 proved to be a major milestone for The Well Asian Information and Advice Centre in Glasgow.

2.6.1 A new webpage has been produced and can be viewed at www.thewell.org.uk

2.6.2 For many years it has been obvious that the current premises were not adequate for the present level of activity, so when the premises next door (42-44 Albert Road) became available, the Council agreed to lease and refurbish these while the search for a more permanent solution to accommodation went on. The new adjunct – fondly referred to as 'The Well 2' – was officially opened by the Moderator of the General Assembly of the Church of Scotland, the Right Rev David Lunan, on 10 December 2008. About 100 people, including centre users, representatives of local agencies, members of local churches and an official representative from Glasgow City Council gathered to celebrate this important development in the life and work of The Well.

2.6.3 The extended premises will ease significantly the pressure on the offices in 48-50 Albert Road, ensure that both the community worker and the women's outreach worker can have their own office, and provide a dedicated room for counselling and private consultations, the lack of which was a major impediment. The extension also includes a relaxed reception area, a craft area and a series of computer stations. A number of grants have been received recently, intended specifically for the purchase of computers, and this will allow the staff and volunteers to offer a more varied programme to centre users.

2.6.4 In the meantime, discussions continue between the Council and the Presbytery of Glasgow, with input from the Council of Assembly, to resolve how best to amend and define 'administrative responsibility' and 'partnership' at The Well, and to guarantee to the project the level of resources that will help maintain its strong identity and fine reputation.

2.6.5 Important though all of the foregoing is, the primary purpose in Glasgow of the Well is to serve 'the Asian Community with Christian love and compassion'. It remains committed to helping people in difficulties, from the relatively simple task of dealing with bureaucracy and filling in forms to the more painful task of supporting and protecting victims of domestic abuse. Rhoda Yarmahmoudi, the Community Worker, and her staff and volunteers remain constant in their heart-felt desire to share Christ's love and to be there for people in need.

2.7 Inter-Faith Support Worker

Iain Stewart is the Council's part-time Inter-Faith Support Worker. The main purpose of the post continues to be to offer advice and expertise to local churches engaging with inter-faith issues. An invaluable resource has been the monthly article called 'Relations With Other Faiths' (RWOF), which assists towards a greater understanding of our neighbours of other faiths and promoting positive and healthy relationships. The article also lists key 'Inter-Faith Events' where Christians have a chance to meet with people of other traditions, sharing the Christian message while learning more about other religions. These can be found on the Church of Scotland website at www.churchofscotland.org.uk/councils/missiondisciple/mdresources.

2.7.1 Other resources currently in development include an Inter-Faith DVD, pointing to examples of inter-faith conversations already under way and encouraging local churches to request help and assistance to take forward the building of relationships with neighbours of other faiths.

2.7.2 A *Children of Abraham* booklet is well advanced, which examines the similar origins of the traditions of Judaism, Christianity and Islam and explains some of the key differences. This particular initiative, once available in its final format, promises to be a useful resource in fostering a deeper respect and understanding of Judaism and Islam, encouraging tolerance, and identifying ways in which Christians may confidently share their faith with people of another faith.

2.7.3 The Inter-Faith Support Worker is available to lead seminars for Kirk Sessions or at congregational conferences, and is keen to undertake other such work to support the life and witness of local communities of faith.

2.7.4 As, for example, at Irvine: Mure Parish Church, where the Inter-Faith Support Worker helped in the development of a local Inter-Faith programme. He offered practical help in the building of relationships and in developing understanding of neighbours of other faiths. This included hosting speakers from the Jewish, Sikh and Islamic faiths respectively.

2.7.5 Or as at the Question Time style event that was held in Pollokshields Church during Scottish Inter-Faith week in November 2008. Here members of the Church and visitors from other traditions had the chance to ask questions of a panel of representatives from different faiths, a format that proved very popular.

2.7.6 Other areas of engagement include presenting

seminars at the Rural Church Conference in October 2008, and the Children's and Youth Assemblies, including at the latter a workshop on the 'Biblical Justification For Inter-Faith Engagement'. Iain has spoken at Dumbarton Presbytery and various churches and Guilds, offered advice to hospital chaplains on, for example, how to be respectful to other faith traditions, and responded to colleagues in the Society Religion and Technology (SRT) Project with information on how other faiths view 'end of life issues'.

2.7.7 The Inter-Faith Support Worker recognises too the need to try and break down some of the ignorance and prejudices that may exist in other faiths towards Christianity, and so his engagements have included a lecture to a Christian and Muslim group at Glasgow University on the 'Church and the Mosque' and addressing the Glasgow University Muslim Association (GUMSA) on 'The Christian Responsibility towards Charity'. In the vicinity of the Buddhist Sam Ye Ling Temple, near Eskdalemuir, there is discussion presently on the possibility of running a Christian and Buddhist information day/evening, where participants can learn from each other.

2.7.8 Joint activities with other faiths for the common good have included repairs to the outside of the Central Mosque in Glasgow and painting of the church hall at Govanhill Trinity Church by a team of volunteers from the Global Unity volunteer organisation and local volunteers. A Celebration of Faith Through Music during Scottish Inter-Faith Week in 2008 provided a chance for both sacred song and the sharing of a common meal.

2.7.9 New initiatives freshly embarked upon are plans for young people from different faith backgrounds to collaborate in local community based activities; and preparations for a 'faith programme' as part of a Scout Jamboree at Auchengillon, near Glasgow, in August 2009, to be attended by 1200 Scouts from all across Scotland and the UK. The Scouts will have the chance to explore 'My Faith' and 'Other Religions' and the 'faith tent', where

this activity will take place, will allow them to meet with representatives of the churches and of other faiths. The Scouting Movement is keen for young people to have a faith in God and to re-connect with the religion of their family.

2.7.10 On looking back over his second year in post, Iain observed:

It is with a tremendous feeling of satisfaction that I note the progress that has been made in the past year in raising the profile within the Church of the importance of Inter-Faith engagement. This can be clearly seen in the increasing demands on my time to help facilitate that said engagement and to speak at events and conferences from various parts of the Church. There is a tremendous energy and good will in recognising the importance of such work and the need to build on what has already been done.

2.8 iMPACT

Graham Allison is the Regional Development Officer responsible for co-ordination of the iMPACT programme, which traces its history from 1934 through Seaside and Summer Mission. Graham has been involved in youth work and parish life for over 12 years and is qualified in Theology, Community Education and Youth Work. For further information, please view www.impactscotland. org.uk.

2.8.1 A principal aim of iMPACT is to assist local churches to reach out to children and young people, characteristically in partnership during a Summer Mission Week. Over time the expectation is that a local congregation will develop its capacity to the point where it need no longer be partnered by an incoming iMPACT team of young volunteers, and the team members thus released can be deployed to 'plant' mission activities elsewhere. Sustainable local relationships are key to the ethos of iMPACT.

2.8.2 Other forms of support on offer include 'home-run' missions projects, where the local church conducts its own programme of events but is affiliated to iMPACT and has access to free equipment. iMPACT provides support in terms of advice, planning and prayer.

2.8.3 In the course of 2008, iMPACT missions took place in a variety of locations, urban, rural and island, some new and some longer established. More information is contained in the iMPACT Annual report, which can be supplied upon request to the Mission and Discipleship Council offices in Glasgow.

2.8.4 Wee iMPACT Groups (WiG) operate in Glasgow and Edinburgh and help maintain relationships and contact between volunteers throughout the year, as well as providing occasions for Bible study and open discussion. Bigger iMPACT is a regular gathering for volunteer support, which attracted about 35 participants at a weekend event at the Ardeonaig Outdoor Centre. The event included worship, fellowship and outdoor activity.

2.8.5 Discussions are currently underway to determine how best to develop iMPACT networks through web sites linked appropriately to the Church of Scotland web pages.

2.8.6 Over 2009 iMPACT will function with approximately 10 teams running in various parts of Scotland. 2009 marks 75 years of this special form of outreach. This will likely involve various events for reflection, as well as many open consultations at local and regional levels on what mission can be in the Church of Scotland. Planning for this is currently underway.

2.9 Mission Accompaniment

One of the means of supporting the local church is the process of Mission Accompaniment, which the Task Group maintains an interest in. In his book *Journey into Growth, the Seven Core Values of a Mission Church*, Terry Tennans defines Mission Accompaniment as, *'a process undertaken*

by a local church… in conjunction with an outsider to help them develop as mission communities.' It is this 'outsider' who is the Mission Accompanier. Tennans goes on to use some helpful phases to help us understand this role of accompaniment.

> *The friendly stranger using the Emmaus story;*
> *the skilful outsider who uses their talent as facilitator;*
> *enablers who release the potential in people;*
> *advisers who signpost a range of resources out there.*

2.9.1 The Mission Accompaniment in Scotland group was set up in 2006 as an ecumenical core group to provide spiritual resourcing and renewal for those working as 'accompaniers', to provide opportunities for training, and to develop a network for learning, support and encouragement.

2.9.2 Over the past year the core group has organised two day events. In November 2008 at the North Queensferry hotel, practitioners met together to look at *Leadership for the Neutral Zone, Between the Trapezes.* Based on the work of William Bridges, asking how accompaniers can understand, and so help, congregations who find themselves in places of transition, between the 'redundant old' and the 'hoped for new'.

> *One doesn't discover new lands without consenting to lose sight of the shore for a very long time*
> (Andre Gide)

2.9.3 The second session explored *Understanding the Principles of the Myers Briggs Type Indicator.* In working with ministers and leadership teams, what role does personality play and how does that influence the dynamic of accompaniment?

2.9.4 The second event being planned is a networking meeting where practitioners will be invited to gather at Carberry Tower for support and encouragement. The speaker will be Rev Ewan Aitken, Council Secretary of the Church and Society Council, who will set the context of the work of accompaniment as the church seeks to witness in 21st Century Scotland.

2.9.5 To find out more about the Mission Accompaniment Scotland group or how Mission Accompaniment please refer to the Church of Scotland website (www.churchofscotland.org.uk/councils/mission disciple). A look at Future Focus in the resources section of the website could also be helpful (www.churchofscotland. org.uk/councils/missiondisciple/mdresources).

2.10 Welcoming Immigrants into the Life and Leadership of the Church
The Task Group hopes to be able to announce to the General Assembly that this material, reported upon in previous years, is now available.

2.11 HOPE Alba
The Task Group has been associated on behalf of the Council with this outreach initiative, which has already seen over 200 churches and other organisations commit throughout Scotland to carrying out 'hours of kindness' in local communities, and has encouraged the development of 'Festivals of HOPE' – a month of service projects culminating with a Family Fun Day.

2.11.1 In 2009 HOPE is sponsoring two national initiatives for local schools: the HOPE Schools Challenge and the 'Global Village' interactive mission exhibit (designed for both schools and churches).

3. Worship and Doctrine
3.1 Seeing the World As Others See It
The Council has been encouraged by the very favourable comments made by those groups in Presbyteries which have taken the opportunity of using this resource. It has proved to be a most worthwhile exercise to produce these studies which endeavour to assist congregations and groups within Presbyteries in exploring the Report to the General Assembly of 2007 entitled 'A Challenge to

Unity: Same – Sex Relationships as an issue in Theology and Human Sexuality'. It is the hope of the Council that many other congregations may use this resource in future and find it beneficial in developing an understanding of this important area. The Report is available to download from www.resourcingchurches.org.uk.

3.2 The Language of the Trinity
The Council has resolved, with the support of the Council, that the instruction of the General Assembly in 2005 to explore the issue of the Language of the Trinity has been fulfilled with the completion of a series of studies on an ecumenical basis through ACTS. These studies will be sent to every minister in the Church. It is the hope that these case studies will enable reflection and clarification of a particularly challenging issue in Theology.

3.3 Congregational Resources
The Council is grateful to all those who submit entries for 'Starters for Sunday', which is used by ministers and worship leaders throughout the world (the resource has received over 100,000 hits on the website between April 2008 and February 2009 – www.churchofscotland.org.uk/worship). The Council commends the continuing publication of *Pray Now 2009* which has had a wide circulation within the Church. The resources magazine for musicians and others interested in congregational praise, *Different Voices*, was launched at the 2008 General Assembly. It has been well received and it is hoped will gain an increasing use within the Church and beyond, thereby ensuring the long term viability of this publication.

3.4 Scots Language in Worship
Resources for various seasons of the Christian year are regularly updated and appreciated by those who wish to include particular dialects in their regular worship services.

3.5 Theology and Safeguarding
The Task Group has continued to be involved in the production of a Report to the General Assembly on 'Forgiveness and Proportionality' in co-operation with the

Safeguarding Committee. The Report will be considered at this year's General Assembly, in association with the Report of the Safeguarding Committee. (on page 6.5/5).

3.6 Holy Communion Working Group

The Council welcomes the production of the Report (Appendix I) on this issue. The Report which is presented to the General Assembly is the result of an enormous amount of research and reflection by the Working Group, involving some regional 'Roadshows' demonstrating a real and important enthusiasm by lay and ordained members for the exploration of the celebration of the Sacrament. The Report will be followed by the publication, in due course, of a commentary on Holy Communion Order One in *Common Order* (1994), with other resources on a CD Rom. It is hoped that this will assist both ministers and congregations in their spiritual development and appreciation of the elements of this Sacrament.

3.7 Human Sexuality Working Group

This Council brings another Report (Appendix II) on aspects on human sexuality to the General Assembly. This Report deals with singleness and the Council believes that it will enable and encourage congregations to affirm the importance of the contribution of single people to the ongoing life and witness of the Church of Scotland. Resources for discussion will be made available to stimulate and support discussion in Presbyteries and Congregations.

3.7.1 With this work, the Working Group completes the second part of its work and its members are thanked for their commitment of time, energy and effort, over a number of years, to the consideration of some vital issues of theology. It is hoped that many of the current group will be involved in the production of a report on marriage and its theological and sociological significance in the early 21st Century.

3.8 Church Hymnary Trustees

The 2008 General Assembly noted the concerns of the Council concerning the *Church Hymnary fourth edition*, and instructed the Council to seek conversations with the Church Hymnary Trustees.

3.8.1 The Council reports that these conversations have taken place and that on that occasion the Council was represented by the Rev Alan Birss, Convener of the Worship and Doctrine Task Group, the Rev Nigel J Robb, Associate Secretary, and the Rev Douglas A O Nicol, Council Secretary.

4. Education and Nurture

4.1 Introduction

The Task Group continues to be aware of just how crucial the work of education and nurture is to the life of the Church of Scotland. Task Group members are motivated by a sense of responsibility to resource individuals and local churches. This conviction is confirmed through encounters and relationships facilitated by the events, projects and resources for which the Task Group and its related staff members have responsibility. Our strongly-held belief is that the mission of the church is driven by the education and nurture of the church. If an individual's faith is not living and growing then that faith is unable to go anywhere and do anything! Education and Nurture is not seen as the mere transmission of knowledge. There is no benefit in knowledge if an individual's development lags behind. The Task Group has committed itself to the endeavour of growing the Church of Scotland's educational work with children, young people and adults. If we are successful the mission of the Church will also be successful.

4.1.1 The staff associated with the Task Group work with individuals and groups from all over Scotland and beyond. There is regular contact with the world church and groups from many parts of the world have shown an interest in various aspects of our work. For example, churches in Ireland, Denmark and Kenya are looking closely at the way we run our National Youth Assembly. Closer to home, our staff team is committed to being on the journey with individuals and local churches as they try to grow into the mission they feel called to be involved in. Most of our work is carried out through conversations where people are encouraged to seize the day, to take risks and to move forward.

4.1.2 The Task Group is aware of the fragile nature of this area of the Church's work. New and fresh thinking can often mean exposing our vulnerabilities. As we interpret and discern God's will for this work today we take careful but risky steps. The notion of setting, interpreting, facilitating and actioning an agenda is developed with gentle care and sensitive attention to the individuals with whom we seek to grow. In this way we are all nurtured together.

4.2 Ministry to and with Children and younger teenagers
4.2.1 Remembering the UN Year of the Child
This year sees the 30th anniversary of the United Nations Year of the Child. Much of 2008 was spent in preparation for this year which will see several new initiatives stemming from a desire to include children fully in our life and work as followers of Christ.

4.2.1.1 The first of these initiatives is the launching of the Child Friendly Church programme. The Child Friendly Church Programme invites congregations to consider why and how we welcome and work with children in our faith communities. It is hoped that every congregation in the Kirk will participate fully in this programme. Information will be sent to every congregation and encouragement is given to participate fully in this programme.

4.2.1.2 The second initiative is to revisit the Children's Forums which were a central part of our own Year of the Child in 2001. Last year at the General Assembly 18 Ambassadors from the National Children's Assembly asked their own questions of the Convener of our Task Group. The children deeply valued that opportunity to be heard and indeed showed all of us that their voices are well worth listening to. The Children's Forums are designed to begin listening again to children. We need as many congregations to join us in this venture so that we are able to analyse the responses to the questions and then build a strategy for ministry to and with children based on the findings of each congregation. We hope to launch a National Strategy in 2010 which will offer signposts for nurture and discipleship along the way for folk working with children and, most importantly, for children themselves.

4.2.2 Worship initiatives
At the heart of our faith is worship and the lack of appropriate music for children has been recognised. We are offering a long-term music programme, 'Sing Out!' Everyone is invited to send us original compositions of songs for children. A small committee of people (including children) will sift through the offerings and will select songs that will 'work'. In return for a very modest fee, congregations will be able to use the songs and will receive them on CD with sheet music and guitar cords. This model has been borrowed from colleagues in the church in Sweden where over the last few years it has successfully increased the amount of quality worship songs for children in the churches there.

4.2.2.1 Alongside this we are currently involved in a tour with Fischy Music and the Music and Worship Foundation where we offer workshops and the opportunity to experience new songs from Fischy Music.

4.2.3 Redeeming Hallowe'en
In 2008 Hallowe'en received a lot of publicity! We want to reclaim that holiday from the fancy dress and confectionary industries and other interested parties. We are working with the Boys' Brigade to host a party on 31 October celebrating the eve of All Saints Day. Fuller details about this event will be available after the General Assembly.

4.2.3.1 We intend to offer as many different ways to play as possible. At the heart of this day will be the recognition of the Saints who have gone before us, who surround us in that 'cloud of witnesses', the Saints who will come after us and the Saints we encounter daily. We will centre this day on an act of worship which we believe will enable the children to rejoice in their childhood and in the One who gives us the gift of life.

4.2.4 The National Children's Assembly
Our second National Children's Assembly took place in early November in Aviemore. Our hope was that many of the children from the North of the country would join us and we were thrilled with the response. We had a great time exploring the theme, 'Small World BIG Faith!'

4.2.4.1 In 2009 we are working with the World Mission Council to bring together 50 children from partner churches and 50 children from Scotland. In this year of Homecoming we are all going 'home' to Iona – for many the birthplace of Christianity in Scotland. Our theme for this event is 'ONE' – one Lord, one Faith, one Baptism, one Body, yet in that oneness is great diversity which we will celebrate! We are thrilled to have the Storytelling Centre collaborating on this event too and look forward to hearing the stories of all the children.

4.2.5 A new confirmation programme
We regularly receive requests for confirmation materials for young people or materials to help facilitate membership classes for young people who are thinking about becoming members of the Church. A small group of experienced youth workers has been working on a year-long confirmation programme for teenagers in S1-S4 which will introduce them to the Christian faith, the way faith is expressed in the Church of Scotland and how it then fits into the wider religious scene in Scotland today. This is a radical new venture for younger teenagers in the Kirk and creates the possibility for congregations to take more direct responsibility for the faith development of young people in this age group. At the time of writing this Report the materials are being piloted in congregations

around Scotland and it is anticipated that they will be available in June of this year.

4.2.6 General Assembly Youth Night
The 2008 General Assembly Youth Night event was a great success. The audience was amazed by the talents of the London Community Gospel Choir who were able to get people out of their seats and dancing around the General Assembly Hall. This year's event took place on Saturday evening at St George's West Church.

4.2.7 Cosycoffeehouse
A few years ago we launched the Cosycoffeehouse – a coffeehouse in a box. This initiative allows local churches to provide safe places for young people to gather and socialise with each other and with folks from the congregations. Cosycoffeehouses are popping up all over Scotland with the one furthest north now taking place in Orkney. There are also coffeehouses being run in a few military bases throughout the country.

4.2.8 The Cosy Youth Work Kit
A companion kit, the Cosy Youth Work Kit (a youth ministry in a box!) has just been produced. The kit contains a compendium of resources for the local church context – a training programme for volunteer leaders, a set of learning materials for Bible class or youth group, invitation cards, posters, guidance books on resources, employing a youth worker and being a volunteer worker in the local church. In addition there's a DVD of a Cosycoffeehouse in action at Boghall Church in Bathgate. The purpose of the kit is to help to make it easier to do youth work with young people in the local church and to provide a set of tools to make the church more inviting and to enable the church to reach out to young people in the local community.

4.2.9 The future of youth work in the Church of Scotland
In 2006 the General Assembly agreed on a Strategy for Young People. It is the belief of the Task Group that the new policy is just one step in a whole series that need to

be taken by the Church of Scotland over the next decade. Over the summer and winter months an Advisory Group, consisting of a number of key practitioners in the youth work arena along with members of the Task Group and Council staff, has been meeting to consider the future of youth work in the Church of Scotland and its preliminary findings are appended to this Report in Appendix III. The Group seeks permission to explore the key themes and possibilities it has identified over the coming months and to consult as widely as possible with a view to returning to the General Assembly of 2010 with a series of proposals that will be ambitious and will encourage the Church to step forward in faith with confidence and hope. It is the belief of the Advisory Group that it is time to change the culture and context for youth work in the Church of Scotland.

4.3   Work with young adults and adults

4.3.1   The National Youth Assembly

The National Youth Assembly continues to grow not just in numbers but also in depth of experience in terms of faith, worship and encounter with the Church. The report from last year's event which was held in Dundee will be considered in its own place at the General Assembly but it is worth noting here that the 2009 and 2010 events will take place at Stirling University affording the opportunity to continue that sense of growth mentioned above.

4.3.1.1 The Task Group would like to record its deep appreciation to the scores of volunteers who work tirelessly over the 4 days of the National Youth Assembly to make it such a success.

4.3.2   World Youth Day

World Youth Day 2008 took place in Sydney, Australia. As in previous World Youth Days, the Church of Scotland was invited by the Roman Catholic Church in Scotland to send a delegation and a group of just under 30 young people and staff made the long trip to Sydney in July of last year. It was an amazing experience and a worthwhile encounter with the world church. Young people were able to make

contact with young people from a local reformed church in the Sydney area as well as being involved in the many events associated with World Youth Day itself.

4.3.2.1 Sometimes people wonder why we encourage young people to get involved in this type of event. We do it because they can encounter the world. We do it because it will be an experience of faith and fellowship that they will never forget for as long as they live. We do it because for most of those who made the trip it will provide a significant step of growth in their journey of faith. Finally we do it because sometimes we have to stand beside people who are different from us to better understand who we are, as well as why we are different from each other, but also what we have in common.

4.3.3   Pilgrimage to Israel/Palestine

In November of 2008 a group of youth workers, Council staff and young adults made a pilgrimage to Israel and Palestine. The journey began in Tiberias and concluded in Jerusalem. Instead of simply focussing on the traditional holy sites, time was spent meeting with the 'living stones' and talking to people from all of the communities there. The members of the group found the experience invaluable. A further trip is planned in late June this year.

4.3.3.1 The Task Group would like to record its appreciation of the World Mission Council in securing accommodation for the group in the Church of Scotland centres.

4.3.4   *Threads*: weaving faith and life in the Local Church

Threads is being launched at the General Assembly. It is an exciting new DVD video resource, rooted in the Church of Scotland, telling the stories of ordinary people living out their lives as Christians in the world.

4.3.4.1 Each 20 minute episode weaves faith and life through the eyes of various people, places and situations – the Kirk's Story; the Sacraments; working in partnership at home and abroad; being ecumenical; involvement in politics and society; being alongside the marginalised; working with HIV/AIDS; exploring the journey of faith through celebration and joy as well as struggle and doubt.

4.3.4.2 Discussion material is provided for each episode making *Threads* an ideal resource for small group discussion: enquirers groups, membership classes, house groups, Lent groups or in schools.

4.3.4.3 *Threads* is available to order from www.madstuff.biz, along with all of the other resources mentioned in this Report.

4.3.5 People with Learning Disabilities

The Council's Learning Disabilities Group, in partnership with the Ministries and Social Care Councils, ran a successful conference last year with the Rev Prof John Swinton as the lead speaker. John's challenging talk on the theology of disability encouraged participants to think through various issues: how can the church claim to be church, if it does not see people with learning disabilities as vital for the faithfulness of its community? What might we learn from people with learning disabilities that can enable us to worship more faithfully? Here is a quote from someone who attended the conference:

By far the best bit of the day was attended by people who have disabilities who were prepared to stand up and be counted and tell us first hand what it is about churches that are off-putting. I personally will change the way I do things and it has challenged me.

Just wanted to let you know how much I learned from the conference. The style of worship was accessible and fun. It was such a worthwhile day.

I was struck by how many of the problems facing people with learning disabilities are very similar to people with physical disabilities who are quite articulate. For instance, I too can't tell you how many times I have felt hurt and loss

at the departure, often sudden, of a carer with whom I had built up a relationship of trust and understanding which seems to be shattered by a rapid career move or something.

4.3.5.1 The Working Group is currently planning more conferences in the coming year for service users and leaders, elders and ministers. It is also looking to write new material providing suitable resources for local churches.

4.3.6 NiteKirk

The Nitekirk ran for a week in Greyfriars Kirk as part of the Edinburgh Fringe Festival. The event was awarded four stars by one review:

This is a cool, quiet, relaxing place to spend an evening. Open until after midnight. Greyfriars plays host to singing, poetry and prayer for the ears and art installations for the eyes. There are different events each night and several of the art installations are interactive, including a cross to nail your frustrations to. It's all quite therapeutic.

4.3.6.1 The main purpose of the NiteKirk was to provide a sacred place of stillness and quiet amongst the busyness of the Fringe Festival and the busyness of people's lives. The church was decked with soft lighting, candles and art installations to create a welcoming and atmospheric place. Throughout the evening the offerings of music, poetry and prayer, silence and hospitality enfolded those who came.

4.3.6.2 Rev Richard Frazer, Minister of Greyfriars Kirk, shares his reflections:

I realised we try to cram things in to people in church. We preach endless sermons and talk of what we believe in the hope that other people will believe what we believe. The NiteKirk was about stillness and space and slowing down. It was about discovering what is already in us rather than putting something in. It has reinforced my growing weariness about religious motivation. What do we really mean by our mission? What are we trying to do to people?

4.3.6.3 The Nitekirk volunteers got as much out of the experience as those who visited. It is their hope that the NiteKirk will continue in the Autumn on a more regular basis. Many who visited experienced a time of spiritual anointing and renewal: to view the experience, log onto www.youtube.com/fidge01.

4.3.7 25+ Network

In the course of the last few months this initiative has had a change of name and is now known as I CAN (Church Adult Network). This is a recognition that this type of loose, relational approach is appropriate not just for the young adults who 'graduate' from the National Youth Assembly, but also to many other people in a wide range of age groups. In the past year people have gathered at a variety of regional events and at the Greenbelt Festival in Cheltenham. Significant friendships have developed between members of the group which drives the work forward on an informal basis as well as within the events organised by Council Staff.

4.3.8 Working with Elders and Leaders

What's in a name? Well it can say a lot or very little! In 2008 the Eldership Working Party (EWP) decided to change the name of 'Elder Trainer' to 'Adult Trainer'. This is to give an indication that many of the training materials originally marketed under the 'Elder' banner, are now used widely within the life of the church.

4.3.8.1 So where are we going with adult training? In seeking to 'build for the future', the EWP has agreed the twin priorities of Leadership Development and Pastoral Care.

4.3.8.2 We will continue to train Elder Moderators and offer support to Session Clerks. In late 2009 and early 2010, 'Leadership Forums' for ministers and session clerks will be offered around the country, seeking to answer the question, *'What should leadership look like in the life of the local congregation in 21st century Scotland?'* This will lead up to a visit by Alan Roxburgh from Canada, author of *The Missional Leader* and *The Sky is Falling Down*, later on in 2010.

4.3.8.3 We will also begin to investigate the important issues of 'mentoring' and bridge building in conflict situations.

4.3.8.4 Developments in pastoral care will focus on a new pastoral care DVD which will look at:
- How to set up and develop a local congregational Pastoral Care Group.
- The pastoral care of young people.
- The pastoral care of children in hospital or ill/recovering at home.
- The pastoral care of people with learning disabilities.
- Issues of terminal care and bereavement.
- Visiting in hospital: what is good practice?
- Dementia and the confused elderly.

4.3.8.5 Before this Assembly there will have been a residential weekend looking at *Bereavement Visiting and Funeral Training*. We have also begun to work with the charity Faith in Older People (FiOP) to look at pastoral care and the spirituality of aging.

4.3.8.6 Tying all of this together will be analysis of a national questionnaire in 2008 which asked Kirk Sessions how they were organised for leadership and pastoral care. The purpose of the exercise was to –
a) Inform the Eldership Working Party that has been given the responsibility to develop the work of the Eldership.
b) Enable the Eldership Working Party to have an overview of how Kirk Sessions are working.
c) Assist the Eldership Working Party in developing new resources for the future.
d) Share examples of good practice with others.

4.3.8.7 Due to the timing of the questionnaire, it is not possible, at this stage, to give any analysis. However, what can be said, in the return of over 650 completed forms, is that congregations in every mainland Presbytery responded, so giving any analysis the credibility of a national geographical spread. We have no doubt that the results of this questionnaire will inform the work of the Mission and Discipleship Council, in the area of Eldership, in the coming years.

4.3.8.8 The EWP seeks to support eldership within the life of the church. Contact details and available training opportunities can be found through our publicity and training leaflets and through the Church of Scotland website, www.churchofscotland.org.uk/councils/mission disciple/mdresources.

- 2009 training leaflet entitled *Adult Training and Leadership Development.*
- *The Eldership Past and Present* reflecting on the history and character of the Eldership.
- A leaflet for new and prospective Elders entitled *WHO ME?*

4.3.9   Concluding remarks

The work involving the Education and Nurture Task Group is actioned and realised through inspired individuals who have a desire to respond vocationally to God's call. The many creative, fresh and illuminating ideas come from a place of discernment and reflection. The filter of discussion and enquiry allow a vigorous process that is always open to the whispers of the Holy Spirit. This work is a gift to those involved directly. May it have been and continue to be a gift to the whole Church.

5.   Publishing

5.1 The Publishing Committee oversees the Church's publishing house, Saint Andrew Press, and the finances of *Life and Work* and *Ministers' Forum*.

5.2   Saint Andrew Press

In 2008, Saint Andrew Press publications included:
- *Insights: Christmas* by William Barclay
- *Insights: Lord's Prayer* by William Barclay
- *More than Words* by the Worship and Doctrine Task Group
- *Glasgow Bible* CD by Jamie Stuart
- *Preacher's A-Z* by Richard Littledale
- *Worship Anthology* by Women Ordained to Word and Sacrament
- *Take Up the Song* CD by CH4 panel
- *Vows of Baptism* by David Hamilton
- *Church of Scotland Diary 2009*
- *Scandal of Grace* by Nick Baines
- *My Father – Reith of the BBC* by Marista Leishman (paperback)
- *The Illustrated Children's Bible* by Imgard Weth
- *Finding Faith* by Nick Baines
- *Pray Now* by the Worship and Doctrine Task Group

5.2.1 The new *Insights* series is designed to provide fascinating insight into the Bible in short books that provide great inspiration. The insights come from William Barclay and guest contributors such as Sally Magnusson, John Bell, Richard Harries and Diane Louise Jordan. The series has already been widely acclaimed.

5.2.2 A number of the above Saint Andrew Press publications and their authors were featured in newspapers, periodicals, radio, television and literary and Christian festivals, raising the profile of the Church's Christian message.

5.2.3 The Church's publishing arm has successfully completed the second year of its rolling five-year business plan, aimed at increasing mission while decreasing costs in a long-term, sustainable way. The five-year plan is designed to further strengthen Saint Andrew Press's position as a key communication tool for the Church and as a force in Christian publishing, giving it greater long-term stability, reducing net costs over time in a sustainable way and giving Christian publications maximum impact.

a) The Church's publishing arm is producing books, Church stationery and printed resources designed to inform, enable and encourage church members and congregations in Christian mission and discipleship. The publishing arm is also expanding on its range of ways to reach the widest possible readership and is maintaining tight budgetary control in a changing market.

b) Saint Andrew Press is expanding its mission by developing new platforms over which to offer its Christian material. In addition to conventional printing, each publication will be considered for Print On Demand. Online download availability and various digital options are being explored. The new diversity of delivery is a key element of the future output of Saint Andrew Press.

c) When books are obtained through the website, www. standrewpress.com, most of the income is retained by the Church and the Publishing Committee encourages the website's use.

d) The Publishing Committee would like to thank the Church's IT Department and the Website Editor, Shirley James, for all their hard work on the website.

e) Four people are employed directly to work on Church of Scotland publishing, for Saint Andrew Press. They are Head of Publishing, Ann Crawford; Editorial Manager, Richard Allen; Sales and Marketing Manager, Jonny Gallant and Administrator, Christine Causer.

f) The Publishing Committee welcomes approaches from all parts of the Church in order to fulfil its remit from the Council of Assembly as the first point of contact for all those agencies of the Church seeking to have work published.

g) Saint Andrew Press is making direct contact with a number of individual churches in a variety of ways in order to establish the most effective methods of ensuring that churches are aware of the resources available and are able to advise Saint Andrew Press of any resources that they would like to see published.

h) Through many kinds of partnership and collaboration, Saint Andrew Press has forged strong ecumenical and international links. Its books are read in many countries

while, at home, Saint Andrew Press is collaborating on projects such as the Scotland's Churches Scheme series of regional guides.

5.2.4 The Publishing Committee and Saint Andrew Press wish to extend their thanks to the Rev Ronald S Blakey, Editor of *The Church of Scotland Year Book*, for another fine edition that, once again, was published well within the deadline.

5.3 *Life and Work*

Life and Work remains the best-selling monthly religious title in the UK. Advertising continues to thrive, bucking the trend of the marketplace. The magazine has once again returned a six-figure net surplus which benefits the Church's income stream.

5.3.1 *Life and Work* is a key congregational resource offering the opportunity to engage with and understand the National Church. The magazine and its letters pages provide a forum for a wide variety of ethical and church issues. 2009 marks the 130th anniversary of the founding of the magazine by Professor Archibald Charteris. *Life and Work* has continually developed and changed throughout its history and in its current 60-page format offers readers a wide variety of content.

5.3.2 *Life and Work* Advisory Committee

The Editor's Advisory Committee has met three times during 2008 and is utilised as necessary between meetings. The Editor continues to be grateful for the support and advice of this important Committee and its individual members.

5.3.3 Circulation and Finance

Life and Work continues to operate in a challenging marketplace but remains the second biggest-selling monthly Scottish-based magazine with a circulation above 30,000. The magazine is predominantly delivered through congregations but is also available by direct mail subscription. A recent reader survey confirms that the magazine is widely shared, indicating that on average two people read every copy printed. The finances of the magazine remain healthy in spite of the cover price being held £1.60 for four years.

5.3.4 Staffing

Editor Lynn McNeil has been absent on maternity leave for a year, giving birth to a healthy daughter at Easter 2008. Deputy Editor Muriel Armstrong has been Editor of the magazine during this period. Day to day staffing has been maintained at four throughout the year – three editorial and one administration.

5.4 *Ministers' Forum*

Ministers' Forum continues to provide a means for ministers to debate issues of concern, as well as sharing resources and ideas which may be helpful to others. It is distributed to people in all types of full time ministry, as well as to retired ministers who request it. Many ministers have contacted the Editor, John Ferguson, to express their appreciation of the fact that they can discuss the highs and lows of ministry, along with various theological and ecclesiastical issues, through the pages of the magazine. The importance of editorial independence is appreciated by the Committee and it will continue to support this.

6. Church Art and Architecture

6.1 Dr Samuel Johnson, the great lexicographer and commentator on life and literature once remarked 'There are only two things certain in this life: Death and Taxes'. Perhaps this needs to be corrected and developed. It could be legitimately argued that there are only three things in life that are certain: death, taxes and change. Change is the essential part of life, and indeed part of the gospel and the Church itself.

6.2 The gospel is about change. From the stories of the covenant in the Old Testament through the teaching of Jesus and the apostles, we are reminded that God intends humanity to change. Change here is the sense of grasping the opportunities for new life and ways of living according to the manner God intended. The message of the scriptures is clear: there is grace offered by God that allows human beings to change. This change creates radical reassessment of priorities and the adoption of new patterns and behaviours.

6.3 Since the earliest of times, buildings of the church have changed. From the development of the house church communities of ancient Rome and the Ancient Near Eastern World, domestic architecture was developed by the leaders of the church to accommodate the growing movement of Christianity. In some instances the church adopted and adapted buildings which had been used for worship of other deities in previous generations. They also adapted several features of 'classical' architecture, and the style of many other public buildings influenced the church buildings of the Roman and the Eastern Empire. The changes which occurred in the early life of the Church continued throughout the centuries, and today we have churches built in the Norman style, the Gothic style, the Georgian style and the Victorian style, and in a variety of architectural approaches in the 20th century, where a number of movements could be seen coming together.

6.4 The Committee believes that the essential element of any exploration of a possible change lies in the question: 'How will these alterations, adaptations and creative developments allow the Church to fulfil its charter as bringing mission and worship to the centre of this community? 'With a flexible building that conceives of worship as its central aim, the Church may engage with the community and endeavour to serve its community, as a secondary purpose of its building. In all times and places, despite differences in geography and circumstances, the Committee are convinced that the purpose of the church building remains the same: 'to be a place where the Faith is caught and the Sacraments are administered'.

6.5 Alongside this trend of change in architecture, we need to recognise also that worship has changed over the centuries. What we do now in the church, though having its roots in the New Testament record, and Jewish religious practice in the time of Jesus and before, would not necessarily be always as clearly recognisable to the early church as we might think. Worship in the Reformed Tradition has certainly changed from the time of the Reformation. Worship today, in the congregations of the Church of Scotland, is distinctly changed from much of what John Knox and Andrew Melville introduced into post Reformation worship.

6.6 The Church of Scotland has always been open to change in its worship, having no prescribed form of liturgy which must be observed at all times and in all places. In particular, during the 19th Century, for a variety of reasons, the worship life of congregations was greatly enriched and transformed.

6.7 Today is another time of change and growth in worship patterns and leadership, with the level of participation in leadership dramatically increasing. All this had and has a direct impact on the way we design and adapt our buildings for public worship.

6.8 There is a need for churches to accommodate more involvement of a wide variety of people in the leadership of worship. There is also a need for more movement and a desire to include those who are able and those who are less physically able in the leadership of worship. Church buildings were not always built with the needs and requirements of those who have physical disability. Therefore church buildings that we are constructing and reordering today, need to be flexible, and ready to adapt to a future we cannot predict.

6.9 We have inherited a number of very fine buildings, which contribute to the ecclesiastical and cultural heritage of Scotland. They lend themselves to worship of a certain tradition and type. However, many of our buildings need to adapt, grow and alter, if we are to accommodate new developments which are exciting, invigorating and enlivening congregations throughout Scotland.

6.10 The Church of Scotland has an important role in maintaining the contribution of its buildings to the wider culture of Scotland. Many of the buildings are of distinct architectural or historic merit and this puts obligations upon the church to be sensitive and careful in its approval of any alteration and development.

6.11 Some changes may relate to financial issues, *eg* the cost of heating is often a challenge; or the different types of worship which are being offered to people today; or the kind of witness to the whole community that a congregation wishes to bring, and the need for flexibility. However, the Committee is convinced that any changes which are introduced must be rooted firmly in theological reflection.

6.12 The Committee on Church Art and Architecture is not, therefore, supporting change for the sake of change alone. Change is a message of the gospel, and a challenge in the preaching of Jesus, for us all to grow more Christ-like. The Committee is convinced that any proposal for change must emphasise the conviction that the mission and worship of the Church need to be central to any proposals. Any church building alteration and adaptation must be based on an appropriate response to the religious changes affecting not only the local congregation, but the church as a whole. The changes which are introduced ought to be informed by sensitivity towards the original design of the building, alongside a desire to provide for the ongoing requirements of the worship and mission of the current congregation.

6.13 The Committee, with the close co-operation of the General Trustees, is committed to assisting congregations as they grapple with the challenge of using and developing church buildings to meet the needs of congregations today and tomorrow. The Committee exists to help congregations think about how a building currently serves the mission of the church, and how the congregation may improve that service through creative and imaginative alteration.

6.14 The Committee is convinced that the buildings of the Church of Scotland are crucial resources for parishes and ministries which may be severely under-estimated. Without a focus and a place to conduct worship and mission, the community of the Church may be severely limited in its work and witness.

6.15 The Committee recognises that church buildings, in pre-Reformation times, were often used as community centres, serving a wide variety of uses. The Committee believes that this is an important option for many congregations to consider today. A flexible church building in a rural, or urban, community, may offer a wide variety of uses and give opportunities for the inclusion of a number of people that remain untouched by the normal Sunday worship and other missionary activities of a congregation. While the Committee recognises that diversification of use is often an important part of the consideration of any planned adaptation, this must only be considered alongside the vital importance of worship and mission. It is also important for congregations to realise that, in many instances, the re-ordering and re-design of a church building may not increase its income base, but instead become more costly in terms of the financial responsibilities created by a multitude of uses.

6.16 The main point of this whole discussion is that the mission and worship of the church should be the primary focus of whatever the congregation is proposing. There is a need to hold the dimensions of change alongside the dimensions of the past, and see how they have shaped and characterised the congregation, alongside the need for change and adaptability in order for the Church to achieve its potential as a future and present servant of the gospel.

6.17 The General Assembly will be aware that there are huge advantages in the Church enjoying the privilege of ecclesiastical exemption in relation to the alteration of its buildings. This important advantage is maintained through congregations remembering to contact the Committee and the General Trustees prior to any development and alteration which affects the fabric of a Church Building. Failure to do so will endanger the Churches ongoing status relating to 'ecclesiastical exemption', and congregations are urged to make early contact so that the Committee might be involved from the beginning.

6.18 The Committee is aware that it needs to take account more of what younger people are saying about the style and content of church buildings. The Committee is, therefore, very grateful to the National Youth Assembly organisers who have graciously offered the opportunity for the Committee to make a short presentation on its work in September, prior to inviting the delegates at the National Youth Assembly to give the members of the Committee some reflections on the priorities they have for the design and arrangements of buildings, and the value many young people place on our historic inheritance. The Committee also appreciates the opportunity to be part of the consultation with the Presbytery representatives of the Mission and Discipleship Council in March to hear what assistance and support might be offered to congregations in future.

6.20 The Committee has looked at the budgetary expectations which have been laid upon the Mission and Discipleship Council, and has resolved that it will meet less often, but perhaps for a longer period, to consider particular cases. Smaller groups with expertise on stained glass, church organs, and other specialisms, have also been formed to expedite the business.

6.21 As a part of the Committee's commitment to ease the work of the congregations, and any delays which they are encountering, in achieving a decision, the Committee requests that all submissions are made by electronic means, so that papers can be circulated to the membership, and an opinion and a result can be communicated quickly on proposals. The Committee is still convinced of the need for regular, if less frequent, meetings to reflect on major works of re-ordering, refurbishment and alteration, but hopes that it might be able to make decisions which reflect the gathered wisdom of the Committee quickly and helpfully to enable congregations to respond to particular needs.

6.22 The Committee is pleased to acknowledge with gratitude the continued support of the Sacramental Vessels project by the Goldsmiths Trust. The Trust has generously granted financial aid to assist in the provision of a survey of all the sacramental vessels of congregations of the Church of Scotland. Over 60% of the survey has been completed and Mr Kirkpatrick Dobie has continued to assist the Church with his willing co-operation and devotion to this important endeavour. The Committee believes the Church will be pleased to recognise the support of the Goldsmiths Trust and congratulate Mr Dobie on his continuing involvement in this work.

6.23 The Committee is also aware of its responsibilities to ensure that the disposal of Sacramental vessels is handled appropriately. While there is an argument to support the sale of some items which may be perceived as 'surplus to requirements', this has to be done sensitively, and with due recognition of the heritage of the Church. The Committee, as directed by the General Assembly, takes all requests seriously and attempts to find an appropriate response to the request those items should be sold.

7. Mission Forum

7.1 One of the responsibilities given to the Council is the development of the Mission Forum of the Church of Scotland. The need for such a Forum was first reported to the 2004 General Assembly in the Report of the former Assembly Council when it was described as an 'informal gathering' which would carry forward the hope that 'a mission-oriented ethos should inform and affect every area of the Church's central administration'.

7.2 In the first phase of its life, seen as four years, the Mission Forum has focussed on supporting preparations for 'Edinburgh 2010', and on reflecting on the lessons learnt from a series of Case Studies designed to raise issues relating to mission in a rapidly changing Scotland.

7.3 The membership of the Forum has been drawn from all General Assembly Councils and all areas of concern of the Mission and Discipleship Council, as well as The Guild, the General Trustees, the Committee on Ecumenical Relations, the Panel on Review and Reform, the Stewardship Department, the Committee on the Parish Development Fund, Action of Churches Together in Scotland (ACTS), and the United Free Church of Scotland.

7.4 On each occasion the Forum has met, either in the Church Offices or on a Case Study, a report has been offered on the progress being made with preparations for 'Edinburgh 2010', and on Monday, 15 September 2008, the Forum arranged a Welcome Dinner for the 2010 World Council meeting in Edinburgh. A Report containing details of the preparations for 'Edinburgh 2010' is contained in the Report of the World Mission Council on page 7/30.

7.5 Over the last three years the following Case Studies have been organised:
- Granton, Edinburgh: 4 May 2006: to learn about new approaches in a parish which was due to grow from 8,000 to 45,000 in a decade
- Glasgow: 14 November 2006: to witness to way in which the Church was welcoming immigrants and asylum seekers in 'The Many Faces of Glasgow'
- Upper Tweeddale: 10 May 2007: to experience life in the rural charge of Upper Tweeddale with four parishes – Broughton, Glenholm and Kilbucho, Tweedsmuir, Skirling, and Stobo
- Dundee: 8 September 2007: to learn about the involvement of the Church with young people through three youth projects in Perth and Dundee and by visiting the National Youth Assembly
- Inverness: 22/23 April 2008: to reflect on 'Mission in the Changing Highlands and Islands' with key note speakers, Rev Prof Andrew T D McGowan, formerly

Principal of the Highland Theological College, and Mr Sandy Cumming, Chief Executive of Highlands and Islands Enterprise

- Arran: 25/26 November 2008: to explore the effects which the decline of heavy industry over recent decades has had on the life and mission of the Church, and to explore lessons that could be learnt for future strategy

7.6 Full reports on each of these Case Studies are available on request from the Council's Edinburgh Office.

7.7 On Thursday, 15 January 2009, the Mission Forum met in the Church Offices to reflect on the Case Studies and in particular to reflect on the key themes that had emerged.

7.8 The key points to emerge from the reflections were:

- The Case studies had given an excellent opportunity for representatives of the central structures to interact with the church at local level.
- The overnight Studies had been particularly valuable in giving time for open discussion.
- Members had appreciated the way in which stories had been honestly shared, and the way in which positive practical outcomes had often followed an engagement with issues. Even where positive outcomes had not been achieved, it had been good to sense an acceptance of 'risk-taking for the gospel' in local situations, and a value in sharing defeats and disappointments as much as success and achievement.
- The overall sense of creativity and positivity was tempered with a general concern over future sustainability and resourcing.
- Stories shared illustrated that local work is not inward looking, but rather had often taken its shape from a consideration of its place in the World Church.

7.9 The common themes which emerged for the mission of the church were:

1. The strategic importance of the local church relating to the community, and not standing in isolation from it – the value of partnership working and the Parish Development Fund – not only does partnership working release resources, it is also best practice in that it involves building relations with others – how can congregations be encouraged to be 'outward-looking' through partnership working?

2. The place of leadership – where there is effective leadership there can be positive action – how can we liberate creative people in congregations throughout the country?

3. The issue of 'belonging' – what do we mean by 'membership' in a generation where large swathes of Scottish society still claim allegiance to the Church of Scotland, though are not recorded on Membership Rolls? How can we recognize such allegiance in a 'loyalty' rather than a 'membership' society?

4. The strategic importance of buildings – witnesses to faith in stone and lime throughout Scotland – the need to develop buildings in town and country to be 'appropriate spaces' and the challenge of maintaining them in areas of low population density – how do we ensure that church buildings are more accessible?

5. The value of good relationships with schools – and the great opportunities of engagement with the young people of a community – how can we encourage every congregation to take up the opportunities afforded to them locally?

6. The church cannot be ahead of change and trends, but must be alert and reactive at a time when rapid change is part of life – the need for example of a fresh definition of Christian marriage and of the marriage ceremony is urgent – what are the changes happening around us today to which we must adapt, without losing the kernel of the Christian message?

7. The strategic value of prayer – and the importance that communities attribute to the church praying for the community – how can we all develop our prayer life?

8. Parishes may mean little now in urban settings, but are still of great importance in rural Scotland – should we be sharing the privilege of our territorial ministry, and the 'duty of care' which it implies, with sister denominations?

9. Need for new models of Church – both developments of existing models, including ecumenical partnerships, and also new 'emerging' patterns – how can we be bolder to take risks for Christ and His Kingdom?

10. Importance of sharing stories – all who had participated in Case Studies had commented on the good work being undertaken that was not normally known beyond the locality – sharing stories can be both an encouragement and a spur to action – what further strategies are needed to encourage 'story telling'?

8. Regional Development Team

8.1 At the heart of the Council's work of preparing and delivering resources to congregations is the work of the Development Team, made up of eight Regional Development Officers, the three Associate Secretaries, and the Council Secretary. The Team meets regularly for day and overnight meetings to plan its work, and Regional Development Officers report regularly to the Council on their work.

8.2 The eight Regional Development Officers are based at four offices:
- Edinburgh: Ms Fiona Fidgin
- Glasgow: Mr Graham Allison, Mrs Lesley Hamilton-Messer, and Rev Linda Pollock
- Inverness: Mr Steve Aisthorpe
- Perth: Rev Andy Campbell, Rev Robin McAlpine, and Mr Robert Rawson

8.3 The Regional Development Officers undertake their work on the basis of a Matrix, agreed by the Council annually in June, which notes the percentage of working time which each Regional Development Officer should spend on 'first point of contact' work with congregations in allocated Presbyteries, on specialist work, and on collaborative working across the Team. A full note of responsibilities is given in Appendix IV. Whether in 'first point of contact' or in specialist work, the focus of the Team's work is in 'congregational resourcing', and much of the work reported on throughout this Report would not happen were it not for the commitment of the Council's Development Team. Indeed, reports from individual Regional Development Officers and letters of appreciation from congregations all bear witness to the significant contribution which the Team is making throughout the Church.

8.4 In 2008, with the agreement of the Council of Assembly, the Council agreed to release Rev Linda Pollock from her 'first point of contact' responsibilities in the Presbyteries of Glasgow and Lanark to enable her to focus, in 2009 and 2010, on her specialist role of Children's Ministry. Objectives for this next phase of Linda's work have been agreed and will be monitored by the Education and Nurture Task Group.

8.5 Two new Regional Development Officers joined the Team in 2008 and reports from them illustrate the variety of work undertaken by all Team members:

8.5.1 Steve Aisthorpe, based in Inverness, writes:
Having started as Regional Development Officer for the Highlands and Western Islands in January 2008 I spent several weeks visiting as many parishes as possible, beginning to build relationships and gradually growing my understanding of the particular opportunities and challenges of different areas. One thing that struck me during those first visits was that, while many areas had congregations that were vibrant, innovative and growing, other congregations, even those most nearby, were often unaware of these encouragements. Partly with this in mind I initiated a regular newsletter for the region –

"Lengthen and Strengthen" – available at www.churchofscotland.org.uk/councils/missiondisciple/mdresources. Through this I share news of encouraging situations, highlight resources that have particular application in the region, and ensure that congregations are aware of my own activities and the support that is available to them.

At the core of my work has been introducing a number of Presbyteries and congregations to the "Future Focus" process: facilitating retreats, conferences and workshops to enable them to look afresh at their own gifts and resources, look afresh at their communities – and, through that, to prayerfully seek the Lord's vision for their future. Follow up to this involves support in managing change and coping with transition – and help in accessing resources.

Another observation from my initial visits around the region is that many ministers in isolated charges experience discouragement and loneliness and often lack relationships of mutual encouragement and support. During 2009 I plan to arrange a series of pastoral retreats for ministers and their spouses in partnership with colleagues in the Ministries Council.

Prayer, effective leadership, shared vision and the mobilization and development of the gifts and involvement of all members are common features of healthy churches in the region, and these are areas I plan to strengthen through training and consultation in 2009.

8.5.2 Lesley Hamilton-Messer, based in Glasgow, writes: *Since coming into post in June 2008, I have spent some time finding out about the area that comes under my remit, and so have in some form contacted every parish minister in the Presbyteries of*

Annandale and Eskdale, Dumfries and Kirkcudbright, Wigtown and Stranraer, Ayr, and Hamilton. I represented the Mission and Discipleship Council at the excellent "Weave" Conference in Langholm in October, and have attended meetings of both the full Presbytery of Dumfries and Kirkcudbright and their Business Committee, as well as the Special Interests Committee of the Presbytery of Wigtown and Stranraer.

I have also been in regular contact with Congregational Development Officers in Annandale and Eskdale and in Hamilton Presbyteries, and have greatly valued their insight and assistance in getting to know their respective areas better. I have been assisting Keith Ross in Hamilton Presbytery in facilitating discussions about staffing needs in six of the East Kilbride churches.

I have been working with the Core Group in Inverkip Parish Church as they continue to work out their strategy developed prior to my coming into post, and have facilitated a Day Conference in Elderslie Parish Church. In meetings with a number of individual ministers, Kirk Sessions and Boards in all of the Presbyteries I have been able to provide information about training events and to exchange information with a view to facilitating networking between churches who are engaged in or exploring similar types of work. As a result of some of these meetings, I expect to be involved in delivering training or facilitating workshops and day conferences in the months to come in several locations, as well as hopefully a larger conference involving more than one Presbytery in 2009.

I have also attended the training sessions for facilitators for "Future Focus" and am available should any congregation wish to explore this further.

9. *Future Focus: a way forward for congregations*

9.1 The 2008 General Assembly welcomed the publication of *Future Focus: a way forward for congregations* and commended it to congregations seeking to use a facilitated resource.

9.2 *Future Focus* is a 'toolbox' of ideas intended to help congregations understand their situation better, to read the signs of the times, and to answer the call of God to be all that God wants us to be in these challenging times.

9.3 The materials have been prepared by a Working Party with representation from the Council, the Ministries Council, the Panel on Review and Reform, Elder Trainers and Regional Development Officers. Detailed work on the materials has been undertaken by Rev Peter Neilson, and the Council expresses appreciation afresh to Peter for his outstanding contribution.

9.4 Since the 2008 General Assembly considerable piloting of the materials has been undertaken, with 22 volunteer facilitators having been trained. Through their work, the *Future Focus* materials have been used in a variety of congregational settings, and the Presbytery of Glasgow has used the materials in a new approach to Five Year Visits to congregations.

9.5 A process of evaluation of the materials has been undertaken in the light of these pilots and minor tweaking has been agreed. Once this has been completed, the materials will be produced in a more permanent loose-leaf format in time for a launch throughout Scotland in the Autumn of 2009.

9.6 In the meantime, use of the materials continues to be developed, and their use both at the time of Five Year Visits and in the annual review of Presbytery Plans is being investigated. It is likely that a Report to a future General Assembly will contain firm proposals on the way in which *Future Focus* can be used to support development in the life and mission of the church today and in the future.

10. Rural Scotland

10.1 Many people in Scotland could be forgiven for thinking that in certain parts of rural Scotland it is difficult to look forward positively and with hope in many areas of life. It was years before the Credit Crunch and the economic downturn that many rural communities felt the effects of restructuring and reductions in essential services. Many who live in rural Scotland have found it more costly to live there, almost paying a premium for the privilege. With a lack of affordable housing, an erosion of services and a reduction in the number of shops and businesses, many feel overwhelmed by fears about the future. However, in the midst of the uncertainty and change, there are many churches which celebrate the positive aspects of living and working in rural Scotland. In some villages, the church provides the only community space where people can gather and celebrate special occasions together. In others, the church provides some of the essential services that otherwise would not be present, from social and pastoral care, cafes and coffee shops, post offices and registrars. The Rural Strategy Team – with a particular emphasis on affirming, supporting and resourcing rural churches – seeks to support churches across rural Scotland as they strive to minister to and serve those within their parish. It is within this positive context that the Rural Strategy Team finds a basis for its work and joins, with many others, to celebrate living, effecting change and making a difference in rural Scotland

10.2 Resourcing the Rural Church
10.2.1 *God's Own Country*
In 2007 the Rural Strategy Team published *God's Own Country* as a resource offered to the church to enable strategic thought on such themes as worship, mission, community planning, children's and youth work, poverty in rural Scotland and ecological awareness. The pack continues to be well received by congregations within the

Church of Scotland, as well as many other denominations across the country. The Rural Strategy Team has been encouraged by the number of rural officers across England who have offered feedback in the positive ways in which they use the resource pack. Orders can be placed by contacting sreeves@cofscotland.org.uk or by visiting www.madstuff.biz

10.2.2 *God's Own Country* – The DVD
Owing to the feedback of the printed resource pack, the Rural Strategy Team is currently in the midst of producing a new DVD to assist congregations and church leaders to think through some of the major issues facing rural churches today. The DVD will contain six short discussion starters to guide thoughts and planning within congregations. It is hoped that this new resource will help in strategic planning.

10.2.3 Rural Church Conference
The fourth bi-annual Rural Church Conference took place at the Scottish Police College at Tulliallan on Friday, 31 October and Saturday, 1 November. The theme of the conference was 'Value Added Church', and encouraged opportunities to consider how and in what ways the life, work and witness of the rural church make a positive difference. The conference benefited greatly from all of the workshop leaders and contributors, particularly Dr Stuart Black, Director of Planning and Development at Highlands and Islands Council, who spoke on the role of the church in rural community life, Rev Ivor MacDonald who offered a Christian reflection on the countryside and Rev Pauline Steenbergen who spoke of the experiences of new styles of ministry within a rural Presbytery.

10.2.3.1 Plans are under way for the next conference to take place in the Autumn of 2010.

10.2.4 *Life and Work* – Rural Series
The Rural Strategy Team is grateful to the support received from the *Life and Work* editorial team. In 2008 the Convenor, Rev Bryan Kerr, contributed a six month series

on life and ministry within Rural Scotland. Through the feedback received, the Rural Strategy Team understands the value of these contributions to ministers and church members and it is hoped that, following the success of the series, further collaborations with the Kirk's magazine might be possible.

10.3 Affirming the Rural Church
10.3.1 Royal Highland Show
The Stand at the Royal Highland Show is a growing and developing partnership of many Christian denominations working together, with staffing mainly being provided by a team of enthusiastic volunteers, and is an annual reminder of the ongoing commitment of the churches to rural life and experience as well as the Rural Strategy Team's remit of affirming churches in rural Scotland.

10.3.1.1 Many visitors to the stand spoke of the work in which their church was engaged, whilst others came for ideas and inspiration. It is a privilege for all of those who volunteer at the stand to meet people from different churches and denominations and encourage them in their ministries.

10.3.1.2 A significant development in 2008 was the introduction of a COSY CoffeeHouse. Those who stopped at the stand were welcome to share in tea and coffee with the volunteers and have a relaxed conversation about the church. Those who took the free coffee were delighted with the 'pit-stop' on their way around the show.

10.3.1.3 The stand resources were significantly upgraded for the 2008 Show. The Rural Strategy Team designed and purchased a display stand for the interior of the tent, and large five metre banners for outside to make certain that visitors to the Show knew that the church was in attendance.

10.3.1.4 Thanks are once again due to the Church and Society Council who provided an excellent series of seminars for school groups on the theme of Fair Trade and Food Miles. This interactive and fun seminar allowed the children and young people who visited the stand to grapple with the issues surrounding fair trade both at home and abroad.

10.3.1.5 The schools seminars are run as a 'satellite' of the programme organised by the Royal Highland Education Trust who provide a learning experience for the children who attend through the Discovery Centre. In 2009, the theme of the Discovery Centre will be '10 of the best' recognising the 10th anniversary of the Trust. The Rural Strategy Team is delighted that it has been asked to provide an interactive display for children and families throughout the show. This is a significant opportunity for the churches to have contact with many thousands of children. Hosting a stand in the Discovery Centre allows an expansion of the seminar programme, with many different agencies providing new content.

10.3.1.6 The 2009 Royal Highland Show will take place at Ingliston from Thursday, 25, to Sunday, 28 June. The annual Sunday morning service will be at the bandstand at 10am, with the Chaplain to the Show taking part. During the period of the Show, prayer requests are invited at the Stand, with short acts of devotion at the beginning of each day and in the late afternoon.

10.3.2   Scottish Churches Rural Group

The Rural Strategy Team is always encouraged by the ecumenical involvement in many of the projects it undertakes. The team acknowledges the importance of ecumenical engagement at a local as well as a policy level. To that end the Church of Scotland, through the Rural Strategy Team, is involved in the Scottish Churches Rural Group. This ecumenical group continues to provide support and encouragement to denominations throughout Scotland. With the aim of the group being 'to engage with God's diverse and changing rural scene in Scotland', a number of issues are currently in progress. It is always helpful to hear of the work of different denominations in order that those stories can be used as

an encouragement within our own denomination and within our congregations.

10.3.2.1 Further information about the work of the Rural Group can be obtained from the Secretary, Mrs Shona Paterson, ACTS Office, 7 Forrester Lodge, Inglewood House, Alloa FK10 2HU Tel: 01259 216980. Email: shonapaterson@acts-scotland.org

10.3.3   Consultations

The Rural Strategy Team believes strongly that local churches in rural Scotland should be affirmed in the work they do. Many churches provide community spaces, and are a point of welcome and contact for local people. In partnership with the Church and Society Council, the Rural Strategy Team took part in a Scottish Government consultation on safeguarding rural schools. In the course of this consultation, the Rural Strategy Team was pleased that the concept of the school building as a place that was important for the community was highlighted. However, during the consultation it was stressed that those who live in areas where a school has been closed (despite transport being provided to the alternative school) should not be penalised for not being able to take part in extra curricular activities because of the transport system and that local authorities should be prepared to make use of other community spaces, including churches, to provide suitable activities for children.

10.3.4   Ministry in Rural Scotland

The Rural Strategy Team has been encouraging the Ministries Council to think of ways in which exposure to rural ministry may be realised during the formation and training period of a minister. It is recognised that issues of relocation and geography are very real concerns of all involved; however, in an age where it is essential that future ministers of the church have the widest possible experience, the Rural Strategy Team feels that this is one area that would benefit the whole church.

10.3.4.1 When a minister serves in a rural parish, it can be very isolating. There can often be large distances between colleagues and the Presbytery may not meet each month. The Rural Strategy Team is committed both to affirming the role that ministers play in rural communities and encouraging ministers serving in a rural parish to reflect on their ministry. With collaboration from the Ministries Council, it is hoped to run a study leave course for ministers in rural parishes from November 2009. The course will take place in the grounds of Balmoral and participants will stay in accommodation on-site. The course will comprise the theology, theory and practice of rural ministry and enable ministers to share their experiences, learn from each other and think through the theological implications and practical outcomes. Expressions of interest in the course, and bookings, can be made by contacting Sheila Reeves at the Church Offices in Edinburgh.

10.4 Supporting the Rural Church
10.4.1 Research Project

As was reported at last year's General Assembly, the Rural Strategy Team is preparing a research project to determine the number and character of rural parishes within the Church of Scotland. It is hoped that this will allow consultation with rural churches to take their perspectives into account, and to determine where its priorities ought to lie in responding to the challenges that those churches face.

10.4.1.1 The identification of possible partners for this research is under way, to be followed by an invitation to tender from organisations and individuals that may be able to carry it out. The Rural Strategy Team is pleased that the General Trustees are supporting the concept of this research, and have agreed in principle to contribute financially to it as the results should help also in the work in which they are engaged.

10.4.2 Farm crisis/rural chaplaincy

Over the last number of years the need has become apparent for a wide ranging information, resource and support service for the farming community. A very successful model already exists in the North East of Scotland and it is hoped that the Rural Strategy Team will be the lead agency in providing a farm crisis and rural chaplaincy service across Scotland in the years to come.

10.4.3 Land and Buildings

Following the General Assembly of 2008 the Rural Strategy Team entered into discussions with the General Trustees regarding the use of glebes. Concern had been raised previously by some that glebes were, in certain cases, not being used to their full potential. Discussions have been fruitful and it is clear that the General Trustees work very hard to ensure that glebes bring great benefit to the church. The use of glebes has traditionally been for agricultural purposes although there are some glebes that are used in very creative ways around the country. For example, glebes have been utilised to help train young people in ways of farming and to provide community space. It should be stated that these types of examples are the exception. The General Trustees have given assurances that all applications to them to use glebes in new ways which might include the provision of affordable housing would be looked at on an individual basis and where there is a strong business case which does not conflict with their trusteeship obligations then a variety of uses are possible.

10.4.3.1 There are many benefits that come from the use of glebes, even in the most traditional of uses. Congregations should be encouraged to see the rental income from a glebe not as a portion of the contribution to Ministries and Mission allocation that they do not have to pay, but rather as a contribution that releases a similar sum of general income to be used in the local parish to further the missionary aims of the congregation.

10.4.4 Finance

The Rural Strategy Team was invited to discuss with the General Treasurer the fact that many rural congregations find it difficult to meet a regular monthly contribution to ministries and mission funds, such is the preferred way of transmitting contributions. However, following those discussions the Rural Strategy Team was satisfied that the local Presbytery can give a dispensation to a congregation to pay in another way, taking account of local income patterns. It should be stated, however, that this dispensation should be given annually by Presbytery and if circumstances in the congregation change they should be taken into account.

10.4.5 Rural issues

The Rural Strategy Team has been regularly involved in thinking about many issues affecting rural Scotland. From churches hosting rural Post Offices following the announcement of closures and restructuring, to thinking about the issues of team ministry and effective parish groupings where geography suggests a sense of isolation, the Rural Strategy Team continues to reflect on how the Church of Scotland can have a vibrant and living presence in many of our rural communities across the country.

11. Netherbow Scottish Storytelling Centre

11.1 The Scottish Storytelling Centre Executive Committee advises the Mission and Discipleship Council on matters relating to the operation and management of the Centre.

11.2 In 2008 over 300,000 people took part in events organised by the Scottish Storytelling Centre and Network. As a people friendly form of communication and of community building, storytelling has become increasingly attractive, while narrative is also the 'name of the game' in the media. The Church is par excellence a community which tells, shares and lives its stories.

11.3 With its strategic presence at the heart of Edinburgh's Royal Mile, the Storytelling Centre became in 2008 a venue of choice for national conversations and conferences on issues of cultural, moral, social and spiritual concern. To listen to each other's stories and

experiences is to gain wisdom and find a common way forward. That the Church should provide such a place of sharing and dialogue is an important expression of our place in Scottish society at this time of change.

11.4 Among the cultural successes of 2008 were the local Old Town Festival in June, and the Scottish International Storytelling Festival (SISF) in October. Supported by the Scottish Government Festivals Expo Fund, the SISF brought together people from over twenty countries including storytellers from Alaska to Finland across the northern hemisphere.

11.5 Much effort was also devoted to assisting the churches in planning for the Year of Homecoming in 2009 and ensuring that the Church, through its cultural centre, would make a distinctive contribution to marketing the 250th Anniversary of Robert Burns.

11.6 The creative opportunities for parishes in the idea of 'Winter Festival' have been clearly modelled by the Scottish Storytelling Centre and taken up in many areas.

11.7 As 2008 proceeded, the recession began to bite and a revised business plan was urgently prepared to tackle the significant challenges of 2009.

12. Strategic Use of Gaelic

12.1 The 2008 General Assembly welcomed a Report from the Council on the Strategic Development of the Use of Gaelic and encouraged the Council to develop is future plans as they were detailed in the Report.

12.2 The Council now reports that progress has been made in delivering these future plans with a number of initiatives, such as the 'Statement on The Church of Scotland and the Gaelic Language' published in the *2008/2009 Church of Scotland Year Book*.

12.3 A Gaelic worship aid, including a collection of popular Gaelic blessings, prayer, and short Scripture passages for use within mainly English services has been compiled by the Rev Dr Roderick Macleod, and will be introduced during the General Assembly.

12.4   Gaelic Worship Aid

This book has a two-fold aim. Firstly, it is intended as a support for the good number of ministers and others within the Church of Scotland who conduct worship, who have some knowledge of Gaelic but feel the need for improving their grasp of the language. It is hoped that the publication of this book will provide inspiration for them to continue to make progress. Secondly, it is anticipated that the publication of this book will encourage leaders of worship throughout Scotland, not just in parishes with a strong Gaelic background, to include some Gaelic content in their services. Where Gaelic mourners are present at a funeral service or Gaelic speakers are among the congregation at a marriage service it is thought to be a matter of courtesy to incorporate some Gaelic material. There is a growing recognition within the Church, as in other bodies, of the important place of Gaelic in Scottish life, and this is reflected in the increasing number of congregations which print some Gaelic in newsletters and orders of service.

12.4.1   Having a CD included with the printed material should help those who have made some progress in learning of Gaelic as well as those with little or no familiarity with the language who wish to achieve an authentic pronunciation of the language.

12.4.2   Summary of the contents

Some have expressed the desire to be able as a minimum to open a church service or another meeting with a Gaelic greeting, and similarly to say a few words in Gaelic by way of a parting message. Short sentences of greeting and farewell are included.

12.4.2.1   The booklet will contain a number of well-known passages from the Gaelic Bible which could be used in services of different kinds, particularly for weddings and funerals. Passages which can be used at such services include the Aaronic Blessing from Numbers 6, Psalm 23, Psalm 121, Isaiah 9:2-7 (for use at Christmas services), the Beatitudes from Matthew 5, selected verses from John 14, Acts 2:1-4, 1 Corinthians 13, selected verses from 1 Corinthians 15, Revelation 21, 22 (for funeral services). The Apostles' Creed in Gaelic will also be printed. Individual verses suitable for a number of services are also included.

12.4.2.2   There is a selection of short prayers for use at ordinary Sunday services and for special occasions. This includes the Gaelic version of the Lord's Prayer, short morning and evening prayers, prayers for baptism, marriage services and harvest festival, including the blessing of a civil marriage, Christmas and Easter prayers, the dedication of an offering, Remembrance Day prayers (to include, They shall grow not old',) blessing of a new home, a prayer for each of the seasons.

12.5   The Council recognises the valuable work also being undertaken in the development of the use of the Gaelic language by the Gaelic Group of the Council of Assembly on page 1/7.

13. Church Visitor and Tourism Strategy

13.1   Through its Strategy Group, which works across departments and committees, the Council has progressed steadily through 2008 implementing the plans previously reported to the General Assembly. The results include:

a) Working with Scotland's Churches Scheme to develop a high quality web-site promoting places of worship in Scotland – www.sacredscotland.org.uk. Each participating church has its own page and web address on the site to which it can link and add further information.

b) Working with Scotland's Churches Scheme, through Saint Andrew Press, to launch a series of regional guides to places of worship in Scotland. The first three volumes of a planned ten are being issued for 2009.

c) Awarding over 40 small grants to assist parish churches

with preparing new websites and leaflets. This scheme is now concluded.

13.2 So far, over 1200 churches in Scotland have participated in these initiatives which will continue to bear fruit well beyond the Year of Homecoming.

13.3 For 2009 itself the Scottish Churches have adapted a shared text 'You welcomed me as if I were an angel' (Gal 4:14) and an official form of invitation agreed with the Year of Homecoming.

13.4 Following on this initiative many congregations, Presbyteries and ecumenical groupings are planning special events through the summer and leading up to St Andrew's Day and Advent.

13.5 The aim throughout is to engage more effectively with
• Those living locally but not directly connected with the Church of Scotland
• Local, national and international visitors and tourists
• Partner churches at home and overseas.

13.6 The Council hopes that these objectives will carry through to 2010 when the Church will mark the 450th anniversary of the Scottish Reformation and the Centenary of the Edinburgh World Missionary Conference.

14. 'Why Believe?'

14.1 This interdenominational Apologetics Group facilitated through the Church of Scotland enjoys renewed vigour as it seeks to help Scottish people engage credibly with the realm of religion and society. The Group has members from main Scottish denominations and several Christian organisations such as Scripture Union, and constantly looks for appropriate new members.

14.2 In June an open conference at Stirling University Management suite attracted a participative audience to 'Mixing with the media', with two main speakers and a time for debate. Professor John Haldane, of the University of St Andrews, focussed on Religion in the Public Square, addressing issues of rationality, the place of faith in politics and how the church might respond to an increasingly aggressive secularism. Rev David Robertson, minister of St Peter's Free Church, Dundee explored the process of hosting discussion forums in establishments such as bookshop coffee areas when topics such as Richard Dawkins published ideas are challenged from a Christian perspective with audiences drawn from a wide belief spectrum. A question and answer session with professionals from the broadcast media including Anna Magnusson was well received.

14.3 Since 2008 was promoted as a national year of reading, 'Why Believe?' ventured into a pilot project in which good and accessible Christian apologetic literature was purchased and gifted to libraries. The use of these books and any responses will be carefully monitored over the period until December 2009 to ascertain if such gifts from the Christian Church are worthwhile. For the pilot study the following types of library were used: Secondary School, University, University Chaplaincy, a city Council and a rural Council library.

14.4 March 2009 saw the launch of an apologetics interactive website www.godsearchscotland.org.uk which aims to meet the needs of both a faithful and a questioning user-group. With resources for churches and individual Christians to assist them in presenting their faith and an interactive area where comments and questions on topical issues can be posted. The Group monitors the website carefully and provides appropriate responses.

14.5 Endeavouring to assist the conversations currently engaged in by Scottish society surrounding end of life issues, echoed in debates at the Scottish Parliament led by Margo Macdonald, along with other euthanasia and life/death discussions, 'Why Believe?' has currently underway plans for regional conferences. These would focus on theological, ethical and medical aspects; the working title at present is 'Life values'. Other projects in hand include an apologetics leaflet on the Science/ Faith discussion entitled '*Galaxy*' and an updated general apologetics information leaflet based on the popular '*What Can I say?*' leaflet.

15. Scottish Churches Community Trust moving on to become *FiSCAF – Faiths in Scotland Community Action Fund*

Life is like riding a bicycle – to keep your balance you must keep moving... (Albert Einstein)

15.1   This has been a momentous year for the continuing journey of Scottish Churches Community Trust and by the end of 2008 the Trust had embraced exciting changes which the Trust's Board of Directors believe will, for the future, build on our capacity to provide grants, support and advice to local faith-based anti-poverty initiatives in both rural and urban areas throughout Scotland.

15.1.1   In present-day Scotland, where many communities struggling against poverty are in a state of constant change, and where people from many different parts of the world live, work and worship alongside each other, the time is right to step forward and reflect the changes in Scotland's communities with a new fund reaching across different faith groups.

15.1.2   After almost two years of careful consultation, discussion and examination of different options for the future development of SCCT, the Board of Directors decided at a specially convened General Meeting held in Perth on 10 December 2008 to merge with Faith in Community (Scotland), an anti-poverty organisation working with and through people of faith. A new fund was launched in the middle of March which is known as *FiSCAF – Faiths in Scotland Community Action Fund*. The various legal changes have been agreed by OSCR – the Office of the Scottish Charity Regulator.

15.2   *FiSCAF* will work with local faith groups as they build hope and struggle against poverty by providing grants and support for their initiatives in Scotland's most fragile communities.

15.2.1   We have been aware of the need to have available to us a management group with both a breadth of skills, and a breadth of commitment from a wide range of faith communities, including those denominations who have supported SCCT so far.

15.2.3   We are also sensitive to the need for fairness, openness and transparency in all our dealings and to take seriously the need for gender and geographical distribution.

15.2.4   We are satisfied that within the governance of *FiSCAF*, our distinctive identity will be honoured and we look forward to the significant extra resourcing which the amalgamation can potentially offer. As we look to the future, the Church of Scotland, with her determination to see 'Good news to the poor' (St Luke 4:18) as the gospel imperative, has the opportunity to continue to take sides with the most fragile, recognising the justice of making real chances and choices a possibility through *FiSCAF*. We continue to do this alongside other denominations, with whom we have had an eight year journey, as well as with other faith communities who share our passion and belief that poverty is an offence to the God we worship.

15.2.5   As we look to the future we are aware of the legacy of the past and remember with thanks steps on the journey; those taken both with the inter-church SCCT (launched in 2000) and before that with the Church of Scotland Priority Areas Fund where the Fund found its genesis and inspiration as a result of a decision of the General Assembly of 1995. We urge the General Assembly to continue its commitment to this valuable work by affirming and supporting *FiSCAF* with generosity.

15.2.6   There is no doubt as to the difference the churches' contributions have made over these eight years.

Almost one million pounds have helped local groups in rural and urban Scotland to lever almost eight times as much funding from other sources. Part of the distinctive support package made possible by the churches has been the training grants which are automatically made available – training grants which arguably not only develop people's skills and knowledge but go towards protecting the overall investment of the Fund.

15.2.7 Let folks from two of the projects speak for themselves of the difference the Fund has made to their lives and the life of their community:

Revival Evangelical Mission International, Glasgow:

…*Since being established in 2003 to meet the needs of Swahili speaking people in Sighthill, Glasgow, REMI has grown to encompass a broad range of people from different cultural backgrounds, many from ethnic backgrounds…As a result… cultural based counselling together with translating and interpretation of information from English into specific mother tongues became a very important and ongoing element of the fellowship – primarily delivered with a view to easing integration into the local and wider community, alleviating discrimination and ultimately promoting equal opportunities… REMI has helped integrate asylum seekers and refugees into the community by providing a supportive, befriending environment through the people and other resources of the fellowship and by working on a one to one basis with families and individuals…Money from Scottish Churches Community Trust has helped provide English classes, life skill classes, computing classes and counselling. We conclude by expressing our sincere thanks to you for the support you have given us without which we would not have gone thus far. We hope we shall continue to be partners in this ministry…*

Community House, Alloa:

…*Community House provides a safe space where children and young people can meet to experience and learn new skills. In doing so we are providing an opportunity to fulfil our mission statement – 'sharing vision, offering choice, a listening place'.…We are an ecumenical, Christian based project open to people of all faiths and of none….Throughout the year we have seen many of the children and young people…grow in self-confidence and self-esteem. Youngsters who in the past have been unable to make choices and decisions for themselves are now able to do so, many making simple choices like who they will play with or what food they will and will not eat, many are now also taking on leadership roles in the Community House…*

15.3 A wide range of projects which SCCT are in the process of supporting with multiyear funding will have that honoured in the future by *FiSCAF*.

15.3.1 As we grow into the future *FiSCAF*, in listening to and speaking with local faith communities, will seek to hear clearly the poverty and inequality they and their local community are facing. We will encourage them to tell us why their faith inspires them to take action, and how they will encourage the widest possible participation.

15.3.2 We aim to be a Fund that is passionate and compassionate, that knows that faith matters, is rooted in the everyday and makes a difference. We believe in people, who they are and who they are becoming. We want to work with them and where appropriate be prepared to take risks with their vision for their communities, trusting and building trust.

15.3.3 We prayerfully and humbly echo the words said at great cost to himself by Oscar Romero:

This is what we are about;

We plant the seeds that one day will grow,
We water seeds that are already planted,
Knowing that they hold future promise.
We lay foundations that will need further
development.
We provide yeast that produces effect beyond
our capabilities.

16. Practical Matters

16.1 Operational Plan

At the meeting of the Council in June 2008 an Operational Plan for 2008/2009 was agreed. This listed all the work instructed by the 2008 General Assembly as well as concise objectives for all the areas of work contained within the Council's remit. The Operational Plan has been monitored throughout the year, and the Council at its meeting in April 2009 reviewed the progress which has been made in the fulfilment of each objective.

16.2 Finance

The Council is grateful for ongoing annual congregational financial support for its work through Ministries and Mission contributions, and for the historic resources available to it through capital designated to aspects of its work over the years.

16.2.1 At present the variety of work detailed throughout this Report is being funded from both these sources, though each year the Council is drawing from capital to maintain the current level of work. Such a course of action is in line with the principled decision of the 2008 General Assembly to use a measure of capital to fund current work, with the firm hope that the resources of the whole Church will grow in the future to ensure that all priority work is funded from congregational contributions and interest on the remaining capital.

16.2.2 For the first four years of its life, the Council has sought to ensure that all the historic stands of work inherited by it in 2005 have been maintained and developed. It is now recognised that there is need for a prioritisation of work, with no pre-conditions, and the Council is committed to bringing the results of that exercise, to be undertaken in the Summer of 2009, to the 2010 General Assembly. Such a prioritisation of work will enable the Council both to operate within the reduced financial resources available, and, where appropriate, to bring a more reasoned case for additional funding to the Council of Assembly.

16.2.3 The Council recognises that its capital derives largely from the share of the Salvesen Bequest designated for 'outreach' in Scotland and offers the assurance to the General Assembly that it believes that all of the capital, and the interest derived from it, is being used in accordance with the original intention of the Bequest.

16.2.4 The Council and its staff greatly appreciate the contribution of those staff of the General Treasurer's Department who offer day-to-day financial support to the Council and its work. Giving such support in 2008 were Mrs Pauline Willder, Mr Robert Archibald, Mr Scott Hamilton, and Ms Kamilla Kocot and warm thanks are expressed to each of them.

16.3 Encouragement of Prayer

The Council reports continuing progress on the development of Prayer Correspondents to encourage the prayer life of the church. A full Report on progress will be offered to the 2010 General Assembly, but in the meantime further information can be obtained from the Rev Andy Campbell of the Council's Perth office (telephone: 01738 630514 or by e-mail: acampbell@ cofscotland.org.uk).

16.4 Special Trusts

The Council has continued to offer grants from Special Trusts to congregations and other Christian groups to support new initiatives in mission and discipleship. A full list of grants awarded is contained in the Council Minutes published on the Church of Scotland website, and further information and an application form can be obtained from the Council Secretary.

16.4.1 Through a grant from these Special Trusts of £500 to purchase uniforms and fund training sessions, the Council has been able to support the establishment of Street Pastors in Perth. The initiative of establishing Street Pastors Groups throughout Scotland is welcome, and the General Assembly is invited to note that 250 Street Pastors have now been recruited in 5 teams and to commend the frontier Christian work they are undertaking on the streets of Scotland.

16.4.2 Full information and an application form is available at www.resourcingchurches.org.uk.

16.5 Society in Scotland for the Propagation of Christian Knowledge

For many years the work of the Society in Scotland for the Propagation of Christian Knowledge had been largely in abeyance, but the Council is now pleased to report that on the 300th Anniversary of its establishment, grants are now being paid from the Home Fund to support mission work in Scotland, with particular reference to the Highlands and Islands. A full report of this initiative is contained in the Report of the World Mission Council on page 7/29.

16.6 Presbytery Representatives

The Council maintains a scheme of Presbytery Mission and Discipleship Council representatives as a means of 'two-way' communication with Presbyteries about its work. Each Presbytery is invited to appoint a representative who is invited to meetings held bi-annually. A meeting was held in the Scottish Storytelling Centre, Edinburgh, on Thursday, 11 September 2008, and another at the new Bankfoot Church Centre, Perthshire, on Tuesday, 17 March 2009. The programmes for such gatherings include input about aspects of the Council's work, as well as an opportunity for Presbytery representatives to share initiatives taking place in mission and discipleship in their own areas. They have proved an invaluable way of ensuring that 'good news' stories are shared widely.

16.7 Regional Offices

The Council maintains Regional Offices at Glasgow, Inverness, and Perth at which Regional Development Officers and Administrators are based. Office accommodation is also made available in Glasgow for the Council's Inter-Faith Officer, and in Perth for a member of the Parish Development Fund staff. Contact details for each of these offices are available in the Church of Scotland Year Book and the Administrators in each are:

- Glasgow: Mrs Wendy Kerr (tel: 0141 352 6946, email: manddglasgow@cofscotland.org.uk)
- Inverness: Mrs Seonaidh Howarth (tel: 01463 731712, e-mail: manddinverness@cofscotland.org.uk)
- Perth: Mrs Gael Coupar (tel: 01738 630514, e-mail: manddperth@cofscotland.org.uk)

16.8 'Church Without Walls' Planning Group and Committee on the Parish Development Fund

In the months prior to the preparation of this Report, the Council has, with the encouragement of the Council of Assembly, been engaged in conversations with the 'Church Without Walls' Planning Group and the Committee on the Parish Development Fund.

16.8.1 The Council recognizes that it would be helpful for both governance purposes and for the integration of all areas of congregational resourcing into the Council's work, if the work represented by the Group and the Committee was fully integrated into the life and work of the Council. An assurance is given that a warm welcome will be offered both to the personnel involved and to the areas of work, and the Council sees no reason why these specific interests cannot be fully honoured as strategic elements of the wide and variety work of the Council.

16.9 Collaborative Working

The Council is pleased to report to the General Assembly that collaborative working is continuing to develop with other Councils. A particular initiative in 2008 with the Ministries Council was the organisation of two Conferences, one for the four Outer Island Presbyteries, and one for Presbyteries facing similar staffing and resourcing challenges. A full report on both these Conferences is contained in the Report of the Ministries Council on pages 3/7 and 3/11-3/13.

16.9.1 The four Outer Islands Presbyteries Conference, and an earlier visit to the Presbytery in March 2008, has led the Council into two areas of collaborative working with the Presbytery of Orkney:

- In order to support the thinking about the way in which one minister might in the future support congregations on three separate islands, including the provision of the leadership of worship by video link, the Council has supported some preliminary investigation work relating to the viability of the use of new technology in this way. It is likely that a future General Assembly will be appraised of the progress being made with this project.
- Noting the considerable progress which has been made by the Presbytery of Orkney in the development of existing buildings and the establishment of new, appropriate places of worship, the Council is in discussion with the Presbytery about the viability of producing a DVD on past and current building projects. A further Report is likely to be offered to a future General Assembly.

16.10 Scottish Bible Society:

One of the responsibilities of the Council is to submit to the General Assembly the names of those recommended for appointment to the Council of Church Representatives of the Scottish Bible Society. Following the resignation of the Rev Andrew McGurk, who has served since 2002, the Council hopes to submit his successor's name at the General Assembly.

In the name of the Council

ANGUS MORRISON, *Convener*
MARK E JOHNSTONE, *Vice-Convener*

ALAN D BIRSS, *Vice-Convener*
LINDA DUNNETT, *Vice-Convener*
DOUGLAS A O NICOL, *Council Secretary*
STEVE MALLON, *Associate Secretary*
ALEX M MILLAR, *Associate Secretary*
NIGEL J ROBB, *Associate Secretary*

In the name of the Committee on Church Art and Architecture

ELEANOR MACALISTER, *Convener*
PETER GARDNER, *Vice-Convener*
NIGEL J ROBB, *Associate Secretary*

In the name of the Publishing Committee

JOHN MACGILL, *Convener*
T DOUGLAS McROBERTS, *Vice-Convener*
ANN CRAWFORD, *Head of Publishing*

ADDENDUM

Rev Dr Angus Morrison
At the 2009 General Assembly the Rev Dr Angus Morrison completes a four year term as Convener of the Mission and Discipleship Council. Vice-Conveners, Council members and staff are united in expressing warm appreciation to him for these years of outstanding service.

As the first Convener of the new Council, charged with bringing together the wide range of congregational resourcing work of former Boards, Committees and Panels, Dr Morrison has had the challenging task of leading the process of uniting many diverse interests together. His friendly manner with all, his gracious chairing of meetings, and his unstinting commitment to both mission and discipleship, are but a few of the many gifts he brought to a role that was seldom straight-forward, and which often required a sensitive balance of discernment. The

Council's staff is particularly in his debt for the support he has offered on visits to the Council's offices in Edinburgh, Glasgow, Inverness and Perth, and to projects and conferences throughout Scotland.

All Conveners of General Assembly Councils and Committees are to some extent aware of the commitment of time required to faithfully fulfil the expectations of the Church. When being a parish minister in Stornoway in the Western Isles is also taken into consideration, a fresh level of commitment is required. Yet Dr Morrison has taken in his stride frequent early morning flights in all weather conditions, occasional ferry journeys across a tempestuous Minch, and many nights away from home and family.

As his term comes to a close, the whole Church joins the Council in offering thanks to Angus for a task well fulfilled, and to Marion and all his family for releasing him so generously to fulfil it.

In the name of the Council

MARK E JOHNSTONE, *Vice-Convener*
ALAN D BIRSS, *Vice-Convener*
LINDA DUNNETT, *Vice-Convener*
DOUGLAS A O NICOL, *Council Secretary*
STEVE MALLON, *Associate Secretary*
ALEX M MILLAR, *Associate Secretary*
NIGEL J ROBB, *Associate Secretary*

*In the name of the Committee on Church Art
and Architecture*

ELEANOR MACALISTER, *Convener*
PETER GARDNER, *Vice-Convener*
NIGEL J ROBB, *Associate Secretary*

In the name of the Publishing Committee

JOHN MACGILL, *Convener*
T DOUGLAS McROBERTS, *Vice-Convener*
ANN CRAWFORD, *Head of Publishing*

APPENDIX I
HOLY COMMUNION AND THE RENEWAL OF THE CHURCH

This paper sets out to locate the central importance of the Lord's Supper to the life and renewal of the church, taking note of the degree of creativity (or not) and the questions being asked in contemporary church life. Alongside other work in progress, it seeks to stimulate discussion and reflection, not just by ministers of Word and Sacrament but by the whole people of God, to whom the celebration of the Sacrament truly belongs.

1.   The context of the debate
'What is distinctive about Christian community derives in part from the act of Communion at its heart, the vivid and compelling presence of Christ in the midst of his Church, the quality of sharing implied in the actions and symbols of Communion, and the pattern of community offered to the world which anticipates the perfect sharing in the Kingdom of God…' This excerpt from the report of the Panel on Worship in 2005 stimulated the formation of a Working Group on the place and practice of Holy Communion, comprising a range of voices attentive both to current practice and thinking within our own Church and more widely than that. We have sought to understand the central place which the Sacrament holds within the life of the church, and to interrogate the range of practices which accompany its celebration. We wish to uphold Holy Communion as key to our mission and a source of constant renewal to us as Christian people.

1.1   The resources available on this subject are vast though, interestingly, not voluminous in the recent history of our Church. The General Assembly has not received a major report on the Sacrament of the Lord's Supper in recent history. Yet the place and practice of the Sacrament has been of huge significance since the days of the early church, underpinning of course well-known scriptural texts and the substance of some of the earliest writings outside the canon. Differences of opinion and order have frequently surfaced in church history, since early days and not merely at the time of the Reformation. A rich diversity of rites developed in both East and West, and reforming spirits long before the nomenclature of Protestant was coined addressed themselves to the issues in hand. Theologians elaborated on the meaning of sacramental practice, and Prosper of Aquitaine coined a most famous reflection on this as early as the fifth century: 'look at the sacred witness of the public priestly prayers which, handed down by the apostles, are celebrated in the same way in all the world and in every catholic church, so that the rule of praying should establish the rule of believing'.[47] And so theology has regularly seen as its task to be reflection on the worshipping life of the church; and, with reciprocity, insofar as liturgical resources and practices have been developed, it has been thought utterly important to align how we pray with what we think and believe. However, in recent decades in the Church of Scotland, in respect of the Sacrament of the Lord's Supper, there has been little in the way of articulated theological reflection to accompany the degree of movement in the construction of liturgical[48] patterns and practice.

1.2 As our recent series of Roadshows demonstrated, questions are plentiful aside from any discussions in committee rooms. What basically is Holy Communion, and how will we explain it? Is it only ministers who are allowed to lead the Communion celebration? Who can assist in distributing the elements – and why is this? Who is allowed to enjoy eating and drinking the bread and wine in Communion? What space is there for children in Holy Communion celebrations? Are there prayers or actions which must be said or performed to turn the sharing of wine and bread into the sacrament of Holy Communion? What (offputting) practices can we be free from, and how will change happen? How important is it for Christian folk to take part in Holy Communion?

2. From the past through to the present

The Reformed tradition has given shape to where the Church of Scotland now finds itself. The centrality of the Sacraments was affirmed powerfully, and with high stakes (literally and offensively), through the period of the Reformation. Those actors and thinkers in the sixteenth century both built on their inheritance and set out some self-consciously novel ways of proceeding. This was fuelled both negatively and positively.

- The perceived idolatry of the Mass was to be shunned, and likewise the customs of its ritual.
- Bread and wine were to be understood as signs and symbols, although that point alone caused many and great debates even amongst the Reformers on its definition.
- Communion was to be a communal action, not of the priest or presbyter alone but of the people gathering together; and there was to be such Communion frequently, which had not previously been the case.

2.1 There was a great flow of theological and liturgical publications, picking up on everything from the preparation of the communicants through to their posture when the bread and wine were shared. For Scotland, the order in English prepared by John Knox for exiles in Geneva, and a matching order in Gaelic prepared by John Carswell in the early years of the Scottish Reformation, gave full and sound direction on the rule of prayer. The Scots Confession of 1560 gave the authoritative interpretation. It was never intended to

---

[47] Quoted in G Lathrop, 'Knowing something a little: on the role of the *lex orandi* in the search for Christian unity', in T F Best and D Heller (eds), *So we believe, so we pray* (WCC, Geneva, 1995).

[48] Liturgy/liturgical refers not merely to set *forms* of worship but firstly simply to the 'work' of praising God, by forms and extempore.

be the case that prayers absolutely followed the same wording at every time and in every place, but there was a 'common order', a holding together of strands both theological and liturgical.

2.2 Behind this, we might note that Orthodox and Catholic church traditions of liturgy, once established in local churches, had tended not to vary very much over centuries. It would be possible to exaggerate this point, in that there were certainly changes over time, but there is certainly a contrast with Reformed church history. When the Western church became so fissured through the sixteenth and seventeenth centuries, both the scope of theological reflection and the various orderings of worship produced something like a new world in which, for all the apparent points of overlap between one worshipping congregation and another, and one theologian and another, the range of diversity became very pronounced. If geography and degrees of relative isolation historically had always produced variation, the possibilities now were of great differences even within a small town or rural area.

2.3 Most churches have tended to locate authority in worship in the hands of the few, usually the ordained. The challenge forever remains of keeping the church 'one, holy, catholic and apostolic', not only in the local setting but across time and space, and it matters to read the many historical debates both over ministerial order and liturgical proprieties in that light. Ultimately the Church of Scotland settled on a Presbyterian polity and a relatively light ordering of how worship should be conducted. While the (still technically current) Westminster Directory of Worship in 1644 offered more specific instruction for the celebration of the Lord's Supper than for most other aspects of worship, the emphasis on a strong degree of freedom from set forms was notable.[49] Variations of practice and theology were bound to increase sooner or later.

2.4 The shifts became more and more notable in the nineteenth century. The explosion of hymn writing and the nineteenth-century liturgical movements on the one hand, the ferment of change caused by secessions and especially the Disruption on the other and, allied with this, the range of post-Enlightenment theological exploration gave a background to a range of patterns being explored. While printings began once again of prayers, and the evocative title of the *Book of Common Order* was published in 1940, both local church traditions and ministerial preferences – the minister being solely trusted under church law with the conduct of public worship – dictated what precisely happened. The pace of experimentation has been quickening through the twentieth century. Nowadays we have our third version of *Common Order*, and in addition an inclination amongst many to make sense for themselves what conduces to good worship. A wide range of resources can be drawn upon. The ordination vow to uphold the forms of worship as authorised in the Church is far from defined in its scope. Alongside the 'McDonaldisation'[50] of society has come, very especially in a Reformed church like ours, and often with interest in ecumenical possibilities, a pick and mix mentality with regard to worship possibilities.

2.5 The undoubtedly rich potential of having options for reforming and ever reforming[51], of modernising and appealing to contemporary taste, of maintaining historic traditions or deliberately trying to sit free of them, is arguably one of the attractions of the Church of Scotland. The spirit of our forebears, who preached so passionately against the dry reading of forms of worship with too little regard as to how much they edified, has been truly honoured. That matter of accountability, however, cannot be overlooked. The point is not so much accountability

---

[49] Before 1645, there had been successive printings of Knox's *Common Order*, presumably in answer to demand, but not once thereafter.

[50] The phrase is from John Drane's work.

[51] There are strengths here, but a distinction is worth making between a desire merely to innovate or update and the principle of *semper reformanda*, which implies being re-formed ever more in the likeness of Christ.

to some penultimate earthly authority – although these, such as Presbytery and General Assembly, have their rightful place within our constitutional framework – as accountability before the throne of grace. The church before and all around us has been led to read its Scripture well and to profess, with enduring rightness, the unity, holiness, catholicity and apostolicity of the church brought into being by the Word and sustained by the Holy Spirit to the glory of God. Therefore, our valuing of a 'Church of Scotland' pattern must of needs be set against a wider vision and calling. Attentive to the way the wind blows, or the Spirit moves, we cannot but enter into dialogue both with one another – our fellow-Christians within our own Church establishment – and with our fellow-Christians wherever we find them, in time and in space. History is part of our ecumenical future, as is the church worldwide, and such an ambitious drawing of the household of faith is ignored to our detriment. So we have to ask, do our celebrations of the Lord's Supper link us truly with the body of Christ, in every sense in which that is to be understood? Or negatively, as Paul was obliged to put it in challenge the Corinthians, is it at times not the Lord's Supper that we eat (cf. I Corinthians 11.20)?

2.6 The Working Group has been keen to study the place and practice of the Lord's Supper for the sake of the renewal of the church. There is no interest here in making partisan points, or in narrowing down what is positive about diversity in practice. It is a matter of delight that for all the historic practice of the Sacrament in the Church of Scotland settled for some centuries on relatively infrequent celebrations, nowadays it is as common as not that in parishes, and in settings both formal and informal, celebrations are happening quite often. But still a sense of urgency has lain behind the task in hand. For why is it that in the one church we clearly experience celebrations so different that they can be felt to be alienating or incomplete; and doubts that they are celebrations? The cause may be variation in wording and/or style, so how does this matter? And why is it that so much energy

can appear to be invested in the communication of the Word without so much enthusiasm for sharing in the Sacrament? Is the Sacrament not hugely important to us as church and hugely important for our world? How perplexing that the church can only offer mixed messages on the communion meal when thanksgiving in faith is unfashionable, when some indulge in food and drink while so many others starve or lack clean water, when close to home loneliness abounds, and inequalities only grow, and suffering is patent, and death is feared! Do we not as church carry a gospel, good news, to the world, and not least the local society in which we have our parishes? The time is ripe, as it has been since Jesus instituted the feast, for us not only to pray and listen to the Word but also to break bread when we come together as church.

3. Work in progress

What follows here is a brief essay touching on the place and practice of the Sacrament of the Lord's Supper in the Church of Scotland today. The hope is both to support and critique our common life and to feed a wide engagement in that. We cannot try to say everything – as indeed such a plan would be in vain in any case; the riches of the Sacrament literally far outpass human telling – nor even to pick up every significant point. The hope simply is to be discerning in relation to regular experience and to encourage others, ministers and people, to take up that work.

3.1 In addition, the Working Group is publishing a theological and practical commentary on the first Order of the Communion service in the 1994 publication, *Common Order*, together with some ancillary resource materials. The purpose there is not to make a judgement about the quality of that particular Order, but to use it as a tool, a means of explicating what happens through Communion worship. This will be of use in the equipping of ordained ministers and again of interest, we hope, to any others who might care to study it. Perhaps also the package might stimulate creativity to put together other forms of sacramental celebrations. The commentary itself is in parallel with work already published by the Saint Andrew Press in 2005 in relation to the standard Order for the Sacrament of Holy Baptism, entitled *By Water and the Spirit*. Nothing has changed in respect of our Church's self-understanding about forms and particular orders of worshipping – they give direction but not prescription – but for the sake both of addressing confusions and building positively on our worshipping heritage, these liturgical commentaries are timely. The seminars and roadshows hosted by the Working Group in 2007-08 only strengthened the sense that there is substantial interest and desire to engage with all sorts of questions great and small in relation to the Sacrament of the Lord's Supper.[52]

4.   The 'place' of the Lord's Supper

Jesus shared meals with his friends on many occasions. Of the Evangelists, John would take us into the hills near to the time of Passover, with a multitude in attendance; Matthew, Mark and Luke would take us especially to the Upper Room, a more intimate coming together. When the apostle Paul had to berate the Corinthians on aspects of their practice, he clearly understood that the church assembled for its communal prayers and eating, and people ate not just in their own houses.[53] Thus from the earliest sources, as well as subsequent evidence in writing, art and architecture, we are invited to have a sense of the 'geography' of the Lord's Supper. And so this is one aspect, though not the only one, of how we might reflect on the 'place' of the Sacrament.

4.1   Church traditions have gone in many ways with this. Great and impressive edifices and the finest art and the most glittering gold have been thought fitting for the celebrations, but so too have open-air spaces and quiet corners. Furnishings have been generously donated and

sometimes also have become the cause of very heated disputes. Long before the current wave of debate about pews, the ordering of church buildings simply in our own Church had definite schools of thought about how to build around the placing of Communion table(s), or not.[54] Contemporary experience, then, offers room for reflection on a multitude of possibilities, including more and more informal settings of the Sacrament, whether in nursing homes or retreat centres, as well as in designed church buildings.[55] The simple and enduring point to be made here is that the Sacrament is an occasion for an assembly, a gathering. We come, we share food, we go. Where the meal is served matters less than the fact it is served, and there is companionship (which means, literally, a sharing of the bread) in the event.

4.2   That obviously then raises the question as to when such a meal is offered. It is well known that many of the early Reformers took the view that it should be a monthly event, the regular rhythm of a Sunday – and by that, not especially on what had in the 'unreformed' church been known as Feast Days.[56] When the arrangement was made, in Scotland as in elsewhere, that a less frequent celebration was in order for practical reasons, the early determination in the *First Book of Discipline* was still to make it a pattern of regular ordinariness, *eg* in towns, the first Sunday of March, June, September and December. As in some places churches have moved to

---

[52] See section 8.

[53] John ch 6; Matthew 26 17ff., Mark 14.12 ff, Luke 22.7ff; I Corinthians 11.17ff.

[54] A single Communion table permanently up at the front may have been a reintroduction for the Church of Scotland in the nineteenth century, but of course it had long pedigree elsewhere. Its symbolic value, even empty, should not be underestimated – witness its deliberate absence, for example in certain hospital sanctuaries for the sake of being inclusive towards all faiths.

[55] Current parallel work on theological issues raised in the re-ordering of church buildings takes up some of these issues more fully. Another separate piece of work in progress is the recording of Communion vessels across the whole of the Church.

[56] The law of the late medieval church was that people were to take Communion at least once a year, and Pascha or Easter was regularly the preferred time.

more frequent celebrations, and with often less hesitancy than our forebears about the dangers of 'superstition' in the observance of particular days in the church year, it is still rare within the Church of Scotland to have a weekly celebration. The attempt to push this around the time of the publication of the 1979 edition of *The Book of Common Order* did not apparently gain much approval, and it remains to be seen whether there will be alteration here. But having not very frequent celebrations raises a number of problems – issues around who attends, and how familiar and integrated the Sacrament is (or is not) in the local church's life and witness. In Scotland, Catholic and Episcopalian practice by contrast has endorsed in the last century a weekly celebration in which the members of the parish may fully participate.

4.3 This is more than just a practical issue. A substantial reflection might dwell on how the Sacraments complete or bring to a fullness the preaching of the Word. The sharing of the gospel of salvation – as we read in Scripture – has its climax in the proclamation of the death of Jesus Christ and his rising again. As well as clearly shaping the writing of the four gospels, and much of the New Testament, such was also the overwhelming focus of the ecumenical creeds in the early centuries of the church and in a great deal of preaching and theological writing ever since. Why therefore come up short in, as Paul would put it, proclaiming the Lord's death until he comes (I Corinthians 11.26)? Can the celebration of the Sacrament of the Lord's Supper, touching as it does human experience beyond the power of words and, as we would understand it, taking us into the richest experience of bodily communion, not reinforce the eloquence or otherwise of the preacher of the day?

4.4 However, the issues of participation are also real and significant. Whenever the Sacrament is celebrated, it has become a church tradition, building no doubt on that extended berating text of I Corinthians 11, for there to be care taken as to the spirit in which one should sit down at the table. There have been a variety of practices here, for example disciplines of catechesis, of initiation, of fasting, of the confession of sin (and in some churches, the order of penance). The place of the Lord's Supper has been very highly conceived, with the insistence on the part of church authority that it should not be contemned, taken for granted in any sense. Historically within our own Church, and of course still mostly in the Highlands, disciplines of preparation have been focused in worship services in advance of the Sunday celebration. To make a universal shift towards weekly celebrations would imply a major change of culture, touching also on patterns of pastoral care where Elders still visit in districts. And there is also the consideration of how suited a Communion service is as a missionary parish in 21st century Scotland seeks week by week to draw in the newcomer.

4.5 What then is the spirit of participation? The Church has had continuing discussions as to what membership implies.[57] In that first recorded occasion of difficulties within a congregation, the Corinthians were obliged to think about the meaning of unworthiness, in regard of their Communion practice. There were stern words about the humiliation of the less well off; there were warnings about divine judgement precisely because there was too much human judging going on. Participation, in the Greek *koinonia*, which is itself sometimes translated as 'communion', refers fundamentally to that which is in common. If that Corinthian situation gave out warnings about the setting up of wealth hierarchies, the principle to be extended is that the place of the Lord's Supper is a place where all boundaries are broken down in Christ. The body of Christ in which we share is the place for encounter of the richest kind; we meet one another in love, and love transforms us, the love of Christ, who

---

[57] Cf the report of the Panel on Doctrine ('Measuring membership', 2002), and continuing present work under the auspices of the Mission and Discipleship Council. The question of a roll of communicants and the smaller issue of Communion cards or tokens of course connects here.

gave himself for us. The spirit of participation then is humility and thanksgiving, openness to God and to one another.

4.6 Thus understood – and before we get to any questions about what the bread and wine convey – the Sacrament is truly a celebration. The early Reformers in more commonly talking about the Sacrament to be 'administered' no doubt were focusing on the point of the leader of worship, the minister, not taking it solely for himself (*sic,* at that time) but giving it to the people, who would give the bread and wine on to one another[58]; nowadays, the notion of 'administration' carries different overtones and is not so helpful in this context. Celebration speaks of the giftedness of the church assembly, that any and all might come together in faith 'to taste and see that the Lord is good' (Psalm 34.8). Even in the most serious demands of Christian witness, 'If God is on our side, who is against us?' (Romans 8.31)

4.7 Are there some who should not participate? The answer would seem to be yes and no. If the required spirit implies taking seriously such disciplines of preparation as are helpful and so coming around the table with a readiness to love as we have been loved, then clearly there are situations and circumstances where an individual will not be there without the danger of hypocrisy. The love of God is poured out upon us with an astounding measure of forgiveness but such forgiveness, with God's judgement of sin lying behind it, is no more to be taken for granted than the invitation to sit down and eat. Where there is no thankfulness, where there is no determination likewise to be forgiving, where there is no anticipation of the love of God accompanying us further on our life's journey, where there is no readiness to work with God for the overcoming of evil (we draw here on the latter parts of the Lord's Prayer and its influence both on Scripture and subsequent Christian theology), then participation is sham. God's love is turned away from, and the understanding of being 'in Christ' is words only. In the lovely though now slightly archaic-sounding notion of the Lord's Supper being a 'converting ordinance', there is the idea that the Supper, and our participation in it, turns us to Christ. None of us is worthy to sit at the table, but there is the invitation which comes from the Lord himself. It is an invitation to everyone, but we would dishonour our host if we come prepared to ignore him.

4.8 The place of the Lord's Supper, then, is that it is infinitely more than a religious ritual. Attendance is not something to be ticked off, as if turning up for school; a ticket is not to be presented as if to be a spectator at a football match where there is not a care which side wins. There is absolutely implied a preparation and a follow-on, as well as the event itself. Regularly, preparation is about more than the work of a few in preparing the space and the food and the vessels; for all concerned, the word, and silence, of encounter with God makes us ready. And follow-on is where the loveliest articulations of the vision of the Sacrament – where all are fed, and joined in company with the saints in heaven and on earth, and we await Christ's coming again – feed into our living between the times. A scholar in a very different geographical context put it like this: beware of 'Sunday Christians who steal chickens on Mondays'.[59] The kingdom work and witness continues where there is no table there to remind us of it.

4.9 There should, therefore, be no sense that the Lord's Supper is purely for Christians, a religious sideshow so to speak. This point might be illustrated thus. We live in a world where there is a great deal of concern about religious hatred, where suspicions abound around those

---

[58] Christ being the host of the meal, the tradition almost certainly continued through the Reformation of the Minister serving himself first. Cf for example Westminster Confession of Faith, ch xxix; Richard Baxter, *The Reformation of the Liturgy* (1661). Variation set in later.

[59] C Giraudo, 'The Eucharist as *diakonia*: from the service of cult to the service of charity', p 132 in K Pecklers (ed), *Liturgy in a postmodern world* (London: Continuum, 2003).

who profess a faith of any kind. At the heart of the Lord's Supper, and the life which is nurtured by it, is not assertiveness, but an appeal and a focus to know ourselves as the community forgiven and forgiving – the opposite of Christian bullishness. A violent crusade there cannot be, only a sharing in the power of the suffering Christ. Or, we live in a world where issues of lifestyle become ever more pressing, in view of global warming, for example, or what leads to happiness. Around the Lord's Supper, and the lives which draw from it, there is experience of the community of self-restraint and sharing. Reckoning with the massive challenges facing a world where there is so much poverty and unrelieved suffering, and wars and rumours of wars, it is around the Lord's Supper and the lives which sing songs of praise that there is a building of courage, a sowing of visions, a glorious path on which to follow until death is no more. Fed by our Lord and Saviour we should have everything to give, as we have had so much given to us. We commit to justice and grace and generosity and sustainability: breaking bread and pouring out wine and seeing Christ in the midst opens up the fullness of life. At the event of the meal, there is and should be (as there has been so often through church history) care for the poorest and least. And though we are all of us vulnerable, still as we go out from the assembly we may be strong.

5. What is the church?

So-called 'communio ecclesiologies' centre the understanding of the nature of the church around the place of the Lord's Supper or Eucharist, as it is called after the Greek word for thanksgiving. These are somewhat foreign to the Reformed church tradition in which we find ourselves, with the rationale being that our own tradition has tended to emphasise much more the event of God's encounter with His people and has been suspicious of suggestions that God's blessing is guaranteed in earthly forms, be it church or sacraments of the church. Though such debate continues, still the significant issue on the place of the Lord's Supper in today's Church of Scotland

is the question as to how integrated we are as a church in this regard. Are Word and Sacrament held together as closely as they deserve to be? Are we drawing, as fully as we are invited to, on the grace of the Lord Jesus Christ, the love of God and the fellowship (koinonia) of the Holy Spirit? Reflection on this would need to consider both the place of sacramental celebrations within regular church life, be it in parish, chaplaincy or wherever (including of course fresh patterns of church[60]) and also its significance on occasions of church courts, whether in meetings for 'business' or for admissions to membership, ordinations, the opening or closing of church buildings and the like. The word 'business' is to be put in inverted commas lest the Church be sucked into a mentality of only functioning efficiently and getting its jobs done, perhaps not for monetary profit but nevertheless as a complex organisation. For the body of Christ, wherever Christians come together, there are strong arguments for there being the richest of encounters one with another and with God, which Word and Sacrament together exist to enable.

6. The 'practice' of the Lord's Supper

The practical theology of Holy Communion aims at doing more than giving a series of hints and tips – though with ritual as with words the detail does matter! The heart of the task however is to encourage critical assessment of practice in the Church, giving weight both to the spoken word and to what is seen and done. And so the faith underpinning the Communion service will be able to speak, we trust, of Christ making himself known to us in the breaking of the bread (cf Luke 24.35)?

6.1 Scripturally the practical focus lies around the blessing and breaking of the bread which is then given to those around the table – but on the back of that

---

[60] Cf the current collaborative work of the Mission and Discipleship Council and Ministries Council in promoting general reflection on 'fresh patterns'.

comes a whole set of questions which can be variously answered, from the type of bread to the means of serving and much else besides. Rather than name all the possible options of practice, it suffices to note that behind these lie historic patterns which we might interrogate theologically. Much may be found to have its basis above all in local preferences, which is neither good nor bad but at the very least permissible to vary. We note that sometimes the sense that it has always been done in a certain way is a regrettable barrier to change which could be helpful; yet on the other hand, a regularity of pattern, and understanding why certain patterns are used and not others, can serve the depth of the mystery at hand. The heart of the Lord's Supper comes as we celebrate the mystery of faith – 'Christ has died, Christ is risen, Christ will come again'.

6.2 Thus, leading considerations will be how to prepare for, how to acknowledge and how to go out rejoicing in the blessing of Christ in our midst. The mystery as one Biblical writer put it is the unfolding of God's purposes 'to unite all things in him' (cf Ephesians 1.10). To follow in the line of the letter to the Ephesians, the pouring out of God's grace is a message of reconciliation, of the breaking down of fundamental barriers between ourselves and God, and nothing must be allowed to conceal that. Those who understand their calling see the need for 'all lowliness and meekness… patience, forbearing one another in love, [to be] eager to maintain the unity of the Spirit in the bond of peace' (Ephesians 4.2-3). Can this be seen in the words and the actions of local celebrations? Does the measure of formal ritual, for example, support or detract from our freedom to praise God and to be richly blessed in our companionship with one another? What is the relative importance of certain words and music and silence, of dress codes and seating arrangements, in this light? Are we caught up in a dying historical tradition or a counter-cultural, joy-filled anticipation of the One who makes all things new?

6.3 Our understanding of Christ's coming as inaugurating the new covenant, the transformation of minds and hearts, pulls apart inevitably the limitations of our ingrained horizons of thought and action. To that extent the knowledge of Christ's love is unsettling at the same time as it is hope-filling: it is not for us to remain the same. This point, as much as any, warns against conservatism in style and approach, lest we settle too readily in our comfort zones. Without taking this argument too far – it is not the case, for example, that we have no recognisable landmarks as we journey on; it is not for us to manufacture something so novel that we completely abandon all that is inherited[61] – there is counsel here for openness to the new. The congregation which always sang 'Ye gates' may modify its pattern, for example, or ways of serving Communion may alter…. How best will Christ's love, and our adoption and being joined in the outreach of that love, be expressed?

6.4 One point which exercised the Working Group in this connection related to the participation of children in the Sacrament.[62] Because baptism initiates us into the moment of Christ's dying and rising again and belonging to the community which lives on account of that grace, is there a case for excluding any so welcomed into being part of the new creation? The discussion tends to focus around issues of maturity and understanding. Yet alongside adults who have become familiar with aspects of local practice, children, less habituated, may bring the gift – as in the Passover ritual – of asking 'why?' And as that is allowed, may we respond using language that can be grasped yet every one of us still owning the mystery? And will we take what we allow beyond words, not only admitting that we are all learners and

---

[61] Gordon Lathrop's reflections on what may be called the *ordo* of Christian worship merit attention – 'The Lima Liturgy and beyond: moving forward ecumenically', in T F Best and D Heller (edd), *Eucharistic Worship in ecumenical contexts* (Geneva, 1998).

[62] See General Assembly Board of Education report and deliverances of 1991, 'Too young to matter?'

would-be disciples but also, for example, mixing adults and children together in the serving of the bread and wine? And the opening here would not be merely for liturgy, important though our patterns of worship are, for it must continue, as has already been noted, so that the celebrations of the Sacrament impact upon all of our living. Children have their place both in preparation and in follow-on, in giving as well as receiving.[63] Permissive legislation has already been passed on the admission of children to Communion, but perhaps its full implications have not been sufficiently recognised. As we have been baptized into the body of Christ, so the Church has a task of drawing out the gifts of her people and bringing all towards maturity. We have to ponder the undesirability of closing doors to any within the covenant at the point when, in Communion, our togetherness with Christ is most perfectly sealed.

6.5 Words play a signal role within the Sacrament, in conjunction with actions. There will be singing, sometimes of the prayers as well as of psalms and hymns. And there will be silence, perhaps lengthy silence (though in past practice, now more commonly laid aside, it used to be that there would be a reading of scriptural texts during the Communion meal; and in some places now, there is music or singing). On the guiding principles of all of this, the *Common Order* style has been to harvest both liturgical texts from the long ago and contemporary patterns of the poetry of prayer. There is much to be said for this, since it signals our belonging to the communion of saints who have gone before us while also intimating our present-day anticipation of the joys of heaven. Some will be inclined to lean most heavily on historic wordings, and others less so. Doubtless there is a need for discernment here, based on awareness of the meanings being conveyed; reference to our liturgical commentary may be of help here.

6.6 There are some key moments which, in the minds of some, might determine a need for absolute adherence to particular forms of wording and which in any case must be attended to. The words of institution (drawing primarily on I Corinthians 11) are a case in point. Every service in any book of order the Church of Scotland has produced has included the Institution. Rooting us, through the imagination, with the earliest days of Christian believers and shaping our own imagination of living, and derived from a context where good practice was under threat, it is hard to downplay its function, even if we might have cause to differ with the understanding, in the Roman Catholic Church, that these words together with the action of the Holy Spirit consecrate the elements of bread and wine and are therefore of uttermost importance within the liturgy. We might tend to use alternative forms cautiously and with good reason, but would resist there being a uniquely priestly moment here. And in the clearly related matter of invoking the Holy Spirit, although there has been important discussion, not least in the light of Eastern church tradition, on words of 'epiclesis', *eg* explicitly praying the Holy Spirit to come upon both worshippers and gifts of bread and wine, again there might be reflection that it may be less the formula and who says it when and rather the conjoined commitment of the worshippers and their ordained leaders which essentially shape the event. In the end there is no question of our worship being simply our own offering: we need to know about Christ offering himself, the Holy Spirit drawing us to Christ, the Father hearing our prayers.[64] Our liturgy and lives will be incomplete if we work simply on our own.

6.7 So far, it may be noticed, we have held back from articulating an interpretation of what exactly happens in the Sacrament of Holy Communion, although certain

---

[63] See essay by R Hamilton, 'A reflection on the implications for celebrant and community when children are present at Communion' [see the Church of Scotland website, www.churchofscotland.org.uk].

[64] Cf how the Reformed theologian John Calvin, for all that he moved away from prescribed verbal formulae (the words of institution excepted, as a warrant for the meal), was clear that it was by the efficacy of the Holy Spirit that we might enjoy Christ and all his blessings. J Calvin, *Institutes of the Christian Religion*, 3.1.1.

points are very much linked with that. Given the depth of controversy on this both historically and in the present day between churches, there is no catch-all option here. The teaching in both the Scots Confession of 1560 and in the Church's subordinate standard, the Westminster Confession of Faith, gives the foundation on which we shall build:

> Our Lord Jesus… instituted the sacrament of his body and blood… for the perpetual remembrance of the sacrifice of himself in his death, the sealing all benefits thereof unto true believers, their spiritual nourishment and growth in him, their further engagement in and to all duties which they owe unto him; and to be a bond and pledge of their communion with him, and with each other, as members of his mystical body.

> The Westminster Confession is at pains to emphasise that the event of the Lord's Supper is an event of a sacrifice of praise, lest anything be detracted from Christ's original and decisive work. Therefore the relationship between the outward elements relate sacramentally to the body and blood of Christ, 'in substance and nature… still… bread and wine, as they were before'. What is sacramental in relationship could be otherwise described as a "spiritual" relationship. In that the names and effects of body and blood are applied to ordinary bread and wine, the "work of the Spirit and the word of institution" guarantee the efficacy, eg the communicants spiritually receiving and feeding upon "Christ crucified and all the benefits of his death". "Christ Jesus is so joined with us that he becomes the very nourishment and food of our souls".[65]

6.8 Thus understood, the Lord's Supper is event as opposed to institution. There can be no lasting adoration of the elements which are shared, since it is the very act of sharing which is holy and a gift from God. There can be no summing-up, no full enough description, of what is involved. Participation is key, and the sharing is not the point at which the participation ends. As well as liturgical proprieties, there is something like a covenantal exchange. Christ offers his life to us and expects us to be offering our lives to him. His love is perfect and our love is to draw from that. Our faithfulness may know suffering unto death, but in dying we shall live. In line with the generations before us, our participation in communion is a real source of strength. Nothing can separate us from the love of God in Christ Jesus our Lord (cf Romans 8.39).

6.9 Therefore, we may return at this point to consider the aspect of celebration. There have been tendencies in practice to turn the Lord's Supper into merely a memorial of things past. This can too easily distance the reality of hope and, in consequence, overplay themes of suffering and failure which are part, but not the only part, of the Sacrament. In addition, if the recital of words and going through of actions is all too like play-acting, and historically quaint, again the dimension of transformation, of inviting glory, is too much passed over. We shall not repeat or emulate Christ's sacrifice but we would do well not to close our eyes to his living power amongst us even now, and most certainly within the Sacrament. There is a depth in the practice of 'remembering'.[66] We shall use imagination, in the fullest sense of that term, to picture all that has been given and all that is yet to come; we shall be part of the communion of saints and thus not only joined

---

[65] Westminster Confession of Faith, chs xxvii, xxix-xxx; Scots Confession, chs xxi-xxii. Note the passion in the latter 1560 document to assert how the bread and wine are not merely 'symbols and nothing more' or 'naked and bare signs', which has encouraged the Church robustly to defend the notion of 'real presence' in ecumenical dialogue.

[66] As in I Corinthians 11. 24-25, where the Greek word translated 'remembrance' (*anamnesis*) has no exact equivalent in English. The ecumenical convergence document, *Baptism, Eucharist and Ministry* dwelt significantly on this point. The sacrifice of praise by the worshipping people, like the sacrifice of self in service and sharing by the Lord Jesus Christ, powerfully turns on its head alternative notions of sacrifice involving violence and blood.

with those who have gone before us but also those who will follow on; we shall pause in anticipation of heaven, on the 'eighth day'[67], as it has sometimes been said.

6.10 In practical terms this is an underpinning for taking time for the Sacrament. Indeed sometimes liturgy can be over-wordy, but the solution is neither to gallop through the many words nor to cut down our thanksgiving so that we stop for as little time as possible. As has been said already, music and silence may well also have their place. Somehow all of history is focused in these extraordinary events of Holy Communion. What we regret and what has pained God must be left behind; where we stand by grace and what God has in store for us is to be affirmed. And our thanksgiving finds its decisive centre in God giving to us His Son.

6.11 Such thanksgiving, as it leads into communion, is an enterprise of prayer and presence. After the Word has been proclaimed, after God has spoken, the celebration of the Sacrament is an intense movement by ourselves into the heart of God's life. We pray so as to know the victory of Christ over sin and death and as we pray, he meets us and assures us of that, giving us to taste of his victory, food for the onward pilgrimage of faith. We pray, and it matters immensely then that we join in prayer, and that whoever may articulate prayers on behalf of, or in dialogue with, the community gathered knows that he or she speaks as one with all. Liturgically the rhythm of congregational response or song is a means of affirming this, and there are in the historical traditions of the church ancient and wonderful forms, such as the Sursum Corda dialogue and the Sanctus hymn.[68] At the very least the people should be encouraged to say 'Amen' to the thanksgiving prayers.

In prayer we offer our presence to God, who will heal and renew us. And it is entirely right that at the same time we will remember before God others who are not sitting alongside us, that our prayers will touch the needs of the world and the witness of the church. As we pray, so we should act, and the opportunity for financial giving at the time of worship and the opportunities for showing mercy and kindness well outside the confines of the church assembly come to enable that.

6.12 At the end, however, it is also the sense of prayer and presence which meets us from the throne of grace that is the cause of our renewal. The invitation to share the meal is in anticipation of feasting with Christ in the kingdom when he comes again. In this interim time, we are assured that his prayers and ours are conjoined and, however it happens, – let us not lose ourselves in historic disputes – he is truly present to us as we eat and drink. He leads us on, not as dead words on a printed page but as the living Word; he has gone ahead of us as the pioneer and perfecter of faith. In this understanding, all human leadership at the time of the Lord's Supper is relativised. The great weight of church tradition is to reserve presidency at the Lord's table to one ordained to that ministry, though, as our forebears took note, at the very same time that person is a receiver.[69] We can give only as we first receive. In practical terms, this can have its bearing on the order in which the table is served but more importantly simply in keeping in due order the aspirations of any who seek too far to control the life of the church. As Christ himself taught, service has greater significance than to be served. Both in the liturgy itself, and in the times of preparation and follow-on, the one who presides is one servant amongst many. There is a place for obedience as well as for creativity.

---

[67] Meeting 'after the week, though of course still in the week, proposes that the salvation of our very times is in a coming grace larger than our times can contain' – G Lathrop, *Holy Things*, p 111.

[68] To 'Lift up your hearts', the response is 'We lift them to the Lord'. The song of the angels to be joined in with is, 'Holy, holy, holy Lord, God of power and might...'

[69] Cf Westminster Confession, ch xxix 3.

7. The challenge of continuing dialogue between traditions

It may be that many practical aspects of the Communion service lend themselves to variation. Reverence and awe may be as profound in the open air by a lochside as in stone-vaulted spaces to the accompaniment of rich harmony and dressed ritual. Understanding and the note of celebration may be as real in the company of children sitting to receive for the first time as amongst those who have over many years treasured the familiar pattern. Prayer and presence is a touching of the human heart and an offering to God both when it draws deep from the wells of historic liturgy and as it is crafted in the moment for and with the people to whom it belongs. What matters is that we are ready to give thanks so as to be empowered to serve, eager to be fed so that we may know better what it means to give to the glory of God.

7.1 Changing days bring changes of experience. If there might be a note of caution raised about rushing into change, it comes in recognition that there have been points of order not merely hotly disputed in the past but with genuine issues to measure up to; and while there has always been great diversity in the life of the worshipping church, diversity has its limits. Debate and difference may be a healthy sign of the high value of the Sacrament of the Lord's Supper. However, there is something strange and even dangerous when people simply forge their own path oblivious to our common belonging. Or, what benefits are there when people experience the Sacrament as off-putting and meaningless because there is neither intimacy nor mystery at its heart? Communion is not sealed on our own terms, however amenable and stylistically pleasing they might seem; the very foundation of the Sacrament hinges on obedience: 'Do this in remembrance of me' is an imperative. Christ cannot be divided.

7.2 In this light, there is not least deep scandal through the divisions into which churches have fallen, unable to recognise one another's celebrations of the rite. Ecumenical awareness (in every sense, between localities and between denominations) offers at one and the same time blessing and challenge. We are drawn towards an appreciation of what we hold in common, and what beckons as a shared inheritance from the apostles. However, we are made conscious of there being demarcated camps of difference. Sadly the way in which churches understand the place and practice of the Sacrament of the Lord's Supper bolster antagonism and distrust at the very point at which the salvation of the world should be clearly proclaimed. It is, in one respect, a sorry witness on the part of Christian people and, moreover, a stumbling-block (in the poor sense of that term) to those who look towards us seeking a message of peace and healing. It asks of us deep searching to locate the sin within and a patient yet urgent hoping in Christ to resolve our difficulties.[70]

7.3 It is a little hard to know what all is happening within the Church of Scotland, though the roadshows have given helpful glimpses. It is clear that there is no uniform pattern of celebrating the Sacrament of the Lord's Supper, but that would be a sign of the impoverishment of imagination. Therefore it remains simply to reaffirm prime elements of what we would hold in common – the interplay of Word and Sacrament; the intimate connection between the Sacraments of Baptism and Holy Communion; the regularity of celebrations; the integral linking of what belongs before and after the rite with the rite itself; the dependence upon the active work of Jesus Christ and of the Holy Spirit, and the significance of the full participation of the people who so depend; and the placing of the Sacrament in a context where it focuses not merely an ancient Christian ritual but God's salvation of the world.

---

[70] 'Our journey, full of the fatigue owing to the overwhelming weight of the past, resembles that of the disciples to Emmaus. It is he who will resolve our difficulties…' Paul Couturier, quoted in G Curtis, *Paul Couturier and unity in Christ*, p 275.

8. Postscript – Reporting the Roadshows

Roadshows were held in Edinburgh, Paisley, Hawick, Aberdeen and Dingwall in 2008 and provided a rich exchange of views and questions. For half of the time brief presentations were given on Church of Scotland practice both within classical patterns and new ways of thinking; in the various locations also an Elder and a Roman Catholic participant were asked to voice something of their perspectives. For the other half of the time – and, additionally, over the sharing of a meal – full participation from those attending was invited.

8.1 Although the following is inevitably painted in broad brushstrokes, we might take note of leading affirmations and concerns on the one hand, and of questions needing answers on the other.

8.2 A regular affirmation was of the value of small-scale and intimate celebrations of the Lord's Supper. Some indeed went so far as to say they found the large-scale occasion unable to reproduce the same intensity of experience. There was at the very least strong support for variety in the style of service and the mood of celebrations. This then extended into perceptions of the depth of the mystery and appreciation of the direct encounter with the risen Christ through the Sacrament. Reference was made both to the communion of saints, *eg* the joining in worship with others in space and time, and of the value of relating the Sacrament to contemporary experience, for example through the form of spoken words, the vivid use of symbol, an honouring of the down-to-earth and simple or with respect to the sincerity and passion of those who participated. An active role for children could be affirmed, not least to unpack the meaning of the ritual, and in connection with that – though extending more widely, for example to those with learning difficulties – the importance of being inclusive as a community of faith. There was the sense that the appreciation of the depth of the mystery would grow over time and through experience – to use traditional language, that Christ and his benefits might be ever more fully received. Respect for the Communion meal and the real presence of Christ in the breaking of bread could strengthen the desire to bless the name of the Lord every time food was shared. Change in the details of celebration could be valuable, though it mattered that these should be well explained, since overall there was a desire for the communion to be an experience of active participation, not something involving, as it were, passive consumers.

8.3 Concerns articulated raised disquiet about the performance of the ritual being a cause of anxiety, both for those in leading roles and those who were less to the fore. Reasons avouched named unfamiliarity with what all was happening and/or a sense of being straitjacketed by outdated traditions. That people might come to the Sacrament out of duty but with little joy was regretted, as were experiences of people sitting in poor proximity one with another. There were opinions that Communion services could be over-formal or just boring, lacking creativity and life; if Communion is such a rare (precious) event, it can feel a relief to have it over with and a return to normality! There was discomfort about some people coming out only on Communion Sundays but otherwise hanging very loosely into the church family. There was a perception that partaking in the Sacrament could seem only a matter of receiving rather than giving and following on in faith.

Such affirmations and concerns deserve our attention. They may be held with differing degrees of passion, but together they speak of the desire to know the Lord's Supper as a rich experience at the very heart of the church's life. The mixture of voices, whether ordained or not, Church of Scotland or not, bore consistent witness to that.

8.4 A large number of questions was also articulated. Some of these related to traditions observed in some places and not in others, or at some points in history and otherwise not. Examples would be questions about the frequency of celebration, or about silence at the time the bread and wine are distributed and about who should distribute. We talked about change and how change could or could not happen in local settings. And there was beyond this an urgency to explore what might be called more fundamental questions. How do we estimate the significance of the Sacrament of the Lord's Supper, as opposed to services of the Word, and how will we best explain its meaning? How satisfactory is it to have Communion worship when the signs of our brokenness, within congregations as well as more widely within the body of Christ, are so conspicuous? What is essential to the power of the Sacrament – is it to do with those ordained to serve, is it the forms of words and actions, or is it the living community of the church? And when then does the impetus to include come up against the need to close in?

8.5 However much the report to the General Assembly printed above or the liturgical commentary may or may not give answers to such questions, the experience of the roadshows underlined the high importance of enabling informed discussion. It was abundantly clear that around the Sacrament there are serious causes of disquiet at the very same time as there are happy remembrances of intense spiritual encounter. We talked quite a lot about preparations for the Lord's Supper, both of the material aspects (bread, wine, space, music, assignment of roles, *etc*) and of journeying in faith and understanding. How far do we in the church, locally or on special occasions, draw on the potential riches of the Sacrament, and how much do we allow ourselves to sell out to almost emptying the ritual? Is the Lord's Supper a celebration of Christ's life in our midst and so the anchoring of our hope, or is it a sad commemoration of a dying faith? We can all recognise our brokenness and need, if we open our eyes, but are we together going to the One who will heal us and feed us or, scarily, being satisfied with limping along and again and again just feeling our hunger and thirst? Participants at the roadshows wanted these words to go out – that

they might find convincing responses in the Church of Scotland's life.

Members of the Working Group
Mr Kirkpatrick Dobie
Rev Dr Peter Donald (Convener of the Working Group)
Rev Fiona Douglas
Rev Leith Fisher
Rev Douglas Galbraith
Rev Roddy Hamilton
Very Rev William McFadden
Rev Robert Pickles
Rev Dr Laurence Whitley

Ex officio members
Rev Nigel Robb, Associate Secretary, Mission and Discipleship Council
Rev Linda Pollock, Regional Development Officer, Mission and Discipleship Council
Rev Andrew Campbell, Regional Development Officer, Mission and Discipleship Council

APPENDIX II
BEING SINGLE: IN CHURCH AND SOCIETY

1   Introduction
2   Contemporary social context
3   Church history
4   Scripture
5   Theological approaches
6   Single life
7   Sex, the single and the church
8   Conclusions

1.   Introduction
This report explores the experience of being single both within and outwith the church. Members of the working group on issues in human sexuality, and others who have been involved in contributing towards and reading earlier work, have from time to time suggested that issues around singleness should be considered by the group.

But it has seldom been a subject for theological reflection in the Reformed Church. Indeed, in eliciting responses on questions of singleness from single people, some have queried the need for any particular focus on single people within Christian theology or church life. Others, however, have welcomed the approach and focus, and have been glad to contribute, and so this report is offered with the conviction that a study of singleness uncovers much of importance for contemporary church and society.

1.1 Why *Being Single: In Church and Society*?

Patterns of relationship, sexual practice and living arrangements are changing rapidly in contemporary society. Being single is increasingly common, which is a significant factor in the rise in the number of people living alone, though of course the two groups are not identical: not all single people live alone, and not all people who live alone are single. Over 10% of Scottish households in the 2001 Census were single-person households, and between 1981 and 2001, the number of these households rose from 393,000 to 721,000.[71] We shall discuss a variety of possible causes in some detail in sections 2.31-2.4 below, but for the moment we simply note that people are settling down later, marrying later, and it is relatively common for people to have a period of living alone between leaving home and moving in with a partner or marrying. We all know something of what it means to be single, but for some people, the period of singleness is extended through life, and may involve living alone for most of life. Furthermore, the high incidence of separation and divorce means that many people are 'post-married', and again may well live alone. It is also typical for those in later life to live alone rather than with children and further generations, and with life expectancy increasing, longevity is more and more common. These various scenarios are known by Christians as much as by society at large.

---

[71] http://www.gro-scotland.gov.uk/statistics/publications-and-data/occpapers/household-change-scotland-in-a-european-setting/scotlands-place-in-the-uk-and-ireland/one-person-households.html.

1.1.1 Under the brief of the working group on issues in human sexuality, this work on issues around being single has naturally included attention to questions of sex and sexuality. The Mission and Discipleship Council therefore sees the guiding questions for this report as follows. What are the patterns of singleness within our society and the church, and what are the influences upon that? What do single people and their lives, including their sexual lives, tell us about God? What is God's word on single people and their lives, including their sexual lives? What is it to be single in today's church and society? Are there particular emphases in Christian faith and life for single people? What does the reality and presence of single people mean for the church? This report more explores issues around being single rather than prescribing how single people should be, yet while it cannot pretend to be exhaustive or definitive, it encourages the Church to take up the opportunity to consider these issues and to reflect on how they impact upon belief and practice. And in exploring the life choices – including sexual choices – faced by single people in their Christian discipleship, some conclusions are offered as to how the Church might promote the spiritual flourishing of single people.

1.2 Definition of terms

Because part of this report's intention is to explore the various different meanings of being single today, it is not proposed in this section to offer hard and fast definitions of terms. Nevertheless, it may be useful to pose some of the questions about definitions which will later be taken up in detail.

1.2.1 A *single* person may be defined, for example in law, as a person who is old enough to be married but is not married. But there are varieties of singleness in these terms: such a person may be single having never married, or be divorced or widowed. Some divorced people are happy to be considered single; others see themselves as essentially married to their (legally) former spouse. Some widowed people may see themselves as single; others believe that such a term disparages their relationship which was parted only by death. Furthermore, someone may be single in the narrow sense of unmarried but living in a marriage-like relationship, living together with a partner, and such a relationship may be of years' or decades' standing; it would be absurd to describe such a person as single. On the other hand, a person may legally be married, but separated in fact, living alone and apart from their spouse. In certain ways, that person is living a single life.

1.2.2 Defining *sex* is equally fraught. There is a huge variety of human behaviour which can be thought of as sexual, with different layers of intimacy, involvement and commitment. There are different sexual activities which different people would understand as being *sex*. Without seeking to impose definitions, this report would recognise that there is more to sex than sexual intercourse between a man and a woman, though sometimes that is what sex means.

1.2.3 And there also come tricky questions about defining sex and the single. For example, young people, some much younger than the age of consent, have sex, but we might hesitate in using the term 'single', given that they are too young to marry. But then again, young people can very definitely work with the concept of being in a relationship. In addition, adults who are single – in the sense of being neither married nor in a long-term partnership – may all the same be sexually active; and those who are married or in a long-term partnership may not be sexually active, with their relationships celibate in a temporary or permanent way.

1.2.4 Given these complications, perhaps it should be admitted that, ultimately, single people are those who understand themselves as being single.

1.2.5 There is also a set of difficulties in defining *celibacy* as against singleness. Celibacy as a term appears to imply a voluntary choice – in the sense that a celibate person

is one who chooses not to have sex. But the term is also regularly used by those who have not chosen a life without sex, but who for one reason or another are in situations where sex does not take place.

1.2.6 Other issues of language arise when describing aspects of life in terms of *aloneness* or *solitude* or *loneliness*. These terms may not admit of simple definitions, and their meanings may shade one into another, though perhaps 'aloneness' is a relatively neutral term compared to 'solitude' which has more positive connotations, and 'loneliness' which tends to be more negative. In discussing the experience of single people, it will be necessary to use this vocabulary, referring to the experience of being alone – its hallmarks, its blessings and frustrations. Still it should be clear that that these aspects of experience are not those exclusively of single people.

1.2.7 As for *marriage*, there is the legal definition, but even that term is complicated by the prevalence of long-term relationships in which couples live together in marriage-like arrangements, often bringing up children together. And is there not more to marriage than a convention in law?

1.2.8 Furthermore, pretty much all these problems of definition apply in a similar way to homosexual as well as heterosexual relationships, where the questions of singleness and celibacy, the activities of young people and the experiences of solitude or aloneness, and the matter of what is legally recognised and what runs more deeply are again pressing.

1.2.9 What matters is to be clear that the patterns of sexual and intimate relationships in contemporary society are complicated, fluid and various. Our theological reflection needs to bear this in mind. There is more to sex than, for example, sexual intercourse between husband and wife, and there is more to singleness than, for example, the bachelor son living on with his parents. It is the variety of ways of being single and of possible

Christian perspectives on that variety which call for careful reflection.

1.3 Previous reports to General Assembly

Singleness has never been the focus of a report to the General Assembly, but in recent years it has been addressed in the context of related subjects. In 1993, the Panel on Doctrine reported on *The Theology of Marriage*. Issues of singleness and celibacy are treated there in the context of marriage in the Old Testament, New Testament, early church, medieval Christendom, the Reformation era, and from the Enlightenment to the Modern Age. The report notes that in the Old Testament, 'there is no notion of committed vocational celibacy in either men or women,'[72] while in the New Testament 'celibacy is in places conceived of as superior.'[73] The report observes that the early church elevates virginity and celibacy, while theology in medieval times and beyond becomes more positive about marriage.

1.3.1 In 1994, the Panel returned to the subject, presenting a further report *On the Theology of Marriage*, which attempted to engage with the contemporary situation in society. Only one paragraph explicitly discusses singleness and celibacy (see section 6.2 below), but there is a sustained discussion of sex outwith marriage, concluding that some non-marital relationships of sexual intimacy may be responsibly chosen by Christian people. Also in 1994, the Board of Social Responsibility presented a report on Human Sexuality which discussed among other things questions of sexuality for people with learning disabilities and physical disabilities, and for elderly people, including the autobiographical testimony of a woman with a physical disability as to her relationships with men.

1.3.2 In 2007, the Mission and Discipleship Council presented a report to the General Assembly entitled *A challenge to unity: same-sex relationships as an issue in theology and human sexuality*. This report focussed on homosexuality, but covered material of relevance to singleness, discussing sexuality in Christian understanding, changes in societal understanding, the church and power, the interpretation of Scripture, and chastity and celibacy for the homosexually-inclined person. It was noted that many Christian homosexual people feel they must strive for a celibate life, given the wrongness, as they see it, of same-sex sexual activity, and that this celibacy and the singleness of many homosexual people leads many to find their lives marked by loneliness.

1.3.3 Although our search could not be fully comprehensive, we did not find substantial material published by other churches on the area of singleness, aside from reflections on vocational celibacy.

1.4 Process

With the encouragement of the Mission and Discipleship Council, the working group began its focus on issues around being single in 2007. This involved reading Scripture and theology, listening to contributions from pastors, theologians and historians, disseminating a questionnaire to some single people outside the group and critical reading of a series of drafts. An advanced draft of the report was then circulated to a panel of readers whose comments further contributed to the group's thought. The report which results is therefore informed by the voices of single people as well as theological reflection and pastoral experience. The group itself is drawn from across the Church of Scotland, and contains women and men, ministers and others, single people and those not single, and Christians of widely differing theological perspectives. Meetings revealed a large area of common ground in Christian reflection on being single, though there were certain points of disagreement. However, there was throughout the sense that in Christ we are one, and that this unity is not dissolved through disagreement on the interpretation of Scripture or the right approach to questions of faithful Christian living.

---

[72] Panel on Doctrine, *The Theology of Marriage*, 1993, section 2.1.
[73] Panel on Doctrine, *The Theology of Marriage*, 1993, section 3.3.

Rather, through debating these issues and understanding the alternative perspectives more deeply – and with the refining of approaches through what others can bring – the group came to a strong sense of the need to affirm thoughtfully God's creative, loving and gracious relationship with people, single or otherwise, and of each Christian's responsibility, single or otherwise, to live a faithful, loving and generous life in response, shaped by the forgiving power of Christ.

2. Contemporary Social Context

Theological reflection on sex and the single person must take account of the contemporary social context. Indeed, it is partly because singleness is a prominent feature of contemporary Western life, including in Scotland, that this report is felt to be called for. This section will describe contemporary patterns of singleness, suggesting some of the principal reasons for the prevalence of singleness and one-person households. Certain other features of contemporary society relevant to sex and the single will be considered, before a necessarily brief overview of the experience of single people in the church.

2.1 Young people's experience of sex

Of clear importance in any discussion of singleness and sexuality is the experience of young people in their teenage years, most of whom will form their first sexual relationships during this time. These years are crucial in their own right, and also as related to the decisions they will make as they grow older and begin in many cases to settle down into longer-term relationships. What must be recognised at the outset is that issues of singleness and celibacy are clearly different for young people than for older people.

2.1.1   Research indicates that sex happens at an earlier stage in relationships than was commonly the case before – though we should note that all statistics in the area of self-reporting are notoriously unreliable.[74] Few people wait for marriage to embark on sexual experience; and the average age for losing one's virginity is coming down. In a 2006 survey of 20,000 16-24 year-old Britons, 30% said they had lost their virginity before the age of 16, the legal age of consent.[75] In terms of having sex, it has been found that young people feel pressure to have sex even if they do not feel ready, although this is related to social class: middle-class girls are more able to resist boys' sexual advances, often drawing their emotional well-being from a group of friends rather than a boyfriend. A 1996/7 survey of 14 year-olds in the east of Scotland discovered that 18% of boys and 15% of girls reported having had sexual intercourse. A fifth of these girls though less than a tenth of the boys reported that they had been 'under some kind of pressure' to have sex. 32% of the girls and 27% of the boys thought that sex had happened too early for them; 13% of girls and 5% of boys wished it had not happened at all.[76] Peer pressure and alcohol have also been found to be the two main outside influences in people's first sexual experiences.[77]

2.1.2   Rates of teenage pregnancy are higher in the UK than anywhere else in Western Europe,[78] and indicate that a significant number of young people – despite school-based education in contraceptive methods – are either inconsistent in using contraception or indeed seek parenthood.[79] Incidence of Sexually Transmitted

---

[74] Johnson AM, Wadsworth J, Wellings K, Field J, *Sexual attitudes and lifestyles* (London: Blackwell Scientific, 1994).

[75] http://www.bbc.co.uk/radio1/bareall/survey_moreresults.shtml.

[76] http://www.bmj.com/cgi/content/full/320/7244/1243.

[77] *Informing Choice: New Approaches and Ethics for Sex and Relationships Education in Scotland* (Edinburgh: Scottish Council for Bioethics, 2004), p 13.

[78] See *Informing Choice*, 10, though they are falling in Scotland: figures for births to mothers 15 years old or younger have fallen from 6 per 1000 births in 1997 to 3 per 1000 births in 2006, the same figure as in the early 1970s. See http://www.gro-scotland.gov.uk/files1/stats/06t3-6.

[79] 38% of 16-24 year-olds don't always use a condom with a new partner, according to Bare All 2006, http://www.bbc.co.uk/radio1/bareall/survey_moreresults.shtml.

Infections is rising.[80] Rates of abortion continue to remain significant.[81] Furthermore, young people tend to have a number of sexual partners before settling into a long-term relationship such as marriage or a marriage-like relationship.[82]

2.1.3 The 2000 National Survey of Sexual Attitudes and Lifestyle gives further data. Young people do not generally accept traditional Christian teaching on delaying sexual intercourse until marriage. Over 85% of 16-19 year-olds considered sex before marriage to be 'rarely/not at all wrong.' However, the same age group was much more disapproving about sex outwith marriage (traditionally, adultery) with, again, over 85% considering it to be 'always/mostly wrong'. Beliefs about one-night stands were more conflicted, with over 40% believing them to be 'rarely/not at all wrong' while over 26% of men and over 44% of women considering them as 'always/mostly wrong.'[83]

2.1.4 Why do some young people have so much sex? Clearly the onset of puberty with biological and hormonal changes lead to the beginning and subsequent increase of sex drive. But there is more involved than satisfying physical urges. Research indicates that psychological needs are a strong motive, such as seeking affection, easing loneliness, confirming masculinity or femininity, bolstering self-esteem, or even expressing anger.[84]

2.1.5 Many parents believe that their influence over their children is increasingly overwhelmed by other voices, such as those of peers, education authorities and the media. Parents may be unsure how sexually active their children are, and also unsure how to encourage sexual behaviour which they feel is appropriate (and how to discourage what is inappropriate). Parenting throughout society has also become less traditional: in some communities, parents often condone and support their children's sexual relationships, from mid-teenage years onwards. The prevalence of marital breakdown is also influential in young people's understanding of sex: their world is one in which a single monogamous relationship sustained across decades is increasingly unusual, a pattern appropriate for their grandparents but unrealistic for their own lives and times.

2.1.6 However, parenting is still influential in young people's sexual attitudes and behaviour. Children of two-parent families are associated with lower sexual activity than children of lone parents. Parental oversight is also related to their children's sexual activity: the more monitoring, the less sex, though it has been shown that excessive monitoring can be counter-productive.[85] Young people's self-esteem is closely bound up with family relationships, and low self-esteem can lead young people to seek peer approval in sexual activity.[86]

2.1.7 If high levels of teenage sexual activity, pregnancy and sexually transmitted infection, alongside emotional immaturity and the huge variety of reasons for sexual activity are dispiriting to a Christian audience, it may make us realise that the church has failed to inspire many young people to a higher calling: in terms of their relationships' quality, endurance and stability, and in terms of the purpose of life. Section 7.21 below indicates areas in which the church can support young people as they navigate adolescence and the sexual pressures which face them.[87]

---

[80] *Informing Choice*, p 11.

[81] *Informing Choice*, p 12.

[82] 43% of 16-24 year-olds claim to have had at least five sexual partners; 18% claim to have had 10 or more, according to Bare All 2006, http://www.bbc.co.uk/radio1/bareall/survey_moreresults.shtml.

[83] See *Informing Choice*, p 13.

[84] *Informing Choice*, 27, drawing on the findings of F Hajcak and P Garwood, 'Quick-Fix Sex: Pseudosexuality in Adolescents', *Adolescence*, 1988 Vol 23.92, pp 755-760.

[85] See *Informing Choice*, 36 and references there.

[86] For this paragraph, see *Informing Choice*, pp 41-2.

[87] The Church of Scotland's Church and Society Council also considers issues of sexual activity, and has recently taken part in consultations over

2.1.8 Although children cannot be considered as being single, it seems appropriate when considering young people and sexuality to consider very briefly the issue of sexualisation of the young. Sexualisation may be defined as the inappropriate imposition of sexuality on a person – which seems clearly to be the case with children. But other aspects of sexualisation are in play as well – that a person's sense of worth comes from his or her sexual appeal or behaviour; that a person is judged as being sexy according to physical attractiveness; and that a person is sexually objectified.[88] It has been widely recognised that popular culture presents sexual images, themes and opportunities to children.[89] Magazines, television programmes and adverts, video games and internet sites, clothes and toys either for children or used by children present themes around sex. Sex sells – and increasingly sex is used to sell to children (and their parents), particularly from lower socio-economic groups. In Christian understanding of sexuality – as in conventional secular wisdom – sexuality is appropriate to emotional maturity, and sees in the sexualisation of children a deliberate corruption of innocence, shortening and narrowing the proper joys of childhood, often for adult material gain.

2.2 What people want

What do people – of all ages – want from sex? What are they looking for? We may start with the instinct which human beings have for sexual pleasure – at least part of what people want from sexual intimacy is sexual pleasure for themselves. Theological handbooks, on the other hand, tend to describe sex as having two main functions – procreative and unitive. Undoubtedly some people have sexual intercourse because they want to have a

child – the procreative function. But the unitive function is central to sex too. In being sexual, in intimacy, in sexual activity and sexual intercourse, people express their love for their partner and try to give them pleasure, deepen their relationship.

2.2.1 There are many other reasons – less laudable perhaps – why people consent to have sexual intercourse. They may feel pressured into trying to impress the other; they may want something from the other person and sex is akin to a payment.[90] There is also the pressure that people may feel to be having sex because it seems that society expects people to be sexually active, or to be having sex regularly, or to be having great sex, akin to earth-moving depictions on film and TV. To some extent, many people are engaged on a project – consciously or not – of constructing their identity, making themselves. To be sexually active in a wonderful sexual relationship may be part of the image of ourselves we are trying to build. Part of this report's purpose is to lay out the possibility of human identity, whether single or not, that sees our identity as creatures of God, shaped by the redeeming love of Christ, in which we are *not* obliged to find our marital state and sexual behaviour as overwhelmingly constitutive of who we are.

2.3 Consequences of contemporary patterns of relationship

Contemporary patterns of sexual relationship are naturally central to any understanding of singleness. There are a number of features which are relevant: the sort of relationships people have as they mature – whether these are sexual, involve living together or marriage; the number of close relationships people have before settling down; the times of singleness between relationships; the prevalence of separation and divorce; patterns of re-marriage and new partnerships.

---

the proposed Sexual Offences (Scotland) Bill as it relates to consensual sex between older children aged between 13 and 16.

[88] http://www.apa.org/pi/wpo/sexualizationsum.html.

[89] See http://www.apa.org/pi/wpo/sexualizationsum.html for the Report of the American Psychological Association Task Force on the Sexualization of Girls. Australia has seen a particularly keen debate on this issue.

---

[90] Of course, those in the sex industry do have sex or perform sexual acts for literal payment.

2.3.1 Marrying/co-habiting later

It is a feature of modern life that many people, particularly middle-class people, are marrying or forming long-term partnerships later, and delaying childbirth until the mother's thirties or forties.[91] Most people are marrying at a later age than their parents did. One consequence of this delay in marriage is an extended length of singleness (in terms of not being married). Typically a couple may marry 20 years after the onset of puberty, and perhaps 15 years after their first sexual encounters. One will expect and be comfortable that one's partner is sexually experienced before meeting. Furthermore, during one's teens, twenties and thirties, one may experience different periods of singleness (as in not being in a couple) between relationships.

2.3.1.1 And it is not simply that people are marrying later, they are marrying less. Even despite second and subsequent marriages, the number of marriages taking place is in decline, a drop of 35% since 1960.[92]

2.3.2 Serial partnerships

Serial partnerships are not new in human society. Before the development of effective medicine, it was of course common to lose one's spouse to death, and the re-marriage of widows and widowers was common. Many women were married a number of times, outliving a series of husbands. But the contemporary picture is as much characterised by separation and divorce as by widowhood. Divorce started to rise slowly from the 1930s, and has risen steeply since the 1960s. Statistics suggest that between a third and a half of contemporary marriages end with divorce, allied to which is the even higher break-up rate for cohabitating couples. There is not the scope in this report to analyse in detail the phenomenon of marital breakdown, but it is clear that

there are many pressures on contemporary marriages, including sex outside marriage, affluence and the desire for a wealthy lifestyle, work and individualism.

2.3.2.1 These pressures will mainly be discussed briefly in sections 2.3.3 and 2.4 below; as for sex outside marriage: it is rare for an extra-marital affair to be treated lightly within an ongoing marriage, and indeed it is not uncommon for extra-marital sex to be a cause to a greater or lesser extent in the break-up of a partnership. It may be a strong sign that the original relationship is foundering, and it almost invariably indicates a loss of trust between partners.

2.3.2.2 Many people thus find themselves single again at a relatively young age, and seek to make new partnerships. Their lives may be a cycle of partnership which may be marriage or singleness with relationships of greater and lesser intensity at different times. Thus those who are single in the sense of not having a lifelong partner may well be sexually active, involved sexually with one or a number of people for periods of various duration. For some this will be as it were a searching for partnership, marriage. For others the intimacy of the sexual experience will be rather more an end in itself.

2.3.2.3 Of course, not all people whose marriages or partnerships end immediately find a new relationship. Some deliberately choose the single life thereafter; others, although open to a new relationship, do not form a new partnership. There are consequently many post-married single people, some widowed, others separated or divorced.

2.3.3 Pressures on relationships

The pressures on contemporary partnerships, marriage and family life which contribute to the high levels of family breakdown, singleness and lone parenting include the increasing affluence of society. In order to have the material possessions and expensive experiences of contemporary affluence, people choose

---

[91] See http://www.gro-scotland.gov.uk/files1/stats/06t7-3 for marriage data and http://www.gro-scotland.gov.uk/files1/stats/06t3-6.pdf for data on birth.

[92] http://www.statistics.gov.uk/cci/nugget.asp?id=322.

particular ways of living. These include working long hours, away from home, both partners working, using childcare, taking on high levels of debt. While much of this lifestyle may be beneficial – people may enjoy work and may be fulfilled in balancing parental with career duties – there are also pressures which come. Financial stability may be precarious. People can become excessively tired. Couples may see very little of each other and their children. Families may increasingly live independent lives. Material wealth may impoverish relationships.

2.3.3.1 Another contributory factor in relationships breaking down, and in the prevalence of singleness more generally, is the priority given to work in contemporary society. People work long hours, work shifts, work away from home for a time, are contactable at home on work matters and bring work home. All of these pressures on time, energy and attention squeezing out one's partner or spouse or children contribute to dissatisfaction with family relationships. (In addition, work may be a refuge for those unhappy at home.)

2.3.3.2 Furthermore, some people may be considered unsuitable for a particular working environment if they have other commitments such as spouse and children. This is particularly the case for women, who may find that being married or having children presents a barrier to promotion or even to being appointed to certain jobs.

2.3.3.3 In other words, it is increasingly difficult – if it was ever possible – to have it all. A single life may allow for a fuller focus on work just as combining work with marriage and family life may involve either a diminished career or estrangement from one's family. We may have moved some distance from medieval patterns of renunciation (see 3.1 below), but renunciation is still an inescapable part of the choices people make in life. And of course for Christians, themes of renunciation, self-sacrifice and dedication are significant ones.

2.4 Individualism

A further feature of contemporary society which has a bearing on issues of singleness and sex is individualism. Recent decades have seen a rise in people's identifying themselves in terms of personal status, appearance, abilities, interests and desires rather than in collective or corporate terms. For example, whereas someone in the post-war period may have called himself a Shell man, he or she would be more likely to say today that he or she is working for Shell, and furthermore, such a person is likely to work for more than one company throughout working life. A person's skills, experience and CV are portable. Or in terms of entertainment, in the post-war period, huge numbers of the population would listen to the same wireless programmes, listen to the same records, watch the same television programmes; today audiences are much smaller, as people pursue individual tastes in music, media and the internet.

2.4.1 These examples could be multiplied. By and large contemporary people identify themselves less with causes or companies than with what they like. Furthermore, there are greater opportunities to satisfy these individual desires – for a particular kind of holiday or sofa or car or form of entertainment. And many people feel free to pursue their own interests. But this of course is freighted with double meaning. In pursuing their own interests, we could mean simply the things that interest them. But we could also mean advancing their own interests over against those of others. And there is a perception held by many that society is becoming more individualistic in that sense too – that we increasingly act selfishly, that we think less of corporate good than our own good, that we behave to suit ourselves. The critique of individualism is strong within the Christian tradition.

2.4.2 Individualism carries consequences for relationships. Some people, perhaps especially women, who might in a previous generation been bound into a marriage, will now remain single, feeling able to pursue their own lives and develop as people unencumbered by the compromises necessitated by sharing a house, decision-making and family ties. Conscious of the unhappiness which marriage often seems to bring to others, they see many more positives than drawbacks in the single life. Others will embark on sexual relationships but with a sense that they do so as autonomous beings, preserving their own individuality fiercely, unwilling to subsume their personal wishes into that of the couple. It may be that individualism in this sense is a contributory factor to the instability of modern marriages, and the rise in separation and divorce.

2.4.3 Yet it is important to reflect that if this rise in individualism is particularly evident in the rise of autonomy in women, men have for centuries essentially led individualistic lives, at least vis-à-vis their wives and families, and this was largely made possible by the subservience and financial dependence of women. If the clash of interests is problematic for society and its coherence, there are few desirable solutions in merely turning clocks back.

2.5 Lone parents

A further feature of contemporary patterns of family life is the phenomenon of lone parenthood. According to the 2001 Census, 22.9% of British children were being brought up by lone parents, and the proportion of children living with only one parent is rising.[93] There are a variety of situations involved. Some are born to mothers who are not in a committed relationship with the father. Other parents, though together at the time of birth, subsequently separate. Consequently, many single people, especially but not exclusively women, have the sole or major responsibility of caring for and bringing up their children.[94]

---

[93] http://www.statistics.gov.uk/cci/nugget.asp?id=348.
[94] See http://www.statistics.gov.uk/CCI/nugget.asp?ID=432&Pos=2&ColRank=2&Rank=528 which shows that 9 out of 10 lone parents are women.

2.5.1 Lone parenthood has extremely significant implications for the single parent's life, with financial, emotional and practical challenges different from couples who parent together. Being a single parent can in some cases impinge on one's ability and willingness to form new long-term relationships.

2.6 Experiences of single people in the church

As with so many aspects of this paper, it is important not to over-generalise in this area. Every single person in the church has a different experience of being single and in the church. Nevertheless, our work would indicate that there are certain patterns of experience which are common to many single people in the church.

2.6.2 First, for many Christians, it is not of particular importance to their self-understanding within the church that they are single. The church is the people of God, and the place where God's people gather for worship, to be inspired to serve in the world. Being single, in terms of their domestic circumstances, may be a contingent fact about one's life but not one which bears particularly upon Christian faith or experience of the church. As one respondent to the questionnaire wrote: 'We're all single at some stage in life. I don't see any issue here. We're all individuals within the church family.'

2.6.3 Indeed, it could be argued that the church predicates much upon individuals finding each their own place within the community. We make our profession of faith as individuals, exist on membership rolls as individuals[95], and very often serve in an individual capacity as, for example, Sunday School teacher, choir member, property convener, elder. Where couples are involved, they have come by and large each in their own right to that point of service. Furthermore, many of our forms of association in the church deliberately separate us from our family: we educate the young separately in Sunday School

---

[95] Note however that the Presbyterian Church in Ireland counts its membership by families.

and youth groups; women gather in the Guild (though men are welcome); men gather in men's associations. And it is often the case that people attend church while their spouse or partner stays at home. Indeed, many people of Christian faith are married to those without faith.

2.6.4　For some single people, the church may offer a fellowship, companionship and community which is not easily available to them elsewhere. Their friends are often their fellow-Christians at church, and worship services, meetings and other forms of service are the times and places they meet their 'family'. This is perhaps true especially (though not exclusively) for the widowed, whose children (if any) may live away, and older people are well represented in many churches. One respondent considered this fellowship as important: 'As someone who is single by choice, I greatly appreciate the friendship and support of my brothers and sisters in the church.'

2.6.5　On the other hand, some single people have the experience of the church seeing them as abnormal. The church's celebrations may remind single people of what is lacking in their lives – Christmas underlining 'the gift' of the child for Mary supported by Joseph; the sharing of news about weddings, and the close families all around the baptism of infants; the language of 'family services'; certain approaches to Mothering Sunday. They may hear in sermons and addresses the lament that there are not more 'young families' in the church and that the church should support families. They may know of the church appointing a Families Worker. They may hear through the preaching that God's will for his people is that they marry and be fruitful. One respondent wrote: 'Some congregations may lay so much emphasis on traditional family that singles feel left out. I've sensed that once or twice when visiting.' Moreover, some respondents clearly felt hurt by an attitude they met in church that to be single was to be pitied: 'I was chatting to a friend the other day after church… She is beautiful, talented, smart and interesting. She is also over thirty and single… One of the

older ladies came along… She said hello, then patting my friend on the hand asked if she had herself a man yet. No? 'Oh well girls, don't you worry – God will have someone for you yet.' It's so insensitive. Is she not adequate as she is? Do all married people think that single people are not whole?'

2.6.6　On the other hand, the opposite extreme – namely the inference that the single person is asexual – is also unhelpful: as one response says, 'the pious attitudes of some Christians that state that if you are single, you have no interest in sex or having a sexual relationship'.

2.6.7　Responses to the questionnaire also indicated that those who are single following separation or divorce may have different experiences of the church from those single in other circumstances. Regarding divorced people, one respondent writes: 'There appears to be an atmosphere of judgement or confusion as to what best to do with this person'.

2.6.8　A related set of issues are around ministry and being single. The advantages and disadvantages of being single, explored in greater depth below in section 6, apply to ministers in particular ways. Ministers work closely with people, hearing stories of great emotional depth, being with people in times of great stress, sharing in administration with people who can be difficult. Ministers make judgments as to what is best in the parish, in worship and in church life, and can often feel exposed, vulnerable and lonely within the work setting. A minister who is single and/or who lives alone cannot straightforwardly share these burdens with another as the married minister can. Friends and family may help, but sometimes are too remote from the situation to be particularly useful. The single minister thus faces the risk of isolation in a particularly acute form. And while the traditional approach of the Roman Catholic Church to this problem – that of priests living in community – is increasingly rare with declining numbers of priests, such an approach for close mutual support amongst those ordained has not been strong in the Reformed Church.

2.6.9 Moreover, one avenue which may be available to other Christians is not straightforwardly available to those who are ordained. As noted below in 3.4, some churches are increasingly comfortable with non-marital partnerships in the church. But there is throughout the Church the view that those in positions of leadership are called to higher ethical standards. To some extent elders, and to a greater extent ministers and other Christians in leadership, are expected to aim at the highest standards in all areas of moral life. Ministers promise in their vows of ordination to 'live a godly and circumspect life'. Sexual relationships outwith marriage are understood by many in the church to be neither godly nor circumspect. At the same time, as we shall see below in 7.13, while many revisionist Christians argue that some non-marital sexual relationships can be appropriate, when they are loving, generous, compassionate and just, for such Christians, particularly those who are ordained, there can be a dissonance between the traditional teaching of the church – reflected in the high moral standard expected of them by their fellow-Christians – and their own theological views on the status of sexual relationships. Any Christian who breaks with the mainstream is engaged in the often painful process of standing out from fellow-believers. But in the case of ministers or other Christian leaders, this process is exacerbated by their public role and public expectations of them, which may lead to their feeling constrained in how they live – not by their conscience but by the expectations of others. And the experience of such constraints may be for many single people in Christian leadership a particular burden.

2.6.10 These reflections have led us to the stage where we must add further layers to our considerations, layers which are fundamental to a specifically Christian approach to being single. Let us step back from contemporary society to see where we have come from.

3. Church History

Having looked at contemporary society's approach to sex and the single person, it will be of use to consider the central approaches the church has taken at different times to issues of singleness, sex and celibacy. For one thing, until the twentieth century, the church's views on sex and singleness were taken as normative for western society as a whole, and so a brief overview of the Christian past will help us understand whether and where society has changed in recent times. Furthermore, contemporary Christian views on sex and the single emerge partly from traditional understandings, which themselves interpreted the scriptural witness to God's relationship with creation. Further sections of the report, on Scripture and theological reflection, will interact with our historical underpinnings.

3.1 Early and medieval Christianity

Based partly on interpretation of key New Testament texts from the life and teaching of Jesus and the letters of Paul in particular (see sections 4.2-4.23 below) practices of sexual renunciation quickly took hold in the Christian community. Clement of Alexandria for example encouraged escaping bondage to desire, but not the rejection of marriage. But by the third century, asceticism was a growing and influential movement in the Christian world. The Desert Fathers and Mothers sought God in solitude, fasting and celibacy, removed from the city as the source of temptation. The ascetic movement saw the increasing centrality of virginity as a spiritual practice, allied to the beginnings of monasticism where celibates began to form a community together. Celibacy began to be lauded as better than marriage, though marriage was itself considered good. The Church in Scotland owes its earliest witness to Columba and others who embraced celibacy.

3.1.1 In time, it was increasingly expected that clergy would be celibate. This was enforced to greater and lesser extents from the fourth century onwards, though it was only from the twelfth century that ordained clergy were no longer permitted to marry in the Western Church. However, alongside the experience of celibacy belonging to priests and religious, the medieval church taught the importance of marriage and procreation. Marriage was the only proper place for sex; there was no divorce; the illegitimate were at a grave disadvantage; there was no scope for women to enjoy sexual licence.

3.1.2   A feature of medieval mysticism was the intensity of erotic discourse, described by celibates, both men and women. Some women mystics envisaged themselves as Christ's brides, their souls given to him and ravished by him; men too spoke in similar terms.

3.2   Reformation

A key aspect of the Reformation was the movement away from a celibate clergy and the practice of religious celibate monastic life. These were accused of being a form of works-righteousness, and the Reformers saw no harm, indeed, they saw positive good in nearly every Christian life in being married and having children. Christian marriage was a spiritual discipline. This was exemplified in the life of Martin Luther himself, who went from being a monk to being married. Reformation thought however still saw sex as requiring close regulation: sex was for marriage alone, as the right place for the regulation of lust. As for celibacy, while it was not promoted officially, in practice nearly all women had to be celibate in order to have independent roles in the church, such as missionary and deaconess, as these became possible in the 19th and early 20th centuries.

3.2.1   However, we might note that for all the Reformed Church has promoted marriage, some of the most influential figures in the Kirk have been single for all or much of their lives, including Mary Slessor, William Robertson Smith, George MacLeod and Donald Baillie.

3.2.2   In regard to marriage, definitions of marriage have shifted historically and there were various conventions for men and women living together and raising families. The boundary between betrothal and marriage was more fluid:

relationships which were not technically formalised as marriages instituted in a wedding ceremony, nevertheless functioned like marriages with equivalent standards of faithfulness, exclusiveness and permanence. Even if not without debate, social determinants have always been at play as much as theological considerations, and with variations of behaviour between social groups.

3.3   The traditional consensus

However, it may be said that from the mid nineteenth until the middle part of the twentieth century, a solid line towards singleness and sex which prevailed within church thinking was highly influential within society as a whole. Marriage was presented as the rightful calling of nearly all people. For women in particular, early life including work as domestic servants was seen as a training ground for marriage. Religious literature gave advice to young women as to how to avoid spinsterhood. Church was a place where young people could meet potential husbands and wives, for example as Sunday School teachers together. Thus the church strongly promoted stable marriages for the bringing up of children. The church condoned and encouraged young women who were pregnant to marry the father, thus making the child legitimate. And the church deplored separation and divorce, pressing couples to stay together. Re-marriage of divorced people was not possible in the Church of Scotland until the latter half of the twentieth century, and it continues to be rarely possible in other churches. Homosexual anal intercourse, illegal until 1967, and homosexual activity more broadly was seen as sinful and deviant and overwhelmingly was not accepted by the church.

3.4   Late twentieth century developments

In the late twentieth century and beyond, there has been an explosion of thinking, change and, in some circles, retrenchment regarding sex and the single, some of which will be reflected in later sections of this report. Fundamental has been the influence of feminism. A great deal of traditional thinking about the proper place of sex had been guided, implicitly if not explicitly, by the assumption that women are the property of men, to be kept chaste until given in marriage; that if unmarried they become 'old maids'; that women's sexuality is threatening and needs to be kept in check. (By contrast, male experience was quite different: typically men chose their brides; were often encouraged to practise sex with older women or prostitutes; if unmarried they remained bachelors largely without any negative stigma; and their sexual incontinence was often overlooked.) However, from the 1960s onwards, women increasingly broke free from traditional assumptions about the roles of women and men, and from the structures themselves – marriage, motherhood, a domestic life rather than career. The single life, and not necessarily a life without sexual relationships, increasingly became possible for women, and desirable to an appreciable proportion of the population. Developments in contraceptive technology caused a mixed response in the churches. Though the Church of Scotland approved the use of the contraceptive pill in 1960, other Christian voices, notably the Roman Catholic Church in *Humanae vitae* (1968), saw artificial methods of contraception as evil. And for many women and men who came to adulthood from the 1960s onwards, the church represented all that was oppressive, mistaken and unhealthy in sexual and societal assumptions.[96]

3.4.1 In theology and church practice, the influence of feminism has in part forced the church to re-evaluate thinking which was patriarchal, sexist and which had confused the gospel with its various cultural contexts. This re-evaluation in theology has been allied to a change in church practices. In Scotland, there have been women elders and ministers since the 1960s, and more recently Moderators of the General Assembly. Women are being seen independently of their relationships to men – their fathers, husbands or sons. This has an impact on how we understand our sexual identities and singleness.

3.4.2 An example of the new-found sexual confidence of women in the church is that women no longer need to choose the path of celibacy in order to exercise ministry. Female elders, readers, deacons and ministers may be married and have children. This does not, however, take away from the real practical challenges which face women managing family and ministry responsibilities which may weigh less heavily with men.[97]

3.4.3 There has been in the church also the partial acceptance of homosexuality as an acceptable Christian lifestyle. The Mission and Discipleship Council's Report to the 2007 General Assembly described an increasing acceptance of homosexual orientation within parts of the church, though it was bound to express the disagreements which remain in assessing the acceptability of homosexual activity. Nevertheless, it is now possible in considering questions of sex and the single to bear in mind the reality that many single people, including Christians, are homosexual, and that any Christian discussion of singleness must take account of the distinctive though perhaps overlapping experience which homosexual and bisexual people have in being single.

3.4.4 Less publicly contentious than questions of homosexuality have been issues around sex outwith marriage and cohabitation. Section 7 below will deal with the theological issues involved. But at this stage it is worth noting that some (though by no means all) Christians and churches have come to accept and even become comfortable with people having sex outwith marriage in long-term committed relationships. Many Christians who are not married but live with their partners attend church, receive communion, serve in many ways and are ordained as elders. The prevalence of separation and divorce has been influential in this regard. Many

---

[96] See Callum Brown, *The Death of Christian Britain* (London: Routledge, 2001), chap 8.

[97] However Christian development agencies often expect their staff to be single or married to someone else working in the same place.

separated or divorced Christians find strength, friendship and sexual intimacy with a new partner, but are hesitant, or are unable legally, to be re-married. In many churches today they do not feel unwelcome, though this is a patchy picture – with churchgoing people in non-marital partnerships sometimes feeling it expedient to keep quiet about living arrangements, or even the existence of a partner if they do not attend church together. Might it be that churches are more tolerant of middle-aged people in sexual relationships outside marriage than they are of sexually active young people? If so, is it because we think that the middle-aged are mature enough to have sex for the right reasons?

3.4.5 Church practice in history and the present day is always informed by its reading of Scripture. Indeed, singleness and its corollaries of marriage and family life are presented throughout the pages of the Bible, and can draw forth rich theological reflection. So let us turn to Scripture.

4. Scripture

The sorts of question which will guide our enquiry are as follows. What patterns of sexual relationship are presented in Scripture as normative? What specifically is said about single people – their status, roles and difficulties? What role does and should the community of faith take in supporting single people? What activities and moral guidelines are commended for single people?

4.1 Old Testament

The Old Testament's presentation of those who are single is essentially seen as part of its understanding of God's purposes for humanity through the covenant relationship with Israel, within which the people are bound together in marriage and child-bearing.

4.1.1 On single life

Texts traditionally seen as foundational for the Old Testament's understanding of human relationships and for the church's understanding of God's purposes are

Genesis 1 and 2. In chapter 1, we read that God created humankind – male and female together – in his own image. Neither the single male nor single female would appear to encompass the image of God, or encompass the nature of humankind.

4.1.2 The second chapter's presentation of the creation of humanity begins with a single human being, Adam. God then makes a garden and puts Adam in it to till and look after it. All so far has been good. But now there is a discordant note: 'it is not good for the man to be alone'. Aloneness, singleness, being without a partner is not good – does not seem to be in accord with the harmony of God's creation, nor the fulfilment of humanity. Wild animals, birds of the air are all formed but are not suitable partners for the human being. It is only the being like himself, formed from his own bone and flesh, that is a suitable partner, and they are described as 'the man and his wife'.

4.1.3 By the end of the second chapter of Genesis, that which was not good in creation has been completed and become good – the human being is no longer alone: he has a partner: the two human beings – male and female – are not alone but have each other. The image of God, found in male and female, finds its full expression in Genesis 2. They are naked but feel no shame: no sin has taken place to spoil the harmony of creation. This presentation of a world before sin shows two human beings in partnership.

4.1.4 However from Genesis 3 the situation is complicated. Sin enters the world through the serpent and the people's disobedience of God. As soon as they sin, they blame each other: 'It was the woman you gave to be with me...' Sin disrupts the harmony of the couple, and they become discordant individuals, with wills at odds with each other's. Of course, the account has Adam and Eve continue together and bear children together, but we are aware that their marriage cannot be perfect in a world marked by sin: their love is flawed, and involves an individualism which cannot be excised from their experience.

4.1.5 Nevertheless, as the Old Testament continues the human story in encounter with God, this foundational account of the mutuality of man and woman seems implicit. For the man not to be alone, women are sought as wives. And men too are sought as husbands, especially for widows such as Ruth. The concern stated many times for widows and orphans is a concern for people disjoined from families. God, according to Psalm 68:6, puts the solitary into families. A life lived alone is an anomaly in Old Testament understanding. As the people of Israel are called into a covenant relationship with God, the Law which issues is steeped in commandments for family and community life. Thus marriage binds people into family and community and being single is best left behind; when it happens through death, it is well remedied through re-marriage or absorption into a larger household. At the same time it should be noted that the Old Testament presents a large number of narratives of marriages which are full of tension, involving dishonesty and sexual incontinence. So while there is no conception of the people of Israel aside from the bonds of family and community, there is cognizance of the difficulty of the holy, obedient life within such bonds, including marriage.

4.2 On family life

In addition to the discomfort the Old Testament feels around long-term singleness is the central importance of child-bearing and descendants. Crucially, God entered into covenant with Abraham *and his descendants*, who would be as many as the stars of the sky. This involved the miraculous birth of Isaac to Abraham and Sarah. Indeed, Sarah is only the first of a series of infertile women whose lives are blighted by their inability to conceive. The Old Testament is clear that this is a curse: barrenness prevents the fulfilment of one's religious duty to give birth, stops the line of descendants and involves the pain of loneliness

and unfulfilled potential. Hannah, for example, while childless calls herself 'heart-broken' and speaks out of the depths of 'grief and misery' (1 Sam 1:15-16).

4.2.1 The theme of infertility is central in the Old Testament's depiction of Israel. Barrenness is a sign of God's disfavour; children a sign of blessing; conception following infertility a sign of the specialness of the child in God's purposes. The people of Israel are compared to a woman – and prophets' own sexual lives are used to exemplify the situation of God's people. Hosea is to marry an unchaste woman to represent God's covenant partner being unfaithful, while Jeremiah is told not to marry in order to represent the barrenness of Israel.

4.2.2 A contemporary Christian reflection on that issue of childlessness may recognise much in these Old Testament emphases which resonates with typical experiences today. Many women and men find their lives blighted though childlessness whatever its cause or causes. Many people echo Hannah's distress. Having children, bringing up one's family, envisaging posterity through one's offspring is seen by many Christians as a significant part of God's blessing in their lives. But a fully Christian and contemporary approach will also question certain Old Testament nostrums. These include whether bearing children can any longer be seen as one's religious duty, whether infertility or childlessness for any reason should be seen as a withdrawal of God's blessing, and whether we should see our destiny as ultimately residing in having descendants. Christian eschatology sees eternal life not in the survival of our blood-line, but in our own person being found in Christ in life, death and beyond.

4.3 On celibacy

The properly religious life in the Old Testament, then, is a family life of marriage and child-bearing. The covenant with Israel is handed on through the generations, through birth. There are narratives of other sorts of life – polygamy and concubinage, for example – but these are not lauded as normative. As for celibacy, this is rarely presented, and there is no word for 'bachelor' in the Old Testament.

4.3.1　But such a view of celibacy is not one which is preserved intact in the New Testament, or in subsequent Christian thought and practice. As we shall see below, the person of Jesus Christ brings a significant shift in the understanding of loyalty, allegiance and family, a shift which continues to this day in Christian understanding of sexuality and being single.

4.4　New Testament

Whereas the Old Testament uniformly sees marriage and procreation as signs of God's blessing and human virtue, both in the order of creation and amongst the covenant people, the New Testament operates with somewhat different assumptions. Disciples are called into relationship with God in Christ, and with each other, and that relationship stands apart from, and perhaps even in tension with, the 'normal' social order of family life.

4.4.1　This differing attitude can in part be explained by how the people of God are to be constituted in the light of the gospel. No longer is belonging seen as genealogical. It is not birth but adoption and belief that defines who belongs. It is mission and not procreation that ensures the increase of God's people. It is baptism into Christ, where there is 'neither male and female', rather than social covenant, that creates human fellowship. Further, whereas the Mosaic Law assumes an intention to regulate the social order of Israel as a whole, the New Testament assumes that God's people will exist as a minority differentiated from the wider social order, a differentiation existing even within the same family structure.

4.4.2　Generally, ancient Greco-Roman society encouraged citizens to marry and procreate not simply as a matter of cultural or moral nicety, but that the city or empire might survive; celibate exceptions are rare and anomalous. Family life indicated investment in, and loyalty to, the civic order. One of the questions then for the early Christians was: how does the Christian community, whose citizenship is of heaven, fit into this social order with its accepted family patterns? Key here are two questions of allegiance – first, to what extent does loyalty to Christ and to the new Christian community call into question loyalty to family (and to spouse)?; and second, to what extent does this new loyalty call into question conformity to the normal social expectations and pressures, including the pressure to marry and have children?

4.5　Jesus and the gospels

Significantly, the gospels present us with a Jesus who is assumed to be single. The Christian role-model is the second Adam but with no corresponding Eve. Further – regardless of the later church's concentration on the Holy Family as exemplars – the Jesus of the gospels seems to stand somewhat dislocated from the life of his own family. Being 'in his Father's house' means not being by his parents' side (Luke 2:41-51). He operates from his own (or Peter's) house in Capernaum. He seeks the companionship of the twelve, rather than of his kin. Traditional familial loyalty is redefined, so that the question 'Who is my mother, and who are my brothers?' solicits the unusual answer 'For whoever does the will of my Father in heaven is my brother and sister and mother' (Matthew 12:46-50). Loyalty to God and the community of disciples appears to subvert the expected primacy of spouse and family.

4.5.1　Nevertheless Jesus affirms marriage as part of God's created order. Indeed, in his rejection of divorcees remarrying on the grounds that the Creator made the two one, he takes a high view of the marital union. It is no less than the Creator who makes husband and wife inseparably 'one flesh', so that Moses' permission for divorce is marginalised, and the remarriage of the divorcee (virtually) forbidden. However, it is this same high view of the permanence of marriage which leads the disciples to ask, 'is it then expedient not to marry?' And Jesus, although stating that his 'teaching is not for all', commends the eunuch as a model of living 'for the sake of the Kingdom' (Matthew 19:11-12). Whatever this enigmatic saying means, it is a further departure from expected norms and from Genesis' procreative imperative. Here the accursed, non-procreative, and dis-engendered eunuch is made a Kingdom model for 'those who can accept it'. Whilst Jesus does not make celibacy a condition of discipleship, he certainly challenges the normal expectations of family life as the accepted religious way of life, and sign of virtue and divine blessing. Jesus here also acknowledges that people may be single (metaphorically eunuchs) for reasons of birth or circumstance, but adds to that the possibility of being so 'for the sake of the Kingdom.'.

4.5.2 This passage does not stand alone in presenting radical Kingdom values and suggesting that the cause of the Kingdom makes new claims on the sexual existence of the disciple. It is, after all, this celibate Jesus who prophesies blessing on the barren women (Luke 23:29), commends those who put Kingdom before 'father and mother' (Luke 14:26), and reconstitutes the family as 'those who do the will of God' (Mark 3:12-15). Of course this should not necessarily be read as a call to abandon family life – Jesus explicitly demands that parents be honoured, and rejects the notion that such obligations may be laid aside for reasons of religious service (Mark 7:9-13) – but it is a relativising of natural (creation) ties for the sake of the Kingdom, and an insistence that devotion to the Kingdom ought to override natural desires and social expectations. To be a disciple is to be among those who give up 'house or brothers or sisters or mother or father or children or fields for my sake and for the sake of the gospel' (Mark 10:30 – and Luke 18:29 adds wives).

4.6 Pauline Writings

In contrast to Genesis' statement that 'it is not good for a man to be alone', Paul can write 'it is good for a man not to touch a woman' (I Corinthians 7:1). Although, in the passage that follows, Paul is at pains to insist that this good does not make marriage bad (sinful), nevertheless his insistence that not marrying is also good. Not only does it run counter to Old Testament assumptions, it also goes against social and civic assumptions about the duty of the citizen, to family, city and empire. The resultant discussion (I Corinthians 7:1-40) of what is good in marital choices itself opens up a new space for discussion – a freedom of choice is implicit, indeed explicit, in the exhortations. Here, marriage too can be a good, indeed it can be a moral necessity – either to avoid immorality (7:2) or otherwise acting improperly to a betrothed. But other than this, there ought to be no compulsion to marry. A choice to be single is a good choice. Here Paul appears to offer his own (implicitly single) lifestyle as a model for believers to follow, wishing that all would be 'as I myself am' (7:7).

4.6.1 The discourse on choice here is significant, particularly that Paul seeks at so many points to make clear that men and women equally have to choose marriage or singleness, and that the Church will consist of those who have made different choices. Yet the choice is not a matter of indifference. The overriding question is: what best demonstrates devotion to the Lord? And here Paul is not neutral. Although he gives no command, his argument is clear: singleness is to be preferred when possible. Other than avoiding immorality, no positive reasons to marry are given. Social pressures (procreation, family duty, civic responsibility) are ignored, perhaps seen as part of the form of a world order that is 'passing away'. Whilst marriage may not be sin, the believer is instructed not to 'seek a wife' and Paul, despite having 'no command of the Lord', then offers a string of arguments for believers to follow his example of singleness. He ends by insisting that whist the unmarried man is concerned with 'the things of the Lord' and 'how to please the Lord', the married man is concerned with 'the things of the world and how to please his wife'. Marriage is thus somehow more 'worldly'. Whilst the married person's interests are divided, 'unhindered devotion to the Lord' is to be preferred.

4.6.2 Perhaps underlying all this is Paul's insistence in the previous chapter that 'the body is for the Lord' (6:13), is a member of Christ, and 'temple of the Holy Spirit' (6:19) and the believer is not altogether free in sexual choices. Paul alludes here to the Genesis 'one flesh' discourse on the union of man and wife and uses it to suggest that even a casual sexual union with a prostitute has deep significance. The argument proceeds by comparing sexual union with its demands on the body, with the believer's spiritual union with Christ and its demands on the body. Here, bodily devotion to the Lord makes a sexually immoral union unthinkable, but it perhaps also suggests a potential tension between being united to Christ and the choice of whether to give oneself to another in marriage. The married believer is said to be 'bound' to the spouse (7:27) who shares authority over the believer's body (7:4), yet Paul wishes not to be dominated by anyone (6:12) as the body is for the Lord. It is difficult to escape the conclusion that Paul here sees marriage and belonging to the Lord as a potential conflict of loyalties. Indeed, somewhat enigmatically, it is only the unmarried woman who is said to be concerned 'to be holy in body and spirit' (7:34). The suggestion seems to be that singleness makes possible a more complete Christian devotion, or even holiness. It is a small step from here to the notion that being a 'Bride of Christ' is an ideal of Christian devotion that spiritually exceeds marriage.

4.6.3 These passages perhaps have the potential to cause other questions to be raised, not just about the benefits of marriage or singleness for Christian devotion, but questions about the underlying pressures to marry. Why is it that the believer seeks to be married? And how far are such desires an indication that the believer is conforming to the expectations and desires of society, rather than seeking devotion to Christ? How far is the person making the choice seeking the 'things of the Lord' rather than 'the things of the world'? The ethical question 'can I?' is answered quickly – marriage is not sin, not marrying is also good – but larger questions of worldview,

freedom and conformity are also raised. Perhaps, picking up on I Corinthians 6:12, they move the question from 'what is permissible?' to 'what is beneficial?' for Christian service.

4.6.4 In Ephesians 5:21-6:9, the emphasis is somewhat different. Here the existence of the Christian household is taken for granted, its relationships to be transformed, rather than called into question, by the believer's new identity in Christ. Ephesians deliberately compares Christ's love and self-sacrifice for his Church to the devotion that the Christian husband should have to his wife. Once again, the Genesis 'one flesh' motif is used both of marital union and of Christ's union with the Church, and used to stress the significance of both. It is used to insist that the wife be treated as part of the husband's own body, just as Christ cares for his body, the Church. However, there is no suggestion here of a tension between these unions, but rather that one should model the other. The union of husband and wife is a mystery that reflects that of Christ and his Church. The danger is perhaps that in suggesting that Christian marriage *can* be beneficial to the believer's expression and demonstration of Christ's self-sacrificial love for his people, a normative analogy is created that might suggest that those in such marriages *are* better able to express or experience the self-giving of Christ. Indeed, just as the Genesis text can be used to suggest the single person is somehow incomplete, only half a person, so too this text could be used to imply that the single person incompletely models the self-giving of Christ.

4.6.5 When we turn to the Pastoral Epistles, we also find marriage and ordered family presented as normative for the Christian. Indeed these letters pour anathemas on false teachers 'who forbid marriage and enjoin abstinence from foods' (1 Tim. 4:2-3). Certainly this is an indication of one ascetic direction in which some Christian teaching could, and indeed later would, go. There appears to be a recognition that Christian teaching has potential to disrupt the order of the family, or certainly to be accused of such by non-believers. The Pastor is particularly nervous about single women, painfully aware of the danger that any accusation of social impropriety might cause for the church. Women too are to be respectable (1 Tim. 2:9-10), 'managed' by their husbands (1 Tim 3:12) and knowledgeable of their place in the hierarchy of the household and the church (1 Tim 2:11-12). The socially anomalous class of widows are treated with special caution. Younger widows are to marry, bear children and manage households so that they 'give the enemy no occasion to revile us' (1 Tim 5:14). Only older widows, who are 'beyond reproach' and have previously discharged their social duties in service and child rearing (1 Tim 5:10), may be given the financial support necessary to remain unmarried. These last comments are intriguing, particularly when taken with references in Acts 6 which indicate that making provision for widows was a significant activity for the early church, at least in Jerusalem. For was this merely an act of charity, or was the church making resources available such there was a new possibility of remaining single for those widows who would previously have been economically forced to remarry? After all, in a different Church context the Pastoral epistles seek to regulate and limit this possibility – although even here it is not eliminated.

4.7 Themes

Putting the New Testament evidence together, the first thing to note is the degree to which living in Christ makes a claim on the sexual body of the believer, and on all of his or her relationships. Teaching about Christian living must not be seen as merely imposing ethical limitations on social conventions and personal choices. Marriage or singleness are not merely permissible choices which the believer happens to make, but the choices themselves are to be surrendered to Christ. Here a canonical balance is required: I Corinthians 7 and Matthew 19 question assumptions about the desirability of marriage. For those who either assume marriage is God's ideal for them, or who feel free to make their own independent choice,

these texts ask the discipleship questions of 'how do I best serve the Kingdom of Heaven?', 'is devotion of Christ my chief end?' and perhaps 'what are the social and cultural pressures, assumptions, and expectations that are influencing my choosing?' On the other hand, Ephesians reminds us of how marriage too can be an act of Christian self-giving and not just one's personal fulfilment – in marriage Christ's love can be modelled. Perhaps the Pastoral Epistles again serve to remind us that the social realities and the contemporary context of the Church cannot be ignored altogether. What is a good witness?

4.7.1 However, one thing that is clear from the pages of the New Testament is the primacy of the Christian community in questions of the social identity of the believer, whether married or single. Certainly a married Christian is to be a dutiful spouse, loving and loyal – covenant obligations to the partner are underlined by both Jesus and Paul – and self-giving is to be the mark of the relationship in Christ. Yet marriage is also relativised in light of the primacy of Christian belonging. Those who are married are somehow to live 'as if not'. The traditional familial bonds of father, brother, sister and child are usurped as this same language is taken to denote the new fellowship of relationship in Christ. Something of the exclusivity of the genetic family appears to be dissolved in this new family of the baptised. It is interesting to note that whilst the New Testament re-uses the language of family love to speak of the Christian community, the Church today so often does the opposite. Passages like I Corinthians 13, or hymns like 'Bind us together' which speak of the communal love of Christians, are easily misapplied when connected specifically to marriage. Key here is the concept of *koinonia*: the new commandment is to 'love one another, as I have loved you'. This is a far stronger concept than friendship or companionship, since it embraces not just those we choose to love or with whom we enter into covenant relationship, but all of those who are bound together in Christ, and by Christ's choice, not ours.

4.8 Scriptural conclusions

This survey of the Bible on issues of singleness reveals central themes. In Old Testament perspective, singleness is anomalous, requiring explanation, as against the basic understanding that God's people are called into marriage, child-rearing and family life. Family is central to God's Law, and to how God's people relates to God. It is in family life that obedience and religious observance is found. Being single is akin to being outside the covenant relationship with God; being childless is consequently a curse.

4.8.1 But the New Testament sees singleness in quite different terms. Marriage is re-emphasised as a good thing, and Christians have to take duties in marriage seriously, but it is not principally in family relationships that God is encountered and obeyed, but in one's following of the way of Jesus Christ and adoption of the values of his kingdom. Consequently, being single is seen as advantageous, allowing a greater attention to the Lord. Childlessness – following the life, death and resurrection of Jesus Christ – drops out of focus.

5. Theological Approaches

It is evident from our survey of Scripture that issues of singleness are not at all incidental to the Biblical witness to how human beings relate to God and to their neighbours – in marriage, celibacy, child-bearing, childlessness, and Kingdom living. We now turn to theological reflection on these issues, bearing in mind the resources of Scripture, and our earlier discussions of the contemporary social situation and church history. We begin with God as relational.

5.1 God as relationship, God in relationship

God is God in relationship. As Father, Son and Holy Spirit, God is Trinity, three persons in perichoresis, the notion being that there is relationship, sharing, mutuality, love and togetherness within the Godhead. And this relationality does not only exist within itself, but reaches out into what is not God, that is, God's creation. We should be careful not to say that God's loneliness drives God into creating a recipient for love. But perhaps we can say that God's love finds further expression in creation, spilling over into an other, an external relation: stars and planets, atmospheres and soil, plants and animals, men and women. God, in love, freedom and wisdom, chooses to be in relationship. The church has been at one in holding that this relationship between God and creation brings God glory.

5.2 Human relationships under the grace of God

Not only is God in relationship with creation, but human beings are in relationship with God, sometimes a relationship acknowledged as the heart of our lives, sometimes observed in the breach. We are the ones capable of faith and prayer, of being spiritual.

5.2.1 Relationships which we have with each other potentially mirror God's relationship with creation, in an outpouring of love, a manifestation and communication of goodness. At the same time our relationships can be marred and damaged, and our lives are also not self-sustaining as is the divine's; aseity belongs only to God. Yet we can say that being in relationship is critical to our development as human beings: beyond the womb into early bonding with those who nurture us; through socialization experiences before school and the learning and making of friendships; within the close family and beyond the family; in romantic relationships, and marriage and/or partnerships; through being parents and grandparents; and being dependent in illness and infirmity. (Of course we do not all have all of these relationships.) Scripture, as we saw above, reflects these social connections in human beings on almost every page: the people of Israel; the centrality of husband, wife and offspring in the patriarchs; loss of family in Job; care for the vulnerable in the prophets; discipleship and the church in the New Testament; the new heavens and the new earth, in Revelation. (Examples could be multiplied.)

5.2.2 So is the love of a sexual relationship, as is

commonly argued, and in particular the love of husband and wife, a strong image of God's love for creation and for human beings? The sexual act, for example, can be seen as an act of complete self-giving. Moreover, the love which develops throughout marriage – passionate, tender, joyful, supportive, patient and forgiving – can be seen as echoing the faithful love which God shows to creation (see 7.12 for further development of this theme with regard to sex and marriage). It is important to note that sexual relationships are just one form of human relationship which reflect God's interaction with creation. Family relationships which are not sexual should also be acknowledged in any account of human flourishing. The relationships people have with parents, grandparents, siblings, children, grandchildren and other family members are important to most people. And in the case of single people, in the absence of marriage or sexual partnership, family relationships may have greater significance than to others. It is possible in a variety of relationships for the love of God to be reflected and experienced.

5.2.3 Friendship, for example, an often under-explored theme in the Christian life, is a central form of relationship for many people, and not least single people. It is evident that friendship can be for many Christians a profound context for their sanctification. Friendships offer relationships of physical and emotional closeness, of trust and of intimacy, relationships that may last for many years, even across a life. As section 4.5 above on Jesus' re-definition of family indicated, friendship with our brothers and sisters in Christ is at the heart of Kingdom relationships, and can be immensely satisfying in providing fellowship and opportunities for trust and service. Friendships for many people are crucial to their identity, giving them a sense of place, honour and importance to others. Such friendship is found within marriage and partnerships, but also in many relationships which do not involve sexual desire or intimacy. Indeed, in no sense does friendship with

people of the sex one desires sexually demand physical sexual expression.[98]

5.2.4 Friendship is certainly of importance in particular scriptural narratives, though it is important to note that both Old and New Testament emphases on friendship spring from different social and theological contexts from our present-day understanding. In the Old Testament, the covenantal friendship between David and Jonathan, for example, is akin to the covenantal relationship between the Lord God and Israel. In the New Testament, friendship is broadened in a number of ways. Jesus wept when his friend Lazarus was dead. 'Friend' is a theologically significant term which Jesus uses to describe his relationship with his followers: 'You are my friends, if you do what I command you' (John 15:14). Here friendship is not so much about spontaneous and loving care, but the practice of obedient discipleship (though also involving love). Furthermore, New Testament understanding of Christian love sees it as being for all Christians, and indeed for enemies, extending far beyond exclusive friendships.

5.2.5 In later theology, the idea of friendship was developed theologically in ways more at home in contemporary patterns of relationship and church life rather than scriptural models and understanding of the church. Friendship was explored especially in the monastic tradition, by for example Aelred and Francis de Sales, while recent feminist theology of friendship emphasises the particular nature and significance of female-female friendship.

5.2.6 The theological significance of friendship can be developed as follows. First, friendship is grounded in the nature of God, which is love. God is the source of friendship, in that the Holy Spirit is the bond of love between Father and Son and is reflected in the bond of

---

[98] Although it is probably a perennial topic of conversation among young people – can men and women be friends without sex getting in the way? This was the question behind the successful film *When Harry Met Sally*.

love between friend and friend. Friendship is possible because God is present in the world by his Spirit in every relationship of those who participate in God in Christ. Second, in friendship there is a movement towards God. To love fellow human beings, created by God, is not merely to love them for their own sake but to love the creator who fashioned and continues to fashion them. As one loves a friend, God who continues to be in the friend through His image, which is always present, is also loved. Our loving our friend is akin to, and so practice for, the love we ought to have towards God. Third, friendships should be conducted according to the model of friendship par excellence which we possess – the friendship which God has with us. This is a friendship which is marked by complete selflessness, without any hint of advantage to God. It is pure gift, sheer grace, and is offered entirely out of love. True friendship, following this model, is not a reciprocal arrangement or a result of bargaining – it is not given for what one receives therefrom. Fourth, friendships here remain unfulfilled, but will be made perfect in heaven. As God is the source of creaturely love and friendship, so in eternity our friendship and love will share unsurpassably the love of God.

5.2.7 Drawing these threads together, the best of human relationships are formed under the grace of God, and may be an image of God's relationship with creation. There may be an intimate sexual relationship or else growth through relationships with family or friends or fellow-Christians and others. The difficulties in our relationships reflect of course the distance our lives have travelled from the goodness of creation. Nevertheless, whether single or not, the pattern of our relationships, part of God's created gift of life, can offer images of God's love, faithfulness and joy.

5.3   The body and sex

The direction contemporary reflection has taken is towards an understanding of sexuality as richly part of God's good creation, indeed part of what is described in Genesis as very good. This is to some extent at odds with the early church's movement into sexual renunciation, monasticism and a celibate clergy, and the high regard for virginity as a spiritual path. Much of the traditional Christian difficulty with sex stemmed in part from an understanding that the human essence, the centre of the human person, was the soul. And the soul could be thought of as being separate from, though located in, the human body: there was debate as to the moment when and how it entered the body, but what was crucial was that it was not contingent on the body, and did not depend on the body for its existence.

5.3.1   This understanding of the soul, influenced by Plato's *Phaedo* among other texts, guaranteed the possibility of life beyond death, conceived as the soul's immortality. It was in the soul that the image of God resided, the soul which related to God, the soul which was the seat of humanity's virtue and the soul which could enter into eternal life after the body had withered and died. The body was thought to be of earth rather than heaven, solid, material, vulnerable to and polluted by sin, and the source of further temptation to sin. The body craved sexual satisfaction, food and ease, and drew the person back towards earth. Given this categorisation of the human person, with the body a temporary if necessary vehicle for one's essence, one's soul, it followed that sex was understood as a bodily requirement and function, which required strict regulation to avoid falling into sin. Note, however, that the church did not altogether dispense with the body, indeed deeming heretical those groups which saw the body as demonic or not part of God's good creation, such as the Gnostics or Cathars; nevertheless, the church saw in the body that which united us simply with brute animals rather than that which united us with God.

5.3.2   Contemporary theology has performed a spectacular volte-face in this area. For much contemporary theology, the human being is created by God as bodily, inescapably so. Talk of the soul is downplayed though rarely jettisoned completely: when the soul does feature, it is understood as emerging in and through the human being's bodily experience. Life beyond death is commonly understood through the frame of resurrection of the body rather than the immortality of the soul. In this theology, as well as re-reading Scripture, has been influenced partly by science, social science and even much philosophy which see human beings principally or indeed entirely as bodies and relegate talk of the soul or spirit to the margins. Whether or not it is sustainable to disregard the ensouled nature of the human being is not central here; what matters is that the human body is understood as God's good creation. And it is not part of its definition that sex is sinful, any more than a hand which can punch but also heal is sinful.

5.3.3 Sex, in the newer theological view, is more than the created means for reproduction, it is also for binding human beings in intimacy. It is a natural and normal part of being human to desire sex, to enjoy sex and to find it a central part of loving relationships. The Song of Songs is now recognised as a Biblical celebration of the goodness of sex, aside from the significance of other possible layers of interpretation.

5.3.4 As section 2.2 observed, sex involves more than a physical instinct (though this is clearly basic and important), but of course involves human beings in emotional and moral spheres. The centrality of sex to art, including poetry, fiction and film as well as the visual arts, bolsters the view that sex involves the whole human person. Sex is interesting because it cannot be reduced to the fulfilment of a biological urge. Sex opens up and often constitutes the drama of human interaction. Thus it is rather important to consider sex as part of human spirituality. The drama of desire, attraction, joy and pain, trust and fulfilment, betrayal and shame which is inextricably bound up with sex in myriad possibilities involves the human being in the depths of human self-understanding and identity, of motive and action, of sin and redemption, of fidelity and grace. Sex and sexuality, no more but perhaps no less than other aspects of our humanity, feed into our relationship with God, our following of Christ, our life in the Spirit.

5.3.5 The basically positive view of human sexuality in contemporary theology thus includes its moral importance. Sex can be the occasion of total self-gift, of generosity, of kindness, of the mutual expression of love, of healing, of intimacy. And it can also be the occasion of selfishness, greed, self-regard, violence, hatred, damage and hurt. Rape, incest and other forms of coercion show that sex can be sinful. And there are questions, dealt with in part in sections 7.12-7.14 below, as to the proper context for sexual intimacy and sexual intercourse: with whom is it appropriate? When is the time to embrace and a time to refrain from embracing (Eccl 3:5)? Sexual intimacy may be part of a loving, consensual relationship, but how are the parties bound to other people in loyalty and fidelity? Such questions have furnished half the Western canon of literature and much popular story-telling: far beyond Christian circles, sex matters morally.

5.3.6 It might be questioned how much the church at large has accepted and promoted this more positive view of human sexuality. Christian teaching about sex and sexuality does take place in sermons, small group discussions and youth work, but probably not as frequently as the importance of sexuality to our lives might suggest. Even marriage preparation meetings and classes tend to focus on other aspects of the couple's life rather than their sexual intimacy. Perhaps this reflects a proper privacy. But on the other hand it may also have one of a number of unfortunate results – either that Christians believe the church's view is unchanged from a frowning distaste for sexuality, or alternatively that the church has nothing to say on sex and sexuality at all.[99]

---

[99] One area of the church's work where sex and sexuality are frequent subjects for conversation is mental health chaplaincy, where patterns of inhibition and taboo are different from other spheres.

5.4 Singleness: theological status

Given our understanding of God as relational and human beings being made in that likeness, and our contemporary confidence that sex and marriage are part of God's good creation, a particular question arises regarding being single. In upholding partnerships for the ordering of human sexuality, does being single run counter to the God-given plan for human beings? For if so, being single – particularly being single throughout life and never marrying – would be a deficiency, an aspect of dishonouring God.

5.4.1 Although such arguments are made in the church, it is our contention that theology and attention to the unique circumstances of each person's life counters sweeping judgments about whether remaining or being single is sinful. There may be a particular circumstance which has prevented someone from marrying: for example, shyness, caused in part by the actions of parents and others in childhood. More often, there are numerous and overlapping factors which influence people not to enter committed relationships. Of course the choices we make, the personalities we are and the circumstances which affect us are inescapably bound up with creaturely sinfulness, but that does not necessarily lead to the conclusion that the single person has turned away from God's call on their life.

5.4.2 And so singleness is not to be regarded as some deficiency or that single people are lesser than their married counterparts or that their lives reflect God's purposes less. Neither the New Testament nor human experience should lead us to see singleness in these terms. Indeed, rather than ask why people are single or whether they should be single, it is more fruitful to view singleness as a vehicle for grace and a state for journeying towards fulfilment and blessing. The best question is to ask how God can best be glorified by those who are single – as well as those who are not.

5.5 Identity and Personhood

What is the role of sexuality in our identity? Theological thinking in this area has known tension between underplaying and overestimating its role. Christians understand their identities in a number of overlapping ways – child of God, follower of Christ, part of the Kingdom, woman, man, Scot, mother, father, child, brother, sister, friend, doctor, hairdresser, and so on. But Christians may also identify themselves in certain key ways to do with their sexuality: as straight or bisexual or homosexual; as married, in a partnership, separated, divorced, widowed, or single. Our identity as Christians is affected by our identity as sexual beings: we follow Christ as the people we are; we relate to God from the identity we have; our worship and prayers reflect the circumstances of our lives; our means and choice of service reflect the opportunities our domestic circumstances allow. The reverse is also true, and possibly more significant: our identity as sexual beings is affected by our identity as Christians: we become the people we are as we follow Christ; our identity is formed by our relationship to God; the circumstances of our lives are shaped by our worship and prayers; our domestic circumstances are shaped by the service we are called to.

5.5.1 And so it would be mistaken to present Christian spirituality in a unified form, as if the married mother of four relates to God entirely as does the single man. They are different personalities with different experiences, including sexual practices: so they differ in their spirituality. And their different Christian emphases and experience of faith affect their approaches to their sexual relationships. Furthermore, the experience of single men and women is often subtly different.

5.5.2 However, a single person's faith is not necessarily vastly different from a married person's. There will clearly be overlap because we share our humanity and are one in Christ, redeemed by the same Saviour, following the same God. (This is surely why a single pastor can understand others' marital problems, why a childless elder can sympathise with the church member with difficult teenage children.) It should also be noted that for many people, sex is simply not that important, whether they are married or single. Other things matter more – work, interests, friends, family, faith. They do not see themselves fundamentally in sexual terms. Nevertheless this runs increasingly counter to a society which appears fascinated, possibly even obsessed, by sex.

5.6 Choice and celibacy

Singleness is not always a deliberate choice. There are many people who, although open to love, relationship or marriage, have not taken that path. The reasons are as many and varied as the individuals. The interplay of circumstances, accidents of personality and character, or abuse experienced in earlier life, may be involved in some people not being able to find or commit to a long-term relationship. Also, there are those for whom physical or mental illness or incapacity can be major factors in the cementing of relationships.

5.6.1 However, no discussion of being single in theological perspective should overlook the ways in which being single can follow from an individual's own choices. It is not only external circumstances that lead some to marry, some to separate, some to remain single. Christians understand that human beings are, essentially, free to enter into unions or to remain single. Of course, as this report points out at greater length in sections 3.2-3.4, the experience of people in the past, especially women, was often one of great coercion and little freedom. And contemporary human beings are still far from the autonomous individuals presupposed in much rationalist philosophy. We are influenced to greater and lesser extents by genetic and other inheritances, environment, experience and circumstance, by coercion and pressure.100 However, the Christian faith, particularly in the realm of moral action, lays emphasis on the gift of freedom and that the human being may make choices which shape our character, experience and relationships, not least with God.

---

100 Recent legislation on forced marriages makes it clear that coercion is still present in many people's lives in this area, particularly women's lives.

5.6.2 In the matter of this report, it follows that (with qualifications) we are free to marry or not, free to enter into sexual relationships or not, free to have children or not. This is, as we have seen, presupposed by the central New Testament discussions in this area, including the teaching of Jesus and of Paul. To marry? whom to marry? when to marry? to be sexually active at all? – are questions which ideally Christians answer as part of their response to God's call in their lives. How to answer these questions involves, so far as one is able, discerning the will of God for one's life. For some Christians, they feel it is the will of God that they remain single. And – even though this may run contrary to certain of their desires – they attempt to follow Christ in this path.

5.6.3 However, one feature of contemporary life to be noted here is what may be described as the pressure to be partnered. There is a presumption in contemporary society that the natural course of a life will involve settling down into marriage or partnership: this is learned by children from a young age from fairy-stories where the hero and heroine marry and live happily ever after, through romanticised images and portrayals of love in adolescent and grown-up fiction. The single are often assumed to be looking for love. The divorced are often assumed to be ready for a new partnership. Newspapers and the internet offer increasingly easy ways for the single to meet new potential partners.

5.6.4 Of course, many single people are looking for the intimacy, companionship and security that they perceive a partnership/marriage will bring them, but this is not true of all single people. Being single seems to many to be the best way of fulfilment, caring for family and friends, and contributing to society – and for the Christian, of following Christ. But there is little emphasis in contemporary conversation, media or societal ideals on the contentedly single. This may make singles increasingly insecure as to the validity of their singleness, whether largely chosen or unchosen.

5.6.5 Indeed, the question of whether or not to remain single is one which is raised in a number of the responses to the questionnaire. For many Christians, being single is a conscious decision, occasioned to a great extent by their Christian discipleship. 'I am single because of my Christian faith. I could easily be in a relationship at the moment, but because of my commitment to Christ, I have chosen to be single'. 'I met someone who did not share my beliefs so would not commit myself'. 'I took the decision to remain celibate when my marriage ended and that was Biblically-based, bringing about a contented lifestyle and a drawing closer, I felt, to an understanding with God'.

5.6.6 Nevertheless, celibacy as the deliberate choice of a life without sexual partnership is not especially common in the church today, particularly in the Church of Scotland.[101] As discussed above in section 3.2, the Reformed Church saw in celibacy a mistaken emphasis on meriting God's favour through denial of sexual expression.

5.6.7 However, the long tradition of celibacy in the church sees it in much more positive terms. As well as the choice of a celibate life as a way of controlling sexual desire, of putting oneself at a remove from particular temptations to sin, Roman Catholic understanding describes celibacy as, fundamentally, a choice for the kingdom of God, to devote oneself to Christ over all other relationships, and thus be able to serve a greater number of people than those with spouse and children. Christ himself is understood as the model of the celibate life, whose life was poured out for others. Celibacy is required for those ordained to particular vocations to priesthood and to the religious life. It is our contention that the choice of a single life, including the commitment to celibacy, far from a turning away from Christian duty as earlier Reformed thought maintained, may be for some a fruitful and rich path of discipleship, bringing blessing to their own lives and to many others, and glory to God.

---

[101] It should be noted, however, that monasteries in the Orthodox Church are currently experiencing a surge of new entrants.

5.7 Asceticism in singleness and marriage

It may seem curious to see marriage as well as singleness as an ascetic practice. For we saw in section 3.1 that asceticism rose in the church among those who renounced marriage and sex, in the desert or a monastic life. And clearly the single life can be one which offers an environment to develop ascetic practices – the absence of sexual intercourse, for one. And there are other practices which may be easier for single people to develop – fasting, emphasis on prayer, going on retreat.

5.7.1 However, marriage and partnership can also be seen as a place for ascetic discipline. All who have lived in such a relationship will know the opportunities it gives for compromise, for self-sacrifice, for devotion to the other, for abstinence from sex at times. It is a false dichotomy to see marriage as a place for sexual fulfilment, while celibacy is the path of self-denial. Rather, both celibacy and sexual partnership call for holiness: self-denial and self-giving to others; repentance and humility; charity to self and others.

5.8 Wholeness in the community of the church and in heaven

Whether single or married, separated or divorced, a parent or childless, Christians do belong to the family of the church. The principal scriptural image for this community is the body of Christ – an intriguing metaphor: the material, sexual body represents God's people. Paul uses this image to affirm that all Christians, despite their different gifts, belong in the same body, the same fellowship, share the same Christ. Indeed, perhaps it is possible to believe that we can find a wholeness within this body, complete within the church. This thinking has been central to the understanding of monastic life: a vow of celibacy yet a community of love. At its best the church offers the company to the single person which they may feel is denied them in family life: fellow-Christians are brothers and sisters in Christ. Some practical outworkings of this insight will be found later in section 7.23-7.24.

5.8.1 But we can go further than this. It is also part of the Christian faith that, different as we are, single, married and so on, we will be united in the perfect community of heaven, where 'every accursed thing shall disappear' (Rev 22:3). All that is imperfect in our relationships, all that sin spoils, all the pains and loneliness will, we hope, be healed in the presence of God.

5.8.2 The question of marriage going beyond death is one that has intrigued Christians. According to Jesus, they neither marry nor are given in marriage at the resurrection, but will be like the angels in heaven (Matthew 22:30). Theologians have tended to interpret this as seeing marriage as a temporary, earthly institution, which is for our time but not for eternity. Consequently, tradition has often questioned whether earthly couples will be couples beyond death. Indeed, speculative attempts to imagine the resurrection body have inferred that it will be without sexual organs. Nevertheless, the doctrine of the resurrection of the body implies that the blessed will be knowable by others, and be social. It may be that there will be no marriage and no sexual activity in the life to come, but rather a perfect community, without exclusive relationships. Perhaps then it is paradoxical that a traditional image for the End is the Consummation, an image particularly developed in the erotic visions of medieval celibates as discussed in section 3.1 above.

5.8.3 However imagined, it is the Christian hope that our imperfect reflection of God's love in our loves will be made complete in the life to come, that our identities will be no longer shifting and insecure but that we will be perfectly known and know others, that we shall know peace after the sometimes gruelling compromises of creaturely life.

6. Single Life

Having explored scriptural and theological perspectives on singleness, it is time to look more closely at the actual experience of single people. This section will identify both positives and negatives found in single people's lives, particularly Christian people, both in terms of their experiences and opportunities for growing in holiness, love and service. In this section in particular, we are conscious that as with all attempts to depict human experience, what is said can only be by way of generalisation. People are different, and the experience of being single may be very different depending on one's age, sex, to what extent singleness is chosen, whether one is single following separation, divorce or bereavement, and in countless other ways. It is clear, for one thing, that experience of being single changes markedly throughout life. Young people may feel their single status keenly, with an extreme sense of loneliness, but this stage is often short-lived. Later in life, the experience of being single may have different levels of expectation, acceptance, happiness or discontent. Furthermore, the positives and negatives of single life overlap with those of life as part of a couple: for example, some couples leave a lot of space for separate friendships, while for others there can be great loneliness within marriage. This section draws significantly on Martin Israel's book, *Living Alone: The Inward Journey to Fellowship*[102] which both describes the experience of living alone, which often overlaps with being single, and offers a way of Christian spirituality which is unique to living alone. In what follows we will be considering those who are single who may or may not live alone, bearing in mind that the experience of being single may be greatly different in ways both positive and negative for those who live with family, flatmates or friends, from those who live entirely alone.

6.1 We are all individuals

Perhaps the best place to start is the realisation that we are all individuals, whether single or married. Israel makes the point that we all in some sense journey through life alone, that life is a constant series of separations:

---

[102] Martin Israel, *Living Alone: The Inward Journey to Fellowship* (London: SPCK, 1982).

from the womb, from parents, from friends, from safe environments, from family, from sexual partners. So while many people may differ from single people in having an intimate partnership, all may experience solitude, all are prey to loneliness. Israel adds that acknowledging our aloneness is a crucial part of gaining a deeper knowledge of God. Indeed, we may encounter our deepest self when abandoned.

6.2   Positives

The Panel on Doctrine report on marriage in 1994 put the point well that singleness can be seen as a gift:

> We believe it is important to affirm that celibacy or singleness is a valid life-choice, gift or vocation. This should not be seen, as it often is in popular assumption or even in Christian attitudes, as second-best, conveying an image of 'failing to find the right person' or pitiable isolation. Single and celibate people may, just as much as married or sexually active people, be involved in rich and deep relationships of friendship and creative interaction.[103]

6.2.1   Let us take this insight forward by exploring what may be positive in single people's lives, drawing partly on responses to the questionnaire which asked What do you see as advantages in being single? In being single and a Christian?

6.3   Time and space for God

The traditional answer, associated with the church's understanding of celibacy as discussed in section 5.6 above, is that being single allows one to be devoted fundamentally to God, in obedience and in guidance. The practical, emotional, sexual and even moral distraction of a partner is absent. For one respondent: 'I'm not obliged to anyone but God… I'm alone so I have to consult God myself in everything for everything'. For another: 'I have the time to spend

with God where and when I want without trying to fit in around another person/family'. This has practical outworkings in a number of ways.

6.3.1   Martin Israel makes the point that the single person who lives alone knows silence more keenly than those who live with others: and there are uses of this silence – to explore one's own personality; to listen to others (paradoxically – the idea is that a person used to silence is one who has a skill to listen); to hear the Holy Spirit leading us into the truth of our condition; to pray for the world. One response emphasised this positive aspect of solitude: 'Space for solitude and reflection'. Another: 'Christ's promise 'Lo I am with you always' and prayer are the mainstay of a single person's life'.

6.4   Freedom for self and others

A further advantage of the single life is that one may be oneself without having to adapt one's characteristics, preferences, pursuits, spending or whole way of being to fit life with a partner, or to children if childless. That does not necessarily make one selfish but it does all go to the making of who one is. Singleness gives one a latitude and possibility of fulfilment denied to those who are not single. One respondent put it this way: 'Freedom to make one's own choices, from small things like what to eat or what to watch on television, to major choices about work, home and lifestyle'.

6.4.1   The other great gift which singleness offers is a width of friendship with both sexes. Marriage is based on love between two people alone, and love of that kind is not found in singleness: it is too exclusive. Instead singleness offers a breadth of friendship, and that is the gift a single person may give to society. One response puts this in terms both of gift and need: 'because I don't have a particularly strong 'love' relationship going on with one person I realize my need to love others and give my self over to them'. Of course the married have friends, but their primary

---

[103]   Panel on Doctrine, *On the Theology of Marriage*, 1994, section 8.7.

responsibility and typically their greatest love is for their spouse and children.[104]

6.4.2 A number of writers and responses to the questionnaire develop this idea that not having the weight of an intimate sexual relationship allows single people greater freedom to give themselves to family, friends and others in need. Indeed these relationships can be wonderfully pleasurable, sustaining and beneficial on all sides. It should be noted, however, that single people who bring up children may have little more freedom, time and opportunity to serve than those in couples.

6.4.3 Martin Israel cautions that although the single person may have more time and space for others, there are complexities – love for neighbour depends partly on costly self-knowledge:

> Living alone provides an admirable means of being available to many people in need. But I would emphasize that this availability is the fruit of a long, bitter, exhaustive encounter with one's own inner nature and a slow working-out of personal difficulties and inadequacies.[105]

6.5 Service

There are many avenues of service which single people may take: Israel mentions being able to be agents of reconciliation because of their detachment, prayer for others, voluntary service, listening to others who are alone, relationships of honesty, respect, loyalty, confidentiality and self-giving love.

6.5.1 Connected to this is the idea that single people may have energies which they would in other circumstances devote to their intimate relationships, but which they are free to give to other projects. The

responses confirm this: for one respondent, being single gives 'more freedom to become involved'. And for another, 'more opportunity to serve'.

6.5.2 These opportunities may recall remarks above about the nature and end of the celibate life. Clearly, while there is a difference between those who are called to a voluntary life of celibacy, possibly in orders, and those who find themselves to be single (and living alone), there is overlap in the quality of experience, opportunities and gifts.

6.6 Negatives

It is evident that there are advantages, blessings and gifts available to the single person and which the single person gives to others. However, we do single people no justice by skating over the particularities of the single life when they may be negative, from some sort of forced theological cheerfulness. For many people living alone and/or being single is not an unqualified good, or, more strongly, makes them miserably unhappy, and naming what is not good is an essential part of a Christian spirituality appropriate to the reality of life. The questionnaire explored this area by asking *What do you see as disadvantages in being single? In being single and a Christian?*

6.7 Loneliness

Perhaps the most obvious issue to be addressed is that those who are single may be lonely. Loneliness is something often experienced, known and recognised when it comes, but elusive to describe. Some people are lonely for brief times, while others may be described as lonely people. (Fiction has the space to convey loneliness in a remarkable way, for example the novels of Anita Brookner, or Brian Moore's *The Lonely Passion of Judith Hearne* or the short stories of William Trevor.) And there are as many lonelinesses as there are people who experience it. But, running the risk of caricature, let us say that people, when lonely, yearn for company and do not have enough or enough of the right kind. They would prefer to spend more time with others rather than

---

[104] It should be noted here, however, that surveys show that most married men cite their wife as their best friend; wives' closest confidante is more often a woman friend.

[105] Israel, *Living Alone*, p 42.

themselves alone. They find a huge range of activities dissatisfying because done alone or with the 'wrong' person, such as a friend rather than a lover. Almost every activity can be an occasion and reminder of loneliness: eating, playing, relaxing, holidaying, sleeping, being ill, going to church, praying, seeing family, seeing friends, Christmas, weekends, shopping, sex. (This list is infinite.) This last – sex – should not be underplayed. For one respondent, a disadvantage of being single is 'lack of touch and physical intimacy, which can sometimes be painfully acute'. For the lonely, it can be hard to find a meaning or purpose to activity, particularly outside work. Joys and sorrows are not shared with 'someone special'. Single people may also feel fear that they are alone when trouble comes: 'Once your parents die there will be no one who weekly checks if you're OK… No one who knows you long term and cares that you exist long term'. This may involve anxiety as to who will look after them in old age, without partner, and for some, without children – though as pointed out above in 5.2, wider family relationships may offer mutual support and care. And perhaps there may also be for some single people a fear of annihilation: 'we fear we will be entirely forgotten when we cease to register in the minds of anyone'.[106]

6.8   Lack of feedback

Single people may be submerged by experience and by memories, especially of past unhappiness. Without a partner to talk through a situation, without a partner whose acceptance of one makes one feel OK, the past (and the present) can prey on one's mind. Margaret Miles puts it this way: the single person can experience a host of internal voices which 'comfort or cajole or scoff at me'[107]: without a partner it is hard to be rid of the internal voices which are most unreasonable and most unhealthy. One respondent wrote in this regard: 'Lack of having someone

'special' to discuss and 'let off steam' when perturbed'. Miles makes a further point which is intriguing:

The other difficulty of living alone is that no one person is continuously available to remove my experience of ambiguity. There is no one when I go home every day to whom I can present an amazingly homogenous picture, convincing to both of us, of myself as an all-reasonable, all good-intending, lovable and worthwhile person.[108]

6.8.1   In other words, single people are more likely to analyse their behaviour, question their motives, doubt their character. Now these are surely rightful elements in the Christian's life, but if they become overwhelming, they may undermine our capacity to flourish.

6.8.2   On the other hand, one respondent suggests that single people who live alone may lack the benefits to character and behaviour which partnership offers: 'to live in the company of another brings checks and balances which go some way to avoiding selfishness and self-righteousness'. Indeed this is perhaps the great risk to which being single is vulnerable. Pleasing oneself in the house, in use of time and money, in choice of activity, in way of life may have a tendency to spill over into character, into relationships with family, friends and others, into one's Christian walk. The holiness to which all are called involves following Christ in his identification with others – even for those whose others do not include a partner.

6.9   Exclusion

Single people can be excluded from social events and opportunities because they are aimed at couples or families. They may be overlooked for anything from dinner parties to weddings because of the 'problem' of not having a partner. As friends settle down and have children, single people can be neglected in favour of other married and new families. One respondent notes

[106] Israel, *Living Alone*, p 28.
[107] Margaret R. Miles, 'The Courage to be Alone – In and Out of Marriage', in Mary E. Giles, ed, *The Feminist Mystic and Other Essays on Women and Spirituality* (New York: Crossroad, 1985), p 99.

[108] Miles, 'The Courage to be Alone', p 100.

that a disadvantage of being single is 'isolation from many of the socially accepted norms'. Moreover, single people may choose not to do certain things they would like to because they do not wish to do them alone and there is no one suitable to share the activity with – eating out, going to the cinema or theatre, dancing, going on holiday. There is an element of self-exclusion here since there is no proscription on doing such things alone, but for many single people, going to the cinema alone, for example, is daunting, because of practical issues and the supposed stigma of being seen to be alone.

6.10 Practical Issues

Being single is expensive. There is only one income, and housing, cooking and holidaying are more expensive for one adult with or without children than for two or more sharing. And being single often means the time-consuming, practical discipline of housework cannot be shared, but falls on oneself. For many, this simply means burdensome chores; but other single people, with no one sharing their space, do not look after their health or environment well. Single men who live alone, in particular, tend to have lower standards in nutrition, hygiene and health than men in partnerships. As for single parents, they may often find that becoming single means having much less time for other family, friends or the church, because so much time is required for working and looking after house and family.

6.11 A limited life?

Single people who have never married or been in a marriage-like relationship may furthermore live with the regret that a whole area of human experience has been denied to them, one which they will never know, and they may feel that their experience as human beings, indeed as Christians, has been limited and incomplete. It may be a matter of great regret or even grief to them that they have never married, never been a husband or a wife, never known what it means to be part of a mutually supportive relationship of love, albeit imperfect, one

which is characterised also by sexual intimacy. Indeed, many single people who have never known a sexual relationship may feel their lives to have been limited by this lack, and may feel their lives to have been too narrow, incomplete, unfulfilled. They may be perceived as a single man or woman, a bachelor or old maid, while inside they may feel themselves to be a sexual man or woman whom circumstances have not allowed to find intimacy in marriage. They may feel unlucky, and become bitter at the seeming ease with which other people fall in love, fall into marriage, and fall out again.

6.12 Childlessness

We saw above in Section 4.12 how painful the experience of childlessness was to a number of Old Testament characters, both men and women. Barrenness is presented as a curse, without redeeming features. In today's society, infertility or the not having of children through the absence of a partner or other circumstances can be equally as painful. The childless may grieve the loss of their unborn children as genuinely as they mourn the loss of other family members, and this grief is one which may be harder to leave behind. Many single people are childless, though of course the two groups are not co-terminous.

6.12.1 Much of the discussion above regarding the gifts and negatives of singleness apply also to singles and couples who are childless. People without children have greater experience of silence, may fulfil their own interests and tastes more easily, can form wider and deeper relationships with friends (although they may feel cast out from friendship with their peers who have children). The childless also have the possibility of living for others, including children, and using the energies elsewhere for good which would otherwise have gone into child-rearing.

6.12.2 But similarly, loneliness may be a feature of the couple or single person without children, loneliness for that particular form of relationship. And whether single or in a couple, the childless may live with the regret that a whole area of human experience has been denied to them, one which they will never know, and they may feel that their experience as human beings, indeed as Christians, has been limited and incomplete, never a parent, never able to bring up a child, never able to fulfil the promises of baptism.

6.13   Discipleship for all

It may be questioned whether the Christian faith encourages single and/or childless people to see their lives as limited. Clearly they do not experience a major sphere of human life. But the Christian understanding of the human person does not begin from assessing *how many* aspects of life are explored, how rich is the panoply of relationships enjoyed. Rather Christian understanding of the human person begins from one's relationship to God and God's interaction with the person. As people being redeemed by God in Jesus Christ, our lives then to a greater or lesser extent reflect God's love in us. God is faithful to us, forgiving of us, generous with us: the Christian life is the attempt to live out in our human ways this divine activity in us.

6.13.1   Given that understanding of the Christian life, it may be argued that all Christians have ample opportunity to live for Christ, for the kingdom, seeking to reflect God's love in every circumstance. Clearly a married person lives the Christian life in the particular crucible of marriage, and parents follow Christ in particular responsibilities of bringing up children. The single person is also called on to reflect God's mercy in the spectrum of life's relationships and circumstances faced.

6.13.2   In other words, it is not part of a Christian understanding of the human person that one has a right to marriage, or sexual fulfilment, or to parenthood. These aspects of life are gifts which depend on God no less than all that is created good. And they are not the only gifts of relevance here: friendship, meaningful work, fellowship in the church, opportunities to serve, the knowledge of God, faith itself – all are conceived in Christian understanding

as God's gift. And so we are called not to lament what might have been, but to accept what is given to us, and follow Christ more nearly in these circumstances. As we saw above in section 6.2, the single life is not second-best for the Christian, but also-good.

6.13.3   One response encapsulates much of this discussion of single life and is worth quoting at length: 'Despite the potential loneliness and cultural isolation of being single, there are positive advantages to being faithful to God's call on our lives, even if that calling is to celibacy (however temporary or permanent that celibacy may be), for while celibate the time and energy that could be devoted to a relationship can be channelled into other things. It can work – with the right attitude, although to be told this by married people can be condescending in the extreme. That doesn't mean that the single person cannot express his or her sexuality – femininity or masculinity can and are expressed in a myriad of ways other than through mere copulation. In fact why not celebrate celibacy and get on with life!'

7.   Sex, the Single and the Church

One central debate which has hovered over a number of areas of this report so far is whether sex outwith marriage can be a legitimate, non-sinful activity. We have seen that people are having sexual relationships younger, marrying or settling down later, separating and divorcing more often, and embarking on new relationships later in life without necessarily re-marrying. We are aware that extra-marital affairs are a contributory factor to marital breakdown. We have recognised that many people in the church, sincere Christians, have sex without being married, and live with their partners outwith marriage. We have also pointed out that some people, who would describe themselves as single, still have sex. It is to this context that we feel it important to give voice to Christian understandings of sex and the single.

7.1   Scripture, tradition, reason, experience

A great deal of this debate mirrors the equivalent

discussion taking place in the church on homosexual sex. Indeed, in preparing the 2007 report *A challenge to unity: same-sex relationships as an issue in theology and human sexuality*, the group was aware of a number of contributions which suggested that homosexual sex was a form of fornication, namely sex outwith marriage. And so methodological questions touched on in the earlier report, such as the presuppositions with which the reader approaches Scripture, the weight placed on reason, experience, tradition and Scripture, and the way one uses Scripture to interpret Scripture, need not be rehearsed in detail here. However, it may be useful to make a brief statement of two general approaches to theological method in this area.

7.1.1 First, traditionalists emphasise Scripture and traditional interpretations of Scripture in their understanding of ethical questions.[109] Scripture is understood as the Word of God, and so has an authority which other texts and influences in theological reflection do not have. Reason is brought to bear on the theological interpretation of Scripture, but an intellectual approach which seems to run counter to the plain meaning of the text cannot easily be adopted. Human experience is also considered in the development of doctrine, but generally insofar as it elucidates traditional interpretations. Scripture then is the authoritative standard by which other theological resources are judged.

---

[109] The terms commonly used for approaches to scripture and theology – 'conservative' and 'liberal' – have been avoided as potentially misleading, particularly given the technical sense that 'liberal' has in the history of theology. Although the issue of sex outside marriage, as with theological debate more generally, does not neatly fall into two parties, the terms 'traditionalist' and 'revisionist' are used in the report as follows. As already noted, traditionalist views reflect the overwhelming consensus of Christian thought which held sway until roughly the 1960s, whereas revisionist accounts of Christian ethics, from about the 1960s, attempted to revise the traditional consensus. The terms in this report refer only to theological approaches in the area of ethics.

7.1.2 A second approach may be characterised as revisionism. Revisionists similarly emphasise Scripture as foundational to their understanding of God and humanity, but are less prone to see narratives as normative. Traditional interpretations are often critiqued for what they reveal of the interpreter and his time (the *his* is deliberate, since the male authorship of Scripture and theology is part of what may be critiqued). A high regard for reason is brought to bear in theological endeavours, and where reason appears to disagree with the plain text of Scripture, it is often accepted that Scripture needs to be re-interpreted or even laid to one side as belonging to the culture when it was written and not of the essence of God's word to us now. Finally, experience is considered as of particular importance in teasing out ethical questions.

7.1.3 Both traditionalists and revisionists believe that God speaks to the church and the world through Scripture and that theology's task is to elucidate that word for the present age.

7.1.4 It should be noted that the debate as explored in this section would be enhanced by a fuller treatment of the Christian theology of marriage (as in the Panel on Doctrine's reports of 1993 and 1994). That remains outside the scope of this report. Nevertheless, a discussion of singleness in Christian understanding requires that questions of sexual activity by single people be raised.

7.2 Sex outside marriage: a traditionalist view
A traditionalist view begins from the view that human sexuality is part of the created order – *created* by God for human beings' enjoyment, intimacy, the building up of relationship and for the conception of children – but made to be enjoyed according to right *order*. And this order can be stated simply as: within marriage. Drawing on the interpretation of Genesis 1-3 outlined above in section 4.11, traditionalists understand sex as belonging properly to a man and a woman united in marriage. This complementarity and exclusivity of relationship reflects the covenantal love of God in creating humanity in

his image and calling a people to be his own. God's relationship with his people is marked by faithfulness – his love is faithful, not capricious, and not turned aside by creaturely infidelity – and uniqueness or exclusivity, since he covenants himself to love his people and requires of his people that they have no other gods but him. Consequently, marriage reflects the essential nature of God's relationship with humankind, and so should echo the hallmarks of that relationship: faithful and exclusive.

7.2.1 The Bible lays out a number of alternative patterns of sexual relationship, none of which reflect God's covenantal love with his people. *Adultery* is sexual activity of someone already married with someone other than his or her spouse. This, as is clear from the Ten Commandments, is contrary to God's Law and is not directed at the fruitful development of human ends (Ex 20:14). It leads to a bad end according to Proverbs 5 – poverty, death, Sheol. Instead, 'Let your fountain, the wife of your youth,/be blessed; find your joy in her' (Prov 5:18). Church tradition has understood the 'adultery' of the sixth commandment as also covering other sexual sins.

7.2.2 Another alternative pattern of sexual behaviour is called in the Bible *sexual immorality*, which older translations call *fornication*: this is for sex outside marriage. Again, the Bible discourages this undisciplined indulgence of the sexual appetite, which does not reflect divine exclusivity and faithfulness in the way that marriage does (Lev 18:6-20 especially v 20).

7.2.3 According to the New Testament, those who commit adultery or fornication are endangering their salvation: they will not possess the kingdom of God (1 Cor 6:9-10); God's judgment will fall on them (Heb 13:4); and fornicators flout the sound teaching which conforms with the gospel (1 Tim 1:10-11).

7.2.4 *Concubinage* and *polygamy*, though not laid out explicitly as contrary to God's Law, are presented in Scripture as leading to disastrous consequences for those

who follow such a path, for example Abraham, David and Solomon.

7.2.5 In other words, it is not so much that a traditionalist approach to sex outwith marriage is opposed to the sexual relationship per se as that the opposition stems from a high valuation of the place of marriage within the purposes of God for humankind. Extra-marital sex is a breach of faithfulness within marriage, while pre-marital sex is a breach of fidelity before marriage, or to the marriage one may subsequently enter. In either case, it is the goodness of marriage which calls for holiness in sexual living before, during and after marriage. Sexual intimacy and union within marriage is a part and sign of the faithfulness, constancy, commitment and forgiveness of the marriage as a whole.

7.2.6 This understanding of marriage is underpinned by the Biblical reference to *one flesh* (discussed above at 4.2). Genesis 2:24 says that a man leaves his father and mother and attaches himself to his wife and the two become one flesh. This teaching is reiterated by Jesus in Mark 10:6-9, who takes the passage as implying that a divorcee who remarries commits adultery. It is further quoted by Paul in 1 Corinthians 6:12-20, who draws the implication that anyone who has sex with a prostitute becomes physically one with her.

7.2.7 Although there are subtle differences of emphasis, most traditionalists interpret *one flesh* as showing that when two people are united sexually, a profoundly important connection is formed, permanent where the physical union is temporary, spiritual although the fleshly union is obviously physical, with consequences for one's deepest reality rather than simply the fulfilment of animal desire. Sex is more than sex: it is a union of two people. And so for traditionalists, the sexual partnership and the marriage partnership cannot be completely distinguished. Those who are united sexually are one flesh; those who are married are one flesh. Although not all traditionalists are comfortable with such language, it is argued that there is a *mystical* relationship which is formed in marriage and in sexual partnership: something beyond and not explicable according to our physical and emotional union alone, rather a unity given by God.

7.2.8 It follows that for the traditionalist a sexual ethic which separates sexual intercourse from marriage is fundamentally mistaken. Sex outside marriage is a pollution of the body, and a violation of that which ought only to be for one's marital partner – indeed, according to Paul, that which ought only to be for the Lord.

7.2.9 Nevertheless critical questions may well be raised. Does 'one flesh' indicate that in Paul's example the man is actually, really, in the sight of God, married to the prostitute? Does it imply that one's first sexual partner is one's spouse for all eternity? The reason we may be unwilling to go this far is that it seems to rest too much on a human action which, as with all human activity, is subject to selfishness, error, immaturity and, indeed, coercion. We can hardly say that someone who loses her virginity in being raped is married to her rapist in the eyes of God. Indeed the appalling seriousness of rape or sexual coercion is conveyed by the phrase 'one flesh': the aggressor forces a despicable unity of flesh.

7.2.10 The difficulty for the traditionalist is in considering non-marital consensual sexual experience, prior to marriage with another. Central to any understanding of this is to see that, in common with all the decisions which make up our being and our character, such sexual experience is open to God's forgiving grace. As people follow the Christian path and become more open to God's truth and will, they turn away from their selfishness, repenting their sin, including sexual experience, and seeking the Spirit's strength in their future living. And in the Christian's relationship with God, the Father of Jesus Christ, this experience is capable of being forgiven, our selfishness healed, our lives set on a path of holiness and generosity, our actions aligned with the Kingdom of God. This allows the possibility of retaining the image 'one flesh', while also understanding that when people do settle down and get married, their marriages have not been nullified by the existence of previous sexual encounters. Nevertheless, there is this concern that a previous sexual experience infringes on the sacredness of what happens properly only within marriage.

7.2.11 This is not to say that all pre-marital sexual experiences are sinful (after all, even holding hands may be considered to be a sexual experience), and all marital sex is legitimate. Marriage, no less than being single, is a realm in which the Christian faces the temptation to be selfish, ungracious and hurtful.

7.2.12 A further question which the traditionalist has to face is the question of marriage-like relationships. If a relationship reflects the closeness, unity, faithfulness, permanence, fruitfulness and exclusivity of God's covenantal relationship with his people, but has not been instituted in public vows, does it remain a relationship in which every sexual act is immoral, or is it essentially like marriage in which sexual activity is proper? The traditionalist may rightly claim that marriage is different from long-term partnership – in law, name, ecclesiastical basis and publicly-expressed commitment. But what is it precisely that makes for the mystical nature of marriage, its one-flesh-ness? For there are relationships, even if not publicly instituted in marriage, which are very far morally from, say, the casual sexual relationship arising from little love or commitment. If there is a spectrum on which human relationships reflect the love, faithfulness and exclusivity of God's relationship with people, marriages and non-marital relationships alike may be at various places on the spectrum. And yet the traditionalist must still retain the view that sex outside marriage is contrary to God's purposes for human relationships.

7.3 Sex outside marriage: a revisionist view

A revisionist view of sex outside marriage includes a critique of the traditional understanding, and the development of a sexual ethic which, while remaining

Christian, is open to the possibility of sexual activity outside marriage being in conformity with the will of God for human beings. Thus the traditionalist understanding is subject to the following critique.

7.3.1 First, scriptural material about marriage and the rightful ordering of sexuality belongs to an overall approach to ethics which contains questionable assumptions. These include patriarchy – the dominance of male over female. Scriptural depictions of marriage depend on and reveal an understanding of the woman being given in marriage to the man, Eve created for Adam. In contemporary theological understanding of marriage which sees a loving partnership of equals, the patriarchal context for marriage in Scripture requires revision. In particular, revisionists argue that in such a context, adultery and fornication are prohibited partly as offences against the man whose property the woman is.

7.3.2 Second, the prohibition on fornication found in Leviticus belongs to the code of prohibitions regarding cleanliness, which it is not clear to us today are of the essence of our moral responsibilities in following Christ.

7.3.3 Third, as well as patriarchal assumptions in Scripture, patriarchal practices in society are also questioned. Marriage in Christian understanding has been subject to a strong feminist critique, which has questioned traditional guiding assumptions – for example, that a father gives away a daughter, that the husband be head of the marriage.

7.3.4 And fourth, the era in which Scripture was written knew little of the delay between puberty and marriage which is typical today. Is it realistic, the revisionist asks, to expect young people to refrain from sex for ten to twenty years while they wait for marriage?

7.3.5 In addition to and partly dependent on this critique of the traditionalist approach, there are a number of revisionist developments of a Christian sexual ethic

which are at variance with the traditional approach on marriage or celibacy. Yet the starting-place is not so very different. Just as the traditionalist sees marriage as reflecting the faithfulness and exclusivity of God's love, so the revisionist draws on these aspects of God's character, and says that where these virtues are found in human sexual relationships, whether marriage or not, then there is a goodness to them. It is the quality of the relationship which is the criterion for the appropriateness of sexual activity. A revisionist approach does not say that anything goes sexually, since for the revisionist sexual behaviour as with all human behaviour is subject to the call of Christ to be holy in our lives as his disciples: loving, generous, compassionate and just.

7.3.6 The framework for justice in relationships, including sexual relationships, is found primarily in the Jesus of the gospels, who encourages his disciples to live in right and just relationships with each other. The marks of such relationships may be found, for example in Gal 5:22-23, where the harvest of the Spirit is adumbrated – love, joy, peace, patience, kindness, goodness, fidelity, gentleness and self-control. However, the critic of such an approach may note that only a few verses earlier, fornication is listed as belonging to the unspiritual nature (Gal 5:19).

7.3.7 To sum up: a revisionist Christian ethic of sex would emphasise that sex be consensual, with adequate provision for contraception, that it involve genuine intimacy rather than a simple physical thrill, that it be generous and self-giving, and that it not involve infidelity to an already-held relationship of trust and commitment. Traditionalists raise a number of questions about the revisionist development of a sexual ethic.

7.3.8 First, the revisionist critique of the traditional theology of marriage based on scriptural understandings has some force with regard to injustice within marriage and the need for our understanding of marriage to take heed of issues in contemporary life. But it does not raise serious doubts about the essence of marriage in theological perspective – as permanent, public and exclusive.

7.3.9 Further, the question of permanence is awkward for the revisionist. To what extent in a revisionist ethic of sex does it matter if the relationship is long-lasting before the couple embarks on sexual intercourse, or the parties intend that the relationship be long-lasting? Here the revisionist may be forced to say that while from the outside it is impossible to say where casual sex ends and sex in a committed relationship begins, most sex clearly belongs to one category rather than the other. Indeed, a relationship may begin casually, but grow into one of commitment, love and even marriage.

7.3.10 The issue of permanence is particularly pointed in the case of young people. Section 2.1 made clear how prevalent brief sexual relationships are among young people. Given the fast-moving emotional landscape of young people's experience, the revisionist Christian ethic of sex outside marriage may be impractical. Such an ethic depends on young people adjudicating their readiness for sex, the quality of their relationship, the presence of love, and the probability of long-term commitment. But it is not clear that young people have the time, wisdom and maturity to make these judgments. The difficulty is being able to turn such an ethic into clear, understandable and practicable teaching for young (and older) people.

7.3.11 And a further traditionalist response is to ask how marriage is related to the new approach. Many revisionists would say that marriage is the ideal sexual partnership, witnessed to in Scripture and confirmed in the experiences of many people, and would strongly encourage couples in long-term committed relationships to enter marriage. But for other revisionists, marriage is simply one vehicle amongst others for expressing commitment. Certainly, some people who live together but do not get married are clearly and explicitly choosing not to get married for all sorts of reasons – for example,

fearing the consequences of marriage or expressing a principled opposition. However, Christians have consistently seen marriage as a good, the making of promises of commitment to each other before God and witnesses. There seems no good reason for most Christians to choose to be in a long-term committed relationship without entering the traditional social, public and ecclesiastical expression of it.

7.4 The nature of the difference

There is a real difference here which cannot be skated over. As with so many debates it is about something much deeper than the surface issue. The question is essentially about God. The traditional view is defended on the grounds of Scripture, while those who depart from it often claim that the traditional view includes the covert desire to maintain sexual power in traditional hands, namely husbands and male religious authority. But the traditional view is really this: God is not a God to bear false witness – not a God to inspire the writing down of his Word, offer himself in covenant to his people, offer himself in the presence of his Son only for humanity to find this Word, this covenant, this Son's teachings unpalatable or unhealthy or unrealistic. If we take God seriously, we develop an understanding of sexuality, the sacrifices of singleness and duties of marriage based on God's Word. And so according to this approach, non-traditionalist interpretations essentially deny God's sovereignty over creation.

7.4.1 But for the revisionist approach too, the question is also about the nature of God. God is not a God to bear false witness, and when a text, written by the hands of human beings, is treated mistakenly as the Word of God only and not also a creaturely text, this narrows God into certain human interpretations, partial, and prone to discrimination and error. If we take God seriously, we develop the capacity to 'read' God's will in tradition, experience and reason, given to humanity by God, and this 'reading' involves the critical reading of Scripture. This then leads to an understanding of sexuality, singleness and human relationship which is not bound to the literal meaning of Old and New Testaments but also follows from the Word of God as interpreted in the light of reason, tradition and experience, and also wherever God's Word is found in other contexts. According to this approach, traditionalist interpretations too essentially deny God's sovereignty over creation.

7.4.2   This may seem to be a real impasse. However, perhaps there is a way out together. Even though Christians disagree over the interpretation of Scripture, we still share the common faith that God is sovereign over creation. Indeed, we share the conviction that God longs for the flourishing of his creation and the proper discipleship of his people – physically, emotionally, sexually and spiritually. Both traditionalist and revisionist develop their understanding of sex within and outwith marriage in the context of holiness, of the proper discipleship of human beings called by Christ to love and to commit to service and to justice. Acknowledging that shared conviction gives a context for our genuine disagreement as to how we should follow Christ in particular issues such as sex outside marriage. We can therefore continue the discussion on the basis that it is a debate which arises out of a shared Christian vision.

7.5   Church life
Although this report is primarily theological, it has clearly recognised that questions of singleness do not belong only in the realm of thought but in lived reality. As the Mission and Discipleship Council offers it as a resource to congregations, this section draws out some implications from the foregoing discussion for single persons in their church life. We must still be aware of the risk of over-generalisation.

7.6   Supporting young people
Following the discussion above in section 2.1 on young people and sexuality, we advocate the church being open and engaging for young people in this area.

Christian Bible-studies, youth groups and drop-in cafés will ideally be places and contexts where young people, exploring faith, identity and reality, can ask about what Christianity says about sex, and receive honest answers. School chaplains may also be invited to speak with children and young people in these areas, and they should accept the challenge. The Christian vision, outlined above, of sexuality as God's gift, not only for the making of babies, but for pleasure, for giving pleasure, for developing intimacy and deepening relationships of love is a vision worth explaining and sharing.[110] The traditional understanding of sex as appropriate only for marriage and the reasons for that are surely worth exploring with young people, who may be astonished at such a view. Given the numbers of young people who feel pressured into early sex, and subsequently regret such experience, the church should speak boldly on the importance of emotional maturity in questions of sexual practice. Furthermore, Christian teachers of the young can share what is positive about being single, perhaps helping to prevent young people rushing headlong into marriage, cohabitation and sexual partnership. In addition the church ought to resist the sexualisation of children.

7.7   Worship and teaching
This report is strongly recommending that in its worship and teaching the church does not privilege the family over against being single, or vice versa. It is clear from reflecting on Scripture and theology that while the Christian faith respects and values family relationships and responsibilities, it also recognises that Christian discipleship involves a commitment to Christ which is fundamental. All that is good and supportive in families may be celebrated and indeed promoted. Indeed, in a number of places, this report has stressed the

---

[110] Indeed the Scottish Government refers to Sexual Health and Relationship Education, indicating that sex education cannot be separated from broader questions of relationships and emotional maturity.

importance of the immediate and wider family in our lives. Nevertheless, such recognition of the blessings of family life need not lead to the disparaging of single life, or of those who are single. One might term a lauding of the family and concomitant disparaging of being single as 'familyism'.

7.7.1 'Familyism' is at best unhelpful, and on occasion an approach which excludes many from full participation and welcome in the church. And so the church needs to consider how to promote the full acceptance of single people inasmuch as they are single. Approaches which exclude single people may at times be blatant, as for example, when a Nominating Committee prefers a married minister, preferably with children (and preferably male) over a single and/or childless candidate. Another possible case is when a church's resources take up a focus on families, say in the appointment of a Families Worker. If such a person is appointed, there should be clear messages that single people are still equally served by the church's ministry. Services styled as 'Family Services', often around the church's main festivals, may well be insensitive to those who are conscious that they do not belong to a family in the sense implied – not being married, not having children. 'All-age' may be a more sensitive alternative, unless it is very clear that the notion of family is referring to the family of God rather than human families. The language and content of worship should reflect the presence and acceptance of single people as well as those who are not single. More insidiously, preaching and teaching may imply that the family is the particular vehicle of God's grace, that marriage is where the Christian's soul is most effectively shaped, that childbearing is a woman's duty, that family life is largely synonymous with the Christian life. One example would be preaching in which most illustrations are drawn from the preacher's own family life. As our reflection on singleness in the New Testament made clear, the human family is certainly not presented there as the principal locus for our relationship with God. Although there are duties to family which follow from our life in Christ, it is Christ himself who draws us into relationship with him, a new family, his body. Single people are not discriminated against in this vision: nor should they be in the visible church. One questionnaire response in this vein says: 'I would like there to be more honesty about the Biblical record and church history with regard to marriage and family values'.

7.7.2 And so as we are thankful that God's love is for all people, that Jesus Christ's life, death and resurrection offer redemption and hope to all people, and that inspired by the Spirit, all people are called to holy living in response to the love of God, the church ought not to teach or imply that being single is second-best, a lesser way of being Christian, a lesser way of being human, nor that being sexually active or being a parent is essential for a full life. Instead, human value is found fundamentally in the saving actions of God in Jesus Christ for every human being. Whatever our marital status, it is for us to offer our response to that.

7.8   Mission

Christianity's message to single people is of course the same as it is to people who are not single. But perhaps a single person may hear the gospel in a particular way. The New Testament vision is of a people called principally into a relationship not with family but with Jesus Christ, called not to go forth and multiply but make disciples of all nations. This is a gospel which offers single people the prospect of community: the fellowship of the forgiven, people conscious of failings, yet bound together by a common faith in maker, friend and love. For those newly single following separation or divorce, the church ought properly to be a place of welcome, of acceptance, even of sanctuary, where we do not judge, but include because God's love includes. And for those newly widowed, fragile, conscious of loss, the church is ideally a place of companionship, of care, of quiet waiting, of comfort and hope.

7.8.1 Moreover, we recommend that the church be aware of what single people can give in their Christian lives, with possibly more time and freedom to devote to Christian worship and service. On the other hand, it is clear that 'being single' does not necessarily mean 'wholly available for the Lord's work'. One questionnaire response says: 'Sometimes people forget that I have a demanding full-time job, and so do not always have the time or energy to do what I'm asked to do. Also I help to look after my Mum and help to run the house'. Moreover, single parents may have very little time for church activities.

7.9   Pastoral care

In this area, it is wise to bear in mind the different support networks which people have. Someone may be single, and even live alone, but still not living in isolation – but rather as part of a family, a network of friends, an internet community, in relationship with God; others may be lonely and struggling.

7.9.1 Churches have traditionally been conscious of their responsibility to single people in terms of pastoral care. Traditional patterns of pastoral visiting have focussed on the bereaved, who are often newly single, and on the ill. A sensitive pastor or pastoral visitor will be aware when someone who is single and perhaps with few close family members needs particular attention. Some ministers, elders and other pastoral visitors make a particular point of visiting single people around Christmas or other times when families often gather.

7.9.2 One respondent to the questionnaire pointed out the importance of pastoral care of single people recognising the immense variety of circumstances in being single – never married, separated, divorced, widowed; content, regretful, lonely, happy, devastated, coping, struggling; and the complexity of emotion after separation and divorce, connected to the nature of the relationship. 'Surely the Church needs to show by its actions more than its words how it can reach out into the local community and heal the broken-hearted'. And so

pastoral care of all people requires sensitivity, but perhaps especially with separated and divorced people. People may be acutely aware of rejection, or worried about what other people may think, or may be feeling guilty. The pastoral encounter in such cases is extremely important, and can go a long way towards helping the love of God be felt, and questions of anger, bitterness, the fear of rejection, regret, contrition and forgiveness be addressed.

7.9.3 In this regard, the questionnaire asked *What would you like to hear the church saying or see the church doing with regard to single people?* Some practical responses were as follows: 'Ensuring they are well-supported in crises'. 'Specific focussed groups/organisations/meetings that deal openly and honestly with the issues that single folks face'.[111] 'Social events especially designed for singles'. 'Ensure that every table [at a social event] has an odd number of chairs so that no single person feels left out'. We might add specific help for single parents by offering childcare at church events. These ideas clearly add to the pastoral care and mission of the church towards single people. Yet there is a tension which may be overlooked. In offering opportunities for single people to gather, as well as the panoply of other church events – worship, service, outreach, administration – the church often, unconsciously, draws those who are not single away from their spouses, partners and families night after night, week after week. This can have a detrimental effect upon marriages and family life: it may be that the church sees people who are *not* single too much as individuals discrete from their domestic commitments. One example may be emblematic: a church has traditionally held a Christmas meal for anybody who wishes to come, but one year the minister's family say, no, this year, let it just be us. The event doesn't go ahead – though then for some singles it's crushing. The same debate which is at play in

---

[111] We learned for example of one group, Heart to Heart, with a Christian ethos which offers a group-based recovery programme in the Stirling area for people affected by the isolation, pain and trauma of divorce or separation.

the New Testament – between the family of Christ, and the domestic family – is still unresolved in many practical situations today.

7.10   What is the Church?

'Who are my mother and my brothers?' (Mark 3:33.) Jesus questioned the importance of traditional, blood-family ties in his Kingdom. This report, in reflecting on Jesus, the Scriptures more generally, and the history of theological development has been led to the realisation that single people are not some adjunct to the people of God, an awkward remnant alongside the married which has to be accommodated, both practically and theologically. Rather, single people reveal something to the whole church as to the nature of what it is to be the church. The presence and reality of single people exemplify the often-overlooked truth that we are all individuals, before God and in the world. The single recall the church to the fundamental nature of discipleship – of the individual following Christ and so finding the community of faith. Single Christians both call for and offer the central pastoral task of the church: loving. Listening to single people reveals the insidious and commonplace heresy which can undermine so much church life, teaching and practice: that the essence of the Christian faith is being respectably married and with respectable families. Instead, being single shows that being Christian is more basic than our patterns of relationship, though it is within these patterns that we are shaped by the forgiving love of God and live out our discipleship.

8.   Conclusions

Being single is a fundamental aspect of every human life. As we are individuals, relating to other people and to God, at the root of every human being is a singularity to the self, an aloneness before others. In a basic sense we are born, live and die alone. Being single is also the basic aspect of our life as regards sexual partnership. It is as single people that we form relationships and enter marriage or not. People are usually single before any committed relationship; many people are single throughout their lives; many others have periods of being single after relationships ended by separation, divorce and death; many die as single people. We are all single, for some or all of our lives.

8.1   Contemporary patterns of relationships mean that more people today experience being single than was the case before. People marry or settle down into couples later, marriage is less common, a high percentage of marriages and long-term partnerships break up, a significant minority of people remain single throughout life. There are pressures on family life which lead in part to many people being single: society's affluence, the rise of individualism, the pressures of work. On the other hand, society and the media place a great importance on people finding fulfilment through sex, romantic love and being part of a couple, while business uses sex to sell to young people and to children – with harmful consequences. Many single people live alone, though others live with family, flatmates or friends.

8.2   Within the contemporary church, single people have a huge variety of experiences, to some extent mirroring society's differentiated view of being single. Among the spectrum of perceptions, some people find in churches the companionship and family they seek; others find in churches' attitudes the implication that being single is a lesser and deficient way of life for the Christian; for others being single barely registers for them at all as an issue in their faith.

8.3   Taking a longer perspective, the church has at different times and in different places promoted marriage or promoted celibacy as the better path. By medieval times, celibacy was enjoined for the clergy and religious, and marriage for the laity. In the Reformation, celibacy was seen as a largely mistaken emphasis for the Christian and marriage was encouraged for nearly all people. Until the mid-twentieth century, being single in the Reformed tradition was considered to be appropriate for women called to forms of ministry, particularly the missionary field and certain professions, but there was a strong consensus that marriage, to be ended only by death, was the most properly Christian way of life – although many single men and women have served the church publicly and influentially.

8.4 From 1960 onwards, the picture has been much more complicated. Feminism, the sexual revolution, more effective methods of contraception, the decline of church allegiance, secularism and youth culture have all affected church life and theology. Being single, being separated or divorced, living in a non-marital relationship with one's partner, being homosexual, being in a civil partnership – these are all possible and in certain contexts accepted within the Christian church.

8.4.1 Drawing on scriptural resources, it is clear that issues of singleness have been at the heart of how the people of God have related to God. Old Testament understanding begins from the conviction that it is not good, not God's desire, for the man to be alone. And so marriage, child-bearing, the extended family are all hallmarks of being Israel, a community called by God into covenant relationship. The Law is bound up with duties to family and neighbour.

8.4.2 In the New Testament, Christ, a single person, becomes the centre of God's revelation, and so it is no longer duties within the immediate family which mark one's obedience to God, but commitment and loyalty to Christ himself, and by implication, his family, his disciples, one's brothers and sisters in Christ, those others of his body. In this view of allegiance, being single can be lauded as a way of being which allows energy, time and commitment to the Lord. However, neither Jesus nor Paul derides marriage as of no value: those who are married are still encouraged to recognise it as a high calling, and one in which the highest moral standards should prevail.

8.4.3 As a whole, Scripture recognises the physical and psychological needs which the human person has for companionship, love and intimacy, while also recommending that these needs are put in the context of our love for God, obedience to his will, and way of holiness in following him. A biblical faith recognises that being single is not in itself good or bad, but rather places importance on how we are single, who we are as single people, and how our single lives reflect the love of God.

8.4.4 Theological reflection draws out some of the implications of the scriptural witness. As God is a relational God, so God's human creation finds pleasure and joy in relationships – family, friendship and sexual. Sex is part of God's good creation. Singleness stands out as a different pattern of being from that of marriage, but it must not be assumed that being single is a deficiency. For both those in and not in a relationship, there is joy and renunciation. Sex matters for the single, the married, indeed for all people; but it is not all that matters, or all that affects our lives, our faith and our spirituality. Whether, when and whom to marry, and when sexual intercourse is appropriate, are moral choices which Christians make as part of their broader path of discipleship. Celibacy remains a genuine option for the Christian, to which some people feel called, as a way of offering one's self more fully to God and others. Sex, as with all of life, will be ravelled up into the fullness of God in the life of the world to come. Both Scripture and tradition imply that sex, marriage and singleness will all themselves be made whole in the perfect society of love.

8.4.5 What is it to be single today, in society and the church? There are many perceived benefits over a life in long-term partnership or marriage. And being single allows people to know themselves, to have time for themselves, to be themselves, to experience silence; they have time for wide friendship and family relationships; they can give themselves more abundantly to others, to causes and projects, to prayer and to God. Being a single parent qualifies many of these features.

8.4.6 But there are many drawbacks which single people experience. Loneliness is easily named but may overwhelm a life; single people may feel strongly the lack of another to give them feedback on experience; they may miss the possibility of sexual intimacy and joy, the depth of a long-term partnership, the experience of bearing and raising children; they may feel culturally isolated, impoverished financially and in time, at risk of selfishness, and they may fear trouble, and death with the particular fear of annihilation.

8.4.7 An integrated, single, Christian life will be one in which the person has recognised both the blessings and curses of being single, faced them, accepted life with its particular circumstances as, ultimately, the gift of God, and gone on to live a life sanctified by the power of the Holy Spirit for holiness, love and generosity.

8.4.8 The church not only faces today a society with a greater range of meanings of being single, but a greater variety of sexual behaviour also. One Christian response, a traditionalist approach, is to maintain that sex is for marriage, reflecting God's love – exclusive and faithful – and hence, pre-marital and extra-marital sex is sinful. Alternative, revisionist approaches stress that many sexual relationships which are not framed by marriage may reflect God's loving nature in virtues of loyalty, faithfulness, generosity, intimacy and joy, and tend to human flourishing. These may be heterosexual or homosexual relationships. These differing approaches, mirroring debates over homosexual practice, scriptural interpretation and other issues in the church, do not admit of easy compromise. They represent genuinely different starting-points, emphases in theological method, and outcomes in Christian and church practice. It is our contention, however, that both approaches to the question of sex outside marriage are held with integrity by Christians who see them as the outworking

of their understanding of God, and that it is our calling as Christians to continue discussing such issues in the unity of our common faith in Christ who draws all who follow him to the way of holiness and love.

8.4.9 Being single has always been the way of life for many in the church. Today it is experienced in some form by an increasing proportion of Christians, whose single lives have much to teach the church of Christian discipleship and flourishing. The church has a crucial role in helping single people flourish in life, faith and service. This can begin in children's and youth work, preparing each generation for the moral decisions which they face in the realm of sex, intimacy and commitment. In its teaching ministry, the church should recognise the presence of many who are single – never-married, separated, divorced, widowed, parents, childless – and help them come to understand themselves not as failures or misfits, but Christians loved by God, shaped by his Son's life-giving love, drawn into fruitful lives by the Spirit. In its mission to the world, the church ought to be aware of how the gospel may be heard by single people. Furthermore the church could further encourage people who are single to serve according to the particular gifts they have, which may in some ways be affected by their being single. In its pastoral care, the church should be particularly aware of the difficulties which single people face, and attempt to care in the name of Christ in ways appropriate to those who are single, appropriate to the reasons for their being single. This may well involve groups for single people to gather; it may also involve opportunities for single people to live in community, itself a witness to the love of Christ in the world.

8.4.10 This report is offered as a word for our times, engaging with contemporary patterns of being single, being sexual and being in partnership, drawing on Scripture, theology, and the experience of single people in the church. May we understand more fully the love of

God for each and all, and the response such love calls from us in faithful, loving lives.

The Working Group

Rev Ian Aitken (from 2007)
Mrs Ann Allen
Rev Dr Peter Donald (Vice-Convener)
Rev Dr Bob Fyall
Rev Gordon Kennedy
Rev Dr Donald MacEwan (Secretary)
Rev Dr Moyna McGlynn
Dr Calum MacKellar (from 2007)
Rev Dr Alistair May
Mrs Doris Meston (resigned 2008)
Rev Dr Angus Morrison (Convener)
Rev Dr Ruth Page (resigned 2008)
Rev Scott Rennie
Dr Heather Walton
Rev Isabel Whyte (from 2008)

Ex officio

Rev Alan Birss, Convener, Worship and Doctrine Task Group

Rev Nigel Robb, Associate Secretary, Mission and Discipleship Council

APPENDIX III
THE FUTURE OF YOUTH WORK IN THE CHURCH OF SCOTLAND

In the gospel we read the story of John the Baptist realising when his time at the centre of the stage is up and that it is his moment to move into the shadows because someone else has arrived who is going to take over the work. Jesus was coming into the foreground and John's disciples were upset because they could sense that things were about to change. John seems to accept his fate and to welcome it. It is the right time.

As we encounter Jesus in the opening years of the 21st century do we have a similar attitude when it comes to the generation of young people who need to hear the old, old story? Will we hold on to our traditions, our culture, our history and heritage because they are of supreme importance to us even if that very holding on costs us the opportunity to make contact with young people? Or will we realise that we are only custodians of the church for a time and that, like John, we must hold on to it loosely so that the reins can slip from our hands into the hands of others?

For too long the agenda relating to our work with young people has been a negative one. This has been discussed at length. In spite of that negative agenda local churches continue to work with significant numbers of young people – tens of thousands. Significant numbers of local churches now employ specialist youth work staff and we can see that this type of investment bears fruit.

In spite of these many encouraging examples it is the conviction of this Advisory Group that it is now time to take a new radical course and in this short paper it outlines a number of key points that it seeks permission to consider further and consult with all interested parties.

The membership of the Advisory Group consisted of people from different backgrounds, theological positions, ages, levels of experience etc, but their discussions led them to be united in one firm conclusion which they bring to the General Assembly today, namely that it is time to change the culture and context for youth work in the Church of Scotland.

Why?

We believe that the question before the Church is not whether it is doing anything for young people but rather if it is doing *everything* it can for young people. There needs to be a sense of urgency underpinning this work. It is vital that we find ways to reach out to young people in our communities and it is just as vital that our congregations have a real welcome for those young people who are already involved and those who will become involved in the future.

The Church must become a voice on behalf of and for the young. That voice should speak with a clarity that will catch the attention of young people and will be listened to carefully in wider society.

The Church must be prepared to transform itself for the sake of the young people in Scotland today. It must seek to transform its structures and its people at all costs to take away the barriers that prevent young people being fully involved in the life of the Church today or for those 'outside' the Church seeing it as having any relevance to them. The returns from the recent Kirk Session questionnaire show that many local churches simply do not know how many young people they are working with and how many volunteers are engaging in this vital area of work. We count the things that are valuable to us.

The church must be prepared to be counter-cultural. It needs to move with the world but also be ready to move the world. It should console and challenge and seek to become a place of beauty and fun for everyone. In putting new energy and resources into work with young people the Church will have the opportunity to be at the forefront of cultural change and by doing this will energise itself and become more dynamic and fit for the purpose of its holy calling.

Put simply, this is our duty. We have a responsibility to do this as the national church in Scotland. The young people of our parishes deserve this from us. They deserve to have us do our best to meet them and to meet their needs.

Finally, it is time for us to agree, once and for all, what it is we think we are doing with young people and, speaking with one voice and walking in time with each other, to set about achieving the task for which we were established.

Some practical possibilities

The Advisory Group seeks to examine some key issues over the coming months:

- Should training of volunteer workers become mandatory?
- Should it relate to the already existing Safeguarding training in some way?
- Should we establish a standard set of terms and conditions for paid youth workers employed by local churches?
- Should there be an agreed set of standards that paid youth work staff should be able to measure up to in terms of experience, qualifications *etc* before they are able to gain positions in the Church of Scotland?
- How can we move beyond the stereotypes that pervade our conversations about young people and sit comfortably with the fact that all young people are made in the image of God?
- How can we recognise the complexities involved in working with young people and therefore respect and affirm those who do that work?
- What should youth work in the local church look like and how should it be supported by the regional and national support systems of the Church of Scotland?

These are just some of the issues that the Advisory Group considered. What is clear is that any proposals that emerge from further discussion are going to be expensive to implement. They will cost us some of our fondly held traditions, they will cost us a sense of security in assumptions we make about young people and the practice of youth work and most likely they will cost us lots of time and money?

It is the hope that at next year's General Assembly the Advisory Group can bring forward a set of radical proposals that will redraw the map for youth work in the Church of Scotland that will ultimately reshape the Church itself. This change needs to be set in a ten year time frame. We know that many churches are having success with young people all over Scotland so we know that the change we seek is possible. It will take a generation to build this new thing but build it we must. Building it will be costly but choosing not to build could cost us even more.

APPENDIX IV
PRESBYTERY COVERAGE OF DEVELOPMENT TEAM

- Mr Steve Aisthorpe (Inverness Office)
  - First point of contact for congregations in the Presbyteries of Inverness, Lochaber, Ross, Sutherland, Caithness, Lochcarron–Skye, Uist and Lewis with specialism yet to be discussed.
- Mr Graham Allison (Glasgow Office)
  - First point of contact for congregations in the Presbyteries of Irvine and Kilmarnock, Ardrossan, Greenock and Paisley, Dumbarton, and Argyll and specialising in 'iMPACT' and Youth Ministry.
- Rev Andy Campbell (Perth Office)
  - First point of contact with congregations in the Presbyteries of Stirling. Dunkeld and Meigle, Perth, Dundee and Angus and specialising in Worship, Doctrine, and Church Art and Architecture.
- Lesley Hamilton–Messer (Glasgow Office)
  - First point of contact with congregations in the Presbyteries of Annandale and Eskdale, Dumfries and Kirkcudbright, Wigtown and Stranraer, Ayr and Hamilton and specialising in Mission and Evangelism.
- Fiona Fidgin (Edinburgh Office)
  - First point of contact with congregations in the Presbyteries of Edinburgh, Lothian, Melrose and Peebles, Duns, and Jedburgh and specialising in Education and Nurture (Adult Education).
- Rev Robin McAlpine (Perth Office)
  - First point of contact with congregations in the Presbyteries of West Lothian, Falkirk, Dunfermline, Kirkcaldy, St Andrews, Orkney and Shetland and specialising in Eldership and Leadership Training and Mission Accompaniment.

- Rev Linda Pollock (Glasgow Office)
  - Focus for 2009 and 2010 on Children's Ministry. The Glasgow Office has become the first point of contact for the Presbyteries of Glasgow and Lanark for this period.
- Robert Rawson (Perth Office)
  - First point of contact with congregations in the Presbyteries of Aberdeen, Kincardine and Deeside, Gordon, Buchan, Moray and Abernethy and specialising in resourcing the Rural Church.

The first point of contact for congregations in the Presbyteries of England and Europe is the Council Secretary.

APPENDIX V
RECOMMENDED SALARY SCALES FOR ORGANISTS

The Scottish Federation of Organists has recommended that the following scales be used by Churches from 1 January 2009 to 1 January 2011, when a further review and revision will have taken place. These salary scales offer an increase of around 10%, bearing in mind that the last recommended salary scale was fixed on 1 January 2006.

a) **Churches Without Choirs**
   Salary £1,450 to £2,240 / Deputy Fee £50 (previously £1,320 to £2,035 / £45)

b) **Churches with choirs making an occasional individual contribution to worship**
   Salary £2,240 – £3,570 / Deputy Fee £50 – £65 (previously £2,035 – £3,245 / £45 – £60)

c) **Churches with choirs make a substantial individual contribution to worship**
   Salary £3,570 – £4,780 / Deputy Fee £65 - £90 (previously £3,245 – £4,345 / £60 – £80)

d) **Churches with complete and competent choirs singing full choral services**
   Salary £4,780 – £7,140 / Deputy Fee £90 – £100 (previously £4,345 – £6,490 / £80 – £90)

e) **Churches employing a full or part-time professional director of music with extensive responsibilities**

are recommended to consider salary scales higher than scale (d)

Salary £7,140 plus Deputy Fee £100+ (previously £6,490 + £90+)

1. There is a uniform approach to Deputy Fees, these now covering all church services, weddings and funerals. Different services contain different emphasis, but all are important and should receive equal treatment.
2. Recording fees remain unchanged:
   Fee plus 50% for sound recording
   Fee plus 100% for video recording
3. These scales are not mandatory. They provide guidelines for churches throughout Scotland.
4. If exceptional situations arise, which are not covered by these scales – for example, the number and nature of services within the Anglican and Roman Liturgies, or within Church of Scotland linked charges – then dialogue and negotiation are recommended as ways towards mutual agreement. Organists should be prepared to be pro-active in such matters and not diffident concerning reference to these scales.
5. These scales exist to provide a working framework and to maintain reasonable standards of remuneration. If there are musicians who are prepared to accept alternative remuneration, or to offer their services on a voluntary basis, then that is a matter for individual decisions and outwith the scope of these recommendations.
6. Churches that are experiencing financial difficulties or who do not wish to subscribe to these scales should not seek to engage deputies who do expect these scales to be observed.
7. It should not be necessary to emphasise that the labourer be worthy of hire. Those who benefit from SFO scales should be competent to do so.
8. Copies of current Income Tax information kindly supplied by the Church of Scotland's Financial Department, may be obtained from the SFO Secretary.
9. The current Church of Scotland contract for organists is now an extensive document containing sections applying to Duties, Salaries, Hours of Work, Holidays, Sickness Benefit, Expenses, Disciplinary matters, Redress of Grievances, Protection of Children and Young People, Dress and Worship.

Not every church will adopt this contract and local variations exist. These matters should be checked carefully before entering into employment. Copies of the contract can be obtained from the Church of Scotland Legal Department at 121 George Street, Edinburgh, EH2 4YN (0131 225 5722).

APPENDIX VI
COMMITTEE ON CHURCH ART AND ARCHITECTURE – MEETING DATES

7 May
25 June
3 September
1 October
3 December

APPENDIX VII
CO-OPTED MEMBERS ON TASK GROUPS AND COMMITTEES

Education and Nurture
Mr Birendra Rongong
Mission and Evangelism
None
Rural Strategy Team
Rev Alex Currie
Mr Bill Harvey
Ms Ishbel McFarlane
Rev Ken McKenzie
Rev Lorna Murray
Rev Brian Ramsay
Mr Lewis Rose
Rev Dr Adrian Varwell
Worship and Doctrine
Rev Karen Watson
Rev Dr Peter McEnhill

Committee on Church Art and Architecture
Mr Campbell Duff
Mr Ian McCarter
Mr Neil Taverner
Publishing Committee
Mr John S Brown
Netherbow: Scottish Storytelling Centre Executive
Members from Church of Scotland:
Jean Findlater
Nansie Blackie
Rev Dorothy Purnell
Margaret Grant
Members from Scottish Storytelling Forum:
D Colin Mackay
Rachel Smillie
Rev Linda Bandelier
David Campbell
Senga Munro
Rev Russell McLarty

'Why Believe?' Group

Church of Scotland:	Rev Dr Alistair Donald,
	Prof Joe Houston,
	Rev Pauline Steenbergen,
	Mrs Alison Carter,
	Rev Jock Stein,
	Mr Mark Stirling
United Free:	Rev Stephen Matthews
Salvation Army:	Mr John Coutts
Scot Episcopal Church:	Prof Wilson Poon
Free Church:	Rev David Robertson
Baptist:	Rev Andy Scarcliffe
Methodist:	Rev Gerald Bostock
Scripture Union:	Mr Stephen Hall

CONTENTS

PROPOSED DELIVERANCES

The General Assembly

1. Receive the Report.
2. Note the work of the Convener, Vice-Conveners, Council and staff in undertaking a challenging remit during the current financial down-turn.
3. Note the need to review the timing of the capital programme in view of the changed financial climate.
4. Note the excellent achievements by service staff in relation to quality, accreditation and qualification targets and encourage the continuation of the programme to encompass all services provided by CrossReach.
5. Urge all congregations to recognise the need for supporting the work of CrossReach especially at this time when funding from local authorities is under extreme pressure.
6. Urge all congregations and presbyteries to continue to support the work of CrossReach in prayer.
7. Encourage congregations and presbyteries to promote the Trading Company and use the online shop.

1.   Convener's Report

The Social Care Council of the Church of Scotland (CrossReach) continues to provide a wide and extensive range of social care services to the people of Scotland. These include services to children and families, to older people, to those with learning disabilities, to those with substance misuse problems, to people caught up in the criminal justice system, to men and women in need of counselling and to those who find themselves homeless.

It is a breadth of service provision that is unique within the Scottish voluntary sector. These services are delivered by a dedicated staff group committed to putting their faith into action and to providing care in Christ's name. We are unashamed to say that the services we provide arise out of our love for and commitment to Jesus Christ.

Of course such a commitment to care in Christ's name has often to be worked out in a challenging context. This past year has been no exception and this year's report highlights a number of these challenges.

There is the challenge of the present economic climate, which has had an effect on our main funding sources and an unwelcome impact on the progress of our capital programme. There is the challenge of changing our business processes to become a more efficient and effective provider of care.

There is the challenge of operating in a competitive environment where risks have to be managed effectively and services delivered within appropriate financial parameters.

There are the environmental challenges that are being met as we seek to operate throughout all levels of the organisation in ways that are *environmentally sustainable, economically feasible and socially responsible.'*

There is the challenge of losing key personnel. This past year has seen the departure of our Chief Executive,

Mr Alan Staff, as well as our Executive Director, Mr Jim Maguire, and we wish them both well for the future.

Then there is the perennial challenge of providing, in Christ's name, the highest quality of service for those in our care. I am pleased to say that this report evidences that this is a challenge that is being risen to by staff at all levels. As a consequence CrossReach is an organisation that is increasingly being recognised for the quality of the care it offers.

This is my last year as Convener and I would like to express my thanks to members of the Social Care Council, the Council of Assembly, CrossReach senior management and staff at all levels of the organisation for their support, hard work and commitment in what have often been challenging times.

It is my prayer that CrossReach will continue to meet the challenges of the future with faith and confidence in the One who has called us to serve and follow him.

2.   Performance against Strategy

The Strategic Plan for 2008 (Appendix 1) laid out 15 key targets which have been a focus of activity throughout the year. These 15 key targets have been cross-referenced to the Government's 15 National Outcomes; CrossReach's main themes taking us through 2009-10 have been identified from these. Targets 1 and 2 related to workforce development and CrossReach has continued to develop its staff training in line with national objectives and organisational targets. This is evidenced by the excellent results in both Care Commission gradings and quality accreditation and achievement of qualifications targets. Target 3 relates to achieving a balanced budget by 2011.

Targets 4, 5 & 6 have been met by our focused commitment to each of the service areas and by the raising of our profile nationally. Although pressure on finances across the sector has not permitted the level of regional networking that we had hoped for, partnership working with churches and local communities remains a high priority and continues to be an objective, despite the mounting pressure on our resources. Particular attention is being paid to establishing partnerships with organisations sharing a similar ethos to allow joint competitive tendering bids.

Fundraising (target 9) has been very challenging this year and is reported on later. Targets 10 and 11 relate to quality and accreditation, an area where CrossReach has achieved notable success in the last year as the result of clear strategic planning around achievement of training targets, quality indicators and external monitoring. The organisation is ahead of its target levels and is a market leader in this field.

Targets 12 and 13 identify Estates issues which are picked up later in the Report but the timing of the capital programme agreed by the General Assembly in 2003 has had to be reviewed due to our changed banking and governance arrangements. There are a number of buildings/services still in urgent need of refurbishment or rebuild if they are to be retained as viable projects, but the current financial position regarding borrowing has required a pull-back from the previous plan which was to complete in 2011. The remaining targets 14 and 15 are being addressed by the Business Review process which is considering smarter working methods and the further development of the Wide Area Network (WAN) as detailed in Section 11.2.

3. Quality

In line with our stated objectives CrossReach invested heavily in training this year and as reported has exceeded our objectives in most areas. While external accreditation is an outward sign of quality and commitment to that quality, it is the gradings given by the Care Commission which can be translated directly into financial benefit and marketability of services. At the end of 2008 the Care Commission published its first report on its activity, giving a benchmark position of all services reviewed. In simple terms any service area that scores below three in any aspect can expect to have their income reduced for at least a year and to have reduced referrals. Conversely services scoring five or six can expect an improved position in marketing terms although not any extra local authority money.

CrossReach performance benchmarked against the national averages are shown below and indicate an outstanding level of care, which is recognised nationally at all levels. The Church should be justifiably proud of the fact that its care provision ranks among the very best in public, private or voluntary sectors.

Sixteen of CrossReach's Residential Homes had been given a grading for each of the categories below.

This is the comparison between CrossReach and Care Commission general grading for Services to Older People in Scotland from 1 April 2008 to 5 November 2008.

5

The graph below illustrates how well CrossReach Older People's Services have performed in the last year in Care Commission inspections.

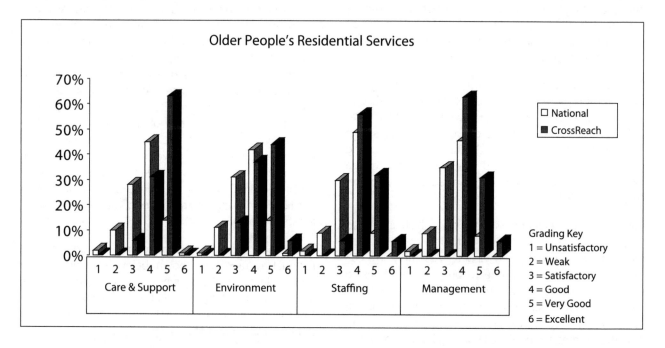

On a national basis it can be seen that some services are still achieving grades at the bottom of the scale with awards of grade 1 and 2.We are delighted to report that none of the CrossReach services have been assessed in that category. All of the CrossReach services in this area of delivery area have been given at least a grade 3, with most being graded as a 4 or 5. It is a major achievement for us to have been assessed as a grade 6 in some areas where nationally no other services have been awarded this grade.

4.   Organisational Structure

The revised organisational structure as laid out in last year's Report, was implemented and its impact reviewed. In the light of financial pressures, especially around central management costs, it was decided to delete the posts of Executive Director and Regional Director (East and Borders) and reallocate their functions across the senior management structure. The Regional Director's responsibilities for Children's Services and the Principal Officer (Children's Services) posts were consolidated into one, that of General & Strategic Manager (Children's Services). The regional responsibilities were taken up by the Director of Corporate Planning.

The loss of James Maguire and Paul Robinson, with 30 and 15 years' service respectively is keenly felt by all and we wish them every blessing in their retirement.

ORGANISATIONAL STRUCTURE
January 2009

SOCIAL CARE COUNCIL

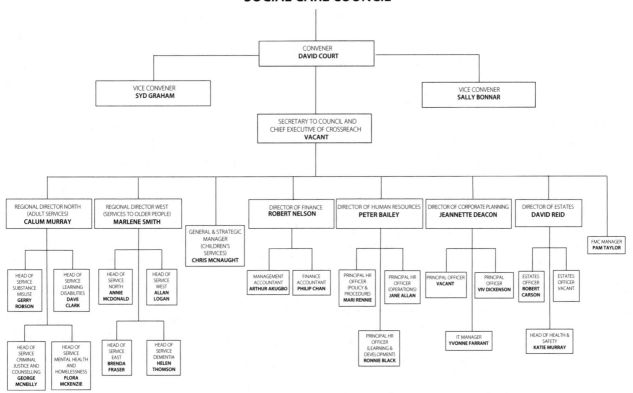

CONVENER
DAVID COURT

VICE CONVENER
SYD GRAHAM

VICE CONVENER
SALLY BONNAR

SECRETARY TO COUNCIL AND
CHIEF EXECUTIVE OF CROSSREACH
VACANT

REGIONAL DIRECTOR NORTH
(ADULT SERVICES)
CALUM MURRAY

REGIONAL DIRECTOR WEST
(SERVICES TO OLDER PEOPLE)
MARLENE SMITH

GENERAL & STRATEGIC
MANAGER
(CHILDREN'S
SERVICES)
CHRIS MCNAUGHT

DIRECTOR OF FINANCE
ROBERT NELSON

DIRECTOR OF HUMAN RESOURCES
PETER BAILEY

DIRECTOR OF CORPORATE PLANNING
JEANNETTE DEACON

DIRECTOR OF ESTATES
DAVID REID

FMC MANAGER
PAM TAYLOR

HEAD OF
SERVICE
SUBSTANCE
MISUSE
**GERRY
ROBSON**

HEAD OF
SERVICE
LEARNING
DISABILITIES
**DAVE
CLARK**

HEAD OF
SERVICE
NORTH
**ANNIE
MCDONALD**

HEAD OF
SERVICE
WEST
**ALLAN
LOGAN**

MANAGEMENT
ACCOUNTANT
ARTHUR AKUGBO

FINANCE
ACCOUNTANT
PHILIP CHAN

PRINCIPAL HR
OFFICER
(POLICY &
PROCEDURE)
MARI RENNIE

PRINCIPAL HR
OFFICER
(OPERATIONS)
JANE ALLAN

PRINCIPAL OFFICER
VACANT

PRINCIPAL
OFFICER
VIV DICKENSON

ESTATES
OFFICER
**ROBERT
CARSON**

ESTATES
OFFICER
VACANT

HEAD OF
SERVICE
CRIMINAL
JUSTICE AND
COUNSELLING
**GEORGE
MCNEILLY**

HEAD OF
SERVICE
MENTAL HEALTH
AND
HOMELESSNESS
**FLORA
MCKENZIE**

HEAD OF
SERVICE
EAST
**BRENDA
FRASER**

HEAD OF
SERVICE
DEMENTIA
**HELEN
THOMSON**

PRINCIPAL HR
OFFICER
(LEARNING &
DEVELOPMENT)
RONNIE BLACK

IT MANAGER
YVONNE FARRANT

HEAD OF HEALTH &
SAFETY
KATIE MURRAY

5. Finance

2008 proved to be a very challenging year financially across the whole sector, with a number of factors combining to slow the CrossReach recovery programme. The effects of the global financial crisis impacted early in the year and continued to cause increasing problems throughout the year.

Key factors influencing the performance were:
- Drop in income from legacies, trusts and fundraising.
- Reduced income from local authorities, as they struggled to balance their books.
- Sudden and unprecedented rise in commodity prices and overhead costs, *eg* fire regulations.
- Holding back on capital improvement projects.
- Loss of value of investments.

Every effort has been made to limit the adverse effect of this downturn, including reducing staff levels and rationalising services which cannot manage within budget. While this has proved successful in bringing both Older People's Services and Adult Services to a position where both should trade within budget (with the exception of Counselling Services) the income to the Schools has continued to give cause for concern. The net effect of the loss of income from Schools and gifts combined to generate a loss of £3m on the budget set for the year. The response to this has been a major review of staff costs including some redundancies, some successful new aspects of work which have begun to generate new income, a raising of charges and a reduction in operational costs. The Schools have begun to show a clear move back towards breakeven but remain a high risk (high cost low volume) area of social care activity, dependant entirely on local authority financial commitments and continued support. The loss of gifted income is reflected across the whole sector, as the levels of legacies fall and the amount Trusts have to give is reduced due to low interest returns.

One of the most significant impacts of the lack of confidence in the financial sector has been the need for us to review the timing of the capital programme which relied on borrowing to refurbish or replace outdated estate and paying this off through sale of earmarked disposable assets. The effect of this is that we maintain a number of otherwise viable services which due to the poor physical condition of the buildings make a loss to the organisation. Some local congregations which have been assured of progress on their local services will be understandably very disappointed with this lack of progress. It is hoped that they will recognise the difficult financial situation and continue to work with us.

A number of adjustments have been made to central costs including some redundancies and deletion of posts, savings on operational expenses and an appraisal of the make up of these services. Currently these costs amount to around 10% of income against 7.5% recoverable from our contracts but include some charges such as higher pension costs and parish support activity not possible to charge to local authorities but important for our role as an arm of the Church. This is an area that will require further review.

While this has been a very disappointing year there are some positives, notably the overall maintaining of income at £47m annual turnover, the improvement in the trading position of most service areas with a lower number of deficit generating services than in previous years and the improvements being made in the business management processes to enable faster and more efficient business reporting and greater local autonomy for Service Managers.

6. Governance

The governance groups for CrossReach are: Finance, Human Resources, Information, Quality Audit, Safeguarding, Strategic Planning, Estates and Health & Safety. This year has seen more members of the Social Care Council serving on these groups and the frequency of meetings of the Finance Governance Committee increased, reflecting the growing need for close scrutiny of the budget.

7. Children's Services

CrossReach Children's Services are undergoing a radical reformation. In 2008 **Geilsland** and **Ballikinrain** Schools combined to create one residential School Service across two campuses with a single management structure.

This and other budgetary measures including the downsizing of both campuses, with a number of voluntary redundancies, reflect the general decrease in the residential school market with the aim of achieving a sound financial basis to support this work.

The function of the new CrossReach 'Include me in' Children's Services at Ballikinrain will draw upon existing skills and motivations across current Children's Services to:

- Improve the well being of children.
- Support families within their communities.
- Locate children and their families firmly within a network of local supports.
- Improve the skill base and employability of those with whom we have contact.

Much work has taken place in communities, particularly North Glasgow and Stirling in supporting families. CrossReach staff, in addition to delivering parenting classes, group work for children and a variety of activities, have also acted as conduits, linking families with existing services and other supports.

The service at Geilsland has gone through a dramatic change and now focuses on providing vocational training for its residential and day pupils. Trainees are able to progress through the vocational training in construction and horticulture, to Geilsland LINKS, which provides real work experience and industry-recognised qualifications. These developments, aimed at improving employability skills, alongside the work of Threshold in this area, formed

the focus of a presentation at the Scottish Parliament, which was well received by MSPs.

The 100 acres of woodland at Ballikinrain has been put to good use and it is used every day as a Forest School. Here, pupils, many turned off by formal education, enjoy learning. Local primary Schools have also used the resource, and it is hoped this link will continue.

Developments at **Mallard**, although slow, will see the introduction of accommodation specifically geared to ease service users through the very difficult transition to adult life. The Mallard was the first of the Children's Services to be inspected by the Care Commission using the new grading system and was rated highly with a number of top marks being awarded.

Other services in this area also reflected gradings at the higher end of the scale and consistently receive positive reports.

8. Adult Services

8.1 Mental Health and Homelessness

Mental Health and Homelessness services continued the work begun in 2007 exploring ways of increasing the involvement of service users. In February and June, service users and staff came together to review how CrossReach could listen better to service users and to explore the development of service user participation at different levels within the organisation.

The predominant theme for CrossReach's Mental Health Services in 2008 has been "Recovery". The idea of recovery can be an elusive one and is not synonymous with "cure". As the very attractive booklet produced by Morven Day Services states: "It is about giving people the tools to become active participants in their own health care – it is about having a belief, drive and commitment to the principle that people can and do recover control of their lives, even where they may continue to live with ongoing symptoms".

As with all Adult Care Services, all those in Mental Health and Homelessness have made good progress in achieving a high proportion of staff qualified and able to register with the Scottish Social Care Council as a result.

Training courses on dealing with aggression were run for staff from both the Mental Health and Homelessness Services. Each member of staff undertook two days' training in the theory of restraint and de-escalation techniques and two days in the practice of Escape Techniques. These staff will go on to be trained as trainers of other staff.

Homelessness Services have been dealing with change in different ways. The loss of Government "ring fencing" around Supporting People monies, has left services which are funded in this way vulnerable to funding reductions. This was most apparent in the case of **Cunningham House** where the City of Edinburgh Council reduced the budget by 7.5% and are now seeking to recover up to 8.5% in "efficiency savings".

Non-accommodation housing support services in Edinburgh went out to tender late in 2008. It is likely that accommodation-based services in Edinburgh will go out to tender in the near future. This will directly impact on the service at Cunningham House. CrossReach is currently exploring with Christian-based voluntary sector partners how best to respond to this challenge.

We continue to support people who have successfully moved on from projects to their own accommodation in partnership with commissioners, one of whom has also enjoyed a successful volunteer placement with the CrossReach Learning and Development Department.

At **Kirkhaven** in Glasgow, the Service Manager, Kathleen Cairns, won the Scottish Care Home Manager of the Year at the Scottish Care Awards. Following a fire at Kirkhaven caused by service users breaching the smoking rules, the Fire Service conducted a thorough investigation. The

project was commended on having its paperwork and processes in exceptionally good order.

Positive Care Commission Reports continue to be received by all services with minimal recommendations made. Further, the planning process for the re-provisioning of **Rainbow House** in Glasgow has continued in partnership with Thenew Housing Association and Glasgow Addiction Services with a new building due by mid-2010.

Service users with learning disabilities and service users with mental health difficulties at **Whiteinch** in Glasgow have successfully moved on and negotiations with Glasgow Addictions Services continue over this facility being re-configured to meet the needs of people with an addiction.

8.2 Learning Disabilities
The contemporary focus of activity in Learning Disability Services has been the consolidation of several smaller services into larger groupings. There have been diverse advantages from this policy, including creating a strategic capacity within services, enhanced career pathways and, critically, savings in staffing structures.

Threshold Glasgow, which had already incorporated the previous Glasgow services of **Cairnhill**, **Saltmarke**t and **Florentine**, now includes those people previously resident at **Westhaven**. The hostel model of Westhaven was no longer required and, after prolonged negotiations, Glasgow City Council agreed to it being re-commissioned as a Housing Support service, which sees service users enjoy the status of tenants with a home of their own.

November saw the launch of **Threshold West of Scotland** consolidating from **Threshold South Lanarkshire** and **Cornerstone**. The residential model of care of Cornerstone is being renegotiated with relevant local authorities, and the Wishaw service should transfer to housing support soon.

Considerable effort has been invested in training staff.

Well over 100 Learning Disability staff have achieved Scottish Vocational Qualification (SVQ) 3 and 4, and two Managers have completed the highly reputable University leadership course, "Leading to Deliver."

Learning Disability Services face considerable challenges in 2009. Last year saw major improvements in the financial position and work is continuing to improve this in 2009. Equally, the tendering culture being introduced by local authorities will challenge our services to retain even existing levels of service.

Financial constraints faced by local Government are also beginning to impact on services, with **Threshold Leven** being asked to reduce the level of service. However, despite the local authority indicating it no longer requires **Choices Short Breaks**, that service continues to prosper.

Services have risen to the challenge by achieving Charter Mark and scoring highly in the recent Care Commission assessment.

CrossReach Learning Disability Services have engaged with, and influenced, the wider care environment: a successful Faith Conference was held in partnership with Aberdeen University Theology Department; we participated in the Mission and Discipleship Conference on Disability; and have supported the production of a training video for new Church elders.

Besides these initiatives, CrossReach Learning Disability Services were thrilled to be able to send a member of staff to represent the Church of Scotland in China, briefing delegates there about autism, based on our direct experience of supporting people with Autistic Spectrum Disorders.

8.3 Counselling Services

Counselling Services continue to be in great demand at all CrossReach locations across Scotland. The need for these services is evidenced by the current uptake: 15,000 counselling sessions are delivered each year, and at any one time there can be up to 118 clients on the waiting lists, 80% of whom are referred directly from health care professionals. They are not merely the 'worried well'; most suffer from recognised depressive or anxiety-induced illnesses. Many express thoughts about suicide, particularly true of postnatal depression services, turning to CrossReach Counselling as a last hope.

Post Natal Depression (PND) services continue to experience a growth in referrals, possibly as a result of awareness raising among Guilds and our telephone helpline, launched last summer in partnership with Parentline Scotland Children 1st. Counselling Services, disappointingly, do not benefit, statutorily, from direct local authority, Health Board or Government funding streams and are mainly supported by charitable giving, a range of grants (some from Health Boards) and trust funding. As such, Counselling Services constitute the main charitable service of CrossReach unlike most of our other services which come with a statutory obligation on local authorities or NHS Boards for funding.

It is important to acknowledge the significant volunteer contribution made within the Counselling Services; that of counsellor and administration personnel equates, in financial terms, to some £1.4m in "contracted staff" time per annum. In consequence of this, every £1.00 invested by CrossReach converts to delivery of £3.00 worth of service evidencing exceptional value for money.

The support of the Church of Scotland Guild Project for the PND work has been invaluable over the past two and a half years. Unfortunately, this source of income will end in 2009 but has been a major contributor to sustaining the continued delivery of the PND service to date.

The successful provision of "Fast-track" access to Counselling Services (this is when clients can opt to pay for the service and subsequently have faster access to a counselling service) operated within the **Tom Allan Centre**, Glasgow, continues to have a high number of

5

referrals. However, the experience of the Glasgow service, although offered in other services, has not been replicated across the country and there appears to be a much lower up-take in the other locations.

Clinical Outcomes in Routine Evaluation (CORE), reported on last year is completing its first full year of operation. The value of this system is currently being evaluated and the intention is to continue with it for a further year. CORE will provide assurance of quality as well as evidence of progress with clients and of outcomes of service provided, which should help with funding bids.

Throughout 2008 every effort has been made to increase income in order to reduce the sum that CrossReach contributes to Counselling Services. The target of £250,000 set has, unfortunately, not yet been achieved and the support of Health Boards and other funders has not been forthcoming, despite evidence that our services are both good value and meet Government targets on Mental Health. A variety of other options is still being explored.

Work has been done throughout 2008 to encourage services in Dunfermline and Dundee to become established as independent Counselling Services in their own right. This has provided easier access to funding due to the smaller financial turnover of the service and has contributed towards reducing the financial deficit experienced within Counselling Services.

8.4 Criminal Justice Services

Criminal Justice Services within CrossReach are represented by the work of **Dick Stewart Project**, Glasgow, the **Visitors Centre**, HM Prison Perth, and **Friarton Young Offenders.**

The Dick Stewart Project celebrated 20 years of service in 2008 providing accommodation for men and women on court orders, bail or returning to the community on licence from prison.

Major changes have taken place in the Criminal Justice

System over the past two years with the introduction of Community Justice Authorities (CJA) across Scotland. CJAs set out three year action plans for approval by the Scottish Government; provision of supported accommodation continues to be part of the current Glasgow City Council CJA action plan. Currently work is being done with Glasgow City Council Criminal Justice Service as they carry out an evaluation of service provision across Glasgow. Recently there has been an increase in the vacancies but generally the service is well used. However, as with most service provision there is an increased interest in non-residential based service provision. In 2009 careful consideration will be given to the service model within Dick Stewart Project and an evaluation of criminal justice service provision and the strategic direction of the service will be reviewed.

The Visitor Centre in Perth has now completed its second year of use of the Centre by visitors has seen a steady and substantial increase over this period of time. The service is now well established and provides support to an average of 275 adults and 30 children each month. Many families become lost in the bureaucracy of the Prison Service particularly in the circumstance where their family member is in prison for the first time; it is often wrongly assumed that family members are familiar with the Criminal Justice System. Visitor Centres can support family members by assisting with practical information about the prison system and by signposting people to a range of other support services pertinent to their need.

This work is about the Church meeting the needs of people, often on the edge of life itself – the place where Christians should be.

Additional funding is being sought in order to extend the service to cover all visit times. Currently the service operates on five days, the aim being to open seven days per week. The Robertson Trust has agreed to provide funding for a third year; however, other sources of funding require to be secured in order to ensure the future service provision. Applications have been made to the Guild Project Committee and the Big Lottery. The Centre operates with a small staff team and is dependent on volunteers for additional service user support. The recruitment of the latter has been a major challenge and substantial efforts continue to be made to recruit sufficient volunteers to support the service.

8.5 Substance Misuse

During the course of 2008, the Substance Misuse aspect of Adult Care Services have worked hard to move from a deficit situation to one where services are projected to be in surplus in the current budget. The funding of such services is constantly under challenge and CrossReach staff continue to be creative in responding to what is a growing problem in Scottish culture – the misuse of alcohol and, increasingly, drugs. To that end, CrossReach Substance Misuse Services is now a full member of the Federation of Drug and Alcohol Professionals, with the majority of its Service Managers achieving individual membership.

In addition to the Scottish Vocational Qualification (SVQ) attainment previously identified, learning and development on professional issues, organised by our Employee Development Officer, continues to ensure that the highest capability exists in this constantly evolving arena. All long-standing staff working directly in the therapy arena have achieved the Primary Certificate in Rational Emotive Behavioural Therapy (REBT). This provides the bedrock for all staff in this category to be professionally qualified and recognised by commissioners of services as such. Further advanced level training will follow, with all senior therapists qualifying to Diploma level by early 2010.

With one exception, all services are operating at full capacity and, at the **Lifestyle Centre** in Stornoway, we have been awarded £24,000 to develop outreach services across Lewis on behalf of the local Drug Action Team. As part of this, preparations are in hand for home-based detoxification services on Benbecula and Uist, taking over from the in-house mental health team.

9. Services to Older People

2008 was a year when Services to Older People continued to raise their standards of care, performance and quality to meet changing needs and expectations of service users and their carers as well as ensuring compliance with Care Commission and Scottish Government Legislation.

Staff in Older People's Services have achieved SVQ Level 2 and 3 in excess of the 60% required by the National Care Contract. This will enable CrossReach units to attract the higher level of funding for quality within that contract.

Two of our staff members, Elspeth McPheat, Manager of **St Margaret's Dementia Unit** in Polmont, and Anna Shavanaz, cook in **Williamwood House Dementia Unit** in Glasgow, were finalists in the Scottish Care Awards. Elspeth also reached the finals of the National Awards in London.

9.1 Quality

The Charter Mark Customer Service Award for Excellence has now been attained by 80% of services and a planned programme is in place to ensure all services have this award by 2010.

Care Commission gradings (see graph in Section 3) are well above the national average, **Adams House** in Renfrewshire has been identified as the top home within that authority. The **Oasis** in Garelochhead achieved the highest grading of a 6. This day care unit continues to have an excellent local reputation in Argyll and Bute and the model of service delivery is one which CrossReach would hope to replicate in other parts of the country.

A partnership model with the local church in Bankfoot has been established and a new day care centre opened there. Discussions are at an advanced stage with Perth and Kinross Council to commence a Home Care Service in that area. This goes some way to assure the people of Pitlochry that CrossReach would attempt to maintain a presence in that area as well as **The Tryst Day Care**.

It was with great sadness that two CrossReach residential units closed in 2008. **Clyde View** in Helensburgh and **Chequers** in Pitlochry but the transition to new homes for the service users went as smoothly as possible and several staff continue in CrossReach employment.

The need to address the timing of the capital programme will affect several units such as **Bellfield** in Banchory; **Budhmor** in Portree; **Eastwoodhill** in Glasgow; and **Wellhall** in Hamilton. Discussions are ongoing to establish the best way forward for these units. The effect of local authority spending cuts is being felt particularly by services commissioned by Glasgow City Council within our Glasgow Housing Support Services to older people.

Ashley Lodge in Aberdeen will close in 2009 and is being replaced by a new state of the art facility for 64 service users at **Rubislaw Park** in Aberdeen. Existing service users and staff will transfer over to the new building.

9.2 Developments

Development ideas for Older People's Services include expanding Dementia Services to provide a service to relatives and all those affected by a diagnosis of dementia from point of diagnosis through the whole spectrum of that journey. Discussions are taking place with East Renfrewshire Council and other purchasers as to the "market gaps" in this area so that local solutions may be implemented.

Palliative care is being delivered by many of our staff – it would be our intention to formalise this service and market it as such.

Local authority strategy is shifting their balance of care to more of a care at home model; CrossReach would seek to be involved with that and also to deliver respite care packages in different ways.

CrossReach Services to Older People seeks to provide care in Christ's Name to older people of Scotland and ensure that our hallmark is one of excellence and exceeding expectations.

10. Human Resources

Human Resources (HR) provided support to the Services as well as developing and implementing new initiatives in line with the overall HR strategy.

The Personal & Professional Development programme (PPD) for main grade staff has been further developed and streamlined to ensure closer integration with the new SVQ in Health and Social Care. We have extended the support mechanisms to help new employees achieve their award in a more effective way. This has involved the introduction of an innovative learning mentor programme coupled with guidance for Managers contained within a half day training session.

We have extended the PPD process to include Operational Managers which provides a streamlined induction to their new post. This process facilitates the process of building working relationships between the Operational Manager and key personnel within Central Services.

We have successfully implemented four out of the planned six Management Development modules which extends beyond the accredited management qualification. These modules have been enthusiastically received by both new and long-standing Managers who are relishing the challenges and putting the learning into practice back in the workplace. Feedback from the course attendees has resulted in the development of bespoke training events on Managing Stress in the Workplace and Emotional Intelligence.

The HR software package has been developed to enable accurate and up to date recording of training and continuous professional development required for the Scottish Social Services Council (SSSC) registration.

Management information can be easily obtained to track progress.

The Personal Quality and Development Planning System (Appraisal) has now been rolled out to all main grade staff and this process will identify accurately all current training needs giving the Learning and Development section the ability to deliver training to meet the needs of the organisation.

Practice teaching is a valuable resource providing great learning opportunities both for Social Work students and our Services. Due to changes in funding we have considered various strategies to increase the viability of practice teaching within CrossReach. Funding has been accessed from the SSSC to enable us to maximise student placements. It is the intention to use Skype technology for supervision to make best use of financial and human resources.

Our annual awards ceremony recognised the achievements of 173 staff ranging from Scottish Vocational Qualification (SVQ) 2, 3 and 4, Registered Managers Award, Verifiers and Assessor Awards, Higher National Certificate (HNC), Counselling & Psychotherapy in Scotland (COSCA) Certificate in Counselling Skills, Post Graduate Certificate in Autism and Administration Awards. At this service CrossReach was also proud to present the first annual Learner of the Year Award.

The focus on recruitment and retention has continued and a CrossReach recruitment open day was held in Edinburgh last year. This year to date we have focused on the Aberdeen area to facilitate recruitment for the opening of the new Rubislaw service. Web based recruitment has continued to be successful and with the introduction of a new facility we are able to track which websites generate the most traffic to our own website and result in completed applications.

Over the last year we have piloted the health and safety e learning modules within eight diverse Services. Overall this was seen to be effective across a number of key areas including: user friendliness, cost effectiveness and a positive learning experience. It is the intention that this will be rolled out to the whole organisation within the coming year. Part of this process has required us to address IT literacy across the organisation and this is an ongoing project.

We have recently developed partnership working with Workers Educational Association (WEA) to provide literacy support, IT training and English for Speakers of Other Languages (ESOL) in the Glasgow area.

Staff in the Employ of CrossReach
at 31 January 2009

	Full-time		Part-time		Total		Full-time Equivalent	
	2009	2008	2009	2008	2009	2008	2009	2008
Operations Staff	608	609	866	854	1474	1463	1176.88	1172.28
Executive, Office & Support Staff	86	88	17	17	103	105	95.95	98.36
					1577	*1568	1272.83	1268.64

*In addition there are 625 people employed as Relief Care Workers (compared to 620 at 31 January 2008).

A group has been established to begin the process of Investors in People (IIP) accreditation. This group has established professional competencies for all office based staff and this combined with the work carried out in focus groups to identify How to Reflect the CrossReach Values provides a solid base for organisational development in our Central and Regional Offices.

Following a competitive tendering process a new Occupational Health Provider was appointed. Their approach will underpin our wish to support staff during illness, while at the same time seeking to reduce the length of absences.

10.1   Safeguarding

Safeguarding is the umbrella term covering child protection and adult protection. The Safeguarding Section was established in March 2007. Although everyone who works for CrossReach has a responsibility for safeguarding, the service is led by the Head of Service, Safeguarding.

Harm can and does occur in *all* social care services, whoever provides them – that includes Christian providers. In everyday language, harm is *'any conduct that you suspect or know is having, or could have, an adverse affect on a person who is unable to protect themselves.'* Harm rather than abuse is the preferred term when speaking about protecting adults. It cannot be eliminated but it must be minimised.

'CrossReach is an organisation which *demonstrates* that it protects children and adults using its services.' We do this by recognising the following:
1.   *Fact:* harm or abuse to service users can happen anywhere
2.   *Aim:* zero tolerance – harm of any type or level is unacceptable. We will minimise the risk of harm occurring
3.   *How?* All staff will be able to recognise alleged, witnessed or suspected harm. They will immediately report it to their manager. Training and support will be provided. Protecting people from harm of abuse is a multi-agency task. We will involve social work and the police where appropriate.

These three statements translate into practical actions which are set out *CrossReach's Safeguarding Strategy*, 2008. Achievements in 2008 include the following:
• The provision by the Head of Service, Safeguarding of safeguarding advice about decision making in individual cases of suspected, witnessed or reported harm. This advice is backed-up with written confirmation within two working days.
• The publication in January 2008 of CrossReach Adult Protection Policy, Procedure and Guidance, a 96-page colour booklet. The booklet includes a clear step-by-step procedure about what to do if harm is witnessed, suspected or reported plus 70 indexed pages of articles on 'best practice' culled from research and Government guidance.
• Implementing this policy and procedure with comprehensive multi-agency adult protection training. Two levels of training are being provided: 1) two-days mandatory intensive training for all staff with line management responsibility which started 13 May 2008 and is due to finish 29 April 2009 when 290 Managers will have been trained and 2) half-day training for all staff and volunteers cascaded by the Managers who have attended the two-day training.
• Ongoing child protection training in our Ballikinrain and Geilsland Schools and two sessions at the Mallard short breaks service for children and young adults affected by disability.
• The provision of support and a comprehensive set of materials for adult protection training to be cascaded to all staff.
• Applying lessons learnt from individual cases of harm or abuse to ensure that there is organisational learning, leading to better protection of service users and improved quality.

- A database of the incidence of suspected, witnessed, or reported harm in all CrossReach Services has been established. This management information will help us improve safeguarding in our services.

CrossReach has improved its systems for identifying suspected, witnessed or reported harm and taking appropriate action to safeguard our service users. We have done this through improved information sharing and communication within CrossReach, the wider Church and with local authority social work departments and the police. This work is being overseen by the Safeguarding Governance Group.

We will continue to develop our safeguarding services in 2009, within existing resources, to ensure that harm or abuse, of whatever type and seriousness, has no place in our services.

11. Corporate Planning

The remit of the Corporate Planning team has been focused on raising the professional and political profile. Professionally it is apparent that, although many areas of Scotland have CrossReach Services within their local communities, few of these communities are aware that the quality services and the support offered in Christ's name is provided by CrossReach. To address this, our starting point was the production of our first Annual Report which was distributed at the 2008 General Assembly. It focused on the eight service areas of support offered and the information included comments by service users and provided an overview of what may be experienced at point of service delivery.

Benchmarking some aspects of the ongoing work provides opportunities to focus future planning and address areas of change. The annual Service Users' Survey gleans vital information from those receiving our services and undoubtedly helps staff deliver improved services. The uptake of the CrossReach Service User Satisfaction Survey 2008 increased by almost 2% to 75.25% and

has recorded an overall increased satisfaction of the service users. Each of the three core areas (Staff, Support and Overall Service Rating) yielded results indicating a rise in the best possible category responses, whilst the percentages at the bottom end of the survey have seen an overall reduction. Care Commission inspections are seeking hard evidence demonstrating service user involvement (without which, top gradings of 5 and 6 are not possible) and the survey results in conjunction with the creation, updating and implementation of resulting quality improvement plans serve as a key component to this process. This was the fourth survey of its kind conducted by CrossReach and the findings support the Organisation's augmented value in seeking external accreditation. The Services engaging in processes such as Charter Mark (now Customer Service Excellence) are primarily discovering an overall increase in the satisfaction amongst their 'clients' with increased positive percentages in all core areas of the survey.

Service user involvement is an increasing focus of the Care Commission and many of our service users across the sector have a vital role in the day-to-day decisions concerning their life choices and CrossReach's professional profile. These roles include active involvement in personal care plans, service user meetings, recruitment of staff and service profiling.

The quality agenda has seen many more services achieve the Government external accreditation of Charter Mark. As previously detailed, this award has changed its name and criteria to meet the increasing service user involvement agenda. The new award is for Customer Service Excellence, reflecting the current thinking of customer involvement and satisfaction. CrossReach has embraced this and a significant number of services are striving to gain this in 2009. Services to Older People aim to have 100% of their services having achieved Charter Mark or Customer Service Excellence by 2010. Other service areas involved in the new award are Learning Disabilities and Mental

Health. At the same time, those services who achieved Charter Mark on the first round have been successfully reassessed, proving quality is embedded in the service delivery of CrossReach.

Other service areas are engaged with external accreditation systems more relevant to their specific needs. In the Children and Young People's services, Ballikinrain has achieved the Investors in People award. Like the others, this evidences the commitment of all to excellence.

Corporate Planning have maintained CrossReach/ Eurodiaconia links with involvement in the working group addressing the European Social Inclusion agenda. This involvement with other faith based non Government organisations ensures the Scottish support models and Service User Involvement strategies are shared with this European network.

Our professional and political profiling has delivered press releases (in particular supporting World Mental Health day) and the hosting of two events in the Scottish Parliament, raising awareness of the social care arm of the national Church. The interest from MSPs and their research assistants has been encouraging, leading to involvement in a number of cross party working groups.

11.1 Conferences
CrossReach has hosted and participated in a number of conferences this year including in April, the International Dementia Conference; our own very successful annual Staff Conference in Dundee; and the Drug and Alcohol Today Conference in Glasgow.

In February 2009, CrossReach hosted a Homeless "Hearing" event to coincide with homeless week. The highlight of the event was hearing from service users how they had been helped by our homeless support services. The audience of services users MSPs, Councillors and providers was well received. Comments below from a sample of attendees:

Jamie McGrigor, MSP –
Letter – "It was an extremely useful and interesting session. I particularly enjoyed hearing about the experiences of the service users directly, as did my members of staff............ The event was informative and a great success."

Billy, Rankeillor ex-service user, now student and service volunteer –
Speaking at the event – "When does my past become my past?"

After the event, in response to CrossReach letter of thanks for speaking – "I've never had a letter like that before."

Ronnie, Cale House service user –
Returning to Inverness after the event, Ronnie told Service Manager Zandra Kinnaird how welcome he was made to feel by everyone there and that he wasn't made to feel like "somebody different".

Pete Cuthbertson, Fundraising Manager, CrossReach
Email – "The feedback I heard in conversation was that it was a very good event that people enjoyed."

11.2 Information Management & Technology
In line with the objectives stated in last year's Report an extensive review of business systems and protocols was commissioned which took evidence from central staff, Service Managers and some external stakeholders. This review concluded that there was a need for updating a complex system which had developed organically over many years into a series of non-integrated manual systems and labour intensive computerised methods. A range of benefits was defined including faster handling of transactions, reductions in administration, paper and postage costs and more accurate real time reporting which could be gained from more appropriate use of the existing software. Council agreed that an investment in business software, training and process management was urgently required and a project team was put in place to manage the project. The cost of this modernisation

in the current year is £400,000 which will be capitalised and included in 2009 budget. It is anticipated that the key benefits will be available from spring 2009 onwards. As part of this process and included in the cost is the roll-out of a Wide Area Network (WAN) which was a part of our previous strategy. This system allows cheaper communications, Skype access across services thus reducing travel, faster and more reliable transfer of data, much improved access for Managers of all their financial and personnel data and direct transaction facility reducing energy consumption and waste as well as time wasted. Focus on this area of work has delayed the intended work on web design and function but a Web Advisory Group has been established and are moving it forward.

11.3 Marketing

The year saw the release of the CrossReach DVD which has proved very popular with church groups in particular, and once again the Bluebell Campaign was seen to have a very high profile. CrossReach had a presence at a number of the larger conferences, and of particular interest was the two day exhibition and reception at Holyrood attended by a wide range of politicians. Other work has included journal articles, the development of a range of new leaflets and service brochures as well as business marketing across local authorities. The issue at last year's General Assembly of our first Annual Report was very well received and attracted encouraging feedback from as far afield as Malawi. This year's review reflects much of this feedback, particularly in that it does not duplicate the information in the Church's Annual Report.

11.4 Fundraising and Communications

On Bluebell Day, 6 June 2008, CrossReach launched a free phone Bluebell Helpline for women affected by postnatal depression and their families. The launch was attended by the Moderator, The Right Rev David Lunan, and Mrs Lunan, along with the Lord Provost of Edinburgh and many local business people. Such a service has not existed in Scotland before. This is a particularly exciting innovation as the service has been possible through partnership working with ParentLine Scotland at Children 1st. The two organisations have forged an excellent working relationship. Statistics are being collated and will be analysed with a view to continuing this service beyond 2009. CrossReach would like to express thanks and appreciation to staff and volunteers at ParentLine Scotland and Children 1st for helping us to make this happen. The telephone number is: 0800 3 457 457.

The Bluebell Campaign for Postnatal Depression continues to build support including runners taking part in overseas marathons. The Bluebell Newsletter is sent to around 3,000 people and this is steadily increasing. We have continued to enjoy huge support from The Church of Scotland Guild and are grateful to the members of The Guild across the country in helping to spread our message and in raising much needed funds.

During 2009, we will be focusing on building our fundraising support across the country and will be seeking to recruit small groups of volunteer fundraisers to help; this will include a youth volunteering strategy. We hope to involve church groups and youth organisations such as the Boys Brigade.

The Circle of Care Trading Company Ltd sold over £100,000 worth of goods in 2008 and continues to expand the online shop to include items for all year round and not only items for Christmas. We thank all our customers for their continued support.

CrossReach continued to take an active part in exhibitions, including attending the Royal Highland Show with the Church of Scotland Rural Affairs group; the annual Church Without Walls events at Aviemore and Ingliston; promoting Bluebell in Livingston; the Baby Show at the Scottish Exhibition Conference Centre (SECC) and Crossover.

5

12. Estates

The work of Estates has focused largely on our residential properties, in particular the properties providing care and support to older people, through the refurbishment of existing premises and the construction of our new flagship care home in Aberdeen. In addition a planned maintenance programme specifically directed at ensuring compliance of our residential establishments with the requirements of recently introduced fire legislation has commenced and is likely to extend through 2009 to achieve completion.

During the course of the year major refurbishment works were completed at **Achvarasdal**, Reay and **South Beach House**, Ardrossan and now offer fully en-suited accommodation to 25 and 39 older people respectively.

Oversteps in Dornoch is one of our care homes that was fully refurbished in 2006/07 as part of the ongoing capital programme. The building was entered into a competition by the architects, White & McGinn, Inverness, and at a ceremony held in Thurso on 14th August 2008, won the award for the category of "New life for old buildings" in the Highland North heat of the Inverness Architectural Association (IAA), Awards for Architecture 2008. The IAA is the northernmost Chapter of the Royal Incorporation of Architects in Scotland (RIAS).

The new care home on the site of **Rubislaw Park House**, Aberdeen, is progressing satisfactorily and will come into service later this year providing 64 fully en-suited bedrooms, where 40 beds will be for the care of dementia sufferers and the remaining 24 for the care of older people.

Capital developments currently in the planning/pre-contract phases have suffered a setback as a result of the need to review the timing of the capital programme. A number of projects are still being progressed in anticipation of an early upturn in the economy. Similarly, the planned programme of property disposals, the proceeds of which would be attributed to capital projects has suffered due to the economic climate.

12.1   Energy and Green issues
12.1.1   Environmental Commitment

We continue to build on the commitment of last year through the development of a green policy in line with best practice and a general commitment to energy reduction. Having signed up to the Carbon Trust last year we have now produced an Environmental Policy that confirms our aims to manage our services and operations in ways that are environmentally sustainable, economically feasible and socially responsible. The aims and objectives include:

- Raising of awareness of staff and service users of CrossReach's environmental objectives and performance through environmental programmes for staff and service users and encouragement of feedback, suggestions and ensuring good practice.
- Implementation of sustainable resource management practices, a carbon management strategy through the uptake of low carbon technologies in buildings, services and equipment.
- Management of waste and recycling including the benefits of the WAN roll out and paperless invoicing.
- The development and management of a green transport plan for CrossReach.
- Consideration of sustainable construction options for new development or major refurbishment projects and to manage the estate with a view to amenity enhancement and biodiversity wherever possible.

12.1.1.1   Ballikinrain received the Green Flag Eco School Award, the first residential school in Scotland to receive this award.

12.1.2   Energy

The work of ensuring energy is purchased at the most beneficial rates and the monitoring of consumptions has continued throughout the year resulting in substantial financial savings as well as a reduction in emissions of harmful greenhouse gasses.

Application to the Energy Saving Trust resulted in the awarding of a substantial grant towards the cost of the provision of the renewable energy heating system incorporated into the new care home in Aberdeen. As reported last year this project is heated by a combined heat and power unit in association with geo-thermal heating.

We have also been successful in obtaining interest free loans from the Energy Saving Trust to replace inefficient heat generating plant, where the saving in fuel costs will offset the loan repayments. At the end of the repayment period we will benefit from reduced carbon emissions and economy savings.

13. Ecumenical and Parish Support Activity

Ecumenically, our services are predominantly engaging with local parish churches and local Roman Catholic churches with various levels of input and involvement. Some services lease church rooms to host day care/counselling facilities such as our Mental Health Services and Counselling Services and others receive support of a more pastoral nature. There have been various types of financial benefits supplied by both the local parish church and Roman Catholic Church to one of our Homelessness Services whilst our Children's Services are leading a Parent's Group in partnership with one of their parish churches. In the Older People's Services, Friends Groups from the national Church play key roles in offering support in a wide and varied way and some services have invaluable input from the local ministers regarding staff recruitment. The Learning Disabilities Services are engaged with the "People with Learning Disabilities Working Group" in partnership with the Ministries Council and also have links with the Aberdeen University Department of Theology.

The Council has continued to provide the Church of Scotland representative in the governance of Scottish Churches Housing Action (SCHA) which is a prime example of ecumenical practice and wholly owned by 13 denominations. A CrossReach Vice-Convener has served as Vice Convener of SCHA and we have continued to provide the Church of Scotland contribution to its core costs and also HR and Property advice.

14. The Year in Review

Jan 29	11 CrossReach services received the prestigious Charter Mark award which recognises 'customer service excellence'.
Jan 30	Scotland's first specialist dementia home, Williamwood House in Glasgow, celebrated its 25th anniversary.
Feb 13	Sunflower Garden in Edinburgh was presented with the 'Spurgeons Network Award for Improving the Lives of Children and Young People' by Christian organisation Faithworks.
Feb 19	Eskmills Project celebrated 10 years of supporting adults with learning disabilities in Portobello, Joppa and Musselburgh.
Apr 30	CrossReach hosted an International Dementia Conference in Glasgow on the theme 'End the confusion – see me, not the illness'.
May 12	Eastwoodhill home in Glasgow celebrated its 60th anniversary.
June 6	Launch of joint Bluebell telephone helpline at Tynecastle Stadium in Edinburgh in association with Children 1st.
Sept 18	20th anniversary of Dick Stewart Hostels in Glasgow which offer support to former offenders to get their lives back on track.
Nov 5	2nd Charter Mark awards held in Glasgow. A total of 21 CrossReach services now have Charter Mark.
Nov 12	Oversteps home in Dornoch held a service of thanksgiving in Dornoch Cathedral to mark its 50th anniversary.
Nov 14	At the Scottish Care Awards, Kathleen Cairns from Kirkhaven in Glasgow was named 'Care Home Manager of the Year'.
Nov 27	Launch of Threshold West of Scotland,

bringing together the work of Threshold South Lanarkshire and the Cornerstone Projects.

Dec 8   CrossReach was awarded the Eurodiaconia Innovation Award at the European Parliament for its programme to protect vulnerable adults receiving social care.

15. Key Events for Next Year

May 15   Ashley Lodge, Aberdeen, 50th anniversary
June   First Carers Conference taking place in partnership with Carers Scotland.
June 15   Kinloch Day Care, Auchtermuchty, 10th anniversary
June 20   Ballikinrain School, Balfron, 40th anniversary
June 30   South Beach House, Ardrossan, 50th anniversary
Aug 5   Walter & Joan Gray, Shetland, 40th anniversary
Sept 18   Whinnieknowe, Nairn, 60th anniversary
Oct 13   Gaberston, Alloa, 20th anniversary

In the name of the Council

DAVID L COURT, *Convener*
SALLY BONAR, *Vice-Convener*
SYDNEY GRAHAM, *Vice-Convener*

ADDENDUM

Retiral of Convener

In 2009 Rev David L Court completes his term of office as the Convener of CrossReach, Social Care Council. David's involvement with CrossReach and the Board of Social Responsibility stretches back to 1996 when he was nominated to the then Board of Social Responsibility. From 1997 he served as the Convener of the Operations Committee and as a member of the Executive Committee.

David served as Vice Convener of the Board from 2001-2004 when he retired from that position at the end of his term of office. In 2005 David was invited back as Convener to CrossReach. Over the years David has been involved in a variety of Christian organisations, including Rutherford House, UCCF and the Bible Society.

A keen and very competitive footballer, David's involvement now mainly focuses on his support of Motherwell FC. While serving at CrossReach David has enjoyed being involved in the 5-aside football league and has used this time to add to his long list of broken bones. As a result it would appear that his competitive playing days are over. His energies are now focused on the golf course where it is said he is a very good golfer, turning out on occasion for the Church of Scotland golf team.

In his service to CrossReach David has evidenced his commitment to the work of the organisation and of his support and availability to staff at all levels. He has shown an understanding of the issues faced in the social care field today. He has debated these issues at length externally on behalf of CrossReach and in a supportive manner which has been an encouragement to all in what have been difficult times.

David was particularly supportive of staff at the sad loss of Ian Manson, our previous Director, and his presence was appreciated by all at that time. CrossReach would like to record its sincere and heartfelt appreciation of David's long and committed service to CrossReach and give thanks to God for his continuing commitment in his service of his Church and his Lord.

In the name of the Council

PETER BAILEY, *Acting Chief Executive Officer*

APPENDIX 1
STRATEGIC TARGETS 2008

1. To build the capacity of the workforce through promoting life long learning for all staff.
2. To equip staff to meet the demands of the changing aspects of social care and support through a development programme which provides them with a variety of skills and qualifications.
3. To achieve a balanced budget by 2011.
4. To deliver services through three main areas of work: Young People and Families, Adult Recovery Services and Services for Older People.
5. To continue to work to realise the aspirations of the 21st Century Social Work Review Report "Changing Lives".
6. To raise the political and professional profile of CrossReach.
7. To develop partnership working with churches and local communities to enable local solutions to local needs.
8. To develop partnership working with other agencies and organisations to broaden the way we deliver our services.
9. To develop Fundraising in CrossReach to meet the current and emerging challenges and demands of an organisation within the voluntary sector.
10. To promote continuous improvement and sustainable change throughout the work of the organisation.
11. To continue to improve quality in practice and service delivery both operationally and corporately, and seek appropriate external accreditation of these areas.
12. To continue to develop existing and new buildings to meet national standards and to provide a safer, greener, smarter and healthier environment for staff and service users.
13. To develop CrossReach's Capital Planning Strategy in order to meet the changing needs of services users and other stakeholders.
14. To develop SMART technology to provide personalised services and promote independence of service users.
15. To develop an Information Technology infrastructure which enables CrossReach to be contemporary in its work and which supports and improves service delivery.

5

SUPPORT AND SERVICES COUNCIL
May 2009

PROPOSED DELIVERANCE

The General Assembly
Receive the Report.

REPORT

The Support and Services Council embraces the Assembly Arrangements, Central Services, Ecumenical Relations, Legal Questions, Safeguarding, and Stewardship and Finance Committees. Each of these six Committees reports separately to the General Assembly, but the Council Convener represents all six at the Council of Assembly.

The Council meets twice annually when brief reports on each Committee's work are shared. Each of the Committees has the opportunity to report annually to the Council of Assembly.

In the name and by the authority of the Council

VIVIENNE A DICKSON, *Convener*
JOHN C CHRISTIE, *Vice-Convener*
GORDON D JAMIESON, *Secretary*

PROPOSED DELIVERANCE

The General Assembly

1. Receive the Report.
2. Approve the Order of Business for the first three days (Order of Proceedings).
3. Appoint Mr Roy Pinkerton to edit the verbatim record.
4. Encourage commissioners intending to move amendments and counter-motions to arrange to have these printed in the Assembly papers.
5. Resolve that the Convener of the Nomination Committee, when not a commissioner, should have corresponding membership of the General Assembly in terms of Standing Order 32.2, with immediate effect; and instruct the Clerks to amend the Standing Orders accordingly.
6. Thank all who contributed to the consultation on the culture and timing of the General Assembly and note that the questions considered at meetings with Presbytery representatives and circulated to Presbyteries and Kirk Sessions are set out in Appendix B and Appendix C respectively.
7. Thank Mr Roy Pinkerton for his analysis of the responses to the consultation and note the findings set out in Appendix D and in section 9 of the Report
8. Instruct all Councils and Committees to ensure that their Assembly Reports are accessible to commissioners and designed to facilitate informed decision making.
9. Instruct the Committee, in consultation with Councils and Committees, to devise systems whereby Councils, and particularly the larger ones, report on the totality of their work over a period of years.
10. Agree with the Committee's conclusions that there is not an overwhelming desire to move the General Assembly to September and that the practical difficulties in the way of such a move suggest that this matter should not be pursued.
11. Instruct the Committee to examine the possibility of using Sunday afternoon for the Lord High Commissioner's Garden Party.

Scottish Bible Society

12. Gratefully acknowledge 200 years of vital practical service to the Church by the Scottish Bible Society.
13. Recognise the Society's role in supplying Scriptures for Christians at home and abroad.
14. Commend local partnerships in using Bibleworld and other resources to stimulate young people.
15. Encourage the Church's support of efforts to provide spiritual sustenance in situations of poverty, disaster and health crises.
16. Appoint Rev Andrew Anderson, Rev Sandy Gunn, Rev Lynn McChlery and Rev Dr Norman Maciver to the Scottish Bible Society's Council of Church Representatives.

REPORT

The Very Rev David Lunan

David Lunan came to the moderatorial chair with a wealth of experience in ministry. Following studies at Glasgow and Princeton he served for six years as Assistant Minister and youth club leader at Calton in the east end of Glasgow. This was followed by a twelve year ministry at St Andrew's-Lhanbryd in Moray. Thereafter he moved back to Glasgow as minister of the city centre congregation of Renfield St Stephen's. Fourteen years later he was appointed Clerk to the Presbytery of Glasgow from where he was called to be Moderator of the General Assembly of 2008. To this varied ministry within Scotland must be added a long standing commitment to the work of Christian Aid. Such a background in youth outreach, rural and urban ministry, the experience of being Clerk to the Church's largest presbytery and a passionate concern for world development issues have all been reflected in the various facets of his moderatorial year.

Maggie Lunan has shared fully in her husband's ministry – not least in her own significant work for Christian Aid and Alternativity. This moderatorial year has been no exception to the partnership principle by which the Lunans live and the Church has also benefited from Maggie's rich experience. Together they have been excellent ambassadors in their visits to the Presbyteries of England, Kirkcaldy, Hamilton and Annandale and Eskdale and in overseas trips to Nepal, Malawi and Zambia. In addition they both played a leading role in the ground breaking Scottish Interfaith Pilgrimage to Israel and Palestine last July.

In speaking, listening and simply being with so many people in so many different places both have been generous with their time and their gifts. They have been gracious witnesses to Christ and worthy representatives of the Church of Scotland.

2. Presbytery Representation

The Presbytery returns show that there are in all the Presbyteries 1,170 Charges, whether vacant or not, and that there are 203 other ministers (excluding retired ministers) who are members of Presbyteries. Representation is calculated for each Presbytery in accordance with Act III, 2000, and the total number of Commissions is made up as follows: 371 Ministers, 371 Elders and 33 Deacons.

3. Business Committee

In terms of Standing Order 15 it is proposed that the Convener and Vice-Convener of the Assembly Arrangements Committee, respectively the Rev David Arnott and the Rev Janet Mathieson, act as Convener and Vice-Convener of the Business Committee. The names of others nominated to serve on this Committee will be found in the Order of Proceedings.

4. Assembly Services

The Assembly Service has been arranged in St Giles' Cathedral on Sunday 24 May at 10 am with the Gaelic Service that day at 12.30 pm in Greyfriars Tolbooth and Highland Church. A service of evening worship will be held in the Assembly Hall the same day at 6.00 pm. The Assembly Communion Service will be held on Friday 22 May at 9.30 am in the Assembly Hall.

5. Notices of Motion and Assembly Papers

The Committee again draws attention to the fact that commissioners wishing to move amendments or counter-motions to deliverances can have these printed in Assembly papers. As a courtesy to other commissioners, and for the convenience of the Assembly, the Committee asks that this be done wherever possible. Clearly situations can arise in the course of a debate where someone wishes to make a motion and such spontaneity is part of the life of the Assembly. However, where people have considered and prepared texts, particularly if these are substantial, it is extremely helpful to have them in the order paper. Certainly, the availability of the screens means that motions can fairly quickly appear in writing and the "behind scenes team" work hard to provide this service. However, when something complex (and clearly considered) suddenly appears it can take time to get it up on the screen and further time for reading and assimilation. There will again be four sets of papers – covering (1) Thursday and Friday, (2) Saturday and Monday, (3) Tuesday and (4) Wednesday. For the first set of papers notices of motion should be sent to the Principal Clerk's Office at "121" by Friday 15 May. For the second and subsequent sets they should handed in to the Clerks' table by 12 noon on the Friday, Monday and Tuesday of the Assembly.

6.   Notice of Questions

A frequent concern raised by Council and Committee Conveners is the difficulty of answering Commissioners' questions that are technical or require some checking of information. Standing Order 45 reads: "It shall be in order to ask questions of the Convener regarding any matter in the care of the Committee to which no reference is made in the Report but in such cases timeous notice shall be given to the Convener." While it is reasonable to expect a reporting Convener to be well briefed on those matters on which he or she is reporting to the General Assembly, there will be some questions of detail that it is not reasonable for a Convener to be able to answer *ex tempore*, even if they relate to the Report being debated (where the Standing Order would not apply). There is no intention to change Standing Orders in this regard, because all sorts of questions can genuinely emerge only in the course of an Assembly debate and it is right that they should be asked. However, any Convener should feel entitled to decline to answer any question of which he or she clearly required notice, and will be supported by the Moderator where necessary; and Commissioners are asked to exercise every possible courtesy and forethought in enabling Conveners to prepare for debates.

7.   Corresponding Membership

The Committee has considered the role of the Convener of the Nomination Committee, and believes that it is vital for this office-holder to be as familiar as possible with the work of the Councils and Committees to which the Nomination Committee suggests appointments each year. Until now the Convener has attended the General Assembly only in year in which he or she has held a commission from Presbytery, and is therefore less familiar with the work of the General Assembly than other Conveners. Both the Nomination Committee and the Assembly Arrangements Committee recommend that the Convener of the Nomination Committee, when not a commissioner, should have corresponding membership in terms of Standing Order 32.2, taking effect for this General Assembly.

8.   Commissioners' Subsistence and Travelling Expenses

The Board recommends the following rates for payment of expenses:

Overnight subsistence
Not exceeding £50.00 for each night

Daily out-of-pocket Expenses
Not exceeding £15.00 per day

Mileage rate, when no public transport is available, 25p per mile

9.   Culture and Timing of the General Assembly

As approved by last year's General Assembly the Committee has undertaken a wide ranging consultation with Presbyteries and Kirk Sessions on the culture and timing of the General Assembly. Last October meetings with Presbytery representatives were held in Aberdeen,

Inverness, Glasgow, Dumfries and Edinburgh. In addition Presbyteries and Kirk Sessions were invited to complete a questionnaire.

The Committee is grateful to Mr Roy Pinkerton for analysing the various responses. His report was received at the January meeting and given further consideration in February. In light of the comments received from around the Church the Committee brings the following observations and recommendations to the General Assembly. The text of Mr Pinkerton's full report can be found at Appendix D.

It is clear that the General Assembly of the Church of Scotland is held in very high regard across the country. The giving of the full title for this gathering is deliberate. It is the General Assembly of the Church of Scotland. This is not a convention of some like-minded church people. This is our General Assembly. This is where the Church transacts its business so that its Councils may go forward with confidence; this is where the Church can showcase its wares by telling the good news stories; this is where the inspiration is found through worship and networking.

We should, therefore, never underestimate the importance of the Assembly in the minds of our members and others. Change and development should never be such that the dignity and significance of the Assembly might become undermined.

Over the years there have been many changes to the General Assembly. Apart from the obvious one with the modernisation of the Assembly Hall itself, a move universally welcomed, we have also changed the starting date. We have altered the length of the Assembly, introduced youth representatives, expanded daily worship, as well as introducing Sunday evening worship in the Assembly Hall. Electronic voting is now a regular feature and the screens are in constant use for a variety of functions. Swipe cards allow us access to the Assembly Hall and open up microphones.

Our research has shown, however, that there is still a desire for further development. While the General Assembly of the Church of Scotland is just that, there is a perception abroad that it is not as accessible as it should be. Reports in the Blue Book are overly long and too unwieldy for the unsuspecting reader. The length and density of some reports make it very difficult, if not impossible, to hold the Councils to account, yet such accountability is one of the major functions of the General Assembly. Some respondents went so far as to suggest that the size of reports led them to suspect attempts to hide difficult and sensitive material in the midst of some heavy-weight writing. While this Committee would not wish to give credence to that kind of comment the Assembly ought to know it was not an isolated remark.

If we are serious about communicating our message we also have to be serious about the ways in which we communicate. It is essential that those we wish to hear what we are saying, are also able to understand. Good communication and credibility go hand in hand. At our meetings with Council Conveners and Secretaries, the first of which was in September 2008, we highlighted the need for the Councils to examine very closely the lay-out of their reports so that commissioners and others could find them more accessible. At the time of writing this report we await with anticipation the fruit of those discussions.

As the appendices show there were many concerns raised in our consultations. The lack of diligence in attendance shown by some commissioners was highlighted in comparison with our youth delegates. However, it was not just their presence that many commented on, but also their preparedness for debate, their readiness to ask intelligent questions. This preparedness is partly due to the fact they gather each evening to discuss the following day's business. Some suggested, therefore, the possibility of a residential assembly, or at least accommodation where commissioners could get together of an evening to discuss business for the following day in a similar fashion to the youth representatives. Some also suggested this ought to be a matter for Presbyteries to deal with before the Assembly begins.

The question of when best to hold the General Assembly fairly divided the respondents. The minority argued passionately for the retention of May while a small majority argued less passionately for the possibility of giving September a try. We are aware that September marks the beginning of the congregational year and is a busy time, especially for ministers. It is also not the best time for those who work the land. We are equally aware that a move to September has very strong backing from the Secretaries of the Councils as they believe this would allow a fuller use of time available. It would also be the preferred option for those who have the responsibility for the Church's accounts.

At present most Councils are able to hold one meeting after a General Assembly in June before a break over the summer months. They then have only until the end of February to complete their year's work and write their report for the General Assembly. Were the Assembly to be held in September the Councils argue that they could begin their work almost straight away and continue through till June, leaving the fallow summer months for the production of the Blue Book.

However, as noted above there are a number of important practical matters to be considered. The Festival Fringe in late August/early September provides a reliable let for the Assembly Hall. Accommodation for commissioners in Edinburgh at such a busy time would also be an issue. The New College session begins in mid September which means that vital accommodation would not be available to the Assembly as in May. There is also the argument that September would not be so suitable for parish ministers.

The Committee believes that a move to September would represent a major change and would require a very

deliberate decision by the Assembly. The Committee is not persuaded by the "give it a try" argument. The General Assembly is a major event in the life of Edinburgh and of the nation as a whole and many people beyond the Church have it "on their radar". Chopping and changing would simply cause confusion and would not reflect well on the Church. If the Assembly thinks such a change would bring significant benefits and wants the Committee to make a thorough study of all the implications then the Committee will be happy to oblige. However, on balance, the Committee does not sense an overwhelming desire for such a change and this, taken together with the practical difficulties alluded to earlier has led us to conclude and recommend that this matter be no longer pursued and that the Assembly should continue to meet in May.

Another topic which emerged was a suggestion that the Assembly meet every other year, with some, as yet unspecified event in the intervening years. A number of Presbyterian Churches around the world have made such a change in recent years.

Again the Committee did not sense an overwhelming desire for such a change and is aware of counter arguments such as reduction of frequency of representation. However, the Committee did warm to the suggestion that Councils, particularly the larger ones, might devise ways of reporting which meant that they did not have to cover everything every year. Indeed it may be that a rota might even be established whereby some bodies reported every other year. This would allow for a continuing annual Assembly but one which was less crowded than can be the case under present arrangements.

The experiment of an outing on the Sunday afternoon last year to East Lothian organised by the Tourist Board was appreciated. It has been expanded this year. The fallow period of much of the weekend, however, did come in for some criticism especially from those who took the opportunity to go back home. Were the Lord High

Commissioner's Garden Party, to which we are all invited guests, held on a Sunday afternoon this would free up the Saturday afternoon for business. The Committee is aware of sensitivities in this area, however, even though food and fellowship are solid Biblical themes, and it would look to the General Assembly to give it clear guidance on this issue.

10. Assembly Hall

The Assembly Hall sub-committee was established in May 2008 to give detailed consideration to and advise the Assembly Arrangements Committee on matters relating to its remits to be responsible for (a) the care and maintenance of the Assembly Hall and (b) all arrangements in connection with the letting of the Hall.

During the year the sub-committee has introduced new procedures to co-ordinate the overall management of the Hall in a more efficient and cost-effective manner.

As a result the sub-committee identified a number of key areas that required attention; these included, among other things, much needed redecoration; repairs to the heating system; improving health & safety; reviewing the telephone and IT systems and updating the insurance requirements. The sub-committee is also pleased to report that, by the time of the General Assembly, work will have been completed to restore the large painting of "Queen Victoria's Chaplains" which hangs in the Lower East Corridor.

The sub-committee continues to enjoy a positive business relationship with Edinburgh First who organise the letting of the Hall. Although the net revenue from letting has been falling over the last couple of years, there are now some very positive indicators that this position could successfully be reversed. During more recent months the Hall has hosted a wider range of events including two large corporate AGMs, the launch of a new album by a leading Scottish music group and several good quality concerts. To take full advantage of these new opportunities the sub-committee is now working closely with Edinburgh First to examine cost-effective ways by which the stage-area, with related facilities such as lighting, could be improved to attract a wider range of events.

In the name of the Committee

A DAVID K ARNOTT, *Convener*
JANET S MATHIESON, *Vice-Convener*
FINLAY A J MACDONALD, *Secretary*

APPENDIX A
REPORT OF THE SCOTTISH BIBLE SOCIETY

'This same good news that came to you is going out all over the world. It is changing lives everywhere, just as it changed yours that very first day you heard and understood about God's great kindness to sinners.' Colossians 1:6 (NLT)

What a privilege to play a part in the spreading of this good news around the world. We thank God that the Scottish Bible Society has been enabled to do this for the last 200 years.

The last year has seen widespread suffering, caused by conflicts (Georgia, Congo, Zimbabwe, Israel/Gaza, Sri Lanka), natural disasters (Burma and China in particular) and the global economic downturn. At least the Beijing Olympics delivered some feel-good moments! One common strand in all of this was the presence of the Bible. It was available free at the chapel in the Athletes' Village, provided as part of co-ordinated relief to victims of the Irrawaddy cyclone and deeply appreciated by congregations in earthquake-stricken Sichuan. The good news about Jesus Christ is indeed going out all over the world.

Thank you

Over recent months the Scottish Bible Society has been

a channel for contributions to many other parts of the world, not least Malawi. The process of translation that began in 1876 with Dr Robert Laws (from Aberdeen) still continues so that people may access the Scriptures in their own languages (such as Lomwe and Yao). Work already done in Chichewa is being extended through a 'Talking Bible' for the blind and a study edition for church leaders lacking reference books. Yet when the Bible Society of Malawi's executive director, Clapperton Mayuni, visited last October, his most important message to us in Scotland was 'thank you' – for the pioneer missionaries, for his own teachers and for all who donate to provide the Word for a growing church.

200 Not Out

We are enjoying celebrating our Bicentenary year. We have given a birthday present to every secondary school in Scotland in the form of 'The Passion' DVD, shown on BBC TV last year and ideal as an educational resource. We've had our own TV appearance when St Michael's Linlithgow was the focus for a BBC 'Songs of Praise' programme (broadcast on May 10) highlighting some key aspects of our work. We've provided a leaflet that churches can offer to 'Homecoming' and other visitors, a DVD-based resource of a Bible Overview and a 'Local Heroes' exhibit showing how Scots played a vital role in the spread of the Scriptures worldwide.

These, along with other events and products aim to raise the profile of the Bible in Scotland and bring it to the attention of those who would not normally take notice of its message. We pray that it will result in changed lives!

At the same time, we continue to look outwards, in particular towards impoverished areas of north-eastern Brazil. In partnership with our colleagues there we plan to provide a bus equipped with medical and dental facilities, as well as Bibles and Bible teaching resources. This type of holistic ministry has been well received along the Amazon over several decades, and is an excellent opportunity for Scots to 'invest' in a long-term service to the needy. The extra cost is very challenging at this time of financial uncertainty, but we trust God to unlock the funds needed.

As we look ahead we do so with confidence that God still speaks through the Bible and that the gospel of Jesus Christ changes lives. To God be the glory and praise!

APPENDIX B

The consultations with Presbytery representatives asked three questions.
What is working well at the General Assembly?
What is missing from the current General Assembly?
What shape should a future General Assembly be?

The most popular responses were:

Working well
- Technology / administration / organisation
- Worship
- Youth representatives

Missing
- Holding councils to account
- Diligence by commissioners
- Participation from elders
- Preparation
- User-friendly Blue Book
- Accessibility to debate

Future Shape to consider
- Midweek
- Accessible Blue Book
- May or September?
- Better use of weekend
- Bi-ennial assembly?
- Biennial reporting?
- Residential possibility

6.1

APPENDIX C
CONSULTATIONS WITH PRESBYTERY REPRESENTATIVES

The consultations with Presbytery representatives asked the following questions:

(1) How do you react to the Committee's summary of contemporary expectations of the General Assembly?

(2) If you find yourself broadly in agreement with it, please comment as to whether and to what extent these three expectations are being met. Please comment in particular on how each one might be achieved more effectively
   (a) Dealing with the business
   (b) Providing opportunities for theological reflection and discussion on themes such as mission, social engagement *etc*.
   (c) Offering inspiration through worship and celebration

(3) If you have additional or different expectations of the Assembly please indicate what these are.

(4) How do you react to the suggestion that the General Assembly might be held in September rather than May?

(5) Please indicate any other changes which you would like to see introduced, *eg* number of commissioners, frequency of meeting, venue, location.

(6) Please indicate any other comments you wish to make – use an additional sheet if required.

APPENDIX D
REPORT TO ASSEMBLY ARRANGEMENTS COMMITTEE: ANALYSIS OF CONSULTATION QUESTIONS ON THE GENERAL ASSEMBLY

1 Introduction
1.1 The basis of the report
The following report attempts to collate and analyse a total of 328 responses. Most of these took the form of completed questionnaires; a small handful addressed the issues in an alternative format. Respondents to the questionnaire were invited to indicate whether they were replying as individuals, on behalf of a Presbytery, or on behalf of a Kirk Session.

1.1.1 234 responses were received on behalf of Kirk Sessions. These in fact represent 236 congregations: in two cases, a single response was sent by a pair of linked or neighbouring congregations.

This represents a response rate of approximately one in six. Four responses do not indicate which Kirk Session they come from, but the remaining 232 show a reasonably representative geographical spread. Only two Presbyteries are not represented, and while the response rate naturally varies from Presbytery to Presbytery in only six (one urban, three urban/rural and two rural) is it lower than one in twelve, *ie* lower than half the national average.

10 of these questionnaires are completely blank, some offering as an explanation the fact that the Kirk Session has had too little experience of the General Assembly to be able to make any useful comments. Many other questionnaires have been only partially completed.

It is clear that these responses vary considerably in the way they were produced. Some result from full discussion at a meeting of the Kirk Session, some have been compiled by one or more individuals and have then been endorsed by the whole Session, some have been submitted by the elder who most recently attended the

General Assembly as a Commissioner. A small number of partially-completed responses carry the 'health-warning' that they have been completed on the basis of very little knowledge of the Assembly, as none of the elders who had taken part in the discussion had ever been a commissioner. Despite the first-person-singular format of many of the replies, they have been considered as Kirk Session responses if the appropriate box has been ticked. There may therefore be some misallocation of responses between the categories of 'Kirk Session' and 'individual', but this did not seem particularly important in the overall context of this questionnaire. Similarly, there may be some repetition and overlap between Kirk Session and Presbytery responses: those submitted by one Presbytery were echoed almost word for word by several Kirk Sessions from that Presbytery, but these have all been counted as separate responses.

1.1.2 84 responses were received from individuals. 20 of these were anonymous, 49 came from elders and 15 from ministers.

1.1.3 10 responses were received from Presbyteries; these ranged from fully completed questionnaires addressing all the issues in depth to extract minutes of brief deliverances covering only a couple of matters.

1.2 The compilation of the report
The questionnaire consisted of five specific areas for discussion, together with a sixth section inviting any other comments. The analysis of these comments has not been altogether straightforward. Not all respondents read the questions before starting to write their answers, those who had read the questions did not always stick to the point, and some of those who did stick to the point were determined to stick to it through thick and thin and emphasise it by frequent repetition throughout their whole response. Section 3, asking for 'additional or different expectations of the Assembly', raised particular problems, with most respondents failing to focus on the word 'expectations' and instead writing comments

which more properly related to one of the other sections. The format of this report is therefore not simply a serial analysis of what has been said in each of the six boxes on each of the returned questionnaires; instead many of the responses have had to be reordered to avoid going over the same ground several times. An attempt has been made to indicate the strength of support for each comment.

While many respondents may not have related their comments to the most appropriate section of the questionnaire, most comments did on the whole relate to the General Assembly. The very occasional complaints about other aspects of church life ('streamline the bureaucracy in 121', 'it takes too long to appoint ministers', 'reduce Councils to a bare minimum', 'restore Presbytery representation to Councils') have been ignored in the following analysis. Also omitted from this analysis are a number of suggestions, no doubt emanating from those who have not been commissioners for some years, asking for something that already exists: introducing hymns and a short talk into morning worship, setting time-limits for speakers, arranging an induction evening for new commissioners just before the start of the Assembly, and other now well-established practices.

Since there is a call (see 2.2.3 below!) for all reports to include a succinct summary with bullet points, the remainder of this analysis might be summed up as follows:
• reduce the business
• reduce the costs

2. Expectations of the General Assembly
(sections 1, 2 and 3)
2.1 Introduction
2.1.1 There was a considerable measure of support for the Committee's summary: 210 respondents (151 Kirk Sessions, 53 individuals and six Presbyteries) expressed agreement, many enthusiastically, others 'broadly' or 'in principle'; a number of these, however, entered the

6.1

caveat that some extra time would be needed if all these expectations were to be met. Only 36 respondents (25 Kirk Sessions and 11 individuals) indicated some measure of disagreement. Most of these (27) felt that only the first of the committee's expectations was appropriate to the General Assembly (one observing that in the General Assembly 'there is little to inspire or stimulate'), while five agreed with the first and third but did not approve of the second. One Kirk Session felt that the Committee's expectations were 'unnecessary' and another thought that they were 'difficult for ordinary members to understand'. One individual felt that they did not 'express real enthusiasm for radical change', another found them to be interesting but unachievable, and yet another considered them to be a 'knee-jerk reaction to something that has been broken for some time'.

2.1.2 A number of respondents picked up on the Committee's use of the words 'court' and 'conference': of the responses which directly contrasted these two words, the majority (34 out of 41) were adamant that the Assembly must retain its principal function, that of 'court', and only seven indicated that they would like to see it become 'more conference than court'. Many others, however, saw merit in what was referred to as 'conference', without directly contrasting it with 'court'. It has to be said that not all respondents made a clear distinction between the 'conference sessions' recently introduced into the business of the Assembly and a 'conference style' which might be more applicable to the 'fringe', and some of the comments in the relevant sections of this report may not have been placed in the correct category.

2.1.3 In attempting to explore in more detail the tension between 'court' and 'conference', views varied from one extreme to the other. One respondent felt that the Assembly should simply take the form of the National Gathering held at Ingliston, while another proposed that a straightforward 'change to the conference type of Assembly' would stimulate greater interest and enable

the Assembly to reconnect with congregations. At the other extreme, two respondents wanted to abandon conference-style 'stage-management' altogether and return to simple debating, noting that 'we do not recognise as divinely inspired the trend towards aping what is done by political party conferences'. However, most of those who raised this issue were somewhere in the middle: while the Assembly was neither 'just another conference' nor 'the AGM of a plc', it was accepted that both formal business sessions and time for discussion should continue to be integral parts of the Assembly and the problem was how to marry the two together. Three respondents pressed for clear lines of demarcation between conference and business sessions, on the grounds that 'it is hard to move from hearing inspirational and staged accounts of how well a council is doing to then criticising how they conduct their business', while another two expressed concern that the movement away from formality should go no further, uneasy at the 'imperceptibly gradual drift' towards the 'procedural trappings' of a conference style. One respondent suggested that much could be learned from the way major ecumenical conferences manage both business and conference sessions. More detailed responses on this aspect of the Assembly are dealt with in section 2.3 below.

2.1.4 A number of more general comments on the ethos of the Assembly were made, which might usefully be brought together here before moving on to section 2 of the questionnaire. A frequent comment was that the Assembly must hold committees and committee members to account much more rigorously than it does at present (9). One Presbytery believes 'that the General Assembly needs to move from a culture of 'reporting', in which a great deal of time and effort is devoted to approving detailed deliverances, to a culture of 'informing', in which Commissioners are enabled to identify with the work being done in their name'. Recent improvements in the way the Assembly is run and the organic way it is developing are to be commended (5), but there is also a feeling that some passion has gone out of it, and any sense of Christian involvement is missing, with the Gospel 'taking second place to political manoeuvring' (2): more 'rapid and radical change' is needed to send commissioners home 'with renewed vigour' (1). The Assembly should capitalise on its unique ability to draw together a wide spectrum of differing opinions and come to consensus decisions and it should therefore be less cautious in discussing and taking decisions on sensitive matters and more willing to live 'on the 'edge' (5). One respondent was appreciative of all the work that goes into the General Assembly and expressed disappointment that it is achieving far less than it should: ways must be found of sharing the 'faith in action' of the General Assembly with the wider church (1). The General Assembly should return to 'the church of the Acts of the Apostles', and develop a more prayerful and visionary focus (4): its organisation should not be determined by 'the agenda of the central administration', by 'the needs of finance departments', or by the 'ceremonial aspects of the week' (4). One respondent who had recently been a first-time commissioner had been 'challenged, confused, but *never* bored', another was 'pleasantly surprised', and a third found the whole process 'arcane but stimulating': words like 'inspiring' and 'energising' crept into many of the responses, and it is clear that despite all its many faults and failings the Assembly means a great deal to a great many people.

2.2 Dealing with the business (section 2a)

2.2.1 A very high proportion of respondents had something to say on this subject, although in most cases their focus was on the second half of the question. Nonetheless, 77 respondents (58 Kirk Sessions, 17 individuals and two Presbyteries) specifically indicated that the business was being dealt with effectively at present. Six indicated that the business could be despatched more efficiently or in a more business-like manner, without going into further details.

2.2.2 The main complaint, expressed in general terms by 29 respondents but implied in the more detailed responses from many others, was that there is too much business, that the business is too unwieldy, and that it should be dealt with more quickly. The opposite view was also expressed: some respondents felt that adequate opportunity was not always given for engagement with significant topics: much of the business was a mere formality, as the Assembly tended to be a rubber-stamping exercise (3).

2.2.3 One respondent asked whether the Blue Book was the best way to present reports, and a substantial number commented on the book and its contents. It should be published earlier (5) and available on the internet or in CD form (3, one of whom argued that this would allow commissioners to search for key words and to avoid having to read it all). The length and detail of reports and deliverances should be reduced and the Blue Book revamped and made more user-friendly (39). Councils should be encouraged to highlight the major issues and not feel obliged to 'account for every decision they have made, no matter how small and trivial'; their reports should clearly distinguish between routine matters which merely needed to be noted by the Assembly and more significant or more controversial matters on which a decision is needed (7). Each report should include a brief bullet-point summary of its contents (5), and one respondent went so far as to suggest that each report should be reduced to a list of key points with the minimum of explanation. A full report should be made available on the website, with only a shorter version, related to the deliverances, printed in the Blue Book (3). Deliverances should be reduced to a maximum of ten on each report (1) and should be more challenging (1). Reports in the Blue Book should be printed in the order in which they are to be taken at the Assembly (1).

2.2.4 Those responsible for planning the business should ensure that it is properly prioritised, with important reports being scheduled for peak attendance times, possibly first thing in the morning (14). Many of those who made this point had unhappy memories of the rather full Monday at the 2008 Assembly. There could be merit in devoting each day to a separate theme: on the day when the Stewardship and Finance Committee reports, for example, the Assembly could also hear from the General Trustees, the Housing and Loan Fund, the Investors Trust, the Pension Trustees, etc. (2). An attempt should be made to avoid the same topic being discussed under more than one report: the example given was Israel (1). When timetabling business, clashes should be avoided between major reports and major 'fringe' items (the example cited mentioned a clash between the Ministries Council and the Highland Meeting) (1); it would also be appropriate not to timetable contentious issues on the same day as the communion service (1). A short break between items of business would be helpful (3, one of whom also suggested that stretch exercises should be offered, as 'sitting for long hours in debate is not good for body or soul'). The opposite point of view also surfaced: one Presbytery and three of its Kirk Sessions issued a plea for 'fewer gaps between, and interruptions of, business sessions'. Care should be taken to ensure that business is not weighted in favour of regular attenders (3). Business should not be allowed to overrun, since this interferes with commissioners' attendance at other events (2). 'Trailers' for the following day's business might prove useful (1). In organising the Assembly, lessons might be learned from how the Youth Assembly and the Lambeth Conference are run, and from how parliament deals with major items of business or how television news channels present important information (4).

2.2.5 Various suggestions were made for reducing the time devoted to business. Not all reports need to be dealt with by the Assembly. All judicial business could be given to other bodies (1), although one Presbytery expressed concern about cases going to the Commission of Assembly and another respondent wanted to see

nothing more delegated to Councils. There is no longer a need for a report from the Guild, since women can now be commissioners (1). Time could also be saved by printing and circulating 'courtesy addresses' (1). Routine business could be dealt with either 'by paper' before the Assembly (1), or at committee level, with only the key policy issues coming to the Assembly (7). Some business could be dealt with during Assembly Week by small groups appointed by and accountable to the Assembly, with reports scrutinised in a 'House of Commons Committee' style (5), or the Assembly could be divided into groups meeting simultaneously to deal with 'non-keynote reports' (1). Some of the more formal reports could be taken as read, a practice that is increasing at Presbyteries (4). Not all Councils and Committees need report annually (9). Supplementary Reports should be discouraged (1), and commissioners should be urged to be more co-operative in ensuring that proposed amendments are submitted in time to appear in the Daily Papers (1).

2.2.6 When presenting reports, conveners should adhere strictly to the proper time-limit (6); conveners of 'minor committees' should not feel that they must use all of the time allocated to them (1) and indeed the time allocated to conveners might vary in relation to the relative importance of the committee (1). Since the full report is printed in the Blue Book, conveners need give only a very brief summary (1) and should listen to the Assembly rather than claim more time for speaking (1). If referring to sections of their report, they should clearly indicate the section concerned (1), and if Acts of Assembly are mentioned in debate, they should be explained (1). The presentation of reports could start with a brief Bible reading and conclude with a prayer (1). Conveners were seen as having too much influence over the decisions of the Assembly, seldom taking note of challenges from the floor (3).

2.2.7 Discussion should be shortened, either by adhering strictly to the time-limits or by limiting the number of speakers and/or the number of questions (18). The alternative view was also expressed: more time is needed for full discussion of major issues and for initiating new legislation (4), more questions should be encouraged (2) and more issues put to the vote (1). There was a feeling that the recent reduction in the number of deliverances had stifled discussion (2). It would be helpful to have designated personnel speaking both for and against major issues (2), with the permanent staff possibly undertaking these roles (1). There should be stricter control of the debate (2), with ways found to deal with those who ramble (3) and with those who speak at every conceivable opportunity (13). It was suggested that those wishing to speak in a debate should indicate this prior to the Assembly (1), and there was also a plea that speakers should not 'state personal views but those of the Presbytery they represent' (2). Two more unusual suggestions were that the discussion should take place 'before the reports are made' (1), and that those who feel nervous about speaking in the Assembly should be shown more tolerance and allowed to send in written comments in advance (2). There should be greater flexibility in standing orders (1). Ways should be found to explain procedures to new commissioners and to encourage more elders to participate in debate, perhaps by producing an explanatory DVD for issue beforehand (13).

2.2.8 To enable more informed discussion at the Assembly, either summaries of reports or a note of their salient points should be sent to Kirk Sessions and Presbyteries for prior discussion, with a summary of their responses made available to the Assembly (6). Councils should issue newsletters throughout the year, or a leaflet similar to 'Praying across Scotland' should be published to keep the church informed of likely topics for discussion at the next Assembly (3). Congregations could be invited to submit their own suggestions for discussion topics at the Assembly (2) and more overtures from Presbyteries should be encouraged (1). As a different way of preparing for the Assembly, commissioners should be encouraged to spend time beforehand in prayer and meditation (1),

and ministers should be allowed two Sundays off to help their preparation (1). There should be better pre-briefing of commissioners, either by Presbyteries beforehand or by Councils holding briefing meetings at the Assembly itself (5). 'Pre-arranged' questions which simply give conveners longer to speak were deplored (1).

2.2.9 The oft-heard plea to use more accessible language made a frequent appearance, coupled with the request to abandon archaic procedures and dress, including wigs (25): the word 'solicitor' was offered as an example of archaic language. Theological language was singled out for adverse comment, with one respondent issuing the reminder that 'theology and plain English are not mutually exclusive'. Business procedures showed too much commitment to 'established formulae' (1).

2.2.10 The use of modern technology to assist in presenting reports is welcome and could be further developed (18), although care has to be taken to ensure that this is not over-done (3): the printed word, being permanent, remains essential (1). The electronic voting system does not inspire confidence (1), and the use of microphones could be improved (2). The use of better technology to capture input from commissioners (such as 'Meetingworks') was recommended (1).

2.2.11 A small number of comments related to the nature of the business to be discussed. Time has to be devoted to strategic planning and not just to the on-going work of the church (1). One respondent complained that there is too much emphasis on matters coming under the Church and Society Council (1), whereas others recognised a need to engage more with the Scottish Parliament and with issues within Scotland and the UK and to recognise that the Assembly can provide a forum for 'a non-partisan national debate on important issues' such as devolution (4).

2.2.12 A small number of comments related particularly to the officials of the Assembly. Since one year is 'not

6.1

enough' for a Moderator, the appointment should be for two years (1) or even for three (1). Moderators 'seem too much part of the central machinery' and 'rarely seem neutral in the whole process' (1); they should be given training in handling a gathering of the size of the Assembly (1). Those allowed to speak from the playpen have an unfair advantage (2). The occupants of the playpen should avoid displaying personal bias (3) and the Clerk should not speak (1). Former moderators should simply retire to the 'back benches', as at Presbytery meetings (2).

2.3 Providing opportunities for theological reflection, etc.

2.3.1   It is perhaps not surprising that of the Committee's three proposed expectations this was the one which respondents found greatest difficulty in addressing: only 24 (20 Kirk Sessions and four individuals) stated that this expectation was currently being met, and the comments offered were somewhat diffuse and imprecise. As mentioned above, it was not always clear whether conference sessions within the body of the Assembly or 'fringe' activities during Assembly Week were being referred to.

2.3.2   Although only a small number of respondents explicitly expressed their satisfaction with the way this issue was currently being treated, the support shown in general terms for the Committee's proposed expectations in the responses under section 1 confirms the importance of theological reflection and the discussion of wider issues, and 20 respondents specifically mentioned the need to devote more time to such matters and to strengthen this element of the whole Assembly experience. There was less agreement, however, about how to do this. 59 respondents felt that at least some part of the conference-style activities of what is now the 'fringe' should become part of the 'mainstream' Assembly, while 44 wished the 'fringe' to remain separate.

2.3.3.1   Many of those who wished to see more time given to discussion of wider issues in the body of the Assembly offered no suggestion as to how this might be achieved. Others were more specific: brief periods for discussion could be set aside during the business sessions, perhaps with a particular slot each day, such as immediately after the lunch-break (5), discussion sessions could be held in the evenings (9) or one day could be designated as a 'conference day', with groups of commissioners each studying one of a number of topics in the morning and another in the afternoon, followed by a plenary session in the evening (2). Those who wished to see a different balance between 'court' and 'conference' suggested that business sessions could be restricted to mornings, with afternoons and evenings being reserved for conference-style activities (2), or even that business could be restricted to a single day, with the remainder of the week given over to 'theologically-informed debate on current issues' (1).

2.3.3.2   The Committee's suggestion of using keynote speakers was welcomed (33), with various pleas that youth and overseas delegates and others from outwith the Church of Scotland be invited as well as in-house experts. One Presbytery, however, urged that keynote speakers be restricted to the 'fringe' and two other respondents wondered about the criteria for choosing 'keynote speakers with a proven track record'. Small group discussions would result in a higher level of participation (16), and videos, posters (as at academic conferences), drama and interviews could also be used (2). Conference sessions could go out live on the internet (1), and video-conferencing could be used to involve a greater number of people (2). Several discussion groups could meet at the same time, with a report back to a plenary session (4). There was a feeling that subjects for discussion should be limited and that each Assembly should focus on no more than one or two quite specific issues (4): commissioned research on social issues could be fed into the discussions (1), or relevant Councils could offer 'starters for discussion' (3). Some felt that conference sessions were not realising their full potential and needed to be improved (2).

2.3.3.3 Those who favoured giving 'fringe' activities a more central role advanced several arguments in support of their views: the Assembly should see itself as not just a decision-making body, but as one that can shape and influence the thinking of Councils before decisions are finalised (1), new commissioners and those apprehensive about speaking in the more formal business sessions might be encouraged to play a bigger part in the Assembly (4), the sharing of ideas and experiences which a semi-informal setting would facilitate was to be encouraged (2), and the discussion of wider issues in a conference setting might be more likely to enthuse commissioners and in turn inspire congregations (5).

2.3.4.1 Those who expressed the opposite point of view and deplored the idea of the Assembly becoming more of a conference seldom elaborated on their answers. A number of respondents felt that the proper place for theological reflection and the discussion of wider issues was elsewhere: separate conferences should be held at different times of the year and in different venues, either as national events or as Presbytery-based occasions (16). Four respondents wanted to see more events run on 'Church Without Walls' lines. One respondent suggested that chat rooms on the web could be used for theological discussion. Others felt that participation in conference sessions was not the only way of experiencing the benefits of reflection and discussion: committees were already fulfilling this function through their reports and could further enhance their activities in this area (5).

2.3.4.2 Arguments in favour of keeping conference-style procedures out of the Assembly ranged from the pragmatic (conference-style Presbytery meetings are badly attended, so why introduce them at the Assembly? (1)) to the paranoid ('conferences, rather than being deliberative gatherings, can too easily be deployed as expensive tools for reinforcing ideas already being fed by keynote speakers on behalf of lobbyists within the various Councils' and a conference-style Assembly would stifle

proper discussion and leave major decisions in the hands of committees (7)).

2.3.5 Responses that focussed specifically on the 'fringe' noted that it would lose one of its most valuable features, its informality, if it became an integral part of the Assembly (3). While the extended lunch-break, allowing greater opportunities for participation in the 'fringe', was noted with appreciation by one respondent, two others requested that 'fringe' events should not occupy lunch breaks, which were seen as valuable times for fellowship and informal networking. A first-time commissioner asked for clearer information about how to locate the 'fringe' activities. Some recommended that only the high-profile aspects of the 'fringe' should be incorporated into the Assembly (8), one respondent suggested that 'tasters' for 'fringe' events could be given to the Assembly and three others proposed that reports of discussions on the 'fringe' be brought to the whole Assembly.

2.3.6 As a final cautionary note to this section, two respondents deplored the fact that so often informal discussions led nowhere and asked for less talk and more action.

2.4 Offering inspiration through worship and celebration:

2.4.1 88 respondents (66 Kirk Sessions, 20 individuals and two Presbyteries) explicitly stated that they find the worship inspirational and energising, many of them couching their responses in highly enthusiastic terms. The central role of worship in the Assembly and the need to continue to develop it was stressed by a number of respondents, one of them making the point that 'as many commissioners are leading worship all year, the opportunity to be led is deeply appreciated and should be further developed.' Recent developments in extending the opening worship each morning and in introducing a greater variety of styles were particularly welcomed, with the 2008 Assembly being specially mentioned by 16 respondents, 11 of these singling out the Sunday evening worship for particularly favourable comment. The involvement of young people was mentioned favourably by five respondents, and the impressive effect of unaccompanied psalm-singing by three.

2.4.2 Various suggestions were made for extending opportunities for worship during the Assembly. In addition to the opening worship each morning, it was suggested that the afternoon sessions also could begin with a hymn, or even just a prayer and silent reflection (4). Each day's business could finish with a short act of worship (5). Evening worship sessions could be arranged (10), and breakfast worship was also suggested (1). There could be a 'final act of worship' at the end of the Assembly, (5): positive encouragement should be given to commissioners to stay on for this (1).

2.4.3 While Moderators each brought their own distinctive style to the worship, there was a plea that they should resist the temptation 'to do something different, regardless of whether it improves on the traditional' (1). The Moderator should perhaps be relieved of the burden of preparing all worship sessions, with worship being led instead by different groups of commissioners, by overseas delegates, by contemporary worship groups, by the councils reporting on that day, by representatives of different types of congregation, or by 'world class thinkers and speakers' (11). The style of worship could be further varied by having greater focus on prayer (4), on inspirational preaching (3) and on evangelical preaching (3). Worship could be more participatory (1) and could make more use of either quiet music providing time for reflection (3) or (at the other end of the auditory spectrum) of sonic percussion (1). The music could be enriched by the use of different instruments or singers from Scottish Opera (1). A 'Songs of Praise' evening could be held (2). An Assembly Worship Committee might be appointed (1), and there could be presentations on worship (3). Commissioners could be assigned to small groups to meet for prayer and informal worship during

Assembly Week (2).

2.4.4 There was a call to review the place and purpose of two major worship events: the Assembly service in St Giles and the Assembly Communion service. The former was seen to be 'stiff' and formal and its place in the Assembly programme should be reconsidered (7): a service in the Assembly Hall or in other churches might take its place (4). One respondent found the Communion service time-consuming, and others questioned whether the Monday morning was the best time: one asked that it be restored to its previous place before the first full day of business and three others wondered whether it would be better to hold it at the start of the Assembly, or at the end, or on the Sunday morning (either at St Giles or in the Assembly Hall)? One respondent wanted two communion services, one at the start and the other at the close of the Assembly (1).

2.4.5 If the purpose of worship is to inspire (and this was queried by several respondents), it was suggested that this purpose would be more successfully achieved by a large-scale gathering held elsewhere: an outdoor event at Ingliston or an open-air witness service in Princes Street Gardens might be more fruitful than trying to extend the worship of the Assembly (6). An alternative suggestion was to devote one full day (or half a day at least) to a 'religious celebration led by a charismatic speaker' (1). Six respondents noted that inspiration can come not only from worship sessions and large celebratory events but from the sense of engaging with difficult and central issues on the business agenda. Two respondents somewhat plaintively noted that inspiration did not trickle down to Kirk Sessions, while another posed the question 'Are we there primarily to be inspired or to ensure the business is done well?'

2.4.6 A number of more strongly negative voices were heard. The worship needs 'more radical redevelopment': in recent years it has not been inspiring, it is 'very traditional' and 'needs to be modernised' and it is a little 'staid and formal' and needs 'more emotional engagement' (5). More needs to be done to make it more inspirational, more varied and more lively (7) with a wider range of worship styles along the lines of the Youth Assembly (2). It should be 'strictly controlled' and kept simple (2), and not extended in either length (4) or frequency (4): the opening worship each day is not the place for either preaching or experimentation (2), and there should be no 'gimmicks' like praise bands (1).

2.5 Additional or different expectations of the Assembly (section 3)

2.5.1 Less than one-third of respondents completed this section, and the vast majority of these offered responses which belonged more properly to other sections of the questionnaire.

2.5.2 The most thoughtful response, outlining a different set of three expectations, is worth quoting in full:

'A: Upward listening: The Assembly gives an opportunity for the Kirk to listen to the concerns and voice of the grass roots membership.

B: Networking: The Assembly is important for both ministers and members to develop a wider network of contacts enabling people to obtain support and encouragement from fellow Christians in other parishes and Presbyteries.

C: Public Relations: The Assembly provides the Kirk's most important gateway to influencing public opinion'.

2.5.3 Each of these alternative expectations was echoed by other respondents. Two others stressed that the General Assembly should 'reflect the faith and views' of its membership and should 'articulate the church's vision'. 10 others welcomed the opportunities it provided for fellowship and for making and meeting friends, resulting in the sharing of experiences and the giving of mutual support. Seven others saw its role to be a 'shop-window for the Church of Scotland', a 'golden marketing opportunity' to share with the nation who we are and what we do and to offer a Christian response to the concerns and challenges of the day.

2.5.4 Two other roles which might be expected of the General Assembly were discernible: it should itself provide support to congregations, especially those in priority areas, offering ideas and help (3), and it should be a body that would be a real source of inspiration to the church, focussing on the centralities of the Christian faith in order to 'challenge commissioners to return home with different ideas' and 'lead the church forward in an ever-changing world with renewed enthusiasm' (5).

3. The General Assembly: practical arrangements
3.1 Timing – May or September? (section 4)

3.1.1 As might be expected, responses to this question varied from those who saw no compelling reason for change to those who felt that the logic in favour of a September Assembly was irrefutable, and from those who welcomed the prospect of a long, leisurely read through the Blue Book during the summer months to those who felt that a holiday was needed after the General Assembly and not before.

3.1.2 The breakdown of the 'voting figures' is as follows:

	Kirk Sessions	Individuals	Presbyteries	Total
retain in May	66	29	4	99
change to September	106	42	4	152
no preference	43	9	2	54
no comment	19	4		23
total	234	84	10	328

3.1.3 Those who preferred the status quo tended to hold fairly firm views that May was the 'traditional' and the 'best' month for the General Assembly, whereas those who favoured a change to September encompassed both those who strongly supported this idea and those who simply expressed a mild preference for a change of date but wished to see a trial run for a few years before it became firmly established in the church's calendar; if September were to be chosen, several pointed out that a date early in the month would be strongly preferred, some even suggesting that late August would be a suitable alternative. Those who expressed 'no preference' did so either because both sides of the argument had gained equal support in discussion or because they saw this as unimportant and were prepared to go along with the majority decision.

3.1.4 By no means all respondents offered arguments in support of their preference. Of those who did, most echoed one or more of the three arguments put forward by the Committee in the 2008 Blue Book in favour of one date or the other.

The 'financial argument' in favour of September was generally accepted, although two respondents stated quite firmly that financial matters should not determine the timing of the General Assembly and three others suggested that a change to the end of the financial year would be a better solution to the problems of timing than a change to the date of the General Assembly. One individual felt that the problem would be solved if accounts and budgets were produced earlier through a combination of 'diligence, hard work and lack of procrastination'. Another made the observation that there was some merit in *not* having full financial information available, in order to avoid acrimonious discussion about levels of funding for individuals' pet projects.

The 'administrative argument' in favour of September was also generally accepted, apart from the eight respondents who disapproved of changes being made merely for the sake of administrative convenience: 'the central administration… exists to service the Church at large' and the rhythm of the parish year 'should outweigh considerations of committee convenience'.

Of the three points made by the Committee in its 2008 report, the 'parish year' argument in favour of May attracted the most comment. 32 respondents specifically mentioned the impossibility of removing ministers and key elders from parishes at the start of the winter session, one making the point that 'only Christmas or Easter would be worse times to call the minister and an elder away'. However, 12 respondents opposed this 'rather spurious' argument and gave strong support to the opposite view: a parish minister noted that 'I now find that May is no quieter a month in my diary or the Church calendar, so to say that September is a busy month carries very little weight', a Presbytery thought 'it makes little difference to ministers who are busy all the time', and a Kirk Session remarked that 'it is easy to over-emphasise the business of the start of the congregations' winter programmes', adding that if September was indeed such a 'key period' in the church's year 'there is something to be said for the Assembly being held to coincide with it'.

3.1.5 Additional arguments in favour of one date or the other surfaced in several of the responses.

3.1.5.1 Several respondents seemed to assume that the Blue Book would continue to be published at the same time as at present: eight welcomed a September Assembly on the grounds that this would allow commissioners more time to assimilate the Blue Book properly, while a further four rejected a September Assembly since this would involve a four-month delay in dealing with committee reports and the previous year's accounts.

3.1.5.2 A number of respondents focussed on the aftermath of the General Assembly and its effect on commissioners. A September Assembly would 'inspire', 'energise' and 'invigorate' commissioners as they enabled the 'buzz and energy' of the Assembly to take immediate effect in their parishes, whereas the impetus of a May Assembly tends to go off the boil over the summer months (12): alternatively a May Assembly provides a 'visionary high' at the climax of the church year and allows commissioners to reflect on its decisions before implementing them in their parish programmes over the following winter (3).

3.1.5.3 May and September have a different 'feel' to them: May is an enlivening, challenging, uplifting and optimistic time of year when the nights are lighter, the weather is better, and commissioners are more 'switched on' (10): on the other hand 'May has an "end of term" feel to it, while people are more apt to be looking forward in September' (1, but this view was also implied in the replies of those mentioned in 3.1.5.2 who favoured the idea of moving immediately from a September Assembly into the work of the new congregational year).

3.1.5.4 The growing involvement of youth delegates in the Assembly led a group of 10 respondents to express strong support for September on the grounds that this would not clash with school and university examinations, a factor which also affects candidates for the ministry and the children of manse families. On the other hand, one respondent noted that a September date would clash with the National Youth Assembly.

3.1.5.5 Other points made by only a very few respondents are as follows:
- Some favoured May on the grounds that preparation for the Assembly, including the publication of the Blue Book, would be more difficult during the summer months and that commissioners would not want to have weighty holiday reading (4).
- Others also favoured May on the grounds that September would clash with party political conferences, resulting in a further reduction in the amount of media coverage (3).
- Rural respondents were divided about how a change of date would affect them. One felt that May would be less convenient for those engaged in crofting, farming, fishing and tourism, while others noted that in September the harvest and the start of the sheep sales would cause problems (5).

- September would allow accommodation to be arranged in university halls of residence (2, though several others mention the possibility of using this kind of accommodation in their responses under section 6 – see 4.9 below).
- September is still for many people part of the holiday season, especially for those ministers without children who cover for colleagues who are obliged to take holidays during the school vacations (2).
- Should there be consultation with the Free Church, given that their General Assembly shares certain 'State activities' with that of the Church of Scotland (1)?

3.1.5.6 Perhaps the last word in this section should go to the respondent who urges a change to September, offering the consolation that 'in a couple of years it would become "aye been"'.

3.2 Timing – midweek or not?
3.2.1 The Committee did not specifically ask for comment on this issue, but a number of respondents chose to raise it. Seven expressed satisfaction with the present arrangements (although two of these expressed the hope that if these were to continue more productive use should be made of the weekend), and 39 (including four of the ten Presbyteries who replied) requested a return to the previous single-week pattern.

3.2.2 The usual reason given for wishing to return to the previous pattern was that a midweek-to-midweek Assembly disadvantages younger commissioners and those in full-time employment in requiring them to take parts of two consecutive weeks off work, one respondent adding that it was also inconvenient for child-minding grandparents if two separate weeks were affected. One respondent felt that the limitation on the kind of people who could attend resulted in the commissioners being an 'unrepresentative clique', while another insisted that the timing of Assembly Week must take account of the needs of younger elders, without being more specific about what these were. One minister, however, pointed out that

6.1

the present arrangements make it easier for ministers in parishes some distance from Edinburgh to be sure of being back in their parishes on the Sunday following the Assembly.

3.3 Frequency (section 5)

3.3.1 Section 5 was phrased in such a way as to encourage a response only if changes were felt to be desirable. It is therefore reasonable to assume that if respondents did not allude to a specific area they were happy with the status quo.

3.3.2 For those who specifically mentioned the frequency of meetings, the breakdown of figures is as follows:

Retain annual Assembly	88
Consider changing	
(but with no other recommendation)	2
Meet less frequently	19
Meet more frequently	7

3.3.3 The vast majority of those who wished to reduce the frequency of meetings (17 out of 19) favoured a meeting of the Assembly every second year, while four of the seven who wished to increase the frequency of meetings suggested two meetings per year. One Presbytery proposed that the Assembly should meet two or three times a year, one individual wanted three meetings per year, and a Kirk Session proposed 'three two-day meetings, to be held throughout the year' (although with the qualifying comment that their discussion was limited by the fact that only two elders [out of a total of 43, according to the 'Year Book'] had ever been to the Assembly).

3.4 Size (section 5) **and other matters relating to elders' commissions:**

3.4.1 As stated above (3.3.1), the wording of section 5 suggests that respondents who did not mention this area in their reply have no desire for change. 76 respondents, however, either mentioned quite specifically that the size of the Assembly should remain unchanged or indicated a general 'no change' in answer to the question as a whole.

3.4.2 There were, however, a number of dissentient voices.

- 26 respondents suggested a reduction in the number of commissioners, mostly for reasons of cost, although in one case the reduction was suggested because many commissioners in any case take no active part in the proceedings; three of these suggested an optimum figure of 600, and one pointed out that the UK parliament managed to do its business with only 640 members. Two respondents were even more radical: one wished to cut the Assembly down by 50% and the other asserted that 'two commissioners from each Presbytery would be enough'.

- 12 respondents suggested an increase in the number of commissioners, although two acknowledged that this would cause logistical problems. Two Kirk Sessions wished to be able to have commissioners more often than current rules allowed: one of these was in a linkage and felt disadvantaged by being able to have a commissioner only once every eight years. Two others suggested that all congregations should be able to send commissioners, one that all ministers should be able to attend, one that congregations in remote areas should be able to send two elders or deacons along with the minister, one that there should be three commissioners instead of two from each congregation represented and another that 'as many commissioners as possible should be there'.

- Two respondents suggested that the size of the General Assembly should be reconsidered, without indicating whether they wished to see an increase or a decrease.

- One suggested, without going into further detail, that the Assembly should be 'a conference for all Presbyteries', who would then hold (presumably similar) conferences for their congregations.

3.4.3 The following additional matters relating to the ways in which commissions are currently organised were raised:

- Six respondents suggested that congregations should be allowed to nominate more than one elder for a commission, so that these commissioners could effectively job-share: this would allow different people to attend for different parts of the business in which they might be interested, might make it easier for elders in employment to take only a couple of days off work, and would ensure that a greater number of elders had the privilege of attending the General Assembly.
- Six respondents suggested that elders' commissions should run for more than one year, to allow for greater continuity in decision-making and to enable commissioners to acquire a greater level of experience: three suggested that a two-year term was desirable, two suggested three years, and the fourth, a Presbytery, suggested that commissions could run for four to five years.
- One Kirk Session had reservations about the use of the term 'commissioner', seeing this not only to be somewhat legalistic and exclusive but also because 'it conceals what should be the real role of members of a Presbyterian organisation, *ie* to represent the views of the members in their church'. Two respondents urged that the role of commissioners be reviewed, noting that too many were merely passive onlookers.
- Five respondents commented on the lack of diligence on the part of some commissioners and expressed 'outrage' that 'part-time commissioners' could claim expenses for full-time attendance. 'Mandatory attendance at all sessions' was urged by one respondent, while others suggested using commissioners' swipe cards to record attendance with a graduated scale of expenses for those who put in less frequent appearances.
- Six respondents expressed concern that the same people seemed to be present every year; it was suggested that a way should be found 'to break the dominance of persistent attenders', ensuring that nobody should be able to attend more than two consecutive Assemblies. Should Presbytery clerks always be present?
- One respondent suggested that Standing Orders should be amended to allow Council Conveners to receive a commission automatically.

3.5 Location and venue (section 5)

3.5.1 Again, there was little support for major changes, with 126 respondents specifically mentioning that the status quo should be maintained, in addition to those who did not feel called to make any comment (see 3.3.1). A handful of respondents admitted that a different location might be desirable, but would not be practical on grounds of cost: some of these suggested that committees or the Commission of Assembly might occasionally meet outwith Edinburgh. It is perhaps worth mentioning that one Kirk Session geographically very distant from Edinburgh emphasised that 'nobody from our Kirk Session felt themselves discriminated against by the Edinburgh location'.

3.5.2 A number of respondents, however, raised the possibility of the Assembly meeting outwith Edinburgh. 17 expressed the desire to see it meet elsewhere, without being more specific about how this might be organised, and a further 23 offered more detailed alternative proposals. Four of these appeared to want to abandon Edinburgh entirely: one for an unspecified destination, one to a more central location such as Stirling or Perth, one to more rural places, and the fourth 'to outlying areas, *eg* Shetland, Dumfries and Galloway, or the North Highlands'. 12 wished to see the Assembly moving away from Edinburgh every few years, possibly to another of Scotland's major cities, three suggested alternating annually between Edinburgh and somewhere else, and a further four wanted the Assembly to have a different location every year, one of these offering the suggestion that each Presbytery could host it in turn.

3.5.3 Many respondents saw no reason to move out

6.1

of the Assembly Hall, especially now that it had been modernised. One, however, described it as 'outdated' and another recommended that it be sold and conference facilities bought in. One felt a pang of nostalgia for the Edinburgh International Conference Centre, in view of its better facilities for the public and the media, and another for the Usher Hall, speaking warmly of the higher level of social interaction it provided. One expressed a desire for better catering facilities and two urged that the Assembly Hall be made more disabled friendly, one of these commenting unfavourably on difficulties of access and parking. Two called for more space to be made available in the public gallery and another for more space in the display area.

3.6 Length

3.6.1 With the cost of the Assembly in mind, 12 respondents suggested reducing its length: an Assembly that lasted from three to five days, possibly over a long weekend, was the most popular suggestion, but one respondent proposed it could be cut down to a single day. On the other hand, one respondent suggested that it be extended by one day, to give a platform for 'keynote speakers on the mission of the church at home and abroad', along the lines of the annual meetings of the Guild.

3.7 New models for the General Assembly

3.7.1 With three separate aims in mind, the desire to give a higher profile to conference-style elements in the General Assembly, the desire to transact the business more efficiently and the desire to reduce costs, a number of respondents suggested a variety of new models for the Assembly.

3.7.2 The simplest of these were merely proposals to reduce the length of the traditional Assembly and hold it either over a 'long weekend' (from Friday to Wednesday or from Thursday to Monday) or in a shorter week (from Sunday to Friday, thus leaving Saturdays free, this being regarded as a 'family day' by many ministers and younger

commissioners, or from Monday until the following Friday or Saturday) (12). One respondent proposed moving the Garden Party to the Sunday afternoon and devoting the whole of Saturday to business.

3.7.3 Two responses offered a more detailed re-ordering of Assembly Week. One suggested that the Assembly should begin with the traditional communion service on the Monday morning, thus enhancing the status of this act of worship, and conclude with the traditional service in St Giles on the following Sunday morning. Those ministers who simply wanted to 'do the business' could leave on the Saturday and need not even miss a Sunday from their own church; elders would need to take only one week off work. While this pattern would involve Sunday travel, those who found this difficult or theologically objectionable could travel on the preceding Saturday and return on the following Monday and should be entitled to additional allowances for so doing.

The second pattern opted for a shorter Assembly over a long weekend, as follows:

Friday:	business in morning, afternoon and evening
Saturday:	business in morning and afternoon, praise event in evening
Sunday:	Communion service in morning in Assembly Hall, fellowship time in afternoon, praise evening in a different style
Monday:	remaining business

3.7.4 More elaborate proposals for holding two distinct General Assemblies also had some support.
- Financial and budgetary business could be transacted at a 'financial Assembly' in September, possibly lasting no more than one day and with only a small number of commissioners (one suggestion was to have as few as three from each Presbytery), while all other business could be taken at the usual meeting in May (4). A variant of this suggestion came from a financial expert,

who expressed the view that budgets did not need to be approved by the General Assembly and that this function could be delegated to a special committee which would meet in October: the Assembly in May could then discuss the various plans of the Councils and approve them 'subject to the overall budget to be discussed and approved in October by the Special Budget Committee'.

- There could be distinct 'business' and 'conference' Assemblies, either in alternate years, thus allowing Councils to operate on a two-year cycle (4), or at different times of the same year (7). Two respondents offered quite similar proposals under this heading. The 'business Assembly' (in 'court' style) would include 'ceremonial, ritual and legal' elements, together with reports; it would have 200-300 commissioners and only a very small number of overseas and other delegates, and would last 2-3 days, possibly over a long weekend to facilitate maximum participation from working elders. The 'conference Assembly' would include 'theological reflection and discussion of vision'; it would be larger (and could even be open to all members and adherents) and would benefit from the input of a wider range of overseas visitors; it would last for 3-5 days, again possibly including the weekend, and could be held in different venues around the country. Holding the 'business' Assembly in September would solve some of the problems raised by the Committee in its report in the 2008 Blue Book, while the May conference could be 'more reflective, free-ranging and unencumbered', 'a forum where more innovative ('blue sky') ideas could be surfaced and discussed without the tensions of having to proceed immediately to deliverances and the attendant tensions of voting'. Councils could use the summer months between the two Assemblies as 'a useful incubation period for continued discussion on contentious topics and proposals'.

4. Other comments (section 6)

4.1 A wide variety of additional comments were made, here loosely grouped into related headings and arranged roughly in order of the number of respondents who raised each issue.

4.2 39 respondents expressed disappointment at the low level of media coverage of the General Assembly and of the church's work in general; many of these recognised that this is not a matter over which either the Committee or the Assembly has any control, but nonetheless hoped that the matter might be investigated. One suggested that better press releases might help to attract more attention from the media, and another that it might help to stimulate interest if forthcoming Assembly business were published in the press.

4.3 The Church is out of touch with the 'grass roots' and needs to reconnect itself with those who are keeping it going at parish level (26): two of these respondents, both Kirk Sessions, made the point that the discussion on the questionnaire had 'highlighted how disconnected many elders feel from the workings of the General Assembly'. There was a proposal from a Kirk Session at a considerable distance from Edinburgh that representatives of the General Assembly be given a 20-minute slot at a Kirk Session meeting to explain why the Assembly was important: it was not clear whether this was an individual request or a suggestion to be implemented throughout the whole country.

4.4 What should happen after the Assembly attracted a number of comments. The church in general needs to communicate its stance on key issues more effectively, and there was strong support for measures to this end to be taken immediately after each Assembly. Information both about the Assembly itself (perhaps in the form of a DVD with highlights, including the Moderator's addresses) and about its decisions (possibly in the form of a brief summary sheet) should be sent out to congregations as soon as possible after the end of the Assembly: this might go some way towards redressing the two-fold feeling that the Assembly is out of touch with the church and the grassroots membership is not interested in the Assembly

(23). A questionnaire should be issued to commissioners to seek their views (1), and Presbyteries should hold debriefing sessions for all their commissioners (1). Three respondents asked that commissioners be urged to report back more fully to their own congregations and Presbyteries. Remits sent down to Presbyteries and congregations for discussion should be more positive, in order to encourage more vigorous feedback: it is not enough to ask that something merely be 'considered' (1). Where Assembly decisions require action, the procedures need to be quicker and more transparent: the Assembly should itself review previous decisions to ensure that they are being implemented (4).

4.5 10 respondents mentioned that it was important to preserve a sense of dignity and tradition, one of these expressing concern that the greater relaxedness of recent Assemblies may be obscuring the need for this. On the other hand, 21 respondents regarded the formality, the ritual and the 'state protocol' as being out of date, stifling, unhelpful, and intimidating to new commissioners. One of these found the opening formalities in particular 'increasingly irrelevant' and expressed little interest in 'the nodding and polite exchanges between Church and State', while another deplored 'all the pomp and circumstance of a state occasion' that accompanied the worship at St Giles, and yet another wanted to 'get rid of all the historic re-enactment stuff'. Where customs are retained, commented one respondent, they should be explained – but is it right to retain them?

4.6 16 respondents mentioned the participation of children and young people in the General Assembly, some positively, others less so. Eight both warmly welcomed recent developments and hoped that youth involvement might increase. Although welcoming the contribution of youth representatives, one respondent voiced the concern that this 'could overwhelm the Assembly', while another two noted that their obvious collaboration on certain issues lessened their impact. Three felt that youth representatives should not participate in 'mainstream debate', while two others took the opposite view and urged that their participation should be extended and that they should be allowed to vote. Two welcomed the presence of youth representatives but not of Children's Ambassadors, one queried the worth of the Youth Assembly, and one expressed concern at the 'disproportionately high profile' given to youth representatives in recent years, given that – unlike elders – their 'position requires no necessity of proven commitment to the cause of Christ'. The inspiration and encouragement provided by overseas and ecumenical delegates was also commented on favourably by a number of respondents, although a question was raised about the possible costs involved.

4.7 The webcasts of the General Assembly were commended and should be both developed further and publicised more widely. There should be greater use of web-based reporting and of the church's website (with news items made available for local newsletters, and with the Assembly's Standing Orders available on the web). Presentations to the Assembly should be accessible afterwards on-line. The video suite could be used more imaginatively, with edited clips of 'mood changing speeches' and interviews with the Moderator about 'the big event of the day', not just 'balanced church journalism' (12).

4.8 The Garden Party came in for criticism from 10 respondents. It was seen as an expensive, but sacrosanct, anachronism: either it should be dropped or its purpose should at least be reviewed. One respondent felt that it does not sit easily 'with a gospel that proclaims its empathy with the poor and disadvantaged': either Edinburgh's homeless should also receive invitations or commissioners should have the courage to practise what they preach and urge that the cost of the Garden Party should be donated to charity. In giving voice to the opposite view, two respondents mentioned the usefulness of the Garden Party as a social occasion.

4.9 In terms of 'looking after' commissioners, it was felt that more detailed information and a better induction procedure is needed for those attending the Assembly for the first time (5), perhaps carried out by Presbytery Clerks (1). More should be done to encourage commissioners to meet together socially, either by arranging more social functions, or by encouraging commissioners to eat together, or by arranging residential accommodation (6). Child-care facilities should be introduced (1).

4.10 Six respondents commented on various financial aspects of being a commissioner: two suggested that church members in Edinburgh might offer accommodation and hospitality to commissioners, one suggested that richer congregations should meet the expenses of commissioners from poorer congregations, another noted that although ministerial commissioners continue to receive their stipend other commissioners might have to make financial sacrifices, for example by using up holiday entitlement, a fifth suggested that an increase in the level of expenses might encourage more younger people to attend, and the sixth pointed out that the costs of the Assembly could be reduced if commissioners' expenses were met by their own congregations rather than from central funds.

4.11 Concern was expressed about falling standards of dress: the absence of the clerical collar worried two respondents (one suggesting a white carnation as an alternative), another considered the wearing of 'tee-shirt and jeans a step too far', while a Presbytery noted that more and more commissioners are 'dressed for an afternoon's work in the garden' and suggested that the Principal Clerk encourage 'respectful dress' in his pre-Assembly letters to commissioners. One respondent's comment that 'dress sense needs to change' could be taken either way, but was in fact a plea for greater *in*formality.

4.12 There were five complaints about legislative procedures: one respondent complained about the

Barrier Act slowing down the decision-making process, one complained in general about the length of time it took for legislative changes to be made, another pressed for a cap on 'the voluminous amounts of new legislation which are constantly being passed and almost as quickly amended again' and urged that new legislation should be formulated only if absolutely necessary, while yet another complained that 'laws are often passed without being put into practice'. 'Let us not get bogged down in legalistic detail,' pleaded the fifth. 'One cannot have a rule for every possible eventuality. Let us encourage common sense.'

4.13 On a different level, activities which might be incorporated into the Assembly were opportunities for 'spontaneous participation', such as a session where questions could be addressed to the new Moderator, and opportunities for 'interest groups' of commissioners to meet together, such as Session Clerks or pastoral elders (2).

4.14 The Church needs a spokesman and should either allow the Moderator to speak more freely or should designate the Principal Clerk as the person best qualified for this role, since he is aware of all decisions of the General Assembly (3).

4.15 One respondent urged that the Assembly be costed in terms of man-hours and not just in pounds.

4.16 Finally, six respondents complained about this questionnaire and similar exercises. One felt that there were too many consultation documents, another that insufficient time was often given for replies, and a third drew attention to the cost of issuing questionnaires. With particular regard to the current questionnaire, one respondent felt that 'the questions asked carry their own agenda for change which may undermine the authority of the General Assembly', and two others complained about the wording in section 2: was the Committee not interested in comments from those who were 'broadly in *dis*agreement' with its summary in section 1? On the

6.1

other hand – to end this report on a positive note – 16 respondents complimented the Assembly Arrangements Committee on keeping the Assembly under constant review and on being prepared to contemplate radical changes, and thanked it for giving the church at large this opportunity to contribute to its thinking.

Roy M Pinkerton
11 January 2009

PROPOSED DELIVERANCE

The General Assembly
1. Receive the Report.

REPORT

1. Introduction

1.1 The Central Services Committee's remit relates primarily to managing the Church Offices in George Street, overseeing the delivery of central services to departments within these Offices and operating as one of the employing agencies of the Church.

1.2 Meetings have been held twice per annum between the Executive Committee and Heads of Department. These meetings have provided a welcome opportunity to discuss matters of joint interest and concern on a regular basis.

2. Human Resources (HR)

2.1 The past year has seen the Committee continue on a pathway of modernising practice and procedure with the input of an ongoing professional HR service. A number of new policies have been put in place and these are outlined later in this Report. Some of these policies have been about bringing in good management practices but they are also about trying to ensure there is consistency of approach to employees of the Committee when looking at issues such as flexible working hours. Some of the significant areas are outlined below.

2.2 Pay and Grading

The pay and grading review (at time of writing) is now almost concluded, with a reduction from seventy-five grades (forty-four of which were in use) to a ten grade structure. A new job evaluation scheme is now in place which will ensure consistency of approach to the evaluation of posts for future employees of the Committee.

2.3 Car Provision

A small number of employees had historically been provided with cars by their respective Councils. In an effort to ensure consistency of approach it was recognised that this was a contractual term that needed to be removed and, after some discussion with the union Unite and the employees concerned, the removal of the vehicles was agreed from the beginning of 2009.

2.4 Policy Update

The following policies have been introduced in the past twelve months: Capability Procedure, Disciplinary Procedure, Adoption Policy, Recruitment and Selection Policy, Learning and Development Policy and Flexible Working Hours Policy. We continue to work closely with Unite on the development of all of these policies and indeed are currently examining the best way forward to develop a Dignity at Work policy.

2.5 Recruitment

2.5.1 The overall staffing count has risen by thirteen in the past twelve months although more than half of these are accounted for by the need to cover absences such as maternity leave and by posts which attract external funding.

2.5.2 In accordance with an instruction from last year's General Assembly, the HR Department continues, in consultation with Council Secretaries and Heads of Department, to consider whether any post advertised should specify a requirement for the post holder to be a Christian. In the last year, it has not been necessary to have any post designated in this way.

2.6 Turnover

The turnover figure for staff for the year ended 31 December 2008 is 10.12%. This is regarded as a healthy figure in terms of turnover and is no cause for concern as an employer. Indeed the examination of Exit Questionnaires from staff leaving our employment does not reveal any points of concern, although this is an area that we will continue to monitor.

2.7 Learning and Development

2.7.1 A learning suite was officially opened by the Moderator on 26 February 2009. This is the first time that a dedicated room has been set aside for learning within the Church Offices, and it is fully equipped to meet the needs of general training courses and IT training courses. It is expected that through time it will also become an open learning centre where staff can attend, for instance, on-line training. There were 483 instances of individual training during the period January 2008 to February 2009. This year will see an increase in this activity with an expected 712 participants in planned learning events including policy training, IT training and general work skills training, as well as a further 400 involved in more informal learning events such as lunchtime learning and a Learning at Work Day. There will also be departmental training which is not accounted for in the statistics.

2.7.2 We have examined the options for the training of managers over the last twelve months with the Head of HR spending considerable time in a coaching role with a number of our senior employees. In order to take the focus on Learning and Development forward for senior staff, Council Secretaries are currently participating in a pilot 360 degree appraisal programme. On completion of this an evaluation will be carried out and it is likely that a programme will be rolled out to other senior staff within the Church Offices. This will afford the opportunity to set clear objectives for staff which can then be filtered down through individual departments identifying Learning and Development needs at all levels.

2.8 Induction

A review of induction processes was undertaken over the past year and as a consequence of this a revised induction programme was introduced in February 2009.

3. Information Technology

3.1 The past year has very much been about taking the opportunity to stop and examine the present IT function. A detailed audit, involving all Heads of Department and Council Secretaries, was commissioned. This has resulted in significant re-focussing of the job description for the IT Manager which went to advert in February 2009.

3.2 The audit confirmed the need to:
- ensure the correct infrastructure was in place before beginning to examine any further developments.
- modernise the network within the Church Offices.
- upgrade to Microsoft Exchange 2003/Outlook 2003 early in 2009.
- upgrade to Microsoft Office 2007, beginning towards the end of 2009, which will include a training programme involving all employees. This will ensure that the Church is keeping up to date in terms of current software applications.
- implement a new virtual server infrastructure through the first half of 2009 which will ensure a much greater degree of longevity for the future. This not only brings us up to date with server technology but will also allow us to expand our infrastructure with minimum cost in the future.
- employ a part time Interim IT Manager from January 2009 to assist in the planning process prior to a new

permanent IT Manager being appointed in Spring 2009.

- set up an IT Steering Group in 2009 to ensure the involvement of users in the future development of IT services.

3.3 In addition to overseeing the work referred to above, the interim IT Manager has been completing a five year IT Strategy to ensure that all staff members are enabled to carry out their roles within the best technological environment which can be afforded.

3.4 A revised budget has also been constructed which puts in place a budgeted programme to 2013.

3.5 A rolling replacement programme is in place to replace supported IT equipment when it reaches the end of its lifecycle or has become unfit for purpose.

3.6 The Applications Development Team is moving forward with projects using *Intrelate* software and significant progress has been made on the FASTi database. A major project is also in progress initially to develop a web based Central Information package for the Church. Both this and the FASTi database are available to view at the General Assembly. The Regional Development Database will be redeveloped using *Intrelate.* The Ministries Council, Safeguarding and Presbytery Clerks' databases were completed in 2008.

3.7 The last twelve months have been challenging for the IT Department and it is important that the employees are commended for their efforts in maintaining services whilst we have taken the opportunity to ensure there is a robust plan for the future.

4. Central Properties Department

4.1 The Central Properties Department has continued to develop its wide ranging brief and has, in the last year in particular, developed the health and safety aspects of the work. The Department has three full-time and one part-time staff member who bring the expertise of the following disciplines through qualification and experience: construction; property management; facilities management; housing management; and health and safety.

4.2 Arbitrations
The Department has responsibility for managing the administration of the Arbitration process in the case of readjustment. Since the last report, the department has attended to two arbitrations.

4.3 Property
4.3.1 The Department has responsibility for the management of 100 properties, the delivery of new build projects and major refurbishment programmes, the management of facilities and procurement of work equipment, and health and safety for the Central Services Committee and other Councils of the Church.

4.3.2 In the last year, the following major projects were completed: major refurbishment of Gilmerton Church; provision of a church outreach facility in Greenock; and provision of additional facilities for "The Well" Asian Information and Advice Centre in Glasgow.

4.3.3 At present, the Department is involved in the following major projects: construction of a new church building for the congregation at Glasgow: Garthamlock and Craigend East and for the congregation at Glasgow: Easterhouse St George's and St Peter's; the purchase/lease of a site for a church building in Dunfermline: East St Paul's; development of a worship space for Aberdeen: Cove; and identification and purchase of a furlough property suitable for the accommodation of persons with disabilities and/or wheelchair users.

4.3.4 Projects awaiting funding include construction of a new church building for Dunfermline: East St Paul's.

4.4 Health and Safety
4.4.1 The Committee has an obligation, as an employer, to comply with the Health and Safety at Work Act 1974.

The staff of the Department includes a suitably Chartered Safety Practitioner and Health and Safety Technician. The development of the Health and Safety strategy continues with advances in a number of key areas including policy, training, communications and implementation. The Committee is delighted to report that the core strategies highlighted in last year's report have all been implemented.

4.4.2 There are many strands to the health and safety process but it may be worth noting the following:

4.4.3　Training
Core training on health and safety was delivered to all staff. This provides the platform for the delivery of training for specific subjects. This training is nearing completion. Health and Safety induction training is now part of the process for all new starts and relocated staff members.

4.4.4　Risk Assessments
A programme of risk assessments is in place and workstation risk assessments for all staff should be completed through 2009.

4.4.5　Fire Safety Risk Assessments
The review of the existing assessments has been completed and variations in requirements are being implemented as and where required.

4.4.6　Accidents
In the period covered by this Report, one accident required to be reported to the HSE. A number of non-reportable accidents occurred but these were of a minor nature. These are dealt with as they arise and where necessary in conjunction with the appropriate Council/Department.

4.4.7　Safety Committee
A Safety Committee was appointed in line with statutory legislation. This meets on a regular basis and comprises representation from management, staff and the union. The Safety Committee has developed a pattern of work

which is positive and contributes to the wellbeing of staff, volunteers and visitors.

4.4.8　Commitment
The Committee is encouraging a positive and inclusive approach to health and safety. It is committed to working in partnership with staff, the union, Councils and departments in continuing the development of the policy which will deliver a healthy and safe environment for all staff, volunteers, visitors, contractors and others.

5.　Facilities Management
5.1　Health and Safety
The tests and inspections of lifts, boilers and electrical distribution boards have all been satisfactorily completed. The Health and Safety training programme is well underway and workstation assessments are being carried out for all staff. The Facilities Manager has attended a Fire Safety Manager's course and is working closely with the Health and Safety Adviser to review the evacuation procedures. Many more members of staff have volunteered for Fire Marshal duty. Four new First Aiders have been trained. An induction loop system is available for use in the Committee Rooms. Extensive Fire Safety compliance works to all the Fire Doors in the Church Offices have been carried out. Emergency exit doors leading from the offices in 123 George Street have now been upgraded.

5.2　Environmental and Waste Management
5.2.1　The introduction of mains fed water coolers by Aquaid has been a great success. The reduction in cost is approximately 30%. Apart from the obvious environmental benefit, another benefit is the link with Christian Aid and Pump Aid. Due to our business with them, we have been able to raise enough money to provide costs towards the installation of a pump in Malawi. We have only recently received photographic confirmation of the pump and plaque displaying The Church of Scotland's name.

5.2.2　Negotiations with utilities suppliers took place at the end of 2008. The rising costs are unavoidable, particularly electricity, but the Department managed to secure competitive fixed deal contracts with both electricity and gas suppliers. This will help with our budget forecast for the next three years. We are currently pursuing energy saving light fittings and have instructed a survey of all the fittings in the office.

5.2.3 Staff members continue to be very supportive of the recycling regime for paper, cardboard, fluorescent tubes and aluminium cans.

5.3 Maintenance Works
5.3.1 The Church Offices continue to be well maintained and meet the requirements of our insurance policy.

5.4 Café Lounge
Albacore was awarded the contract to provide catering and hospitality on 31 March 2008. Since then, there has been a marked improvement on the Service. The Healthy Eating Award from Edinburgh Council was presented to Albacore for this site in November. The annual review of the contract will be carried out in April.

5.5 Design Services
A new Senior Graphic Designer, Claire Bewsey, joined the Design Team in April 2008. The Department is now able to offer a full graphic design service to departments within the Church Offices and to the wider Church organisation. Some of the new business this year included the Annual Report, Church of Scotland Logo, Safeguarding Logo and the Church and Society and Parish Development Fund Newsletters. We very much hope to attract more business and continue to encourage other departments to consider the Design Team for their design requirements. The hourly rate has had a modest uplift, in line with inflation, and with this increase and extra resource we are very confident that we will be able to continue to improve the service overall.

6. Media Relations
6.1 An internal audit relating to the implementation of the Communication Strategy concluded that the Church is developing a generally effective approach to communication.

6.2 Last year, the Church's first Annual Review was launched at the General Assembly and widely distributed. Feedback, together with numerous requests for additional copies, suggests that the Review was well received. The Communication Adviser also worked on promotional material relating to the Year of Homecoming and it was heartening to note that a spin off from this was an increase in requests for the Introductory Leaflet.

6.3 The Church at national and local level continues to be of interest to the media and enquiries from journalists remain steady in terms of volume and varied in content.

6.4 During the year, the Moderator started a weekly blog on the website which has proved successful and attracted a consistently high number of readers each week. Work has also been done with several groups within the Church to redevelop existing content or produce new material. All local congregations have been asked to provide some information about whether they have their own websites, and some of the issues they face in getting online or keeping their sites updated, with a view to looking at what help the Church might be able to provide.

In the name of the Committee

STEWART ROY, *Convener*
PAULINE WEIBYE, *Vice-Convener*
DOUGLAS PATERSON, *Vice-Convener*
PAULINE WILSON, *Administrative Secretary*

6.2

COMMITTEE ON ECUMENICAL RELATIONS
May 2009

PROPOSED DELIVERANCE

The General Assembly
1.   Receive the Report.
2.   Pass an Act amending Act II 1984 anent Presbytery Visits to Congregations (as amended), as set out in Appendix II to the Report.
3.   Adopt the protocols in relation to the Covenant with the United Free Church (Appendix III).
4.   Welcome the report of the Conversation with the Free Church of Scotland (Appendix IV).
5.   Approve the delegates to Assemblies, Synods and Conferences of other Churches as detailed in Appendix V.
6.   Approve the appointments to ecumenical bodies as detailed in Appendix VI.
7.   Approve the contributions to ecumenical bodies as detailed in Appendix VII.

REPORT

1.   Introduction

1.1 *We believe that it is time to think of the total church life in Scotland in terms of a woven fabric, a cloth for the cradle, a robe for the king. We believe that the woven fabric is best envisioned, for us, in terms of tartan. As we know, tartan has one or two basic colours through which strands of other colours are woven, giving the tartan its unique individuality. We aspire to such an understanding of Scottish Church life where each colour, large and small, has its importance in the final design.*

1.2 With these words the Ecumenical Policy, approved by the General Assembly in 2004, drew to its conclusion. The policy clearly stated that the model of ecumenism adopted by the Church of Scotland was not one of a melting pot, but of churches together. It set out a model in which the churches hold out to each other what is important to them, in the expectation that this will be respected. The churches commit themselves to one another in such a way that authority remains with the churches and is expressed differently by the churches. The churches take responsibility for the agenda. (Para 8.2)

1.3 **The policy set out what is required of us as the Church of Scotland in five distinct areas:**
(a) **Commitment to supporting and resourcing UK and International ecumenical structures** through financial contributions, participation in conferences, councils and assemblies, appointment of delegates and a commitment to rationalising the European and International ecumenical bodies.
(b) **Commitment to and resourcing of Action of Churches Together in Scotland (ACTS)** through what was then called the Scottish Churches' Forum (now the ACTS Members' Meeting), participation in the ACTS Networks and, when instructed by the General Assembly, through bilateral or multilateral discussions and agreements with other denominations, thus maximising the use of resources and strengthening our capacity to provide the "ordinances of religion" across the whole of Scotland.
(c) **Commitment to and support of local ecumenism** through Presbyteries, parishes and chaplaincies supported by a network of Presbytery ecumenical contacts.

(d) Commitment to and support of the National Sponsoring Body for Local Ecumenical Partnerships and its Advisory Groups as the channel through which to address matters of legislation, practice and procedure which can make such partnerships difficult.

(e) Commitment to ecumenism within the revised central structures of the Church of Scotland through the role of the Ecumenical Officer and the composition of the Ecumenical Relations Committee and how each relates to the Councils of the Assembly.

1.4 The policy is due to be reviewed in 2010. In preparation, the Committee this year has taken a look at the current climate affecting ecumenical engagement.

2. Ecumenical Climate

2.1 In 2006, in Porto Alegre, the member churches of the World Council of Churches committed themselves to a deepening and a broadening of the Ecumenical Movement. There was to be a deepening of the commitment of the churches to work together in addressing both the needs of the world and the doctrinal issues which continue to divide the churches. By broadening the movement, more churches would be involved, particularly from the Evangelical and Pentecostal backgrounds.

2.2 These commitments were given against a changing background. The traditional faith and order agenda, through which churches address their differences either through bilateral or multilateral dialogue, continues as a specialist area. It is seen by many to have little relevance to the day-to-day life of churches in local communities. On the other hand, an increasing amount of the joint action of the churches is being done through new, light-structured organisations that can respond quickly in a focused and targeted way. There has been a blossoming of organisations *eg* ACT International which allows

Christian aid agencies to co-ordinate their work, thus avoiding unnecessary duplication when responding to emergencies. ACT Development has evolved to do a similar task in the area of longer term development work, ensuring the place of the Christian voice in addressing the needs of the world's poorest communities. The Ecumenical Advocacy Alliance has been co-ordinating the voice of the churches against injustice in the areas of HIV/AIDS and trade justice. In the next years the focus on trade justice will change to the global food crisis.

2.3 The broadening of the Ecumenical Movement to include Evangelical and Pentecostal churches has led to the formation of the Global Christian Forum which also includes the Roman Catholic Church, the Orthodox churches and the World Confessional bodies e.g. the World Alliance of Reformed Churches. The Forum had its first global meeting in Nairobi in 2007 and a second one is planned for 2011. At the moment, a series of regional meetings are being held in different parts of the world. One of the keynote speakers at the Nairobi Forum described the context in which the Forum had arisen:

> *"the old 'mainstream' ecumenical paradigm is dying and nothing less than a re-birth of ecumenism is needed to embrace the challenges of the new faces, the different worldviews and the new voices of non-Western Christianity. Those wishing to create a new space for Christian unity need to undergo a process of conversion and all of us from the North, the South, the East and the West need to die to old assumptions regarding each other."*

2.4 The World Council of Churches is part of the Global Christian Forum. Within the Ecumenical Movement the World Council of Churches remains a privileged instrument because of its expertise and leadership in global ecumenism. In the Global Christian Forum it works alongside the World Evangelical Alliance, the Pentecostal World Fellowship and churches and organizations belonging to the Charismatic,

Evangelical, Holiness and Pentecostal movements. The emphasis of the Forum is on sharing faith journeys, getting to know one another and to building up trust. It has not attempted to face contentious issues on which it is known that the churches divide.

2.5 This reconfiguration of the Ecumenical Movement has implications for the World Council of Churches as it makes adjustments in the way it works. There are financial implications too as member churches from the global north, already facing financial constraints, reconfigure the distribution of their contributions to the ecumenical bodies.

2.6 Another part of the reconfiguration process relates to a change in attitude to the purpose of the Ecumenical Movement. While there is still emphasis on the goal of Christian unity, more energy is being put into strengthening the distinctive denominational voices.

> *"Only a minority of Christian communities would openly question or resist the call to greater fellowship. On the other hand, we see an increase of denominationalism in all parts of the world and the tendency among churches to affirm particular identities and to strengthen their institutional profile. In most churches ecumenism no longer seems to have the quality of a vision which mobilises people to transcend inherited traditions and to engage in acts of renewal."* (Konrad Raiser, *Reformed World*, Vol 55, No 2, June 2005 Geneva p 77)

2.7 All this feeds into the shift of emphasis that is inherent in the "Churches Together" model that is the basis of the Ecumenical Policy.

2.8 Another change that is affecting the ecumenical movement as we have known it over the past 60 to 100 years is the growth of the "fresh expressions" or "emerging church" movement. New initiatives are being taken which are given a freedom from the accepted denominational structures to find new ways of being the church which engages with today's generation who know little or nothing about the church. Denominational identity is less important and freedom to pick and mix from the Christian tradition opens up new ways of doing things. Only time will tell what long-term effect the emerging church movement will have on the overall shape of the church of the future. What is clear is that it cannot be ignored and it presents challenges both to mainstream denominations and to the ecumenical bodies as they have developed in the past century.

2.9 This complex and shifting picture in which church and ecumenical life as we have known it appear fragile and vulnerable, presents challenges to our ecumenical policy which will need to be taken up in the review next year. At the same time, the current model does give a strong sense that we are travelling along a path with others, seeking the best way to be faithful to our calling as followers of Jesus Christ. The commitment to work together, to cross the boundaries of our historical divisions and to make visible the unity we have in Christ continues to inspire and energise conversations between churches, to lead to the signing of covenants at local level and to many aspects of joint work which are reported on more fully by the several Councils of the Assembly.

2.10 The next section of this report gives an overview of how the policy is working in relation to the ecumenical organisations to which we belong – the World Council of Churches, the World Alliance of Reformed Churches, the Conference of European Churches, the Community of Protestant Churches in Europe, Churches Together in Britain and Ireland and Action of Churches Together in Scotland.

3. Supporting and Resourcing UK and International Ecumenical Structures
3.1 The World Council of Churches (WCC) (**www.oikoumene.org**)
Much has already been said about the changing global context and the place of the WCC within it. This will

6.3

have implications for the way in which we engage with ecumenical work at global level. While continuing to meet our membership contribution we will need to take a look at how particular pieces of ecumenical work can be supported. The Ecumenical Relations Committee is in the process of opening up a conversation with the Councils of the Assembly which is posing the question how, as Councils, they can support and resource UK and International ecumenical structures. In some instances, this is work already in progress. In other cases, it is hoped that new opportunities will be taken to link the work of the Councils with the wider ecumenical agenda. Specifically related to the World Council of Churches, the Committee will be hosting a meeting in November with staff members responsible for the programmatic work of the WCC and Council Conveners and Secretaries to explore this further.

3.2   The World Alliance of Reformed Churches (WARC) (www.warc.jalb.de)

3.2.1   The merger of WARC with the Reformed Ecumenical Council in 2010 to form the World Communion of Reformed Churches will effectively reduce duplication of effort within the Reformed family of churches and our general support for this development fitted well with our commitment to seek a rationalising of International ecumenical bodies in terms of their role and function.

3.2.2   Tension is increasing within WARC in the area of resourcing. The work is concentrating in the South while the funding is coming from the North. More could be done to engender a sense of partnership in determining the agenda.

3.2.3   It is anticipated that the Church and Society Council will participate in briefing the delegates attending General Councils in the areas of economic justice and environmental issues which remain key issues on the WARC agenda.

3.3   The Conference of European Churches (CEC) (www.cec-kek.org)

3.3.1   CEC, which will celebrate its 50th anniversary at its Assembly in Lyons in July, keeps open relations between the churches in East and West Europe, between the Reformation Churches in the West and the Orthodox Churches in the East. It is not always a comfortable space, with incompatibilities evident not just on the positions taken but also on questions of process. The *Charta Oecumenica* has provided a valuable benchmark document for neighbourly relations. (See General Assembly 2002, p24/39.) It was agreed by all the main European Churches and is evoked in discussions between churches and with outside bodies.

3.3.2   The Dialogue Commission in Geneva is well placed to concentrate on exploring relations with the Orthodox churches. The Church and Society Commission in Brussels is consolidating its position as a credible and sought-after partner with the European institutions. At the Lyons Assembly a third Commission will be added with the integration of the Churches Commission for Migrants in Europe. The churches will then have better access to the lobbying and educational work of this Commission.

3.3.3   However, having two strong Commissions in Brussels increases the imbalance between the two administrative centres of CEC in Geneva and Brussels. Also, the holding together of East and West is perceived to be at the cost of sharpness of position. This has led some churches to want their own voice and office in Brussels and to the development of the Protestant voice of the Community of Protestant Churches in Europe.

3.3.4   The Church of Scotland supports CEC well. Here, too, with an increasing amount of project funding, opportunities for involving the Councils of the Assembly in supporting and resourcing the work of CEC are opening up. The Church of Scotland is well-represented on the Central Committee (Alison Elliot) and on the Church and Society Commission (David Sinclair). We have also been participants on Working Groups on Social Issues and Bioethics and Biotechnology. In the past year, we participated in a conference for church lawyers and a meeting organised by the Dialogue Commission on theological education.

3.3.5 The "Scottish model", as it has become known, of paying for a staff person has been appreciated and is used as an example to others who wish to make appointments or set up offices in Brussels. As Matthew Ross returns, the Church and Society Council have sought to strengthen the relationship with the Church and Society Commission through this mechanism.

3.4 The Community of Protestant Churches in Europe (CPCE) (www.leuenberg.net)

3.4.1 The Leuenberg Fellowship of Churches, now the Community of Protestant Churches in Europe, exists to strengthen the voice of Reformed, Lutheran and Methodist Churches in Europe. It does particular pieces of doctrinal work and, under the umbrella of CEC, has taken forward discussion between the Orthodox churches and the Reformed and Lutheran churches. In recent years, it has strengthened its input to the church and society agenda with the appointment of a staff person to Brussels who works alongside the CEC staff.

3.4.2 The Church of Scotland is invited, from time to time, to participate in consultations. Currently, we have been asked to participate in a study on "The Protestant Understanding of Ministry and Episkope". The CPCE also works in Regional Groupings. A new Grouping is being set up for Northern Europe which will include the United Kingdom and Ireland, Denmark, Norway and Sweden. This group has yet to meet but it will allow us to strengthen our links with some of the Nordic Churches who, through the Porvoo Agreement, also relate to the Anglican Churches in Britain and Ireland.

3.5 Eurodiaconia (www.eurodiaconia.org)

Eurodiaconia brings together those involved in the social service and health care provision organisations of churches across Europe. The Church of Scotland's participation in this is through the Social Care Council.

Once again, the contribution of the Church of Scotland is greatly appreciated and is made visible in the fact that the former Chief Executive Officer of CrossReach was the President of Eurodiaconia.

3.6 Churches Together in Britain and Ireland (CTBI) (www.ctbi.org.uk)
Action of Churches Together in Scotland (ACTS) (www.acts-scotland.org)
Churches Together in England (CTE) (www.churches-together.net)

3.6.1 Following the last round of funding negotiations when it was apparent that there would be less money available to support the ecumenical instruments in Britain and Ireland, CTBI has been through a very difficult period, reducing the number of staff, while trying to maintain a co-ordinating role at four-nations' level.

3.6.2 Costs have also been cut by transforming the Commissions on Mission, Racial Justice and Inter Faith Relations into networks which are light on staff but ensure that those with similar responsibilities across the four nations maintain contact with each other and seek ways of co-operation. The Global Mission Network has now completely integrated what were traditionally classed as "home mission" and "overseas mission". The Racial Justice and Inter-Faith Networks have been recently constituted. Similarly, the Church and Society Forum has become a network. In all cases, the Church of Scotland seeks to be represented by the people with the appropriate level of responsibility and skill.

3.6.3 The next round of funding negotiations are under way and it is clear that, once again, there is likely to be a reduction in the amount available to support the ecumenical instruments in Britain (Ireland is separately funded). This is being addressed. CTBI is looking again at the original vision set out in the "Marigold Book" for a lightly structured organisation at four-nation level. Proposals will be brought to the Trustees in the Spring and to the Senior Representatives' Meeting at the beginning

6.3

of May. These proposals, if accepted, will do away with the common pot which CTBI administered on behalf of the national instruments and will mean a return to direct negotiations between the churches and the instruments. These proposals have been reflected in the table in Appendix VII.

3.6.4　The Church of Scotland makes the second largest contribution to the ecumenical bodies in Britain and Ireland and continues to benefit from the sharing of experience with churches in all parts of Britain and Ireland.

3.7　Commitment to and Supporting of ACTS
3.7.1　For over two years the agenda of ACTS has been dominated by issues relating to Scottish Churches House and to the development of a new constitution and governance structure to comply with the requirements of the Office of the Scottish Charity Regulator (OSCR). There is now a new structure in place and financial capital has been accrued beyond all expectation which has enabled a programme of major refurbishment and development of Scottish Churches House to be put in place. A new director, Carol Stobie, has been appointed to the House and a new Board of Trustees to manage the running of the House is to be appointed. The property is owned by the Trustees of ACTS.

3.7.2　Once again, the pattern already noted in relation to the other ecumenical bodies is becoming apparent in relation to ACTS in that much of its work is done in short to medium term, time-limited projects. These receive support from project funding available to ACTS or from direct contributions of those churches that commit themselves to particular pieces of work.

3.7.3　The ACTS Networks are well-established. The Church of Scotland endeavours to appoint those with experience and who can speak with authority and knowledge about the work of the Councils. In this way, we play an active part in shaping and moving forward the

agenda of the churches together in Scotland.

3.7.4　ACTS embodies the "Churches Together" model which is central to our ecumenical policy and strategy. At its best, it has brought the member churches together with common purpose and cemented friendships and deepened understanding between the churches. However, it has created a comfort zone which has failed to address the significant differences that exist between the churches and to challenge the churches to theological engagement on the path to unity.

4.　Commitment to and support of local ecumenism
4.1　While it has not yet proved possible to set up a network of ecumenical facilitators among the Presbyteries, the Committee continues to rejoice in the amount of local co-operation and partnership that exists in many places. Local churches together groups continue to encourage congregations to journey together, sharing in joint acts of worship and prayer and engaging in joint projects in the community. The annual October Conference and information sent in to the newsletter, "Groundswell", allow for stories to be told and experience to be shared.

4.2　Through the Duncan McClements' Trust the Committee is able to give small grants to assist local people to deepen their ecumenical experience. In the past year this included enabling a member of the Student Christian Movement (SCM, www.movement.org.uk) to attend the International gathering of the World Student Christian Federation (WSCF, www.wscfglobal.org).

4.3　A new area of relationships is opening up as we become more aware of migrant churches in Scotland. The Romanian community in Scotland has been overwhelmed by the generous welcome they have received in Shettleston Old where they have been able to consecrate the church hall as a Romanian Orthodox Church. The Scottish Churches Racial Justice Group together with the Assistant General Secretary of ACTS have begun a mapping exercise to enable us all to see more clearly the number of migrant churches in Scotland. As small congregations, often representing large churches abroad, they have much to offer us and to enrich our understanding of the Christian faith. We are beginning to seek ways in which that gift can be shared both locally and nationally.

4.4 A significant area of local support is provided by the National Sponsoring Body for Local Ecumenical Partnerships.

5.   Commitment to and Resourcing of the National Sponsoring Body for Local Ecumenical Partnerships (NSB)

5.1 Under the umbrella of ACTS is the National Sponsoring Body which was set up in 2005 to encourage local church unity through formal and informal agreements and partnerships. It provides a means whereby those involved in local ecumenical partnerships (LEPs) can share stories and learn from one another. It also acts as a reference and support body providing advice and guidance to those who wish to develop LEPs.

5.2 In addition, it initiates a biennial gathering for those involved in LEPs and which is hosted by one of the established LEPs. In November 2008, the second of these was hosted by Oakshaw Trinity in Paisley under the title of "Threads".

5.3 A series of Regional Advisory Groups was set up in five areas of Scotland to support the work of LEPs. They have been variable in their implementation and practice as well as in their effectiveness. Where they do function well, they have begun to implement a Review Process, approved by the NSB and which draws together the requirements of all the participating churches so that congregations involved in LEPs do not have to be separately reviewed by each of the participating denominations. In the Church of Scotland, this ecumenical process has been affected

by the "bedding in" of parish groupings which were, by and large, not seen as an opportunity for ecumenical working. Now, however, the Committee has been able to work with the Legal Questions Committee to seek the incorporation of the ecumenical review into the superintendence procedures of the Church of Scotland and an Act is appended to this report. The Ecumenical Review will apply to congregations involved in either single-congregation LEPs ("ecumenical charges") or churches in covenanted partnership LEPs. The Review is to be carried out by a representative appointed by each denomination. For the Church of Scotland this will be someone appointed by Presbytery, normally from the Committee charged with Superintendence. The resulting report will be presented to Presbytery. In this way the Ecumenical Review will respect the normal powers of superintendence exercised by the Presbytery. (Appendix II)

6.   Bilateral Conversations

We continue to be involved in a number of bilateral conversations and are in the process of developing two new ones with churches in Germany.

6.1 The United Free Church of Scotland (www.ufcos.org.uk)

6.1.1   The Covenant Monitoring Group is concerned at how many people are unaware of the existence of the Covenant between the two Churches and the commitments for co-operation that it encourages.

> We commit ourselves to encourage local congregations to enter local covenants as a means of moving towards an ever deeper sharing of resources for mission and service to the community. (Commitment 4)

6.1.2   To this end, the Committee has been happy to produce a DVD of the very successful partnership at Canonbie as a resource to encourage further co-operation in other parts of the country. A section of the deliverance also encourages Presbyteries to take the Covenant into account when doing their forward planning.

6.1.3 It is the intention of the two Churches to continue the process of biennial review of the Covenant with alterations being put into immediate practice and being incorporated into the reworking of the Covenant every five years. The renewed Covenant would be signed by the Moderators of the General Assemblies, alternating between the Churches, thus also ensuring that the Covenant is given a high profile within both Churches.

6.1.4 As requested by the General Assembly in 2008, a set of protocols have been drawn up which will take immediate effect. (Appendix III)

6.2 The Free Church of Scotland (www.freechurch.org)

A joint report, detailing the outcome of the discussion with the Free Church is appended in Appendix IV. There are uncertainties about the goals of the conversation but all who are involved believe that the fact that there are talks is significant and can only be beneficial in seeking ways to build on the co-operation that exists in many places at local level and at national level in, for example, the Scottish Churches Parliamentary Office Advisory Group.

6.3 The Roman Catholic Church (www.bpsconfscot.com)

6.3.1 The Joint Commission on Doctrine was pleased with the way in which the document on *"Baptism: Catholic and Reformed"* has been received. It has been widely distributed and there have been requests for further copies.

6.3.2 The Joint Commission agreed to organise a symposium to mark the 500th anniversary of the birth of John Calvin. The symposium, *"Calvin: Catholic and Reformed",* is to be hosted by Scotus College and will include four papers relating to Calvin, two from Church

of Scotland speakers and two from Roman Catholic contributors. The day will finish with a meal. Church leaders and final year divinity students have been invited to the Symposium.

6.3.3 Consideration is also being given to finding an appropriate way to mark the 450th anniversary of the Reformation in Scotland. This anniversary offers the possibility of reconciling the memories of a particularly sensitive period in our shared history.

6.3.4 The main focus of the Joint Commission's work has been the report of the third phase of the International Dialogue between the World Council of Churches and the Vatican, *"The Church as Community of Common Witness to the Kingdom of God".* The Joint Commission was particularly fortunate in having with them two Scottish members of the drafting Committee, Prof Alasdair Heron and Rev Dr Harry O'Brien. It is the intention of the Joint Commission to produce a joint response to this document for submission to the WCC's Faith and Order Commission and the Pontifical Council for Promoting Christian Unity.

6.4 The Church of England (www.cofe.anglican.org)

6.4.1 There are two ongoing conversations with the Church of England. There is the biennial consultation that shares experiences around the respective responsibilities and experiences as national churches. The twelfth consultation took place in Edinburgh last October. Jointly chaired by Dr Alison Elliot and Most Rev Dr John Sentamu, the consultation shared a general overview and particular developments relating to changing patterns of ministry, apologetics, International mission (including the proposed celebration of the centenary of the Edinburgh Missionary Conference of 1910) and issues relating to church and state relations.

6.4.2 The second conversation happens annually and involves the Joint Working Group on Faith and Order. At its meeting last November, it was agreed to bring a joint report to our respective governing bodies in 2010. This report will effectively round off this series of conversations and leave the way open for another series which would include representatives of the Scottish Episcopal Church along with the Church of England because it is recognised that any faith and order agreement with the Church of England would necessarily have implications for our relationship with the Scottish Episcopal Church.

6.5 The Evangelical Lutheran Church in Bavaria (ELKB) (www.bayern-evangelisch.de)

The relationship with the Evangelical Lutheran Church in Bavaria seeks to build on already existing relationships between Bavaria and Scotland. There is a well-developed Edinburgh Presbytery/Munich partnership which comprises biennial exchange visits and theological reflection. There are possibilities of developing the twinning arrangements between Perth and Aschaffenburg and between Aberdeen and Regensburg. Alongside this there are developing partnerships in ministry placements in Dundee and Orkney. These have been extremely well received and it is the wish of the ELKB to extend such opportunities. Encouragement is given to Church of Scotland ministers to seek short-term appointments in Bavaria.

6.6 The Evangelical Church of Westphalia (EKW) (www.ekvw.de)

In February 2009, we hosted a visit of representatives of the Evangelical Church of Westphalia. The Westphalian Church is seeking closer relations with a church in Western Europe which has a similar role to its own. The delegation met with representatives of various Councils and a return visit is being planned for August 2009. This relationship is still very much at an exploratory stage but there are good signs of there being plenty of scope for journeying together for a time.

7.   Commitment to Ecumenism within the Councils of the Assembly

Built into the revised structure of the Church of Scotland is an ecumenical remit affecting every Council. In order to support this, the Committee on Ecumenical Relations includes five core members who each relate as a full member of one of the Councils. These members monitor the way in which the ecumenical dimension is acknowledged and developed.

7.1 Church and Society Council

Much of the work of this Council is undertaken with an ecumenical dimension. Four representatives from the ACTS member churches serve on the Council on a rotational basis. Staff attend ACTS' networks as part of their core activity. People from other churches are co-opted onto its working groups according to their particular expertise. The work of the Scottish Churches Parliamentary Office is done with the assistance of an Advisory Group that draws its membership from most of the member churches of ACTS plus the Baptist Union and the Free Church. Mention has already been made of the Brussels post which is supported by the Council and which will continue in a way that strengthens the relationship between the Council's work and the work of the Commission in Brussels. The Society, Religion and Technology work continues to work ecumenically. Eco-congregations Scotland, which the council already heavily supports, has always been ecumenical in nature. It is soon to become a separate charitable company limited by guarantee and the new constitution will embed that ecumenical commitment.

7.2 Ministries Council

Amid all the work on governance, the ecumenical dimension of the work of the Ministries Council is most noticeable in the work done in priority areas and chaplaincies. Consultations have taken place with the Church of England and Methodist Church on "fresh expressions" and with other churches as part of the review of ministries' training.

7.3 Mission and Discipleship Council

The Mission and Discipleship Council carries a wide remit,

working through a variety of specific task forces. From rural church issues, to worship and doctrine, to explorations and new patterns of mission and discipleship within Scotland, the various task forces seek to work with other church partners. Through this, they have gained the experience of other churches as they have sought to address contemporary issues and trends, and have engaged with other churches in seeking to address issues facing the Church in Scotland. On a number of occasions, the Council has sought to suggest that work be undertaken through ACTS. While this has created difficulties in meeting General Assembly remit reporting dates, it has had the advantage of addressing an issue which commends itself to the churches in Scotland *eg* "*The Language of the Trinity*"). On the whole, the Council is seeking to work ecumenically, and is to be encouraged in and commended for working in this manner

7.4 Social Care Council
CrossReach provides care to people of all faiths and of none and the care is delivered by people from many Christian backgrounds and, in that sense, the Council works ecumenically. When exploring new areas of service the possibility of working ecumenically is always explored and local support groups for care homes are always open to the participation of people from different church backgrounds. As already noted, the Chief Executive Officer was President of Eurodiakonia where the Council has for many years engaged with issues relating to service provision across Europe.

7.5 World Mission Council
The review of the strategic plan of the World Mission Council highlights the areas where ecumenical working has been a success but it also notes that there are areas in which "resources, finance and unforeseen factors can have an impact on areas where progressive ecumenical work has been instigated." The projected plan continues to retain a strong emphasis on ecumenical issues and aims "to establish viable and fruitful ways of working

with the ecumenical bodies in which the Council plays a part." The targets for each area of the Council's work all mention relevant ecumenical bodies as a key interface for the progression of the work and the section on networking highlights the importance of maintaining active participation in ecumenical networks.

8. Overlapping Areas
There are several events which are providing the opportunity for ecumenical engagement across a number of Councils. These include:

8.1 The Calvin Quincentenary – 2009 (www.calvin500.org)
This significant anniversary has allowed us, together with other churches, to examine the legacy of John Calvin and to assess his influence on Scottish society and culture.

8.2 The 450th anniversary of the Scottish Reformation – 2010
This anniversary provides the opportunity for a sensitive marking of the occasion that avoids a triumphalism and allows for a clear statement that, through the ecumenical engagement of the past century, the churches in Scotland are in a different place now than they once were. It also allows the churches together to address the changed context in which they minister and bear witness to the Gospel of Jesus Christ and to find common ways of expressing their shared Christian identity and calling.

8.3 Edinburgh 2010 (www.edinburgh2010.org)
The centenary of the World Missionary Conference of 1910 presents the opportunity for the churches to celebrate different aspects of belonging to a world church, to welcome people from across the world to our country and to seek ways to refresh and enthuse our churches with a vision of renewal and hope that, together with churches around the world, we can bring a Christian voice into work with people of all faiths and of none as we seek a more just, more equitable and more peaceful world for all. (For a fuller report, see under World Mission Council.)

9. Conclusion

What becomes clear from this survey is that, despite the difficult and uncertain context within which ecumenical relations take place, there is much that is being done which is exciting and full of life. The churches together model works locally, nationally and internationally. Local ecumenical partnerships continue to mature and develop new work, revising their commitments and covenants. Churches do seek opportunities to work together and to take the time to share information and learn from one another. Through it the local seeks support, encouragement and resourcing from the national and international and links are made between nations and, in all cases, across denominations. This way of working, which we have called "the churches together model", leaves us less challenged to move beyond the security of our denominationalism. It encourages co-operation and commitment across denominational lines. It keeps before us the fact that we are bonded in baptism to all who confess the name of Christ and are called to serve in mission together in the one Church. The threads of the churches together model run horizontally and vertically, weaving a colourful tartan where, as we said in 2004, "each colour, large and small, has its importance in the final design".

In the name of the Committee

WILLIAM D BROWN, *Convener*
LINDSAY SCHLUTER, *Vice-Convener*
SHEILAGH M KESTING, *Secretary*

ADDENDUM

Rev William D Brown completes his term as Convener of the Committee on Ecumenical Relations. Bill brought a wealth of local ecumenical experience to the task which he used not just to encourage others in their local ecumenical relationships but also to bring clarity and relevance to relationships at national and international levels. He carefully guided the Committee as it encouraged the implementation of the Ecumenical Policy across the Church. His thoughtful leading of worship, his natural enthusiasm and gentle chairing created a good atmosphere within which to work. The Committee expresses its thanks to Bill for the way he tended and nurtured ecumenical relationships at all levels and continued to remind the Church of Scotland of its ecumenical commitment and wishes him well in his continued ministry in Murrayfield.

On behalf of the Committee

LINDSAY SCHLUTER, *Vice-Convener*
SHEILAGH M KESTING, *Secretary*

APPENDIX I
ACRONYMS

ACTS	–	Action of Churches Together in Scotland
CEC	–	Conference of European Churches
CPCE	–	Community of Protestant Churches in Europe
CTBI	–	Churches Together in Britain and Ireland
ELKB	–	Evangelical Lutheran Church in Bavaria
LEPs	–	Local Ecumenical Partnerships
NSB	–	National Sponsoring Body for Local Ecumenical Partnerships
OSCR	–	Office of the Scottish Charity Regulator
WARC	–	World Alliance of Reformed Churches
WCC	–	World Council of Churches

APPENDIX II
ACT AMENDING ACT II 1984 ANENT PRESBYTERY VISITS TO CONGREGATIONS (AS AMENDED)

Edinburgh, 23 May 2009, Sess. IV

The General Assembly hereby enact and ordain that Act II 1984 as amended is hereby further amended by the addition of a new section 11 as follows:

6.3

11. In the case of a Single Congregation Local Ecumenical Partnership (LEP) and Churches in Covenanted Partnership, which are recognised to be such by the National Sponsoring Body for Local Ecumenical Partnerships (NSBLEP), an Ecumenical Review in the form approved by the NSBLEP on 14 March 2008 shall be deemed to fulfil the requirements of this Act for the purposes of the Church of Scotland. For the avoidance of doubt, this is without prejudice to the general right and responsibility of the Presbytery to exercise superintendence in other ways, and it is without prejudice to the requirement of the regulations of any other denomination which is a partner in the same LEP.

APPENDIX III
PROTOCOL TO THE COVENANT BETWEEN THE CHURCH OF SCOTLAND AND THE UNITED FREE CHURCH OF SCOTLAND ON TRANSFER OF CONGREGATIONS AND MINISTERS BETWEEN THE CHURCHES

1. The Church of Scotland and the United Free Church of Scotland agree the following Protocol, which shall be regarded as a statement of good practice and implemented as far as possible by both Churches.

2. The Protocol shall be reviewed along with the Covenant, in terms of Commitment 7 of the Covenant document.

3. Transfer of Congregations
a) Where a congregation seeks to be admitted to membership of either party to the Covenant ("the receiving denomination"), and its current or last known denomination was the other party ("the releasing denomination"), this Protocol shall apply.
b) The Ecumenical Officer and the relevant Presbytery Clerks of both Churches shall confer together, and consult where necessary with the Solicitors, Principal Clerks or other relevant officials of either denomination.
c) The releasing denomination shall advise the receiving denomination whether any matters of Church law and discipline, or of civil law, remain to be resolved in respect of the congregation, and shall undertake to inform the receiving denomination when such resolution has been reached.
d) The receiving denomination shall not recognise the congregation in its membership until it has considered the advice received in terms of 3(c) above, and should explain to the releasing denomination its reasons if it decides to admit the congregation before the resolution of those matters.

4. For the avoidance of doubt, with the agreement of both denominations, a Congregation of the releasing denomination may be admitted to membership of the receiving denomination notwithstanding issues relating to ownership of heritable property remaining unresolved between the Congregation and the releasing denomination.

5. Transfer of Ministers
a) The transfer of ministers between the Churches shall be subject to the law of each Church.
b) Where a congregation transfers its membership from one denomination to the other, as described in 3 above, and there is a sitting minister (or other member of a ministry team) in place, the normal rules of transfer of ministry shall apply, subject to the provisions of 5(c).
c) In the circumstances referred to in 5(b) the receiving denomination shall take particular care to discover whether any disciplinary or other legal processes are in process to which the minister or other individual is a party. In the event of such proceedings the normal rules of transfer shall not apply until the releasing denomination has informed the receiving denomination of the individual's good standing.

6. Interpretation of Protocol

If the Ecumenical Officer and the Principal Clerks of the two Churches disagree on the interpretation and implementation of this Protocol in any case, the Covenant Monitoring Group shall advise on the matter and each denomination shall implement its own interpretation of the Protocol, so far as possible in the spirit of the advice received and of the original Covenant.

APPENDIX IV
CHURCH OF SCOTLAND – FREE CHURCH OF SCOTLAND DIALOGUE

1. Introduction

In 2007, the General Assemblies of both the Church of Scotland and the Free Church of Scotland warmly endorsed a Joint Statement. This Statement began with the recognition, so important to churches of the Reformed traditions, of Scripture as the "supreme rule of faith and life". It acknowledged the common confessional basis we have in the Westminster Confession of Faith. It confessed the scandal of the continuing divisions within our Presbyterian family and called for a mutual recognition of each other as churches; mutual acknowledgment that each church needs the other and cannot be the Church to the exclusion of the other; mutual commitment to cooperate as far as possible in the advancement of the kingdom of God; and it called for the provision of a framework within which ongoing discussion could be accommodated and which would facilitate frank exchange of views. The Joint Statement then went on to suggest ways in which these aspects could be lived out in practice, acknowledging that there are already good examples that make visible what we believe and confess.

It was with great joy that the Conveners of the two Churches' Ecumenical Relations Committees addressed each other's Assemblies. That crossing of the road was hailed as "a small step for a Christian but a giant step for the Church". The Joint Statement expressed the hope that the two churches would grow in prayer for one another

and identified areas of cooperation – evangelism and church planting, theological education in continuing professional development, moving from cooperation to commitment in local structures through formal links, joint social projects, joint conferences and fellowships, social events and representations to governments and public bodies.

The joint statement also committed the churches to ongoing dialogue and continued exchange of views in the hope of developing greater understanding and of expanding the framework for dialogue in the future beyond the Ecumenical Relations Committees.

Following the Assemblies of 2007, the Dialogue Group returned to consider the respective understanding of the two churches relating to the Word of God and Holy Scripture. The Group has endeavoured to identify more clearly those areas of common ground on which there is unanimity and those areas in which differences of opinion still provide a significant stumbling block to further co-operation.

2. Seeking Consensus on an Understanding of the Word of God and Holy Scripture in the Church

Following the Assemblies of 2007, the Dialogue Group returned to consider a revised paper which spelled out *The Constitutional Position of the Church of Scotland with respect to the Word of God and Holy Scripture*. A responding paper was presented setting out *The Constitutional Position of the Free Church of Scotland with respect to the Word of God and Holy Scripture*.

The two churches share a common history and a common theological heritage. Up to the later decades of the nineteenth century there was little divergence in the way in which the Word of God and Holy Scripture were understood. Divergence came as a series of unions led first to the formation of the United Free Church in 1900 and then to a reunited Church of Scotland in 1929. During that period the Free Church underwent a crisis on the very issue of the doctrine of Scripture and those who remained in 1900 felt unable in conscience to do other than maintain a separate, more strict witness to the *Confession* and to the doctrine of Scripture. This means that when it comes to discussing the Word of God and Holy Scripture it is to touch a very sensitive area for the Free Church – that of its historic identity. Nevertheless, by examining the shared theological heritage, it was hoped that there might be clarification of the shared understanding of the nature of the Word of God and the nature of Holy Scripture. It was also hoped that such an examination might clarify our understanding of the Church as the community of the people of God that, at one and the same time, hears the Word of God, and translates and communicates that Word to the community of all who are made "in the image of God".

3.　A shared theological heritage: *The Westminster Confession of Faith*

The *Westminster Confession of Faith* states that "Holy Scripture" is "given by the inspiration of God to be the rule of faith and life". (I.2) The *Confession* also affirms that: "We may be moved and induced by the testimony of the Church to an high and reverent esteem of the Holy Scripture." (I.5) In addition, it is clear from the *Confession* that Scripture is set within a broader context of divine revelation.

> *Therefore it pleased the Lord, at sundry times, and in diverse manners, to reveal Himself, and to declare His will unto the Church; and afterwards, for the better preserving and propagating of the truth… to commit the same wholly unto writing: which maketh the Holy Scripture to be most necessary; those former ways of God's revealing His will unto His people being now ceased.* (I.1)

The *Confession* establishes, as a principle of interpretation, that the "infallible rule of interpretation of Scripture is the Scripture itself", (I.9) with the "supreme judge by which all controversies of religion are to be determined" being "no other but the Holy Spirit speaking in Scripture." (I.10)

The authority of Scripture and the grounds upon "which it ought to be believed" are not to be found in the Church, according to the *Confession*. (I.4) The Church can provide "testimony" as to the efficacy of Holy Scripture, but the "decrees and councils" and the "opinions of ancient writers" are alike "to be examined" by "the Holy Spirit speaking in the Scripture". (I.10) That is not to say that "councils" have nothing to contribute to our understanding, but the *Confession* makes it clear that:

> *All synods or councils, since the Apostles' times, whether general or particular, may err; and many have erred. Therefore they are not made the rule of faith, or practice; but to be used as a help in both.* (XXXI.4)

It is clear that in the *Confession* Scripture is placed over and above the Church, and that the "traditions of men" provide no possibility of insight into the counsel of God. (I.6)

Therefore in the *Confession* we find an affirmation that the testimony of infallible Scripture, interpreted by Scripture itself, is entirely consonant with the work of the Holy Spirit. Thus, the inner testimony of the Holy Spirit, conjoined to the Word of God, unite to produce in the heart of the believer the experience of the power of God.

The relationship of the Church of Scotland to the *Westminster Confession of Faith*

The relationship of the Church of Scotland to the *Westminster Confession of Faith* is set out in the *Basis and Plan of Union* (1929) and, specifically, in the *Articles Declaratory of the Constitution of the Church of Scotland in Matters Spiritual*. The *Basis of Union*, as regards "Doctrine", places the *Confession* in a relationship with the *United Presbyterian Church Declaratory Act* (1879) and the *Free Church Declaratory Acts* (1892 and 1894), as well as *The Church of Scotland Act on the Formula* (1910). Equally, with respect to the "General Constitution" of the Church, the *Basis of Union* places the "subordinate standard" in a relationship with the *United Free Church Act anent*

Spiritual Independence of the Church (1906) (Weatherhead, 1997:154-179)

Within the *Articles Declaratory* we find embodied the spiritual constitution of the Church of Scotland, as found in *The Church of Scotland Act, 1921*, and as adopted by the Church in 1926. The *Act* is an acknowledgement by Parliament of the spiritual rights inherent within the Church of Scotland, as *a* Church that is a branch of *"the Holy Catholic or Universal Church*, rather than as *the* Church of *Scotland*. The *Articles*, and in particular *Article I*, embody the "evidently cardinal doctrines" of the Church, and identify those doctrines "which were clearly fundamental and essential to a Christian Church". (Weatherhead, 1997: 26; Sjölinder, 1962: 252-308, 363-374, 386-391; Murray, 2000: 63-114) Thus, while it is granted that: "The Church has the right to interpret theses Articles, and ... to modify or add to them", (*Article* VIII) it is stated that this act of interpretation takes place "always consistently with the provisions of the Article hereof, adherence to which, as interpreted by the Church, is essential to its continuity and corporate life". (*Article* VIII) In this way a clear distinction is made in the *Declaratory Articles* between "what is fundamental (*Article* I), and what is expedient and may be altered by the Church (all the other *Articles*)". (Weatherhead, 1997:5-6)

Following a description of the Church of Scotland as "part of the Holy Catholic or Apostolic Church", a narrative of the work of Christ allied to the promise of the Holy Spirit, *Article* I gives a statement of the Church's identity and its relationship to Scripture:

> *The Church of Scotland adheres to the Scottish Reformation; receives the Word of God which is contained in the Scriptures of the Old and New Testaments as its supreme rule of faith and life; and avows the fundamental doctrines of the Catholic faith founded thereupon.*

There follows in *Article* II the statement that

> *The principal subordinate standard of the Church of Scotland is the Westminster Confession of Faith approved by the General Assembly of 1647, containing the sum and substance of the Faith of the Reformed Church.*

Equally, the "Preamble" to the Ordination to the office of the Holy Ministry affirms that:

> *The Church of Scotland holds as its subordinate standard the Westminster Confession of Faith, recognising liberty of opinion on such points of doctrine as do not enter into the substance of the Faith, and claiming the right, in dependence on the promised guidance of the Holy Spirit, to formulate, interpret, or modify its subordinate standards; always in agreement with the Word of God and the fundamental doctrines of the Christian faith contained in the said Confession – of which agreement the Church itself shall be sole judge. (Weatherhead, 1997: 163; Murray, 2000: 168-171)*

The relationship of the Church of Scotland to the *Westminster Confession of Faith* as constituted in 1929, and thereafter, differs from the relationship which existed before 1929. This is exemplified with respect to the *Preamble* cited above, with its reference to "recognising liberty of opinion on such points of doctrine as do not enter into the substance of the Faith", and the 1929 *Formula* which is set out in terms consistent with *The Church of Scotland Act on the Formula (1910)*. The latter, as found in the *Basis and Plan of Union (1929)*, follows on from the *Preamble* and affirms, in relation to the *Westminster Confession of Faith*, that:

> *I believe the fundamental doctrines of the Christian faith contained in the Confession of Faith of this Church. (Weatherhead, 1997: 165)*

Thus, there is an affirmation of the place of the *Confession*, albeit that this is qualified with the recognition of "liberty of opinion".

This may be contrasted with *Formula* previously used; essentially that of 1889, as modified in 1901 and 1903, and construed in terms consistent with the *Act for Settling the Quiet and Peace of the Church 1693 (c.38)*. This affirmed, in relation to the *Westminster Confession of Faith*, that:

> I declare the Confession of Faith, approven by former General Assemblies of this Church, and ratified by law in the year 1690, to be the confession of my faith, and I own the doctrine therein contained to be the true doctrine, which I will constantly adhere to. (Mair, 1904: 530-532)

This *Formula*, declaring the Westminster Confession of Faith *"to be the confession of my faith"*; whose doctrine we own to be true, may be said to differ in character from the *Formula* enshrined in the *Basis and Plan of Union (1929)*.

From this survey the relationship of the Church of Scotland to the *Confession* four points are to be noted:

1. The primacy of *Article* I in the *Declaratory Articles*.
2. The placing of the *Westminster Confession of Faith* as the "principal subordinate standard" of the Church of Scotland in *Article* II.
3. The stating of the relationship between the Word of God and Holy Scripture ("the Word of God which is *contained* in the Scriptures of the Old and New Testaments").
4. The terms under which the relationship of the Church of Scotland to the *Westminster Confession of Faith* is to be understood in relation to the *Preamble* and *Formula*.

The Word of God and Holy Scripture in the Church of Scotland

As a Church in the Reformed tradition, the Church of Scotland is a confessional church. The *Scots Confession* (1560) established the principle of the primacy of Scripture over *Confession*, when it affirmed that anything found in the *Confession* that is "contrary to God's Holy Word" was to be subject to correction by Scripture. ("The Preface" to the *Scots Confession*). In this way the doctrinal formulations of a Reformed Church are, in principle, open to clarification and correction in the light of Scripture, perhaps the principal distinguishing characteristic of a Church in the Reformed tradition.

Commenting on the relationship between the Word of God and Scripture as set out in section I.1 of the *Westminster Confession* (see above), H.J. Wotherspoon and J.M. Kirkpatrick write:

> *The Confession of Faith* here recognises the Holy Scriptures as the written Word of God to men in and through which it is God Himself who speaks in person, but it recognises also that Revelation was precedent to the Scriptural record. Thus in regard to the New Testament the Revelation was mediated and apprehended, the Christian faith existed and was stated and believed and taught, before the various scriptures it contains were in being… The Faith did not make its first appearance in a written but in an oral form: it existed, was preached, believed, and transmitted for some time before it began to have expression in inspired writings. When these writings appeared, they did not supersede the unwritten Faith which the Apostolic witnesses communicated to the Church, nor did they add to it. They are a photograph of that Faith in the process of transmission, and thus became the standard of reference for verifying the content of the Faith. (Wotherspoon and Kirkpatrick, 1960: 56-57)

While the extent to which Wotherspoon and Kirkpatrick express the authorial intention of the framers of the *Confession* may be open to debate, they do formulate an understanding of the relationship between the Word of God and Holy Scripture which is adequate as a description of the process whereby the Apostolic faith was first stated and thereafter expressed in Scripture. In addition, they see the function of Scripture as providing a measure for the adequacy of attempts to describe the normative content of the Christian faith. They also make clear that the context within which the Word of God is heard, the Apostolic faith is stated, the faith is expressed in Scripture, and its doctrinal content is described, is that of the Church.

There is, therefore, no absolute identification of the Word of God with Scripture, but an affirmation that it is through Scripture that the Word will be heard. It is understood that the framers of the *Articles Declaratory* made this distinction between the Word of God and Scripture and desired to avoid any equation of the two. (Sjölinder, 1962: 167-182; Murray, 2000: 63-114) The Word of God and Scripture relate to one another in a constant and unbroken relationship in which they mutually inform one another. Weatherhead writes:

> This *Article* does not make a verbal identification of the words of Scripture with the Word of God, but states that the Word of God is "contained in" the Bible, thus leaving scope for the application of the phrase "as interpreted by the Church", and also for liberty of opinion. (Weatherhead, 1997: 19)

So, in relation to the place of the Word of God,

1. The Church of Scotland stands within the Reformed tradition, with respect to its understanding of Scripture.
2. The Church of Scotland affirms the principle of the primacy of Scripture.
3. The Church of Scotland acknowledges that the Word of God "is contained in the Scriptures of the Old and New Testaments".

That having been said, it was acknowledged within the Dialogue Group that the precise sense in which the Word of God was "contained in the Scriptures of the Old and New Testaments" remains open to a variety of interpretations within the Church of Scotland.

The Constitution of the Free Church of Scotland

Two important features of the Free Church's constitution, in its own view and in the view of civil law, are the *Confession of Faith* and the Questions and Formula answered and signed by office-bearers at their ordination.

Office-bearers answer affirmatively the questions:

1. Do you believe the Scripture of the Old and New Testaments to be the Word of God, and the only rule of faith and manners?
2. Do you sincerely own and believe the whole doctrine contained in the *Confession of Faith*… to be founded on the World of God…?

The Free Church affirms chapter I, Section 2 *Confession*:

> Under the name of Holy Scripture, or the Word of God written, are now contained all the Books of the Old and New Testaments… all of which are given by inspiration of God, to be the rule of faith and life…

In addition, it is pointed out that the *Confession* also states:

> The authority of the holy Scripture, for which it ought to be believed and obeyed, depends not upon the testimony of any man or church, but wholly upon God (who is truth itself), the author thereof; and therefore is to be received, because it is the Word of God. (I.4)

From this basis the Free Church holds, as a constitutional principle, that the Scriptures are the Word of God. It takes issue with the Church of Scotland position stated in the *Articles Declaratory* that it "receives the Word of God which is contained in the Scriptures of the Old and New Testaments as its supreme rule of faith and life: and avows the fundamental doctrines of the Catholic faith founded thereupon", because this can be interpreted to mean that there may be Scripture that is not the Word of God. It understands that when the framers of the *Shorter Catechism* used the phrase "contained in the Scriptures of the Old and New Testaments" they would not have meant anything different from what was said in the *Larger Catechism* ("The holy scriptures of the Old

6.3

and New Testament are the Word of God"), or that they used the word "contained" in a different sense from that in the *Confession* when it says that all books of the Old and New Testaments "are contained" under the name of Holy Scripture.

While welcoming the references in the Church of Scotland paper to those sections of the *Confession* which relate to the authority and infallibility of Scripture, the Free Church response highlights the area of the identity of Scriptures with the Word of God as the area of profound disagreement. "The Church of Scotland says they are not identical and the Free Church says they are." From the Free Church perspective this question is foundational. If all of Scripture is not "God-breathed" (*ie* the Word of God) all Christian doctrine is uncertain.

The Free Church is not reassured by the non-negotiable statement of faith in the first *Article Declaratory*. It welcomes the positive statements on the Trinity and the Person of Christ. On the other hand it finds the phrase "glorifying in His cross and resurrection" too vague a statement which says nothing about the meaning of these events whether by way of atonement, redemption or justification.

Summary of points of agreement and disagreement
The following points emerge from the discussion on the Constitutional positions of the two churches in respect to the Word of God and Holy Scripture.

A. Areas of Agreement
1. Both churches stand within the Reformed tradition with respect to their understanding of Scripture in that both churches affirm the primacy of Scripture.
2. Both churches draw on the doctrinal statements of the *Westminster Confession of Faith* as their principal subordinate standard.

B. Areas of Disagreement
1. Both churches acknowledge the constant and unbroken relationship between the Word of God and Scripture but the Church of Scotland's relationship to both Scripture and the *Confession* are defined within *Declaratory Articles* whereas in the Free Church they are not.
2. The Church of Scotland allows "liberty of opinion" in relation to matters that do not enter into the substance of the faith. The Free Church's problem with this is that "the substance of the faith" is not defined.

Relations at Local Level
The doctrinal discussions can be seen against the background of good relations that are developing between local ministers and their congregations. Presbyteries in the North and West were invited to give a picture of what was happening on the ground. The following responses were received:

1. Presbytery of Caithness
Wick – Pultneytown and Thrumster – relations cordial. There were some differences which were respected *eg* the Free Church insistence on the use of Psalms only in worship. This presented problems when joint services were suggested. The local Free Church minister (together with the Baptist Church and Salvation Army) took part in the Good Friday March and Open Air Service. The parish minister felt this was an important public witness of the unity of denominations in Wick. The Free Church minister also attended joint meetings for ministers in the area. Free Church members attend special events in other churches and members of other denominations accept the Free Church's invitations to attend their special Psalmody evenings.

Lybster – The Free Church Missionary and the Church of Scotland Deacon conducted the Remembrance Service together annually and took it in turns to visit Dunbeath and Lybster primary schools. They have on occasion conducted funerals together. They organise a holiday club together and have a good personal relationship.

Thurso – The Church of Scotland and Free Church of Scotland ministers are part of the chaplaincy team at the High School. They meet up at a regular fraternal, together with other ministers and priests in Thurso. Apart from the annual ecumenical Remembrance Day Service, the Free Church is not involved locally in church services with the CofS. However, the relationship is cordial.

Reay – All three Free Church ministers attend a monthly prayer meeting in Reay which is also attended by the local Church of Scotland minister. When Luis Palau comes to Inverness a local one-day event is being planned involving the Free Church, the Church of Scotland and other denominations.

2. Presbytery of Sutherland

"There is a slow, though sometimes tentative, improvement in relations with the Free Church – partly because the division in the Free Church some years ago removed the more conservative element to the Free Church Continuing."

3. Presbytery of Lochcarron and Skye

Relations are good in the **Lochalsh** area. There are often midweek joint meetings in each other's halls followed by the usual tea/coffee and food. Meetings are intimated in each other's churches. In one part of Lochalsh the Free Church has no building and use the Lochalsh Church after the Church of Scotland service on a Sunday morning. The Church of Scotland minister has conducted worship in Gaelic in the Free Church and the Free Church minister has conducted a Preparatory Service in the Lochalsh church. They hope that the good relationship will continue.

Strath and Sleat: there are joint monthly joint services with the Free Church in the parish, (alternating monthly in the two churches premises). Elders and other members take services in the Free Churches in Skye and area. There is an annual Joint Elders' Conference. There has been a Joint visitation (over two years) to every home in the Strath and Sleat parish, which both churches serve.

Two joint services bringing both the **Poolewe & Aultbea** and the **Gairloch** Free Church congregations together with the **Gairloch & Dundonnell** Church of Scotland will take place on Sunday 31 August. There will be a visiting preacher over that weekend, Dr Sam Gordon, who used to be a broadcaster with Trans World Radio and has written several Bible commentaries. There will also have been a shared community evening on Saturday 30th involving the Inverness and District Male Gospel Choir, raising funds for Blythswood in the process.

4. Presbytery of Uist

Benbecula – enjoy extremely cordial relations with the Free Church. Each month the Free Church minister joins the Church of Scotland ministers from Benbecula and North Uist for a ministers' fraternal and prayer time. Church of Scotland members often join with the Free Church for missionary, evangelistic and/or prayer meetings in FC centre. The Free Church minister preaches annually in Church of Scotland – Gaelic Communion preparatory service (with Free Church elder precenting); the Church of Scotland minister has preached in Free Church. The Free Church, Roman Catholic and the Church of Scotland clergy work jointly as chaplains in the local Primary and Secondary schools (on rota). The Free Church, Roman Catholic and Church of Scotland plan/lead annual community Christmas carol service in local primary school.

Carinish – The Free Church minister form Benbecula and South Uist preached at the communion services. The Church of Scotland buildings were used for the induction and ordination of the Free Church minister for North Uist, Grimsay and Berneray. There is a joint weekly Youth Mission with North Uist "Urban Saints" which includes leaders and workers from both churches. Church of Scotland ministers meet with Free Church ministers on a monthly basis for fraternal rotating around different churches and manses. The Church of Scotland minister has been the guest preacher in the North Uist Free Church preparatory service.

Berneray and Lochmaddy – theological compatibility is noted, making co-operation possible. The Church of

Scotland ministers have a prayer time, usually once a month with the minister(s) of the Free Church. In relation to more practical aspects, ministers, elders and members seek to support each other at times of funerals, and they work together with "Urban Saints". When needed, there are several within the Free Church who are willing to help out with pulpit supply.

Manish-Scarista – Relations are good. There has been a marked improvement in this area since the Free Church split a few years ago. At a personal level relationship between the ministers are very good. The Free Church minister has preached twice during a recent Church of Scotland Communion Season. (He also preached at the recent Tarbert (Harris) Communion Season). The Church of Scotland minister was invited to preach at Free Church service but unable to accept because of prior commitment. In acts of worship at times of death and the funeral services, elders and members of both denominations support each other by helping with leading of prayers and precenting. "Urban Saints" meet weekly in the Church Hall in Leverburgh and it is led by the Free Church minister.

5. Presbytery of Lewis

Back – Church of Scotland ministers are now being asked regularly as supply and guest preachers in the Free Church congregation.

Knock – There is a Joint Youth Program: *Point to Life*, including input from Church of Scotland and the Free Church. The Free Church minister conducted a joint Remembrance Day service.

Ness – The relationship is cordial and the Free Church minister recently took part in a Remembrance Day service with the Church of Scotland. The ministers also invite each other to participate in funeral services.

Carloway – There is a joint youth programs, a joint youth worker and joint "congregational fellowship" at communion times

Stornoway – Relationships are cordial. There is joint participation in funerals. A ministers' fraternal has been started.

Barvas – The relationship is cordial and there is joint participation in funerals.

Kinloch – during a recent vacancy, the Free Church minister regularly conducted mid week services in the Church of Scotland congregation. Relations are cordial.

Lochs – There is regular interaction between the two ministers and the relationship is cordial.

Scalpay – The Free Church gets the use of the Church of Scotland building and the relationship is cordial.

Where from here?

There is no question that the two churches regard each other as belonging to the Church of Jesus Christ. However, it seems that the points of divergence in relation to the identity of Scripture and the Word of God remain a serious stumbling block to co-operation, far less uniting. The words of the late John Murray of Westminster Theological Seminary provide a continuing challenge to the two churches:

> Though the diversity which manifests itself in differentiating historical developments might appear to make ecclesiastical union inadvisable or even perilous in certain cases, yet the biblical evidence in support of union is so plain that any argument to the contrary, however plausible, must be false. (*Murray, 1976: Vol. 1 269f.*)

Both churches acknowledge that the continued divisions within the Presbyterian family in Scotland are a scandal and that the existence of separate congregations within the same community, with ministers who have sometimes little to distinguish them theologically, is a situation that is both unsustainable and gives a bad witness to the world. Nevertheless, while it is clear that co-operation will continue to take place and be developed in places where local congregations and ministers have a shared view of Scripture, it will take sensitivity to work out areas where the two churches can work together both locally and nationally on a broader front.

Bibliography:

Mair, W. (1904) *Digest of Church Laws* (3rd ed.) (Edinburgh: Wm. Blackwood & Sons).

Murray, D.M. (2000) *Rebuilding the Kirk: Presbyterian Reunion in Scotland 1909-1929* (Edinburgh: Scottish Academic Press).

Murray, J. (1976) *Collected Writings of John Murray* (Edinburgh: Banner of Truth Trust).

Sjölinder, R. (1962) *Presbyterian Reunion in Scotland 1907-1921* (Edinburgh: T&T Clark).

Weatherhead, J.L. (1997) *The Constitution and Laws of the Church of Scotland* (Edinburgh: The Church of Scotland).

Wotherspoon, H.J. & Kirkpatrick, J.M. (1960) *A Manual of Church Doctrine according to the Church of Scotland* (2nd ed.) (London: OUP).

APPENDIX V
DELEGATES TO OTHER CHURCHES

The following have been appointed as delegates to the Assemblies, Synods and Conferences of other Churches:-

Presbyterian Church in Ireland – The Moderator, Chaplain and Elder

Presbyterian Church of Wales – The Moderator

Church of England – Rev D Galbraith

United Reformed Church Scotland Synod – Rev I Wilkie

Scottish Episcopal Church – Rev M Pearson

Methodist Synod – Mrs M Crawford

United Free Church of Scotland – Rev L Schluter

Baptist Union of Scotland – Rev A Kerr

APPENDIX VI
ECUMENICAL BODIES

The following serve on Assemblies and Committees of the ecumenical bodies of which the Church is a member:-

World Council of Churches

Central Committee	Mr G McGeoch
Faith and Order Commission	Rev Dr P H Donald

World Alliance of Reformed Churches

Executive Committee	Rev A G Horsburgh

World Alliance of Reformed Churches/ Reformed Ecumenical Council

Uniting General Council (2010)	Rev Dr A Falconer, Rev A G Horsburgh, Very Rev Dr S M Kesting, Mr I McLarty, Rev L Schluter

Conference of European Churches

13th Assembly (July 2009)	Dr A Elliot OBE, Very Rev Dr S M Kesting, Rev Dr J L McPake, Miss A Watson
Central Committee	Dr A Elliot OBE
Church and Society Commission	Rev Dr D Sinclair

Community of Protestant Churches in Europe (Leuenberg Church Fellowship)

Rev Dr J L McPake

Churches Together in Britain and Ireland

Forum of Senior Representatives	Very Rev Dr F A J Macdonald

Action of Churches Together in Scotland

Members' Meeting

Voting member: Convener of the Committee on Ecumenical Relations (alternate voting member: Convener of the Council of Assembly), non-voting members: Secretaries of the Mission and Discipleship Council, Church and Society Council and the Ecumenical Officer

(alternate non-voting members: Secretary of the Ministries Council, General Secretary of the Guild and the Moderator of the Youth Assembly)

6.3

Networks:		*Mission*	Mrs L Dunnett,
Church Life	Rev R Dobie, Rev A Paton,		Miss L Hamilton-Messer,
	Rev F Penny, Rev N Robb,		Rev A Millar, Rev J Reid,
	Rev A Scobie, Mrs N Summers		Mr J K Thomson
Church and Society	Rev E Aitken, Mrs S Aitken,	*Finance Committee*	Mr A McDowall
	Mrs H Fairgrieve, Mr G Lumb,		
	Dr M Macdonald, Mr A Shaw,	*Network of Ecumenical*	
	Mr J Thomson, Mrs A Twaddle,	*Women in Scotland*	Rev V Allen, Mrs K McPherson
	Mr R Whiteman		
		Joint Liturgical Group	The Very Rev Dr G I Macmillan,
Faith Studies	Rev A Birss, Rev E Cranfield,		Rev N Robb
	Rev N Robb, Rev J Scott,		
	Mrs M Whyte		

APPENDIX VII
CONTRIBUTIONS TO ECUMENICAL BODIES

	2009 £	2010 £
Churches Together in Britain and Ireland	176,000	15,000
Action of Churches Together in Scotland		160,000
Churches Together in England		1,000
World Council of Churches	45,382	46,000
World Alliance of Reformed Churches	24,057	24,400
Conference of European Churches	21,286	21,600
	266,725	268,000

PROPOSED DELIVERANCE

The General Assembly
1. Receive the Report.
2. Pass an Act amending Act VIII 2003 (as previously amended) as set out in Appendix I (Section 4.1).
3. Adopt the Overture anent Discipline of Elders, Readers and Office-bearers, as set out in Appendix II, and transmit the same to Presbyteries under the Barrier Act, directing that returns be sent in to the Principal Clerk not later than 31 December 2009 (Section 4.2).
4. Note the Revised Guidelines on Arbitration, set out in Appendix III (Section 5).
5. Approve the Guidance Note on Voting in Cases, set out in Section 6 of the Report.
6. Pass an Act amending Acts VI 1997 (as amended) and VI 2007, as set out in Appendix IV to the Report (Section 7).
7. Commend the new Trustees Indemnity Insurance scheme and instruct all Financial Boards to participate in it (Section 10).

REPORT

6.4

Church-State questions

1. Act of Settlement
The Committee has been monitoring recent debate surrounding aspects of the Act of Settlement and the 1707 Union. The Solicitor has kept abreast of the introduction of the Royal Marriages and Succession to the Crown (Prevention of Discrimination) Bill.

2. Jurisdictions Working Group
2.1 The Committee maintains a small working group with the remit to monitor the current operation of the Church of Scotland Act 1921, especially in relation to developments in civil law, both through legislative change and relevant case law. The Group monitors cases affecting other denominations, in order to advise the Committee and the wider Church if judgements are made that would affect the Church of Scotland in areas like employment law or the guaranteeing of human rights in the field of religion.

2.2 During the past year, the main work of the Group has consisted of a conversation with the Office of the Scottish Charity Regulator, to clarify the relationship between the operation of the Church's independent spiritual jurisdiction in terms of the 1921 Act, and OSCR's implementation of its responsibilities in an appropriate and proportionate way in terms of the Charities and Trustee Investment (Scotland) Act 2005. The group believes that there is no threat in the 2005 legislation to the right of the Church to make decisions in the area of the spiritual jurisdiction subject to no appeal to civil authority.

Church Law questions

3. Resourcing and teaching:
3.1 Advanced Church Law Course
The Depute Clerk, with assistance from several Councils and Committees, ran this three-day course in the summer of 2008. The course was designed for people

whose involvement with Church law and procedure went beyond the content of the basic course delivered to all probationers, and it was attended by almost all of the many new Presbytery Clerks who have taken up appointment in the last two years, along with other individuals identified by their Presbyteries as having possible future roles in implementing Church law at quite an expert level. Topics covered included appraisal and vacancies, education for the ministry, and complaints and discipline of ministers. The Committee believes that in another two or three years there may be demand for the course to be refined and repeated for a fresh group.

3.2 The Legal Systems of Scottish Churches

As reported last year, Dundee University Press invited the Committee to produce a small volume for a legally-aware readership, describing the system of Courts and Commissions of the Church and their operation and giving guidance especially to those representing parties in judicial business. At the time of writing the manuscript has been completed, and includes a substantial contribution on the legal system of the Scottish Episcopal Church, and a much shorter note about the Roman Catholic Church (shorter because it is very unusual for secular lawyers to appear before their Tribunal in Scotland, so the contribution had a much more limited purpose). By the time of the General Assembly, the marketing of the book will be under way, and its availability will be intimated to Commissioners.

3.3 McGillivray: Introduction to Practice and Procedure

The Church owes a great debt of gratitude to the former Depute Clerk of the General Assembly and Clerk of Edinburgh Presbytery, Rev Gordon McGillivray, for many years of teaching Church law to candidates for the ministry. This he did originally in his lecturing role with New College students, and latterly through his loose-leaf *Introduction* which has provided a very reliable successor

to Dr Herron's earlier publications, but with the significant advantage of annual updating of the text. This has been an unselfish labour of love by Mr McGillivray.

Upon Mr McGillivray's retirement from this publishing task last year, the Clerks have taken over the project and are continuing it as an entirely web-based resource. Subject matter experts amongst the Church's senior staff will assist in providing and updating material year by year, and users will find a complete text on the web-site each summer, which they may use on-line or download in its entirety. Using the text on-screen, rather than printing it out, has the additional advantage that computers' 'find' functions provide a much more thorough method of navigation than any printed index; and this is further assisted by the extensive Table of Contents.

These materials now constitute the most reliable and up-to-date source of everyday, routine Church procedure. Non-routine questions are best directed to Presbytery Clerks or, where appropriate, the Assembly's Clerks.

4. Proposed Legislation:

4.1 Ballot-papers in vacancies

The legislation regulating vacancy procedure (Act VIII 2003 as amended) provides the form of voting paper to be used when electing a minister. At present the Act gives the Interim Moderator no discretion in a situation where the intention of a voter is obvious but the voting paper has not been filled in exactly according to the instructions printed on its face. An amending Act, printed at Appendix I to this Report, provides a more sensible flexibility and discretion to the Interim Moderator and Kirk Session, and tidies up the wording printed on the Voting Paper generally.

4.2 Discipline of elders, office-bearers and readers

4.2.1 Staff in the Principal Clerk's Office and Law Department are asked from time to time to advise on the procedure to be followed where an office-bearer is accused of behaving in an inappropriate manner, which requires action to be taken by the Church.

4.2.2 This area has not received the same attention in recent years as the equivalent question relating to clergy, which was addressed principally through Act III 2001 (as now amended). The position is complex and possibly rather inconsistent in some areas, which can present difficulties for officers of the lower courts. Inconsistency is perceived especially in the following three areas:

4.2.3 Court of first instance

The choice of court of first instance is determined by the nature of the offence committed. If the presenting issue involves a 'dispute or disturbance' in the congregation and an elder appears to be involved, the Kirk Session must report the matter to the Presbytery, which becomes the initiating authority (Act III 2000 s.38). If the presenting issue involves apparent 'bullying' or 'discrimination', the case is regulated by Act IV or V (respectively) of 2007 and handled throughout by the Presbytery. In all other cases, however, the Kirk Session would appear to remain the court of first instance, and the relevant legislation would appear to be the Form of Process (Act XI 1707) and the related Act XIX of 1889: the former of these is laid out in no modern textbook while the latter appears as an Appendix in Dr Weatherhead's *The Constitution and Laws of the Church of Scotland*. The Kirk Session would appear to remain the court of first instance in, for instance, a situation of gross immorality by an elder or other office-bearer, or where he or she has been convicted of a very serious criminal offence. In such circumstances, it is likely that a Kirk Session may feel diffident and possibly unsure how to proceed, although it would probably rely on common sense, good advice and local wisdom.

4.2.4 Relationship between courts

Cox's *Practice and Procedure in the Church of Scotland* complicates things further by suggesting some rules of process for those cases which do belong to the Kirk Session. Where the accused is willing to submit to discipline, however serious the offence, the Session is meant to issue the case in its entirety. In a situation where the alleged offence is serious and not admitted, the Session is to refer it to the Presbytery, which in turn authorises the Session to proceed to proof (a trial before the court of which the accused is a member, something the Church abandoned in respect of ministers and some others in 2001). The Session, having fulfilled this part of the process, should then refer the matter back to the Presbytery for the imposition of censure. Dr Weatherhead (p63) wisely suggests that the Kirk Session in such difficult cases will probably use the mechanism of Reference to move the whole process up to the Presbytery; and while most Presbyteries might agree that was the correct thing to do, they might also feel rather inadequate to the task themselves.

4.2.5 Censures

The most recent summary of the censures available in general disciplinary cases is provided by Dr Weatherhead, whose list may be paraphrased thus:

- repentance by the guilty party, to which the relevant court would make appropriate response
- resignation by the guilty party
- suspension pending repentance
- deposition from office.

The use of the word 'office' is always rather problematic: some people understand by it the occupation of a particular active role, and others would understand it to mean the holding of a more general status, like that of minister or elder, which does not of itself imply the occupation of any particular role. It is not obvious which is meant here.

A more satisfying list was devised during the framing of Acts IV and V 2007:

- instruction to the Respondent, on pain of guilt of contumacy where the instruction is not fulfilled
- reprimand, probably accompanied by counsel
- removal from office
- removal of status.

Here the use of 'office' is clearer, because it is separated from the question of status.

The latter list seems preferable, because it gives the court a range of disposals, none of which depends on the prior action of the Respondent. The older list is premised on the behaviour of the guilty party in three of its four options.

4.2.6   Act IV 2007

The Committee looked more generally at Act IV 2007 anent Bullying in seeking a way to clarify this somewhat obscure area of Church law. Act IV is clearly modelled to some extent on Act III 2001 anent Discipline of Ministers (and others), but has been adapted to allow for the fact that individual Respondents will be volunteers with no professional or patrimonial interest to be considered. It describes a robust investigatory process, opportunity where appropriate for mediation, adequate opportunity for the statement of defence, location of the disposal of the case and its censure at Presbytery level, limitation of the grounds of appeal and a clear statement that the Church should not be required to fund the process.

The Committee believes that Act IV can be used as a model for a more general process for the discipline of elders, readers and office-bearers. In particular, the Committee believes it is time to remove any remaining doubt and locate all such cases with Presbytery as the court of first instance. The Committee also believes that it is highly desirable to have a single type of process and range of censures for as many types of case as possible.

4.2.7   Readers

The Committee takes this opportunity to include the office of reader in this legislation. They are not mentioned in Act III 2001. Most of them are elders, and therefore will be subject to the new legislation in that capacity. However, some readers are not elders, and in any case an allegation may arise out of the exercise of the office of the readership. Since the new legislation re-locates the court of first instance from the Kirk Session to the Presbytery,

and since readers are accountable in that capacity to the Presbytery, the new Act would resolve the question of where an allegation should be directed in the case of a reader who is also an elder.

4.2.8   Overture anent Discipline of Elders, Readers and Office-bearers

The Committee therefore presents an Overture under the Barrier Act, which is set out in Appendix II of the Report. It contains many of the provisions of Act IV 2007 along with some provisions from Act III 2001. It does not attempt to incorporate the whole terms of Acts IV or V 2007, because they deal with more specific types of mischief, and in any case they apply not only to individuals but also to Church courts and committees.

4.3   Clerking of Commissions

The General Assembly currently has three Commissions acting with devolved powers to hear most of the Church's judicial cases, especially Appeals. The Judicial Commission is regulated by Act II 1988, the Commission of Assembly by Act VI 1997 and the Ministries Appeals Panel by Act VI 2007. Act II 1988 provides for the appointment of a Clerk to the Judicial Commission in the event that neither of the Assembly Clerks is available. However the Ministries Appeals Panel has expressed some concern that no equivalent provision exists in Act VI 2007, and that a potential difficulty is placed on its work. The Committee agrees with this concern, observing that provisions exist to cover the duties of Procurator and Solicitor in the event of vacancy between Assemblies, but no general provision in respect of Clerks. The Committee proposes the amendment contained in Appendix III, which extends the solution contained in Act II 1988 to Act VI 2007, and extends it also to Act VI 1997 to benefit the Commission of Assembly in exactly the same way.

5.   Arbitration

5.1 Last year the Committee reported that it had established a small working group to review the use of arbitration when local parties are unable to resolve the choice of buildings to be used following readjustment. The Group was convened by the Rev Dr Ian McLean, former Vice-Convener of the Legal Questions Committee and comprised representatives of that Committee, the Committee on Church Art and Architecture, the Central Property Department, the Planning and Deployment Task Group of the Ministries Council, the General Trustees and individuals with considerable experience of conducting arbitrations.

5.2 In his *The Constitution and Laws of the Church of Scotland* James Weatherhead observes: "The best advice to congregations and presbyteries in this matter is that congregations should not agree to a Basis with an arbitration clause if they are doing so only in the belief that the arbiters will choose their own building; and are not really prepared to accept the possibility of a different decision; and presbyteries should be careful about advising an arbitration clause if they suspect that such an attitude is prevalent." The fact is that this good advice is frequently ignored and, while the outcome of the majority of arbitrations is accepted, in some cases it is vehemently rejected with very damaging consequences for local communities.

5.3 Arbitration does, however, appear to be the only practical solution where there is local deadlock on the questions of buildings. Accordingly, the Committee has expanded the preliminary advice it offered last year into a set of guidelines which can be made available where arbitration is being considered. The Committee further considered that were arbiters to be selected for each case from an Assembly appointed panel that might also add weight and authority to their determinations.

5.4 The Guidelines are set out in Appendix IV and the Committee commends them to the Assembly for approval.

6. Guidance on voting in cases

The Committee believes there is exists some uncertainty about voting during appeal cases, especially those heard by the Commission of Assembly.

It is a well-established tradition in the courts of the Church that no motion is accepted which is the direct negative of an existing motion or counter-motion before the Court. The prevailing motion is put 'for or against' at the very end of the debate, which gives opportunity for the Court to support its direct negative. The effect of such a negative vote is that the Court has effectively done nothing on the issue, even despite quite a lengthy debate on several motions; and in that case the *status quo,* as it pertained before the appeal and if it can be clearly identified, continues in force.

There has been a tendency in Commission meetings for only one motion (in favour of one or other party) to be moved, but for some members of the Commission to vote against it. Assuming that no-one in the Commission is intending that no decision should be arrived at by that body, it has to be inferred that those individuals are intending to support the other party. However, no motion has been proposed in support of that other party. Happily there has been no case in which those voting against the motion have prevailed, since in that case the Commission of Assembly could be interpreted as having failed to resolve the dispute before it in either direction.

The Committee suspects there may be some confusion between a new motion which is the direct **opposite** of an existing motion, and a new motion which is the direct **negative** of an existing one. Where a member of any Court of Commission hearing a case wishes to support one particular party at the voting stage, it is necessary for him/her to ensure there is a suitable, positive motion (or counter-motion) to support. If there is only one motion available in a judicial process, it will normally be the case that the voting body is giving itself the choice of doing that one thing, or doing nothing at all; and while that is very often a legitimate choice when faced with a legislative or executive decision, it is rarely a legitimate

6.4

outcome in an appeal situation where the dispute must be resolved somehow.

The Committee hopes the General Assembly will share its interpretation, so that this note may be used as guidance in all those Courts and Commissions hearing cases.

Civil Law questions

7.　Interfaith Legal Advisors Network

In the last year, the Convener attended the two further meetings of the Interfaith Legal Adviser Network, which was established in December 2007 by Cardiff Law School's Centre of Law and Religion. The Network includes representatives from UK Christian denominations as well as Jewish, Hindu, Sikh, Muslim and Humanist participants. The topics considered by the Network included interfaith and interdenominational marriages, the impact of the Equality Act (particularly in the field of discrimination), ongoing developments in Charity law and arbitration and recognition of frameworks within faith groups as a means of alternative dispute resolution.

8.　Law Commission – Unincorporated Associations

The Scottish Law Commission has undertaken a consultation on the subject of Unincorporated Associations, and the Church retains this form of status in civil law. The Committee has submitted a response, drafted by the Procurator with assistance from the Solicitor of the Church.

9.　Personal liability of Kirk Session and Financial Board members

The General Assembly of 2007 approved a statement that the charity trustees of a congregation comprise the parish minister and elders who sit on the Kirk Session and also – if there is a separate Financial Board – the members of the Board (however termed). This coupled with the enactment of the Charities and Trustees Investment Act 2005 which "coined" the term "charity trustee" has, perhaps naturally, produced considerable apprehension among some office bearers as to what liabilities, financial and other they might potentially incur. Although the Committee is not aware of any case where a Church of Scotland office-bearer has been sued in a personal capacity, it accepts that, given our increasingly litigious culture and the overall increase in regulation to which congregations are subject, such a risk cannot be discounted. It has accordingly reviewed the insurances carried by congregations and investigated with the Church of Scotland Insurance Company ("COSIC"), the availability of Trustee Indemnity insurance. Following discussions with the main providers of this type of insurance, a scheme has been devised which will provide cover at a very reasonable cost for all those working for a congregation in a voluntary capacity against any claim made against them in a personal capacity. Any damages awarded against an office bearer as a result of a wrongful act carried out in that capacity and also the cost of defending the claim will be covered. Also covered will be costs incurred in obtaining legal advice and representation in the defence of any criminal proceedings in respect of environmental matters or for government investigations of any kind. As is usual with such policies penalties by way of civil or criminal fines are not however covered. The level of indemnity for each claim will be £500,000 with an aggregate limit under the policy of £5m. With all congregations participating, the premium per congregation is very substantially reduced compared to congregations seeking equivalent cover on an individual basis. It is therefore proposed that, as with public liability and office bearers breach of duty cover, the insurance be made mandatory which it is anticipated will result in the premium per congregation (including tax) being less than £35 per annum. Further details of the policy terms will be made available to congregations by COSIC.

APPENDIX I
ACT AMENDING ACT VIII 2003 ANENT VACANCY PROCEDURE

Edinburgh, XX May 2009, Sess. YY

The General Assembly hereby enact and ordain that Act VIII 2003 as amended shall be further amended as follows:

1. By the addition of a new sub-section 23(3) to read as follows:

    "A voting-paper shall only be considered as spoilt and the vote not counted where the intention of the voter is unclear, and in no other circumstances. It shall be for the Kirk Session, on the recommendation of the Interim Moderator, to determine whether the intention of the voter is clear."

    with consequent re-numbering of sub-sections (3)-(5) as (4)-(6).

2. By the amendment of Schedule I to read:

"I   VOTING-PAPER – Section 23

| FOR Electing [*Name*] | |
| AGAINST Electing [*Name*] | |

Directions to Voters – If you are in favour of electing [*Name*] put a cross (x) on the upper right-hand space. If you are not in favour of electing [*Name*] put a cross (x) in the lower right-hand space. Mark your voting-paper in this way with a cross, and put no other mark on your voting-paper or your vote may not be counted.

Note: The Directions to Voters must be printed prominently on the face of the voting-paper"

APPENDIX II
OVERTURE ANENT DISCIPLINE OF ELDERS, READERS AND OFFICE-BEARERS

The General Assembly adopt the Overture the tenor whereof follows, and transmit the same to Presbyteries under the Barrier Act, directing that returns be sent in to the Principal Clerk not later than 31 December 2009.

The General Assembly, with the consent of a majority of Presbyteries, enact and ordain as follows:

1. For the purposes of this Act:
    (a) 'disciplinary offence' shall mean:
        (i) conduct which is declared censurable by the Word of God, Act of the General Assembly or established custom of the Church or
        (ii) a breach of a lawful order of any court of the Church;
    (b) 'Respondent' shall for the purposes of this Act only mean an elder, reader or other office-bearer against whom a complaint has been made;
    (c) 'office-bearer' shall for the purposes of this Act only mean an individual who serves on a Congregational Board, Deacons' Court or Board of Management, or any other body deemed by the Presbytery to form part of the governance arrangements of the congregation, or on any committee of any of these bodies or of a Kirk Session or Presbytery, and shall for the avoidance of doubt include all Clerks and Treasurers whether or not such individuals serve as voting members of any such governing body;
    (d) 'complaint' shall for the purposes of this Act only mean a complaint that a disciplinary offence has been committed;
    (e) 'Presbytery' shall mean the Presbytery in whose bounds is the congregation of which the Respondent is a member;

6.4

(f) 'Committee of Presbytery' shall mean a Committee of Presbytery of three persons, of whom at least one will be a minister and one an elder, and any one of whom may be a member of another Presbytery appointed for this purpose in terms of Act VI 2002 (as amended) section 2.

2. For the avoidance of doubt it is declared that any proceedings under this Act are part of the exclusive jurisdiction of the Church and in accordance with the Articles Declaratory of the Constitution of the Church of Scotland in Matters Spiritual, as hereby interpreted by the Church.

3. For the avoidance of doubt, where an individual against whom an allegation of a disciplinary offence is made is a minister, licentiate, deacon or graduate candidate, the provisions of Act III 2001 anent Discipline of Ministers, Licentiates, Deacons and Graduate Candidates shall apply and the Presbytery shall proceed in terms of that Act.

4. For the avoidance of doubt, where an individual against whom an allegation made in terms of this Act is an employee of any court or committee of the Church, and that allegation arises within the context of that individual's employment, the provisions of civil employment law shall apply.

5. Where an allegation is made to which the provisions of Act IV 2007 anent Bullying apply, this Act may not be invoked.

6. When in the course of proceedings under Act II 1984 (anent Presbytery Visits) or Act I 1988 (anent Congregations in an Unsatisfactory State) the Presbytery receives notice of circumstances indicating that a disciplinary offence may have been committed by an elder, reader or other office-bearer, it may either proceed simultaneously in terms of this Act or resolve to initiate proceedings under this Act following the completion of the existing proceedings.

7. A Presbytery shall initiate investigatory proceedings as soon as it comes to the notice of the Presbytery that the name of a person over whom it has jurisdiction has been placed on the Sex Offenders' Register or included on the Disqualified from Working with Children List (DWCL) kept by Scottish Ministers under Section 1(1) of the Protection of Children (Scotland) Act 2003.

Allegation of Disciplinary Offence

8. On receiving notice of circumstances indicating that a disciplinary offence may have been committed, the Superintendence Committee of the Presbytery shall within seven days appoint a Committee of Presbytery, as defined in section 1(f). For the avoidance of doubt it is expressly declared that in so appointing the Superintendence Committee shall have all the powers of Presbytery.

9. At the request of the Committee of Presbytery, or on its own initiative, the Presbytery may at any time impose upon the Respondent an administrative suspension, being an instruction by the Presbytery to the individual to abstain from the exercise of all the functions of his or her office until proceedings under this Act are finally disposed of; and it shall not constitute a form of censure.

10. If at any stage of proceedings under this Act the Respondent admits to any or all of the allegation(s), and the Committee of Presbytery is willing to accept such an admission and abandon its consideration of any part of the allegation not admitted, the Committee shall, with the consent of the Respondent, produce a Report for Presbytery recommending summary disposal of the case in terms of section 24.

(1) In the event that the Presbytery approves the decision of the Committee, the Presbytery shall

proceed to dispose of the case in terms of section 24.

(2) In the event that the Presbytery does not approve the decision of the Committee, it shall give such further instruction to the Committee as is necessary.

11. The Committee of Presbytery may sist proceedings pending the outcome of any criminal proceedings which relate to the allegation or part of the allegation. Where the allegation made to the Presbytery is the same as a charge brought against the Respondent in criminal law, a criminal conviction shall be deemed by the Presbytery to satisfy the standard of proof, for the purposes of this Act.

12. The Committee of Presbytery shall meet separately with the complainer (if any), with the Respondent, and with any other individuals the Committee believes it appropriate to meet. The purpose of these meetings shall be to ascertain a preliminary account of the circumstances.

13. The Committee of Presbytery shall, if it believes it is appropriate to do so, institute steps to effect mediation or conciliation between or among the parties, and these steps and their outcome shall be reported to Presbytery through the Superintendence Committee. The report to Presbytery need not contain the names of any of the parties in the event that the steps have, in the opinion of the Superintendence Committee, resolved the complaint without the need for further action on the part of the Presbytery.

Investigation of Complaint

14. In the event that the complaint has not been resolved through the steps referred to in section 13, the Committee of Presbytery shall consider whether to carry out an investigation.

15. The Committee of Presbytery shall intimate in writing to the Respondent the nature of the offence alleged and the nature of the evidence purported to exist in support of the allegation and shall offer him or her the opportunity to make any answer thereto, provided that he or she shall not be obliged to answer.

16. In considering whether to carry out an investigation the Committee of Presbytery shall have regard to all the relevant facts, and in particular

(a) the bona fides of any person making an allegation that a disciplinary offence may have been committed;

(b) any representation by the person who is the subject of the allegation;

(c) the preliminary account ascertained in terms of section 12;

and

(d) the gravity of the alleged offence.

For the avoidance of doubt the standard of proof throughout proceedings shall be the balance of probabilities.

17. If the Committee of Presbytery decides that it is not appropriate to carry out an investigation in respect of all or any of the allegations made, the Committee of Presbytery shall report that decision to the Presbytery for its approval.

(1) In the event that the Presbytery approves the decision of the Committee, it shall recall any administrative suspension imposed in terms of section 9. Without prejudice to its existing powers of superintendence, the Presbytery may issue an instruction to the Respondent regarding his or her conduct. Any disobedience of that instruction may be treated as a disciplinary offence.

(2) In the event that the Presbytery does not approve the decision of the Committee, it shall give such further instruction to the Committee as is necessary.

18. If the Committee of Presbytery decides to initiate investigatory proceedings it shall:
    (a) give notice to the Respondent of the decision to investigate the case and of the allegation or allegations which are to be investigated;
    (b) give notice to the Presbytery of that decision and of the allegation or allegations which are to be investigated; and
    (c) give notice to the Legal Questions Committee, which shall appoint a legally qualified assessor to advise the Committee of Presbytery on matters of law and procedure, if it has not done so by invitation at an earlier stage.

19. On receipt of the notice referred to in section 18(b), the Presbytery shall make such arrangements as appear to it appropriate for the provision of pastoral support for the Respondent and his or her family, for the person or persons who made the allegation and for any witnesses within the bounds of the Presbytery.

20. The Committee of Presbytery shall carry out such investigations as it deems necessary to determine whether a disciplinary offence may have been committed, and shall keep a Record Apart of the investigatory proceedings.

21. Before reaching any conclusion, the Committee of Presbytery shall make known to the Respondent the substance of the complaint made against him or her and the nature of the evidence existing in support of the allegation and shall offer him or her the opportunity to make any answer thereto; provided that he or she shall not be obliged to answer.

22. Upon consideration of the allegations and evidence submitted and of any answers given, the Committee of Presbytery shall be entitled to resolve that no further investigation shall be carried out if there is no case to answer. In that event, it shall report to the Presbytery for approval.

(1) In the event that the Presbytery approves the decision of the Committee, it shall recall any administrative suspension imposed in terms of section 9. Without prejudice to its existing powers of superintendence, the Presbytery may issue an instruction to the Respondent regarding his or her conduct. Any disobedience of that instruction may be treated as a disciplinary offence.

(2) In the event that the Presbytery does not approve the decision of the Committee, it shall give such further instruction to the Committee as is necessary.

23. In the event that the Committee of Presbytery decides to proceed further in terms of this Act, it shall bring a report to the Presbytery in numbered paragraphs stating its findings in fact and a recommendation as to disposal of the case. The Presbytery shall hear and dispose of the Report.

Disposal of Complaint

24. The Presbytery shall dispose of the case as seems appropriate to it. The disposals available to the Presbytery shall include the following, and may consist of a combination of elements:
    (a) instruction to any party regarding future conduct; disobedience of such instruction constituting the disciplinary offence of contumacy;
    (b) reprimand, which shall be an expression of disapproval of particular behaviour with counsel regarding future conduct;
    (c) removal from a particular office held, including removal from membership of a Kirk Session;
    (d) deprivation of status as an elder, subject to future restoration by the Presbytery, or or of status as a Reader, subject to future restoration by the Presbytery in consultation with the Ministries Council.

Miscellaneous

25. All decisions made by Presbyteries in terms of this Act shall (subject to the provisions of section 26) be subject to the normal rights of appeal to the Commission of Assembly, but such appeal can be brought only on one or more of the following grounds: (a) that there were irregularities in the process, (b) that the final decision was influenced by incorrect material fact, or (c) that the Committee of Presbytery acted contrary to the principles of natural justice.

26. An appeal brought by any party against any actions taken in terms of sections 8-21 inclusive of this Act shall be regarded as an intermediate appeal and shall not sist the Committee of Presbytery's process.

27. No legal expenses in connection with proceedings under this Act shall be met from the funds of the Church.

Consequential Amendments

28. Act XI 1707 (the 'Form of Process') and Act XIX 1889 (Act on Forms and Procedure in Trial by Libel and in Causes Generally) shall cease to apply in relation to proceedings under this Act.

29. Act III 2000 (Consolidating Act anent Church Courts) (as amended) is hereby further amended by the addition in sub-section 37(1), after 'execution,' of the words 'and, subject to the provisions of Act YYY 2010,'

30. Act VI 2002 anent Co-operation by Presbyteries (as amended) is hereby further amended by the removal in section 2 of the word 'or' and the addition, to the end of section 2, of the words 'or YYY 2010'.

APPENDIX III

ACT AMENDING ACTS VI 1997 ANENT THE COMMISSION OF ASSEMBLY (AS AMENDED) AND VI 2007 ANENT THE MINISTRIES APPEALS PANEL

Edinburgh, xx May 2009, Sess. XX

The General Assembly hereby enact and ordain as follows:

1. Act VI 1997 anent the Commission of Assembly (as amended) is hereby further amended by the re-numbering of section 5 as 5(1) and the addition of a new section 5(2) reading as follows:
"The Clerks of the General Assembly shall act as Clerks to the Commission of Assembly, though not members thereof, but the duties may be carried out by one of them. If neither of them is present, the Commission of Assembly shall appoint a substitute, whether or not a member thereof, to act as Clerk of the Commission during the sittings thereof, and the oath de fideli shall be administered to him or her and recorded."

2. Act VI 2007 anent the Ministries Appeals Panel is hereby amended by the deletion of the final sentence of section 2, the re-numbering of section 2 as 2(1), and the addition of a new section 2(2) reading as follows:
"The Clerks of the General Assembly shall act as Clerks to the Ministries Appeals Panel, though not members thereof, but the duties may be carried out by one of them. If neither of them is present, the Ministries Appeals Panel shall appoint a substitute, whether or not a member thereof, to act as Clerk of the Panel during the sittings thereof, and the oath de fideli shall be administered to him or her and recorded."

6.4

APPENDIX IV
REVISED GUIDELINES FOR ARBITRATIONS

1. It should be clearly understood by all parties that, while external arbiters will give reasons for their decision, that decision is final and binding on the parties.

2. Accordingly the involvement of independent arbiters in deciding the question of buildings following parish appraisal should always be seen as a matter of last resort.

3. No congregation should agree to arbitration unless they are prepared to accept that their building may not be the one chosen.

4. Act VII, 2003 [Section 5(2)] brings consideration of future use of buildings into the Presbytery planning process. Presbyteries should therefore take early opportunity of discussing these matters with the congregations concerned. If thought desirable such discussions could include representatives of the Ministries Council's Planning and Deployment Task Group.

5. Where choices have to be made between or among church buildings it is much to be preferred that the decision should be made by the congregations themselves, in consultation with the Presbytery. Arbitration should always be seen as a last resort.

6. Recognising that local affection for church buildings is such that consideration of their future use raises emotional and pastoral issues every effort should be made to engage effectively with such members of the congregations as are willing to be involved in the process of weighing the options for the future mission of the Church in the area and developing a buildings strategy designed to serve that mission effectively. In this respect it should be noted that the General Trustees are available and willing to give advice and guidance in connection with feasibility studies and buildings surveys. It should be further noted that such advice would require to be given prior to and not as part of any arbitration process.

7. Given the importance of church buildings to the wider community it is also recommended that steps be taken to help that community to understand the issues and the hard choices facing the Church with regard to buildings.

8. Where pastoral efforts to secure local agreement on the building issue have failed the Presbytery may refer the matter to binding arbitration. In doing so the Presbytery should keep in mind the need for continuing pastoral care during the arbitration process.

9. As a precursor to this step the congregations shall be given the opportunity of voting on the Basis of Adjustment which shall include a clause specifying that the choice of buildings will be determined by arbiters.

10. In taking this step the Presbytery should recognise that, in effect, the arbiters' decision is its decision and as binding upon it as upon the congregations in question.

11. Given the importance of the role of Interim Moderators in representing the Presbytery and facilitating the process in a neutral way the Presbytery may wish to consider the appointment of a new Interim Moderator who has not established relationships within the congregation before the matter goes to arbitration.

12. On the report of the Nomination Committee the General Assembly shall appoint a panel of twenty arbiters. For each situation a Convener and Vice-Convener shall be appointed along with three others identified by the Head of the Central Properties

Department. Care will be taken to exclude any potential arbiter who has any connection with the case or is a member of a congregation within the bounds of the relevant Presbytery.

13. Where a Presbytery decides to seek arbitration it shall refer the matter to the Central Properties Department at 121 George Street, Edinburgh which shall appoint a panel in terms of section 12 above.

14. The Central Properties Department will provide literature to the Presbytery for distribution amongst the members of the congregations. This literature, prepared by the Department, will set out clearly what is involved in the arbitration.

15. In addition the Central Properties Department shall advise the Presbytery on the question(s) to be put to the arbiters and the nature of the decisions required of the arbiters, for example, whether is it an option to make continuing use of more than one building; whether it is an option to decide that neither building is suitable; whether the practicalities of disposing of the building not chosen should be addressed.

16. It should be clearly understood by the arbiters that where a determination involves significant building work this should be realistic having regard to the resources available.

17. It shall be open to the Presbytery and congregations to commission survey reports and offer these with such other submissions as are desired to the arbiters. On receiving such documentation from the congregations the arbiters shall be entitled to specify what further information is necessary. Where surveyors are appointed by the Presbytery this should be done on the basis that they survey all relevant buildings and that, in the event of arbitration, these survey reports will be passed to the arbiters.

18. The arbiters shall ensure that the submissions and documentation considered by them are made available to all parties.

19. The arbiters shall give written reasons for their decision within 28 days and that decision shall be final and binding on all the parties.

6.4

SAFEGUARDING COMMITTEE
May 2009

PROPOSED DELIVERANCE

The General Assembly
1. Receive the Report.
2. Instruct Kirk Sessions to adopt and use the Safeguarding Panel Model to manage confidential safeguarding matters. (Appendix 2)
3. Instruct Kirk Sessions to adopt the 'integrating those who pose a risk' policy. (5.1)
4. Instruct the Safeguarding Committee to prepare a Code of Good Practice for integrating those who pose a risk in congregations, and distributed to Kirk Sessions as soon as possible. (5.2)
5. Instruct the Council of Assembly to ensure appropriate financial resources are made available to enact the policies and procedures required by the Protection of Vulnerable Groups (Scotland) Act 2007. (Appendix 1)
6. Encourage Presbyteries to provide appropriate support and resources to their local Safeguarding personnel.

REPORT

1. Introduction

1.1 The Safeguarding Office continues to manage and minimise risk on behalf of the Church of Scotland by developing systems to prioritise the safety of children and vulnerable groups in our congregations as well as responding to legislative demands and ongoing potential developments in safeguarding practice.

1.2 Safeguarding has travelled a significant distance since the office was set up in 2005 marking, as it did, the transition from Child Protection to Safeguarding which in turn had happened because of the rapid and ongoing changes to the legislation introduced by both the Scottish and the United Kingdom Governments. Sometimes it feels as though there is a constant pressure to change, adapt and develop to meet new circumstances and changing attitudes in the light of both legislation and experience on a monthly basis.

1.3 Gerrilyn Smith says *'Sexually abusive behaviour is unacceptable and we all need to do everything we can* *to make sure it is not allowed to flourish. Only organised networks of protecting adults will effectively out manoeuvre sex offenders'*[1] Recognising this the General Assembly has, since the Child Protection Unit was formed in 1997, been both supportive of and encouraging to everyone involved in maintaining the high standards of safeguarding in the Church's congregations.

1.4 The network of safeguarding associated with the church includes Volunteers; Congregational Coordinators; local Safeguarding Panels; Presbytery Contact and Trainers, and indirectly – though essentially – those who allocate budgets and respond with appropriate resources to ensure the task is achievable. The commitment of all of them to safeguarding children and young people cannot be too highly commended. Each person in this Church-wide network, in his or her own way, contributes to making the Church as safe as it can be in a world where

---

[1] Gerrilyn Smith in 'The Protectors' Handbook page 183

there are those who would strive to target, groom and abuse children, young people and adults at risk The Safeguarding Committee is more appreciative of each one of them than words can say.

1.5 The work of the Forgiveness and Proportionality Task Group, the subject of a separate report, has taken much time. The Committee expresses its gratitude to Nigel Robb, Secretary of the Mission and Discipleship's Worship and Doctrine Task Group, and its staff for the significant contribution to the Forgiveness and Proportionality Working Group. Importantly, for the Safeguarding Committee, that task has increased rather than diminished the awareness of the necessity of safeguarding within the Church.

> *"Most People advocate stringent child protection measures in society but they struggle with the principle of establishing them at church. The argument is that we shouldn't need them, God's house is sacred, we might offend someone, we have to show Christ's grace and, anyway, we're all good eggs at church, we wouldn't do such a thing. This mentality is exactly why paedophiles target churches."* [2]

Meantime, the day to day task of protecting children, young people and adults at risk continues through a network of safeguarding that is committed to 'out manoeuvre sex offenders.'

1.6 The task of the Safeguarding Office ensures that, so far as possible, no child or adult should ever be placed in a situation of danger or abuse or of abuse itself. Robust recruitment procedures as well as good links to statutory agencies assist the Safeguarding Office to execute this important task on the Church of Scotland's behalf.

1.7 The 'In the Beginning Bible'[3] tells the story of Jesus' imperative *'Let the children come to me and do not stop*

them' in a dialogue. *'Let them come here,'* said Jesus. *'Jesus,'* the girl asked, *'can children live in God's land too?'* *'Children?'* said Jesus, and he lifted the girl onto his shoulders, *'Children above all are allowed to live in God's land. Because God's land is specially meant for children.'* The values expressed here underpin the Safeguarding role and remit and will continue to do so as the safeguarding task evolves to include all Vulnerable Groups.

1.8 The Safeguarding Office liaises closely with external, statutory agencies to minimize risk within congregations as well as promote the work of the Church of Scotland in this sphere. This continued liaison will be crucial in relation to the monitoring of sex offenders in congregations as highlighted in the Forgiveness and Proportionality report.

2. Administration and Finance

2.1 The network which safeguards children, young people and the vulnerable on behalf of the Church of Scotland is expanding each year. In total we have 1,828 Safeguarding Co-ordinators across Scotland who voluntarily undertake this work.

2.2 Since the 2008 General Assembly the Safeguarding Office has processed 4,346 Disclosure Scotland applications. There have been 27,489 Disclosure Scotland checks processed in total since the introduction in 2003.

2.3 The Safeguarding Advisory Panel has met 5 times over the last year to consider blemished Disclosures (*ie* those containing conviction and non conviction information) with on average six cases being dealt with on each occasion.

2.4 In order to support the Safeguarding Co-ordinators in their work, there were 18 Co-ordinator Training events in 2008.

2.5 The Safeguarding Advisory Panel is piloting a new risk assessment protocol which is being used to consider blemished Disclosure checks. The development and

---

[2] Barbara van Pelt and Erika Cotteleer in 'In the Beginning Bible' page 191
[3] Rebecca Andrews in 'Policing Innocence' page 91

professionalism of existing systems has ensured that a more robust and accountable risk assessment process is in place in advance of the implementation of the Protection of Vulnerable Groups (Scotland) Act 2007 ("the PVG Act").

2.6 The Safeguarding Office deals with numerous enquiries in relation to the practical application of the Disclosure process and training matters. In addition, the Advisory team which consist of the Head and Assistant Head of the Safeguarding Office, deal with between 15 and 20 substantive enquiries per week. These may be general or related to particular situations of risk, and include questions in relation to the implementation of legislation, the application of policy and good practice guidelines as well as questions in relation the potential risk of harm within congregations and liaison with statutory agencies.

2.7 The Safeguarding Office under the legal requirements imposed by the Protection of Children (Scotland) Act 2003 made three referrals to the Disqualified from Working with Children List held by Scottish Ministers since the 2008 General Assembly.

2.8 The Safeguarding Committee has met three times over the last year to provide support and direction to the Safeguarding Office as well as respond to current political developments.

2.9 The Safeguarding Committee continues to be appreciative of the tireless professional support given in a voluntary capacity to the Advisory staff by its former Vice-Convener Ms Anne Black.

2.10 A new logo has been designed to provide a corporate identity for the work of the Safeguarding Office and ensure a professional approach to all external correspondence and training materials.

This logo was launched in the winter 2008.

2.11 As well as other means of communication, the Safeguarding Office also promote the use of their area of the Church's website and regularly post information that may be of interest to Co-ordinators, Trainers and interested colleagues.

2.12 The Safeguarding database was designed and installed in autumn 2008 by the Church of Scotland IT department. This has enabled the Administration staff to streamline and structure the processing of data in advance of the evolving legislative demands. It also ensures the necessary degree of Data Protection security required when handling such sensitive and confidential information.

2.13 In terms of finance, the Safeguarding budget remains healthy as a result of the involvement and support of a vast network of volunteers throughout the Church of Scotland.

2.14 The implementation of the PVG Act anticipated to occur in 2010 which will encompass the safeguarding of protected adults as defined by the Act, as well as children and young people will require an increase in budget expenditure to ensure adequate resources are available to those charged with this additional task.

2.15 Whilst safeguarding finances ended 2008 with a small surplus, due to slightly less expenditure on staffing costs than expected because of staff turnover, it is anticipated that, as a result of changes in legislation, costs will be higher in 2009, because materials will require revision, and in 2010, because additional staff will be needed to handle increased numbers of Disclosure checks.

3. Recruitment and Staffing

3.1 The Safeguarding Office has now reached a full staff contingent having carried two administrative vacancies since February 2008 which were subsequently filled in autumn 2008 by one full-time and two part-time staff.

3.2 This has eased the pressure in terms of handling and processing confidential information within the timescales required by the Central Registered Body in Scotland (CRBS).

3.3 The Safeguarding Office also continues to process the Disclosure Scotland checks on behalf of the Boys and Girls Brigade in Scotland.

3.4 As part of the third phase of the scoping exercise undertaken in 2005 which looked at the Safeguarding Office becoming a church wide resource, the Safeguarding Office now administer checks on behalf of the Ministries Council as part of its rolling process of Disclosure checking. This covers all those involved in the recognised Ministries of the Church.

3.5 As well as this, it is anticipated that the Protection of Vulnerable Groups (Scotland) Act 2007 (PVG) legislation will require Disclosure checks for all those working with vulnerable groups as defined by legislation. This has implications for the Safeguarding Office as well as staffing and the resources to undertake the increase in workload.

3.6 It is anticipated that new Training Materials will be devised as a consequence of the forthcoming changes in legislation as well as new Handbooks, Fact Files and Policy documents.

3.7 The Safeguarding Advisory staff is involved in consultation with the Scottish Government via the Voluntary Sector Issues group and is instrumental in the shaping and subsequent implementation of the PVG Act in relation to vulnerable groups. The Committee hopes that a proportional response can be achieved which also reflects the needs of all faith groups. A summary of the new Scheme which the Act will introduce is contained in Appendix 1 of this report.

3.8 The Safeguarding Office promotes a robust recruitment protocol which includes two references, a job description, an interview as well as a Disclosure Scotland check. This provides a degree of protection for all those recruiting staff into child care positions and minimise opportunities for those who wish to have access to children or adults at risk with ulterior motives.

3.9 For a full list of child care positions where this recruitment protocol applies, please refer to the list of designated child care positions in the 2003 blue book. This complies with civil and criminal legislation as well as Church law.

3.10 The Safeguarding Office would wish to convey their appreciation and thanks to all the Volunteer Co-ordinators who give their time and attention to ensuring that the systems in place are fit for purpose and make the Church of Scotland a safer place.

4. Training

4.1 The 2008 Safeguarding Trainers' conference was held in October in Tulliallan Police College. The title of the conference was the "Spirit Level" to reflect the theme of balance and proportionality in the safeguarding task.

4.2 Presbytery Contacts attended the full conference this year which reflects their increasingly important role within the Safeguarding team developing in many Presbyteries.

4.3 Each Presbytery is encouraged to have a Safeguarding Presbytery Contact. There are eight Presbyteries without a Safeguarding Trainer. 16 of the 44 Safeguarding Presbytery Contacts are also Trainers.

4.4 There are 64 Trainers of whom 13 are Trainers in Training and not yet accredited. Of the 51 accredited, 15 are due for re-accreditation and three resigned during 2008. As new legislation in relation to vulnerable adults is enacted, the Committee anticipates that it will require an increase in the pool of existing trainers.

4.5 The Safeguarding Committee would commend the commitment of those in our congregations who volunteer to become Co-ordinators and Trainers as their investment both in time and energy should not be underestimated. The Safeguarding Committee would also like to note their appreciation to all the volunteers who diligently complied with the demands of safeguarding over the last year.

4.6 During 2008, 72 training courses were held for volunteer children's workers and 18 training courses were held for Congregational Co-ordinators covering the whole of the Scottish mainland, Shetland and the Western Isles. Training courses were also held in Amsterdam, Paris and Lisbon.

4.8 As the vast majority of congregations now have a trained Safeguarding Co-ordinator, the demand for courses for new Co-ordinators is diminishing. However, a cycle of refresher training is now being undertaken by those who completed the course initially and there is always a need to provide training opportunities for retirement or other natural turnover.

4.9 Those wishing to be considered as a Trainer must be prepared to have their presentation skills assessed and be guided as to the standard required.

4.10 A training package is presently under development to reflect the wider roles and responsibilities of Youth Workers. It is hoped that this can be piloted in the near future.

4.11 The demand for Safeguarding Training for Ministries Council is increasing and we now provide input to courses for Candidates, Readers and Ministers in the admissions process.

4.12 Following the 2008 General Assembly deliverance, there is now increasing awareness of and demand for Kirk Session Training. Courses are being organised by Presbytery contacts for individual sessions or for cluster groups, depending on the numbers likely to attend.

4.13 The Assistant Head of Safeguarding, Jennifer McCreanor has completed training to become a CEOP (Child Exploitation and Online Protection) ambassador and can now offer training on internet security and online protection. It is hoped that Jennifer will cascade this training throughout the organisation as well as to our Safeguarding colleagues at CrossReach.

4.14 As a result of the changes and developments, the Safeguarding Office is charged with producing and disseminating new materials to each congregation, Co-ordinator, Trainer and Presbytery Contact as required.

4.15 It is proposed that the Safeguarding Handbook be rewritten and circulated as well as new sections produced for the Fact File. Policy and guidance notes will follow to ease the implementation process.

4.16 Since the 2008 General Assembly, the numbers of enquiries from congregations concerned about particular situations have risen as those charged with the responsibility of safeguarding in congregations become increasingly aware of the issues.

5. Report by the Forgiveness and Proportionality Working Group

5.1 Following the work undertaken by the Forgiveness and Proportionality Working Group (see separate report) the Safeguarding Office will be providing appropriate information, policies and guidance notes in terms of implementing Covenants of Responsibilities. These protocols will allow sex offenders to worship in congregations without compromising the safety of others.

5.2 A new code of practice will emerge from this work which will ensure all sex offenders worshiping within the Church of Scotland are identified and comply with civil as well as church legislation.

In the name and by the authority of the Committee

JOHN C CHRISTIE, *Convener*
FIONNA MISKELLY, *Head of Safeguarding*

6.5

APPENDIX 1

The Protection of Vulnerable Groups (Scotland) Act 2007

1.1 The Scottish Government is taking forward a comprehensive implementation programme to deliver the provisions outlined in the Protection of Vulnerable Groups (Scotland) Act 2007 (PVG).

1.2 The PVG Act delivers the principal recommendation of the Bichard Inquiry Report which was undertaken following the murders in Soham in 2002. This recommendation called for a registration system for all those who work with children and protected adults.

1.3 Proposals to strengthen and streamline Scotland's Disclosure system so that unsuitable people are excluded from work with vulnerable groups and end the need for multiple Disclosure applications have been published by the Scottish Government.

1.4 The proposals are in response to a detailed consultation on the steps required to implement the new Vetting and Barring Scheme, introduced through the Protection of Vulnerable Groups (Scotland) Act 2007.

1.5 The PVG scheme will:
- ensure that those who have regular contact with vulnerable groups through the workplace do not have a history of abusive behaviour.
- deliver a fair and consistent system that will be quick and easy for people to use, ending the need for multiple, written Disclosure applications.

1.6 The scheme will exclude people who are known to be unsuitable, on the basis of past behaviour, from working with children and protected adults – either paid or unpaid – and detect those who become unsuitable while in the work place.

1.7 It builds on what has been learned from the current Disclosure system to deliver a robust, strengthened, streamlined service for people who work with vulnerable groups.

1.8 Protection for adults will be improved, as the PVG Act creates, for the first time in Scotland, a list of those who are barred from working with protected adults, complementing the safeguards introduced through the Adult Support and Protection (Scotland) Act 2007. The PVG Act defines a protected adult as an individual, aged 16 or over who receives one or more type of care or welfare service. This definition recognises that some adults may always require protection due to the nature or frequency of services they receive, while others may do so only for short periods. The purpose of the term 'protected adult' is to distinguish the category of an adult requiring protection and to avoid labelling adults solely on the basis of having a specific condition or disability. Defining adults in this way is intended to help employers identify the services that make an adult 'protected' and therefore, assess which posts will constitute regular work.

1.9 The Act introduces a scheme membership system for people who work with children and protected adults. If a person is considered unsuitable to work with children, protected adults or both, they will be unable to become a scheme member in relation to either workforce or both. It will be an offence for an organisation to permit someone whose name appears on either the Disqualified from Working with Children List or the Disqualified from Working with Adults List and has thus been barred from undertaking such work.

1.10 Scheme membership will end the need for employees (paid or unpaid) to complete multiple written Disclosure applications which is a cause of frustration with the current Disclosure system. Scheme records will be updated automatically when member's circumstances change, for example if they move to a different job or if they are convicted of a crime. It is hoped that this scheme is computer based and therefore paper free.

1.11 This will enable the employer to do a simple check to verify that a person is a scheme member and therefore not categorised as unsuitable. As well as providing an enhanced tool to help employers to make and (in the vast majority of cases) speedier recruitment decisions, scheme membership will save overall costs and reduces bureaucracy. Checks for volunteers working in the voluntary sector will continue to be paid by the Scottish Government.

1.12 The PVG scheme will be managed and delivered by Disclosure Scotland as an executive agency, which will continue to deliver the other types of Disclosure. A new team with Disclosure Scotland will receive and consider referrals and take decisions, on behalf of Scottish Ministers, about those people who may be unsuitable to work with children or protected adults. The team will gather and assess all relevant information to make expert, fair and consistent decisions.

1.13 The Scottish scheme dovetails with the system being developed in other parsts of the UK, through the Safeguarding of Vulnerable Groups (2006) Act, to ensure a consistent and UK wide approach to Vetting and Barring. This means that someone who is barred from working in the relevant workforce in Scotland would also be barred throughout the rest of the UK and vice versa.

1.14 The Scottish Government has published the response to consultation on policy proposals for secondary legislation. A date for the scheme to 'go live' is still to be determined and the Scottish Government has given a commitment that the date will be announced well in advance to allow organisations adequate time to prepare. In the meantime, implementation plans are continuing, in partnership with a range of groups and organisations. This includes the development of a comprehensive package of guidance and training.

APPENDIX 2

The Safeguarding Panel
Kirk Sessions are now required to appoint a Safeguarding Panel to manage confidential and delicate safeguarding matters on behalf of the Kirk Session.

The benefit to the Kirk Session is that information which for legal reasons cannot be shared in a larger group can be managed on their behalf by the Panel.

Membership of the Panel
In 1998 the Child Protection Unit (now the Safeguarding Office) recommended the development of Child Protection Panels. Now called Safeguarding Panels the suggested membership is:
- Safeguarding Coordinator
- Minister
- One other church member with relevant experience

There should be at least three Panel members but can be more to include key relevant responsible persons. Some congregations have decided not to include their Minister on the Panel as they believe that doing so may compromise him/her in undertaking their pastoral care role. This is a matter for the Kirk Session and the Minister to decide. Many congregations include their Session Clerk as a member of the Panel.

The purpose of the Panel
A Panel has six key functions which are to:
- Represent the Kirk Session in matters relating to their church's child protection/safeguarding policy and its implementation.
- Assist the Co-ordinator in procedures of recruitment and selection of children's workers and the promotion of training.
- Ensure that procedures are followed and records maintained to the satisfaction of the Presbytery.
- In Liaison with the Safeguarding Office discuss and manage allegations of harm on behalf of the Kirk Session.

6.5

- In liaison with the Safeguarding Office discuss and manage the safe inclusion of sex offenders in the congregation on behalf of the Kirk Session.
- In liaison with the Safeguarding Office implement the Church's Disciplinary Code on behalf of the Kirk Session.

Training for Panel Members

It is important that Panel members are encouraged to attend child protection training.

Maintaining confidentiality

Panel members must understand the importance of maintaining absolute confidentiality. This will mean that the sharing of details about any matter discussed will be restricted and not discussed at Session meetings.

STEWARDSHIP AND FINANCE COMMITTEE
May 2009

PROPOSED DELIVERANCE

The General Assembly
1. Receive the Report.
2. Receive the 2008 Report and Accounts of the Unincorporated Councils and Committees of the General Assembly.
3. Welcome the decision to offer the paid-consultancy level of support from Stewardship Consultants to all congregations free of charge, and urge Kirk Sessions and Financial Boards to embark on the 'Gifts for God' programme with this support.
4. Urge Presbyteries to be proactive in encouraging Kirk Sessions and Financial Boards to challenge members and adherents to give as generously as possible to enable the sharing of the gospel through the worship, mission and service of the Church.
5. Resolve to work towards a more sustainable use of financial resources than that represented by a situation where 35% of charges support the cost of parish ministers in the other 65%.
6. Approve the revised Regulations for Ministries and Mission Contributions from Congregations as set out in Appendix 3.

REPORT

1. Stewardship

1.1 Pilot Programmes for a National Stewardship Initiative

1.1.1 Preliminary results for the pilot programmes in the Presbyteries of Ardrossan and Falkirk have shown increases in the number of members giving through the Gift Aid scheme and giving by bank standing order, both of which are positive changes. In most of the participating congregations there were indications of immediate increases in the offerings. However, the number of congregations participating in the pilot programme was under 60% of the total. The number of congregations participating in the second phase, in the Presbyteries of Hamilton, Perth, Gordon and Moray, has not exceeded this percentage.

1.1.2 The Committee is concerned that in many of the congregations in these six Presbyteries, and in other Presbyteries, there is an unwillingness to talk about the Christian giving of money. Sometimes congregations refuse to embrace stewardship in any form. Sometimes congregations emphasise the fact that stewardship is about more than money. This is correct, but the comment often means that congregations will address the Christian giving of time and talent, but are unwilling to address the Christian giving of money.

1.1.3 What has been learned from the pilot programmes is that where congregations address the Christian giving of money with the support of one of the Church's Stewardship Consultants, there are positive results. This support amounted to the number of planning and training meetings normally provided only in a paid consultancy. It has been increasingly difficult to justify providing this level of support free of charge in some Presbyteries and charging a fee in other Presbyteries.

The Committee decided that from January 2009 the Stewardship Consultants would offer seven meetings for planning, training and assessment purposes free of charge to all congregations embarking on the 'Gifts for God' programme, provided they were adhering to one of the three objectives in that programme:

(a) to increase the regular, committed giving of money;
(b) to increase involvement through better giving of time, talent and money;
(c) to raise a large sum of money for a particular project.

The Committee anticipates the Stewardship Consultants receiving a significant increase in requests for assistance from congregations in all Presbyteries.

1.1.4 While the methods outlined in the above paragraph address the needs of congregations which wish to challenge their members on their Christian giving, they do not deal with the situation in congregations which refuse to issue this challenge to their members. The fact that some congregations make little or no effort to increase their Christian giving of money while others make a considerable effort is a matter for Presbyteries to address. Proposals in section 2.2 of this report will give Presbyteries additional powers to address this in relation to Ministries and Mission Contributions, by ensuring that congregations which make an effort to increase giving are not penalised by those who make no effort.

1.1.5 Some congregations have used the present economic climate as a reason for not participating in a programme about the Christian giving of money at the present time. While some members and adherents are adversely affected by the present economic climate, others are not. If the Church is to continue to share the gospel through worship, mission and service throughout Scotland and beyond, there is a need for all members and adherents to give as generously as they possibly can. Generosity is always giving from what we have. Some may need to give less at the present time. Others could give more. Doing nothing about the Christian giving of money until the economic climate improves is a luxury which most congregations, and the Church as a whole, cannot afford.

1.2 Gift Aid

The Committee's Supplementary Report to last year's General Assembly welcomed the decision of the Chancellor of the Exchequer to maintain the tax recovery on Gift Aid offerings at 28% until 5 April 2011, despite the reduction in the basic rate of income tax from 22% to 20% from 6 April 2008. During 2008 congregations requested over 30,000 stewardship leaflets. It is interesting to note that approximately 18,000 of the leaflets requested were Gift Aid leaflets. This indicates that congregations are still seeking to increase the number of their members and adherents who sign Gift Aid Declarations and enable the Church to increase the value of their offerings by 28%.

1.3 Legacies

The Committee reported to last year's General Assembly that it intended to formulate a strategy for promoting legacies for the work of the Church – local, national and global. This is a very sensitive area and continues to be a work in progress.

1.4 External Funding

Last year's General Assembly instructed the Committee, in consultation with the Council of Assembly, to explore the appointment of an External Funding Adviser. The Committee has pursued the issue of external funding in a different way by subscribing to 'GRANTfinder', a web-based product which indicates possible sources of funding for particular projects. The Head of Stewardship and the Stewardship Consultants all have access to 'GRANTfinder' and are able to make use of it, where appropriate, in their work with congregations. The Parish Development Fund staff have been made aware of this resource. The cost of a three year subscription to 'GRANTfinder', at less than £10,000, is a more efficient use of resources than a salary for the same period.

2. Ministries and Mission Contributions

2.1 Contributions to 31 December 2008
(Appendix 2)

2.1.1 By 31 December 2008 congregations had remitted £41,259,161 as Ministries and Mission Contributions for 2008. This is 97.9% of the total required. The shortfall of £898,995 will be reduced by late payments made during 2009. Late payments to the Parish Ministries Fund and the Mission and Renewal Fund for 2007 and previous years, which were made during 2008, amounted to £467,625. The Committee wishes to record its thanks to congregations for meeting their financial obligations in this way.

2.1.2 The Committee is pleased to note, in respect of Regulations I 2008 section 2, that over 75% of congregations are now remitting all or most of their Ministries and Mission Contributions by monthly standing order. This greatly assists cash flow as money is paid out to Councils and Committees on a monthly basis throughout the year. Congregations which are unable to remit contributions by monthly standing order are reminded that they must apply annually to their Presbyteries if they require dispensation from this regulation. The Committee is aware that this regulation is not being fully implemented in all Presbyteries, and is pursuing this matter with the appropriate Presbyteries.

2.1.3 In addition to Ministries and Mission Contributions, congregations contributed £15,133 in general extra contributions to the Mission and Renewal Fund and £144,883 in specially designated extra contributions.

2.2 Review of Regulations for Ministries and Mission Contributions from Congregations (Regulations I, 2008 and Appendix 3)

2.2.1 Last year's General Assembly, on the report of the Special Commission on Structure and Change, gave the Committee the following instruction:

The General Assembly resolve that the present system of Congregational allocations based on income is revised to provide greater incentive to local Congregations to raise funds through Stewardship and other means for local purposes, and instruct the Stewardship and Finance Committee to bring to the General Assembly of 2009 proposals for implementation in 2010 of the recommendations contained in sections 12.1 to 12.5 of the Report without compromising the Church's often repeated commitment to its poorest congregations.

In pursuit of this instruction the Committee formed a task group of nine, including Professor Ian Percy, a member of the Special Commission on Structure and Change, and the Rev Dr George Whyte, one of those who petitioned the General Assembly of 2006 on 'A Voice for the Local Church'. The key areas in which the task group brought recommendations, which the Committee endorsed, included communication, income base and Presbytery involvement.

2.2.2 To provide clearer information to members and adherents, the Committee has introduced the sending of an annual letter to Session Clerks, giving details of how their own congregation's Ministries and Ministries Contribution is used for Parish Ministries, Mission and Renewal, and the general support and services to Councils and congregations. This information has been provided in a format which is designed for communication to all who belong to the congregation. The letter makes it clear whether the congregation is meeting the full cost of its ministry and supporting the cost of ministries in other parishes, or is being supported by the contributions of other congregations in terms of the cost of its ministry.

2.2.3 This letter is in addition to the annual leaflet on Ministries and Mission Contributions produced by the Committee. This year's leaflet *Belonging to a Sharing Church* provides a fuller picture than previous leaflets. As much of the work of some Councils is funded by income other than Ministries and Mission Contributions, the leaflet takes account of payments for CrossReach services and central income which Councils receive from

6.6

investments and other sources. It is important to note that effective communication with members and adherents is not only a matter of clear information being provided by an Assembly Committee but also the information being passed on by Ministers, Session Clerks and Treasurers.

2.2.4 In reviewing the process for calculating Ministries and Mission Contributions, three criteria were seen to be fundamental:
(1) The process must be fair to all congregations.
(2) The process must not be a disincentive to promoting Christian giving.
(3) The process must continue to have input from Presbyteries.

2.2.5 To be fair to all congregations, the average income base, from which Ministries and Mission Contributions are calculated, must continue to be calculated annually on the basis of actual income. The recommendation that the average income base in one year should have increases in line with inflation applied to it in the next two years is a departure from dealing with actual income, would be unfair to congregations whose income is decreasing or increasing at less than the rate of inflation, and would introduce considerable problems in returning to actual income at the end of a three year period. In recent years the annual increases for most congregations have been lower than the rate of inflation. Most of the congregations with higher increases have been those whose Ministries and Mission Contributions are below the scale amount appropriate to their average income bases. To be fair to all congregations, as many congregations as possible should be asked to contribute the appropriate scale amount.

2.2.6 In recent years the graduated scale used in the calculation of Ministries and Mission Contributions has become a 'flatter' scale. In 2007 a congregation with an average income base of £100,000 was expected to contribute 66% as its Ministries and Mission Contribution. This percentage reduced to 62% in 2008 and to 59% in 2009. Where average income bases exceed £100,000,

congregations are expected to contribute a lower percentage than those stated above. This trend has become possible because the Council of Assembly has insisted that other sources of funds available to Councils and Committees are included in their budgets, and congregational Ministries and Mission Contributions are meeting a smaller proportion of the total budget approved by the General Assembly.

2.2.7 The Committee is conscious that an income-based process can be a disincentive to promoting higher levels of Christian giving. While a few congregations may be in situations where there is little scope for increasing income, the Committee believes that most congregations have the potential for higher levels of Christian giving. If a congregation continues to do nothing to improve its Christian giving, its Ministries and Mission Contribution is likely to stay around the same amount or decrease. This outcome is unacceptable. Congregations which make an effort to improve their Christian giving must be affirmed through action being taken by Presbyteries to encourage other congregations to make similar efforts, thus benefiting all congregations.

2.2.8 Encouraging higher levels of Christian giving should be motivated by a desire on the part of members and adherents to enable the sharing of the gospel through the worship, mission and service of the Church. It is important that members and adherents know that 87% of Ministries and Mission Contributions is supporting Parish Ministries in 2009 and that a considerable amount of the remaining 13% is supporting, directly or indirectly, the work of congregations. The Committee is of the opinion that it is not helpful to distinguish between local and central in Church finance, and that financial resources should be seen to enable the whole work of the Church – local, national and global.

2.2.9 Section 14 of the current Regulations gives considerable scope to Presbyteries to reduce the proposed Ministries and Mission Contributions for particular congregations each year. The Committee believes that this provides a necessary local input to the process as Presbyteries are in the best position to assess the different situations and needs of their congregations.

2.2.10 There was considerable discussion in the task group about giving Presbyteries the power to increase Ministries and Mission Contributions where these were significantly below the appropriate scale amount or where congregations were deemed to have the potential for much more generous giving. The 'Revision Schedule' model of the former Committee on the Maintenance of the Ministry led the task group to favour a negotiated 'Giving Agreement' with the trustees of congregations. This approach was preferred to the alternative where Presbyteries make arbitrary decisions to increase particular Ministries and Mission Contributions above the proposed amount without discussion with the trustees of congregations.

2.2.11 The proposed new section 15 in the Regulations for Ministries and Mission Contributions from Congregations (see Appendix 3) would give Presbyteries power to increase the Ministries and Mission Contributions of congregations through a negotiated 'Giving Agreement', which would apply to the following three financial years and be approved by the trustees of the congregation and Presbytery. This would enable Presbyteries to bring Ministries and Mission Contributions to the appropriate scale amount more quickly and/or would enable Presbyteries to challenge those congregations which have the potential for much higher levels of giving. To encourage Presbyteries to use the facility of a 'Giving Agreement', any increase in total Ministries and Mission Contributions from congregations in a Presbytery would be added to the 3% already available to the Presbytery for reductions.

2.2.12 The Committee also noted that the annual maximum percentage increase referred to in section 12 of the Regulations has been applied to the final amount for the Ministries and Mission Contribution for a particular congregation in the previous year, and not to the initial proposed amount sent to Presbytery. To prevent congregations falling below the appropriate scale amount, the annual maximum percentage increase will in future be applied to the initial proposed amount. If Presbyteries feel that certain congregations need assistance through the 3% discretion for more than one year, they should make these decisions on an annual basis.

2.2.13 While this report is not proposing radical changes to the process for calculating Ministries and Mission Contributions from congregations, the Committee has found the instruction to review the process to be a very worthwhile exercise and has greatly appreciated the input from the two members of the task group who were not members of the Committee.

2.3 Other Discussions

2.3.1 Within the task group and in meetings with the Ministries Council and the Special Commission appointed to consider the relevance of the Third Declaratory Article in today's Scotland, there was considerable discussion of the fact that in 2008 there were 408 charges (35%) whose Ministries and Mission Contributions provided sufficient money to meet the costs of their own ministers, *ie* stipend, employer's national insurance and pension contributions, and support the cost of ministries in the other 745 charges (65%) whose Ministries and Mission Contributions did not meet the cost of their own ministers.

2.3.2 There is general agreement that, in a sharing Church, those with the greater financial resources should support ministries in the priority area parishes and in the more remote parts of Scotland. However, an examination of the statistics shows that there are urban areas where there are a number of congregations, some or all of which are being supported, in terms of the cost of their ministry, by the 408 charges mentioned in 2.3.1 above. At a time when the Church is wishing to develop new forms of ministry and new approaches to mission, both of which require considerable financial resources, the Committee invites the General Assembly to endorse the view of the Committee that the current situation is not the best stewardship of the Church's precious financial resources and to resolve to work towards a more sustainable position.

2.3.3 The Committee hopes that the letters to Session Clerks in 2.2.2 above will clarify the current situation for all congregations and that some congregations will make a determined effort to improve their Christian giving to the extent that their Ministries and Mission Contributions will meet the full cost of the ministry provided.

2.3.4 The Committee is conscious that much of section 2 of this report will only be effective if Presbyteries are proactive in their own stewardship of the Church's resources through realistic and imaginative Presbytery Plans and in encouraging congregations to improve the level of their Christian giving.

3. Accounting Matters

3.1 Central Accounts for 2008

As in previous years, separate sets of Accounts for 2008 have been produced for each of the following:

The Church of Scotland Investors Trust
The Church of Scotland General Trustees
The Church of Scotland Trust
The Church of Scotland Pension Trustees
The Unincorporated Councils and Committees

The first three of the above bodies are statutory corporations and the Pension Trustees are an unincorporated body constituted by the General Assembly. These four bodies are responsible for producing and approving their own Accounts.

The Stewardship and Finance Committee is responsible, on behalf of the General Assembly, for preparing and approving the Report and Accounts of the Unincorporated Councils and Committees, which comprise Ministries Funds, Mission and Renewal Funds, Social Care, and Miscellaneous Funds.

3.2 Attestation of Presbytery Accounts

After the Accounts have been approved by Presbyteries at the end of each financial year, they have to be submitted for attestation to the Committee, which then has to report to the General Assembly. The Committee has attested the 2007 Accounts of 41 Presbyteries. Despite numerous reminders, at the time of completing this report the 2007 Accounts of the Presbyteries of Dundee and Moray had not been submitted.

3.3 Presbytery Attestation of Congregational Accounts

3.3.1 Presbyteries are required to attest the Accounts of congregations within their bounds and to report to the Committee that they have completed this attestation and details of their findings. The 2007 Congregational Accounts were the first to be prepared under the provisions of the Charities Accounts (Scotland) Regulations 2006. The Committee was encouraged to note that the reports from 38 Presbyteries on the inspection of these Accounts and the analysis undertaken within the General Treasurer's Department indicated that the vast majority were found to be compliant. Despite numerous reminders, at the time of completing this report the Committee had not received reports on the Attestation of 2007 Congregational Accounts from the Presbyteries of Duns, Glasgow, and Lewis.

3.3.2 The Committee fulfilled the instruction from last year's General Assembly to re-examine the attestation process and has issued a revised template to Presbyteries for the inspection and attestation of 2008 Congregational Accounts.

By the authority of the Committee

VIVIENNE A DICKSON, *Convener*
RICHARD BAXTER, *Vice-Convener*
IAIN W GRIMMOND, *General Treasurer*
GORDON D JAMIESON, *Head of Stewardship*
FRED MARSH, *Administrative Secretary*

ADDENDUM

Mrs Vivienne A Dickson, CA, Convener

Vivienne Dickson has brought to the Stewardship and Finance area of the Church's work a deep personal faith, a firm commitment to Christ and his Church, and the professional skills of a Chartered Accountant. She had a long association with the Board of Stewardship and Finance from 1986 when she became Stewardship and Finance Convener in the Presbytery of St Andrews. In 2001 she was appointed Vice-Convener, and in 2005 became the first Convener of the Stewardship and Finance Committee. During this long period, Vivienne has been equally competent talking about the teaching of Christian giving, the calculation of congregational contributions, or the finer points of Congregational or Presbytery Accounts.

In 2007 she was also appointed Convener of the Support and Services Council. This gave her the opportunity to play a full part in the Council of Assembly and its Budget and Governance Groups.

Vivienne's service in the Church has not been confined to Assembly Committees. As an elder in St Leonard's Parish Church, St Andrews, she has served as Congregational Treasurer and Session Clerk. In the Presbytery of St Andrews she has played a full part over many years, including terms as Stewardship and Finance Convener, Presbytery Treasurer and Moderator.

The Stewardship and Finance Committee is greatly indebted to Vivienne Dickson for the leadership she has provided and for the support she has continually given to members of staff.

APPENDIX 1
LEGACIES TO CENTRAL FUNDS OF THE CHURCH

	2008 £	2007 £	2006 £	2005 £	2004 £
Social Care (CrossReach)	894,393	1,193,078	1,561,849	1,318,143	1,411,547
The Church of Scotland (Unrestricted)	562,065	751,130	982,078	362,418	870,042
New Charge Development	196,964	2,538	–	86,681	42,408
General Trustees	182,800	350,000	243,103	64,519	30,386
World Mission	105,406	135,219	408,905	304,346	495,386
Ministries	81,935	551,251	462,179	316,231	398,423
Pension Funds	71,350	120,095	50,088	652,281	210,171
Housing and Loan Fund	51,193	110,000	101,979	283,204	134,361
Mission & Discipleship	3,400	14,985	118,233	87,797	38,956
Ecumenical Relations	2,912	74	6,847	–	2,700
The Guild	500	–	–	–	90
Mission and Renewal Fund	107	237	–	12,703	5,378
Christian Aid	–	–	–	83,815	–
Diaconate	–	–	–	–	500
Total Legacies to Central Funds	2,153,025	3,228,607	3,935,261	3,572,138	3,640,348

APPENDIX 2
MINISTRIES AND MISSION CONTRIBUTIONS

Year	Total to be Contributed	Received by 31 December		Shortfall in Year	
	£	£	%	£	%
2004	41,235,964	40,349,129	97.8	886,835	2.2
2005	42,251,504	41,546,738	98.3	704,766	1.7
2006	43,588,762	42,836,513	98.3	752,249	1.7
2007	43,713,751	42,997,314	98.4	716,437	1.6
2008	42,158,156	41,259,161	97.9	898,995	2.1

Notes:
1. Until 2005 there were separate contributions for Ministries Funds and the Mission & Renewal Fund. These have been added together above.
2. Late contributions received subsequently have significantly reduced the shortfalls shown above.

6.6

APPENDIX 3A

(To be moved by the Convener if the Joint Report of the Stewardship and Finance Committee and the Council of Assembly has been approved by the General Assembly)

Replace Regulations I, 2008 with the following:

Regulations for Ministries and Mission Contributions from Congregations

General

1. All congregations, with the exception of single congregation Local Ecumenical Partnerships, are required to make a Ministries and Mission Contribution in terms of these regulations. For the avoidance of doubt, single congregation Local Ecumenical Partnerships are required to make an equivalent contribution in terms of Regulations I, 2007.

2. Each congregation shall transmit its required contribution in ten or twelve equal monthly payments during the financial year by bank standing order, unless permission is granted annually by Presbytery to allow payments to be made under some other arrangement. Each Presbytery shall advise the Stewardship and Finance Department annually by Extract Minute of any such individual arrangements.

3. It shall be the responsibility of the Financial Board of each congregation to inform the members of the congregation of the required Ministries and Mission Contribution and the ways in which this contribution enables the worship, mission and service of the Church.

4. Ministries and Mission Contributions shall be credited to the Parish Ministries Fund and the Mission and Renewal Fund in proportion to their budgets, as approved by the General Assembly. Any shortfalls in contributions shall be borne by the Parish Ministries Fund and the Mission and Renewal Fund in proportion to their approved budgets.

5. The Stewardship and Finance Department shall annually inform Presbytery Clerks of shortfalls in Ministries and Mission Contributions from congregations within their bounds, and also shortfalls in respect of reimbursement by congregations of ministers' travelling expenses, both for the latest financial year and any accumulated totals for previous years. Each Presbytery shall record all such shortfalls annually in the Minutes of the Presbytery and shall consult with the office-bearers of the congregations concerned.

Process of determining Ministries and Mission Contributions

6. To facilitate the process of calculating the required Ministries and Mission Contribution for each congregation, Financial Boards shall be required to send annually by 31 March to the Stewardship and Finance Department a copy of their Congregational Accounts for the previous financial year.

7. The required contributions shall be calculated from a graduated scale, which is related to each congregation's Income Base (see paragraphs 8 and 9 below) and provides the total budget for the Parish Ministries Fund and the Mission and Renewal Fund to be met from congregations, as approved by the General Assembly.

8. The Income Base for each congregation shall include:
   (a) General Fund income;
   (b) Ministry income (including glebe rents, Consolidated Stipend Fund income and local stipend endowment income);
   (c) Fabric Fund and Reserve Fund income (including income in Fabric Funds held by the General Trustees);
   (d) Net property rental income;
   (e) A percentage of contributions from outside

agencies for the use of premises, if in excess of a sum to be determined by the Council of Assembly;

(f) Any other regular income which is available to meet ordinary expenditure.

For the avoidance of doubt, legacies or capital receipts, such as the proceeds from the sale of property or investments; special collections for other charities; income in temporary capital funds for major projects, such as the refurbishment of the church or the building of a new hall; or income from external funding sources which is specifically to meet the costs of a specialist worker, shall be excluded from the Income Base.

9. The Council of Assembly shall appoint a Panel to adjudicate on any appeals from congregations relating to the application of paragraph 8 above.

10. The average of the Income Base figures for the latest three years, calculated as specified above in paragraph 8, shall be the base figure for calculating the required Ministries and Mission Contributions from congregations.

11. If a congregation's scale contribution will be less than its stipend endowment income, the required contribution shall be increased to equal the amount of the stipend endowment income plus a sum sufficient to ensure that the stipend endowment income shall be applied solely for the Parish Ministries Fund part of the total contribution.

12. The Council of Assembly shall determine each year a percentage for annual maximum increases in proposed contributions for individual congregations issued to Presbyteries. Presbytery shall also have the right to increase a required contribution by more than the maximum percentage permitted where a congregation received a reduced required contribution in the previous year.

13. The total of the approved budgets for the Parish Ministries Fund and the Mission and Renewal Fund to be met from congregations plus 3.75% shall be the total proposed Ministries and Mission Contributions for congregations. The Stewardship and Finance Department shall send to each Presbytery Clerk by 31 August each year a list of proposed Ministries and Mission Contributions for congregations within the bounds of that Presbytery.

14. Presbyteries may reduce the proposed contributions required from congregations by 3% of the Presbytery total. Presbyteries may use the 3% permitted reduction in any or all of the following three ways:

(a) To reduce the proposed contributions for individual congregations before they are finalised for the following year, in the light of local knowledge of the current situation in congregations within the Presbytery;

(b) To reduce the actual required contributions of individual congregations during the year to which they apply if changes in circumstances arise which the Presbytery decides would justify this course of action, and provided such reductions are communicated by Extract Minute to the Stewardship and Finance Department not later than 31 October each year;

(c) To pay off shortfalls from previous years for individual congregations where the Presbytery considers this course of action to be appropriate, and provided such payments are communicated by Extract Minute to the Stewardship and Finance Department not later than 31 October each year.

If any of the 3% is not used in these ways, Presbyteries may not carry forward, after the end of the year to which it applies, any balance for use in future years.

15. Presbyteries may increase the proposed contributions for individual congregations where these are substantially below scale or where Presbyteries deem

6.6

that there is considerable potential for increased giving by completing a 'Giving Agreement' with the trustees of the congregation which will indicate the agreed contributions for the following three financial years and will be recorded in the Minutes of the Presbytery. Any agreed increase in the proposed contributions will be added to the 3% available to Presbyteries in terms of paragraph 14 above.

16. The percentages stated in paragraphs 13, 14 and 15 shall be reviewed from time to time by the Council of Assembly.

17. Presbyteries shall notify their congregations, with the exception of single congregation Local Ecumenical Partnerships within their bounds, of their required Ministries and Mission Contributions for the following financial year not later than 15 November each year. Presbyteries shall also communicate by Extract Minute the required Ministries and Mission Contributions for congregations within their bounds for the following financial year to the Stewardship and Finance Department not later than 15 November each year.

18. The Stewardship and Finance Department shall then issue to Congregational Treasurers in December each year confirmation of the required Ministries and Mission Contributions for the following financial year.

19. Where a congregation has a ministerial vacancy, an allowance, within limits determined by the Ministries Council, shall be given towards extra costs incurred for locum provision during the vacancy. Allowances in respect of ministerial vacancies shall be charged to the Parish Ministries Fund.

APPENDIX 3B

(To be moved by the Convener if the Joint Report of the Stewardship and Finance Committee and the Council of Assembly has <u>not</u> been approved by the General Assembly)

Replace Regulations I, 2008 with the following:

Regulations for Ministries and Mission Contributions from Congregations

General

1. All congregations, with the exception of single congregation Local Ecumenical Partnerships, are required to make a Ministries and Mission Contribution in terms of these regulations. For the avoidance of doubt, single congregation Local Ecumenical Partnerships are required to make an equivalent contribution in terms of Regulations I, 2007.

2. Each congregation shall transmit its required contribution in ten or twelve equal monthly payments during the financial year by bank standing order, unless permission is granted annually by Presbytery to allow payments to be made under some other arrangement. Each Presbytery shall advise the Stewardship and Finance Committee annually by Extract Minute of any such individual arrangements.

3. It shall be the responsibility of the Financial Board of each congregation to inform the members of the congregation of the required Ministries and Mission Contribution and the ways in which this contribution enables the worship, mission and service of the Church.

4. Ministries and Mission Contributions shall be credited to the Parish Ministries Fund and the Mission and Renewal Fund in proportion to their budgets, as approved by the General Assembly. Any shortfalls in contributions shall be borne by the Parish Ministries

Fund and the Mission and Renewal Fund in proportion to their approved budgets.

5. The Stewardship and Finance Committee shall annually inform Presbytery Clerks of shortfalls in Ministries and Mission Contributions from congregations within their bounds, and also shortfalls in respect of reimbursement by congregations of ministers' travelling expenses, both for the latest financial year and any accumulated totals for previous years. Each Presbytery shall record all such shortfalls annually in the Minutes of the Presbytery and shall consult with the office-bearers of the congregations concerned.

Process of determining Ministries and Mission Contributions

6. To facilitate the process of calculating the required Ministries and Mission Contribution for each congregation, Financial Boards shall be required to send annually by 31 March to the General Treasurer a copy of their Congregational Accounts for the previous financial year.

7. The required contributions shall be calculated from a graduated scale, which is related to each congregation's Income Base (see paragraphs 8 and 9 below) and provides the total budget for the Parish Ministries Fund and the Mission and Renewal Fund to be met from congregations, as approved by the General Assembly.

8. The Income Base for each congregation shall include:
   (a) General Fund income;
   (b) Ministry income (including glebe rents, Consolidated Stipend Fund income and local stipend endowment income);
   (c) Fabric Fund and Reserve Fund income (including income in Fabric Funds held by the General Trustees);
   (d) Net property rental income;
   (e) A percentage of contributions from outside

agencies for the use of premises, if in excess of a sum to be determined by the Stewardship and Finance Committee;
   (f) Any other regular income which is available to meet ordinary expenditure.

For the avoidance of doubt, legacies or capital receipts, such as the proceeds from the sale of property or investments; special collections for other charities; income in temporary capital funds for major projects, such as the refurbishment of the church or the building of a new hall; or income from external funding sources which is specifically to meet the costs of a specialist worker, shall be excluded from the Income Base.

9. The Executive Sub-Committee of the Stewardship and Finance Committee shall adjudicate on any appeals from congregations relating to the application of paragraph 8 above.

10. The average of the Income Base figures for the latest three years, calculated as specified above in paragraph 8, shall be the base figure for calculating the required Ministries and Mission Contributions from congregations.

11. If a congregation's scale contribution will be less than its stipend endowment income, the required contribution shall be increased to equal the amount of the stipend endowment income plus a sum sufficient to ensure that the stipend endowment income shall be applied solely for the Parish Ministries Fund part of the total contribution.

12. The Stewardship and Finance Committee shall determine each year a percentage for annual maximum increases in proposed contributions for individual congregations issued to Presbyteries. Presbytery shall also have the right to increase a required contribution by more than the maximum

6.6

percentage permitted where a congregation received a reduced required contribution in the previous year.

13. The total of the approved budgets for the Parish Ministries Fund and the Mission and Renewal Fund to be met from congregations plus 3.75% shall be the total proposed Ministries and Mission Contributions for congregations. The Stewardship and Finance Committee shall send to each Presbytery Clerk by 31 August each year a list of proposed Ministries and Mission Contributions for congregations within the bounds of that Presbytery.

14. Presbyteries may reduce the proposed contributions required from congregations by 3% of the Presbytery total. Presbyteries may use the 3% permitted reduction in any or all of the following three ways:

    (a) To reduce the proposed contributions for individual congregations before they are finalised for the following year, in the light of local knowledge of the current situation in congregations within the Presbytery;

    (b) To reduce the actual required contributions of individual congregations during the year to which they apply if changes in circumstances arise which the Presbytery decides would justify this course of action, and provided such reductions are communicated by Extract Minute to the Stewardship and Finance Committee not later than 31 October each year;

    (c) To pay off shortfalls from previous years for individual congregations where the Presbytery considers this course of action to be appropriate, and provided such payments are communicated by Extract Minute to the Stewardship and Finance Committee not later than 31 October each year.

If any of the 3% is not used in these ways, Presbyteries may not carry forward, after the end of the year to which it applies, any balance for use in future years.

15. Presbyteries may increase the proposed contributions for individual congregations where these are substantially below scale or where Presbyteries deem that there is considerable potential for increased giving by completing a 'Giving Agreement' with the trustees of the congregation which will indicate the agreed contributions for the following three financial years and will be recorded in the Minutes of the Presbytery. Any agreed increase in the proposed contributions will be added to the 3% available to Presbyteries in terms of paragraph 14 above.

16. The percentages stated in paragraphs 13, 14 and 15 shall be reviewed from time to time by the Stewardship and Finance Committee.

17. Presbyteries shall notify their congregations, with the exception of single congregation Local Ecumenical Partnerships within their bounds, of their required Ministries and Mission Contributions for the following financial year not later than 15 November each year. Presbyteries shall also communicate by Extract Minute the required Ministries and Mission Contributions for congregations within their bounds for the following financial year to the Stewardship and Finance Committee not later than 15 November each year.

18. The General Treasurer shall then issue to Congregational Treasurers in December each year confirmation of the required Ministries and Mission Contributions for the following financial year.

19. Where a congregation has a ministerial vacancy, an allowance, within limits determined by the Ministries Council, shall be given towards extra costs incurred for locum provision during the vacancy. Allowances in respect of ministerial vacancies shall be charged to the Parish Ministries Fund.

PROPOSED DELIVERANCE

The General Assembly

1. Receive the Report.
2. Give thanks for the life and witness of overseas staff who have died, salute those who have completed their period of service overseas, and uphold in prayer all overseas staff who continue to serve.
3. Reaffirm the Church's commitment to respond in obedience to Jesus' command to "go into all the world and proclaim the good news to the whole creation"; and instruct the Council to continue working with partners on contextually appropriate initiatives in evangelism.
4. Welcome the six new mission partner appointments made during 2008; and urge Presbyteries and congregations to take all possible steps to bring opportunities for overseas service to the attention of members and adherents.
5. Salute the courage of the people of Zimbabwe, particularly the witness of the United Presbyterian Church in Southern Africa Presbytery of Zimbabwe; pray for the day when the forces of oppression and impoverishment will be defeated; and assure the Presbytery of the continuing solidarity of the Church of Scotland during extremely trying days.
6. Recognise that the conflict in Israel and Palestine cannot and will not be resolved by force; and assure partners who live and witness in the Holy Land of the determination of the Church of Scotland to journey with them until the day when "righteousness and peace kiss each other".
7. Give thanks to God for the training base for mission, global and local, which has been provided by St Colm's College in Inverleith since it was opened in 1909.
8. Encourage the preparations being made internationally to mark the centenary of "Edinburgh 1910" and, together with sister churches in Scotland, look forward to welcoming world church representatives who travel to Edinburgh in June 2010.

REPORT

Good News to Share: Evangelism with Global Horizons

"How then will they call on him in whom they have not believed? And how are they to believe in him of whom they have never heard? And how are they to hear without someone preaching? And how are they to preach unless they are sent? As it is written, 'How beautiful are the feet of those who preach the good news!'" (Romans 10:14-15)

The news about Jesus Christ is so good that it has to be shared. This impulse has prompted the outreach of the church not only in its own locality but widely across the face of the earth. This year, the lead theme of the Council has been its evangelistic commitment. In this, it has taken renewed inspiration from two notable centenaries – the 1910 World Missionary Conference and the birth of Lesslie Newbigin in 1909. It has also been encouraged and energised by consultation with partners with whom it has walked together through the past century and with whom it shares a commitment to work together on evangelism in today's world.

2008 – A Year of Consultation with Partners

When significant changes, driven not least by a substantially reduced budget, were made to World Mission's way of working in 2005, a commitment was made to partners to undertake a review in 2008. This was particularly important for those who became locally supported partners in 2005. For many of them it was a painful experience to see valued expressions of partnership, such as the appointment of mission partners or the award of grants to support strategic work, come to an end. Yet it was also an opportunity to pioneer new ways of working, particularly through the development of local-to-local links or "twinnings". A consultation was therefore held with representatives of locally supported partners at Scottish Churches House, Dunblane, from 30 April 2008 to 2 May 2008 in order to explore together "what the Lord requires of us" as partners in Christian mission.

Final Statement of the Dunblane Consultation
What does the Lord require of us?

Building on Partner Church Consultations held at St. Andrews in 1999 and Carberry in 2005, we rejoiced that, during the challenging early years of the 21st century, we have begun to discern together an emerging shape of a new form of partnership while remaining open to other models.

In renewing our commitment to journey together:

- *We reaffirm the strategic commitments of the Council as agreed in 1999 and 2005:*
  - *Local involvement in global mission – as an overarching theme*
  - *Evangelism – working with partner churches on new initiatives in evangelism*
  - *Reconciliation – working for justice, peace and reconciliation in situations of conflict or threat*
  - *The Scandal of Poverty – resourcing the church to set people free from the dehumanising effects of poverty.*

- *We recognise that the local-to-local way of working is a mode of mission whose time has come. In welcoming the growth of Twinning arrangements we are challenged to:*
  - *acknowledge the limited nature of our understandings of church and critically review them under God until they better serve God's mission to the whole of creation;*
  - *acknowledge and respect the historical, cultural, social, political, economic and ecclesiastical differences that exist within our partnerships recognising always the possibility of greater understanding and mutual enrichment;*
  - *reaffirm the need to foster effective working between national offices and local congregations. National offices should be pro-active in developing local-to-local links and promoting good practice. Local congregations should report regularly to their national offices on the progress of their links so that appropriate monitoring and support is provided;*
  - *acknowledge the value of networking within regions and the need to develop regional coordination;*
  - *recognise the need for careful thought to be given to the appropriate use of spiritual, financial, human and other resources in partnership;*
  - *ensure, on a decentralised model of partnership, that there is a balance between initiative and ownership at local level and necessary accountability;*
  - *explore how best to provide appropriate training and education for those embarking on Twinnings; and*
  - *ensure that the aims, methods and scope of our partnerships inspire and enable congregations to participate more fully in God's mission to the whole of creation.*

- *We recognise the call to women and men together in the churches to ensure:*
  - *a) the provision of strong Christian nurture and education for young people;*
  - *b) gender justice within the home, church and in society; and*
  - *c) the support of healthy family life.*

- *We recognise the challenge, pain and opportunities presented by large-scale migration of people and the need to examine more fully the following aspects:*
  - *the implications of the loss of people to churches and communities;*
  - *the loss of necessary skills;*
  - *the support and integration of a diverse immigrant population – both in the life of the society and the life of the church;*
  - *the need to overcome xenophobia and discrimination;*
  - *the contribution to church and society brought by immigrants, notably those who are people of faith; and*
  - *the potential enrichment of the church at local level as immigration brings to congregational life a new mix of cultures, races and backgrounds.*

As representatives of churches partnered in the mission of Christ, we commit ourselves to commend this statement to our churches.

We have been inspired by our worship together and encouraged by the depth of our fellowship in Christ. We have heard and received the call to forge a new pattern of partnership for our time. We give thanks to God and seek Christ's strength to meet the challenges discerned through the power of the Holy Spirit.

In order to confer also with centrally supported partners, a consultation was held during the 2008 General Assembly when delegates from all CSPs were present. This consultation considered the shape of our partnership in mission, the ministry of presence, sharing people in mission, the growth and potential of twinnings, communication, and networking within regions. It reaffirmed the strategic commitments made by the Council and called for a deepening of partnership work aimed at putting them into effect.

A Century of Evangelism: Remembering Edinburgh 1910

Scotland enjoys the privilege of having hosted perhaps the most remembered World Mission conference ever to have taken place. At the time of Edinburgh 1910, the Conference chair John R. Mott described the occasion as "the most notable gathering in the interest of the worldwide expansion of Christianity ever held, not only in missionary annals, but in all Christian annals." After 100 years, it remains a stand-out event. Often recognised as the starting point of the modern ecumenical movement, it is also a landmark in the history of evangelisation. Edinburgh 1910 covered many themes but there can be no doubt that at its core was a passion for evangelism. It was motivated by the possibility, which appeared to be within the grasp of the churches, of taking the gospel to every part of the earth for the first time.

The delegates were ready to sacrifice themselves for this purpose and they inspired many others to do so. They had discovered that Christian faith is not a matter of looking after yourself but of giving yourself for the sake of others. And they were affirmed at the Conference when no less an ecclesiastical leader than the Archbishop of Canterbury, Randall Davidson, stated that "the place of missions in the life of the Church must be the central place, and none other: that is what matters".

A century later, the World Mission Council continues to cherish this vision. Its focal theme for the year 2008-09 has been "Good News to Share: Working with Partner Churches on New Initiatives in Evangelism." The 100-year period since Edinburgh 1910 provides a framework within which to assess the progress of evangelism worldwide.

Though "the missionaries" have often been caricatured for their supposed excessive religious zeal, cultural insensitivity and complicity in Western imperialism, their achievement speaks for itself. Whereas before the missionary movement Christianity was largely confined to Europe and North America, its impact has been such that Christianity has become a faith with more adherents in the Global South than in its historic heartlands. While many European churches saw a decline in membership numbers during the 20th century, developments on the continent of Africa formed a dramatic contrast, with the number of Christians increasing from around 10 million in 1900 to some 360 million at the end of the century, an unprecedented rate of church growth. Latin America and parts of Asia have also witnessed dynamic expansion of the churches. For all its faults, the Western missionary movement was the detonator through which this dramatic change was accomplished. The world's religious demography has been transformed while Christianity itself has discovered new character and direction.

Qualitative assessment of the missionary movement which effected this change can come from unexpected sources. Matthew Parris, in the opinion piece in *The Times* of 27 December 2008, wrote: "Now a confirmed atheist, I've become convinced of the enormous contribution that Christian evangelism makes in Africa: sharply distinct from the work of secular NGOs, government projects, and international aid efforts. These alone will not do. Education and training alone will not do. In Africa, Christianity changes people's hearts. It brings a spiritual transformation. The rebirth is real. The change is good."

Recognition of the centenary of Edinburgh 1910 does not imply an unqualified approval of all its guiding ideas. Many of these have proved to be mistaken. It was guided by a territorial idea of Christian expansion – "carrying the gospel from the Christian to the Non-Christian World". It was unable to avoid a degree of complicity with imperialism and colonialism. It made use of a military metaphor for mission which appears shocking today. It took an often patronising attitude to the emerging churches in the Global South. Its confidence that it stood on the brink of a great age of world evangelisation proved to be ill-founded. Within a few years of the Conference, the energies of the Western "Christian" nations would be consumed by a war more destructive than any experienced hitherto, and a great deal of the worldwide evangelistic effort would be put on hold. Nor was this to

prove to be a temporary interruption. Edinburgh 1910 which understood itself to be on the brink of a great new surge of missionary advance was, in fact, the high point of the movement. Never again would the Western missionary movement occupy centre-stage in the way that it felt it did at Edinburgh. The scenario envisaged by the Edinburgh delegates never came to pass.

Nonetheless, despite all its blind-spots and weaknesses, the 20th century has witnessed a vindication of a fundamental conviction of Edinburgh 1910: that the good news of Jesus Christ can take root in every culture across the world and produce fruit in church and society everywhere. Vigorous and numerous expressions of Christian faith are to be found on all six continents today. Though we are now very much aware of the primary role played by local people in the spread of the faith, there can be no mistaking the importance of the Western missionaries as catalysts of change. Inasmuch as Edinburgh 1910 was the occasion on which the vision of the modern missionary movement found its most concentrated expression, it can be remembered with thanksgiving as a vision fulfilled. However imperfect its conceptual equipment, the Edinburgh conference anticipated the transformation through which Christianity would become a truly worldwide faith.

The Church of Scotland has played its part in the vast accession to the Christian faith which has taken place in the Global South. Mission stations which had attracted a few dozen or a few hundred converts in 1910 have today grown into Churches which, in some cases, number their members in millions. Can it ever cease to be a source of wonder and profound thanksgiving to God that a small national church on Europe's north-western seaboard should have been blessed with the privilege of sharing the good news of Jesus Christ with people in distant lands to such remarkable effect? It is a striking reality that the witness of the Church of Scotland has borne so much fruit in situations so far away from our own shores.

Besides being an occasion for thanksgiving, the upcoming centenary asks questions of us. Can the memory of Edinburgh 1910 provoke us once more to take stock comprehensively of the church's progress in relation to its evangelistic mandate? Can Edinburgh 2010 help to identify and stimulate the new vision and the fresh energy which will shape church and mission in the 21st century? So far as the challenge of world evangelisation is concerned, it is worth observing that though the number of Christians has greatly increased, the proportion of Christians in the world population has remained fairly constant. So far as the direction of missionary endeavour is concerned, the movement "from the West to the rest" may be going into reverse as Christians from the Global South approach Europe as a mission field.

Lesslie Newbigin 1909-1998

"There is no participation in Christ without participation in his mission to the world." (*The Open Secret*, p. 1.)

Among the many outstanding missionaries appointed by the Church of Scotland during the 20th century, it would be hard to find any who were more influential in shaping our understanding of church and mission than Lesslie Newbigin. After studies in Cambridge during which he came to faith in Jesus Christ, Newbigin served for three years on the staff of the Student Christian Movement in Glasgow. It was there that he met Helen Henderson whom he married in 1936. The same year, they sailed, as Church of Scotland missionaries, for Madras. After learning Tamil and recovering from the shattering of his leg in a serious bus accident, Lesslie began his work as a district missionary in Kanchipuram. He played a leading role in the church union discussions which led to the formation of the Church of South India in 1947. Newbigin himself was consecrated as one of the first bishops of the new church and was given episcopal responsibility for the new diocese of Madurai and Ramnad.

Over the next twelve years, he combined his ministry in India with a key role in ecumenical developments, including the formation of the World Council of Churches in 1948 and preparations for the integration of the WCC and the International Missionary Council in 1961. This led to his becoming General Secretary of the IMC in 1959 and, from 1961, director of the WCC Division of World Mission and Evangelism. In 1965 he returned to India and became bishop in Madras where he served until reaching retirement age in 1974. He then began what some have considered to be his most significant missionary work – thinking through, from the perspective of a foreign missionary, "… what would be involved in a missionary encounter between the gospel and this whole way of perceiving, thinking and living that we call 'modern Western culture'?" (*Foolishness to the Greeks*, p. 1.) He taught at Selly Oak Colleges for five years and then became minister of a small United Reformed Church in inner city Birmingham. During his final years he was based in London, continuing to write and lecture until he died in 1998 at the age of 88.

Throughout his life, Newbigin displayed an extraordinary prescience, often ahead of his time in identifying the key questions for church and mission. On such matters as the Trinitarian basis of mission, contextualisation, pluralism, church unity, the rise of Pentecostalism, and mission after Christendom, he opened up areas of discussion of vital importance for the witness of the church. His biographer Geoffrey Wainwright likened Newbigin's work to that of the Church Fathers, identifying significant similarities with the great bishop-theologians who gave definition to the Christian faith in its early centuries. There is a widespread consensus that the centenary of his birth offers an opportunity to assess the relevance of his work to today's context. The Church of South India has planned a year-long celebration, culminating

7

in a major event in December 2009. In the UK, Churches Together in Britain and Ireland are leading the organisation of a series of day conferences, to be hosted in London, Birmingham and Edinburgh in late 2009, which will consider the meaning of Newbigin's thought for today's world.

Partners in Evangelism

In terms of partnering together for evangelism, a recurrent observation offered by partners is that actions speak louder than words. Living out the gospel is of the utmost importance in making Christ known. Without this, the words of the proclamation will soon be exposed as hollow. In an age of much "bad religion", few will be convinced by verbal proclamation of the gospel until they have seen it lived out in loving action and sacrificial service. This note will be struck repeatedly in the accounts of our overseas partner churches which follow.

Lesslie Newbigin offered this reflection on his experience as a young missionary – "I was in a very sacred Hindu city. It is a place which has almost less Western influence than any other city in India, the ancient capital of the Pallava Empire, with a thousand temples and hundreds of thousands of pilgrims who come there every year. And I used to do a lot of street preaching. And I often used to think to myself, 'Now does this do any good? Is this just words?' And I used to reflect that it was because people there know that we who are standing up and preaching like that are also healing their sick in the hospital, and are also teaching their boys and girls in the schools, and are also helping the village people to do something about their desperate poverty, and are also involved in attempts to make a more just society; it is because they know that, that the words will have some meaning. In other words, that the words without the deeds lack authority! The deeds without the words

are dumb, they lack meaning. The two go together." ("On Being the Church for the World" 1988)

Zambia

The United Church of Zambia (UCZ) understands itself as the product of the "vigorous evangelistic programmes" undertaken by the churches and missions, including the Church of Scotland, which united to form the UCZ in 1965. Its hopes to appoint full-time evangelists have not been realised on account of financial constraints, and it is concerned that this could let it lapse into maintenance mode. The high levels of poverty in the country present another challenge – the good news has to be for the poor. In this context, the Church finds that actions speak louder than words. Congregational committees mandated to care for the needy have made a great impact in many communities. The Church has undergone rapid numerical growth, throwing into relief the need for growth in faith and commitment.

At a full Synod meeting in June 2008, Rev Chrispin Mbalazi and Rev Mulumbwa were elected General Secretary and Synod Bishop respectively. The leadership has to deal with a financial crisis which has led to an erosion in confidence in the leadership of the church. Deficits mean that clergy in some presbyteries have not been paid for months. A group of expert laymen is implementing a strategy to eliminate the deficit and re-introduce sound financial management to the church.

Yet this is a Church of 3 million members (about a quarter of the population) that is growing, with new congregations being established regularly. Fewer than 200 ordained ministers serve congregations in each of Zambia's nine provinces. Much of the life of the church depends on a cadre of trained elders. Resplendent in their red jackets at churches across the country, these men and women have completed courses run by Theological Education by Extension in Zambia (TEEZ). Kangwa Mabuluki,

Director of TEEZ and a team of colleagues work with UCZ and eight other denominations to equip lay people for church leadership through courses on preaching, leading meetings, counselling, *etc*. These courses are being reviewed to take account of changing contexts, *eg*, gender issues, HIV and Aids and contextualisation. All courses are being redesigned to make them less knowledge based and more formational.

> Lesslie Newbigin once wrote that "A theological seminary is seen as a sort of Sandhurst where an officer class is trained, thus creating a chasm between 'clergy' and 'other ranks'. The style of training in the Church …ought to be more akin to that of a 'citizen army' – something that is available to all, which is not confined to one initial period, which continues all through life as members show growing capacity to profit by training and to exercise wider leadership." (*Ministerial Formation* No. 4, 1978, p. 4.)

In April 2008, the Church of Scotland was one of six overseas partners who participated in a pastoral visit to UCZ. The visit was an opportunity to hear the 'voice of the church' and reflect this back to the leadership of United Church of Zambia ahead of the Synod meeting.

The pastoral team had three objectives:
• to understand the nature and challenge of Christian leadership in the present socio-political and economic context in Zambia;
• to explore the key challenges in terms of ministry, mission, witness and service faced by the church in Zambia today; and
• to discuss the internal and external institutional and ecclesiastical issues facing the UCZ today.

In a message to Synod, the partners said: "The UCZ is a united church but unity within the Church needs to be nurtured and actively promoted to achieve solidarity within and among all ten presbyteries. This requires sharing of resources, caring for the weak and vulnerable in society and standing for social justice and dignity for all." They also called for the UCZ to develop its prophetic voice for justice in the country and to use its resources to maximum effect in the diaconal service of God's people.

A peaceful Presidential election resulted in Rupiah Banda being elected as Zambia's fourth President. His Government faces considerable challenges, not least the economic and social collapse which has occurred across the Zambezi in Zimbabwe. The UCZ seeks to offer critical solidarity to the Government.

Ecumenical mission partners are involved in key ministries within the UCZ. Rev Colin Johnston teaches at UCZ's Theological College in Kitwe where his experience and pastoral gifts are appreciated by staff and students alike. Keith Waddell teaches at Mwandi Basic school which he describes as "a typical rural school with 25 teachers for the 900 pupils, aged between 6 and 20." Ida Waddell is a nurse at the 82-bed hospital and runs the HIV and Aids programme that includes awareness raising, voluntary counselling and testing and distribution of antiretroviral drugs.

Malawi

April 2009 marks the major milestone of the 150th anniversary of the first contact between Scots and Malawians when David Livingstone visited the area which is now Malawi in the course of his Zambezi Expedition. It is expected that the Moderator will visit Malawi to celebrate 150 years of what has proved to be a very special relationship for both nations.

It finds expression today not only in a church-to-church partnership but also in an inter-Governmental Agreement and in a wide range of civil society activity coordinated through the Scotland-Malawi Partnership. Under the Scottish Government Malawi programme, the Council received a grant of £265,405 to support the work of the CCAP Nkhoma Synod Safe Motherhood programme. Meanwhile, the Church of Scotland plays a prominent role

7

in relations with Malawi as congregations twin with their counterparts in Malawi, creating a steady flow of visitors to and from Scotland. With a Faithshare Visitors grant, two members of St Fillan's Aberdour were able to visit Alumenda, a Blantyre Synod congregation, and nurture a growing friendship between two rural congregations.

Our links with all three synods of the Church of Central Africa Presbyterian continue to grow and develop. Helen Scott continues to serve as Deputy Headteacher at Ekwendeni Girls High School, while Dr Andy and Fliss Gaston returned to the UK after 11 years service at Ekwendeni Hospital and Livingstonia Synod Aids Project (LISAP). Nkhoma Synod requested the Church of Scotland to recruit medical workers to serve at the synod hospital, and there are opportunities for service at Zomba Theological College and LISAP.

In August 2008, Rev Levi Nyondo succeeded Rev Matiya Nkhoma as General Secretary of the Synod of Livingstonia while Rev Maxwell Mezuwa Banda was elected as Moderator. In another development, the Synod has appointed its first Training Chaplain, a need that was identified during strategic planning. Rev Henry K Mvula will deal with all issues related to training of clergy and lay people. Livingstonia Synod sees its health, development and educational work as being integrated with evangelism in holistic mission. It also promotes annual evangelistic campaigns when large numbers of Christians gather in one area to proclaim the gospel. One-to-one personal evangelism is encouraged throughout the year. World Mission and Mission & Discipleship Councils worked together to facilitate two delegates' participation in the Synod of Livingstonia Youth Conference in July.

With the support of the Scottish Malawi Foundation, Scottish Churches World Exchange is helping to develop a volunteer programme in Malawi for Malawian students. Tiwonge Mzumara, the SCWE Field Officer for Malawi, is co-ordinating the pilot phase of the project which will see thirty Malawian student volunteers working in rural schools and communities during their vacation. Scottish Churches World Exchange expects to continue to support this development and in the near future to go one step further and facilitate the exchange of volunteers between developing countries.

Scottish Churches World Exchange has won funding from the Scottish Government for youth and leadership training courses based at Likhubula House on Mt Mulanje in Malawi. Several hundred young people from all the churches in Malawi, and from other faiths as well, will spend a week together on the mountain learning about leadership and co-operation. The redevelopment of Likhubula House has been a major project for Scottish Churches World Exchange in partnership with the CCAP Blantyre Synod who own the property. In the last four years, over £250,000 has been raised by Scottish Churches World Exchange from sources outside the churches to develop and manage the project.

At the time of writing, it is hoped that the three Synods will meet with overseas partners in April 2009. Two of the main items on the agenda will be support for Zomba Theological College and the boundary dispute between the Synods of Nkhoma and Livingstonia which has resulted in serious division within the CCAP.

Mozambique
The Council was pleased to welcome Rev Constatino Mugema, the General Secretary of the Igreja Evangélica de Cristo em Mozambique, (IECM) to the Partner Church Consultation at Dunblane. After seeking advice from their partners, including the Church of Scotland, on the role of presbyteries, IECM has established its own presbyterial structure. The three presbyteries of Nampula, Malema and Niassa will help the church to manage its life and work more effectively. This is an essential step for a church that has 50,000 members meeting at hundreds of places of worship every Sunday but with a very small number of ordained ministers. The church must now decide if it will also change its name to reflect its Presbyterian structure.

With its final grants to Mozambique, the Council has been able to support the training of a cohort of ministers at Ricatla Theological College. While the new ministers are very welcome, the question arises as to how to provide for ministerial training in future. Despite these concerns and a chronic lack of resources, IECM is working on a range of projects including literacy, clean water, AIDS awareness, and church extension.

South Africa

A key figure in enabling transition in the relationship of the Church of Scotland and the Uniting Presbyterian Church in Southern Africa (UPCSA) has been Rev Dr Vuyani Vellem, the General Secretary. Most recently, he played an important role in the Partner Church Consultation in Dunblane and also the Church Without Walls National Gathering at Ingliston. The new shape of the relationship is exemplified by the link between Pirie Mission and Blackhall St Columba's which was strengthened by another successful visit, from South Africa to Scotland, in October 2008. Working together on the Zimbabwe crisis has also renewed the bonds uniting the two churches (see below). Dr Vellem has been appointed Deputy General Secretary of the South Africa Council of Churches where he is working on the role of the churches in public life, especially in respect of the church's relationship with the state. His successor, Rev Jerry Pillay, took up office in February 2009. A Moderatorial visit to the UPCSA is being planned to mark the 10th anniversary of the union which was enacted in 1999. Becoming a truly united church has been, and remains, a massive challenge, given the immense social and economic divisions which mark South African society, even in the post-apartheid era. Nonetheless, the union has held and secessions have been limited to a very small number of congregations. So there is much to celebrate and affirm through the Moderatorial visit.

Zimbabwe

It has been a year of extreme suffering for the people of Zimbabwe as their democratically expressed wish for a new kind of Government has been frustrated by the determination of Zanu-PF to cling to power at any cost. Death, rape, injury and torture have been the fate of those who have been suspected of disloyalty to the ruling regime. With the 2009 election having resulted in a political impasse, a power sharing agreement was brokered by Thabo Mbeki and finally implemented in February 2009. Morgan Tsvangarai was sworn in as Prime Minister with the rest of the cabinet following shortly after. It is against this background that Morgan Tsvangarai must now try to assert his authority and begin to rebuild Zimbabwe. With members of the MDC still being arrested and held incommunicado even as the new Prime Minister started work, the prospects for the new Government did not seem hopeful.

Meanwhile, the economy has undergone a collapse of unprecedented speed and scale. By November 2008, the rate of inflation had risen to 1,600,000,000,000,000,000,000%, effectively making the money in people's pockets worthless. Unemployment reached 80%, leaving many struggling to survive. Everyday items like bread or petrol could be bought only with US dollars. Public sector employees like teachers, nurses, doctors and police officers, went unpaid. Failed rains and an exceptionally poor harvest meant that food shortages reached catastrophic levels, with the World Food Programme predicting that up to 5 million people would be dependant on food aid by the beginning of 2009. The Council heard of parents eating only on alternate days to ensure that their children were fed. In late 2008, with essential services, like health and sanitation, having completely broken down, cholera struck. By February 2009, the World Health Organization was publishing a daily update showing the number of cases rising by more than 1000 each day. The total number of cases had risen from 20,000 at the end of 2008 to 80,000 by February 2009 with the total number of deaths rising to 4,000 over the same period.

With our partners in Zimbabwe facing these crises, this has not been a year for the Kirk to remain silent or inactive. Working together with leaders from other British churches, the Moderator wrote to the late President Mwanawasa of Zambia, then chair of the Southern African Development Community (SADC), urging Zimbabwe's neighbours to take action on behalf of the people of Zimbabwe. In subsequent letters to front line heads of state and in an article in *The Scotsman,* the Moderator made the case for an African solution to an African problem. Effective help for the people of Zimbabwe must come from within the region, not least because the crisis is spilling over into neighbouring countries.

In July, the Council was represented at a summit in Johannesburg that was co-hosted by our partner church the Uniting Presbyterian Church in Southern Africa (UPCSA) along with the Council for World Mission and the United Congregational Church in Southern Africa. The summit, entitled "Overcoming Fear by Faith", sought to encourage the Church in Zimbabwe to find a prophetic voice. Allan Boesak, a veteran of South Africa's struggle against Apartheid, urged the Christian community to speak out: "The painful, bitter truth is that the ZANU-PF regime… is now oppressive, violent, not worthy of the trust of the people, illegitimate. The time has come for the churches [in Zimbabwe] to say so." The summit also set out to identify the priorities for partners of the Zimbabwean churches:

1. *With South African congregations as the channel, partners will seek ways to supply food and medicines to Zimbabwean congregations and the communities in which they live. A particular emphasis was laid on the importance of an adequate supply of seed maize for the next planting season, to remedy the current desperate shortage of seed.*
2. *Sensing that, within the Zimbabwe Council of Churches (ZCC) itself, and between the ZCC and the Christian Alliance, there are tensions over*

how to address the political circumstances of Zimbabwe, stress was laid on the urgent need to secure a single and united voice from the churches of Zimbabwe.
3. *Perhaps again with South African congregations as a channel, the partner churches pledged themselves to secure and supply supplementary funds for pastors and church workers in Zimbabwe.*

The Council has provided moral and material support in response to the conclusions of the Summit. An emergency grant was received by the Presbytery as a "God-send", and they have also appreciated enormously the willingness of volunteers to live and work with them. The twinning between UPCSA's Presbytery of Zimbabwe and the Presbytery of Greenock and Paisley offers an opportunity to provide very practical help and support. This year, the twinning has focused on strengthening the relationship and collaborating with other international partners, like the Presbytery of Denver in the USA, to examine the question of how partner Presbyteries can best offer meaningful support to the Presbytery of Zimbabwe at this most troubled time.

Kenya
The Presbyterian Church of East Africa's (PCEA) Board of Social Responsibility (BSR) took the lead role in the church's response to the violence that followed Kenya's disputed Presidential election. By April 2008, when a government of national unity was formed, the BSR was helping to care for almost 3,000 families who had been forced to flee from their homes. Many of these people moved to camps like the one at Molo which was visited by Stewart Gillan, the Council's Vice Convener. At this camp, and at another in Mathare (one of Nairobi's largest slums), Stewart saw what the BSR had achieved with the support of international partners. The BSR was especially grateful to those partners, like the Church of Scotland, who had responded quickly, making it possible for them to provide help when it was most needed.

The Church was able to provide the displaced families with shelter and food, and perhaps most importantly, a place of safety at the camps. At Molo and Mathare, Gibson Gitchuki, the BSR's Director, stressed that the Church was helping anyone who had been affected by the violence. While the focus at Molo had been on the displaced Kikuyu population in Mathare, the relief work had responded to the needs of Luo. For all of Kenya's churches the crisis had been cathartic, with an admission that they had been partisan, and that they had failed to speak with a united voice, so the coordination of relief, and the help provided to the victims of violence, were important signs that they were trying to heal divisions amongst themselves. The whole crisis will be investigated by a special commission that is to be set up by Parliament so the process of healing the wounds that were inflicted on Kenyan society will continue.

The PCEA has responded to the concept of twinning with enthusiasm and have identified a member of their secretariat to be the facilitator at national level. It is encouraging to report the development of several new twinnings, including Colinton Parish Church twinned with Umoja Congregation, and Birse and Feughside twinned with Icaciri Congregation. Meanwhile existing links such as the congregations of Hope Park twinned with Murera, and Maxwelltown West twinned with Mathia Congregation continue to develop the initial friendship and work towards a twinning agreement. The twinning process is not always an easy one and communication is often a major hurdle. The embryonic twinning of Chalmers Ardler and Kayole congregations have struggled with this problem in 2008. A highlight in 2008 was the visit of young folks from Kibera to their twinned congregation of Barrhead Bourock and their joined participation in the National Youth Assembly where they were able to share their experience of living through the post-electoral violence where their church building was razed to the ground and lives were lost.

Sudan

In recent years, the Council has reported on the factionalism and controversy that have prevented efforts to reunite the two halves of the Presbyterian Church of Sudan (PCOS). Despite the opportunity afforded by the end of the civil war between the government in Khartoum and the Sudan People's Liberation Army (SPLA) in the south, the church was unable to resolve its own internal differences. The Council, along with other international partners, came to the conclusion that external involvement with PCOS had not helped the situation.

In April 2008, the PCOS met in General Assembly at Malakal. The General Assembly was attended by both parts of the church. Guests at the Assembly included members of the state government, including Dr Riek Machar Teny. Dr Machar addressed the Assembly offering government support for the church as it sought to find a united way forward. The Assembly went on to adopt a new constitution and to agree on the division of new presbyteries for the whole church.

The Rev Peter Makuac Nyak was then elected Moderator of the united church and Rev Paul Bol Kuel became vice moderator, while Rev Gideon Tai Tudeal was appointed General Secretary. The Assembly went on to establish the departments and offices of the church.

The difficulties faced by the reunited church are considerable, not least as they seek to renew their mission and rebuild their infrastructure. Writing from Loki, after the Assembly, the new Moderator said: "I sincerely request your spiritual prayers and moral support because the work I begin now I don't know where to start but through your prayers I believe God will give my way with your help I will start."

Meanwhile tensions continue to trouble the relationship between the government in Khartoum and the Sudan People's Liberation Movement (SPLM) government in southern Sudan. The peace agreement has foundered on several occasions in recent months with both sides

7

mobilizing troops. There will be many challenges for the reunited PCOS in the years ahead.

Nigeria

The General Assembly of the Presbyterian Church of Nigeria (PCN) met in August 2008 and elected Rev Ndukwe N. Eme as Principal Clerk. The Assembly expressed concern about the high levels of youth unemployment in the country and called for Government action to address this problem, called for serious attention to be paid to the need for development in the Niger Delta region, stressed the importance of probity and resistance to corruption among those holding public office and expressed concern about political developments in Zimbabwe, condemning the "sit-tight syndrome of political leaders in Africa". The Church has plans to establish the Hope Waddell University (named after one of the first Church of Scotland missionaries in Nigeria) in Ohafia, Aba State, in order to contribute to the development of education and the formation of future leaders. During the Assembly the new Principal Clerk urged the church to "demonstrate more commitment to mission and evangelism" and proposed a bold three year plan to triple membership and to plant 1000 new congregations. This is a plan that will call for the active participation of every church member: "Every Parish Session should work toward opening more congregations and mission outstations… We must take the Gospel to hospitals, schools, prisons and universities… every Presbyterian youth and adult should talk to at least three persons about Jesus each week."

PCN is keen to develop twinnings, sending a number of profiles from Nigerian congregations hoping to link with counterparts in Scotland. Interested congregations are invited to contact the Associate Secretary (Local Development) – cfinlay@cofscotland.org.uk Pioneering work in this regard has been undertaken by Banchory Ternan West which has forged a fruitful link with PCN's urban health centre in Aba. The centre is hoping to open a new unit that will provide extended services to the community.

Ghana

The General Assembly of the Presbyterian Church of Ghana (PCG) has taken the initiative in evangelism by urging each congregation to work for a membership growth rate of 10% per annum. The Assembly has invested in outreach to the general public by committing to weekly production of an evangelistic television programme. The PCG also runs a fleet of eight evangelism vans which operate nationwide, particularly in areas where there are no churches. A new development is ministry to street children through the establishment of foster homes. Some former street children have entered higher education and have powerful testimonies.

The maturity of democracy in Ghana was apparent in a closely fought Presidential election and in the peaceful transfer of power from the outgoing President, John Kufuor, to his successor John Atta Mills. The churches play an important role in civic education and in promoting a democratic culture.

The Presbyterian Church of Ghana has been a pioneer in the development of twinnings. The idea has been met with real enthusiasm and an abundance of congregations have volunteered to be twinned with congregations in Scotland. In the words of Rev Dr Samuel Ayete Nyamapong, PCG's Ecumenical and Social Relations Director, "Our enthusiasm is based on the fact that local congregations are being offered the opportunity to be directly involved in designing the kind of partnership that would challenge them to share their wealth of Christian experience, gifts, graces, stories and hopes with their sister congregations, all for the mutual benefit and for the building of God's kingdom." The Council has also welcomed the efforts of the Evangelical Presbyterian Church (EPC) to initiate twinnings. One of the newest opportunities for twinning is amongst the EPC's congregations in the Volta region. Whether it is the longstanding link between the PCG's Kwamebikrom community and Murrayfield Parish or the newer connection between the EPC Maulwi Estates and Boghall congregation, it is apparent that no two twinnings are ever the same, and that even the most well established can develop and change.

It was with great sadness that the Council learned in June 2008 of the death of Rev Professor Kwame Bediako, Rector of the Akrofi Christaller Institute of Theology, Mission and Culture at Akropong. A graduate of the University of Aberdeen and a frequent visitor to Scotland, Professor Bediako did much to connect Scotland and Africa at the level of theological thinking. A Memorial Service was held in Edinburgh in September 2008 at which Andrew Walls offered the assessment that: "Kwame Bediako was the outstanding African theologian of his generation…. He did perhaps more than anyone else to persuade mainstream Western theologians and mainstream Western theological institutions that African theology was not an exotic minority specialization but an essential component in a developing global Christian discourse." As Bediako himself wrote, in his ground-breaking book *Christianity in Africa*: "It may also be part of the 'surprise story' of Christian Africa in the twentieth century that having emerged largely as a result of the impact of the West, African contributions to Christian scholarship may now become a benediction to the West … By overturning virtually every negative verdict passed on African primal religion by an ethnocentric Western missionary enterprise, Africa's Christian theologians have contributed in no small measure to reaffirm the place of *religion* itself in the Christian theological enterprise. By all indications, in Africa it is religion – and the findings in the history and phenomenology of religion – which have become the handmaid of theology." (author's italics) (pp. 259, 261)

Pakistan

The Church of Pakistan recognises the fact that Pakistan is an Islamic country where conversion from Islam to Christianity is prohibited. At the same time, it takes seriously the responsibility it has to share the love of Christ with all. In this context, it is practical action and the demonstration of God's love in the lives of Christian believers which speaks louder than any words. This finds expression particularly in such institutions as schools, hospitals, drug rehabilitation centres and centres for the mentally handicapped. In Karachi, services of healing at the Holy Trinity Cathedral attract people from every faith and the Diocese reports that it enjoys good relations with Muslim friends and neighbours. This is seen *eg* in inter-faith meetings which provide the opportunity for dialogue, questions and clarification. The Diocese of Hyderabad has a particular emphasis on tribal evangelism, outreach which is underpinned by programmes of education, healthcare and development work.

Currently, news from Pakistan often focuses on Taliban atrocities in the tribal areas bordering Afghanistan. The Church of Pakistan's Diocese of Peshawar covers this area and Bishop Mano Rumalshah speaks of the "privilege that we as a church are present in perhaps the world's most hostile and vulnerable areas at the moment. God has allowed us to be there in his name to serve humanity, especially people who despise and hate us by cleaning their wounds and nurturing the children." Bishop Mano had thought that was the reason why the social service centres run by the diocese have not been attacked. However, in December 2008 threats were made against staff and students at Elizabeth Girls College in Peshawar while the previous month two missiles damaged Pennel High School in Bannu. The missiles were believed to have been fired by militants retaliating against attacks by US drones.

In November 2008, Rt Rev Samuel R. Azariah, a special delegate at the General Assembly in 2008, was elected Moderator of the Church of Pakistan Synod. Mission partners were withdrawn from Pakistan in 2002 but a security review has cleared the way for new appointments, and two dioceses, Hyderabad and Raiwind, have requested World Mission to recruit mission partners.

7

India

The last year has been the worst since independence in terms of violence being directed against the Christian community. Particularly serious has been the situation in Orissa where the murder of a Hindu leader, Swami Laxanananda Saraswati, in August sparked a wave of attacks on Christians. The National Council of Churches in India (NCCI) condemned the murder, which was apparently carried out by Maoist terrorists. Nonetheless, extremist Hindu groups attacked villages, displacing thousands of people. Hundreds were beaten and some died, often after their homes or church building were set on fire. Priests and ministers were attacked, and, in one notorious case, a nun was raped. The Church's response to the violence, and its efforts to bring aid to those affected, were hindered by the indifference of the state government and the indecision of central government. As the violence spread beyond Orissa to states like Madhya Pradesh, Kerala, Karnataka and Chattisgarh, the Church of North India (CNI) Synod, meeting at Pathankot in the Punjab, declared that the violence was "a naked attack on article 25 [of the constitution] which guarantees citizens the right to 'practise, preach and propagate their faiths'. We appeal to the Central and State governments to ensure that Muslims, Christians and Sikhs, and other minority religious communities are not denied this fundamental right." Despite these calls, and the affirmation of Prime Minister Manmohan Singh that "Christianity is part of our national heritage", the attacks continued until late 2008.

Our partners view the attacks on Christians as one expression of the "communalism" which threatens the very fabric of Indian society. Despite these extreme pressures, they continue to proclaim the gospel and they remain committed to the fight against poverty and the struggle for social justice. But the churches have warned that inter-communal violence is damaging efforts to overcome India's most pressing problems.

In a report received by the 13th Ordinary Synod of the Church of North India, in October 2008, a Special Evaluation Commission explained why witness is so important for the Church: "Christian witness embraces a life of reverberating testimony about Christ's earthly mission, the reality of love and redemption for human kind through suffering on the cross and later enlightenment through the Holy Spirit." The report went on to say "witness assumes its brilliance in times of persecution due to intolerance and fundamentalism…" It noted that "the Christian way of witness is through concrete acts of love and social justice in our personal lives."

Other reports received by the Synod, including those submitted by their 25 dioceses demonstrated how that witness is put into effect, for example in the social empowerment programmes of the Diocese of Marathwada where church membership is highest among the Dalit community, or in the outreach to the children of sex workers in Siliguri, in the Diocese of Eastern Himalaya, and a similar scheme for street children in Nagpur. The Council has been able to offer some help to programmes like these through the Boys Brigade World Mission project which offered support for a centre for rag-pickers in Nagpur; and through the annual stamp appeal which has helped girls to return to education in Kalimpong. The congregation of St Blane's, through its stewardship campaign, has supported the Diocese of Eastern Himalayas livelihood project.

CNI recognises the need to engage the whole church in this mission and so it inaugurated the Congregational Renewal for Effective Engagement in Mission (CREEM) to "empower local congregations for the task of holistic mission in the 21st century." CREEM envisages a "radically bottom up approach to 'doing' mission" by beginning with local congregations. Two rural and two urban congregations from every diocese (a total of 100) have been selected for the first phase of the scheme working on five priorities: liturgy, service, preaching, teaching and fellowship.

For the Church of South India, this has been a year of transition, with new office bearers appointed in early 2008. The new moderator, Bishop John Gladstone participated in the Partner Church Consultation at Dunblane in May 2008. Plans are now well advanced to celebrate the centenary of Bishop Leslie Newbigin with a year-long programme expected to culminate in December 2009. Meanwhile the Presbytery of Edinburgh has entered into a twinning process with Bishop Newbigin's former Diocese of Madras and welcomed the visit of Rev John Vadiangadu and Mrs Sheila Lawrence in November 2008.

Nepal

The United Mission to Nepal (UMN) is the Church's principal partner in this Himalayan country. Since 1954, UMN has worked to "minister to the needs of the people of Nepal in the Name and Spirit of Christ and to make Christ known by word and life, thereby strengthening the universal Church in its total ministry." UMN works with local implementing partners in five geographical locations in eight areas of work (Education, Women and Children, HIV/AIDS, Food Security, Enterprise Development, Disaster Management, Peace & Conflict Transformation and Advocacy). UMN staff train local partner organisations so they can deliver services more effectively and become more sustainable. When Rt Rev David Lunan undertook the first Moderatorial visit to Nepal, he saw how this approach can transform people's lives. UMN Dhading Cluster, based three hours west of Kathmandu, has worked with Jagat-Jyoti Community Development Centre on food sovereignty and enterprise development for three years. UMN's food sovereignty officer had successfully introduced the idea of growing coffee in nurseries to increase farmers' income. JCDS has worked with two Dalit communities since 2006. At first, the people would hide from strangers but they welcomed the Moderator into their village with garlands, proudly showing the community vegetable garden that has improved the nutrition and health of the community. As the Moderator wrote in *Life and Work*:

I asked what was the biggest change in their lives since they'd started working with UMN. 'That we can meet you and talk to you.' For generations they have been shunned and would hide if anyone other than a Dalit came near them. The transformation in their attitude, their self-esteem, their way of life was total…They were no longer afraid, the future held hope for them – it was as though we were witnessing a small part of Mary's hymn of praise for the coming of the Messiah – 'He has filled the hungry with good things'.

World Mission is implementing a new strategy for recruiting people to serve with UMN. As well as featuring a link to www.umn.org.np on the Church website, there will be a quarterly focus on one particular post that will involve advertising in the national and specialist press and websites.

World Mission is developing new partnerships with two Bible colleges in Kathmandu. The Nepali church is perhaps the fastest growing in the world – in 1959, there were just 29 Christians secretly living in Nepal and today the number of Nepali Christians has grown to an estimated six hundred thousand – but there is a shortage of well-trained pastors. Some of the church growth is due to splits and schisms but it is also true that "Nepali Christians are good at converting people, though weak at teaching." World Mission's partnerships with Nepal Institute of Theology and Nepal Ebenezer Bible College offer an opportunity to share our resources in the building up of the still young church in Nepal. The Hope Trust funded library books for NIT and NEBC and there are opportunities for further cooperation, including faculty development.

Bangladesh

Bishop Paul Shishir Sarker is the new Moderator of the Church of Bangladesh, succeeding Bishop Michael Baroi who will retire later in 2009. With some 18,000 members, the Church of Bangladesh is a small church in the world's seventh most populous country, yet carries out a wide range of social and development work across Bangladesh.

7

The vulnerability and resilience of the people of Bangladesh is demonstrated in the village of Karia Nagar near Mongla at the head of Bangladesh's Sundarban nature reserve. The Christian community there was established over a century ago. They depend on fishing and are susceptible to the vagaries of the weather and natural disasters. In November 2007, Cyclone Sidr flattened 34 of 35 houses in the village. Rev Sanjib Bala, the pastor responsible for the sub-parish of Karia Nagar, had seen the cyclone warning on TV. Mongla was at alert level 10, the highest on the scale. Rev Bala phoned his parish to pass on the information, saving many lives as a result. 150 people crammed into the two-storey church and school-cum-flood shelter for four days. One couple there were George and Shanti. Their son was born in the church shelter and is named Sidr. This community has rebuilt houses and returned to fishing. They testify to the importance of their Christian faith and worship. They show no self-pity or bitterness, rather they witness to the gospel of grace and embody the kingdom values of the Beatitudes.

The Church of Bangladesh gives priority to the marginalised. The Garo people mainly live in the north and are nearly all Christians. The Church of Bangladesh is working to affirm and preserve their distinct culture which is being threatened by outward migration driven by poverty and lack of opportunities and the homogenisation of cultures caused by globalisation and mass media. It takes hours to drive on narrow mud roads between fields and forests to Panihati (where Angus Presbytery is supporting a new clinic), Thanarbaid and Dhorati. These are isolated places where the government does not deliver health or education services, and even the basic health and education provision from Church of Bangladesh and other NGOs is vital for these marginalised communities.

The Church of Scotland is a member of the Church of Bangladesh Group. This ecumenical body coordinates the work and sharing of resources between seven churches and mission organisations in the UK and Europe. There are four mission partners currently serving in the development sector and the Council aims to recruit a staff member to teach at St Andrew's Theological College in Mirpur, Dhaka.

Sri Lanka

The story of evangelism in Sri Lanka is bound up with the varying political and economic circumstances which have prevailed over the centuries. The adoption of Christian faith by families and communities has often been a response to social and educational realities, with the result that the dynamic of receiving and sharing the gospel has only found expression to a limited extent. Today, the Presbytery of Lanka is sensitive to the multi-racial, multi-religious and multi-cultural character of the Sri Lankan nation. In a context where offering care to the needy can lead to accusations of unethical evangelism, outreach to the community has to be developed with great care. For example, it is the church's work amongst the poor that is most likely to draw allegations of unethical conversion, with the suggestion that converts are bribed. Many believe that Christians only ever engage in social action in order to entice the vulnerable. These fears were apparently confirmed in the report of a congressional commission in January 2009. The report claimed to have found overwhelming evidence of unethical practice and forced conversion. This prompted a renewed effort to introduce legislation that will outlaw "forced" conversion.

For our own partners this has raised questions about the very nature of witness: what does it mean to speak of evangelism and conversion in a multi-racial, multi-cultural, multi-religious society? In a letter to parliamentarians church leaders recognized that there had been "insensitive and even thoughtless… behaviour," and "the need to learn new lessons of respectful co-existence" but they also asserted their constitutional right to practise their faith, and their calling to serve the community. The leaders offered to adopt a voluntary code of practice and, as an alternative to legislation on "conversions", they proposed a representative Inter-Religious Council with the power to mediate and to strengthen the ties between the faith communities.

The churches in Sri Lanka understand the need for a common voice in these circumstances, but they also understand that their most effective witness is in the work which they do together on the ground amongst the people, the work that leaves them most open to these charges. In Advent 2008, the Protestant Churches were able to set up a Confederation which will enable them to collaborate more effectively both in their work with the people and in their response to any proposed changes in the law relating to religious practice.

The Presbytery of Lanka is a founder member of the Confederation of Christian Churches in Sri Lanka – a significant source of strength to what is a very small denomination. St Andrew's Colombo, now a charge of the Presbytery of Europe, has enjoyed its first full year as an associate member of the Presbytery of Lanka. The value which St Andrew's offers to the Presbytery was indicated by the election of its minister, Rev John Purves, as Deputy Moderator of the Presbytery. The new Moderator is Rev Saman Perera, a former Church of Scotland bursar, whose own congregation in Kandy has been active in developing twinning relationships with congregations in Scotland.

The intensification of the civil war over the past year has caused great suffering, with the poor and vulnerable being hardest hit. Church life is marked by severe tension and constant anxiety, yet the harsh circumstances yield a deeply impressive vibrancy of faith. Analysis of the political, social and military situation is offered in the Report of the Church and Society Council (pp. 2/112 Paper 6)

Burma/Myanmar

In early 2009, it was reported that authorities in the former capital, Rangoon, were warning pastors from leading congregations that their regular Church services would be banned. The services take place in residential apartments as the government had long since stopped issuing permits for the possession of land and building churches. In response, churches had begun to meet in apartments many of which were bought in the name of private owners. At a meeting with leaders of 50 congregations, officials said that churches could be sealed off if worship was not stopped. The order could affect up to 80% of Christian groups meeting in and around Rangoon. One Christian who e-mailed the Mizzima News Agency explained that: "Only a few churches have their own land. Most churches use rented buildings, houses and office style rooms for worship." Meanwhile the authorities have kept Aung San Suu Kyi under house arrest for more than thirteen years and prospects for a political solution seem to be as far away as ever.

China

2008 was a year of great celebration and great sadness for China. The great celebration came in the form of the Olympics held in Beijing in August. The great sadness came with the devastation and loss of life in the Sichuan Earthquake which happened on 12 May. Both of these events touched the entire Chinese nation in a way not seen for many years.

The Chinese people saw the Olympics as a way to show the rest of the world the progress that had been made in their country. While many of us may have had questions about the amount of money being spent by the hosts, those same concerns were met with surprise by a peasant family. They may have been living in a very remote area that required hours of walking to reach and they may have had no kitchen or bathroom, but they did not want money diverted from the Olympics to be spent on them – their pride in China's achievement as host was all that mattered.

7

The plight of those affected by the earthquake galvanised support and assistance throughout the country. Within the first 23 days, RMB43 bn (approx £4.3bn) had been donated, much of it from within the country. Students, office-workers, seminarians, people from all walks of life organised collections or offered practical help and support *eg* Shengjing Hospital in Shenyang, one of the Scottish Churches China Group's main partners, offered specialist medical care to some of the survivors. The Amity foundation had a member of staff in the region within hours of the earthquake to coordinate its response. Outside the city of Mianzhu, 100 "Meeting Points" and the Christians who attended them were lost in the Earthquake. A newly rebuilt Church in the city itself was so badly damaged that it will need to be torn down, but this did not stop the local congregation meeting in the courtyard every evening to worship and to offer basic food, water and blankets to anyone in need.

Different as these two events were, the Church and Chinese Christians were an obvious presence in both. The Amity Printing Press was given permission by the Government to print 50,000 Bibles, with the Olympic logo on them, to be given out to Olympic competitors and officials. Shenyang hosted the football competition, so the local government gave the Catholic Cathedral RMB4m (approx £400,000) to refurbish the building so that visitors would have somewhere "nice" to worship.

The Faithshare Programme supported Alan Gibson, a staff member of Crossreach, who travelled to China under the auspices of the Scottish Churches China Group to speak at a conference on disability and deliver a series of training workshops for partners in Nanjing. Meanwhile Nessbank congregation continue to develop their twinning relationship with Meishan Gospel Church in Nanping.

South Korea

The 93rd General Assembly of the Presbyterian Church of Korea (PCK) was held in Jeju Island last September and celebrated the centenary of the first mission to the island by Rev Lee Ki-poong in 1908. The centenary was not only celebrated by PCK. When Rev Lee Ki-poong arrived, there was only one Presbyterian denomination. Over the last 60 years, however, the Presbyterian Church in Korea split many times over theological issues. In order to celebrate the mission to Jeju together and enhance the spirit of unity, all the commissioners of four major Presbyterian denominations gathered together for the first time since the church split, prayed hand in hand, repenting the sins of dividing the body of Christ and not having been the light and salt of the world. PCK hopes the Korean Churches will go on to unite with each other and to serve the world in the name of our Lord.

While the PCK takes seriously its commitment to the Great Commission, the twin challenges of stagnation of church growth and the economic crisis have struck, which has affected Korea and the church there. They have started a new movement for church growth, "the PCK 3 Million Believer's Movement", with the goal to increase the number of congregations by 10 per cent within 2 years. Yet, this is not just about numerical growth, for what the PCK hopes to achieve is to revitalise mission and evangelism within the church and to give the message of hope and compassion to Korean society with "servanthood" as the new keyword for the movement. Although developing slowly, the Presbytery of Lanark's twinning with the Presbytery of East Seoul in the Presbyterian Church in the Republic of Korea (PROK) has seen the first step toward congregation-to-congregation links, following the visit of members of Carluke St Andrew's to South Korea.

Taiwan

In 2006, the Presbyterian Church in Taiwan (PCT) set "identity, commitment and growth" as the goal of its evangelism in the following decade. As Rev Andrew Chang, the General Secretary explains, "Our plan is to start with our family and then expand our sphere of evangelism to church, society, our nation and the world." Recognizing that mission is more than simply "proselytizing for Christianity", the church has adopted six dimensions of holistic mission as guiding principles for their evangelism. The dimensions are: proclaiming the gospel, nurturing God's people, serving with love, transforming society, caring for creation and gospel and culture. These essential facets of a healthy church are the focus of PCT's evangelism because "church health is key for church growth. A healthy church naturally becomes the body of Christ serving the world."

That service takes many different forms. For example, 2008 was chosen as the "Aboriginal Missions Year". Many of the indigenous population have moved into Taiwan's cities, which means that tribal churches lose members, and those that move to the cities often lose contact with the church. Through a Partnership in Mission programme, PCT is encouraging city churches to work with the indigenous community in their own parish, and through them to form partnership with the communities and churches from which they originally moved. As it reaches out to indigenous communities, PCT is also sharing their concerns, for example over the use of tribal land whether that be for a proposed nuclear waste disposal plant or national park projects in areas given to the aboriginal community.

Jamaica

As Council member Rev George Lind and Locally Supported Partnerships Officer Neill Crawford discovered during a visit to Jamaica, the challenges facing the Uniting Church in Jamaica and the Cayman Islands (UCJCI) are not so different from those confronting the churches here in Scotland and Europe. Society in general seems to be increasingly secularized. Mainline church membership is falling while independent congregations are growing. The church finds itself questioning its role, and trying to understand its mission in a changing context.

At a special meeting of the UCJCI Synod in July 2008, the church set out its response to these challenges. "The

Agenda For Change" aims to equip congregations for their role in witness and evangelism in modern Jamaica. In Jamaica, as in Scotland, the church has recognised that the local congregation will have a leading role to play in meeting the work that lies ahead.

The 200th anniversary of the abolition of the slave trade was an important date for Jamaicans. There is a new awareness of the past and indeed many have become conscious of the role that Scots played in the slave trade. That awareness also feeds concern about modern slavery. In amongst the beaches and tourists of towns like Negril, human trafficking has become an issue.

Despite the wealth of tourist centres like this, local young people often leave school long before they have acquired the skills to survive. There is a real danger that they end up enticed into the sex trade. The Theodora project is the churches' response to the problem. Led by Margaret Fowler, a former mission partner of the Church of Scotland, the project focuses on adult literacy, basic maths skills, and vocational training.

The 2008 hurricane season was especially severe, with the impact of hurricane Gustav being particularly heavy in Jamaica. Many roads were closed, crops damaged or destroyed, and there were some injuries. It is, perhaps, telling that the UCJCI's response to the storms was to offer support where it was needed. A group of churchwomen from the Cayman Islands flew to Cuba to help their counterparts who suffered so much more after hurricanes Ike and Hanna.

In 2008, Crown Church in Inverness welcomed visitors from their twinned congregation, North Street United Church in Kingston. Early in 2009, Rev Jim McDonald of Crieff Parish visited Shortwood congregation in Kingston to further their relationship and also to spend time with the UCJCI secretariat developing procedures that enable congregations to build their relationship. The engagement of the UCJCI and other partners helps in this process, giving us much needed advice on developing guidelines for congregations.

Trinidad

The Presbyterian Church of Trinidad and Tobago has seen a significant rise in the number attending worship over the past two years. It is estimated that total average attendances on Sundays have risen from 17,000 to 25,000. This revitalisation of the worshipping life of the Church is integrally related to the consolidation of the work of its schools, with teachers playing a key role in the community. A highlight of the Church Without Walls National Gathering at Ingliston was the address on "21st Century Discipleship" given by Rt Rev Elvis Elahie, the Moderator of the PCTT, who also spoke challengingly at "Re-energize 4" in Aviemore in January 2009.

Israel and Palestine

Of all the areas of the world in which the Council works, there is none more subject to constantly changing circumstances than that of Israel and Palestine and the wider Middle East. Working in a region of such uncertainties, responsible for a considerable level of resources, both human and property, inevitably creates a high level of risk for both the Council and the Church at large. Risk, in all its guises, requires detailed management virtually on a day-to-day basis and occupies a large proportion of the time of staff directly responsible. To provide added strength to our management capability "on the ground", the Council has appointed Mr James Laing to the new position of Regional Manager for the Council's work in Israel and Palestine. Based in Israel, Mr Laing, working closely with the Church's senior staff in the area, has responsibility for the day-to-day management of the Centres. Through the life of the Centres, the Council seeks to embody the good news of Jesus Christ in the form of hospitality – a quality that is sorely absent from much of the interface between different communities in the Middle East. The life of the Centres gives expression to a vision of justice and peace which springs from faith in Christ as Saviour.

Of profound concern to the Council has been the conflict in Gaza. The death and devastation caused through an inability and unwillingness by both sides to sit and resolve their long-standing political differences has the result of once again creating victims out of the innocents. The round of strident accusations continues with no-one, seemingly, able or willing to break the circle of claim and counterclaim. Appeals from the international community and church leaders in Israel and Palestine and from around the world fall on deaf ears, and the killing goes on. During this period, we are constantly in touch with our partners in the region, the Diocese of the Episcopal Church in Jerusalem and the Middle East. Bishop Suheil Dawani noted: "Of immediate concern is the urgent medical services needed by the victims of this violence. The immensity of providing care for the injured and wounded is overwhelming a healthcare system struggling to provide essential healthcare services for 1.5 million Palestinians, most of whom live in refugee camps. Our Al Ahli Hospital, located in the heart of Gaza City is providing essential frontline medical and emergency humanitarian services to those coming or being brought directly to it. Additionally, it is receiving patients transferred by UNRWA from the Government Hospital Al Shiffa for emergency inpatient and surgical treatment of the wounded and injured. As a non-partisan, well-established Hospital, we are receiving patients from all directions." The Council's response was the provision of an emergency grant of £25,000 to enable the purchase of medical supplies, fuel and food.

As Dr Bernard Sabella, a delegate to last year's General Assembly noted: "The conflict in Gaza, and in fact in Israel and Palestine, cannot and will not be resolved by force. Only the victims pay the price and politicians are left to weigh the advantages to their positions, especially at the eve of upcoming Israeli elections. In the long run, however, what is right is right, and violence will not move us in this land towards an acceptable end of conflict." The Palestinian community and the Palestinian Authority are divided between Hamas and Fatah while the Israeli society is currently seeking to elect a new government which can command the respect and confidence of the electorate, unlike its predecessor. Until both parties to the conflict can put in place strong representatives mandated to resolve the conflict with a political solution, the region seems destined to continue in the suicidal path of death and destruction.

After some time, the worldwide economic decline caught up with Israel and Palestine threatening the financial wellbeing of the area. For a region of the world which relies so heavily on revenue from tourism, the impact of a serious decline in visitors whether for economic reasons or political instability will have an equally serious consequence not only for the region as a whole but also for the Church's Guesthouse and Hotel, both of which rely heavily on "external" visitors. While we have evidence to show that there is usually a quick recovery in the rate of visitors upon the cessation of open conflict, we are in unknown territory in the event of a long-drawn-out global economic decline. This constitutes a risk which requires very careful monitoring and appropriate action when necessary.

Parish Grouping
St. Andrew's Scots Memorial Church, Jerusalem with St. Andrew's Church in Tiberias form the basis of a Parish Grouping which, over the past eighteen months, has been faithfully served with a number of Locum Ministers, to whom the Council would want to pay tribute for their commitment to the ministry of both congregations and to the wider community in Israel and Palestine. The Council is pleased to have made the appointment of Rev George Shand to the post of Minister of St. Andrew's, Jerusalem and also the appointment of an Associate Minister in Tiberias.

In addition to nurturing the Church's wider ministry in Israel and Palestine, whether within the Council's own Centres or in the community at large, a major role for the Grouping is the development of the formal partnership the Church of Scotland has with the Diocese of the Episcopal Church in Jerusalem and the Middle East. In April 2008, members of the Council's Middle East Committee met with representatives of the Diocese in order to re-establish and put new life into the relationship. Following this three day meeting, an agenda was set for the newly formed Partnership Working Group which now meets in Israel on a monthly basis to continue the process of development.

Meanwhile, relationships continue to be maintained and developed with other Churches and Church related bodies, including support where possible, for example the Lutheran Media Centre in Bethlehem, Sabeel, Al Ahli Arab Hospital in Gaza, the Department of Services to Palestinian Refugees (DSPR), Near East Council of Churches in Gaza, Al Shurooq School for the Blind, Atfaluna Society for Deaf Children and the YWCA.

The Council is grateful for, and appreciative of, the continuing spiritual and financial support of The Society of Friends of St. Andrew's, Jerusalem towards the work and witness of St. Andrew's Church and Guesthouse in Jerusalem.

Tabeetha School, Jaffa
Recognised by the Israeli authorities as a unique multi-faith, multi-ethnic educational establishment providing a model for other schools to follow, Tabeetha School continues to give evidence that it is possible to provide the positive and secure environment which allows young people to be educated, to develop and to grow together within a mixed community which, beyond the walls of the school, is a community of fear, suspicion and hatred.

The Council appointed Mr Antony Short as the Principal of the School and is delighted to put on record its appreciation that, led by the School's Senior Management Team under Mr Short, the School continues to enhance its reputation not only within the local Jaffa community but also in the larger educational community.

A major development for the school is its registration as an Amuta, a charitable trust. This legal status within the State of Israel will serve the school in many ways, including its legitimacy to continue to receive funding and other support from the Ministry of Education.

A recent development has been the appointment of a Chemistry Teacher from Scotland. As a Mission Partner, the new appointee will add to the Christian presence within the School and will be a valuable asset in developing its Christian ethos.

St. Andrew's Scottish Guesthouse, Jerusalem

Following the completion of major renovation work, the Guesthouse has experienced a remarkable demand by many visistors, both local and from overseas, to stay. The reasons for its popularity are varied. Being in the heart of Jerusalem close to the Old City, it is ideal for Pilgrim Groups, for family and individual tourists from outwith Israel and Palestine and also for local Israelis visiting the area on business or simply sightseeing. What is common to all who have used the Guesthouse, in one way or another, is the response to their stay.

It would be very rare indeed to hear other than compliments from visitors appreciating as they do the attentive and welcoming staff, the warm and pleasant ambience, and facilities and surroundings which mark out the Guesthouse as one of the desirable places to stay in Jerusalem. With very little funds being spent on advertising, the level of occupancy reached an impressive 91% in 2008 against a budget of 83%. The net operating profit for the year of £131,600 exceeded the target by £53,500, an increase of 68% over budget. In financial terms, these outcomes for 2008 exceed any past records for the Guesthouse and are very much a reflection of its popularity among the many who keep coming back to spend time in this special place set aside from the busy world around, where people, regardless of culture or creed, are made to feel welcome within a Christian setting. During 2008, 24 pilgrim groups made use of the Guesthouse.

Scots Hotel, Tiberias

Of its style, the Hotel continues to be one of the most popular in Israel. Led by its enthusiastic General Manager, Shimon Kipnis, the multi-faith, multi-ethnic staff team work hard at trying to do something which is rare in the standard Israeli hotel, make people feel welcome. The Scots Hotel has the feel of a "family hotel" renowned both within Israel and Palestine and beyond for the fact that, whatever the tensions and problems between the different communities outwith its walls, the community life of the Hotel bears witness to the fact that people from such communities can work and play together. While the percentage occupancy for the year was reduced from the target of 72% to 67%, the net operating profit was increased from its budget projection of $141,700 to $200,100.

Working closely with the Minister, the Hotel management continues to develop and promote the Christian presence and ethos of the Hotel. During the year, some 244 pilgrim groups from around the world used the Hotel, many of whom were repeat visitors. An increasing number of local Christian groups and individuals visited, whether for rest and recreation or to participate in seminars, conferences or the like. To encourage and facilitate such use of the Hotel and its facilities, the Church, working with the Hotel, offers significantly discounted rates. One sadness is the difficulty the Hotel experiences in being able to welcome potential visitors from within the West Bank and Gaza because of imposed travel restrictions. On the other hand, from time to time, the Hotel has hosted groups from nearby Jordan. In consultation with our partner Episcopal Church, plans are currently being developed for a Peace and Reconciliation Centre which will utilise the facilities of the church and hotel.

Syria and Lebanon

Early in 2008, the then Moderator, the Very Rev Dr Sheilagh Kesting, was delighted to receive an invitation to visit from the National Evangelical Synod of Syria and

Lebanon (NESSL). Not only was it an opportunity to learn at first hand about the work and witness of the Synod, it was also an opportunity for the Moderator to affirm the solidarity extended to the Church by the Council following the Israeli-Hezbollah war; and to see the reconstruction work completed by the Synod with the help of much appreciated emergency grants from the Church of Scotland. At a time of considerable tension in the region, the Moderator confirmed the concerns of the Church of Scotland for a just and enduring peace. In response the Synod looks forward to the future development of the partnership and expressed its desire to explore the development of twinnings and the placement of volunteers. While in the area, the Moderator was able to visit Shatila refugee camp in Beirut and see the work of Christian Aid's partner Association Najdeh amongst the Palestinian refugees.

Egypt

Relationships with the Evangelical Presbyterian Church of Egypt, Synod of the Nile, were revitalised when Council staff made a brief visit in December 2008. The Synod is engaged in a multi-faceted outreach within Egypt's predominantly Islamic society. It sustains a major commitment to educational and medical work, with 30,000 children in its schools, two hospitals and a network of clinics that are open to all. Every bed in the hospital is supplied with a Bible which patients often request to retain when they are discharged. Church members make pastoral visits to the hospitals and are often invited to pray with the patients. For historic reasons, the Presbyterian witness is concentrated in certain districts of the country while in others there is no active church life. This poses the question as to whether it is possible to develop a mission strategy which embraces the whole country. As in many other contexts, evangelism takes place primarily through personal relationships as Christians live out the gospel and share it with their friends. In a context where family, community and religious identity define one's life, some Muslims have been drawn to faith in Jesus Christ as Saviour while remaining within an Islamic religious and cultural identity. The Synod is active in promoting Muslim-Christian dialogue, both at the formal and theological level and at the level of everyday life in the community. The Evangelical Theological Seminary in Cairo provides a vital training base not only for Egypt but for the wider region, a resource from which the Council hopes to benefit as it develops its new bursary strategy which is based on students undertaking their courses within their own region.

Europe

The Council holds reserved funds for use within Europe. Consultation with partners has revealed that a priority for them is the award of scholarships for a period of study in Scotland. Therefore, though the Scottish-based bursary programme has been discontinued, arrangements have been made for bursars from European partner churches to study in Scotland on the basis of receiving a grant award and making their own arrangements. The Council therefore looks forward to welcoming bursars from the Hungarian Reformed Church and the Evangelical Church of Czech Brethren in the 2009-10 academic year.

At the end of 2008, the Council bade fond farewell to Bertalan Tamás on his retirement as Ecumenical Officer of the Reformed Church of Hungary. "Berti" served for many years as minister of the St Columba's congregation in Budapest and has remained a constant friend and adviser to the Church of Scotland. The Council looks forward to working with his successor as Ecumenical Officer, Balázs Ódor. A notable event in the life of the Evangelical Church of Czech Brethren (ECCB) was the 90th anniversary of the formation of the Church at which the Council was represented by Europe Convener Catherine Buchan and Scots Kirk Paris minister Alan Miller. Partnership with the ECCB has been revitalized by inspiring twinnings and the participation of young Scots in the annual ECCB Youth Camp. The Synod of the Waldensian Church met in August 2008 and grappled with issues raised by the increasingly pluralistic society in which it bears witness. Amongst the many immigrants arriving in Italy at this time are Protestant Christians with whom the Waldensians share a common understanding of the faith but often experience a wide gulf when it comes to culture and language. The Council has been pleased to help support the work of Alex and Dorothy Cairns at the Waldensian English Speaking Congregation in Turin which has provided a place of welcome and worship for a great diversity of immigrants to the city.

Overseas Charges

In fulfilment of legislation passed by the 2008 General Assembly, the charges of Christ Church, Warwick, Bermuda and St Andrew's Colombo, Sri Lanka were admitted to the Presbytery of Europe and a smooth handover of responsibilities took place. The introduction of Rev John McLeod to St Andrew's Nassau has brought fresh impetus to the aspiration to form a Presbyterian Church of the Bahamas, initially comprising the Church of Scotland charges. A notable expression of the Covenant in Trinidad was the ordination of Denyse Rattansingh by the Presbyterian Church of Trinidad and Tobago for service in the Church of Scotland charge.

Whom Shall I Send and Who Will Go for Us?

Over two centuries, much of the Council's work has revolved around the sacrificial service of mission partners who have gone to serve overseas for periods of time. It has been a matter of regret to the Council that their numbers have been steadily falling over the past fifty years and it has recognised that it now reaches a crisis point. Without decisive action to turn around the drastic decline in mission partner numbers, the Council will very soon be lacking this backbone of its overseas partnership work. Enabling church members to serve overseas for periods of time remains at the core of the Council's purpose. Therefore developing new models which are more relational, collaborative, varied, flexible and open is a matter of the utmost urgency for the Council. It has

committed itself anew to recruit, send and support the people who will be at the forefront of developing mission strategy and will give life to its relationships with partner churches in the years to come.

The benefits of 'Saying it with people' are enormous. Whether an individual or a church is involved in the sending of or the receiving of a mission partner, the outcome is good for their faith, and for the health of the church as a whole. Here are some reasons why:

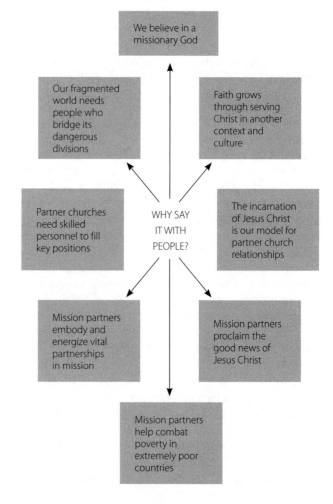

We believe in a missionary God

Our fragmented world needs people who bridge its dangerous divisions

Faith grows through serving Christ in another context and culture

Partner churches need skilled personnel to fill key positions

WHY SAY IT WITH PEOPLE?

The incarnation of Jesus Christ is our model for partner church relationships

Mission partners embody and energize vital partnerships in mission

Mission partners proclaim the good news of Jesus Christ

Mission partners help combat poverty in extremely poor countries

Lesslie Newbigin urged: "We cannot faithfully discharge our missionary responsibility to our own people unless we are willing to listen for what the living God says to us through his servants in other cultures. We need all the saints, and the foreign missionary is not a temporary but an abiding necessity for the life of the church, provided always that the movement of missionaries is multi-directional, all churches both sending and receiving. The word of God is to be spoken in every tongue, but it can never be domesticated in any." (*Foolishness to the Greeks*, p. 147)

Tasting the Fruits

While the fruits of mission can be encouraged to grow by those engaged in mission in different ways – short visits, twinnings, projects, volunteer placements *etc* – the mission partner has a particularly valuable role to play. The fruits of his/her service can be understood in the following terms:

We believe in a missionary God

When we think of Christian mission, our first conviction is that it is the mission of God. The Bible, from beginning to end, tells us of a God who has a purpose of salvation. This purpose finds its full and final expression in the coming of Jesus Christ. When we encounter him, he says: "As the Father has sent me, so I am sending you." At the core of the experience of coming to faith in Jesus Christ is the sense of being sent, not on a mission of our own making but as "co-workers with God". Since God's mission comprehends the whole world, our horizons are stretched and we are challenged to think of whether we could make a contribution somewhere far from home.

Faith grows through serving Christ in another context and culture

There is undoubtedly an element of sacrifice involved in accepting appointment as a mission partner. It provides few material rewards and often a good deal of discomfort and disturbance. Yet the great majority of those who have served have described their time as a mission partner as the best years of their life. A Czech proverb states that "as often as you learn a new language, you become a new person." Not only maturity of faith but a great sense of personal growth is very often the experience of those who embark on the adventure of serving as a mission partner.

Mission partners embody and energize vital partnerships in mission

People who enter into the life and language of an overseas partner church play a major role in sustaining and developing the relationship. Such mission partners become bridges across which effective communication and interaction between the two churches takes place. This opens up the possibility of many people becoming involved in the partnership, enabled and strengthened by the longer-term mission partners who function as the spine of the relationship.

The incarnation of Jesus Christ is our model for partner church relationships

The best way God could find to express his love for us was to become human and live among us for a time. Could we find any better way in which to express our love for our sisters and brothers in other lands with whom we are united in the gospel? Mission partners are appointed to a specified job but also to much more. Taking the model of the incarnation, they share in every aspect of the life of the community to which they go, learning to live on terms set by others. As was the case with Jesus, this is highly costly but also infinitely rewarding.

Partner churches need skilled personnel to fill key positions

The good news of Jesus Christ first reached Europe, we are told, because the apostle Paul had a vision of a man of Macedonia begging him to "come over to Macedonia and help us." The Church of Scotland still receives such messages from partner churches in other parts of the world. When they identify an aspect of their mission

7

which could benefit from the contribution of a mission partner from overseas, they send a request. It may be a specific professional skill which is needed or it may be an area of ministry which could be refreshed and enhanced through the contribution of someone from outside the situation who brings a new perspective to it.

Our fragmented world needs people who bridge its dangerous divisions

A church which witnesses to reconciliation in Christ today meets a world which is sorely divided. Cultural, religious and political fault lines create alienation and hostility. In order to embody the message of reconciliation it is necessary for some people to cross the divide, *eg* between the West and the Orient, between first-world power and neo-colonial subjugation, or between Western and Islamic societies. Creating teams of people whose commitment to Jesus Christ brings them together across such divisions is a strategic witness in today's world. This offers a challenging yet strategic opportunity for mission partner service.

Mission partners help combat poverty in extremely poor countries

A great gulf is also set between rich and poor as we live through a time when the rich are getting richer and the poor are getting poorer. A church comfortably placed in the rich world is obliged by the gospel to express solidarity with partner churches who face a situation of extreme poverty. Nothing is more appreciated than the presence of mission partners who share at first hand in the challenges of living amidst poverty. In a number of countries nobody is better placed than the church to deliver programmes which counter poverty, and suitably skilled mission partners have a key role to play.

Mission partners proclaim the good news of Jesus Christ

The news about Jesus Christ is so good that we cannot keep it to ourselves. In fact, there is a mandate in the New Testament which directs us to share it not only close to home but also "to the ends of the earth". Mission partners have been described as "the agents of the help which one part of the church sends to another for the discharge of the common missionary task" (Lesslie Newbigin). What was once a movement "from the West to the rest" is now a mission "from everywhere to everyone". Still the need remains for people to accept an assignment which takes them far from their comfort zone with the primary objective of making Jesus Christ known. It is when the gospel of Christ crosses a cultural frontier that it is seen in sharpest relief.

The Council has identified four patterns of service overseas which it seeks to encourage and affirm:

Long-Term Mission Partner: The Council will recruit long-term mission partners for service in strategically chosen contexts. An initial contract of four years and eight months can be renewed with further contracts of two years and four months. In this category of service, staff will be generally expected to learn the local language and become familiar with the culture and society of the country where they serve. Positions will be identified through discussion with overseas partner churches. There will be two routes to appointment.

In the case of people selected for overseas service through the selection school process, the Council will consult with partner churches with a view to identifying a suitable post (note: it cannot be guaranteed that this effort will succeed). Alternatively, a post identified through consultation with a partner church, will be publicly advertised with appointments being made through a competitive interview process.

Short-Term Mission Partner: The Council will recruit short-term mission partners for service in strategically chosen contexts. Normally these appointments will meet a need for specific skills to be brought to a project which will be completed within a short period of time. Contracts will be for 1-2 years, depending on the requirements of the overseas partner. Positions will be identified through discussion with overseas partner churches. There will be two routes to appointment. In the case of people selected for overseas service through the selection school process, the Council will consult with partner churches with a view to identifying a suitable post (note: it cannot be guaranteed that this effort will succeed). Alternatively, a post identified through consultation with a partner church, will be publicly advertised with appointments being made through a competitive interview process.

Volunteer: There remains great potential in using volunteers for the development of partnership in mission at this time. Partner churches and institutions are requesting volunteers. People are prepared to serve as volunteers. A change from the past is that greater flexibility is required – longer-term and shorter-term, one-off and recurrent patterns of volunteering are being requested. This is demanding in management terms and issues of risk and liability have become difficult to navigate. However, the Council believes that these are not reasons to discontinue volunteering but rather challenges to be met with determination and creativity. It holds to the view that the best way to do this is through Scottish Churches World Exchange as an instrument dedicated to supporting volunteering in a church context.

Mission Associate: In order to recognise and support Church members who are involved in overseas mission through agencies other than the Church itself, the World Mission Council will name as "mission associates" those who accept such status and satisfy the Council that their work overseas is broadly in line with its objectives.

Discerning the Signs of the Times – Openness to new Possibilities: While the Council is at full stretch in offering the above four possibilities, it remains open to new possibilities and new mission imperatives which may emerge through the advance of God's kingdom. To this end, the Council has its ears always open to the voice of the people of the Church of Scotland and will consider any reasonable request from those engaged in mission to reconsider its geographic and thematic priorities. A template has been prepared for the use of any who would wish to make such a request.

New Appointments Made; More Vacancies Advertised

After a number of lean years, the Council is delighted that it was able to make six mission partner appointments during 2008. It is determined to sustain this momentum and nine vacancies have been advertised during the winter of 2008-09. The Council is also developing a "one-stop-shop" approach to assist any Church members or adherents who are considering service overseas. Open Days are planned for 6 June in Edinburgh and 31 October 2009 in Glasgow. Details are available from Sarah-Jayne McVeigh sjmcveigh@cofscotland.org.uk who also welcomes enquiries about overseas service at any time. These new initiatives are driven forward by a Recruitment Task Group which is reporting to the Council on a six-monthly basis.

Scottish Churches World Exchange

Volunteering remains an excellent opportunity for meaningful involvement with the world church and the Council is grateful to continue to work through the dedicated agency of Scottish Churches World Exchange (SCWE). Through SCWE, the Council has provided valuable volunteer support to partner churches in India, Burma, Malawi and Zimbabwe this year. The hospitality, faith and commitment of individual members of our Partner Churches have a profound impact on the lives of the volunteers who are sent. Young people from Scotland have returned to their churches with greater enthusiasm and a deeper understanding of what is meant by the whole gospel for the whole world.

Scottish Churches World Exchange is developing a new series of international ecumenical study visits designed to offer younger volunteers from the Scottish churches a well-managed and encouraging experience of the life of Christian churches in another part of the world. These visits will explore the life and witness of churches acting together to address social, economic and environmental issues. In 2009-2010 they propose to lead visits to Malawi, north-east India and Ghana.

St Colm's International House

17 October 2008 saw St Colm's filled with former students and friends to celebrate the centenary of the laying of the foundation stone by the then Moderator, Dr Laws of Livingstonia. Six services were held throughout the day, celebrating the commitment to mission and evangelism which had been at the heart of the house and in the hearts of so many women (and men) who studied there since the College opened in 1909. The first students entered the partly finished building in Inverleith in May 1909, to prepare for service in Africa and Asia, almost exactly 100 years ago. To celebrate the centenary a friend of St Colm's made a gift to Scottish Churches World Exchange to meet the cost of inviting women from churches in the developing world to come together at St Colm's for a working seminar on "Women, Ministry and Mission".

World Mission Scholarships

The World Mission Council's Scholarship Programme offers opportunities for postgraduate study to candidates recommended by partner churches and organisations. One of the main purposes of this programme is to build capacity within the partner church or organisation. Successful applicants study in their home region which allows for visits home for holidays or research. Students also visit Scotland to facilitate building relationships with the church here. In 2008-09 scholarships were given to seven students from Malawi, Nepal, Pakistan and Zambia for post-graduate study in theology, water engineering and medicine. In 2008, the Council adjusted its policy to allow for up to one-third of its budget for bursary awards to be devoted to locally supported partners in particularly needy situations. This recognises that not all

partners are able to accommodate twinnings at this time and leadership development in some cases is the most strategic expression of partnership.

Local Development

"How can this strange story of God made flesh, of a crucified Saviour, of resurrection and the new creation become credible for those whose entire mental training has conditioned them to believe that the real world is the world which can be satisfactorily explained and managed without the hypothesis of God? I know of only one clue to the answering of that question, only one real hermeneutic of the gospel: a congregation which believes it." (Lesslie Newbigin, "On Being the Church for the World", 1988)

The number of twinnings has continued to rise steadily throughout the year and it is heartening to hear the stories of how twinning with a congregation or presbytery overseas creates mission opportunity here in Scotland. Such acclamation as "having the focus of the twinning link with friends in Lubuto has recalibrated my faith" or "the response of the community here in Portobello to our link with Ghana has been overwhelming" or "being able to pray meaningfully for the situation in Zimbabwe because we have personal friendships there" reinforces the notion of twinning as a missional model for today's church. While the Council welcomes all linkage with the world church, it concentrates its resources on the Church's long-term partnerships where twinning is part of a wider ongoing relationship. A growing area of work for the Council is the Faithshare Visitor Programme (see Appendix V) which has proved to be an invaluable resource for congregations undertaking exchange visits with their overseas partners.

During the latter part of 2008, the Panel of Review and Reform, working with World Mission Council have begun a piece of research from which it is hoped a deeper and wider picture of the connection with the world church at grassroots level will be seen (see Report of the Panel on Review and Reform pp. 19/3 Section 3). It is also envisaged that the results of the study will form a resource and be used to shape tools for the future of twinning.

The appointment of Gillian McKinnon as the new communications officer has seen steady development of audio, digital and printed resources. The Council commends to all ministers and members of the Church the weekly email Update which brings up-to-date news and requests for prayer support from partners around the world. This is a simple yet highly effective means of keeping informed about key developments amongst our overseas partner churches as they happen. It is free of charge and anyone can subscribe. The popular WM magazine has been remodelled on a slightly reduced frequency and offers vivid and thought-provoking insights into the life and witness of the church worldwide. For both publications, anyone can subscribe free of charge by contacting wmeditor@cofscotland.org.uk or writing to the Department at 121 George Street, Edinburgh.

Christian Aid

The work of Christian Aid is needed more urgently than ever with the threat to the poor from global warming a major focus and the "Cut the Carbon" march a significant campaigning event in 2008. Working through local partners, Christian Aid has been the agent of high-quality development work as well as effective response to crises such as the floods in Bihar, India, the cholera outbreak in Zimbabwe, the civil war in the eastern Congo and the food crisis across Africa.

The extent to which Christian Aid supports work on the frontlines was highlighted when the Israeli Air Force attacked and destroyed a clinic run by Christian Aid partner the Near East Council of Churches during its military action in Gaza in January 2009. With the Obama Presidency raising hopes, Christian Aid is taking the opportunity to intensify its long-running campaign for justice in the working of the global economy. With the

global economic downturn hitting the poor hardest, particularly through sharply rising food prices, progress in regard to fair trade and tax justice is more urgently needed than ever. Also at the heart of this campaign is advocacy for the international community to take decisive action on cutting carbon emissions through the UN climate summit in Copenhagen in December 2009.

As a primary point of connection in the relationship between the Church of Scotland and Christian Aid, the Council has been made aware of concerns widely felt in the Church about the current direction of the organisation. In November 2008, these were raised at the Christian Aid AGM which has asked its Board to initiate a process to engage with them, in consultation with its sponsoring churches. Meanwhile, together with Christian Aid Scotland, the Council has initiated a series of "conversations" to address such concerns. Following two small-scale conversations during 2008, a larger occasion is planned for 2 March 2009.

Society in Scotland for the Propagation of Christian Knowledge (SSPCK)

On 25 May 2009, the SSPCK will celebrate its tercentenary, Queen Anne having signed its charter on 25 May 1709. The Society began operations in 1712, aiming to dispel the "ignorance and superstition" which were then prevalent in the country. By 1800, it had opened almost 300 schools and was the principal provider of education in many remote areas. Also included in the original aims of the Society was the propagation of Christian Knowledge overseas in North America and the Indian Sub-Continent. Following the passing of the 1872 Education Act, two-thirds of the Society's capital was transferred to the Highlands and Islands Trust. One third was retained by the Society, divided roughly equally between the Home Fund and the Foreign Fund. Today, these funds are not large but still yield income which can be used strategically to support Christian mission undertaken by the Church of Scotland, both at home and overseas. Over the past two years, the Society has been revived and organised in line with current requirements for charitable bodies. Details of the grant application process are available on the Church of Scotland website or by writing to SSPCK, c/o the World Mission Department. Two competitions will be launched through *Life and Work* to celebrate the tercentenary: the first involves the composition of a hymn set to a familiar Scottish tune while the second involves the writing of a prayer of no more than ten lines. The Society has chosen the Sower as its emblem and this has been incorporated in its 300th anniversary logo.

Preparations for Edinburgh 2010

Since 2006 the Council has been reporting annually to the General Assembly on preparations to mark the centenary of this great milestone in the history of Christian mission. The work of the Scottish Towards 2010 Council proved to be a catalyst which led to the launch of an international initiative directed by a General Council which is probably more representative of world Christianity than any group which has previously been formed. This has created a framework for celebrating the centenary which is both immensely promising and hugely challenging (see www.edinburgh2010.org). The Council is deeply grateful for the work undertaken by Rev Andrew Anderson, its former Vice-Convener, who serves as Chair of the General Council.

During the past year, much work has been done by nine study networks which will feed considered reflection on the key issues facing Christian mission today into the centenary conference. Meanwhile, plans are taking shape for the international conference to be held in Edinburgh from 2 to 6 June 2010. Clearly, the occasion is inspired by history but it will aim to be thoroughly forward looking in the hope of doing for the 21st century what Edinburgh 1910 did for the 20th: setting out a compelling missionary vision for our times. The event is conceived on a world scale but in Scotland we can look forward to the particular opportunity, as well as the great responsibility, which

Edinburgh 2010 represents for the host nation. While the preparations at international level are coordinated by the Edinburgh 2010 office, based at New College in Edinburgh, the Scottish dimension is being organised by the Scottish Coordinating Team (SCoT), a broad coalition with ACTS as the lead agency. It is organising a prayer network to support the international delegate conference and developing plans for "Edinburgh Local" which will enable Scottish participation around the international conference. Within the Church of Scotland, the Mission Forum has provided an arena for engagement with Edinburgh 2010, with residential meetings in Inverness and Arran during 2008 providing the opportunity for Presbyteries to feed reflections on mission into the study process.

Christians Suffering Because of Minority Status

Interaction with partners during the year has underlined the wisdom and timeliness of the instruction the Council received from the 2008 General Assembly "to ascertain how best the Church of Scotland can be an effective partner to churches in situations where Christians suffer because of their minority status". However, the magnitude of this question has persuaded the Council that it would not be possible to prepare an adequate report for the 2009 General Assembly and it therefore presents only this brief interim report with the commitment to report much more fully to the 2010 General Assembly. At the time of writing, a major day conference is being planned, to be held in Perth on 4 March 2009, with the Rt Rev Mano Rumalshah, Bishop of Peshawar in Pakistan, as the main speaker.

Principal Aims 2009

The Council's principal aims for 2009, elaborated in detail in its Strategic Plan, are as follows:

1. To implement the outcomes of the 2008 Review by developing an effective Committee structure covering all areas of its work.
2. To implement the outcomes of the 2008 Review by

introducing a new Departmental staff structure and achieving its effective operation.

3. To develop a coherent strategy for the support of twinnings while continuing to deliver the mentoring and facilitation required by congregations and Presbyteries already engaged in, or embarking on, a twinning.

4. To continue to develop effective publicity and to strengthen links with Presbyteries and congregations nationwide.

5. To implement the recommendations of the Recruitment Task Force Report, to put a strong system of recruitment in place, and to see a steady stream of new recruits.

6. To induct new staff to serve in Israel and Palestine, to continue the renewal of partner relationships in the Middle East region and to make substantial progress in the development of strategic properties.

7. To implement successfully the new arrangements for the bursary programme.

8. To establish viable and fruitful ways of working with the ecumenical bodies in which the Council plays a part.

9. To contribute appropriately and effectively to the preparations being made to mark the centenary of Edinburgh 1910.

Co-opted Committee Members

Rev Elisabeth Cranfield has served as a co-opted member of the Overseas Charges Committee; Mrs Judith Walker and Rev Elijah Obinna as co-opted members of the Africa and Caribbean Committee; Rev James Macdonald and Rev Iain Cunningham as co-opted members of the Local Development Committee; and Mr Ken Mathewson as a co-opted member of the Middle East Committee.

Today's Missionary Frontier: Can the West be Converted?

The delegates who gathered at the World Missionary Conference in Edinburgh in 1910 looked out from what they regarded as "fully missionised" lands to the "non-Christian world" to which they aspired to "carry" the gospel. In the course of a century, a great reversal has taken place. Many of the lands once described as "the mission field" have become heartlands of the faith while in Europe there has occurred a recession of Christian faith which is unprecedented in its extent and severity. Lesslie Newbigin liked to quote General Simatoupong of Indonesia – "Of course, the number one question is: can the West be converted?" Surveying the emerging world situation in terms of evangelism he observed: "What we call the modern Western scientific worldview, the post-Enlightenment cultural world, is the most powerful and persuasive ideology in the world today. The Christian gospel continues to find new victories among the non-Western … cultures of the world, but in the face of this modern Western culture the Church is everywhere in retreat. Can there be a more challenging frontier for the Church than that?" (*A Word in Season*, pp. 66-67.)

As the Church stands at that frontier it is not alone. A remarkable worldwide network of partners in the gospel offers resources of fellowship, prayer, experience and shared faith on which we may draw, both locally and nationally, as we engage with the missionary frontiers of our time. Moreover the vibrancy, diversity and freshness of the world church is coming close to home as a growing number of minority churches use Church of Scotland premises for worship. The opportunities offered by today's world for believers to share with one another what they have discovered of Jesus Christ opens up boundless new possibilities for evangelism. Could it be the Church's worldwide mission engagement which is the key to a fresh encounter with Christ in today's Western culture?

In the Name of the Council

COLIN RENWICK, *Convener*
LEON MARSHALL, *Vice-Convener*
D STEWART GILLAN, *Vice-Convener*
KENNETH R ROSS, *Council Secretary*

Mr Leon Marshall
Retiring Vice-Convener

Leon Marshall retires at this General Assembly following three years as Vice-Convener of the World Mission Council. As a chartered accountant and former Convener of the General Assembly's Board of Stewardship and Finance, Leon has brought a great breadth and depth of knowledge to the work of the World Mission Council as Vice-Convener and as Convener of its Finance and Overseas Charges Committees. His expertise has always been given freely, with quiet authority, and with great grace. He has ably represented the Council on visits to Malawi and Sri Lanka. His incisive analysis has often proved key to resolving debates and enabling the Council to take sound decisions.

Mindful of the fact that Leon has undertaken this additional work in the midst of a busy professional life and his deep involvement in his own congregation at Kilmacolm: Old, members of the World Mission Council express their deep gratitude to him, and wish him God's blessing in all that lies ahead.

In the Name of the Council

COLIN RENWICK, *Convener*
D STEWART GILLAN, *Vice-Convener*
KENNETH R ROSS, *Council Secretary*

APPENDIX I
STAFF AND FAMILY MEMBERS OVERSEAS BETWEEN 1 JANUARY AND 31 DECEMBER 2008

ASIA
Church of Bangladesh

Dr Helen Brannam	Doctor	Bollobhur Hospital (Ecumenical appointment)
Mr David Hall	Development Consultant	Church of Bangladesh (Ecumenical appointment)
Mrs Sarah Hall	Education consultant	Church of Bangladesh (Ecumenical appointment)
Rebecca		
Reuben		
Mr James Pender	Environmental/ Conservation Work	Church of Bangladesh, Social Development Programme Meherpur (Ecumenical ppointment)
Mrs Linda Pender		

CARIBBEAN
Bahamas

Rev Scott Kirkland	Minister	Lucaya Presbyterian Kirk, Colombo
Mrs Anita Kirkland		
Pricilla and Sarah		
Rev John Macleod	Minister	St Andrew's Presbyterian Kirk, Nassau
Mrs Carol Macleod		
Bethany and Andrew		

Trinidad

Rev John Bacchas	Minister	Greyfriars St Ann's with Arouca and Sangre Grande
Mrs Claudette Bacchas,		
Kerri-Ann and Shena-Marie		

Middle East & North Africa
Israel/Palestine

Mr James Laing	Regional Manager	Israel
Mrs Nicola-Jayne Laing		
John		
Rev John Cubie	Locum Minister	St Andrew's Scots Memorial Church, Jerusalem with St Andrew's Church of Scotland, Galilee (Parish Grouping)
Mrs Moira Cubie		
Mr Anthony Short	Principal	Tabeetha School, Jaffa, Israel
Mrs Darya Short		
Joelle and Ezra		

7

Mrs Jeneffer Zielinski	Programme Director	St Andrew's Scots Memorial Church, Jerusalem with St Andrew's Church of Scotland, Galilee (Parish Grouping)
Rev Ian Clark	Locum Minister	St Andrew's Scots Memorial Church, Jerusalem with St Andrew's Church of Scotland, Galilee (Parish Grouping)
Rev Colin Anderson	Locum Minister	St Andrew's Scots Memorial Church, Jerusalem with St Andrew's Church of Scotland, Galilee (Parish Grouping)
Rev Colin Douglas	Locum Minister	St Andrew's Scots Memorial Church, Jerusalem with St Andrew's Church of Scotland, Galilee (Parish Grouping)
Mr Donald Marshall	Locum Programme Director	St Andrew's Scots Memorial Church, Jerusalem with St Andrew's Church of Scotland, Galilee (Parish Grouping)
Ms Elizabeth Pattullo	Volunteer	St Andrew's Scottish Guesthouse, Jerusalem

SUB-SAHARAN AFRICA
Church of Central Africa Presbyterian, Malawi

Dr Andrew Gaston	AIDS Control Programme Co-ordinator Programme ended October 2008	Livingstonia Synod Ekwendeni
Mrs Felicity Gaston Katy and Daniel		
Miss Helen Scott	Teacher	Ekwendeni Girls Secondary School

United Church of Zambia

Rev Colin Johnston	Tutor	United Church of Zambia Theological College, Mindolo Campus, Zambia (Ecumenical Appointment)
Mr Keith Waddell	Mission Support Partner (Education)	Mwandi UCZ Mission, Mwandi Royal Village, Western Province, Zambia (Ecumenical Appointment)
Mrs Ida Waddell	Mission Support Partner (Medical)	Mwandi UCZ Mission, Mwandi Royal Village, Western Province, Zambia (Ecumenical Appointment)
Ms Jenny Featherstone	Trainer	Mindolo Ecumenical Foundation, Zambia (Ecumenical Appointment)

APPENDIX II
DEATHS

Rev Robert Philp	2 March 2008
Rev Ian Donald Fauchelle	11 March 2008
Rev John Nelson	11 April 2008
Mrs Jean Wilkinson	6 May 2008
Miss Evelyn Gall	10 July 2008
Rev Dr Andrew Ross	26 July 2008
Rev Richard Baxter	7 February 2009

APPENDIX III
BRITISH AND IRISH AMITY TEACHERS' GROUP (BIATG)

BIATG Teachers currently working in P.R. of China:

Long Term Teachers
2007 –
Ian Groves, Jiangsu Institute of Education, Nanjing, Jiangsu Province

Short Term Teachers
2006 –
Christine Green, Wuwei Occupational College, Wuwei, Gansu Province

David Clements, Northwest Normal University, Lanzhou, Gansu Province

2007 –
Kath Saltwell, Youjiang Teacher's College for Nationalities, Baise City, Guangxi Province

Gordon Paterson, accompanied by his wife Hilary, Liuzhou City Vocational College, Guangxi Province

APPENDIX IV
WORLD EXCHANGE VOLUNTEERS OVERSEAS 2008

Catriona Anderson	India
Chris Barr	Burma
Kieren Barnes	Malawi
Judith Craig	Malawi
Blodwin Farquhar	Malawi
Norma Forbes	India
Fiona Grimmond	Malawi
Fiona Hutchinson	Malawi
James Hutchinson	Malawi
Kevin Kilty	Malawi
Dorothy Martin	Malawi
Ross Muiry	Malawi
John Miller	Zimbabwe
Mary Miller	Zimbabwe
Alistair Macdonald	Zimbabwe
David Taylor	Malawi
Catriona McDonald	Malawi

World Exchange Scotland Volunteer

Trudi Newton	Hoy, Scotland

APPENDIX V
FAITHSHARE VISITORS 2008/2009

Mrs Annie Banda, Mr Mayor Chirwa, Rev Norman Hara, Mrs Anna Sichinga, CCAP, Muchengawatuwa Congregation, Synod of Livingstonia, Malawi. Henderson, Kilmarnock, Scotland. (22 April to 6 May 2008).

Mrs Teresia Karanja, Mr Samuel Muhoro, PCEA, St Peter's Ihindu, Kenya. St Mary's, Haddington, Scotland. (5 to 19 May 2008).

Mr Stephen Chege, Mr Charles Wanjiku, PCEA, Megina Congregation, Kenya. Avonbridge linked with Torphichen, West Lothian, Scotland. (12 May to 4 June 2008).

Mr Gregory-Paul Campbell, Mrs Elaine Christie, Rev Nigel Pusey, Mr Donald Reynolds, UCJCI, North Street United Church, Kingston, Jamaica. Crown Church, Inverness, Scotland. (14 to 23 May 2008).

Rev Arthur Christie, Mr Liam Christie, Mrs Elizabeth Geddes, Ayr Presbytery, Scotland. CCAP, Bandawe Presbytery, Synod of Livingstonia, Malawi. (3 to 23 June 2008).

Ms Fellen Hara, Ms Loyina Hara, Mr Gift Lowole, Mr James Ngulube, Mr Mike Nsini, Ms Len Shonga, Baula, Malawi.

7

Ruchazie, Glasgow, Scotland, Together for A Change. (4 to 25 June 2008).

Mrs Cynthia Dayes, Mr Clinton Dayes, UCJCI, Montego Bay, Jamaica. Rubislaw, Aberdeen, Scotland. (10 to 24 June 2008).

Ms Ruth Astbury, Mr Ivor Butchart, Ms Elizabeth Farr, Dunblane Cathedral, Scotland. CCAP, Likhibula, Mulanje, Blantyre Synod, Malawi. (13 June to 6 July 2008).

Rev Dr Iain Barclay, Aberdeen Presbytery, Scotland. CCAP, Blantyre City Presbytery, Blantyre Synod, Malawi. (24 June to 10 July 2008).

Dr Malcolm Adamson, Gundrun Shah, Dalgety Church, Dalgety Bay, Scotland. CCAP, Engcongolweni Congregation, Synod of Livingstonia, Malawi. (7 to 23 July 2008).

Mr Iain McLarty, Miss Hannah Pickles, COSY, Mission and Discipleship Council. CCAP, Synod of Livingstonia, Youth Conference, Malawi. (21 to 30 July 2008).

Mr Ross Campbell, Mr Steven Paterson, COSY, Mission and Discipleship Council. ECCB, Youth Camp, Czech Republic. (26 July to 4 August 2008).

Mr Angus Adam, Miss Catherine Hay, Rev John McMahon, Church of Scotland HIV/AIDS Project. XVII International AIDS Conference, Mexico. (29 July to 9 August 2008).

Mrs Janette Ferguson, Rev Elizabeth Fisk, Mrs Margo Henderson, Mrs Nicolette Lynch, Ms Lynn Scotland, Miss Natasha Scotland, St Ninian's, Dunfermline, Scotland. ECCB, Orlova Congregation, Czech Republic. (2 to 10 August 2008).

Mrs Leah Githinji, Rev Peterson Githinji, PCEA, Mai-a-Ihii Congregation, Kenya. New Pitsligo linked with Strichen and Tyrie, Scotland. (7 August to 5 September 2008).

Mrs Margaret Ogg, Mr David Slater, Trinity College, Glasgow University. PCG, Trinity Theological Seminary, Accra, Ghana. (18 to 26 August 2008).

Mrs Violet Chavura, Ms Grace Kulupando-Saka, CCAP, Chigodi Women's Training Centre, Blantyre Synod, Malawi. Child Survival in Malawi (Scotland). (26 August to 15 September 2008).

Mr John Karuoya, Rev Benjamin Kimanzi, Mr James Macharia, Ms Beatrice Mathenge, PCEA, Mathia Congregation, Kenya. Maxwellton West, Dumfries, Scotland. (27 August to 9 September 2008).

Ms Martha Gachanja, Ms Hannah Karanja, Mr David Karingithi, Mr James Munga, Mr Michael Wambui, Ms Naomi Wambui, PCEA, Emmanuel Congregation, Kenya. Barrhead: Bourock, Glasgow, Scotland. (29 August to 15 September).

Mr Zebedee Chiumia, Mrs Charity Nyirenda, CCAP, LISAP, Synod of Livingstonia, Malawi. Presbyteries of Argyll, Buchan and Glasgow. (31 August to 18 October 2008).

Mr Andrew Cumming, Mr Peter Cumming, Miss Kimberly Patterson, Aberdeen Presbytery, Scotland. CCAP, Blantyre City Presbytery, Blantyre Synod, Malawi. (2 to 17 September 2008).

Mr Mubanga Chisanga, Miss Chungu Kafwimbi, Ms Martha Lungu, Mr Flywell Thole, UCZ, Lubuto Congregation, Zambia. Dunscore linked with Glencairn and Moniaive, Dumfries, Scotland. (9 to 26 September 2008).

Rev Isaac Asara, Colonel Henry Ofosu-Apea, PCG, Akrapong Christ Church, Ghana. Howe Trinity, Alford, Scotland. (11 to 25 September 2008).

Rev Iain Cunningham, Mr Graham Houston, Mrs Irene Houston, Mr William Scott, Presbytery of Lanark, Scotland. PROK, Presbytery of East Seoul, Korea. (7 to 21 October 2008).

Mr Alan Gibson, Crossreach with Scottish Churches China Group. Leading Training Workshops and Seminars,

Amity Children's Development Centre, Nanjing, China. (9 to 27 October 2008).

Mr Shepherd Kashe, Mrs Memoria Lubambo, Mrs Nombeko May, Miss Sisanda Xotyeni, UPCSA, Pirie Mission, South Africa. Blackhall St Columba's, Edinburgh, Scotland. (10 to 18 October 2008).

Mr Alexander Waugh, Mr James Wyse, St Fillan's, Aberdour, Scotland. CCAP, Alumenda Congregation, Blantyre Synod, Malawi. (27 October to 6 November 2008).

Mrs Sheila Lawrence, Rev John Vadiangadu, CSI, Diocese of Madras, India. Edinburgh Presbytery, Scotland. (29 October to 12 November 2008).

Mr Freedom Chawinga, Mr Jeffrey Dindi, CCAP, Lusangazi Congregation, Synod of Livingstonia, Malawi. St Kenneth's, Kennoway, Scotland. (17 November to 1 December 2008).

Rev Ernest Asare, PCG, Kwamibikrom, Asante Presbytery, Ghana. Murrayfield, Edinburgh, Scotland. (17 November to 12 December 2008).

Mr Ian Lochhead, Mr Colin Proctor, Colinton, Edinburgh, Scotland. PCEA, Umoja Congregation, Kenya. (21 November to 1 December 2008).

Mrs Izolismaria and Mr Manasses Villaca, PCB, Igreja Presbiteriana Maanaim, Brazil. St James, Broughty Ferry, Scotland. (29 December 2008 to 22 January 2009).

Ms Carleen Knowlton, Rev Ian Manson, Church of Scotland, Geneva. CCAP, Ekwendeni Hospital Aids Project, Synod of Livingstonia, Malawi. (7 to 22 January 2009).

Rev Elvis Elahie, United Church of Trinidad and Tobago. CWW Re-energise Conference, Aviemore, Scotland. (10 to 16 January 2009).

Mr Gift Ndau, Miss Elita Nyambose, CCAP, Ekwendeni Hospital Aids Project, Synod of Livingstonia, Malawi. Church of Scotland, Geneva. (22 January to 5 February 2009).

Rev James MacDonald, Crieff Parish Church, Scotland. UCJCI, Shortwood Congregation, Jamaica. (2 February to 9 March 2009).

Miss Gemma Burns, Miss Melissa Sim, South Leith Parish Church, Edinburgh. UCZ, Chipembi Girls School, Zambia. (11 to 25 March 2009).

Mr Benjamin Nkansah Antwi, PCG, Dwerebease Congregation, Ghana. Portobello Old, Edinburgh, Scotland. (19 to 31 March 2009).

Ms Nola Box, Mrs Isola Campbell, Ms Carrol Kerr, UCJCI, Montego Bay Congregation, Jamaica. Rubislaw, Aberdeen, Scotland. (7 – 21 May 2009).

7

CHURCH OF SCOTLAND HIV/AIDS PROJECT GROUP
May 2009

PROPOSED DELIVERANCE

The General Assembly
1. Receive the report, and thank the members of the Project Group and the Project's partners around the world.
2. Instruct the Project Group, in consultation with other Councils, to develop material and resources that will help the church to reflect and respond appropriately to the issues surrounding HIV and Aids, and jointly with other Councils to consider the use of an 'HIV-competent Church' programme.
3. Instruct the Project Group to work together with the Ministries Council in exploring ways in which HIV and Aids education can be offered as part of the candidates training programme.
4. Thank the Very Rev David Lunan for his leadership in launching "The Moderator's Challenge", and encourage all Presbyteries to set up a fund-raising goal averaging at least £10,000 (according to size) for the Church of Scotland HIV/AIDS Project.
5. Invite congregations to observe Sunday 10 January 2010 as a day of worship, reflection and fund-raising on the theme of the Church's response to HIV, and instruct the Project group to produce worship resources to enable congregations to hold "Souper Sunday" services and events.

REPORT

1. Introduction

"Stop AIDS. Keep the Promise." – the campaigning slogan for World Aids Day 2008 and its theme of 'leadership' seems a good place at which to start this report. It is hard to believe that 2008 saw World Aids Day, established by the World Health Association in 1988, 'come of age'. Individuals and organisations all around the world came together on 1st December to bring attention to the global Aids epidemic for the 21st time. The theme challenges everyone to demonstrate leadership and deliver on promises made in the response to HIV and Aids. Those making the promises and those making them, are not just governments, and organisations such as UNAIDS or the Global Fund but are you and me. The Church of Scotland HIV/AIDS Project, one of a wide range of Faith Based Organisations (FBOs) is involved in the continuing struggle to ensure justice and equity for those infected and affected by HIV and Aids.

The 17th World AIDS Conference held in Mexico in August 2008 witnessed a dramatic sign of change in attitudes towards FBOs summarised in the words of Peter Piot, the retiring Executive of UNAIDS "when I started this job I saw religion as one of the biggest obstacles to our work…but I have seen great examples of treatment and care from the religious community, and lately prevention." UNAIDS recognises that as 70% of the world's people identify themselves as members of faith groups, such communities play a major role in influencing people's behaviour and attitudes and in providing care and support for people living with HIV. This is a major step forward.

The Ecumenical Advocacy Alliance, of which the Church of Scotland HIV/AIDS Project is a member and contributor, has produced a resource called Exploring Solutions: How to talk about HIV Prevention in Church. This aims to help people in churches to talk openly, accurately and compassionately about why HIV spreads and what we as individuals and communities can do to help stop it in its tracks. For over two decades Aids has led to the deaths of millions of people and devastated families, communities, and the social and economic fabric of many countries. Although there is no short term prospect of any cure, today we know how to treat HIV and Aids and how to prevent the transmission of HIV. And yet the virus continues to spread because so many of us don't talk about it.

Much of the focus of the work of the Project Group in 2008/09 has been to build on the strength of being a FBO and the opportunity to work with and challenge national and international governments and organisations yet provide the tools necessary for presbyteries and congregations to continue the journey of HIV prevention locally and globally.

2.   Strategic plan

The newly developed strategic plan for the Project emphasizes the importance of theological reflection as we continue to raise awareness of HIV in Churches in Scotland. We recognise that Christ's compassion and courage and acceptance of people as he reached out to them, and his dying on the cross for all, mean that the Gospel compels us both to challenge the stigma associated with HIV, and to offer practical care for people living with or affected by HIV. We plan to facilitate theological discussion relating to HIV and Aids by directing people to relevant worship and study resources, some of which will be informed by the experiences of our partners. We will develop targeted training resources for ministers and elders and we will produce resource material for Councils and Presbyteries and the wider Church. We aim to equip a group of volunteers throughout Scotland who will be able to lead workshops, worship or take part in awareness raising events. In our communication strategy we aim to help people understand the Gospel imperative to respond positively to people affected by HIV and the need for our Project to be a whole Church Project, engaging every Council and every church member in its work.

Our current strategic plan also reaffirms our priority to raise money to support partners as they respond to needs in practical ways. We will continue to support projects overseas and in Scotland which offer peer education, theological education and practical care and will support partners as they develop income generating schemes for people who are HIV+ to help them purchase nutritious food which is so important for the effective taking of ARV medication. We will work cooperatively with our current partners in Scotland and seek to develop ever more authentic relationships with our international partners. We aim for partnerships which are built on honest and open communication, the genuine sharing of ideas and on mutual understanding.

3.   INERELA+

In following up from the General Assembly report of 2008 and the charge to the Project group to be represented on the steering group of Inerela+ Scotland, we are pleased to report that the formal launch of INERELA+, the international, interfaith network of religious leaders – both lay and ordained, women and men – living with or personally affected by HIV, took place in Mexico City on 2 August 2008. The 5 year anniversary of ANERELA+, the African Network was celebrated at the same occasion. Recognising the realities of the HIV epidemic in the rest of the world, it was decided to create 4 regional networks based on shared elements of history, language, culture and religion. Scotland would be part of the Europe/Central Asia region. At its February 2009 meeting, the INERELA+ Board completed its search for a new Executive Director who is expected to be in office by 1 May 2009.

In just under five years, the two networks have grown to encompass over 3,500 members across five continents. It is hoped that within five years of INERELA+'s launch, the networks will increase their worldwide membership to over 6,000. These new members will mobilize their respective faith communities to provide accurate information and other services to an estimated 2.5 million people around the world, helping to reduce HIV-related silence, shame, stigma and discrimination and thereby reducing the number of new infections. Marion Chatterley, Chaplain to People living with HIV, Waverley Care, reports that at present, rather than having our own organisation, Scotland is to be part of INERELA+ UK and some progress is being made to ensure joined up thinking at an International level while recognising the specific needs of particular countries.

4. A Global Overview

Perhaps the best overview comes in the form of the UNAIDS 2008 Report on the global AIDS epidemic. Published mid 2008, it marks the halfway mark between the 2001 Declaration of Commitment and the 2015 target of the Millennium Development Goals to reverse the epidemic by 2015, and is also two years before the agreed target date for moving as close as possible towards universal access to HIV prevention, treatment, care, and support. It is therefore a good time to assess the HIV response and to understand what must be done to ensure that nations are on course to achieve their HIV commitments. As a church, this report and the more recent UNAIDS – Letter to Partners, are important documents to influence our advocacy work. We must keep HIV and Aids at the top of the political and economic agenda and our government should be challenged to keep the promise they made in the setting of universal access targets for 2010. The Church must continue to be a voice for the voiceless.

But has progress been made? There is no doubt that the nearly 4 million people on antiretroviral medication believe this to be so. The annual number of new infections worldwide dropped from 3 million in 2005 to 2.7 million in 2007, young people in many parts of the world are waiting longer to become sexually active and millions of children orphaned now have access to appropriate care and protection.

What are the trends for some of our Project Partners? It is important to note that most epidemics in sub-Saharan Africa appear to have stabilised, although often at very high levels, particularly in southern Africa. In Malawi and Zambia there is some evidence of favourable behaviour changes and there are signs of declining HIV prevalence among women using antenatal services in some urban areas. The estimated 5.7 million South Africans living with HIV in 2007 continues to make this the largest HIV epidemic in the world. In parts of Mozambique, HIV prevalence among pregnant women is increasing and in some of the provinces in the central and southern zones of the country, adult HIV prevalence has reached or exceeded 20%, while infections continue to increase among young people (ages 15–24).

In Asia, the epidemic is of a more disparate nature. In Burma/Myanmar and Thailand there is decline in HIV prevalence, however the epidemic in Pakistan is growing rapidly. New HIV infections are also increasing steadily, although at a much slower pace, in highly populated countries such as Bangladesh and China. As well as the variation in prevalence across the continent, the modes of HIV transmission make Asia's epidemic one of the worlds most diverse. Injecting drug use is a major risk factor in several Asian countries. And the overlap of injecting drug use and sex work is a worrying phenomenon particularly in India, Pakistan and China where an increasing number of women are injecting drugs and also selling sex. Many male injecting drug users also buy sex, and often do not use condoms.

A high HIV prevalence has been found among sex-trafficked females who have been repatriated to Nepal, and also up to half of the females trafficked to Mumbai, India.

Interestingly, Thailand's epidemic has diminished but has also become more diverse, and HIV is increasingly affecting people traditionally considered to be at lower risk of infection.

7.1

In Scotland, during the year since the previous meeting of the General Assembly, there have been a number of developments at both national and local levels. HIV now has a clear profile within Scottish Government priorities. Strategic positioning of HIV firmly within the remit of its sexual health team reflects the reality of the epidemic as it stands in Scotland. Ministerial lead of the National Sexual Health and HIV Advisory Committee (NSHHAC) places HIV at the centre of the health agenda. The progress is most evident in the work to develop a comprehensive and integrated HIV Action Plan. This is based, firstly, on a thorough Scotland-wide needs assessment of HIV treatment and care, and, secondly on the expertise of clinical services, community agencies and service providers. By the summer, Scotland will begin to see the first nation-wide social marketing campaign addressing sexual health and HIV awareness. Unlike the threateningly hopeless tones of the icebergs and tombstones of the 1987 campaign, this will take a positive approach to providing information and resources that support safer sex and wider health improvement. The Church and faith communities have a role to play at all levels in this respect.

Emerging challenges have been identified. Reducing rates of transmission of HIV, making it easier for individuals to test for HIV, and improving the co-ordination and evaluation of our efforts encompass a number of other challenges. How to make condom use consistent and effective depends upon frank sex and relationships education. But it also requires awareness and support in relation to the effect of factors such as relationships, mental health, or alcohol related problems. Successes in tackling the spread of HIV among injecting drug users in the 'Trainspotting' years point us in the direction of pragmatic rather than dogmatic approaches to real life dilemmas.

Collaborative effort across boundaries and borders is a force for change and delivery. Work shared between the Church of Scotland and partner agencies has developed steadily. HIV Scotland's role in this includes Eunice Sinyemu's membership of the Project's Steering Group. Strategic lead at national level sees Rob Brown, the Kirk's representative round the table with leading HIV experts on NSHHAC. On a daily basis, Waverley Care's various support projects draw upon the deep seam of spiritual nurturing that's to be found in parish ministry as well as through its chaplain, Marion Chatterley.

Clarity, challenge and collaboration are crucial characteristics of any organisation with the needs of individuals and communities at their heart. We may often fall short or feel inadequate for the task, but our strengths lie in commitment and compassion.

5. Ecumenical Advocacy Alliance (EAA) and XVII International AIDS Conference, (IAC) 2008: MEXICO CITY

The project group sent The Rev John McMahon, (Project Group member), Angus Adams and Catherine Hay (youth representatives) to represent the Church of Scotland in Mexico City, at both the EAA's pre-conference and the IAC, in July and August 2008. The overall theme of the IAC was 'Universal Action *Now*' and this was reflected in the ecumenical pre-conference call: 'Faith in Action *Now*!' (Fe en Acción ¡Ahora!). For excellent reports and resources from the ecumenical pre-conference, please look at their website: http://iac.e-alliance.ch/.

This was the first time the IAC convened in a Latin American country, where over 20,000 delegates gathered. High profile speakers, including Ban-Ki Moon, General Secretary of the United Nations and Mexico's President Calderon, urged leadership as the key to achieving the action (now!) required to realise the UN commitment of reaching universal access to prevention, treatment, attention and support for HIV and Aids by 2010. Roy Kilpatrick, Chief Executive of HIV Scotland, reminds us that, "In Scotland, we need to ensure that the leadership which is the key to success is levered, supported and where necessary challenged." The churches and other faith-based organisations have a significant role to play.

> If there is such a thing as inspired leadership, it's equally true that most leadership qualities can and need to be worked at. Leaders sometimes need to be picked out from the crowd, encouraged, trained and let loose! The African HIV Policy Network [in Scotland] recently ran a series of 'Vital Voices' leadership courses, an example that could be emulated. A key learning point from healthy respect was the value of local 'champions' in schools, churches and sports clubs.

The ecumenical pre-conference was an excellent showcase of genuine, grassroots, faith-based involvement in the lives of those living with HIV and Aids. It was apparent that this faith-based response was so pivotal to the success of many HIV stories and yet, sadly, the voice of faith-based organisations was somewhat muted at the IAC, perhaps reflecting the scientific and clinical nature of IAC's initial establishment. Clearly, however, alongside the need for prevention, research and treatment, the psycho-social support and care (much of which is provided, although not solely, by faith-based organisations) needs to be more evident on IAC's programme. This requires action (now!) on the part of faith-based groups, submitting abstracts and presentation proposals for the next IAC (in Vienna, 18-23 July 2010), so that the good work evidenced and shared at the ecumenical pre-conference reaches a wider and, therefore, more influential audience.

Of particular interest at the ecumenical pre-conference was a seminar on 'Becoming an AIDS Competent Church'. Whilst the project group has celebrated success in working with our partner churches and agencies overseas, it might be true to say that much work remains to be done here, in Scotland, building upon what has already been achieved but helping the church, as a whole, to place HIV and Aids at the heart of our work

and witness. Many of our partner churches and agencies are already HIV 'competent' and we have much to learn from them.

> The concept of "HIV-competent church" relates to the ability of a given faith community to deal with the challenges posed by the HIV and AIDS pandemic in an appropriate and compassionate manner. An HIV-competent church staunches the spread of HIV, improves the lives of those living with and affected by it, mitigates the impact of HIV and ultimately restores hope and dignity.

The success, for example, of Eco-Congregations in Scotland is perhaps indicative that, through education and awareness-raising, congregations can be enabled to become more knowledgeable and involved, and the project group believes this approach to HIV 'competency' would present to the local church, and the communities in which we serve, an opportunity and a challenge. In other words, faith in action, *now*!

Crucial in helping the church and our congregations best understand the issues around HIV in Scotland, and the world, is to educate and equip our leaders at local, regional and national level. The project group, therefore, proposes to work with the Ministries Council in helping to develop material on HIV and Aids education, initially for those in ministerial training but to be made available to the whole church. If there is no HIV leadership amongst our leaders, there is no leadership in HIV. We believe this response, in keeping with the IAC's theme of 'Universal Action, *Now*!', will help the church to care and support more effectively.

6. Working with our partners – two snapshots

The United Mission to Nepal (UMN) is a co-operative effort between the people of Nepal and a large number of Christian organisations from 18 countries in four different continents. Established in 1954, it seeks to serve the people of Nepal in the Name and Spirit of Christ. The

7.1

Church of Scotland has been a member of UMN since its inception.

Since 2004, the Church of Scotland HIV/AIDS Project has been working with UMN in their overall aim of reducing HIV Transmission rate and improvement of quality of life of people infected and affected by HIV/AIDS in Nepal. UMN continue to support the prevention and control of HIV infection at the national and local level through partnerships and building the capacity of partner organisations. One example of such support is in the training and equipping of peer educators who work in their local community. Here is one of their stories…

> *"Mamata is an extraordinary girl. She lives in the town of Itahari in Sunsari district and although only 21, she has been able to break the cultural barriers and openly speak about the spread of HIV through risky sexual behaviour. In Nepal, where the subject of sex is largely taboo and hardly mentioned in public, young people like Mamata are making a difference in their communities.*
>
> *Mamata confesses that at the beginning it was difficult to talk about sex and HIV, but after receiving HIV and AIDS training from Naba Jiwan Samaj Sewa, a faith –based UMN partner in Itahari, she gained the confidence to speak to her friends and others about the spread of HIV. She is now an active peer educator and has spoken to more than 150 students and also addressed church leaders in Itahari on the importance of speaking out and taking action.*
>
> *"Because of the understanding that I now have about HIV and how it is spread, I know how to protect myself from getting infected, but many of my friends and relatives do not. It is because of this that I need to speak out" says Mamata"*

UMN, through its partner organisations also gives courage and hope to people infected and affected by Aids. Radhika Pun became infected through her husband who was a seasonal migrant worker. She says…

> *"I lost my job and was shunned, neglected, persecuted and depressed. I gave up all hope of life. Then one day, at a social event, I noticed everyone behaving differently towards a group of people. These people were HIV-infected. I immediately felt pity for them and started talking to them. Eventually in 2005 we formed Sakar Samuha Nepal (SSN), a self support group.*
>
> *During an HIV and Aids workshop, we came into contact with UMN, who took an avid interest in our group. Through our partnership since mid 2007, UMN has not only supported us but also inspired us to realise that being HIV-positive does not denote the end of life but the beginning of a new one"*

Joel Gijinthi, UMN's HIV/AIDS Technical Advisor, who had opportunity to meet with the moderator during his recent visit to Nepal, Maggie Lunan spoke of their meeting, *"It was a real delight to meet with Joel Gijinthi and his family when we were in Kathmandu; the first impression was of the warmth of his welcome and his appreciation that we might spend time with him. When he began to tell his story it was we who were humbled; initially he had come to Nepal for two years, leaving behind his wife and children in Kenya – it's a sacrifice I can hardly contemplate. His ongoing commitment to HIV and Aids work with UMN and his professionalism was evident. We were proud to be associated with World Mission Council who had had the foresight to fund his post, recognising the skills and experience he brought."*

Ida Waddell, a Church of Scotland Mission Partner with the United Church of Zambia, working in Mwandi Hospital as the Aids Relief Coordinator tells the story of one of her colleagues who is HIV+ve.

> "Peter has been married for 2 years to Mary who is HIV –ve and practices safe sex using condoms. He and his wife wanted children so came to the clinic for advice. Peter's blood was checked to make sure he was taking his antiretroviral medication properly and the virus levels in his blood were as low as possible. Mary's monthly cycle was monitored to work out when was the best time to conceive. They had unprotected sex on only one occasion but it was enough to give them a healthy baby boy 9 months later. Both Mary and the baby remain HIV –ve."

7. Promoting the Project in Scotland
Children's Assembly 2008

It was a real pleasure for the Project to be involved in the second Church of Scotland Children's Assembly, staged at Aviemore in November 2008. While the subject of HIV and Aids is one which might not seem ideally suited to an audience of 10–12-year-olds, we were keen to play our part in making a difficult issue come alive in a reasonable and responsible way for young church members. Staging six workshops, each involving around 20 assembly participants, the Project team highlighted key issues involving nutrition as they affect people who live with the virus. The aim of each session was to provide the youngsters with an understanding of what antiretroviral drugs achieve and the importance of regular nutrition in making this medication work to its fullest potential. The feedback received from participants and organisers was very heartening, including several of the children taking the message back to their own congregations, raising awareness there and also raising funds for the project

The Moderator's Challenge

Working closely with the Right Rev David Lunan during his moderatorial year has been a great privilege for our Project, not only because of his deep understanding of the issues involved in HIV and Aids, but also because of his personal commitment to keeping the Project in the Church's attention. In particular, we were very pleased that the Moderator took the initiative in stimulating awareness-raising and fund-raising at presbytery level. During the autumn, Rev Lunan (himself a Presbytery Clerk) launched his "Moderator's Challenge" to each presbytery, in the hope that each might commit itself to raising an average of £10,000 for the project. The focus of the launch was a World AIDS Day Reception at the Moderator's Residence to which all Presbytery Moderators were invited. There they were told of the good news from the work of the Church of Scotland HIV/AIDS Project and its partners worldwideó stories of hope and challenge in a situation which all you often hear about is pain, vulnerability and despair. The Moderator said: *"It is together with our partners that we are able to make a difference over the last 6 years we have been able to support projects financially with over £600,000 raised by the people of Scotland. The challenge now is to continue to support partners by increasing their capacity and self sustainability, but we cannot do that without committed funds......Why not challenge your Presbytery to be innovative, and let us seek to reach that first £1,000,000".*

It is our hope that all presbyteries will, indeed, rise to Rev Lunan's challenge in the months to come, so playing a vital part in our work.

"Souper Sunday 2009"

One presbytery-wide activity which should be noted is the Lothian Presbytery event entitled "Souper Sunday", which was staged in many of the congregations across Midlothian and East Lothian on Sunday 11 January. Each congregation had been equipped for the day with an order of service which could either be used, word for word, by congregational elders, or else adapted to reflect local needs

7.1

and interests. Hymns, prayers, readings and three short addresses on the theme of "new beginnings" were offered in the worship resources, which were enthusiastically adopted by many Kirk sessions. Following the services, worshippers were invited to stay in church for a simple soup-and-bread lunch, with donations invited to benefit the work of the Church of Scotland HIV/AIDS Project. As a result of the services and lunches, £5,600 has been raised towards the Presbytery's £10,000 goal. Such was the enthusiasm for "Souper Sunday" across Lothian Presbytery that the Project is proposing its adoption across the Church of Scotland as a whole (see Deliverance, section five).

Mothering Sunday

This year's Mothering Sunday Starters for Sunday material was developed by the Project, following an instruction from last year's General Assembly. In considering HIV and its impact on family life throughout the world, it is impossible to ignore the fact that so many young lives have been lost as a result of the virus's devastating effects. This, in turn, means that many households are cared for not by mums and dads, but by grannies, grandpas and even children.

The HIV/AIDS Project asked the Church to pause on Mothering Sunday, giving thanks to God for mothers the world over, but also remembering that in many parts of the world today there is a "lost generation" of parents, whose families do not know the kind of family life many of us take for granted in Scotland.

Faith and HIV in Action

At the time of writing the report plans are well under way for a training workshop for Christian Faith leaders at which Waverley Care will offer the opportunity for faith leaders to learn how to use a toolkit called 'Breaking the Loud Silence of HIV'. This resource, developed for use in church activities, explores ways to tackle the stigma and discrimination experienced by people living with HIV. The Project supported Waverley Care's Celebrate, Reflect and Remember event in St John's Church, Edinburgh, part of the World Aids Day activities, 2008, and around this time Waverley Care distributed a flyer with the ministers mailing bringing the needs of people living with HIV to the attention of every church in Scotland.

8.   Project Management

At the time of writing, the process of interviews is taking place for the position of full time Project Co-ordinator and a part time Project Administrator. It is hoped that both positions will be filled by the time of publication of this report. Despite a period of more than a year with temporary staffing for the project, the project Group have continued to drive forward the work including the process of taking the project to the next stage of its life, post December 2010. Consultation has begun with the Council of Assembly Governance and Budget Groups and with the Council Secretaries of the various Councils in regard to this. It is planned to report to the General Assembly of 2010.

Conclusion

Although potentially the past year could have been a fallow one for the Project, it has in fact been one when there has been much activity. It has been an opportunity to reflect and respond. The prospect of a new beginning – looking forward to the future beyond 2010 – working together with each partner to enable it to respond to its particular situation is challenging but hugely rewarding.

During the recent US election campaign, President Obama's "Yes we can" approach is perhaps one that we as a Church should emulate. As people of faith we must have the courage to be leaders as we continue to "Stop AIDS. Keep the Promise". In this way we can play our part to empower our global community to treat all people, including our sisters and brothers living with HIV, with love and respect.

In the name of the Project Group

ROBIN HILL, *Convener*
CAROL FINLAY, *Acting Co-ordinator*

Webography

Global campaign to promote "HIV-competent" churches
http://latin-america.waccglobal.org/lang-en/noticias-/11-Global-campaign-to-promote-\

HIV-competent church (WCC)
http://www.oikoumene.org/en/programmes/justice-diakonia-and-responsibility-for-creation/health-and-healing/hiv-competent-church.html

Exploring Solutions : How to Talk about HIV Prevention in the Church
http://www.e-alliance.ch/en/s/hivaids/publications/exploring-solutions/

Universal Access Now.
http://www.hivscotland.org.uk/index.php?controller=Default&action=ShowContent&pageid=39

Leadership is the Key: an article for World AIDS Day
http://www.hivscotland.org.uk/index.php?controller=Default&action=ShowContent&pageid=44

Report on the Global AIDS Epidemic 08
http://viewer.zmags.com/showmag.php?mid=wwfwwq#/page0/

7.1

PROPOSED DELIVERANCE

The General Assembly:

1. Receive Report
2. Affirm the support and thanks of the Church for all who serve in Her Majesty's Armed Forces as Chaplains and thank them for their spiritual and pastoral care of sailors, soldiers and air personnel and their families.
3. Affirm the commitment and support of the Church to our continuing Chaplaincy of Word and Sacrament in the Armed Forces.
4. Encourage the Church to uphold in prayer those who face particular danger and separation during service on Operational Duties, particularly in Afghanistan.
5. Commend to Ministers of the Church consideration of service in the Royal Navy, Naval Reserve or Sea Cadets, Regular Army, Territorial Army or Army Cadet Force, Royal Air Force or Air Training Corps.
6. Note with thanks service to both the Church and the Royal Air Force of the Reverend Peter Mills QHC and wish him well in retirement as Chaplain in Chief and Principal Chaplain Church of Scotland and Free Churches.

REPORT

1. Introduction

1.1 Ask a group of military Chaplains to complete the sentence, 'Chaplaincy is ......' and their replies might include: 'being alongside others wherever they are in their lives'; 'being a walking sacrament'; 'being the servant where others, not the Church, sets the agenda'. Military chaplaincy is many things: the personal, the pastoral, the institutional and often with those who have little or no faith. It demands that the Chaplain is immersed in the community he/she serves. Chaplains often wear the same uniform as their parishioners, share the same tensions, dangers and celebrations for, where their parishioners go, they go – be it to war or other duties. Like everyone else in the Forces, they never stay in one place for very long. Their work is infinitely varied and can be immensely rewarding. The Chaplain is called upon to be priest, pastor and prophet; standing alongside soldier, sailor, marine and airman/woman in critical solidarity and pastoral availability as counsellor to the powerful and advocate for the powerless. Chaplains nourish communities of worshipping Christians with Word and Sacrament, yet spend much of their time with people who usually never come inside a church, helping the human spirit to develop. Ministering in the constant tension of being disciples of the Prince of Peace while living as members of the military community, Chaplains bring 'humanity to an often inhuman situation'. Therefore, in our Report, the General Assembly's Committee is honoured to pay tribute to all who serve the Church of Scotland and our Country in military chaplaincy, both regular and volunteer, for their faithfulness, humanity and dedication.

1.2 Recruitment

1.2.1 The potential recruitment of a Chaplain for regular service with the Royal Air Force is welcome news. The footprint of the Church of Scotland in RAF Chaplaincy is currently much diminished from former years and a matter of concern for the Committee, especially as forthcoming retirement will affect present numbers even more. Since last Assembly, the Rev Hector McKenzie and the Rev Dr James Francis have been inducted to regular chaplaincy with the Army and we look forward to a third entry later in the year. The Rev Alison Britchfield has left the Royal Navy in order to become Minister at the Parish of Lecropt near Stirling. We thank Alison for 16 years of distinguished service and wish her and her husband, Mike, well. The Rev Dr Scott Shackleton has also come to the end of 16 years service and, along with his wife Gillian, returns to parish ministry in Scotland, having been called to Downfield South Church in Dundee. The Committee greatly appreciates the dedication and service given over those years and wish them well.

1.2.2 Applications made for service with the Territorial Army have been well received by the Committee as have those for the Army Cadet Force and Royal Naval Reserve. However, there continue to be vacancies for eligible Chaplains in each of these organisations. Ministers considering such application should please contact the Convener on 01698 853189 or by email, jamesmgibson@msn.com or Douglas Hunter, Secretary. Exchange Tower, 19 Canning Street, Edinburgh, EH3 8EH, telephone 0131 228 2400 or email, dhunter@hbj-gw.com.

1.2.3 During last year's Assembly, commissioners again enquired why no mention is given in the Committee's Report to chaplaincy in the Air Training Corps. This is because Chaplains in the ATC do not hold the Queen's Commission and, therefore, do not come under the remit of the Assembly's Committee. Nevertheless, the Committee gladly commends the invaluable work of ATC chaplaincy to the Church's ministers.

1.3 Interdenominational Advisory Group
The Interdenominational Advisory Group (IAG) is usually an annual meeting of senior representatives from the five groups of Sending Churches – Church of England, Roman Catholic, Methodist Church, United Board and Church of Scotland and Free Churches. Over the past year however, various meetings have been held to discuss a Roman Catholic proposal to introduce Lay Chaplaincy to the military to ease their increasing difficulty with the recruitment of ordained priests. The adoption of such a proposal would have fundamental consequences for

the future nature of military chaplaincy for all Sending Churches and so discussions are ongoing. The Committee is grateful for advice given by all specifically consulted and, in particular, by retired senior Chaplains, the Executive of the Ministries Council, the Church's Chaplaincy Task Group.

1.4 Visits and Events
1.4.1 During the past year, the Convener represented the Committee at the Service of Thanksgiving held at the Armed Forces National Memorial, Alrewas, Staffordshire for all who had served in the Bosnia Campaign; attended the Commemoration Service held in St Paul's Cathedral for the end of 'Op Banner' (Northern Ireland); attended the annual Armistice Day Service held at the Scottish National War Memorial, Edinburgh Castle; visited Chaplains at Aldershot and at York; preached at the annual St Andrew Patronal Service in the Garrison Church, Aldershot and at an Interdenominational Service of Thanksgiving held in the Kirk of the Holy Rood, Stirling for the lives of all Scottish servicemen and servicewomen who have died or been injured while on Active Duty in Iraq or Afghanistan; and attended the 90th Anniversary Service for 'Combat Stress' held in St Giles' Cathedral. The Vice-Convener represented the Committee at a service to mark the 50th Anniversary of St Clement Danes Church London being dedicated as the church of the Royal Air Force.

1.4.2 The Committee is indebted to the Right Rev David Lunan, Moderator of the General Assembly for attendance at military events held over the past year and for his official visit to the Royal Air Force with his wife, Maggie.

1.5 Changes in Senior Posts
1.5.1 The Committee notes the retirement later in the year of the Rev (Air Vice-Marshal) Peter W Mills, QHC BD RAF from the post of Chaplain-in-Chief, Royal Air Force and Principal Chaplain (Church of Scotland and Free Churches). Pete will be much missed for his forthright manner, ready humour and caring humanity. Supported by his wife Sheila, he has served within the RAF with great distinction. The Committee is particularly pleased to note

the conferment on Pete of a Doctorate of Divinity degree by the University of Aberdeen. We extend to them both our thanks for all he has achieved in his chaplaincy and our best wishes for whatever their future may hold.

In the name of the Committee

JAMES M GIBSON, *Convener*
ANDREW V M MURRAY, *Vice Convener*
DOUGLAS M HUNTER, *Secretary*

APPENDIX 1
REPORT ON CHAPLAINCY IN THE ROYAL NAVY

The Naval Service – A Force for Good
It has been another busy year for the Naval Service. (Royal Navy, Royal Marines and Royal Fleet Auxiliary). Our primary aim remains to support the UK's contribution to the continuing operations in Iraq and Afghanistan.

For the last three years we have had significant numbers of personnel in Afghanistan, and 2008/09 was no different. The Royal Marines, Naval helicopters, Harriers from the Naval Strike Wing, Naval Special Forces and numerous augmentees from logisticians, engineers, medics and Chaplains, and both Royal Naval and Royal Marines Reserves are or have been taking part in demanding and intensive operations; 3 Commando Brigade Royal Marines are back once more for the winter deployment. Yet again, we are providing the lead and majority of UK military forces in southern Afghanistan. We must not forget the true cost of these operations and tragically, a number of our Servicemen have paid the ultimate sacrifice in Afghanistan; with Church of Scotland Chaplains being involved in the care of the bereaved, both in theatre and with the families in the UK.

In Iraq, a Royal Marine General is commanding the Divisional HQ at Basrah, and the Naval Transition Team at Umm Qasr is training the Iraqi Navy and Marines, supported by training in the UK for Iraqi Navy officers. It is also very pleasing to see that the Iraqi Navy's ability to defend the two offshore oil terminals is maturing.

Away from combat operations, the surface flotilla, submarine service, Fleet Air Arm, Royal Marines and Royal Fleet Auxiliary all continue to contribute to the defence of the UK, protecting our maritime trade across the world, reassuring legitimate users of the sea, exerting influence on behalf of the UK Government through a programme of engagement and presence, and building trust, co-operation and friendships.

Our maritime security patrols have enjoyed conspicuous success through the year in the Arabian Gulf, North and South Atlantic, Indian Ocean, Mediterranean and Pacific, restricting piracy and disrupting weapons smuggling, human trafficking and the drugs trade. Our counter-narcotics successes in the Caribbean are well publicised, but we have also had a good measure of success off Africa and in the Arabian Gulf.

Admiral Sir Jonathan Band, the First Sea Lord, said recently, "It has been a tough, busy, even challenging year. None of the activity and operational success would have been possible without the professionalism and dedication of the 34,500 men and women of the Naval Service, who continue to display outstanding resilience, courage and pride on all the operations we are engaged in. The 'fighting spirit' within the Service is as strong as ever. Our people have made a significant contribution to the defence of the United Kingdom. We cannot take this for granted, however, and we will need to work hard to recruit and retain our people without forgetting the utterly vital contribution their families make in support. We owe much to the men and women of the Naval Service and their families and this reinforces our resolve to look after them in the manner they deserve".

Naval Chaplains, both Regular and Reserve, continue to serve in the front line, at sea and on land operations.

8

It is our privilege to take the ministry of the church, and indeed the message of the Gospel, to the Service community wherever they are serving in the world today. Naval Chaplaincy continues a long tradition of care for the seafarer, and in being the friend and adviser to all onboard.

I am grateful to the Church of Scotland Committee on Chaplains to Her Majesty's Forces for their support through the year, their wise counsel and ongoing pastoral care of Chaplains and their families.

The number of Church of Scotland Chaplains in the Navy today is critically low. Any Minister who would like to explore this area of ministry, either full-time or as a Reservist, please do make contact with me or with the Convener. We can normally recruit up to age 49 on an initial commission of 6 years, but there is flexibility too. (scott.brown943@mod.uk or call 023 9262 5552).

CHAPLAINS SERVING TODAY IN THE RN AND THE RNR

The Rev Scott J Brown QHC Royal Navy

I continue to serve in the Navy Command Headquarters as the Principal Church of Scotland and Free Churches Chaplain (Naval) and as Director Naval Chaplaincy Service (Capability). I am based in Portsmouth.

The Rev Alison E P Britchfield Royal Navy

Alison left the Royal Navy in April 2009 after 16 years of loyal and fruitful service. She finished her career as the Chaplaincy Team Leader at Her Majesty's Naval Base Clyde at Faslane. We wish Alison and her husband Mike every blessing back in parish ministry.

The Rev Dr Scott J S Shackleton Royal Navy

Scott left the Royal Navy in April 2009 after 16 years of loyal and faithful service, much of it spent in the Royal Marines community. We wish Scott, Gillian, and their family, every blessing in parish ministry.

The Rev Stan Kennon Royal Navy

Stan continues to serve in HMS RALEIGH, the Royal Navy's initial training establishment which is situated near Torpoint in Cornwall, a short ferry ride across the River Tamar from the city of Plymouth. As Chaplaincy Team Leader, he teaches and offers pastoral support to new trainees whilst co-ordinating the work of the Chaplaincy Department, one of the busiest in the Royal Navy. Church of Scotland worship takes place every Sunday in St Andrew's Church within the establishment and is attended by around seventy trainees who come from Presbyterian, Baptist, Methodist and also non-Christian faith backgrounds and many who have none at all: an eclectic and energetic mix. With an average age of nineteen, they generally appreciate Church as a time in the week where they have a special space to become 'human again' amid their frenetic military training.

The Rev Mark Dalton Royal Navy

Mark Dalton has been kept busy throughout the year at a large naval air station. Earlier in the year he took up a new appointment to face the challenges of a training establishment and he very much looks forward to returning to sea sometime in the future.

The Rev Stevie Thomson Royal Navy

"HMS SULTAN continues to be a challenging environment at the forefront of a caring, teaching, and pastoral Ministry to all personnel, whether civilian or military, who live and work on the establishment. We have a pastoral oversight of military nursing staff at Haslar Royal Hospital, together with that of the Armed Forces Pay and Pensions organisation at HMS CENTURIAN and the Fleet Manpower and Supply Unit at Gosport. "On a personal note during May 2008 I was persuaded to attend "Bavarian Surprise", the Royal Navy Adventurous Training week in Germany, where I surprised myself by Kayaking, White Water Rafting, Rock Climbing, Abseiling and Klettersteiging (Climbing up cliffs on wires)".

At the time of General Assembly Stevie will be on Exercise LONG LOOK in either Australia or New Zealand, a 4 month exchange programme with the Royal Australian or Royal New Zealand Navies. He will return to sea-going ministry later in 2009.

The Rev Alen McCulloch Royal Navy

Alen completed an operational tour of Iraq in May 2008. He passed on to the RN, Army and RAF personnel in the Contingency Operating Base at Basra the prayerful best wishes of many congregations and individuals across the Kirk, as well as the large number of boxes of biscuits they donated. This support was very much appreciated by all. He then began a new assignment with the Commando Logistic Regiment Royal Marines (CLR), a large unit based at Chivenor in North Devon. After going on the 3 Commando Brigade RM Mission Rehearsal Exercise on Salisbury Plain in July, he flew to Afghanistan in September. As Chaplain to CLR he deployed on a Combat Logistic Patrol to two of the Forward Operating Bases in Helmand Province; as Garrison Chaplain for Camp Bastion he began a congregation in "Bastion 2" for the large number of UK personnel who live there. The British Chaplains enjoy fellowship there with Chaplains from the USA, Denmark and Estonia. The last two months of his tour were spent as Garrison Chaplain for Kabul. He expects to return to sea in March 2009 on frigates based in Devonport, initially in HMS PORTLAND, and then in HMS MONMOUTH and HMS SUTHERLAND.

The Rev Dr Marjory MacLean Royal Naval Reserve

Marjory passed the Advanced Command and Staff Course (Maritime Reserves) at the UK Defence Academy in summer 2008. In addition to her pastoral care of reservists at HMS SCOTIA in Rosyth and Dundee, she has served as Staff Officer for Operational Capability of Chaplaincy in the Maritime Reserves, an appointment within the RNR command which doubles as Chaplaincy Team Leader (Maritime Reserves) within Naval Chaplaincy Service management.

The Rev Ross McDonald Royal Naval Reserve

Ross continues to serve the men and women of the Naval Reserve at HMS DALRIADA in Greenock. The Reserves play an increasing role in operations, with the RNR Chaplain playing a key role in their care and the care of their families.

SCOTT J BROWN QHC, *Principal Chaplain*

APPENDIX 2
CHAPLAINCY IN THE ARMY

Church of Scotland Chaplains exercise their ministry within the Royal Army Chaplains' Department in all categories: as Regular Chaplains, as Chaplains to the Territorial Army and to the Army Cadet Force, and as Officiating Chaplains. The continuing operational commitment of the Armed Forces means that this ministry is in acute demand, both with soldiers deployed in Iraq, Afghanistan and elsewhere and also with units and families who live with change and uncertainty at home. Recruiting to the Department remains a priority if these challenges and commitments are to be met. The past year has been encouraging for recruiting, with candidates emerging especially for Regular and ACF Chaplaincy, but vacancies remain in every category. Prospective applicants for this rewarding and exciting ministry are most warmly encouraged to contact the Convener or Secretary of the Committee. There is always a requirement for new Regular Chaplains, and specific vacancies within other categories are identified in the list below.

The new Chaplain General, the Ven Stephen Robbins QHC, assumed post in June 2008. The Rev Dr David Coulter QHC continues as Principal of the Armed Forces Chaplaincy Centre at Amport House. Dr Coulter is now Denominational Representative Chaplain for the Church of Scotland, in which capacity he organised an excellent Denominational Chaplains' Conference in early December. The Rev Peter Eagles continues as Assistant Chaplain General 2nd Division with overall responsibility for recruiting, provision and administration of chaplaincy across Scotland, Northern England and Northern Ireland.

8

The military ministry of the Rev Alex Forsyth concluded this year, after 26 years of service to the TA and 25 years to the Cadets. Recruits to the Department included the Rev Dr Jim Francis and the Rev Heather Rendell as Regular Chaplains, the Rev Christopher Rowe to the Territorial Army, the Rev Messrs Roderick MacDonald and Fraser Stewart to the Army Cadet Force and the Rev Neil Gardner as an Officiating Chaplain. Another candidate for Regular Chaplaincy is currently in process.

The celebration of the Centenary of the Territorial Army included a sequence of public services of worship with military involvement across Scotland. Military Chaplains were able to participate and to preach, and this was a reminder not just of the unity of the Regular and the Territorial Army but also of our roots as soldiers and Chaplains in the community and in society. Our ministry as Chaplains is both immediate and universal, and perhaps this is best illustrated in the following narrative, a conflation of Chaplains' diaries for this year:

'As the Battalion Chaplain my role was one of sharing in the varied experiences: the incredibly hot days, the dust, the anxious moments of waiting for a Chinook to take me to my next location, the danger, the presentation of new colours to the Battalion by HRH Prince Andrew, the solemn and dignified repatriation services of fallen soldiers, the times of laughter and good humour. The Church at Camp Bastion was used on a daily basis, and many soldiers visited to light a candle or enjoy the peace and quiet of its surroundings. Since then it has been a time of transition with our emphasis on quality of life including sport and adventure training and also daily routine. A successful multi-cultural evening included foods from Fiji, South Africa, Ireland and Scotland, with pipes and drums, gaelic singing and Fijian dancing. On the horizon is the summer exercise in Kenya. This is a tremendous opportunity to train … (last time) a few members of the battalion ran a marathon, which included crossing the equator, for the rescue centre for street children. In the brigade, Chaplains have this

year produced a Chaplaincy Bulletin and resources for Remembrance for civilian parishes and run an open day for interested clergy. I have attended most of the (Army Cadet Force) Company weekend camps, exercising a ministry far beyond the traditional muster parade worship on a Sunday morning. At the Army Training Regiment, we saw just under three thousand recruits last year; a surprising number choose to attend Church on a Sunday morning, and there is opportunity to encourage those who come with Christian faith and to welcome those for whom meeting an Army Chaplain is their first real contact with the Church. This brings to me most of all a deep sense of gratitude to God for the privilege of serving Him in such a rewarding calling'.

This reflects the work of chaplaincy over the year. Although the Regular Army, the Territorial Army and the Army Cadet Force will all have their own specific context, the challenges and opportunities are the same. The conclusion of the paragraph above defines the ethos of military chaplaincy.

CHURCH OF SCOTLAND ARMY CHAPLAINS – FEBRUARY 09

Rev B J A Abeledo	2 Bn The Royal Regiment of Scotland (RHF) Glencorse Barracks Milton Bridge Penicuik EH26 0NP
Rev J W Aitchison	HQ 101 Log Bde Buller Barracks Aldershot GU11 2BY
Rev D Anderson	Bn The Royal Regiment of Scotland (BW) Fort George Ardersier Inverness IVI 2TD

Rev D Connolly

27 Regiment RLC
Travers Barracks
Aldershot
GU11 2BX

Rev Dr D G Coulter
QHC

AFCC
Amport House
Amport
AndoverHants
SP11 8BG

Rev J C Duncan

2 MERCIAN
Holywood Palace Bks
BFPO 806

Rev D V F Kingston

CSFC Chaplain
RAF Akrotiri
BFPO 57

Rev H MacKenzie

4 SCOTS & 2BN REME
St Barbara Barracks
BFPO 38

Rev C A MacLeod

DACG
HQ 15(NE) Brigade
Imphal Barracks, York
YO10 4HD

Rev J MacGregor

5 Regiment RA
Marne Barracks
Catterick
DL10 7NP

Rev S L Mackenzie

ATR
Bassingbourn Barracks
Royston
Hertfordshire
SG8 5LX

Rev R N MacLeod

1 Bn The Royal Regiment of
Scotland (RS)
Dreghorn Barracks
Edinburgh
EH13 9QW

Rev D J MacPherson

Assistant Chaplain
RMA Sandhurst
Camberley
Surrey
GU15 4PQ

Rev D K Prentice

3 RIFLES
Redford Barracks
Colinton Road
Edinburgh
EH13 0PP

Also serving from the Presbyterian Church of Ireland

Rev N G McDowell

Senior Chaplain
ITC(C)
Vimy Barracks
Scotton Road
Catterick Garrison
North Yorks
DL9 3PS

Rev Dr S P Swinn

JSC & SC
Defence Academy
Shrivenham
Swindon
Wilts
SN6 8LA

Rev M Henderson

British Forces Episkopi
BFPO 53

Rev S W Van Os

DST
Normandy Barracks
Leconfield
East Yorkshire
HU17 7LX

Location of Territorial Army Chaplains

6 Bn The Royal Regiment
of Scotland

Rev S A Blakey

7 Bn The Royal Regiment
of Scotland

vacancy

8

Queens Own Yeomanry (V)	Rev Dr J Francis
105 Regiment Royal Artillery (V)	Rev D J Thom
32 (Scottish) Signal Regiment (V)	Rev C Rowe
71 Regiment Royal Engineers (V)	Rev R R Adams (Baptist Church)
Scottish Transport Regiment (V)	Rev J Smith, MBE, TD (Congregational Church)
225 GS Med Regt (V)	Rev Miss N Frail
225 GS Med Regt (V)	**vacancy**
225 GS Med Regt (V)	**vacancy**
205 (Scottish) Field Hospital (V)	Rev L Kinsey, TD
205 (Scottish) Field Hospital (V)	**vacancy**
205 (Scottish) Field Hospital (V)	**vacancy**

Location of Army Cadet Force Chaplains

Angus & Dundee Bn	**vacancy** **vacancy**
Argyll & Sutherland Highlanders Bn	Rev R D M Campbell, OStJ, TD **vacancy** **vacancy**
Black Watch Bn	Rev Dr I C Barclay, MBE, TD **vacancy**
Glasgow & Lanark Bn	Rev J E Andrews **vacancy**
1 Bn The Highlanders	Rev I C Warwick, TD Rev F Stewart

2 Bn The Highlanders	Rev I A Sutherland Rev T Bryson
Orkney (Independent) Bty	**vacancy**
Shetland (Independent) Bty	**vacancy**
Lothian & Borders Bn	Rev A Hughes (C of E) **vacancy** **vacancy**
West Lowland Bn	Rev D M Almond **vacancy** Rev R Macdonald
Cumbria ACF	Rev D J Thom

Location of Officiating Chaplains to the Forces

Rev R A Whiteford	Resident Battalion, Fort George
Rev Canon D McAlister (SEC)	Resident Battalion, Fort George
Rev Dr I C Barclay	Aberdeen Universities Officer Training Corps
The Rev Dr J Walker	Tayforth Universities Officer Training Corps
Rev A R Mathieson	Resident Battalion, Dreghorn & Glencorse Barracks
Rev N Gardner	Edinburgh Universities Officer Training Corps
Rev S Blakey	HQ 51(Scottish) Bde and Glasgow Universities Officer Training Corps
Rev T A Davidson Kelly	Army Personnel Centre, Glasgow

APPENDIX 3
CHAPLAINCY IN THE RAF

The Royal Air Force continues to deliver capabilities to the UK's operations around the world with 7.2% of its strength (2860 personnel) deployed at the time of writing. For the last 17 years the Air Force has been continually engaged in operations in the Middle East, with some personnel on their twentieth deployment to the region. There are few parts of the front-line that are not feeling the pressure of such sustained commitment and the Chief of the Air Staff recently highlighted the contribution of the Air Transport force, the helicopter squadrons, the Tornado, Harrier and Nimrod forces and the Royal Air Force Regiment. Additionally, the Royal Air Force operates a number of Critical Care Air Support Teams in Iraq and Afghanistan, a unique medical asset, responsible for the repatriation of the most critically ill and injured from the battlefield to the field hospitals.

Approximately 7% of Royal Air Force Chaplains are also deployed on operations at any one time and they provide vital support to personnel undergoing the mental, emotional and spiritual rigours of deployment. At the same time, Chaplains provide vital support to families in the UK and to those feeling the pressure of such prolonged exposure to the operational tempo. Of note is the additional burden placed upon the chaplaincy team at Royal Air Force Lyneham where the dead are repatriated and most weeks, sometimes more frequently, ceremonies are held where families receive the bodies of their loved ones. Chaplains, as well as those from the units involved (Navy, Army or Air Force), are always present with each family before and during the ceremony and then afterwards for those who wish to spend time in a purpose built chapel of rest.

Recruitment remains a challenge and currently there are vacancies for both full-time and part-time Chaplains. When the Rev P W Mills retires from his current post as Chaplain-in-Chief later this year, there will be only 2 full-time and 1 part-time Church of Scotland Chaplains left in the whole of the Royal Air Force. This cutting edge ministry of spiritual leadership, moral guidance and pastoral care is as challenging as it is rewarding. It demands sacrifice and a mixture of robustness and godliness, but every so often one has to stop and marvel at the extraordinary opportunities and encounters that are the bread and butter of Armed Forces chaplaincy.

Church of Scotland Chaplains

The Rev P W Mills is Chaplain-in-Chief and is responsible to the Chief of the Air Staff for the delivery of all chaplaincy throughout the RAF.

The Rev G T Craig is Director Chaplaincy (Training and Operations) and is responsible to the Chaplain-in-Chief for training and operational policy and for the station level and operational delivery of all chaplaincy throughout the RAF.

The Rev S Munro is the Force Chaplain at Mount Pleasant Airport in the Falkland Islands.

The Rev I McFadzean is a Reserve Chaplain who has a yearly commitment of 29 days. He is currently engaged in raising the profile of RAF chaplaincy among Church of Scotland clergy.

Presbyterian Church of Ireland Chaplains

The Rev D Edgar is the RAF Director at the Armed Forces Chaplaincy Centre at Amport House. He works as part of a Tri-Service chaplaincy team under the leadership of the Principal, currently an RAChD and Church of Scotland Chaplain.

The Rev J Wylie is the Church of Scotland and Free Churches Chaplain at RAF Support Unit located at the USAF base in Ramstein, Germany.

8

PROPOSED DELIVERANCE

The General Assembly
1. Receive the Report and thank the members of the Trust for their diligence.
2. Re-appoint the Very Rev Dr Finlay Macdonald and the Rev Prof Kenneth Ross as members of the Trust from 1st June 2009.

REPORT

The Church of Scotland Trust, which was established by Act of Parliament in 1932, submits its Seventy seventh Report to the General Assembly.

1. The Work of the Trust

(a) General

The function of the Church of Scotland Trust is to hold properties outwith Scotland and to act as a trustee in a number of third party trusts. During the year it has dealt with various matters which have arisen regarding these properties and trusts. Matters of particular significance are noted hereafter.

(b) Third Party Trusts

The Trust is currently trustee of 47 third party trusts which benefit different areas of the Church's work. In 2007 the Trust instigated a Rolling Review Programme for these trusts. The Trust's Secretary and Clerk undertakes a review of the trusts annually, producing reports on half the third party trust portfolio to each of the February and September Trust meetings.

(c) Israel

The Trust continues to be consulted by the World Mission Council regarding ongoing and future developments relating to property in Israel. The Trust is represented on the Designated Supervising Group for Tiberias.

(d) Pakistan

The Trust regrets that it must report again that little progress has been made with the transfer of all the Trust's remaining property interests in Pakistan to a suitable body in terms of the Church of Scotland Trust Order Confirmation Act 1958. As previously reported the Trust appointed Dr Peter David, a Pakistani Christian resident in the UK, in February 2007 to help progress the transfers. Dr David was reappointed as an attorney, for a further term, in 2008 with Jamshed Rahmat Ullah, a Supreme Court lawyer based in Lahore. Both Attorneys are assisting the Trust in achieving its objectives in relation to their interests in the Diocese of Sialkot but progress has been hampered by amongst other things the political instability in Pakistan, *ie* the assassination of Benazir Bhutto; problems with the State elections; suspension of the Chief Justice and strike action paralysing the Pakistani Courts. Considerable efforts continue to be made to establish the actual position regarding the properties vested in the Trust in Pakistan. At its February meeting the Trust appointed representatives to meet with representatives of the World Mission Council to discuss their future joint strategy in relation to Pakistan. The Trust is grateful to its attorneys for the time and energy given to their duties.

As reported for a number of years, the Trust continues to be a party to a number of court cases involving its property interests in Pakistan. No substantive progress has been made regarding these actions during the last 12 months. The Trust is legally represented in these cases but, due to the nature of the Pakistan legal system, it is anticipated that these cases will be ongoing for some time.

2.   Accounts for 2008

The Trust's Accounts for the year to 31 December 2008 have been independently examined and copies thereof are available on request from the General Treasurer.

3.   Membership

In accordance with the constitution of the Trust, the following two members retire by rotation on 31 May 2009 but are eligible for re-appointment: the Very Rev Dr Finlay Macdonald and the Rev Prof Kenneth Ross. It is suggested to the General Assembly that the Very Rev Dr Finlay Macdonald and the Rev Prof Kenneth Ross be re-appointed.

In the name and by authority of The Church of Scotland Trust

ROBERT BRODIE, *Chairman*
CHRISTOPHER N MACKAY, *Vice-Chairman*
JENNIFER M HAMILTON, *Secretary & Clerk*

PROPOSED DELIVERANCE

This body will bring a brief report to the General Assembly. At the time of preparation of this volume, up to date information is not yet available. Therefore, this report will be printed in Assembly papers in due course.

PROPOSED DELIVERANCE

The General Assembly:

1. Receive the Report.
2. Commend the Church without Walls (CWW) Planning Group for their innovative and creative use of conferencing over the past five years, not only in bringing together Christian teachers and thinkers from diverse parts of the theological spectrum but by helping the Church to begin to move to a greater appreciation and understanding of the diversity and gifts of God's people.
3. Encourage the successors of the CWW Planning Group to:
    (i) continue to motivate, inspire and model the vision of Church without Walls through the medium of creative events such as the National Gathering and Regional conferences;
    (ii) prepare study materials for congregations to help them engage with the on-going vision of Church without Walls;
    (iii) keep the vision of the "Sending" firmly in view of the whole Church and collaborate with the World Mission Council to bring about a greater awareness of the benefits that come to local congregations through mentoring, maintaining and promoting networks that involve visiting their overseas partnerships;
    (iv) hold to the four key themes of the 2001 Church without Walls Report as they continue to carry forward the vision;
    (v) examine the themes arising out of the conversation with the Councils of the Church and use them to help inform the preparation of future conferences and events;
    (vi) continue to model the relational legacy of the CWW vision within the CWW National and Regional Planning Groups set up to carry forward the vision of the "Regional Dimension".
4. Commend the CWW Planning Group for their innovative use of technology in creating an on-line forum which is allows the work of the Group to be accessed by a larger audience and for the development of the on-line booking system for all Church without Walls events.
5. Commend all the congregations who participated in the National Gathering and especially those who invested in the purchase of a tent, and recognise the generous help received from the Blythswood Trust and the Scottish International Relief Agency who arranged for the tents to be shipped to China to support the victims of the 2008 earthquake.
6. Encourage the Mission and Discipleship Council to continue to recognise the priority and importance of effective resourcing of congregations and the role that Church without Walls can play in bringing this about through their experience in organising events and conferences.
7. Instruct the Mission and Discipleship Council to adopt the Plan of Action as laid out in the Report as an important shaper in developing the role that CWW will fulfill in the revised priorities of the Council.

8. Thank and discharge the CWW Planning Group for their work over the past years, invite the Mission and Discipleship Council to form a task group in order to carry forward the work of Church without Walls and instruct the Nomination Committee to bring forward the relevant names so that their work within the Mission and Discipleship Council can begin immediately following the General Assembly.

A Vision to Direct our Energies
The vision of the Church of Scotland is
to be a church which seeks to inspire the people of Scotland and beyond
with the Good News of Jesus Christ
through enthusiastic, worshipping, witnessing and serving communities.
[General Assembly 2006, Panel of Review and Reform]

Core Values to Shape our Life Together
To be followers of Jesus Christ as encountered in the Gospels.
To engage in creative and life-giving mission in our communities and our culture.
To develop friendship with neighbour, stranger and seeker, locally and globally.
To release the gifts of God's Spirit among God's people in God's world.
To live in the grace of God and to live out the grace of God.
[Based on the "shapers" of Church without Walls]

Introduction

In 1999 the Presbytery of Edinburgh, feeling that there was a need for the purpose of the Church to be articulated clearly, brought an Overture to the General Assembly of the Church of Scotland requesting the Assembly to set up a special commission entitled *The Commission anent Review and Reform*. This Commission was to be made up of a multi-disciplinary group of people and was invited to "re-examine in depth the primary purposes of the Church and the shape of the Church as we enter into the next millennium." They were invited "to initiate a process of continuing reform to consult on such matters with the other Scottish Churches and report to the General Assembly of 2001."

It became known as The *Church without Walls Report*. It was received with acclaim and has surprised us all in the way the Spirit has used it to stimulate the missional imagination of congregations across Scotland – and across the world.

It was seen as a "permission-giving" statement that gave affirmation to the creative innovators and gave courage to many to paint pictures outside the lines of traditional expectations. It allowed congregations to rediscover the importance of local empowerment. There were at least three aspects of this empowerment: resourcing, relationships and relevance.

The report highlighted the need for resourcing of the local congregation by the redistribution of monies from the centre. It encouraged the whole Church to re-examine its structures developing the ability to become more relational and interdependent on each other and the communities we serve. The third area of empowerment called the Church to listen to the people we live and work alongside and discover how we can connect to enable a post-modern world to encounter the relevance of the gospel.

At a time when the Western Church speaks of new churches "emerging" for our culture, and when the Church of England has invested heavily in encouraging "fresh expressions" of church, the Church of Scotland's contribution to this global conversation has been *Church without Walls*. It has proved to be part of something bigger than any of us could have imagined ten years ago.

Conferencing as a Means of Auditing and Inspiring the Church

The 2001 report made provision for a future conference in 2005 to celebrate the effects of the Church without Walls report on the Church. The inspiration for this event found its roots in the 1931 Conference of Unity held to celebrate the union of the Church of Scotland and the United Free Church. It took place in St Andrew's Halls in Glasgow. More than 70 years later, the Church met in conference again this time in Edinburgh and it proved to be of great value to all who attended. The excitement and the creativity of the day was only exceeded by the wonderful spirit of unity that descended on all who attended. It proved that the Church still had a willingness to celebrate and believed it had a future.

Using the idea of events and conferences has turned out to be a very effective way of bringing inspirational people, projects, concepts and ideas, which might lead to reform, before the Church. It has also been a very practical way of displaying a public audit of the extent to which CWW deliverances have been implemented within the Church at large. It has shown the theological breadth of the CWW movement in the Church of Scotland, as Christian teachers and thinkers from diverse parts of theological spectrum of the Church have shared together and worked together to live out the principle of a Church without Walls.

Using Technology to Connect Wider

The development of the online forum www. cwwresources.org.uk as part of our strategy of listening to congregations has given an opportunity for a wide group of people to engage with the work of the Planning Group. The fact that all major contributors to our conferences and events can have their presentations downloaded allows a much wider group of people to participate in our conferencing and means we can disseminate material to a much wider audience. Our use of e-mail to communicate with congregations and the online booking system for all events has meant that we have been able to cut our administration costs to the minimum.

Creating a CWW Community

The interest in these events continues to connect with new people. At the fourth Re-energise Conference held in Aviemore in January this year, over 53% of churches attending had never been to one of our events and of those attending 75% of them had never been to any event before. We find this encouraging because it means that we are still connecting with congregations who up until now have for what ever reason not been involved. It also seems to substantiate our belief that we have connected with the early adopters and we are now beginning to connect with the next group of interested congregations.

Learning, engaging and networking with each other at a practical level has been the hallmark of CWW events. This is best demonstrated by the creative use of tents at The National Gathering in 2008. Around 200 tents became part of the event as congregations the length and breadth of the land shared their stories of faith and hope and even of disappointment.

The tented village, as it was called, became one of the most effective theological statements of the weekend. The National Gathering attracted over 8,000 people to a weekend that sought to ask the Church to consider not what we take forward but what it is that we cannot leave behind. The answer was obvious for all to see as the symbol of water and word, bread and wine, and the cross formed the backdrop of the main stage. It was a reminder to all that our identity did not depend on buildings but on relationships. It demonstrated to all that we were a pilgrim people with 'no abiding city'. It was a massive statement to all concerned that we lived in a world without walls and that the tents would be used to help house some of the poorest citizens of the world. For us this was a symbol of the reality that Church without Walls must understand itself as part of a world community.

The following week all 500 tents were sent to China under the auspices of the Scottish International Trust and the Blythswood Trust. We are indebted to both these organisations for working together to bring this about.

The Sending

In our report last year we highlighted the importance of congregations developing closer links with overseas projects and creating partnerships. We are delighted to hear that the research commissioned by the Panel Review and Reform relating the effects of such partnerships on the life and witness of congregations is under way. We look forward to the results of this research and continue to commend congregations to make arrangements to send representatives of their congregations in 2010 abroad to cement their current overseas partnerships. This was one of the inspirational ideas that caught the imagination of many of the delegates at the last Re-energise Conference in January 2009. We hope that this work will be further facilitated within the proposed new structure of CWW.

Keeping Reform to the Forefront of the Church's Agenda

It is important to understand that Church without Walls's original remit was one of initiating a process of continuing reform. It is rooted within a ten year vision to ensure that the current Church in an age of transition keeps before it the primary purposes of its calling.

At all the events the four core themes of the report have been held before the Church, reminding us that we are shaped by the gospel, shaped by friendship, shaped by the gifts of God's people and shaped by locality. It is from these themes that the whole notion of reform and renewal has been understood.

Nearly eight years after the first report, the challenge of reform and change continues to exercise the Church. The great danger is that we become distracted by reforming structures rather than reforming mindsets and relationships. Structures will only work when we have the right relationships and we have developed an element of trust that allows us to take risks. As new plans are being developed for the shape of the Church regionally, we too have been developing our strategy for the next four years.

Proposals for Transition

The General Assembly of 2008 instructed our group to network across the Councils and to bring to the Assembly of 2009 proposals that would allow the Church to continue on its journey of transition. We were privileged to meet with representatives of all the Councils over a two-day period.

We found these meetings to be insightful and indeed inspirational. We were encouraged by the level of engagement we entered into with all of the representatives. All understood the significant role CWW was playing in the renewing of the Church and each Council expressed a desire to be included in the planning of all future events.

The following topics will give a flavour of the range of our discussions. It is important to note that these were in the spirit of creative conversations and what is expressed may not always represent the firm position of a Council. The conversations brought out significant themes, which the Church needs to address in coming years.

These conversations will allow CWW to align future events with local themes and also national strategic themes. In doing so, we hope that we can offer a more joined-up way of thinking about conferencing throughout the Church.

Themes Arising from Conversations with the Councils

Regional Church

There was universal concern that Presbyteries are not functioning effectively, and had remained untouched by the core values of CWW. It was suggested by the representative of the Council of Assembly that we need regional church centres as a real presence on the high street.

Ministries Council suggested that, if Presbyteries took the CWW values into their lives as a way of working, that would make a significant difference. The Panel of Review and Reform is exploring new models for Presbytery. The General Trustees see the need for Presbyteries to have the capacity to make decisions with "courage and accountability". The discussion on the Third Article Declaratory might be resolved by affirming that we are called to touch "all areas of Scottish life". (Council of Assembly)

Missional Issues

Ministries Council posed the question: "How do we help the Church to cope with what God is doing?"

Church and Society encouraged CWW to remain a cutting-edge dimension to their work whilst at the same time being an integral part of the whole Church.

They identified their key issues as
- ecology
- the credit crunch
- personal economics
- child-friendly society and church

World Council identified the global issues of
- the environment
- human trafficking
- minority Christians under persecution
- 2010 World Conference
- highlighting our place in world Christianity

Ministries Council identified
- new forms of ministries and the review of ministry formation
- emerging church and emerging ministries
- focus on workplace ministries

Mission and Discipleship are focusing on
- children and young people
- emerging church
- "Future Focus" resources for forward planning
- interfaith issues
- rural church
- "why believe?" apologetics being reinstated
- sexuality and singleness
- Holy Communion
- integrating sex offenders

General Trustees spoke of
- options' studies on buildings
- need for creative options without buildings
- need for radical reassessment of buildings usage and location

Ecumenical Relations spoke of
- financial challenges
- OSCR restrictions on ecumenical groupings
- challenges of developing a cohesive response to the 1910 anniversary celebrations
- encouraging an ecumenical matrix in our planning

The Guild spoke of the effectiveness of
- staying with core themes for three years
- women's spirituality

Conversations with the Mission and Discipleship Council about the Future of the CWW Group

When it came to discuss the work of CWW, the general tone of the conversations was one of appreciation for the

11

positive influence of CWW, recognising that there was a section of the Church still untouched – or disinterested. The following bullet points summarise the thoughts of the various Councils regarding Church without Walls:

- CWW has helped congregations see themselves differently.
- The Guild spoke of "investment balance" – where do we invest our energy as a key to how we might work – rather than "power balance" since we represent a "way of doing" rather than a new structure?
- Embody the values and embed them in the Church at all levels.
- Continue to inspire and motivate.
- Take place in the institution and reshape the corporate culture from within.
- Stay close to the edge but be accountable.
- Be a critical friend and a "stone in the shoe".
- Engage with the conversations about a Scottish Greenbelt.
- Become normal – so that CWW has merged naturally into the whole Church life in the next five years.
- Operate ecumenically – encourage people to "talk to your neighbours", and use Ecumenical Relations as contact for networks.
- Social Care highlighted a range of ways of engaging with their issues: ambassadors, supporters, practitioners, lobbyists, resources, rooms for counselling, fundraising, marketing and partnerships.
- CWW is a safety net for people who may go independent, so if CWW is institutionalised, where do they go?

In the future, Church without Walls was encouraged to move in two directions: to maintain that place on the edge where we listen to the creative voices and continue to embody and embed these fresh ways of working; to engage with the institution in such a way that some of the ethos of CWW begins to inform and reshape the Councils. The challenge is to maintain the role of being like a "stone in the shoe" and not be muffled or muzzled by the dominant culture.

The suggestion of regional events was affirmed in which we would make more intentional connections with national strategic themes and changes, and so form strategic partnerships with the Councils on the journey of transition.

Issues Arising from Conversations with Congregations

As we continue our conversations with a wide number of congregations there is a continued need to consolidate and support the work of reform. We are aware that our present strategy within the CWW Planning Group has had its limitations. At present discussions are taking place which will allow us to have a greater input into congregational resourcing and the renewal strategy of the Mission and Discipleship Council.

We are looking forward to taking part in the overall review of the Mission and Discipleship Council's work and hope that our Plan of Action can find a secure and integrated place within the priorities of the Council.

The three key aspects of our work identified above (resourcing, relationships and relevance) find strong resonances within the original report and it is our sense that the Church still has some way to go to seeing this become part of the DNA of the whole Church.

Developing Resources

Essential to developing resources for the Church is a role that the Parish Development Fund can continue to play in strengthening the creative innovators within congregations.

There is little doubt that the work of the Parish Development Fund has been the source of resourcing many innovative projects that would never have got off the ground. The CWW Report enabled such creativity by establishing this Fund and releasing hundreds of thousands of pounds into local congregations, who in turn discovered matched funders from many different sources. This one Fund alone may have generated well over ten times its initial investment.

In the Joint Report of the Ministries and Mission and Discipleship Councils to the 2009 General Assembly, it is suggested that some of these early projects, some seven years later, may well be considering themselves as new expressions of what it means to be church. To read such words when the Church in so many areas is in the mindset of managing decline, is truly remarkable and uplifting and must surely be described as "gospel shaped". However there are many churches who found themselves disappointed because the Fund was unable to support their work.

There is little doubt that the distribution of resources is still a major challenge to the Church of Scotland. Resources continue to be one of the major topics that are discussed during our networking opportunities in our conferences.

Creating a Relational Ethos

A "Relational Church" struck many chords as people began to unpack the idea of a church without walls in a more profound way. The sheer simplicity of the words of Jesus, "Follow Me" which were in the report, encouraged many to see that church is not about stone buildings but rather about building upon each other as "living stones" with Christ as the cornerstone holding our "relational" building together.

The phrase "journeying with Jesus at the centre" encouraged many to understand Christian growth and discipleship as a conversation with Jesus on the move, rather than faith as a piece of second-hand dogma encountered in an immovable space. From these ideas and many more, the Church without Walls Report was simply seeking to reiterate what the primary purposes of the Church has been all along, the relational model inspired by "Following Jesus".

For many, this relational model has been refreshing, as they have encountered it within the structures of our CWW Planning Group. The fact that we take time to invite each other to share from our personal lives and pray for each on a regular basis has allowed us to build strong bonds of friendship within the many groups that operate and report to the CWW Planning Group.

Renewal Calls for Relevance

If the church of the twenty-first century is to engage with the post-modern culture and be resourced and relational, it surely has to have a passion to engage with the significance of "locality"? The 2001 report still holds up in today's climate challenging the slow pace of reform which is taking place within our Kirk Sessions and Presbyteries while we are failing to connect with a rapidly growing unchurched generation.

The CWW Planning Group encourages all Church leaders to seek to engage with the work that the Ministries and Mission and Discipleship Councils are exploring in the area of Emerging Church. We see one of our roles in this area to be that of a bridge working within the traditional Church structures enabling Church leaders to be permission-givers acting as supportive guardians to those who wish to explore a new way to be church. We believe this to be important pioneering work helping the Church to establish links with those who are creating patterns of church beyond the walls. Church without Walls does not see itself as Emerging Church but as one of the many roots through which Church leaders can begin to engage with creative church patterns helping the whole church to understand the changes that might mark the future church.

Core Vision for Renewal – the Regional Dimension

Many congregations have begun to recognise the road to renewal but many more need to start out on the journey. During the past two years we have engaged with over 600 congregations who have sent representatives to our events.

It is out of this experience and also listening to the wider church that we now intend to develop a regional programme of national events that will attract more congregations within regions to participate in these gatherings and conferences and through these experiences become convinced that they can become the agents of change in their churches and communities.

Continuing on the themes affirmed by the General Assembly of 2001, we have a vision that, by 2015, we would like to see the Church of Scotland

- connecting with the missing generations of all ages where they are
- engaging and equipping more "Jesus-followers" for the twenty-first century
- nurturing children and young people in a 10-20 year partnership strategy
- encouraging people to listen to Scripture and explore how to pray
- expressing a spirit of hospitality to the stranger in our community
- promoting parallel Christian presences as "new alongside the old"
- working with other partners for the evangelisation of the nation
- offering models of reconciliation and mediation in a fractured world
- leading the way in environmental responsibility and global justice
- reshaping and relocating our buildings for the needs of this century
- reshaping and retraining our leadership (in all roles) for these tasks

Towards the Vision

A process that would achieve this vision would include the need to:

- raise awareness of the social changes and spiritual roots of our current condition
- come to an agreed understanding that our Christendom assumptions of church and ministry are no longer appropriate for a society after Christendom

- trust that the Spirit of God is at work among the people of God
- stimulate the imagination with Scriptural and contemporary stories of hope and transformation
- provide regional support systems for innovation and transition
- encourage multiple experiments on the edges which may in time facilitate a change in the culture of the Church
- explore the shift from the legal structures of institutionalism to the relational networks of a missional movement
- align systems and legal procedures to the new reality.

Church Without Walls – Plan of Action

The contribution of CWW to such a process would be to continue to develop such a vision with those congregations ready to face the challenges of being a relevant, relational and resourced church. This would involve us:

- Returning to the grass-roots as we continue to embed the core themes of CWW across the Church.
- Creating motivational gatherings that are regionally located but nationally accessible in areas such as Borders, Clyde, North East, South West, Forth and Tay, Highlands and Islands.
- Organising these inspirational regional events to highlight key themes and key resource people. This will have a regional locus, but national catchment. [Note: The Glasgow East by-election was won because 500 SNP supporters gathered to help seeing it as a "national" event. Can we foster that sense of a national movement of mutual encouragement?]
- Establishing a National Planning Group to oversee the strategy and development of Church without Walls, as well as a Regional Planning Group with responsibility to develop the regional events.
- Working with Church Councils in the development of the events and to support their work, listening to the outcomes of the gatherings and shaping policy according to emerging opportunities and challenges.

- Beginning to engage with Presbyteries in the development of the unfolding vision of a more regional church and supporting them towards such an expression of their life together through the regional events.
- Identifying key people throughout the regions who could be seconded from their congregations in order to build around them a team of people who will work over a 12-18 month period around the regional events in order to facilitate the transitions necessary in their regions.

Summary of Discussions with the Mission and Discipleship Council

Keeping all this in mind, we engaged in conversations with the Mission and Discipleship Council outlining our proposals to continue our work for the next four-year period. While we recognised areas of commonality, it became clear to us that the role CWW has within the Church of Scotland and across Scotland is quite unique.

The 2001 report of the Special Commission anent Review and Reform continues to be the most quoted of the General Assembly reports and continues to engage with large numbers of congregations. We have come to the conclusion that there is a creative opportunity to allow our work to be involved in the review of the work of the Mission and Discipleship Council.

Under the direction of the Council of Assembly we have come to see that, for instance, having a vice-convenership within the Mission and Discipleship Council may well give us a greater ability to influence the equipping of congregations, presbyteries and councils. We believe there are enough areas of synergy to allow us to create with the Mission and Discipleship Council a department that will promote and engage with the ongoing vision of the CWW National Planning Group while allowing us to continue to report to the General Assembly.

The CWW Planning Group has always recognised that review is an essential part of achieving goals and aspirations. In our discussions with the Council of Assembly regarding the continuation of our work, we have come to an agreed position that we can operate our present remit and perhaps develop it by becoming an integrated part of the Mission and Discipleship Council.

While we believe that the present accommodation for CWW has worked and delivered some of the most successful events that the Church has organised in recent years, there are always new and alternative ways to deliver ideas and programmes. We are now willing to take this additional step and move into a much more integrated structure. In doing so we pray that our views on the importance of resourcing, relationships and relevance will continue to impact upon the life and structures of the Church.

We propose that we take forward into the review process within the Mission and Discipleship Council our work as laid out in our Plan of Action. We are encouraged that the funding for the first two years of our plan has been ring-fenced by the Central Budget Group and we look forward to seeing how, during such a period of review, the remaining work may be resourced.

Looking to the Future

The Church of Jesus Christ in the Western world is being reconfigured by the Spirit of God for the purposes of God in our time. We are learning to be attentive to what the Spirit is saying to the churches, and responsive to the Spirit's call. As the Gospel has been translated and incarnated into many cultures across the centuries and across the world, so we are learning to flesh out the Gospel for our times in our nation.

Amidst the wider discussions about post-modern living and the post-Christendom context for the Church, Church without Walls envisages a church that touches the Scottish psyche with the Gospel of Christ offering deep healing for our nation:

- the grace that invites us to dare to believe we are special in God's eyes

11

- the call to "follow Christ" which challenges the pressures to conform
- the focus on local community that affirms our Scottish love for "the land"
- the invitation to Christ-like friendship which speaks to our communitarian spirit while challenging our tendency to sectarianism
- and the celebration of God's gifts among us that stimulates our proven capacity for inventiveness and entrepreneurial adventure.

Across the Church in Scotland there are congregations and other Christian communities who are working to be faithful followers of Jesus who will make a difference in their communities and across the world. These pioneer disciples require the support of a wider network of fellow-travellers, for the receiving and giving of mutual support and stimulus.

As Church without Walls has evolved in the past eight years, it has provided one such network for many thousands of people through the gatherings to celebrate and to be "re-energised". We believe it is essential that such networks of support continue to be developed in the coming years in parallel with the other institutional supports offered by our Church. We are confident that as we move forward into a new operating pattern that we will be able to bring the best of the past in order to create with others an enduring transformation that is always continuing, a transformation in the way we distribute our resources, engage in our relationships and consequently discover the relevance of the good news for the twenty-first century.

The Group would like to thank all who over the years have given outstanding service and commitment to the process that has allowed the work to develop to its present place, and record their appreciation to Guy Douglas, Neil MacLennan and Valerie Cox for their outstanding administrating gifts which have helped to make our role as a Planning Group enjoyable and our work successful.

In the name of the Planning Group

ALBERT BOGLE, *Convener*
SUSAN BROWN
PETER NEILSON
DAVID C CAMERON

PROPOSED DELIVERANCE

The General Assembly
1. Receive the Report of the Delegation of the General Assembly and thank it for its work.
2. Continue the appointment of the Delegation with the same powers as hitherto – the Principal Clerk of the General Assembly to be Chairman and the Depute Clerk of the General Assembly to be Vice-Chairman.
3. Remind congregations of the need for them to take immediate steps to ensure that their constitutions comply with civil law and, if they do not, again urge them to adopt either the Model Deed or Unitary Form in terms of Act XIX 1964 (as amended).

REPORT

The Delegation has to report that during 2008 it granted, in virtue of the powers conferred upon it by the General Assembly, seven additional Model Deeds of Constitution.

The present amended Model Deed of Constitution was approved and adopted by the General Assembly on 21 May 1994 for issue to each congregation whose temporal affairs were then administered by a Congregational Board under the Model Deed and for granting to each congregation thereafter adopting it. Some amendments to it were approved by last year's Assembly to take account of changes required by charity legislation.

The General Assembly of 2003 also permitted congregations to adopt, as an alternative to the Model Deed of Constitution, the Unitary Constitution either by Resolution of the congregation or by Basis of Adjustment. 50 congregations adopted the Unitary Constitution during 2008, compared to 31 in 2007 and being a substantially larger number than in preceding years.

A number of the congregations adopting a new form of constitution have done so prompted by the Deliverance of the General Assembly of 2008 instructing congregations to review their constitutions. The Secretary is currently corresponding with a number of congregations who are contemplating moving from their current constitution. However, it is apparent that some congregations, mainly those originating in the former United Presbyterian Church and the pre 1900 Free Church, are still operating under constitutions which are either unwritten and/or which contain outmoded provisions and have yet to take appropriate action.

In the name and on behalf of the Delegation

FINLAY A J MACDONALD, *Chairman*
JANETTE S WILSON, *Secretary*

PROPOSED DELIVERANCE

The General Assembly:-

1. Receive the Report and Accounts of the General Trustees.
2. (a) Appoint Rev David W Clark, Mr William A Hall and Mr Alan F Nisbet as General Trustees (1.3).
   (b) Re-appoint Mr W Findlay Turner as Chairman and Rev Dr James A P Jack as Vice-Chairman for the ensuing year and authorise the making of a payment of £1,420 to each of Mr Turner and Dr Jack as Chairman and Vice-Chairman for the past year (1.4).
3. Remind congregations to seek the appropriate approvals under the Work At Buildings Regulations prior to undertaking work at their buildings (3.2).
4. Remind those congregations and Presbyteries which have not yet done so to instruct insurance revaluations with a view to completing matters by the deadline of 30 June 2010 (4.1).
5. Urge those congregations which have only the basic "fire" cover to consider extending cover to include damage caused by "special perils" (4.2).

REPORT

1. Introduction and Composition of Trust

1.1 The Church of Scotland General Trustees submit to the Assembly their eighty-second Report since the passing of the Church of Scotland (Property and Endowments) Act 1925.

1.2 The Trustees report the retirement at this Assembly of four of their number. Mr A Stewart Chalmers FRICS was one of their longest-serving members having been appointed to the Board in 1970. His professional expertise in land and estate management contributed hugely to the work of the Glebes Committee of which he served as Convener from 1989 to 2002. The Church as a whole owes a great deal to his unstinting time and effort in ensuring that it received maximum benefit from its glebe land. Joining the Board in 1998, Miss Elizabeth A Bayne-Jardine brought to the work of the Glebes Committee her extensive farming experience. Mr John V M Jameson OBE DL BSc FRICS was appointed a Trustee in 2003.

His longstanding connections with the south-west of Scotland in particular and his professional expertise made him an invaluable member of the Glebes Committee. Rev Martyn R H Thomas CEng MIStructE was appointed to the Board in 1993 serving as a member of the Fabric Committee. Mr Thomas undertook much deputation work and many congregations benefited not only from his expertise as an engineer but also from his pastoral encouragement.

1.3 Aware of the impending retirals from the Glebes Committee, the Trustees sought new members and, after due process of induction, Mr William A Hall of New Blainslie, Galashiels and Mr Alan F Nisbet FRICS ACIA were co-opted as Advisory Members to the Glebes Committee with effect from December 2008. Mr Hall has run his own farm for 37 years and also has practical experience of ensuring efficient and effective use of property in a wider community context. Mr Nisbet is a well-respected

Chartered Surveyor who brings with him special expertise in the rural sector. For a number of years, the Trustees have benefited from Rev David W Clark MA BD serving as a Corresponding Member representing the interests of Parish Appraisal, latterly as Convener of the Presbytery Planning Task Group. Following his retiral from that role he was co-opted as an Advisory Member. The Trustees respectfully recommend that these three persons should be appointed as full members of the Board.

1.4 The Trustees further recommend that Mr W Findlay Turner CA and Rev James A P Jack BSc BArch BD DMin RIBA RIAS be appointed Chairman and Vice-Chairman respectively for the ensuing year and that for their services as Chairman and Vice-Chairman for the past year they should each receive remuneration of £1,420 as authorised by Section 38 (1) of the 1925 Act.

1.5 Full details about the Trustees' structure, governance and management, their objectives and activities, the Funds under their administration and their achievements and performance can be found in their Annual Report and Financial Statements for the year ended 31 December 2008, copies of which are available from the Secretary's Department. The following are the particular matters which the Trustees wish to bring to the attention of the Assembly.

2.   Fabric Funds
"… grants totalling £1,647,000…"

2.1   Central Fabric Fund
2.1.1 The Fund, the capital of which stood at £12,656,000 on 31 December 2008, provides financial assistance to congregations towards the cost of repairing and improving the buildings for which they are responsible. During 2008, the Trustees agreed to make available new standard loans totalling £4,542,500. The standard rate of interest on loans is 5% per annum but a number of loans were made available at 3% per annum or on an interest-free basis where the Trustees

were satisfied that this was justified by the circumstances. For many years, the Trustees have been able to make bridging finance available to congregations based on experience that manses are generally sold without much difficulty. With the downturn in the property market, an increasing number of manses have remained unsold with the result that the Trustees are no longer in a position to make available open-ended bridging finance but only where missives have been concluded for the sale of the property. The total amount of bridging loan facilities made available during 2008 was £4,573,082. From January 2009, the rate of interest charged on new bridging loans is 0.5% above the standard rate.

2.1.2 By the end of 2008, grants totalling £1,647,000 were made available from the Fund. The amount available for giving grants is financed from a combination of periodic transfers of surpluses on the Trustees' General Fund, interest charged on loans, investment income, an annual allocation from the Mission & Renewal Fund and the half share which the Trustees receive from the operation of the 10% levy on property sale proceeds.

2.1.3 Of the total, £105,071 comprised priority grants to congregations working in areas of deprivation.

2.1.4 In 2008, the Trustees' share of the 10% levy amounted to £139,000. Under the 2008 Regulations, this amount is ring-fenced to help provide the priority grants referred to.

2.1.5 Mission & Discipleship Council's Rural Strategy Team representatives have met with the Trustees in light of the two deliverances on the Council's Report to last year's Assembly regarding the best use of glebe land and the provision of Central Fabric Fund assistance to areas of rural need. Reference is made to the details contained in the Council's Assembly Report. The Trustees are happy to continue close liaison with the Team on these issues.

2.1.6 A synopsis of loans and grants made from the Central Fabric Fund during 2008 is shown in Appendix 1.

2.2 Consolidated Fabric Fund

2.2.1 The Fund had an approximate value of £61,153,000 as at 31 December 2008 making it the largest Fund under the Trustees' administration. It now comprises two distinct elements, one amounting to £41,003,000 being capital (and accrued revenue) derived principally from the sale of redundant properties and from time to time by the transfer of monies from congregations' holdings in the Consolidated Stipend Fund. Congregations can apply their holdings of capital and revenue towards a wide range of fabric-related expenditure on the buildings for which they are responsible. The second element is a new feature represented by the capitalised value of certain heritable assets as now required by accounting regulations. The value of these assets, based on historical cost, as at the end of 2008 was £20,150,000.

2.2.2 The investment needs of congregations with holdings in the Fund will differ, some being in a position to invest for the long-term while others may require access to their funds more immediately. Through their congregational treasurers, Financial Boards are regularly reminded that they have the authority to advise the General Trustees if they wish to make changes to the investment mix of their capital holdings in light of their Boards' specific needs. Such requests should be given in writing to the Secretary's Department.

3. Fabric Matters

> "… significant transformation
> …in Scotland's poorest areas."

3.1 Good

As indicated earlier, the Trustees have given substantial grant assistance to congregations operating in deprived areas as a practical outworking of the Gospel imperative that the Church's resources should be directed towards the disadvantaged. Working in tandem with the Priority Areas Committee to ensure that these resources are used to best effect, the Trustees are confident that priority grants to congregations such as St Paul's, Cranhill and Pollokshaws in Glasgow have assisted in the significant transformation of buildings for the mission of the Church in Scotland's poorest areas.

3.2 Bad

For many years, the Church of Scotland has operated a comprehensive system of approval for work at churches, halls and manses. The Trustees are concerned that there are a significant number of cases where various projects have proceeded without approval having been given by Presbyteries and/or the Trustees under the Work At Buildings Regulations 1998. While few would challenge the good intentions behind such work, it is important that proper scrutiny is given to fabric projects and congregations are therefore reminded that they should seek the appropriate consents before the start of work. This ensures good stewardship of resources and also seeks to avoid members of Boards and Sessions having to face claims for breach of trusteeship obligations.

3.3 Ugly

Many congregations have undertaken major repair and improvement projects but in some cases the completion of these has often come at a price: ministers and officebearers have faced opposition and have come under great stress as they have sought to develop projects and to lead congregations through major change while in other cases congregations have struggled to assess the future for their buildings and have ultimately been unable to convert their hopes into reality. Concern over this situation has prompted the Trustees to begin a process of investigating what sort of help and guidance might be available to congregations at an early stage of project development and how this might best be delivered. They hope to report in more detail to next year's General Assembly.

3.4 Care of Ecclesiastical Properties

In terms of the relevant legislation, Presbyteries are required to report diligence with regard to the care of ecclesiastical properties within their bounds. The returns from 35 Presbyteries (out of 44) to hand at the time of the preparation of this report revealed that in the year to 30 June 2008, 1,018 Property Registers out of 1,067 had been examined and that all had been found satisfactory. In the same period, the properties of 148 congregations had been inspected.

3.5 Energy
3.5.1 Procurement
The Trustees' Energy Consultants, Argyle Energy, recently re-negotiated the arrangements for the supply of electricity and gas to congregations at preferential prices which should result in substantial savings for those congregations which elect to be involved. For a variety of reasons including the uncertainty of the market, the new arrangement under which British Gas will supply both gas and electricity will last for an initial period of one year from 1 April 2009. The operation of the arrangement will be monitored and a decision taken in due course as to whether it should be extended for a further period or re-negotiated.

3.5.2 Conservation
A whole industry has grown on the back of the rising awareness of environmental issues offering advice and guidance on energy conservation much of it confusing. Discussions have continued between the Trustees and Church & Society Council on how best to ensure that all congregations and not just those in the Eco-Congregation Scheme have access to practical, easy-to-understand and effective tools to measure and reduce their carbon footprint, this being recognised as a useful yardstick to judge efficient energy use. The Trustees and the Council aim to report in more detail to next year's Assembly on progress. In the meantime, Mr Andrew MacOwan, the Trustees' Heating Consultant continues to carry out surveys of ecclesiastical buildings incorporating advice on how to save energy costs and to improve the standard of comfort. The Trustees provide grants to meet around one-third of the cost of such surveys. By the end of 2008,

Mr MacOwan had carried out 33 surveys including repeat surveys of churches and halls as well as 7 surveys of manses. Since the inception of the scheme, a total of 1924 initial and repeat surveys of churches and halls and 192 manse surveys have been undertaken.

3.5.3 Renewable Energy Projects
At last year's Assembly, the Trustees reported on the outcome of their investigations into the provision of financial assistance for renewable energy projects. Following the outcome of an Options Study funded by them in respect of the existing buildings, the Trustees were closely involved in discussions with the Colston Milton Congregation in Glasgow on the type of replacement building and the materials to be used in its construction. They were encouraged by the considerable positive publicity in the national press which was given to the prospect of a community church building made from old beer cans as much as by the substantial funding made available from the Scottish Climate Challenge Fund to cover the cost of employing a firm of architects to undertake further research and design work.

3.6 Lighting and Sound Consultants
During the course of 2008, the Trustees in liaison with the Committee on Church Art and Architecture, began the process of considering the appointment of a number of lighting-design consultants who would be available to assist congregations in working up re-lighting schemes especially of sanctuary areas. A Sound Systems Consultant, Mr John McDonald, is able to provide advice to congregations for a reasonable fee. Details are available from the Secretary's Department.

3.7 Lottery Funding
Representatives of the Trustees and the Priority Areas Committee have met with senior representatives of the Big Lottery Fund and have given a presentation of the vital work being undertaken by many congregations especially in areas of deprivation. In these cases, congregations often represent the only stable institution in situations

where many in the community lead chaotic lives. It is hoped to persuade the Fund to allow congregations to have access to lottery funding for building projects where the re-ordering of premises will provide the appropriate facilities for both congregational and community involvement.

3.8 The Trustees continue to have concerns about not only the level of funding available from Historic Scotland and the Heritage Lottery Fund to congregations seeking to undertake repairs to listed church buildings but also the arbitrary nature of the twice-yearly batching process whereby the success of grant applications (on which significant professional costs will have been incurred in their preparation) seems to be dependant on how many cases are presented from congregations of all denominations in Scotland. Contrary to conservation interests which tend to regard buildings as an end in themselves, the Trustees' view is that churches and halls should be a resource for mission at a local level. To achieve this, there is a need for greater flexibility in the planning process to allow alteration to and even demolition of listed buildings. This is especially so when the total proportion of external funding available for repair schemes is now usually less than 40% of the cost. Equally, Presbyteries and congregations need to take seriously the selection of redundant buildings as part of the Presbytery Planning process. The Church is in a weak position to argue for greater flexibility when it cannot always identify which of its buildings it wants to dispose of or retain.

4. Insurance Matters

4.1 Insurance Revaluation Programme
The Trustees are pleased to note that at the time of preparation of this report, 13 Presbyteries have completed or have instructed the carrying out of revaluations for insurance purposes of congregational buildings within their bounds following the instruction from last year's General Assembly. Five Presbyteries on their own initiative had already carried out such revaluations within the previous five years. A further ten Presbyteries have contacted the valuers seeking quotations for the cost of undertaking revaluations. All revaluations must be completed and the recommendations as to the level of cover implemented by 30 June 2010. In order to achieve this, it will be essential for those Presbyteries which have not already done so to instruct revaluations by the end of November this year. Those congregations which have still to implement revised levels of cover must take steps to do so without further delay.

4.2 Scope of Insurance Cover
The standard policy from the Church of Scotland Insurance Company Limited offers cover against damage caused by fire, lightning and explosion but over three-quarters of congregations opt to take out cover against damage caused by other perils such as storm, flood, burst pipes and malicious activity. The Trustees would encourage Financial Boards who carry only the basic 'fire cover' to consider extending their policies to include other perils. Further information and guidance can be sought from the staff of the Insurance Company.

4.3 The Church of Scotland Insurance Company Limited
4.3.1 The Company is owned by the General Trustees and is authorised and regulated by the Financial Services Authority. The Company either by itself or as an intermediary provides cover for all classes of insurance and continues to insure the majority of Church of Scotland congregations as well as the congregations of other denominations.

4.3.2 During 2008, 8 new fire claims were submitted in addition to 11 fire claims which had been brought forward from previous years. The overall cost to the Company was £29,834. The Directors propose to distribute a total of £1,521,385 under Gift Aid to the General Trustees representing the Company's net profit in the year to 31 December 2008. Of this total, £375,000 had been paid over by the end of 2008. The Trustees have agreed that the sums received from the Company in respect of 2008 and credited to their General Fund should be allocated to the Central Fabric Fund to assist them in giving grants to congregations.

4.3.3 In accordance with current accounting requirements, the 2008 Annual Accounts of the Company have been consolidated with those of the Trustees.

4.3.4 The Trustees wish to record their appreciation of the very significant financial contribution made by the Company towards the Trustees' work. The profits generated by the Company are credited to the Trustees' General Fund. The Trustees also wish to acknowledge the work done by the Directors of the Company. None of the General Trustees who are Directors receive any remuneration for their services.

5. Stipend Matters
5.1 Consolidated Stipend Fund
5.1.1 This Fund is administered for the benefit of the 1,400 or so congregations with holdings in it and is the second-largest Fund under the Trustees' administration. The capital of the Fund is derived principally from the sale of glebeland but also by transfers from the Consolidated Fabric Fund and from the investment of new monies by individual congregations. With the backing of the Assembly and the Ministries Council, the Trustees operate the Fund as a permanent endowment and are thus able to set their investment strategy as being for the long term. Professional advice has confirmed that the Fund should be invested primarily in equities which, over the long term, have consistently provided capital growth with income yield. The Fund had a capital value of £53,366,000 at the end of 2008.

5.1.2 In last year's Report, the Trustees indicated that the rate of dividend of £0.2095 for 2008 was possible as a result of the receipt of special dividend income in 2007. The Trustees are pleased to report that following receipt

of special dividend income in 2008 they propose, with the concurrence of the Ministries Council, a dividend rate of £0.2173 for 2009. It should be noted that there is unlikely to be any special dividend income received during 2009. In light of this and the economic climate, it is certain that the dividend to be declared for 2010 will be at a reduced level.

Statistics reflecting the income and dividend position are as set out in Appendix 2.

6. Glebes
The vast majority of glebeland is leased for agricultural or amenity purposes. The Trustees endeavour to increase rents where appropriate while at the same time being mindful of the prevailing economic climate. Net rental income in 2008 was £327,000 compared with £329,512 in 2007. The collapse of the market for housing development saw a number of potential glebe developments being deferred or cancelled. By the end of 2008, glebe sale proceeds totalled £225,300 compared with £3,085,405 in 2007. Income from glebe rents and glebe sale proceeds are credited to stipend. In certain circumstances upon the recommendation of Presbyteries and with the concurrence of the Ministries Council, it is possible to reallocate surplus stipend capital for fabric purposes and a number of such reallocations can be seen in Appendix 4.

7. Determinations Under Act VII 1995
The Trustees report that under Act VII 1995 (anent powers delegated to The Church of Scotland General Trustees) as amended by Acts XIII 1996 and IV 1998, they have made 69 determinations as set out in Appendix 3.

8. Reallocation of Endowments
The Regulations anent the application of stipend and fabric endowments (Regulations V 1995) provide a mechanism to reallocate the capital held by the General Trustees for the benefit of congregations in the Consolidated Fabric and Stipend Funds. Details of the reallocations made during 2008 are contained in Appendix 4.

9. Finance

9.1 Accounts

The General Trustees' Accounts for the year 2008 as audited by the Auditor of the Church will be laid on the table at the Assembly. Copies of the Annual Report and Financial Statements are available from the Secretary. The Trustees intend that the firm of registered auditors appointed to audit the accounts of the Assembly Councils and Committees for 2009 should also be appointed to audit their accounts for that year.

9.2 Investment performance

The bulk of the Trustees' non-property assets have been invested through the three investment funds offered by the Church of Scotland Investors Trust – the Growth, Income and Deposit Funds. At the start of 2008, the market values of these investments were:

Growth Fund	£85,551,000
Income Fund	£ 7,722,000
Deposit Fund	£38,317,000

During the year the value of the shares in the Growth Fund fell by 27.1% and in the Income Fund by 23.8%. By way of comparison, the FTSE All-Share Index fell by 32.8% over the same period. In each case the single biggest fall occurred in September. More detailed information on investment performance is contained in the Annual Report and Accounts.

9.3 The Annual Accounts for the first time contain a valuation of the glebeland currently in the Trustees' ownership as a major step in complying with new accounting requirements. Following consultation with OSCR and with the Auditors, the Trustees have adopted an historical cost basis of valuation. The Trustees will continue with the process of capitalising heritable assets in their Accounts in respect of churches, halls and manses again on an historical cost basis.

On behalf of the General Trustees

W FINDLAY TURNER, *Chairman*
JAMES A P JACK, *Vice-Chairman*
DAVID D ROBERTSON, *Secretary and Clerk*

APPENDIX 1
SYNOPSIS OF CENTRAL FABRIC FUND GRANTS AND LOANS VOTED IN 2008

		Churches/Halls		Manses		Total	
		no	*amount*	*no*	*amount*	*no*	*amount*
Grants	Priority	12	£105,000	0	nil	12	£105,000
	Standard	136	£949,000	43	£593,000	179	£1,542,000
							£1,647,000
Loans	5%	40	£3,290,500	10	£765,000	50	£4,055,500
	3%	4	£235,000	3	£75,000	7	£310,000
	Interest free	4	£171,000	1	£6,000	5	£177,000
							£4,542,500
Bridging Loans				15	£4,573,082		£4,573,082

APPENDIX 2
CONSOLIDATED STIPEND FUND

Capital	Total Value	Value of Share
31 December 2004	£54,422,320	£3.9254
31 December 2005	£61,204,475	£4.3384
31 December 2006	£67,189,816	£4.7009
31 December 2007	£69,607,174	£4.7722
31 December 2008	£53,365,154	£3.5154

Revenue	Income	Shares Issued at 31 December	Rate of Dividend
2004	£2,340,577	13,864,038	£0.1694
2005	£2,367,778	14,107,493	£0.1646
2006	£2,436,204	14,292,869	£0.1657
2007	£2,962,031	14,586,116	£0.1773
2008	£3,306,958	15,180,264	£0.2095

During 2008 the sum of £2,696,408 was admitted to the Fund in exchange for 594,148 shares.

APPENDIX 3
DETERMINATIONS MADE UNDER ACT VII 1995

1. General Sales: In the following cases, the General Trustees made determinations authorising the sale or let of the property concerned and directed that the proceeds should be credited to the benefit of the congregation in the Consolidated Fabric Fund:- Aberdeen: Garthdee – manse; Aberdeen: Kirk of St Nicholas Uniting – East Kirk; Aberlour – part of manse garden; Auchaber United – Inverkeithny church; Ayr: St Columba – manse; Ayr: St Columba – retirement house; Birsay Harray and Sandwick – Twatt church; Bonnybridge: St Helen's – manse; Buckie: South and West – manse; Cadder – manse; Carstairs and Carstairs Junction – manse; Cellardyke – manse; Coalburn – ground at church; Craigrownie – hall; Dalkeith: St Nicholas Buccleuch – Alms Collection House; Dalmellington – ground at manse; Dornock – manse; Douglas Valley – ground at hall; Dumfries: Northwest – Lincluden church; Dumfries: Northwest – Holywood church; Dundee: Barnhill St Margaret's – manse; Dundee: Craigiebank – manse; Dunfermline: Townhill and Kingseat – manse; Dunnichen Letham and Kirkden – ground at manse; Dunoon: High Kirk – former manse; East Mainland – St Nicholas' church; Edzell Lethnot Glenesk – manse; Foveran – church; Glasgow: South Carntyne – manse; Hoy and Walls – manse; Huntly: Cairnie Glass – St Andrew's church, Glass; Innerleithen Traquair and Walkerburn – Walkerburn church; Inverkip – manse; Inverness: East – manse; Kilwinning: Mansefield Trinity – manse; Kinross – manse; Kyles – Kilbride church; Lochgoilhead and Kilmorich – Carrick Castle church; Marnoch – outbuilding at church; Maybole – manse; Methil – manse; Methilhill and Denbeath – ground at manse; Methven and Logie Almond – manse; Mochrum – manse; Motherwell: South – former South Dalziel church and hall; North West Lochaber – manse; Old Kilpatrick: Bowling – former Bowling church and hall; Orwell and Portmoak – manse; Paisley: Martyrs' – manse; Penicuik: St Mungo's – manse; St Colmon – manse; Stirling: St Mark's – ground at church; Stranraer: High Kirk – manse; Torrance – manse; Tranent – manse; United Church of Bute – former St Brendan's church; Wishaw: South Wishaw – manse.

2. Glebe Sales: In the following parishes, the General Trustees made determinations authorising the sale of Glebe subjects and directed that the proceeds should be credited to the benefit of the congregation in the Consolidated Stipend Fund:- Aberfoyle; Applegarth Sibbaldbie and Johnstone; Burntisland; Caputh and Clunie; Drumoak-Durris; Dunbarney and Forgandenny; Gordon; Guthrie and Rescobie; Noth; Walls and Sandness.

3. Miscellaneous The General Trustees made the following miscellaneous determinations:

(a) Banchory-Devenick and Maryculter/Cookney – discharge of trust conditions for Ardoe Hall;

(b) Glasgow: Barony Ramshorn (Dissolved) – sale of retirement house and transmission of proceeds equally among Central Fabric Fund, New Charge Development (Ministries Council) and Housing & Loan Fund;

(c) Glasgow: Wallacewell – sale of manse and transmission of proceeds to Ministries Council.

APPENDIX 4
DETERMINATIONS MADE UNDER REGULATIONS V 1996

The reallocations made as a result of determinations during 2008 were as follows:-

(a) Cromdale and Advie – £100,000 from fabric to stipend;

(b) Dirleton – £275,000 from stipend to fabric;

(c) Edinburgh: Corstorphine Old – £178,436 from stipend to fabric;

(d) Edinkillie – £75,000 from fabric to stipend;

(e) Foulden and Mordington – £34,000 from fabric to stipend;

(f) Glassary Kilmartin and Ford – £10,000 from fabric to stipend;

(g) Kenmore and Lawers – £30,000 from fabric to stipend;

(h) Kilbrandon and Kilchattan – £100,000 from fabric to stipend;

(i) Killearnan – £60,000 from fabric to stipend and £40,000 to the Minimum Stipend Fund;

(j) Kirkmichael Tinwald and Torthorwald – £35,000 from stipend to fabric;

(k) New Machar – £81,000 from stipend to fabric;

(l) St Madoes and Kinfauns – £500,000 from stipend to fabric.

CHURCH OF SCOTLAND GUILD
May 2009

PROPOSED DELIVERANCE

The General Assembly

1. Receive the report.
2. Commend the Guild for highlighting the importance of the spiritual life and encourage the movement, at all levels, to keep this as a priority.
3. Commend the Guild's contribution to the ministry and mission of the Church through its support of projects during the 2006-9 Programme, *Let's live: body, mind and soul*; and encourage the Guild in its new 3 year programme of themes and projects under the title, *What does the Lord require of you?*
4. Recognise the Guild's work in raising awareness of human trafficking and encourage their continuing efforts, while urging Presbyteries and Kirk Sessions to be alert to the possibilities of this abuse occurring in their area.
5. Recognise the value of the Guild's contribution to the ecumenical group on domestic abuse and welcome the extension of the group's membership to include representatives of other faiths.
6. Urge ministers and Kirk Sessions to be supportive of local guilds, particularly with regard to initiatives connected with Guild Week.

REPORT

More things are wrought by prayer than this world dreams on. (Alfred Lord Tennyson, The Idylls of the king.)

1. Introduction

1.1 If you were to ask Guild members what they remembered most from the 2008 Annual Meeting in Dundee, many would choose the Moderator's words about the value of prayer. David Lunan spoke candidly and movingly about his own dependence on the simple discipline of regular prayer. His commendation of the pattern of thanksgiving, petition, confession, and then the importance of listening for God's word to us, will long remain in the consciousness, and the practice, of Guild members. Along with Irene Howat's challenging faith journey through physical pain to unexpected blessings and Fiona Squires' musical stepping stones through life, this provided a richly rewarding launch for the Guild's 2008-9 session, with its affirming theme: *He restores my soul.*

1.2 When preparation days were offered around the country in March 2008 to prepare local leaders for this theme and the associated discussion topic, *The search for spirituality*, some had misgivings. Years 1 and 2 of the *Let's live: body, mind and soul* programme had been safely negotiated and found to be stimulating as the body and then the mind provided the focus, and issues such as the church as the body of Christ, body image, Christian education and lifelong learning were explored. But the soul seemed to present more of a challenge – wasn't this the preserve of the theologically educated? What business had we dipping a toe in the increasingly mentioned, but still mysterious, area of spirituality?

1.3 This hesitance had been apparent in the Programmes and Resources Committee and meetings to prepare the theme material were difficult, as different understandings and experience of church and liturgy were shared. The result was a larger than usual resource pack, which has helped guild groups to explore that part of our humanity that enables us to commune with God at the deepest level. At the time of writing, reports are being received in Guild Office on how the material has been used. While there are references to the initial unease: *our guild feels these things are "better felt than telt"*; *"the thought of discussing spirituality was rather daunting"*, there are reports of real engagement with the significance of spiritual nurture and refreshment. Comments included: *"it was challenging and took us outside our Church of Scotland comfort zone"*. This was probably in response to the encouragement guilds were given to explore the tools used in other Christian traditions : pilgrimage, icons, labyrinths, and to look at what many people find attractive in other faiths and alternative spiritualities.

1.4 Whatever new paths may have been discovered in this year of the soul, the grounding of it all has been in that verse from Psalm 23: *He restores my soul*. The shepherd who feeds, protects and guides his sheep also provides for their needs at the deepest level. This third year of the *Let's live* programme has brought a real sense of that abundant life that Jesus came to bring. Throughout the 2006-9 period it has been a privilege for guild members to play a part, through its projects, in bringing others closer to that fullness of life.

2. Prayer supported projects

2.1 The six current projects in the scheme come to the end of their partnership with the Guild at the 2009 Assembly. Details of the amounts raised in support of these projects is given in Appendix IV, but more highly valued than the money involved are the prayers which have accompanied every fund-raising effort and which will continue to bind us to those we have come to know and care about. A brief account of the work done is all there is space for here, but for countless people it

represents understanding of past trauma and tragedy, support and advocacy in present difficulties, and new opportunities for life in a more hopeful future.

2.1.1 *Borderline, supporting homeless Scots in London*
The Guild's partnership with Borderline ensures they are able to provide support for those who are homeless and require help and advice. The three years of their link with the Guild have given their work a high profile in churches around the country. In a twelvemonth period, they have made over 3,900 contacts with clients and agencies – finding accommodation; supplying grants for training or accommodation; accessing birth certificates; enabling clients to travel to interviews or family visits; and helping some return to Scotland.

2.1.2 *Christian Aid, Action for the Adivasi , Bangladesh*
The Guild Project has enabled the Christian Commission for Development in Bangladesh (CCDB) to extend its work among some of the poorest people in that country – the Adivasi or tribal people. It works to address the lack of representation of the poor and marginalised, especially the unequal development of men and women, where women and girls are more likely to lose out on healthcare and education. Training in new skills is offered by CCDB, and some have gone on, in turn, to train others. One was encouraged to set up a social movement to campaign against child marriage and dowries. There has been an increasing number of women participating in forums and taking on leadership roles in their communities.

2.1.3 *CrossReach , Beyond the Blues Bluebell project*
Guild support has ensured raised awareness of postnatal depression (PND), enabling the project to take the real story of PND and its effects into all parts of the country. The service in Glasgow, launched in 2006, is the youngest PND service and it alone has dealt with 130 families and now runs outreach groups elsewhere in the region. The newly launched telephone helpline has also provided much needed support to those living in areas without a Bluebell service.

2.1.4 *Leprosy Mission Scotland, Walking in the light, Nigeria*

With Guild support, TLMS is making a huge difference to the quality of life of people disabled by leprosy across the whole region. This support has enabled a number of local people to be trained in the production of prosthetics and the related skills required. Some of those trained have themselves experienced leprosy and previously attended the centre as clients. The training and deployment of more technicians means that desperately needed help can be delivered much more locally and many more people can be helped towards independent living.

2.1.5 *Lydia Project, Miriam: Changing the World together, Eastern Europe*

The Guild has enabled Lydia to support a number of projects in 16 countries in Eastern Europe. By the end of the Soviet era, in the 1990s, there had been no charitable organisations or volunteer-based culture of social outreach for a period of half a century. New groups have been developing and have encouraged women to carry out their hopes for transformation in their communities with greater knowledge and confidence. Social isolation of the elderly and child exploitation are among the issues tackled and many people have been helped, from the vulnerable young to elderly people on very restricted incomes.

2.1.6 *Scottish love in Action, Touching the Untouchables, India*

The work with the Dalit children in Tuni continues to grow thanks to Guild support. Two new part-time headmasters have been appointed and classes are provided for pupils of all ages. Five students have moved on to higher education. An immunisation programme is about to be started and, as hoped, the new extension to the boys' accommodation has now been opened, giving the boys more comfortable sleeping quarters and improved toilet facilities. The addition of the home/school at Hyderabad is providing accommodation for another 62 children and another 93 attend the school from the local area.

2.3 While the Guild looks forward to a new set of partnerships for 2009-12, there is a sense of sadness as the current group comes to a close. Many new friends have been made with the staff and supporters of partner organisations and we wish them well for the future, particularly those who are seeking new sources of funding for their work. Partnership with the Guild is highly valued and our partners are aware of the increased profile they enjoy as a result of it. Many donations for the projects have been channelled through the Guild Office from sources beyond the Guild's own membership, as Kirk Sessions, Sunday schools and youth groups become aware of, and inspired by, the projects being promoted by the Guild.

3. A chain of prayer for peace

3.1 An undoubted focal point for this increased awareness of all that the Guild is involved in is Guild Week, now firmly established in the calendar each November. Ideas packs are circulated and help is offered with display material, but Guild Week is very much a local affair, with each guild choosing how to mark it within its congregation and community. Often guild members will lead worship on the appropriate Sunday and many host social events to which they invite friends to come along and hear about the Guild's activities. One of the most frequently reported comments is "I never knew the Guild was involved in so many different issues." Although the local group is at the heart of Guild Week, the 2007 experience of having a national focus on a particular issue, human trafficking, proved so effective that it was agreed to repeat the idea of a national initiative in 2008.

3.2 This time the focus was on a Chain of Peace, an idea based on the Caravane de Paix, an initiative of the Community of Churches in Mission (CEVAA), which had been shared with us by a sister Guild in Mauritius. Again prayer emerged as a key element of this movement, as messages and symbols of peace were passed from guild to guild across and beyond Scotland. A special prayer was written by the National Convener and it was a joy to have the Moderator and his wife lead a memorable service in Perth to launch the event. Candles and prayers were passed on at various services and meetings, or simply from friend to friend. The National Convener's Guild Week itinerary was publicised and she was able to meet members informally, which was very much appreciated, particularly in rural areas.

3.3 The feel good factor of participating in the chain of peace came through clear and strong in the feedback following Guild Week. But, though valued and precious, that was only a by-product of the whole initiative. The value added in terms of fellowship and confidence within the Guild was an unintended, albeit welcome, consequence of something more outward looking and fundamental. It is significant that Guild Week coincides with the 16 Days campaign of action against gender violence. This annual focus on human rights abuses, particularly abuse against women and children, is a global movement, secular in its origins, but nevertheless one to which the Guild is pleased to add its voice. Our contribution is to offer a call to "pray for a change" and on each of the 16 days from 25 November – 10 December attention was drawn to a factual statement about violence or abuse, followed by a prayer and Bible verse for reflection.

4. Prayer sustained action

4.1 In promoting its Chain of Peace and offering a prayer resource for the 16 Days campaign, the Guild was not retreating into a pious world far removed from the painful reality of many people's lives, but was rather tapping into the power of prayer to inform and sustain effective action across a variety of issues in which it has been involved. Current concerns include:

4.2.1 Domestic abuse : the ecumenical group hosted by the Catholic Church's Commission on Social Care has continued to work in this area with committed input from the Guild. In October a further conference was held

in Perth : "Sharing experience, sharing concern", which looked specifically at the effects on children of living with domestic abuse. An excellent programme included expert speakers, but the most powerful insights were those quoted from the children:

"I think my face must be unvisible else someone would see my scaredness"..."Please…SOMEONE… notice".

Membership of the group has been widened to include representatives of other faiths who bring their particular cultural experiences to the shared goal of tackling a problem that affects and concerns us all.

4.2.2 Human trafficking: The task of working with Presbyteries and others to keep this issue front and centre continued. The General Secretary was invited to address the Presbytery of Edinburgh and encouraged them to take the issue forward, welcoming the initiative to work with Lothian & Borders Police and seek support from other churches. In September the convener of the presbytery's Social and Community Interests committee was among those invited by the Guild to meet Lt Col Dawn Sewell, the Salvation Army's Anti-Trafficking Response Co-ordinator. This was an extremely helpful, if sobering meeting, as Lt Col Sewell outlined her work both in service provision through the Army's accommodation for recovering victims of trafficking, and at strategic level as one of the government's advisors on human trafficking. While it was encouraging to hear of the work of the UK Anti-Trafficking Centre and the success of recent police operations, there was no doubting the serious and dangerous nature of work in this area. The Salvation Army has established an international day of prayer on the theme of trafficking and the Guild was able to share some of the excellent resource material, "Reduce, Restore, Respond", during its National Committees' Conference.

The government's welcome ratification of the Council of Europe's Convention on Action against Trafficking in

Human Beings in December 2008, means commitment to further measures and provision of safe housing and support for victims and the Guild will be alert to any opportunities where the church might be of help. A commitment to act ecumenically with sister organisations resulted from a round table meeting at the Scottish Parliament, when the issue was debated in February.

4.2.3 Prostitution: The call endorsed at last year's General Assembly for an informed debate on the connection between prostitution and trafficking has been taken forward at every opportunity. Invitations have been received from a number of organisations, including the Society of Religious in Scotland and Soroptimists International. Amnesty's report "Scotland's Slaves" published in the summer brought the matter close to home and the debate has featured prominently in the press and broadcast media. The models offered by the very different legal contexts of Sweden, where prostitution is outlawed, and the Netherlands, which has a much more liberal approach, have often been the focus of news comment, and there are signs of an attitude shift, even in the capital of sexual tolerance, Amsterdam. Here's what the mayor of Amsterdam had to say recently about the red light district in that city *"Often people go to the museums and then to the red light district – it's part of the image of tolerant Amsterdam"* but the easy tolerance that characterised Amsterdam is giving way to growing concern about the organised criminal activity that goes on behind all those lighted windows. *"It took some time before we realised the extent of the trafficking and abuse that was going on."* And who is providing the demand that draws trafficking rings to Amsterdam? Tourists from other European countries including Scotland – business men on an away day, lads on a football weekend, or even a stag night.

The debate will go on, and many, including some women and sex workers, will continue to characterise prostitution as a business transaction like any other. But any discussion of trafficking for the sex industry must look beyond the factors of poverty and gender inequality that affect *supply* and focus equally on the nature of the *demand* for this "product"; on the responsibility of those who buy women in prostitution and the strategic role they have in the chain of trafficking.

4.2.4 Gender equality: through its membership of the Scottish Women's Convention and the Women's National Commission, the Guild has frequent opportunities to comment on government proposals and campaign for policy changes. Some of the issues reported above have been the subject of consultations in which the Guild has been able to take part. The Guild particularly welcomed the opportunity to contribute to the WNC's consultation in Glasgow in February, prior to the UN meetings of the Commission on the Status of Women and the Commission to Eliminate all forms of Discrimination Against Women. Through its membership of Engender, and its relations with the women's section of the STUC, the Guild has also had the chance to learn more about issues of equal pay and employment conditions. These stimulating connections have also led to valuable networking through which the Guild has become involved with "Gude Cause", a movement established to mark the centenary of the Women's Suffrage procession which took place in Edinburgh in October 1909 and played a significant role in the campaign for women to have the vote. The Guild plans to be part of the 2009 event which will celebrate women's contribution to society, culture and all aspects of public and private life in 21st Century Scotland.

4.2.5 HIV/AIDS: from the inception of the Church of Scotland's HIV/AIDS project, the Guild has been a strong supporter. One of its first set of projects under the partnership scheme was an AIDS education project in Malawi and in 2005-6 it made HIV/AIDS its special topic for discussion. The strong links which the Guild has always had with the world church have perhaps underpinned this interest, as we have shared concerns about the pandemic with sister organisations in Africa and India. During the 2006-9 focus on fullness of life, it was felt that an update on the work being done to help people living with HIV and AIDS would be a helpful addition to the Guild's programme and Project Convener Rev Dr Robin Hill was invited to address the annual conference of Council Conveners in June. The response to Robin's talk and to the contribution from Rosemary Msofwa from the United Church of Zambia was one of renewed commitment to support this vital work, not least in prayer.

4.2.6 Climate change and sustainability: The Guild's National Committee members were privileged to welcome to their annual Conference, the distinguished scientist Professor Roger Leakey, who spoke about alternative methods of agriculture in the developing world and more effective ways of achieving the millennium goals. The scientific and economic arguments were complex, but the issue was grounded in the local and domestic: how best to use local knowledge and skills to identify and cultivate native fruits and nuts, and how to teach hitherto unknown skills of preserving to improve shelf-life and facilitate trade. In order to enable Prof Leakey to reach a wider audience the Guild organised a seminar in the Church Offices attended by representatives from the World Mission and Church and Society Councils, as well as Christian Aid and Tearfund.

5. Time together in conference

5.1 This breadth of interest and involvement in important issues is largely initiated from the national office by the leadership team and the staff support team, but the leaders at Presbyterial Council and local level are key players in motivating the members of the Guild to become involved and take action. When Council Conveners and members of the National Committees each meet in annual conferences at the beginning of each session, matters of business and policy are discussed, but a more reflective element, based on the theme, is always built into the programme. So this past session has had a significant emphasis on the spiritual nurture of individual members and the need for that restoration of the soul.

Similar events are mounted for other groups of people with key roles in the life of the Guild: Project Co-ordinators, Education representatives and Ecumenical representatives. The annual conferences mounted for each of these groups are characterised by an outward looking programme, involving partnership with other organisations and Church departments.

5.2 The 2009 Conference for Project Co-ordinators sees the launch of six new projects under the Guild's chosen theme for 2009-12 "What does the Lord require of you?" Preparations for this have been underway since the selection of the new projects in October 2008. The Projects and Resources Committee received 24 submissions for consideration – a testament to the success of the Project Partnership Scheme. The criteria for selection covered both the relevance of each proposal to the strategic programme of *What does the Lord require of you but to act justly, to love mercy and to walk humbly with God?* and the sustainability of an effective partnership. Those which were unsuccessful were offered feedback, which was taken up by several and very much appreciated. The links established through this process are valuable and there will be opportunities for sharing information and concern with those organisations whose projects were not selected on this occasion.

5.3 The Mission and Discipleship Council works closely with the Guild in preparing the programme for the Education Representatives' annual conference each April. In 2008 this took a different format with Guild "Ed Reps" sharing in a much wider All-Partners residential conference held by the Council at Carberry. This got mixed reviews from the Guild members who, while valuing the contact with a wider range of people involved in Christian education and nurture, missed the opportunity for more time together as a group. In 2009, the format will revert to a day conference specifically for Ed Reps and with a clear emphasis on issues of justice as the focus turns to the first of the themes for 2009-12 *Called to act justly.*

5.4 Recognising that Guild ecumenical representatives formed a significant part of the constituency for their annual conference, the Ecumenical Relations Committee adopted the Guild's 2008-9 theme, *He restores my soul*, as the title for their event in October. Sessions included challenging questions about how we pray and witness together, with features on the work that is being done in priority areas and on the plans for Edinburgh 2010, the event planned to mark the centenary of the World Missionary Conference which was so significant for the ecumenical movement.

6. Partners in prayer and action

6.1 These various connections with other Councils and Committees of the Church reflect the Guild's commitment to its identity as a component part of the Church of Scotland. Through its office bearers and staff it contributes to:

Mission & Discipleship Council
   Mission Forum
   Interfaith Forum
World Mission Council
HIV/AIDS Project
Church & Society Council.
Ministries Council
   Priority Areas Forum
Ecumenical relations committee

6.2 The Convener and General Secretary were also invited to make a presentation to the Council of Assembly on the Guild's work programme. This was a valuable opportunity to signal the Guild's willingness to link with the Councils of the Church as partners in the Project Scheme. Recent submissions from Councils had not been of a sufficiently high standard to compete with external bids and they were urged to consider carefully their submissions for the 2009-12 round. We are pleased to report that this had the desired effect and there was a marked improvement in the quality of bids received from the Councils. A further invitation to meet the Council of Assembly in April 2009 has been accepted.

6.3 It has been a great privilege to be included in all these areas of work, particularly this past year in the Mission Forum and the Priority Areas Forum, which give opportunities to see the kind of grass roots initiatives which paint a picture of the church energised for action at local level. One factor which works against the effective witness of the local church is conflict within the fellowship. The Guild welcomes the efforts being made by the Ministries Council to address this, and was pleased to be invited to participate, in January, in the planning of a major conference on peace-building and conflict resolution scheduled for November 2009.

6.4 The Guild has also been invited to consultations with the Panel on Review and Reform and with the Church Without Walls group. The chance to reflect with these groups on the Guild's experience of change and development has been mutually helpful. It was particularly worthwhile to share with the CWW Group, the Guild's experience of developing ideas and resources centrally, which are offered to local groups for use according to local needs and contexts. The flexibility of resource material, such as that provided for Guild Week, and the increased opportunity for choice and engagement through the Project Partnership Scheme and the Initiative Fund have shifted the balance of investment between the national and the local in recent years. The national office now has a lighter touch, providing the framework on which local guilds can build their local witness and wider service.

6.5 Beyond the Church of Scotland, the Guild connects with the work of ACTS and its various networks, particularly the Network of Ecumenical Women in Scotland, which fosters good relations and communication with equivalent organisations in other denominations. This formal connection is enhanced by the warm invitations to office bearers to share in the fellowship of each other's annual meetings and conferences. The Guild is also represented on the Scottish Committee of the World Day of Prayer and many of its members contribute significantly to the services held across the nation each March.

6.6 The General Secretary of the Guild is one of the alternate representatives on the Church Members' Meeting of ACTS and there are other representatives on the Church and Society and Church Life networks. The Guild has used the facilities at Scottish Churches' House and looks forward to the next stage in the development of the House and its programmes.

6.7 One of the current Co-Conveners for Scotland of the Ecumenical Forum of European Christian Women is a Guild member, and it was a great privilege to be involved in the Forum's meeting in Dunblane in April, when members from several European nations met to discuss *Women and Theology : A reformed perspective.*

7. Committed members; faithful leaders

7.1 From international connections and global concerns to local groups and outreach to individuals, the Guild depends, for all its activities, on the support of the members. In financial terms, the annual contributions from members form the bulk of the Guild's operating income (See Appendix II). Details of current membership are given in Appendix I and details of the amounts given in support of the wider work of the Church are listed in Appendix III. In non-financial terms an immeasurable amount is given by Guild members to the ministry and mission of the Church in practical energy and in prayer support.

7.2 Local Guild leaders are key people in preparing programmes that motivate the members and provide for fellowship alongside opportunities for the exploration and expression of the faith. Their willingness to serve in this way is greatly valued by the national team and

their gratitude goes to all of them, particularly this year to treasurers. They have been on a steep learning curve as they have responded to the requirements of OSCR and changes to the way in which accounts are presented. Thanks must go, for the support and advice received over the year, to Archie McDowall, of the General Treasurer's Department, and Jennifer Hamilton of the Law Department who have answered numerous queries with patience and clarity. As a result of some of these changes, the National Executive Committee agreed to set up a Constitutional Review group to look at various aspects of the Constitution and its guidelines for practice. This work has begun and any substantive changes to the Constitution will be brought to a subsequent General Assembly for approval.

7.3 The quality of its leadership at national level is a vital part of the success of any organisation and the Guild is blessed by a succession of dedicated and willing leaders. The National Convener, Esme Duncan, of Caithness Council, must have covered more miles than most. Having a camper van at her disposal, and a general preference for the wide open spaces, Esme has undertaken visits to many local groups, some very small and in scattered rural communities. But she has not neglected the larger towns and cities as her travels have taken her from Ayr to St Andrews and from Aberdeen to London. Esme's background in locum ministry and as a Reader has given the Guild a rich vein of inspired worship and reflective prayer at key points in the year, which has been an important element in the journey through the year of the soul. Her supportive Vice-convener, Betty Dunn, from Glasgow North Council, has shared in the representative duties, taking a particular interest in the events surrounding the celebration of Nelson Mandela's 90th birthday. This involvement led to further networking on the issues emerging from the worsening situation in Zimbabwe and the opportunity to support women there through the work of ACTSA (Action for Southern Africa).

7.4 The current leadership team of committee conveners is completed by:

Margaret Broster (Ardrossan Council), Project and Topics;

Mary Notman (Aberdeen Council), Marketing and Publicity;

Dorothy Ramsay (Paisley Council), Programmes and Resources;

Catherine Robb (West Lothian Council), Finance and General Purposes.

In addition to convening their respective committees, this group has met to discuss policy issues and to plan training days and the annual meeting. A diverse group, with a variety of talents, it has thrived on humour and been sustained by prayer.

7.5 Former National Conveners also continue to offer their experience as members of the Bield group, available to advise and support local guilds and Councils, and as advocates at large for the Guild. Each year we celebrate these champions at an annual lunch and it is wonderfully inspiring to see those long "retired" passionately debating the issues of the day. Two of this great company died during the past year and the lives of Elizabeth Grant Anderson and Daphne MacNab were remembered with affection and justifiable pride.

7.6 The staff team remains unchanged since Lesley Blyth took up post in the General Office last year and quickly learned to answer all manner of queries with courtesy and charm. She works well with Maureen Morrish, who has kept track of the finances, during a difficult time of changes to computer packages, with her usual calm efficiency, and Ann Anderson who continues to manage the General Secretary's diary and decipher her handwritten notes. Fiona Punton's work as Information Officer is a vital link between the members and the national office. In addition to her work in support of the projects scheme, she produces Newsletters, Guild Week material and an eclectic weekly email to those adventurous enough to sign up for it. General Secretary, Alison Twaddle, records her thanks to all of them for enabling her to have time and space to look outward from the Guild Office and represent the organisation in the wider church and social context.

8. Worship, prayer and action

8.1 The Guild's Aim is to invite and encourage women and men to commit their lives to Jesus Christ, and enable them to express their faith in worship, prayer and action. During the past year, the prayer strand has been particularly strong, but this does not mean that the year has been one of contemplative inaction. Prayer has been the sustaining and motivating source of energy for all that is reported above and this truth has been the great rediscovery of the year.

In the name of the Guild

ESME DUNCAN, *National Convener*
ALISON TWADDLE, *General Secretary*

APPENDIX I

Membership statistics

Members	29,706
Affiliated groups	1,054

(Figures based on most up-to-date figures available at the time of preparation of this report.)

APPENDIX II

Operational Income and Expenditure 2008

General fund income	£	General fund expenditure	£
Members' contributions	211,907	Management and admin.	174,537
Sales of goods	17,858	Objects expenditure	34,789
Donations and grants	18,076	Cost of sales	14,529
Project support	18,349		
Other	21,373		
Total	£287,563	Total	£223,855

APPENDIX III

Amounts given to Church

Sums given by guilds in 2008 were as follows :

To Ministries and Mission Funds via congregations	£127,075
To Congregational Funds	£440,119
To Work of the Church (including projects)	£315,028
To Work outwith the Church	£108,910
Total	£991,132

APPENDIX IV

Project donations (since June 2006)

Borderline: Supporting homeless Scots in London	£124,558
Christian Aid: Action for the Adivasi	£69,734
CrossReach: Beyond the blues, Bluebell project	£115,687
Leprosy Mission Scotland: Walking in the light	£108,764
Lydia Project : Miriam, changing the world together	£78,417
Scottish Love in Action: Touching the untouchables	£127,969
Total	£625,132

The Statement of Accounts and Financial Report for the Guild, for the year ended 31 December 2008, is available from the Guild office or on the website: www.cos-guild.org.uk

Guild funds are incorporated in the Church of Scotland accounts.

ADDENDUM

Esme Duncan retires as National Convener of the Guild at the close of this Assembly. We would want to record the appreciation, not just of the leadership team and staff with whom she has worked most closely, but of the entire membership from every corner of Scotland and beyond. Esme has met so many of us individually on her travels and her mixture of energetic enthusiasm and spiritual depth has kept us all buoyant and motivated. Her talks at meetings large and small, her worship at conferences and committees and her upbeat contributions to Newsletters have given life and heart to the Guild. There is a great deal awaiting Esme back home in Caithness as she retires, but we hope there will be time for her to reflect on a great year and perhaps write up some of those special moments. We suggest as a title "Travels with Morven" (a very Guild friendly dog).

ELIZABETH DUNN, *National Vice-Convener*
ALISON TWADDLE, *General Secretary*

TRUSTEES OF THE CHURCH OF SCOTLAND HOUSING AND LOAN FUND FOR RETIRED MINISTERS AND WIDOWS AND WIDOWERS OF MINISTERS
May 2009

PROPOSED DELIVERANCE

The General Assembly:
1. Receive the Report and thank the Trustees and Staff.
2. Reappoint Mr J G G Lees as a Trustee.

REPORT

1. Aim of the Fund

1.1 The Fund exists to support retired Church of Scotland ministers, and widows, widowers, and separated or divorced spouses of Church of Scotland ministers, in need of help with housing. The Trustees endeavour to provide assistance by way of either a house to rent or a house purchase loan in accordance with guidelines set, and regularly reviewed by, the Trustees. Guidance Notes incorporating these guidelines are available on the Church of Scotland website or can be requested from the Secretary at the Church offices. The Secretary is always happy to meet with potential applicants to discuss their particular situation, and the assistance which the Trustees may be able to provide to them.

1.2 The Trustees own, and regularly acquire, additional houses for leasing at concessionary rents to those with insufficient resources to enable them to purchase houses for themselves. Alternatively, loans at favourable rates of interest are granted up to 70% of a house purchase price, subject to an overriding normal maximum of £25,000 for Standard Loans, and £122,500 for Shared Appreciation Loans.

2. Housing Transactions : 2008

2.1 Assistance provided during 2008 to ministers, widows and widowers, and separated and divorced spouses, is detailed in Appendix 1 annexed to this Report. The percentage of those eligible to apply, and who were granted assistance, is similarly shown in Appendix 1. All those who applied and who fell within the financial parameters of the Fund were provided with assistance.

2.2 The Trustees owned 253 houses at the end of 2008. The houses purchased and those sold by the Trustees during that year, are detailed in Appendix 2, which also shows the average price of the houses so purchased, and the average price of the houses disposed of. At the end of 2008 four houses were still being marketed for sale.

2.3 Apart from leases granted prior to 1989 (where rents continue at unchanged rates of 70% of fair rents for ministers and 35% for widows or widowers of ministers), rents charged for houses provided by the Fund are at a level of 50% of the open market rent for ministers, and 25% for widows and widowers of ministers.

3. Loan Transactions : 2008

3.1 The Fund provides loans by way of Standard Loans, Shared Appreciation Loans, and Short Term Bridging Loans.

3.2 Standard Loans are granted up to a normal maximum limit of £25,000 at a rate of interest of four per cent for ministers and two per cent for surviving widows or widowers of ministers.

3.3 Shared Appreciation Loans, which link loan values over their term to the value of the property concerned over the same period, may be granted up to a normal maximum limit of £122,500. Currently rates of interest for such loans are two and half per cent for ministers and one and a quarter per cent for widows or widowers of ministers.

3.4 Short Term Bridging Loans are granted for a fixed period, and in specific circumstances, at the discretion of the Trustees. Interest is charged at a rate equivalent to that permitted by H.M. Revenue & Customs without liability for benefit-in-kind taxation. At the time of writing this was six and a quarter per cent, but was due to be reduced to four and three quarters per cent at the beginning of March 2009.

3.5 Details of each of the three types of loan outstanding as at 31 December 2008 are given in Appendix 3.

4.   H.M. Revenue & Customs
4.1 Commissioners will recall from the Supplementary Report to the General Assembly of 2008, that negotiations were ongoing with H.M. Revenue & Customs concerning the taxation of the benefit-in-kind, perceived by H.M. Revenue & Customs to be implicit in the rates of interest charged by the Fund on its various Loans. Despite representations and offers of negotiation having been made by the Church's Tax Consultant to H.M. Revenue & Customs, no effective progress has been made as at the date of the submission of this Report.

5.   Donations, Bequests etc.
5.1 The Trustees have to report that during 2008 they received a total sum of £54,798 by way of donations, bequests and gifts.

6.   Funds
6.1 In accordance with the requirements of the charity regulator (OSCR), significant modifications in the preparation of the annual accounts have taken place. The net cost of house purchases less house sales during 2008 was £541,920. The net increase in long-term loans during 2008 was £675,450.

6.2 Investments at market value, and cash balances, at 31 December 2008 amounted to £3,378,666. Due to the downturn in the global financial markets, unrealised investment losses for the year amounted to £782,370.

7.   The Future
7.1 Those ministers who are within five years of retirement are encouraged to contact the Fund if they feel they may need to avail themselves of the Fund's assistance. Similarly the Trustees always welcome an initial approach from those who are within five to ten years of retirement. Such approaches not only assist the Trustees with financial forecasting, but can help to alleviate some of the anxieties which ministers and their spouses may experience in respect of housing as they contemplate their future after retirement. Details of commitments for the provision of either a house to rent, or a loan, during the next five years, and approved at 31 December 2008, which will require to be met from funds can be found at Appendix 4. Further, the number of ministers due to retire within a five to ten year period from 31 December 2008 and whose names have been placed on the Preliminary Applications List for assistance can also be found at Appendix 4.

7.2 Mindful both of the current state of the housing market, and equally of its obligations towards the Church and the proper and appropriate stewardship of its resources, the Trustees considered carefully the parameters for granting assistance with housing to rent, and assistance by way of housing loans, in December 2008. As a result, and particularly bearing in mind the marked slowing of the housing market in Scotland generally, and the decrease in house prices, it was agreed that the parameters for 2009 would include a maximum price for a house to rent of £175,000 and the maximum price, or value, of a house in respect of which a loan would be given of, similarily, £175,000. The Trustees remain satisfied that such parameters will enable appropriate housing to be purchased for rental, or with the aid of Fund loans, in the current housing market.

8. Diligence

8.1 The Trustees confirm that the Staff have routinely and progressively monitored their stock of rental housing, and housing over which loans have been secured, and have continued to support all of their tenants and borrowers. No significant problems have been identified or encountered.

9. Budget Allocation

9.1 The Trustees will, as previously reported, require to continue to draw down £500,000 per annum for each of 2010 and 2011 from Congregational Contributions to the Parish Staffing Fund, an amount still within the two per cent of stipend limit allocated by the General Assembly for use by the Fund previously.

10. Staff

10.1 The Trustees wish to place on record their indebtedness to the work of the Staff of the Fund, and in particular the care and support afforded by Staff to all those who apply to, or have been assisted by, the Fund.

In the name of the Trustees

J G Grahame Lees, *Chairman*
Lin J Macmillan, *Secretary*

ADDENDUM
Mr R D Oakes, CA, ACMA, MCIM

The Trustees were greatly saddened by the death in January 2009 of Mr Ronald Oakes, who as Secretary of the Baird Trust had served as a Trustee of the Housing and Loan Fund since 1997. Ronnie was well known throughout the Church community because of his involvement with a number of different bodies and organisations all of which he served with enthusiasm and diligence. His wise counsel and his quiet sense of humour at the meetings of the Housing and Loan Fund will be greatly missed.

J G Grahame Lees, *Chairman*

APPENDIX 1

Assistance provided

	2008	2007
Number of Ministers retiring (and therefore eligible to apply to the Fund)	48	50
Percentage assisted with a house to rent	15%	30%
Percentage assisted with a house purchase loan	19%	14%
Total percentage assisted	34%	44%
Percentage of individuals eligible to apply who fell within the Fund's financial parameters and who received assistance	100%	100%
Instances of assistance provided*		
Retiring Ministers	16	16
Ministers already retired	3	5
Widow(er)s	3	4
Spouses of Ministers	1	2
Total	23	27
Tenants as at 31 December		
Ministers	159	158
Widow(er)s	78	76
Spouses	8	8
Commercial rental	1	0
Vacant	7	7
Borrowers as at 31 December		
Ministers	86	80
Widow(er)s	56	55

* Assistance may not be provided in the same calendar year in which the Minister actually retires

APPENDIX 2

Rental Housing

	2008		2007	
Total number of houses owned at 1 January	249		236	
Houses purchased during year	11		17	
Total cost of purchases		£1,761,830		£2,896,459
Average house price		£160,166		£170,380
Houses sold during year	7		5	
Total amount realised		£1,219,910		£778,260
Average proceeds		£174,273		£155,652
Houses bequeathed/gifted during year	0		1	
Houses relet during year	1		2	
Total number of houses owned at 31 December	253		249	
Average market rent of property purchased during year	£7,255		£7,029	
Average rent of new tenancies – Ministers/Spouses	£3,633		£2,812	
Average rent of new tenancies – Widow(er)s	£1,440		£1,560	

APPENDIX 3

Housing Loans

	2008		2007	
Long term loans outstanding at 1 January	135		139	
Value of loans outstanding		£4,176,950		£4,086,265
New loans granted during year	12		6	
Additional loans granted during year	1		2	
Value of loans granted		£815,500		£324,000
Loans fully repaid during year	7		10	
Loans partially repaid during year	4		6	
Value of loans repaid		£140,050		£233,315
Long term loans outstanding at 31 December	140		135	
Value of long term loans outstanding		£4,852,400		£4,176,950
Short term Bridging Loans outstanding at 1 January	2		4	
Value of Bridging Loans outstanding		£92,000		£130,000
Bridging Loans granted during year	10		4	
Value of Bridging Loans granted		£595,000		£570,000
Bridging Loans repaid during year	8		6	
Value of Bridging Loans repaid		£504,000		£608,000
Short term Bridging Loans outstanding at 31 December	4		2	
Value of Bridging Loans outstanding at 31 December		£183,000		£92,000

APPENDIX 4

Outstanding Commitments

	2008	2007
For next 5 years		
Houses to rent	47	45
Housing Loans	30	29
Value of outstanding commitments	£11,225,000	£11,178,500

Preliminary Applications

	2008	2007
For those retiring between 5 – 10 years	9	6

THE CHURCH OF SCOTLAND INVESTORS TRUST
May 2009

PROPOSED DELIVERANCE

The General Assembly
1.   Receive the Report.
2.   Appoint Mr A W T Gibb as Vice-Chairman of the Investors Trust from 1 June 2009.
3.   Approve the re-appointment of Mr S R Auld as a member of the Investors Trust from 1 June 2009.
4.   Ratify the co-option on 16 March 2009 of Mr B J Duffin, Mr R H Nisbet and Mr G R Young and approve their appointments as members of the Investors Trust from 1 June 2009.
5.   Receive the Annual Report and Financial Statements of the Investors Trust for 2008.

REPORT

The Church of Scotland Investors Trust, which was established by the Church of Scotland (Properties and Investments) Order Confirmation Act 1994, submits its fifteenth Report to the General Assembly.

1.   Introduction

The function of the Investors Trust is to provide investment services to the Church of Scotland and to bodies and trusts within or connected with the Church. The Investors Trust offers simple and economical facilities for investment in its three Funds: (a) Growth Fund; (b) Income Fund; (c) Deposit Fund. Investors receive the benefits of professional management, continuous portfolio supervision, spread of investment risk and economies of scale.

The bulk of the Church of Scotland's investments are held on a long term basis, for the purpose of generating recurring income to support the Church's work. An increase or decline in the capital value of investments does not necessarily have a corresponding effect on income receivable.

Ethical considerations form an integral part of the investment management process and the Trustees have given guidance to the investment managers, taking into account views expressed by the General Assembly. At their own meetings, the Trustees regularly review and consider matters arising in respect of ethical investment. Investment is avoided in any company whose management practices are judged by the trustees to be unacceptable. In particular, investment is avoided in any company substantially involved in gambling, tobacco products, alcohol, armaments and other activities which are felt to harm society more than they benefit it. In general, investment is sought in companies that demonstrate responsible employment and good corporate governance practices, have regard to environmental performance and human rights and act with sensitivity to the communities in which they operate.

2.   Investment Performance in 2008

The total value funds invested through the Church of Scotland Investors Trust decreased from £363.0 million at 31 December 2007 to £296.7 million at 31 December 2008. The decrease is the result of adverse market movement.

After three positive years, investment returns were negative in 2008, where the major market for the Growth Fund, the UK, as measured by the FTSE All Share Index, fell by 29.9%. The negative performance of the equity and property markets was to the detriment of the Fund. Total Return was -22.9% against the benchmark of -21.7%.

The Income Fund does not have an overall benchmark and the poor performance of the equity and corporate bond markets resulted in a return of -18.2%.

The market outlook for 2009 can be characterised as one of continuing volatility and illiquidity. However, opportunities are likely to exist for investors able and willing to take a longer term perspective.

3.   Income Distributions

The Growth Fund's distribution rate was targeted to be maintained at not less than16.0p per unit for 2008. The distribution rate for 2007 was16.0p per unit and in addition, a special and non-recurring distribution for 2007 of 2.5p per unit was paid in May 2008. Income from the equity portfolio has for the third consecutive year exceeded expectations as a result of the Managers investing the Fund in companies capable of supporting sustainable dividend growth from strong cash flow. This has enabled the Trustees to declare a total distribution of 16.5p per unit for 2008. A target distribution of not less than 16.5p per unit has been set for 2009 but this will be dependant upon there being no further unforeseen deterioration in financial markets.

Lower interest rates had made it difficult for the Income Fund managers to maintain past income levels and the Trustees concluded in 2002 that the Income Fund's target distribution should be reduced gradually to 67p per unit. The distribution in 2008 was 67.0p per unit, the same as 2007. The target distribution of the Income Fund in 2009 is 67.0p per unit but this will not be achievable if there are material defaults in the bond holdings.

The average rate for 2008 declared by the Deposit Fund was 5.6% whilst base rate averaged 4.7%. This was as a result of the Fund Managers, within investment parameters set, having followed a strategy of placing funds out for longer periods to take advantage of the higher prevailing yields at the longer end of the market. Now that base rate has fallen, this strategy has delayed the adverse impact on the level of revenue earned by the Deposit Fund. The rate payable in 2009 will, as usual, depend on movements in the money market but will decline steadily from the 2008 levels.

4.   Office Bearers

Mr D M Simpson demits office as Vice-Chairman and it is recommended that Mr A W T Gibb be appointed Vice-Chairman as from 1 June 2009.

5.   Membership

In accordance with the terms of the Constitution, the following three members retire by rotation at 31 May 2009: Mr S R Auld, Mr P J Burnet and Mr J Skinner, the latter two having indicated they did not seek re-election. It is recommended to the General Assembly that Mr S R Auld be re-appointed as a member as from 1 June 2009.

Mr B J Duffin, Mr R Nisbet and Mr G R Young were co-opted as members of the Investors Trust on 16 March 2009. It is recommended to the General Assembly that this co-option be ratified and that they be appointed members of the Investors Trust as from 1 June 2009.

6.   Annual Report and Financial Statements for 2008

Copies of the Annual Report and Financial Statements for the year to 31 December 2008 are available to download from The Church of Scotland website or can be obtained from the Secretary.

In the name and by the authority of
The Church of Scotland Investors Trust

I J HUNTER, *Chairman*
D M SIMPSON, *Vice-Chairman*
F E MARSH, *Secretary*

REPORT OF THE IONA COMMUNITY BOARD
May 2009

PROPOSED DELIVERANCE

The General Assembly
1. Receive the Report and thank the Board.
2. Affirm the commitment of the Iona Community to mutual economic accountability and sharing through its economic discipline and its ongoing work.
3. Commend the involvement of the Iona Community in the Ecumenical Accompaniment Programme of the World Council of Churches in Palestine and Israel (EAPPI).
4. Welcome the renovation of the Community's shop on Iona with additional facilities for welcome and interpretation and thank the Church for its support of the Growing Hope Appeal which has made this possible.
5. Approve the updated description of the relationship of the Iona Community to the Church of Scotland through the Iona Community Board.
6. Note with interest the fact that through the report of the Board the Iona Community is represented by the Church of Scotland to the whole Church.
7. Congratulate Rev Peter Macdonald on his election as Leader of the Iona Community from August 2009; and thank Rev Kathy Galloway for her outstanding contribution as Leader for the past seven years.

REPORT

General

1. The daily Act of Prayer of the Iona Community prays for its members 'gathered and scattered' and this is a constant reminder that it is both a worldwide movement, with members and groups everywhere from Malawi to Michigan, from Cumbria to Cuba and from Perth, Scotland to Perth, Australia, and a movement rooted in local realities. The Community is where the members are, scattered yet gathered by the strength and inspiration of its Rule, its prayer life, its local member and associate groups and its local church and community involvements. The Community was born as a practical response to the needs of a community struggling with the challenges of poverty and unemployment – Govan, during the Depression. Ever since that time in the 1930s, the commitment to economic justice and the inclusion of the poorest and most vulnerable in society have been central to the Community's life and work.

This is expressed first of all through the Community's economic discipline. The commitment to sharing and mutual accountability for money has been a part of the Rule of the Iona Community since it was first formulated in the early 1940s. Members commit themselves to tithing of income, of which 60% is given to the wider work of the church and the common good and 40% to the Iona Community, of which 25% is then given away. Members further account to one another for how they use the other 90% of income. They also account for their energy use. In this, the Community is extending into the personal and individual sphere its belief in the sovereignty of God over all aspects of life, including the economic and what is normally considered to be 'private' in western society.

Stewardship, the faithful management of the household resources, is one of the pillars of the Community's economic discipline. Christians inherit gifts from the past of language, story, sacrament, knowledge, art, music, the built environment; from the present, of people's time, talents, money, commitment, prayer, goodwill – and the Community has had these in abundance. How these are ordered in the service of Jesus and in solidarity with God's purposes of justice and love is a central concern of Christian faith. The idea that there is any such thing as private money is quite illusory; on a par with the illusion that slavery did not hugely profit our economies at the expense of the enslaved, or that our energy-profligate lifestyle is our own private business. This privatization has simply contrived to avoid responsibility, as the world has so painfully seen of late. Good stewardship in a Christian context should never be about maximising profits, share returns or property holdings. It should always be about ordering the household so that all its members, including the weakest, can grow and flourish. In their mutual accountability, members are practicing the most down-to-earth spiritual discipline possible, testing their priorities with the help of their brothers and sisters who, they trust, will be challenging and yet supportive, assisting them to place all of life under the sovereignty of God.

This commitment to mutual economic accountability has been expressed variously by Community members; through church extension, service in countries of the global south and youth programmes on islands and mainland. More recently, it has found expression through anti-poverty campaigning, working with young offenders, asylum seekers and vulnerable young people at Camas. As Britain, along with the rest of the world, is entering economic recession, it is all the more important to maintain this commitment. The Community is by no means exempt from these challenges and had a difficult year financially. This led to some staffing cutbacks, cuts in the proposed 2009 budget and an appeal to its constituency, magnificently answered. Though the Community does not use credit, its Access Fund, interest from which subsidises the costs of people on low income

staying in its island centres, will be radically reduced in 2009, and will necessitate drawing down capital.

2.   The Community's Justice and Peace Commitment commits members to prayer and action for justice, peace and the integrity of creation; members continue to be active both locally and nationally in anti-poverty campaigns, in particular through our association with Christian Aid and with Church Action on Poverty. The Community's two-year engagement with the theme of Place has led to the decision to include mutual accountability for energy and resource use, as well as money, as part of its Rule. Given the long association of Community members in Israel/Palestine, most recently through the Ecumenical Accompaniment programme of the World Council of Churches (EAPPI), much activity has been focussed on the critical situation in Gaza. This has given a timely aspect to the Community's forthcoming two-year programme emphasis on peacemaking at every level.

3.   The Community's **Growing Hope Appeal** has continued and has now enabled the Community to proceed with the renovation of its shop with improved welcome and interpretation opportunities. However, the Community recognises that in an economic downturn, fundraising will continue to be an ongoing and essential part of its work, and this is being recognised by the incorporation of fundraising into its governance structures.

4.   The Council of the Iona Community, which is the Community's governing body, has been revising and updating its **Memorandum and Articles of Association** to take account of more recent companies legislation as well as changes in the procedures of the Community. The Community incorporated as a Company limited by guarantee and not having a share capital in December 1985. The Council of the Iona Community is the Board of Directors of the Community.

In 1991, a Special Resolution was passed by the Annual General meeting of the Iona Community concerning the ecclesiastical relationship of the Community to the Church of Scotland. As the membership of the Community has become increasingly ecumenical and Church of Scotland membership of the Community currently stands at around 40%, the Special Resolution is somewhat anomalous. This was recognised at the time of the Church of Scotland's structural reorganisation in 2005, which at the 2006 General Assembly constituted the Iona Community Board as an advisory body with designated ecumenical representation. The Iona Community Board now seeks the approval of the Assembly for new wording describing this special relationship to be incorporated into the Memorandum and Articles of the Iona Community in place of the Special Resolution.

5. The Leader of the Iona Community, Rev Kathy Galloway, completes her seven-year term of office at the end of July 2009. The Board is pleased to announce the election of Rev Peter Macdonald, currently minister of St George's West Church, Edinburgh, as the new Leader from August 2009.

Islands Work

6. The usual busy season on **Iona** was greatly enabled by a strong and committed staff team, who coped with the usual challenges of illness, staff changeover and shortages with characteristic grace and competence. This was helped by a greater emphasis on flexible team working. Occupancy rates were 90% in the Abbey and 70% in the MacLeod Centre, which was encouraging given a 13% drop in visitors to the island overall. The very early date of Easter meant that bookings were quiet at the beginning of the season. However, the introduction of two winter quiet weeks during Advent has been a great success, and both were full with waiting lists. Because guests overwhelmingly state the importance to them of community-building with people of many backgrounds, nationalities and religious traditions,

the new programme has an emphasis on this. The common life is still a vision and aspiration for many in a dangerously fragmented world. The Community's international Volunteer Programme reinforces the value of what George MacLeod called the 'demanding common task' which alone builds community. The Community is grateful to its volunteers and staff. Its MacLeod Centre Deputy Warden, Rowena Aberdeen, finished her contract and has returned to Australia. Rev Jamie Schmeling, a minister of the Reformed Church of America who has been working with the Wild Goose Resource Group for several years has been appointed as new Deputy Warden. Upkeep and maintenance of the Community's properties on Iona is an ongoing challenge, given the extremes of damp and wind, the difficulty of getting appropriately skilled people to carry out work and the lack of continuity in maintenance personnel. A coherent and coordinated maintenance plan for the buildings on Iona has now been drawn up following an extensive survey .

7. Plans for the renovation of **the Community's shop** on Iona finally received all the necessary permissions and work began in December 2008, finishing in time for the beginning of the 2009 season in late March. This work will greatly improve the space and layout in the shop itself, give improved and additional office space and incorporate a welcome and reception area which will allow for better interpretation of the Community's life and work beyond Iona. The Abbey Front Office will be given over to Historic Scotland.

8. **Camas** is the Community's outdoor education centre on Mull, with an emphasis on environmental sustainability, community-building and adventure activity. It serves primarily though not exclusively a youth constituency, especially appropriate for young people from disadvantaged backgrounds. With an excellent team of staff and volunteers, the various youth weeks were very successful and the garden flourished. In order to make the resources of Camas more widely available, four adult

weeks, with environmental and creative (storytelling and traditional music) themes were introduced at the start and end of the season and this is being further developed in 2009, including a week for people interested in learning about what it means to live *Off Grid, Off Oil*.

Mainland Work

9. The **Council** of the Iona Community has been reviewing its governance structures and as part of this has incorporated its Publishing Committee into a new committee with the wider remit of Communications and Fundraising. It has also revised and updated its Memorandum and Articles.

10. Youth Development The Jacob Project, which offers young offenders and ex-offenders positive alternatives to re-offending, has had its first full year, including a very successful briefing event at the Scottish Parliament. All the young men on it have done well and none has re-offended. We are grateful to the Church of Scotland Parish Development Fund which has supported Jacob; however, this kind of work is costly and it is facing major funding difficulties. Schools work in both non-denominational and Catholic schools continues, including an innovative graffiti project at Bellahouston Academy which was reported in Glasgow newspapers and significant work has been done with the Community's Youth Associates which has resulted in several of them applying for full membership of the Community.

Communications and Outreach

11. Wild Goose Publications, www.ionabooks.com have published the following new titles: *We Walk His Way: Shorter Songs for Worship (book and CD)* by John L Bell, *Thinking Out Loud: Collected Scripts from Thought for the Day* by John L Bell, *Christ of the Celts* by Philip Newell, *Bare Feet and Buttercups: resources for ordinary time* by Ruth Burgess, *Between High and Low Water: Sojourner Songs* by Jan Sutch Pickard, *The Tenderness of Conscience* by Allan Boesak, *Going Home Another Way: Daily readings and resources for*

Christmastide by Neil Paynter and new editions of *Living a Countersign* by Ian M Fraser and *Bridging the Gap: Has the Church failed the poor?* by John Harvey. There has been growing interest in *Living the Questions* for which Wild Goose Publications is the UK distributor. Web sales, and overseas editions and distribution have held up well, and the website has been updated. The major and innovative project of digitisation is continuing surely but slowly, partly because there is no standard format as yet for e-books.

12. The Community's magazine **Coracle** has maintained a high standard of editorial and content from across the Community's life and work, and beyond. An exciting new development is the introduction of a monthly **e-coracle**, which will allow much more interactivity and immediacy.

13. The Wild Goose Resource Group. In addition to the monthly Holy City workshop and worship evening in Glasgow, the Community's team of worship and reflection resource workers has offered weekend programmes for those interested in holding their own Holy City event in their own city, and, in conjunction with Strathclyde University Chaplaincy, for those running or interested in *Living the Questions* (faith explorations for progressive Christians). Holy City continues to offer this course in Glasgow. John Bell continues to be in great demand for music and worship consultancy across the world.

14. At Greenbelt, the Christian Arts Festival, a successful new venture in partnership saw the Iona Community Wild Goose Resource Group and youth team, along with Members, join forces with Church Action on Poverty and Fischy Music in a larger venue under the title of Northern Lights, to offer a full programme of hospitality, sales, workshops, worship, talks and music.

Membership

15. Seven new members were hallowed into full membership at Community Week in August, including a second Dutch member, and there are 22 people on the current New Members Programme. Their denominational affiliation is: Church of Scotland/United Reformed/ Dutch Reformed, Anglican/Scottish Episcopalian, Methodist, Salvation Army, Baptist and Independent.

Full membership currently stands at 270, Associate membership at around 1800. In addition to at least 30 Associate/Iona groups in the UK, there are also now groups in Ireland, the Netherlands (5), Switzerland, Germany (5), Sweden (3), Cuba, the United States and Canada, and a group is in the process of forming in Malawi. The Community retains strong links with Wellspring, its sister community in Australia. The Community also mourned, with the Corrymeela Community in Northern Ireland, the death of its former Leader, Rev John Morrow, a member of the Iona Community (1958-71).

16. Plenary meetings in Glasgow and Iona and 5 regional plenaries began to engage with the new focus on Peace, and in particular with *Glory to God and Peace on Earth*, the thematic areas for the forthcoming WCC International Ecumenical Peace Convocation to be held in Kingston, Jamaica in 2011. A member of the Community, Professor Alison Phipps, is on the Spiritual Life Committee for this event. Both the summer and autumn Community Weeks were lively events. Rev Mitchell Bunting (URC) represents Ecumenical Renewal Agencies on the WCC Continuation Committee of Ecumenism in the 21st Century. The Community also mourned the deaths of five members: Jim Hughes, a distinguished Scottish businessman and academic; Donald Rennie, whose accomplishments in faithful ministry in Scotland and in music were much valued; Keith Dowding, a former Moderator of the Uniting Church in Western Australia; Tom Graham, who, at the time of his death was Librarian of Newcastle University and Richard Baxter, former missionary in Malawi and Warden of Scottish Churches House. Every 31st day of its monthly prayer cycle, the Community remembers those members who have died since its formation in 1938 and prays 'tell them we love them and miss them.' In the communion of saints, an ever-present reality for the Iona Community, we are not divided. We give great thanks.

In the name of the Board

MAXWELL CRAIG, *Convener*
KATHY GALLOWAY, *Leader, The Iona Community*

APPENDIX

Company Number : 96243

EXTRACT OF SPECIAL RESOLUTIONS OF IONA COMMUNITY

At the Annual General Meeting of The Iona Community held at the Pearce Institute, Govan, Glasgow on the First day of June Nineteen hundred and ninety one the following Special Resolutions were passed amending the Memorandum and Articles of Association as follows:-

The Memorandum of Association shall be altered by the addition of an additional clause to be added at the end of the Memorandum to read as follows:-

1.   Nothing in this Memorandum is to be construed in a manner inconsistent with the fact that the Community is for all ecclesiastical purposes subject to the jurisdiction of the General Assembly of the Church of Scotland.

The Articles of Association shall be altered as follows:-

At the end of Clause 3 thereof there shall be added the following wording:

> For the avoidance of doubt it is declared that all members are required to adhere to the corporate loyalty of the Community to the presbyterian government of the Church of Scotland and the corporate acceptance by the Community of the fundamental doctrines of the Church of Scotland, and the Council may admit to membership persons who are not members of the Church of Scotland provided that they agree that, as members of the Community, they will do nothing prejudicial to the said corporate loyalty and corporate acceptance, and provided also that they accept membership on

such other terms and conditions and with such rights as may be determined by the Council and approved by the Community in Plenary meeting.

At the end of the Articles of Association the following additional Clause shall be added to read as follows:-

52.   Nothing in these Articles shall be construed as removing the Community from the ecclesiastical jurisdiction of the General Assembly of the Church of Scotland as exercised through the Iona Community Board appointed by the General Assembly or as conferring any right on the Community in Plenary meeting or on the Council to act in a manner inconsistent with the said jurisdiction or contrary to the relevant provisions of the General Assembly of 1951.

Proposed new wording to replace the above:

> The Iona Community originated within the Church of Scotland. Members of the Iona Community who are also members of the Church of Scotland remain subject to the ecclesiastical jurisdiction of the General Assembly of the Church of Scotland, as do all other members of the Iona Community remain subject to their respective denominations. In recognition of these historic links and in furtherance of the ecumenical objectives of the Community, the Church of Scotland has constituted the Iona Community Board as an advisory body to the Community and as the means whereby the Community reports to the General Assembly and to the British churches. The Iona Community Board remains subject to the ecclesiastical jurisdiction of the General Assembly of the Church of Scotland.

NOMINATION COMMITTEE
May 2009

PROPOSED DELIVERANCE

The General Assembly
1. Receive the Report.
2. Make alterations to Standing Committees and Councils as set forth in the Report. (Section 3)

REPORT

1. Charity Governance

The Committee has continued to monitor its procedures in light of the requirements of charity governance, a matter on which it reported fully last year. In October the Convener met with the Council of Assembly's Governance Group when the main points of discussion covered transparency of process in the identification of conveners and vice-conveners, succession planning, the need for nominations from Councils and Committees to be considered alongside nominations from the wider Church and the importance of ensuring that those appointed had the requisite skills and were able to give the necessary time to their duties.

2. Statistical Information

2.1 Last year the Committee, for the first time, provided some statistical details as a means of highlighting the actual engagement of the Church as a whole with the Nomination Committee process. As this was felt to be helpful this information is again provided and done so in such a way as to enable a comparison to be made with last year:

- For the second year running, approximately 3,000 letters inviting nominations were sent out.
- The number of nominations received prior to the meeting was 176 (126 in 2008).
- The number of vacancies to fill was 143 (126 in 2008).
- 41 nominations came from 37 Ministers (44 from 36 in 2008).
- 34 nominations came from 33 Kirk Sessions (29 from 26 in 2008).
- 21 nominations came from 6 Presbyteries (45 from 16 in 2008).
- 3 nominations came from the Guild (2 in 2008).
- 16 nominations came from the Nomination Committee (26 in 2008).
- 61 nominations came from Councils and Committees (57 in 2008).

3. Nominations for Appointment to Councils and Committees

The Committee recommends the following appointments:

Arbitration Panel

Ministers Appointed Ian Black (Grangemouth: Zetland), H Taylor Brown (Kilmarnock: St Ninian's Bellfield l/w Kilmarnock: Shortlees), Elizabeth Kenny (Carnock and Oakley), Hilary McDougall (Cambuslang), Eleanor McMahon (Paisley: St James'), Alistair Malcolm (Inverness: Inshes), Betty Smith (Fauldhouse: St Andrew's *retired*)

Members Appointed Diane Ashton (North Queensferry), Patricia Kingston (Edinburgh: Gorgie), George Lawson (Airdrie: The New Wellwynd), Arthur McDonald (Stirling: Allan Park South), Alan Muat (Grandtully, Logierait and Strathtay), Michael Ramsay (Edinburgh: Cramond), Bill Steele (Alvie and Insh), Fred Stephen (Glamis, Inverarity and Kinnettles), Bill Wishart (Paisley: St Ninian's Ferguslie)

Assembly Arrangements Committee

Minister Retiring Agnes Moore
Ministers Appointed Derek Browning (Edinburgh: Morningside), Neil Gardner (Edinburgh: Canongate)
Member Retiring Vivienne Macdonald

David Arnott, *Convener*
Janet Mathieson, *Vice-Convener*

Central Services Committee

Convener Resigned Anne Lithgow
Convener Appointed Stewart Roy (Glasgow: Jordanhill)
Vice-Conveners Appointed Douglas Paterson* (Edinburgh: St Colm's), Pauline Weibye* (Edinburgh: Craigmillar Park)
Minister Appointed Rosemary Frew (Kirkcaldy: Abbotshall)
Member Retiring Archie Cameron
Members Appointed Fergus McLellan (Renton: Trinity), Angus Macpherson (Edinburgh: Palmerston Place)

Stewart Roy, *Convener*
Douglas Paterson, Pauline Weibye, *Vice-Conveners*

Committee on Chaplains to HM Forces

Ministers Retiring Thomas Davidson Kelly, Iain McFadzean, Rory MacLeod, John Thomson
Ministers Appointed Clifford Acklam (Avonbridge I/w Torphichen), Iain Barclay (Aberdeen: Torry St Fittick's), Andrew Jolly (Chaplain to the Oil Industry), Scott Rae (Old Cumnock: Trinity)
Member Retiring Michael Taitt
Members Appointed Margery Paterson (Old Cumnock: Old), Jo Young (Perth: St John the Baptist's)

James Gibson, *Convener*
Andrew Murray, *Vice-Convener*

Church and Society Council

Ministers Retiring David Graham, John McMahon, James Walker
Minister Resigned Fiona Lillie
Ministers Appointed Janice Faris (Innerleithen, Traquair and Walkerburn), John McMahon* (Chaplain, NHS Lothian),

Matthew Ross (Conference of European Churches), Christopher Wigglesworth (St Andrew's College, Selly Oak *retired*)
Members Retiring John Berkeley, Vivienne Macdonald, Calum MacKellar, Sinclair Scott
Member Resigned Grahame Smith
Members Appointed Eleanor Anderson (Auchaber United), Calum MacKellar* (Edinburgh: North Leith), Iain Mitchell (North Queensferry), Sinclair Scott* (The Douglas Valley), Glenn Walker (Carluke: St John's)

Ian Galloway, *Convener*
Alexander Horsburgh, *Vice-Convener*

Committee on Church Art and Architecture

Members Retiring Campbell McKenzie, Crawford Mackenzie
Members Appointed Sarah Jane Bogle (Bo'ness: St Andrew's), Edward Hawke (Quarter), Campbell McKenzie* (1 year) (Stornoway: St Columba's)

Eleanor Macalister, *Convener*
Peter Gardner, *Vice-Convener*

Church Without Walls Group

Convener Retiring Albert Bogle
Convener Appointed David Cameron (Maxwell Mearns Castle)
Member Resigned Lauren Yule
Members Appointed Kate Aitchison (Edinburgh: Newhaven), Sarah Elliott (Livingston: Old)

David Cameron, *Convener*

Ecumenical Relations Committee

Convener Retiring William Brown
Convener Appointed Alan Falconer (Aberdeen: St Machar's)
Minister Retiring Bruce Thomson
Ministers Appointed Peter McEnhill (Kilmacolm: Old), Matthew Ross (Conference of European Churches), Bruce Thomson* (2 years) (Scone: Old)
Member Retiring Vivienne Macdonald

Alan Falconer, *Convener*
Lindsay Schlüter, *Vice-Convener*

Judicial Commission

Ministers Retiring David Arnott, Ian Black, Sheila Blount, Keith Hall, Alan McDonald, David Randall, Gordon Savage, Duncan Shaw, Norma Stewart

Ministers Appointed Neil Combe (Hawick: Teviot and Roberton), Elinor Gordon (Cumbernauld: Kildrum), Ian McLean (Montrose: Old and St Andrew's), Ian Murray (Blair Atholl and Struan l/w Tenandry)

Elders Retiring Andrew Bell, Maggie Mackay, Michael Meston, Alan Thomson

Elder Resigned Lorna Paterson

Elders Appointed Douglas Allan (2 years) (Edinburgh: Greenbank), Jean Broadwood (2 years) (Edinburgh: Fairmilehead), Robert Carr (North Berwick: St Andrew Blackadder), Alexander Corner (Deer), Steuart Dey (2 years) (Kilmarnock: Laigh West High), Myrtle Gillies (Thurso: West), Jamie Grant (Inverness: Hilton), Marshall Halliday (Mearns Coastal), Robert Nimmo (2 years) (Dundee: Dundee (St Mary's)), Douglas Risk (Aberdeen: Holburn West), Richard Scott (Edinburgh: Mayfield Salisbury), Anne Walker (2 years) (Cumbernauld: Old)

Aileen Nimmo, *Chairman*
Alasdair MacFadyen, *Vice-Chairman*

Legal Questions Committee

Minister Appointed Sheila Kirk (Alyth)
Member Retiring Andrew Bell

Carole Hope, *Convener*
Alan Hamilton, *Vice-Convener*

Ministries Council

Vice-Convener Resigned Barry Dunsmore
Vice-Convener Appointed Ian Dick (Aberdeen: Ferryhill)
Ministers Retiring Colin Anderson, Ian Strachan, Bruce Thomson
Ministers Resigned Karen Watson, Peter White
Ministers Appointed Ian Aitken (Aberdeen: New Stockethill), Bruce Thomson* (2 years) (Scone: Old)
Member Retiring Judith Taylor

Members Appointed Leonard Cazaly (Culloden: The Barn), Frank Dunn (Stonehaven: Fetteresso), Lorna Paterson (Bridge of Allan), Richard Roberts (Stirling: Church of the Holy Rude)

Graham Finch, *Convener*
Ian Dick, Neil Dougall, Lezley Kennedy, Muriel Pearson, *Vice-Conveners*

Mission and Discipleship Council

Convener Retiring Angus Morrison
Convener Appointed Mark Johnstone (Kirkintilloch: St Mary's)
Vice-Convener Appointed Neil Pratt (Glasgow: Martyrs')
Ministers Retiring Anne Brennan, Rachel Dobie, Alan Falconer, Kenneth Petrie
Minister Resigned Christine Houghton
Ministers Appointed Peter McEnhill (Kilmacolm: Old), Kenneth Petrie* (Aberdeen: Craigiebuckler), John Purves (Glasgow: Drumchapel St Andrew's)
Member Retiring Pauline Hunt
Members Appointed Shirley Billes (St Andrew's-Lhanbryd and Urquhart), Esme Duncan (Canisbay), Brian Fraser (Eaglesham), Mary Gargrave DCS (Glasgow: Carnwadric)

Mark Johnstone, *Convener*
Alan Birss, Linda Dunnett, Neil Pratt, *Vice-Conveners*

Nomination Committee

Ministers Retiring Ranald Gauld, Ian Hamilton, Bryan Haston, William Hogg, Ben Johnstone, Andrew McGurk, Alan Ward
Ministers Appointed Alastair Cherry (Glasgow: Penilee St Andrew's), Alastair Donald (Maud and Savoch l/w New Deer: St Kane's), Alistair Malcolm (Inverness: Inshes), Agnes Moore (Bellshill: West), Alastair Younger (Clerk of Inverness Presbytery)
Members Retiring Margaret Anderson, Albert Davidson, Angy MacDiarmid
Members Resigned James Greig, Lorna Paterson
Members Appointed Elizabeth Anderson (Montrose:

Melville South), Elva Carlisle (Glasgow: Pollokshields), Myrtle Gillies (Thurso: West), Dorothy Kinloch (Callander), Rona Lannigan (Newton Mearns), Helen Longmuir (Langton and Lammermuir Kirk), Iain McLarty (Edinburgh: High (St Giles'))

Colin Sinclair, *Convener*
Ian Black, *Vice-Convener*

Committee to Nominate the Moderator
Members Retiring Fiona Cameron, Ann McCarter
Members Appointed Jean Brannigan (Glasgow: Partick South), Elspeth Dale (Kilmarnock: Laigh West High)

Parish Development Fund
Vice-Convener Retiring Mary Miller
Vice-Convener Appointed Rolf Billes (St Andrew's-Lhanbryd and Urquhart)
Members Retiring Alison Henderson, Helen Hughes DCS
Members Appointed Helen Hughes DCS* (Glasgow: Springburn), Isabel McDerment (Glasgow: Scotstoun), John Macpherson (Edinburgh: Palmerston Place)

Martin Fair, *Convener*
Rolf Billes, *Vice-Convener*

Personnel Appeal Panel
Member Appointed David McClements (Blackbraes and Shieldhill)

Solicitor of the Church, *Secretary*

Publishing Committee
Convener Appointed John Macgill* (1 year) (Haddington: St Mary's)
Vice-Convener Resigned Doug McRoberts
Vice-Convener Appointed Kenneth Forrest (Paisley: Sandyford (Thread Street))
Minister Retiring Peter Johnston
Ministers Appointed Peter Johnston* (Blantyre: St Andrew's), Graham Smith (Livingston: Old)

Member Retiring John Henderson
Member Resigned Brian Osborne
Members Appointed Rhona Arthur (Hamilton: West), William Findlay (Bishopbriggs: Springfield)

John Macgill, *Convener*
Kenneth Forrest, *Vice-Convener*

Panel on Review and Reform
Minister Resigned John McPake
Minister Appointed Gordon McCracken (Howe of Fife)
Members Resigned Graham Roddick, Sheilah Steven
Member Appointed Fiona Campbell (Crieff)

David Cameron, *Convener*
Marina Brown, *Vice-Convener*

Safeguarding Committee
Convener Appointed John Christie* (1 year) (West Kilbride: St Andrew's)
Minister Retiring Alastair Cherry
Ministers Appointed Sheila Mitchell (Chaplain, NHS Ayrshire), Karen Watson (Edinburgh: Marchmont St Giles')
Members Retiring Susan Maclaren, John Taylor
Member Appointed Bill Gillis (Dumfries: St Mary's Greyfriars)

John Christie, *Convener*
Ranald Mair, *Vice-Convener*

Social Care Council
Convener Retiring David Court
Convener Appointed Sydney Graham (Iona I/w Kilfinichen and Kilvickeon and the Ross of Mull)
Vice-Convener Appointed Ramsay Shields (Milngavie: St Luke's)
Members Retiring John Burgoyne, Irene Gibson, Jane Ingall, Gillian Neilson, Jim Rendall
Members Appointed John Adamson (Lochalsh), Adrian Bark (Troon: St Meddan's), Matthew Struthers (Abdie

and Dunbog), Bill Usher (Burnside Blairbeth), Deirdre Yellowlees (The Stewartry of Strathearn)

Sydney Graham, *Convener*
Sally Bonnar, Ramsay Shields, *Vice-Conveners*

World Mission Council

Vice-Convener Retiring Leon Marshall
Vice-Convener Appointed Shirley Brown (Edinburgh: Murrayfield)
Minister Retiring William Howie
Ministers Appointed Fiona Gardner (3 years) (Glasgow: South Shawlands), William Howie* (2 years) (member of Aberdeen: High Hilton)
Members Retiring Eileen Bishop, Robbie Mochrie, Jean Pattie, Catherine Seaman
Member Resigned Robert Leitch
Members Appointed Jennifer Dodds (Annan: Old), John McArthur (3 years) (Lenzie: Union), Leon Marshall* (Kilmacolm: Old), James Mitchell (Pitlochry)

Colin Renwick, *Convener*
Shirley Brown, Stewart Gillan *Vice-Conveners*

* denotes second term

Please note that the Committee will bring a Notice of Motion in the Assembly Papers which will include nominations for any appointments required as a result of decisions taken by this General Assembly, including decisions taken on the Joint Report of the Council of Assembly and the Stewardship and Finance Committee.

In the name of the Committee

COLIN SINCLAIR, *Convener*
IAN BLACK, *Vice-Convener*
FINLAY MACDONALD, *Secretary*

18

PANEL ON REVIEW AND REFORM
May 2009

PROPOSED DELIVERANCE

The General Assembly
1. Receive the Report.
2. Discharge the Panel from its monitoring of the Church without Walls Group, recognising the latter's location within the Mission and Discipleship Council.
3. Invite Rural and Highland and Island Presbyteries to select congregations to participate in the facilitated Presbytery Visits to Congregations Pilot Scheme.
4. Invite Kirk Sessions to consider the Pilot Scheme for Presbytery Visits to Congregations and submit reaction and comment to the Panel by 30 November 2009.
5. Urge Councils, Presbyteries, congregations and agencies of the Church to incorporate the vision statement of the Church of Scotland on all correspondence and publicity material. (Section 9.7).
6. Invite Presbyteries to consider the models and questions for discussion in preparation for regional consultation with the Panel during 2009 (Section 10).
7. Invite Kirk Sessions to consider the models and questions for discussion and submit comments to the Panel by 30 September 2009 (Section 10).

REPORT

1. Introduction

He gave some to be apostles, some to be prophets, some to be evangelists, and some to be pastors and teachers, to prepare God's people for works of service, so that the body of Christ may be built up until we all reach unity in the faith and in the knowledge of the Son of God and become mature, attaining to the whole measure of the fullness of Christ.

Then we will no longer be infants, tossed back and forth by the waves, and blown here and there by every wind of teaching and by the cunning and craftiness of men in their deceitful scheming. Instead, speaking the truth in love, we will in all things grow up into him who is the Head, that is, Christ. From him the whole body, joined and held together by every supporting ligament, grows and builds itself up in love, as each part does its work. (Ephesians, 4: 11-17, NIV)

1.1 The Panel on Review and Reform emerged out of the restructuring proposals brought by its predecessor, the Assembly Council, which was discharged by the 2004 General Assembly. Since then, it has concentrated on its remit "to listen to the voices of congregations and Presbyteries, to present a vision of what a church in need of continual renewal might become and to offer paths by which congregations, Presbyteries and agencies might travel towards that vision."[1]

1.2 In collaboration with the Mission and Discipleship Council, we have continued to take forward the Pilot Scheme for Presbytery Visits to Congregations with particular emphasis on the process by which

---

[1] Assembly Council Report to the General Assembly 2004, 10/24, Appendix 2

congregations plan for the future and on how a record of planning for future mission can be incorporated effectively into the reporting procedures associated with the five-yearly Presbytery Visits.

1.3 The Panel, in partnership with the World Mission Council, has also begun research into the effect of overseas mission on the life of local church communities.

1.4 In addition to its work on vision, leadership and planning and following the report of the Special Commission on Structure and Change, the Panel was instructed by the 2008 General Assembly to:

bring to the General Assembly of 2010 proposals for an alternative Presbytery structure, including size, devolved powers, staffing, and appropriate budgets, along with the resources necessary to facilitate and sustain such changes.[2]

The Panel has focused on this remit during the last year.

1.5 Church without Walls Planning Group (CWW)
1.5.1 In its report to the General Assembly of 2008, the Mission and Discipleship Council was "pleased to welcome within the family of Mission and Discipleship the Church without Walls Planning Group."[3]

1.5.2 Since 2004, the Panel has continued to monitor the progress of CWW recommendations reporting various initiatives undertaken by the Group in its reports to the General Assembly. By its listening and reflecting, the Panel has helped to inform and encourage the Church to think creatively about how congregations might engage with the CWW ethos as they seek to be a changing church in Scotland today. Since the Mission and Discipleship Council is to take responsibility for the oversight of the CWW Planning Group, the Panel seeks to be discharged

from its monitoring role.

2. Superintendence
2.1 Forward Planning and the Presbytery Visit
2.1.1 The Panel reported to the General Assembly of 2008 the results of a questionnaire sent to all Presbyteries and Kirk Sessions. These had shown that there was widespread support for the practice of forward planning. In addition, there was equally strong support for this topic to be included in the report prepared for Presbytery following the Quinquennial Presbytery Visit.

2.2 Consequently, the Panel was instructed by the General Assembly "In consultation with the Mission and Discipleship Council and Legal Questions Committee to monitor and review the 'Future Focus' Pilot Scheme with Glasgow Presbytery and selected congregations with a view to bringing legislative amendments to Act II 1984 to the General Assembly in May 2009."[4]

2.3 Accordingly, the Panel has been involved in the piloting of "Future Focus", with particular emphasis on the process by which congregations plan for the future and on how a record of planning for future mission can be incorporated effectively into the reporting procedures associated with the five-yearly Presbytery Visit. As the Panel said in its report to the General Assembly of 2008: "The Panel suggests that the 'Basis for preparation by Congregation and discussion between Visiting-team and Office-bearers' includes a section on forward planning which would be discussed and formally recorded during the course of Presbytery visits. This would go some way towards helping to ensure that sourcing needs at congregational level are included in the preparation or review of Presbytery Plans."[5]

---

[2] Special Commission on Structure and Change, Deliverances of the General Assembly 2008, 28, section 4
[3] Mission and Discipleship Council, Report to the General Assembly of 2008, 4/42, 16.9

[4] Panel on Review and Reform, Report to the General Assembly 2008, deliverance section 11
[5] Panel on Review and Reform, Report to the General Assembly 2008, 19/15, 4.5.5

2.4 From the development of "Future Focus" there emerged a working model for the preparation and conduct of Presbytery Visits as well as a recommendation for the form of final report.

2.5 The pilot scheme for the actual visitation suggests a three-stage process:

1. *The Preparatory Phase* This involves the completion by the congregation of a comprehensive questionnaire "Advance Questions for Congregations" followed four weeks later by a brief meeting of the Visiting Team with the local planning group.

2. *The Consultation Phase* This recommends three separate visits by the Visiting Team:
   Evening No 1: The Healthy Church
   Evening No 2: The Timeline and Mapping our Community
   Day Event: Glimpsing New Horizons

3. *The Reporting Phase* This allows for the completion of the draft report which will be checked with the congregation for accuracy before submission to the Presbytery Superintendence Committee.

2.6 A copy of the document (see Appendix 1) describing in detail how the quinquennial visits might be carried out, including the sheet entitled "Advance Questions for Congregations" and a template for the final report was circulated to all Presbytery Clerks in November 2008. A copy of this document was also sent to the Depute Principal Clerk. Responses were requested by the end of January 2009.

2.6.1 Sixteen replies were received, and the Panel is grateful to those who took time to give a measured response to what was a challenging document. Responses from individual Presbyteries are outlined in Appendix 2.

2.6.2 The positive aspects identified were:
• They encouraged and facilitated visionary thinking and future planning.
• They provided a more thorough evaluation of a congregation's well-being than the current process.
• The Advance Questionnaire was seen to be very helpful in this respect.
• The document was a good tool to work with.

2.6.3 The negative aspects identified were:
• The document contained too much jargon and "management speak".
• The carrying-out of the proposed process would be hard to resource in terms of both manpower and time, putting extra stress on already hard-pressed ministers.
• The procedures were too complicated.
• For rural areas and island Presbyteries the suggested procedures would be unworkable because of the distances involved and the time needed to make the necessary visits.
• One respondent described the process as "administrative hoops" to be negotiated.

2.6.4 Many pointed out that training would be essential for those who visited.

2.7 The Panel recognises that amendments to the current proposals would be necessary, in particular to meet the special needs of the rural and island areas. The demands of resourcing the process in terms of time and personnel still have to be evaluated.

2.8 Consequently the Panel proposes that it should continue working with the Mission and Discipleship Council and the Legal Questions Committee as the pilot process proceeds in Glasgow Presbytery in order to address the various concerns that have been expressed. A final proposal would then be brought to the General Assembly of 2010 containing the necessary legislative amendments to Act II 1984.

3. Overseas Mission Partnership Project

3.1 The 2008 General Assembly agreed the Church without Walls Planning Group's invitation to the Panel and the World Mission Council to:

commission a study into the effect of overseas mission on the life of local church communities where they have an interactive partnership with an overseas project and consult with the appropriate bodies to ensure that financial resources can be made available to fund the study.[6]

3.2 The Panel met with representatives of the World Mission Council and the Church without Walls Planning Group to consider the nature and scope of the work and how it might be funded.

3.3 Dr Virginia Cano, an academic researcher with a proven background experience of World without Walls overseas partnerships was commissioned to work with Ms Carol Finlay, Associate Secretary (Local Development), World Mission Council whose work remit is to facilitate and encourage church twinnings with overseas partners.

3.4 A research methodology was agreed whereby an "in-depth case study analysis of the involvement of 12 Church of Scotland congregations and three Presbyteries in overseas interactive partnerships" would be undertaken under the Panel's supervision. The 15 partnerships to be studied were selected by Dr Cano and Ms Finlay to cover a range of experience and duration. As well as individual partnerships, Presbytery partnerships were included as were links established between urban, town and rural congregations both in this country and overseas. The work would involve face-to-face interviews where possible on an agreed set of indicators.

3.5 This work was begun in autumn 2008. The initial interview stage with the partners in Scotland has been completed and the work involved in contacting overseas partners is underway at the time of writing. The collation of the resulting information will allow for assessment of the impact of partnership for both participants. The second

phase of the project will be an on-line questionnaire to allow a wider participation from congregations who have relevant interactive overseas partnerships. Congregations and Presbyteries are invited to complete the questionnaire which will be hosted on the Panel's page of the Church of Scotland website http://www.churchofscotland.org.uk/councils/reviewreform/index.htm.

3.6 The Panel will report the outcome of this study to the 2010 General Assembly.

4. A Changing Church

4.1 The Assembly Council's proposals for structural change which was accepted by the 2004 General Assembly said, "… the Council is now bringing proposals that we believe will provide a more effective structure for strategic planning and the determination of priorities. It will also allow for a greater efficiency, increased flexibility, necessary rationalisation, and a clearer focus on resourcing the life and mission of local congregations."[7]

4.2 With the emphasis on the "central" (*ie* 121 George Street) resourcing the "local" and enabling the Church to be more focused on mission, the complicated structure of Boards and Committees was rationalised according to areas of work. This was both affirmed and criticised by the Special Commission on Structural Change at the 2008 General Assembly. The Commission stated that some of the disquiet that had been encountered about the centralisation of decision-making may have less to do with changes that have occurred and more to do with changes that have not occurred. Change at the centre has not been paralleled by change at Presbytery level.[8]

---

[6] [1] Church without Walls Planning Group, Report to the General Assembly 2008, 11/1, Deliverance section 8

[7] Assembly Council, Report to the General Assembly 2004, 10.7, 2.5.2
[8] Special Commission on Structure and Change, Report to the General Assembly of 2008, section 6.1

4.3 In general when proposals for change are articulated against what is familiar there are inevitable blocks to progress:
- fear of change;
- a lack of confidence allied to a sense of vulnerability or failure;
- too much negative thinking and not enough challenging;
- entrenched in the past with an over-dependence on Church law which results in the Church's trying to sell what is no longer attractive;
- a fear of losing control at all levels;
- power issues – on the one hand negative ("it can't be done"), on the other a lack of knowledge of how to empower;
- a lack of purpose which produces a watered-down sense of commitment.[9]

4.4 Some we have met in our consultations and discussions have described the church in general as being a "church in exile". The Exodus stories are an example of a time when God tipped history in a new direction and in so doing transformed Israel from a divergent group of slaves into a new kind of people. God chooses to create new futures in the most surprising places.

4.5 The church matters today. The period of change in which we find ourselves requires an adaptable church which can 'let go and let God' instead of holding on anxiously to what is familiar and within our comfort zones. The witness of the Bible points to a God who calls his people out and on from where they are, not knowing where they are to go. The true image of the church is the community of the future and not of the past. Exodus, exile, dispersion, pilgrimage – that is the church's experience and its life. It is the tradition of the Church of Scotland to adapt to change, sometimes radically, yet to retain its identity and its sense of calling and purpose as God's people.

5. Shared Vision For Reform

"Where there is no vision the people perish." (Proverbs 29:18, AV) *It impacts upon us and upon our world; we are never the same again once we determine exactly where it is we are trying to go. It influences our learning, our resources and how we use them, as well as affecting our relationships.*[10]

5.1 The consultation carried out by the Special Commission on Structure and Change asked a simple question: "Where is the Church of Scotland heading if we maintain our present course?"[11] The responses highlighted the absence of a coherent vision and a sense of despondency in the local church about the direction the national church is taking.[12] The Panel is firmly of the view that ownership of a shared vision and clear strategy for forward direction for the Church is the key to a strong future. The vision statement which the Panel introduced to the General Assembly in 2006 was distilled from a conference on the theme "God's vision for the Church of Scotland in the twenty-first century":

> *The **vision** of the Church of Scotland is to be a church which seeks to inspire the people of Scotland and beyond with the Good News of Jesus Christ through enthusiastic, worshipping, witnessing, nurturing and serving communities.*[13]

5.2 Any proposal for change in the structure at a presbytery level should facilitate the achievement of the vision for the Church of Scotland. It should facilitate worship and inspiration, a more comprehensive oversight of resources, and relational support for local mission.

---

[9] Panel on Review and Reform, Report to the General Assembly 2006, 19/5, 3.1.5

[10] Panel on Review and Reform, Report to the General Assembly 2005, 11/1, 1.1
[11] Special Commission on Structural Change, Report to the General Assembly 2008, 25/11 6.2
[12] Special Commission on Structural Change, Report to the General Assembly 2008, 25/11 6.2
[13] Panel on Review and Reform report 2006, 19/11, 8.1.2

The single biggest reason organisational changes fail is that no-one thought about the endings or planned to manage their impact on people. Naturally concerned about the future, planners and implementers usually forget that people have to let go of the present first. They forget that while the first task of change management is to understand the destination and how to get there, the first task of transition management is to convince people to leave home. [14]

5.3 Any proposed structure and all elements within it should be in harmony with the vision and it should always be possible, even during implementation, to demonstrate that this is the case. Placing shared values at the core of proposals for change emphasises that our values are fundamental to the development of all the critical elements of any presbytery structure. The Church's structure, strategy, systems, style, staffing and skills all stem from the call to follow Christ into service, the core purpose of the church.

6.   Structure and Change

6.1 The Panel has reviewed the available material on various proposals to reform the Church's structures since 1973:

> The Committee of Forty, 1973-79
> Abolition of Synods, 1992
> The Special Commission anent Review and Reform, 2001
> The Presbytery Boundaries Committee, 2001-2003
> The Council of Assembly and restructuring of the central administration of the church, 2004
> The Special Commission on Structure and Change, 2008

6.2 The Special Commission on Structure and Change commented that the reason power is concentrated at the

centre is "because there is no adequate repository for it elsewhere."[15] The deliverance of the General Assembly of 2004 on the report of the Assembly Council affirmed that the primary purpose of the Church's central administration was to equip, resource and support the local communities of faith in their worship, witness and service and beyond that, to enable the Church nationally to act, care and speak in ways that cannot effectively be done by congregations or Presbyteries alone, and to provide the support services required to sustain the necessary organisational infrastructure of a large denomination."[16] The Commission was convinced that entrusting Presbyteries with powers to raise and spend budgets would empower the local church in its missional activity. Determining the best structure at the regional level would be for the Church as a whole to decide.

6.3 Several responses to the questions posed by the Special Commission concerned the size of Presbyteries. Reducing the number of Presbyteries was clearly seen by some as a way for the Church to centralise decision-making. While there was some interest in co-operation between neighbouring Presbyteries, there was no great enthusiasm for mergers. However, several Presbyteries believed that change was necessary for a cohesive vision to be realised as small presbyteries may not have the skills or manpower to cope with greater responsibilities. One Presbytery was insistent that the present situation of 46 Presbyteries is untenable and suggested a reduction to around 15. Several responses suggested that larger presbyteries might facilitate greater devolution from the centre, although some warned against a "one size suits all" solution. Rural presbyteries tend to cover large geographical areas, and some responses felt that fewer presbyteries would present greater difficulties for travel and communication. Some suggested that the

---

[14] Bridges, William, *Managing Transitions*, Nicholas Brealey, 2003

[15] Special Commission on Structural Change, Report to the General Assembly 2008, 25/11, 6.2
[16] Special Commission on Structural Change, Report to the General Assembly 2008, 25/11, 6.2

role of Presbytery Clerk be made a full-time one. There was a clear feeling from the responses that rural and island Presbyteries believe that recent changes have affected their ability to influence policy. Presbyteries seemed to be evenly divided for and against larger groupings. However, some were in favour of a return to the pre-1992 synods. Whether or not the size of presbyteries remains unchanged, there was enthusiasm for devolving some resources to them. On such a sensitive matter there is always going to be a wide variety of views. Other Presbyteries expressed strong views on the following matters:

- the recent changes in structure were generally approved, with the proviso that it is too soon to judge any improvements;
- the Church without Walls's vision of a "church upside down" has not yet been realised;
- the question of communication between the three courts of the Church must be addressed, in particular communication from central administration;
- there is no consensus on the future size and responsibilities of presbyteries, but a general desire for devolution of resources was expressed;
- wish for greater responsibility for financial budgeting and allocation at local level;
- while the process of Parish Appraisal was generally recognised as necessary, some Presbyteries felt that relationships had been damaged and congregations demoralised;
- moving from a maintenance/decline mindset to missional thinking is essential, but it is necessary to have that vision articulated.

7. Ecclesia Reformata Semper Reformanda?

7.1 The Panel believes the unifying narrative for the Church can only be one of renewal – reformed and always reforming. There is organic vigour in the Church today but only in some parts and in contrasting styles. The Panel actively encourages the drive for a more cohesive vision for the Church to be realised, but our sense at the moment is that this is more a hope than a reality.

7.2 While the Panel has been asked to present proposals for an alternative presbytery structure, it recognises that structural change of Presbyteries on its own is not enough and will not solve the problems of the Church. There are issues of leadership, mindset, people, process, and a need to seek a more effective way of "being church" locally, regionally and nationally.

7.3 Many congregations have made positive changes and reached out to their communities despite secularisation and the numerical decline of the Church. Nonetheless, we are out of touch with a significant majority of the Scottish population despite our constitutional commitment to mission. The four hundred and fiftieth anniversary of the Reformation and the centenary of the Edinburgh World Missionary Conference in 2010 serve to frame the challenge for us today – for whom does the Church of Scotland exist – the people in the Church or God's people out in the world?

7.4 The Panel invites the whole Church to join together in redesigning its future driven by a visionary purpose and commitment commensurate with the theology of the reformed tradition. "The re-formation of the Church today is about freeing God's people from itself."[17] The first reformation was about freeing the Church, the second reformation is about mission: not structural change, but renewal and engagement within and beyond existing structures. There are different structural possibilities but the Panel feels that regional identity with specific functions could provide an energising and interconnecting dimension that would empower parishes, decentralising agreed functions to enable better focus locally. It would provide forums where enabling mission would take precedence over administration or judicial proceedings.

7.5 There is of course a caveat. If more functions were devolved from the central administration, it would be necessary to identify leaders with skills and experience who would manage and be responsible for each of them.

---

[17] McNeal, R, *The Present Future*, Jossey Boss, 2003, p 43

8. What Is Presbytery For?

8.1 The Committee of Forty Report of 1977 affirmed the functions of presbytery as
1. The proclamation and communication of the Gospel.
2. The mutual support and strengthening which congregations, people and Ministers ought to have from each other; and
3. Proper oversight of all aspects of the life and work of the Church. [18]

8.2 These functions are closely connected and should not be carried out in isolation from one another. The Committee saw the task of presbytery to be the proclamation and communication of the Gospel: worship, mission, teaching, encouraging the presbytery itself "to recover the sense of being not only an administrative body but a company of men and women brought together to wait upon God and learn together what the true priorities are." [19] It is especially important that the presbytery should become the focus of the Church's missionary task.

8.3 At present Presbyteries are expected to fulfil the following key functions, (which for this exercise have been listed by the Principal Clerk's Department):

Planning Related
Approval of the annual update of the Presbytery Plan in terms of Act VII 2003
Changes to Presbytery Plan produced by unexpected circumstances
Implementation of Presbytery Plan as vacancies arise
Vacancy work in terms of Act VIII 2003, by Vacancy Procedure Committee
Vacancies issues referred under s 2 of Act VIII 2003

Ministry related
Some elements of supervision of trainee ministers in terms of Act X 2004 (and all equivalent legislation for deacons, auxiliaries, readers)

Practising Certificates (most at the same time of year, but new applications may arrive at any time, and must be dealt with timeously to enable the applicant's ministry to continue)
Ministries flow: ordinations, inductions, demissions, deaths and tributes
Admission and Re-admission, Presbytery element of Act IX 2002

Supervision related
Routine superintendence functions, especially Act II 1984
Non-routine superintendence functions, especially Act I 1988 (unsatisfactory state), Act IV 2001 (ministers and public office), Act XV 2002 (illness), Act XIII 2000 (NCD), Act VI 1984 (changed state) – and note that many of these functions require more than one meeting of the Presbytery
Non-routine disciplinary functions: *eg* Act V 2000 (sacraments), Acts IV and V 2007 (bullying and discrimination), and to a limited extent Act III 2001 (discipline of ministers and others)
Congregational Constitutions see Act XIX 1964

General Assembly related
Commissions to the General Assembly (currently requires more than one meeting)
Consideration of Overtures under the Barrier Act
Consideration of other remits addressed to the Presbytery by the GA

Finance related
Mission and Renewal contributions (may require more than one meeting)

Property and finance – supervisory tasks largely delegated, see *eg* Act VII 1995

Presbytery administration
Election of Presbytery Moderator, and appointment of committees
Commissions by Kirk Sessions to Presbytery (most at the same time of year, but may arrive at any time depending on

---

[18] Committee of Forty Report, 1997, 483 ff
[19] Committee of Forty Report, 1997, 483 ff

circumstances, and must be dealt with timeously)

Appointment of Presbytery Clerk, or any other paid post which is vacant

Examination of Presbytery records

Judicial

Judicial tasks: appeals, dissents and complaints, overtures, petitions

Miscellaneous tasks relating to the court itself, its relations to other courts, and the ministry, in terms of Acts II and III 2000

Policy making

Pursuing issues of public interest – may sometimes require Presbytery action

8.4 What we focus on becomes our reality. If many Presbytery courts have become little more than business meetings which deal with the necessary administration and legislation, then what has happened to the Presbytery as focus for inspiration, renewal and mission?

8.5 There is a sense that in some areas that the present structures are not working. Repeated attempts to urge the Church to consider an alternative presbytery structure suggest that there is some unease with the one we have now. Throughout the Church, we hear that many of our ministers and members are tired – of the ever-increasing burden of administration, of diminishing resources, with "yet another matter we have to discuss, debate and report on".

8.6 During the course of the Panel's consultations and discussions, we have met with enthusiasm, creativeness, a genuine willingness to work positively to discern a better structure – and cynicism ('all the other attempts have failed so …'). What the Church should have is a structure that supports and feels supported, works efficiently and is focused on a shared vision for its future. All of us want a church which is vibrant and renewing, and serves God and the community.

9. Regional Church Conference

9.1 The first consultation towards fulfilling the remit was with Presbytery and Council representatives in September 2008.

9.2 The Panel presented the following statements and the subsequent hypothesis for discussion:

The vision of the Church of Scotland is:

to be a church which seeks to inspire the people of Scotland and beyond with the Good News of Jesus Christ through enthusiastic worshipping, witnessing, nurturing and serving communities.

(Panel on Review and Reform, Report to the General Assembly, 2006)

One vision of the future, developed by the Panel was:

- *2,000,000 people put their faith into action across Scotland and beyond.*
- *Regional centres resource thousands of faith communities.*
- *After fifty years of CWW, the final wall has tumbled.*
- *Fabric of the church is founded on relationships rather than bricks and mortar.*

The Third Declaratory Article states that, as a national Church representative of the Christian faith of the Scottish people it acknowledges its distinctive call and duty to bring the ordinances of religion to the people in every parish of Scotland through a territorial ministry.

The Panel's hypothesis is:

"Given the above as our context – IF 121 CLOSES IN 2015, AND PRESBYTERIES NO LONGER EXIST – what is the best way to achieve this Vision?"

9.3 The participants went on to discuss and develop thinking based on the question:

Within the ideas which we have begun to create today, how will we best ----------------------?

9.4 Each group chose one of the following themes:
- *Worship*
- *Witness*
- *Nurture*
- *Service*
- *Involve young people in Christian faith*
- *Enable ministry*
- *Enable mission*
- *Put faith into action within communities*
- *Train for ministries of the future*
- *Distribute financial resources*
- *Distribute human resources*
- *Relate ecumenically*

9.5 Participants were urged to focus on the things they would look for in any future structure using the Panel's vision statement as a stimulus for thought. The key questions were designed to elicit enough information to help us understand the complexity of our task and to derive something more concrete to work with in the months ahead.

9.6 From the 44 Presbyteries and Council members represented, it emerged that there was a willingness to take risks, try new things and seek change to the current system of governance. Participants welcomed the opportunity to share and discuss their ideas with others.

9.7 There was a strong feeling that the Panel's vision statement should be more strongly promoted throughout the Church, perhaps appearing on Church newsletters and in publicity material.

9.8 The Panel was encouraged to explore the following in more depth:
- possibilities for devolved powers
- effective communication
- the role and size of presbytery
- resourcing – financial, human, support and training
- management and administration
- buildings used creatively and effectively

- the importance of building fellowship
- encouraging ecumenical links/resourcing
- encouraging the gifts/talents of all people
- identifying and encouraging key leaders
- discerning the community needs
- developing a shared 'resource bank' of gifts and specialisms

9.9 For any proposal for change to be taken forward, it was recognised that
- we need clear guiding principles
- worshipping communities need to be flexible
- ministry and mission are key to all we do
- we need effective community church collaboration
- we need clear devolved responsibility for budgets and resourcing
- we need a clear framework of governance, accountability and authority

10. A Variety Of Models

10.1.1   There is no one single or normative model of church life. The agreed model/s for an alternative presbytery structure should take careful account of the particular time and circumstance into which God's people are called. For example, Highlands and Islands, central belt, urban, suburban, priority area and rural charges will have a common operating structure but require sufficient flexibility according to regional and local need. The Panel recognises that "one size fits all" would not work and invites Presbyteries and congregations to join with them to consider a more dynamic model for the Church that will.

10.1.2   To set that process in motion the Panel proposes to set up regional forums to debate and develop the models during the summer and autumn of 2009. Each forum will examine what functions might be devolved from "121" to any alternative structure and which might be passed from the current presbytery structure to a central administration. The conclusions will be collated and brought to the General Assembly in 2010, along with specific recommendations. The hope would be the regional church, duly reshaped, would help revitalise the Church and enable it to reconnect with Scottish society.

10.1.3   The Panel offers five potential models to assist discussion based on the information gathered from our 2008 Regional Church Conference and other meetings and discussions we have been involved in. The models range from the current presbytery pattern of working to a fully devolved regional structure.

10.1.4   At the moment, the information provided is minimal, drawn from the information that was offered to the Panel. We invite Presbyteries to help us provide more detail, more 'meat to the bones', from your own areas of local knowledge and expertise. We have an open mind on what might emerge from this important stage of the process.

10.1.5   Each model is outlined below with a simple diagrammatical structure and some key features. It must be stressed that the models are presented in the barest outline to give the General Assembly a flavour of where the Panel's consultations may or may not lead. The Panel will continue to consult with the whole Church to add more detail to the models, from which a firm proposal for an alternative presbytery structure will emerge.

Model 1
Current Presbytery Pattern

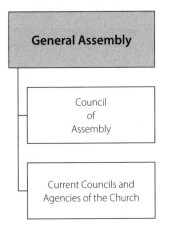
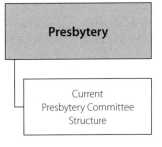
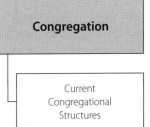

Key Features:

This is the "Do nothing" model, in which structures and functions remain unchanged. If the Church decides to maintain this model, how is the vision to be achieved?

Model 2
Presbyteries Model

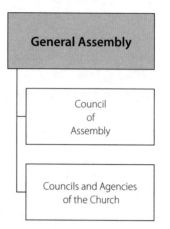

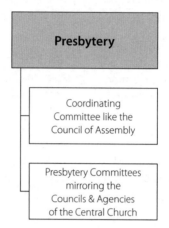

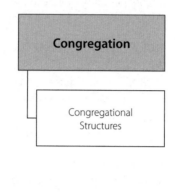

Key Features:

This is to take the current presbytery pattern a stage further with a focus on re-energising it to perform effectively across the Church, and to share and promote effective practices for the benefit of all. There is no change to the structure, instead an emphasis on reforming the existing Presbyteries so that they all become models of excellence in oversight and mission.

This will be achieved by systematically examining what all Presbyteries do, with a view to enabling Presbyteries to function well both administratively and as mission enablers, helping to facilitate local congregations in their worship, witness, nurture, and service.

More collaboration within Presbyteries and between Presbyteries will be encouraged as will the sharing of expertise, good practice and leadership.

If any structural change is involved, it is where Presbyteries operate under the current Council of Assembly template by forming committees that correspond to the work of Councils of the General Assembly. It is hoped this will allow for a more holistic approach in the way the Church defines its work, with central structures and presbytery structures that complement one another.

The central Church will be encouraged to resource the local church with the presbytery identifying where resourcing is to be targeted within its bounds. For Presbyteries to function well there will be a focus on identifying training needs and supplying those needs as well as trying to identify and match the right people for the right tasks.

As Presbyteries develop it may be that they will be better able to take responsibility for some devolution of key functions from the central Church and the responsibility and accountability that goes with that. The main thrust of this model will be to do what we already do but do it better.

Model 3
Regional Councils Model

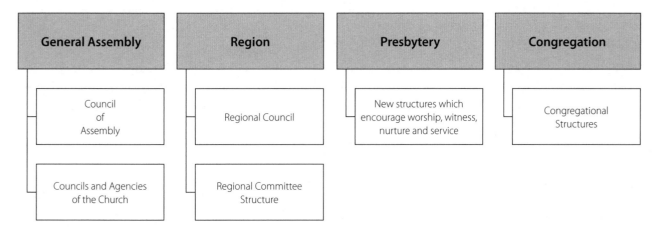

Key Features:

This model again retains the current presbytery pattern but groups presbyteries into a number of distinct geographical regions, each with a regional council. The exact number of regions is for the whole Church to decide but for the sake of discussion let us imagine the formation of five geographical regions.

Each regional council would take responsibility for key tasks from both presbyteries and from the central Church. With administrative functions removed from presbytery and relocated within the regional council, Presbyteries would be able to focus more on support and encouragement in order to facilitate local congregations in their worship, witness, nurture, and service.

With the devolution of key tasks from the central Church agreed powers will be devolved from the centre to the regions making some decision-making more local eg the resourcing of ministries could be devolved to a regional council bringing such decision-making and responsibility closer to presbyteries. It is hoped that regions would take on the responsibility of resourcing presbyteries who in turn may be better able to resource the congregations within their bounds.

In essence, some central functions would be devolved to regional councils while administrative functions would be taken from presbytery and dealt with by regional councils. This would mean that presbyteries remain as the current pattern but perform a different function ie are freed to worship, witness, nurture, and serve.

19

Model 4
Presbytery Region Model

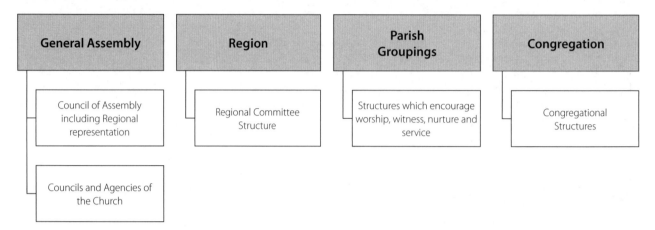

Key Features:

The fourth model involves structural change of presbyteries. The number of presbyteries would reduce with the formation of a number of presbytery regions. Again the exact number of regions is for the whole Church to decide but for the sake of discussion let us imagine the formation of around 8-15 geographical regions each of which may be likened to a kind of "super-presbytery".

Within each region, parish groupings would be developed to encourage local relating and collaboration. The size of these groupings could be increased or reduced to suit local geographical considerations. It is envisaged that they would be around the size and shape of the current Presbyteries. These parish groupings would be responsible for worship, witness, nurture and service while the regions would be responsible for the administrative tasks and agreed key functions devolved from the central Church.

A significant difference in this model is that each region would be represented on the Council of Assembly so that both central and regional functions could have clear open lines of communication encouraging the pursuit of a shared vision across the Church.

The pattern of meetings would be decided locally but in order to reduce the amount of time spent in administration, it is suggested that a region would meet just twice a year with much of the work being undertaken executively with accountability to the region similar to what currently happens with the General Assembly.

Each region would be responsible for resourcing ministry and mission according to the local needs of their parish groupings.

Model 5
Parish Model

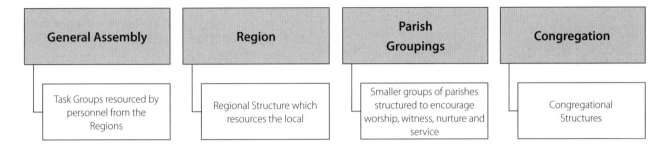

Key Features:

Of the five models presented this model involves the most radical change. It works on the principle of local groups which ensure local relating between congregations and is driven by congregations in parish groupings, supported by regions which perform the functions of the central Church. There is no central church as we currently know it, no "121", but rather all operations are devolved to the region. This means working with a shared vision at local level and sharing resources in a greater way than we do at present.

Presbyteries would amalgamate to form a number of regions. Once again the exact number of regions is for the whole Church to decide and these could vary in size.

Within each region, parish groupings would be developed to encourage local relating and collaboration. The size of these groupings would depend on local considerations but they would be much smaller than current Presbyteries and there would be a greater number of them (*ie* a large number of smaller groupings to ensure greater sharing and interaction between parishes). These parish groupings would be responsible for worship, witness, nurture and

service while the regions would be responsible for the administrative tasks and all functions of the central Church which would be devolved as there would be no "121".

Although there would be no central church as we currently know it, the Church of Scotland would have a national presence so national functions of the Church would be carried out by members of the regions coming together to resource such functions. Where national strategy or oversight was required members of the regions would come together to resource these tasks. Thus we would have a church turned upside down where the local resourced the national.

Specialists would be relocated in regions and would work for the regions with a proportion of their time set aside for central tasks. This is a model currently operated by the Mission and Discipleship Council in the deployment of Regional Development Officers (RDOs) where each RDO is located in a region but also offers their speciality to the central Church. This would ensure equity of standards across the Church in areas of work where that was required and would prevent duplication of effort in each region.

10.2 What makes a good model that will work for the Church?

10.2.1 To help facilitate that discussion, the Panel invites all Presbyteries to discuss the five models and engage with the following questions:

1. Remembering your entire experience at your Presbytery, when were you most alive, most motivated and excited about your involvement? What made it exciting? Who else was involved? What was your part?
2. What do you value most about your Presbytery? What functions are most important? What are the best features of your Presbytery?
3. Make three wishes for the future of the Presbytery.
4. What needs to happen to make that vision happen?
5. What are the first practical steps that you need to take?
6. Where do we look for the sources of energy to initiate these changes?
7. What is the cost of implementing these changes? Financial and Ministry resources?
8. What resistance do you anticipate?
9. If your Presbytery were to move towards the vision you imagine, what support would you value from the Church?
10. How might the Presbytery be shaped and organised to enable better engagement with the people of Scotland?

11. Conclusion

> Polity is the architecture of mission. Missional polity places the congregation in the forefront of the church's witness because it is the place where the church engages the world. The councils of the church (ie sessions, presbyteries … and the General Assembly) exist to guide, support and govern the work of the congregation and to connect and co-ordinate that work with other congregations, so that the whole church may witness more effectively to the activity of God in the world.

> The Presbytery is responsible for the government of the church throughout its district and for assisting and supporting the witness of congregations to the sovereign activity of God in the world, so that all congregations become signs in and for the world of the new reality God has made available to all in Jesus Christ.[20]

11.1 "It is helpful to have such a reminder of our core business which resonates with the Special Commission's call not just for a new presbytery structure but for a new presbytery agenda which is less about maintaining an institution and more about witnessing to the activity of God in the world."[21]

11.2 We have an exciting opportunity to reconsider what presbyteries might become. Already some Presbyteries have adopted a different way of working. The Panel's remit provides us all with the opportunity to work collaboratively to achieve a radical change in the shape and function of the regional church, to provide relational support to strengthen ministry and resource missional opportunities, for worship and inspiration, and to ensure comprehensive oversight of church resources. The reshaping of Presbyteries should reflect so far as is possible the nature of the church as God's people and the body of Christ *joined and held together by every supporting ligament, that grows and builds itself up in love, as each part does its work.*

In the name of the Panel

DAVID S CAMERON, *Convener*
MARINA D BROWN, *Vice-convener*

---

[20] Keynote Address Regional Church Conference, Crieff 2008, the Very Rev Dr Finlay A J Macdonald
[21] Keynote Address Regional Church Conference, Crieff 2008, the Very Rev Dr Finlay A J Macdonald

APPENDIX 1
THE PRESBYTERY OF GLASGOW
A PILOT PROCESS FOR QUINQENNIAL VISITS
USING
"FUTURE FOCUS":
A WAY FORWARD FOR CONGREGATIONS

Background

> **How to use these Notes**
>
> Pages 1-5 are to be sent to the minister in advance of the meeting with the Planning group with a letter of explanation about the process and the timetable. This alerts the congregation to the scope of the consultation and the focus of the report.
>
> Pages 6-7 are to be issued after the initial conversation with the Planning Group and to be returned within four weeks of the first evening.

What? Why? How?

In consultation with the Panel on Review and Reform, who have been evaluating the process of Quinquennial Visits across the Church of Scotland, the Presbytery of Glasgow has agreed to pilot an alternative process during 2008-09. This process is designed to help congregations discern God's calling for the next five years, and to give the Presbytery a better handle on the decisions relating to support and mission planning.

The resource materials are extracted and adapted from a congregational resource called "Future Focus– A Way Forward for Congregations". This material was commissioned by the Mission and Discipleship Council and is being piloted more widely across Scotland. The Glasgow Pilot Scheme is therefore part of a two-track initiative to help congregations take a serious look at their calling at this time – one broader scheme which is entirely voluntary, and this more specific version which is designed to be integrated into the regular work of Presbytery support and oversight.

The process involves some advance preparation by the congregation and with the visiting team. The team will be expected to meet the congregation on two evenings and over the course of a day to "glimpse new horizons" together. In the light of these explorations of the congregation's life, the facilitator and visiting team will prepare a report for the Presbytery modelled on a suggested template to ensure some consistency in the reporting.

These notes outline:

1. The preparatory phase – a brief meeting with the local planning group to explain the process, and to issue the congregational questionnaire to be returned four weeks before the first evening.

2. The consultation phase
   Evening No 1: The Healthy Church
   Evening No 2: The Timeline and Mapping our Community
   Day Event: Glimpsing New Horizons

   A meeting with the Minister will be arranged on Evening No 1 and a meeting with the Treasurer and Fabric Convener will be arranged with the appropriate team members on Evening No 2 (or as is convenient).

3. The reporting phase – the completion of the draft report, to be checked with the congregation for accuracy and submitted to the Presbytery Superintendence Committee within six weeks of the final visit.

Who? – The Facilitator and Team

As Churches take a fresh look at their future, it helps to have a companion to share the journey. The one thing the facilitator cannot do is to anticipate the destination. It is not the role of the facilitator to impose a particular shape which would be his or her desired outcome. That is between the congregation and God. However, the facilitator will ask challenging questions along the way to stimulate, encourage and confront issues that emerge.

The Presbytery Facilitator will be accompanied by members of the Support and Development Team appointed for that congregation. On the first evening, the team will arrange to meet with the minister on the same evening as The Health Check. On the second evening, team members will meet with the Treasurer and Fabric Convener at an appropriate time. The whole team will be present for the day conference and be responsible for the final report.

With whom? – Congregational Leadership

This process is directed at "the leadership" of the congregation – elders, office-bearers and others with significant roles of leadership. We do not meet with the elders and financial court separately. This is an open process where various stakeholders help the congregation to gain "future focus".

The Preparatory Phase

In order to ensure that dates are lined up in diaries, the Facilitator will contact the minister of the congregation three months in advance by phone to outline the process, to suggest dates and to fix a date for meeting a planning group. This initial contact will be followed up by letter confirming the arrangements.

We suggest that the congregation appoints a small Planning Group consisting of the minister and no more than six other office-bearers. In order to explain the new process in detail, and to confirm the sequence of dates for the consultation times, it is recommended that the visiting team meet briefly with the Planning Group two months ahead of planned visits.

The Planning Group will be responsible for completing the questionnaire which is to be found in Appendix No 1. This will be issued after the initial conversation and returned at least four weeks before the visit.

Conversation Starters

The conversation with the Planning Group relates the congregation's story, setting, style, strategy, structure and spirituality. This will give early indicators of the congregation's life, health and missionary opportunities.

- Think back over the last ten years. Share the recent story of your congregation – the celebrations, the struggles and the dreams. Where have we seen God at work among us?
- Looking ahead for the next five years, what changes are we experiencing in our communities? What challenges and opportunities do these changes present to our congregation? What would Jesus do here?
- As we look at our congregational life, what encourages us? What concerns us?
- Review the general facts about membership, worship attendance, leadership structure, fabric and finance. What story do they tell to us – and to the outside observer? [Introduce the questionnaire which asks for more detail about these issues and ask for it to be returned four weeks before the first evening visit.]
- How is the spiritual life of people in this congregation being deepened? What biblical passages or themes shape the life of the congregation?

Key Question
In the light of this conversation,
what question – if answered – would help you
share more effectively in God's mission in your
community at this time?

- Presbytery Plan: what are the interim steps and 10 year conclusions for your congregation in the Presbytery Plan? How do you see these working out?

The Consultation Phase

There are no short-cuts to vision, but we have identified a starting route which offers some analysis, reflection, vision-building. Since this material is extracted from a larger range of resources, we call this "The Green Route":

- The Health Check
- The Timeline
- Mapping our Community
- Glimpsing New Horizons

Note: The order of the first two evenings is optional. The timeline and mapping are more interactive in eliciting the local story. This may be a better place to start for some congregations. That choice can be discussed at the meeting with the Planning Group.

The Reporting Phase

Presbytery Focus

Since this exercise is being undertaken on behalf of Presbytery, the team will require to consider some strategic questions and decisions that may have to be made. The following questions are a guide to the questions which the team may want to ask as they prepare their report.

Where the congregation is thriving

- How can the Presbytery affirm and nurture this life further?
- How can the Presbytery encourage the sharing of this vitality with others?

Where the congregation is facing up to specific challenges (internally or externally)

- What changes are needed in attitudes, relationships, strategy or structure?
- What specific resources are needed to meet this challenge *eg* developing worship, discipleship, practical skills in finance/fabric, deepening spirituality?
- What are the potential partnerships with other agencies, other churches?
- What support is needed to resolve internal conflict/dysfunction?

Where the congregation can no longer sustain this model of church life or engage in effective mission

- What other form of Christian presence would they consider?
- What other partnerships would they consider?
- What resourcing is needed to equip the congregation for a new future?
- What is the pastoral process of closure and/or dissolution?

Where the congregation is no longer in synch with the community

- What long-term process is needed to help them reconnect?
- Who will be the facilitator of the process?

The Report

The report will be written in two stages. The congregational dreams and goals articulated at the vision day will be summarised and relayed back to the congregation as a collation of their ideas and suggestions. There will be a rich mixture of big ideas and small steps which must not be lost for the congregation. This can be used as a reference point for implementing the specific recommendations of the Presbytery Team.

The second stage is writing the report for the Presbytery Superintendence Committee and the Mission Strategy Committee, consisting of 2-3 sides of A4. This will include specific visions and goals agreed by the congregational group present at the "vision day", and also any specific recommendations from the visiting team regarding a Presbytery response.

The report will include comment on the Presbytery Plan. The recommendations will include specific points for the Mission Strategy Committee to update the

Presbytery Plan if required *eg* in terms of appraisal, partners, personnel, buildings, noting the effect of these recommendations on the grouping.

The Presbytery Report should follow the following template:

A. Reference Information
1. Charge and Ministry Team
2. Team visiting
3. Timetable of visits

B. Background Information
1. Brief historical background
2. Significant local factors

C. Executive Summary
Summarise key conclusions in 100-200 words.

D. Conclusions
1. Identify the vision and goals articulated by the congregation.
2. Identify any specific areas for encouragement or concern
3. Identify any Presbytery response required.

E. Recommendations (as appropriate)
1. For the Kirk Session
2. For the Minister/Ministry Team
3. For the Financial Court
4. For the Presbytery – for Superintendence and Mission Strategy (Presbytery Plan)
5. For the Councils of the Church

Appendices (to be retained in the Superintendence files, but not presented to Presbytery)
1. The response to the Advance Questionnaire
2. Any interim reports/notes of the various stages of the process.
3. The current audited accounts

The Timetable
The following timetable should be strictly adhered to and any delay reported to the Committee member responsible for overseeing arrangement for Quinquennial Visits:
•   within two weeks of completing the process – facilitator to complete the first draft
•   within three weeks – to clear the report with other team members
•   within four weeks – to clear factual accuracy of the Presbytery report with the Session Clerk and send a report of the summary of the congregational responses to "Glimpsing New Horizons" for information and appropriate action.
•   within six weeks – to submit report to the Presbytery office.

Presbytery of Glasgow
Pilot Scheme for Quinquennial Visits
"Future Focus": A Way Forward for Congregations
Advance Questions for Congregations

Congregation ....

Dates of Consultation ....

Facilitator ....

Support and Development Team ....

Return to ....

Return by ....

When the visiting team meets with the planning group they will engage in a conversation that allows you to share something of you story with your encouragements and concerns, and to identify some of the challenges which you face as you face the future. The conversation will help the team understand a bit more of the way this congregation operates and the spirituality that shapes your life together.

Factual Questions
These deeper issues are best dealt with in conversation, but it also helps to know a few facts. In order to help us all make the most of this consultation process, please provide information and appropriate comment on the following areas of your church's life:

1.   Membership: graph of statistics for the past ten years, age profile (estimated)
2.   Worship: average attendance over a month (numbers, age groups, gender), style, musical range, use of visuals, innovations
3.   Pastoral Care: baptisms, weddings, funerals per year, specific demands of the situation, ways of sharing responsibilities
4.   Christian Nurture: numbers involved in Christian nurture: children, young people, young adults, adults; resources used
5.   Mission: specific mission initiatives – local or international, school involvement or other chaplaincies, evangelism training and strategies, communication
6.   Leadership: staffing, numbers of office-bearers, training, structure, constitution
7.   Buildings: usage, state of repair, suitability, projects
8.   Finance: accounts, budget, allocations, shortfalls, Christian giving plans, special projects, graph of giving over ten years
9.   Support for Minister: administrative support, travelling expenses, study leave, additional staff needs
10. Wider Church: relationship with Presbytery, Councils of the Church and ecumenical relationships
11. Presbytery Plan: what are the interim steps and 10 year conclusions for your congregation in the Presbytery Plan? How do you see these working out?

Legal Questions

We are required to check that certain legal regulations are being fulfilled:

1. Safeguarding requirements: Child Protection Policy, Child Protection Officer
2. OSCR requirements: copy of accounts
3. Presbytery Plan

Key Point

What key issues would you like to discuss with the visiting team?

APPENDIX 2
A PILOT PROCESS FOR QUINQUENNIAL VISITS

SUMMARY OF REPLIES FROM PRESBYTERIES
(AS AT 20.02.09)

Stirling

Positives: Forward planning; advance questions seem searching and appropriate; Scheme should help all congregations to look closely and honestly at where they are and where they are going.

Negatives: a need to watch jargon and the questions (health check, synch, mapping, timeline, getting a handle on *etc.* not necessarily all helpful expressions).

Comments: Where will the resources come from to help Presbyteries, work where churches need considerable help? Training necessary for Visiting Teams and Facilitators.

Irvine and Kilmarnock

Positives: shows a more thorough evaluation than at present, gained through directed, guided questions, all of which were felt sensible; focus on future planning and mission felt, in the long term to be helpful to congregation.

Possible negatives: process will be expensive in terms of personnel time; a question of whether there would be sufficient people with the necessary skills for the new process to work well.

Comments: Any authority should lie with the Presbytery and not with the facilitator and Support and Development Team. Good relationships are important and in a smallish Presbytery it was recognised that there may be difficulty in challenging a congregation which has no future plans. Perhaps there is a role here for a reciprocal arrangement between neighbouring Presbyteries to carry out Presbytery Visits.

"The principle of what we have been presented with is right – an expansion of what we do at present. It has the potential to encourage new thinking in our Presbytery. But care should be taken not to make it so authoritative that folk are discouraged or feel overwhelmed by the recommendations."

Kirkcaldy

Positives: It is a good tool for our teams to work with. I look forward to hearing more about it at the Presbytery Clerks' conference.

Comments: It requires a good structure and trained people in place to work effectively. In Kirkcaldy I think we now have that.

Lochcarron – Skye

Positives: Would repair the deficiencies in our current QV arrangements.

Negatives: Manpower requirements would present difficulties; the number of visits envisaged by the scheme would also present difficulties, as the distances between certain parishes require a return trip of 246 miles.

Comments: We believe an amended scheme could be produced for smaller Presbyteries where parishes are remote from one another. We look forward with interest to the results of the Glasgow pilot scheme.

Argyll

Negatives: We have reservations about the practicalities and methodology of the draft scheme in so far as rural and island Presbyteries are concerned. Adoption of the draft scheme would be impractical on account of the large number of rural and island charges. Adoption of the draft scheme would be inordinately expensive due to the amount of travelling required.

Comment: "The Presbytery of Argyll is of the opinion that if the draft scheme is to be made mandatory, it should be road tested in more than one rural and island Presbytery before legislation is drafted."

Orkney

The Resources Committee have decided to adopt the Questionnaire of the pilot scheme, the page of the reporting process and made another few alterations to the existing guidelines. This material is now offered for use by Visiting Teams and visited congregations.

Comments: While special training of the visiting teams is desirable, it was felt that a preparatory meeting of the team would have to suffice for practical reasons.

The many helpful ideas in the "Future Focus" Pilot Scheme run in Glasgow were acknowledged but the intensity of the process made it very cumbersome and hard to resource in small Presbyteries and those handicapped by geographical location, *eg* islands.

Uist

Positives: none mentioned.

Negatives: Geography made it difficult to facilitate all the required meetings; small scattered congregations would lead to poor participation; the limited number of personnel would make it difficult to staff; Kirk Sessions have a better understanding of what is possible in their own congregations; Presbytery could not envisage what tangible benefits could be gained from the time, energy and resources that would be required to carry out the process.

Jedburgh – This was a personal opinion and not necessarily the view of the Presbytery

Positives: The Panel is well-intentioned.

Negatives: Ministers and elders forced to jump through extra administrative hoops; Pressures on ministers already great without ratcheting up "the scale of congregational and presbyterial management; where is the time coming from for these super-quinquennials? The extra demands on the visitation team, the minister and office-bearers of the congregation seem not to have been taken into account; the idea of a Day Conference? (with proposals such as these) "the Kirk risks stumbling toward the strangulated ineffective nightmare that Ron Ferguson….. foretells in his Clarence McGonigall series."

Abernethy

Positives: Looks helpful and creative.

Negatives: Finding time to implement it is going to be difficult.

Sutherland

Positives: Process forces congregations to think out their vision for the future.

Negatives: Not sufficient information; timetable too rigid. Too time consuming and too much travelling. Process is cumbersome.

Comments: Complete Pilot and then ask for comments on the report. Mechanics do not fit a rural area. It would be better to set down the principles and what is to be achieved and then let local areas find ways to accomplish that. Process should run in every Presbytery for ten years.

Perth

Positives: Requirement to identify and establish future goals.

Comments: The Consultation Phase can be achieved on one evening and the Visit Day. Not necessary to have separate meetings with Treasurer and Fabric Convener.

West Lothian

Positives: None

Negatives: Shallow in ideas. Lacking in an historical awareness and theology of the Church and its ministry. Management speak! Process too complicated and too time-consuming. (There are several questions all negative in tone.)

Presbytery of Europe

Positives: none mentioned

Negatives: Difficult and expensive to carry out the required meetings.

Comments: Currently, congregations give information about worship over a period of a month. Since 1992 the Presbytery has conducted a survey every four years to examine attendance and other information such as age profile, denominational background, nationality about those in worship one particular day, as a snapshot of the congregation across the Presbytery. This has allowed a picture to be built up of each worshipping community over the past 15 years.

Lothian
Comments: Urge the Panel to make specific provision for good ideas and innovative projects to be briefly described (along with contact details) in the new style of Presbytery report, and also to consider developing a national Church of Scotland "innovation database" to share ideas and experiences as widely as possible throughout the whole Church.

In some cases current reports do not mention areas where criticism is merited, it being difficult for some ministers who rely on fostering good relationships with their colleagues to be critical of them.

Caithness
Positives: "Advance Questions for Congregations (Appendix 1) are an excellent idea, ahead of the Quinquennial Visitation."

Comments: A series of suggested amendments to terminology.

PROPOSED DELIVERANCE

The General Assembly

1. Receive the Report.
2. Recognise the way in which the Fund has continued to make possible new and exciting ways of the Good News being lived out - ways that involve congregations and projects engaging more fully with their wider communities in meeting real needs.
3. Given the almost wholly positive findings and recommendations of the evaluation of the work of the Fund which was carried out this year, encourage the PDF Committee, along with other relevant parties, to learn as much as is possible from the evaluation report concerning best practice in the matter of funding community-based project work.

REPORT

1.1 The Church Without Walls report in 2001 imagined a fund which would function as an *"independent, grant awarding body working in close collaboration with the other Boards (Councils) of the Church…directly responsible to the General Assembly."* The vision was for a fund which would *"create levers for change in the mindset of the church,"* and would signal to local congregations that the General Assembly was willing to invest substantial amounts of money in local communities and parishes.

1.2 It is our view that, for the 135 congregations who have so far benefited from this funding, to a very great extent this vision has been realised. It is also our view that there remains huge potential for many more congregations, and their communities, throughout Scotland to benefit.

1.3 The story of the Parish Development Fund is a **Good News story** for the Church of Scotland.

1.4 It is a story which is unfolding and developing and, if it is to continue as a Good News story, the Church will want to ensure there is **sufficient investment** in the Fund over the coming years.

1.5 It is the story of six years, so far, of making about £500,000 per year of funding available to congregations to enable them to live out the Good News of the Gospel in **very practical** ways within their communities.

1.6. It is the story of two years of administering the Priority Areas Staffing Fund (since January 2007), seeking to get **additional resources** of around £450,000 per year into the very poorest churches and communities in Scotland.

1.7 It is the story of ordinary folks who have been encouraged to get involved and to get into their neighbourhoods, to engage with their communities and to get in touch with the very **real needs** of the people around them.

1.8 It is the story of local churches and others **working together** across boundaries and across denominations, working with other organisations and agencies, expressing the love of God in action.

1.9 It is the story of churches **taking risks**, doing things differently, breaking the mould, looking beyond their walls.

1.10   It is the story of the Church returning nearly £3.5 million to 135 local congregations and communities across Scotland, and those projects attracting up to **four times as much additional money** into their communities.

1.11   It is the story of **people being transformed** – those who help to make projects happen and deliver the work, as well as those who benefit from the initiatives. Time and again the reports we receive from projects we fund tell us of individuals, churches and communities who have discovered a renewed sense of self, who have achieved things they never thought possible, of people who have come to faith or returned to faith as a result of their involvement.

1.12   It is the story of the Fund **supporting projects struggling through adversity**: dealing with funding problems, struggling with issues of management, coming to terms with the responsibility for large sums of money, sorting out staffing difficulties, facing unexpected obstacles.

1.13   It is the story of **growth and renewal**, for individuals, for congregations, for communities:

1.14   And it's a story that everyone in the Church can be part of and that **the whole Church can be proud of!**

2.   Significant Events/Developments in 2008
2.1   External Evaluation
2.1.1   The General Assembly 2008 agreed the following deliverance:

> *"The General Assembly instructs the Council of Assembly, in consultation with the Committee, to review the Parish Development Fund in the light of the expiry of the current funding arrangements in 2010, and bring proposals for its future to the General Assembly of 2009."*

2.1.2   2008 represented the sixth full year of grant funding by the Committee. Whilst the Committee has previously commissioned, in 2006, research into the

spending by the Fund on youth and children's work, there has never been a full external evaluation of the Parish Development Fund. In the light of the aforementioned deliverance, the Committee considered the time was right for such an objective examination of the work of the Fund to take place.

2.1.3   A detailed brief was drawn up, in consultation with the Council of Assembly, and this was sent out to nine potential candidates for the work. Four candidates were invited for interview, with three attending, and the contract was awarded to Dr Eleanor Logan.

2.1.4   The Executive Summary and the Final Conclusions from Dr Logan's report are appended to this report (Appendix 2). The main highlight of Dr Logan's report is the strong affirmation that the Fund has had a hugely significant impact across churches and communities – all of which has resulted in the growth of skills and capacity within churches, enabling them to develop and run organisations, employ staff and support vulnerable people. In so doing, the initiatives of the churches have impacted on the lives of many people in their congregations and communities. The report suggests that the funds invested in 2008 brought benefits to around 19,000 people at a cost of £27 per person, indicating how cost effective the Church's investment has been.

2.1.5   Within the report Dr Logan makes a number of recommendations relating to the day to day running and administration of the Fund and these are now being considered by staff with a view to implementation.

2.1.6   The report recommends *"that the funds made available to the Parish Development Fund be increased,"* (Sect 6.9 Final Conclusions) with Dr Logan concluding that the strong recognition of the Parish Development Fund at the local level is not currently mirrored by the Church as a whole. She suggests that this is something which should be addressed. The final paragraph of her

Executive Summary clearly indicates why she has reached these conclusions:

> "Whilst the Church of Scotland like many institutions across Scotland is operating within tough economic circumstances, the value for money in delivering social change achieved through the Parish Development Fund should be recognised as a significant good news story for the Church of Scotland. As already highlighted it enables the Church to continue to evidence its charitable nature, but crucially the PDF is delivering the core mission and purposes of the Church of Scotland in the heart of congregations across Scotland."

2.2 Grant Awards

During 2008 the Parish Development Fund Committee made 31 main grant awards and 5 small grant awards totalling £772,350. More detail of the awards is given later in this report.

2.3 Project Support

The Parish Development Fund is much more than merely the administration of and distribution of money. Staff members have a crucial role to play in supporting churches at all stages of their project development, both pre-grant and post-grant.

2.3.1 Pre-Grant

2.3.1.1 Often, when churches have no more than a vague idea about what they want to do in their community, staff can give advice on developing a vision, undertaking a community audit, identifying needs within communities or clarifying priorities.

2.3.1.2 In 2008 staff responded to enquiries from 41 churches. In some cases the contact did not go beyond the initial phone call, it being clear from the outset that the Parish Development Fund was not the appropriate source of finance. In these instances staff offered advice and 'sign posted' the enquirer in a more appropriate direction.

Often, the initial phone call led to staff visiting the church to meet with the minister and/or key local people to explore in greater detail their ideas and aspirations. In some cases these initiatives have already come to fruition with an application to the Fund, in others work will continue at the local level to a point where contact is once again made with staff requesting further support.

2.3.1.3 For churches and projects who are moving towards the stage of making an application, staff will offer advice and guidance based on the specific requirements of each potential applicant.

2.3.2 Post-Grant

2.3.2.1 One of the most important ways in which we provide post grant support is through the personal contact from staff. As with the pre-grant support, staff will offer advice and guidance as required, always mindful of the need to avoid dependency.

2.3.2.2 In 2008 a number of additional resources were introduced to enhance the support offered to funded projects.

2.3.2.3 A **Project Information Pack** was introduced and distributed to all projects. This pack provides a range of information for projects about the Parish Development Fund and the support we provide, about other relevant sources of support and some brief details on currently funded projects.

2.3.2.4 Two **Induction Days** were held for newly, or recently, funded projects which offered representatives from projects, both management and workers, the opportunity to meet with the Parish Development Fund staff, to find out more about the support we provide and to network with other personnel from other projects. These were well received.

2.3.2.5 In November 2008 we held a two day **residential event** for project workers at Carberry Tower. A number of sessions and workshops were offered on issues such as volunteer recruitment, fundraising, and evaluation. Perhaps as important was the opportunity provided for project staff to network and make contacts with other staff doing similar work in different parts of the country.

2.3.2.6 In December 2008 the first edition of the Parish Development Fund **Newsletter** was produced. This was sent to all projects and was distributed to churches via the minister's mailing. The newsletter included stories from a number of funded projects as well as other relevant information. It is intended that this will be produced every six months, following each funding round, and will be another method of keeping churches and projects in touch with the life and work of the Fund.

3. Grant Awards During 2008

3.1 Main grants totalling £765,000 (2007 – £726,700) over periods from one to three years were awarded to 31 projects. Of this amount £239,000 was awarded from the Priority Areas Staffing Fund. The total cost of the work being carried out as a result of these grant awards is approximately £3.5million, with the balance of funding required being sought from charitable trusts, additional local giving, statutory agencies and locally held funds.

3.2 In addition, 5 small grants totalling £7,350 (£7,900) for training, research or small-scale action were awarded.

3.3 For an analysis of the grants awarded by the Fund over the past four years, please refer to the Appendix 1.

3.4 Community Outreach and Development (£247,000/32% of total awarded)
Edinburgh: Holy Trinity Church – Wester Hailes Christians Against Poverty Centre – grant of £30,000 from PASF over three years towards salary costs of Personal Debt Counsellor
"Holy Trinity is a church committed to serving its community – this is seen through a community café, an emergency food store, a counselling service, groups for single mothers (MOPS) as well as the individual support given by this active congregation

to those with drug and alcohol abuse problems or housing issues. We are developing a Christian debt counselling service in response to the needs of the community. We envisage through CAP to have burdens of debt lifted, people learning how to budget and to have the support of the church to keep to it."

Regional: Ayr & Ardrossan – ALTERnativity – continuation grant of £5,000 over two years towards core costs of the service
"Participation in the ALTERnativity sessions allows congregations to become aware of the possibilities for more spiritually involved worship at Christmas. Our experience has shown, and our continued hope is, that they will be able to make changes to their worship and approach to Christmas to improve spiritual growth and fellowship."

Glasgow: Cranhill Parish Church – Out of the Box – grant of £24,000 from PDF over three years towards the costs of an Arts and Faith Worker
"The project is about bringing people together using the creative arts to stimulate reflection, discussion, celebration and events which will allow folks to explore questions of identity, faith and the meaning of life as they see it. A creative arts group will allow us to better involve children and young people in worship."

Glasgow: Pollokshaws Parish Church – grant of £24,000 from the PDF over three years and a grant of £45,000 from the PASF over three years towards the costs of a Development Worker
"At Pollokshaws Parish Church we believe passionately that our church should have a more central role in the life of the whole community. Through the development of our building and initiatives – led by the development worker – we hope to find new ways to share the Gospel with the local community."

Glasgow: The Village Storytelling Centre, Pollok- continuation grant of £8000 funding over two years for core costs from the PDF; grant of £45,000 over three years from the PASF towards the costs of a full-time Storyteller
"It is always at the heart of our work that we seek to improve

the quality of life for people in greatest need in our community. We have found storytelling provides a wonderful medium for developing new and exciting ways of working. Our new Storyteller project will enable us to explore working with other artforms to create ground-breaking work."

Hamilton: Uddingston Burnhead Parish Church – The Edge Project – grant of £29,000 from PASF over three years towards salary costs of the Project Manager
"The project is part of the congregation's Mission and Outreach for the parish. It seeks to improve the life of its parishioners by providing beneficial facilities, advice and information and by providing premises and opportunities for health professionals and others to work within the community. It is a joint project, a partnership between the church, the community, local companies and local and national service providers."

Perth: Auchtergaven & Moneydie Parish Church, Bankfoot – grant of £37,000 over three years towards staff salary costs
"This project is a church working with many different groups to the benefit of every area of the community offering great benefits in quality of life to local residents. It addresses the areas of greatest need in the community and works with the community in innovative and creative ways to provide hope and a vision for the future where church and community work hand in hand."

3.5 Children and Young People (£430,000/56% of total awarded)
West Lothian: Basics Trust, Uphall/Broxburn – continuation grant of £16,000 over two years towards the salary costs of youth workers
"This project has brought together three churches (who previously did very little youth work together) into a full, committed partnership with a local Christian Trust, to share resources and ideas. The project has provided opportunities for the members of our congregations to put their faith into action, in the schools, the streets, the sports fields and community centres of our towns and hamlets, all as outlined in the Church Without Walls report."

Lothian: Gorebridge Opportunities Youth Project – continuation grant of £4000 over two years towards project costs
"It is the mission of GO to provide life-enhancing opportunities that are accessible for all 11-18 year olds in the Gorebridge area. Through offering a menu of diversionary activities the GO users are able to be involved in developing and expanding the work of GO. In doing this, they benefit from achieving goals, increased self-esteem, investing in a community project that will benefit themselves and the future youth of Gorebridge."

Ayr: St Andrew's Parish Church – The Upper Room Youth Project – grant of £21,000 over three years towards salary costs of youth worker
"St Andrews is an ageing congregation, where a year ago there was no apparent cross-generational working. Now the older members are getting used to having youngsters in church, with the challenges this presents. The young people enjoy older folks chatting to them! One youngster was surprised when an older woman at church knew his name. When asked, "How do you know me?" she replied, "because you are part of our church family."

Irvine and Kilmarnock: Irvine Fullarton Parish Church: Youth & Community Project – continuation grant of £7,000 over two years; grant of £45,000 from PASF over three years towards the salary costs of a development worker
"The walls created by poverty, deprivation, low self-esteem, generational alienation, and a church distanced from the real needs of people are walls we aim to further break down. The Project targets young folk & their families, who are in greatest need in the community & country and. has a major emphasis on developing the imagination, creativity & ability of young folk to express themselves."

Glasgow: Junction 12, Ltd – Youth Project – grant of £18,000 over three years towards salary costs of project worker
"Members of the local congregations will provide practical support to some J12 events and J12 staff and young people

20

will be involved in some congregational activities. This will allow for relationships to begin to develop between congregations and young people in their parish. It is hoped that stereotypes can be broken down and effective ways of these groups working together will continue to develop."

Hamilton: Calderwood & St Leonards Youth Project – Nu U, East Kilbride – £18,000 over three years towards cost of youth worker

"We hope that our diversionary youth work would reduce the number of young people on the streets, reduce the levels of youth crime and anti-social behaviour thereby improving the image that the community currently has of young people. We also hope that the project would be seen as a community resource, creating a more positive relationship between the church and the wider community."

Hamilton: The Machan Trust, Larkhall – youth work-continuation grant of £20,000 over two years towards the salary costs and training of workers and volunteers

"Communities have been given hope and particularly those which are disadvantaged because their young people now have positive choices which divert them from damaging practices; congregations have hope because Christ's Church is active in the communities in greatest need; staff, volunteers and sessional workers have encouragement that the quality of their work makes a difference; but most of all children and young people are being valued, developed and experiencing Christian love and the planting of the seeds of faith."

Dumbarton: Route 81 Youth Project, Garelochhead – continuation grant of £12,000 over two years towards youth worker salary costs

"Route 81 has allowed many members of the congregation to become involved, not only to develop relationships with the young people of the area but also to provide help on a voluntary basis for their varied activities. This has improved the opportunities and activities for the young people as there is little in the village at present for that age group. It has also changed the "mind set" of many of the adult members towards this generation."

Dunfermline: The Initiative – continuation grant of £10,000 over two years towards salary costs of youth worker

"Through our programme of activities we actively seek to improve the quality of life of our Young People by giving them an awarness of the possibilities open to them. Through our volunteer network we encourage the local congregations to become involved with the Youth of their community. The project is open to the involvement of the other local Churches in the area and works in partnership with local agencies and charities."

Dunfermline: Talk Matters – Headroom – grant of £32,000 over three years towards the salary costs of a youth project worker

"Headroom works with Headteachers and GP's to provide a counselling service for children 11 – 18 years old, who are presenting difficulties that are outwith school resources to handle. On referral no background information is given and the children form a voluntary agreement with their Counsellor who gives them unconditional acceptance, hope of change and strategies to help them cope. Weekly counselling sessions take place mainly in schools."

Dunfermline: Tulliallan and Kincardine Parish Church – Kinship Bridges – grant of £11,000 for one year towards the salary costs of a youth worker

"We are aiming, through a one-year pilot project, to explore how partnership with Fife Council and/or other agencies could develop the present Kincardine Youth Project into a new programme to build bridges for young people to the church and the community, and between old and young."

Kirkcaldy: Kirkcaldy Area Reachout Trust (KART) – £30,000 over three years towards the salary costs of a Children's/Youth Worker

"This project allows the local church community the opportunity to work together. The work is being developed to reach children and young people with the Christian message, and to provide a means whereby their emotional, social and behavioural needs can be supported in a non-judgemental way."

Dunkeld & Meigle: Breathe Youth Project, Aberfeldy – £30,000 over three years towards core costs

"Breathe will function as an expression of God's love to the wider community. Creating a safe environment where young people can explore their spirtiual, physical and emotional wellbeing. It will be mainly based in the Church Centre and other locations in Highland Perthshire."

Perth: Kinross Parish Church – The WEB Project – continuation grant of £11,000 over two years towards the salary costs of a trainee worker

"The Project works with young people aged 10 – 24 surrounding risk behaviours such as drugs, alcohol and sexual health. The project has succeeded at changing the views of the young people using the service who, prior to our involvement, would not have thought about how their behaviour affected the rest of the community. This not only benefits the congregations and church but benefits the whole community."

Dundee: Food on Friday Association – grant of £45,000 from PASF over three years towards the salary costs of staff

"The whole project is living the gospel in risky ways, and interpreting the love of Christ creatively. We believe that working through food not only emphasises health but is a non threatening way to show our Christian commitment and Love. Involving children further means that we will be reaching out to all the most vulnerable people in the community and is also an innovation in this parish and congregation."

Dundee: Hot Chocolate Trust – continuation grant of £8000 for one year towards core project costs

"We will continue to develop the community-based Christian youth work already established, for the purposes of helping marginalised young people realise their potential in a holistic manner, working alongside churches, the City Council, other community agencies and businesses, to the benefit of all involved."

Aberdeen: The Samuel Trust – grant of £36,000 over three years towards the salary costs of staff

"The Samuel Trust exists to engage children, specifically those who have little other meaningful church connection, with the gospel primarily through running high energy kids clubs and engaging with them on their 'territory', including both home and school. Our core activity is a weekly term time children's club at a central point in the community to which we run buses from a number of sites."

Kincardine and Deeside: Portlethen Parish Church Focussed Youth Initiative – grant of £36,000 over three years towards the salary costs of a youth worker

"Portlethen Parish Church is currently the only church of any denomination in the town, and as such is committed to playing a key role in the life of the community. The Youth Worker Project is one way in which the local church endeavours to work with others within the community (individuals and groups) to the benefit of that community. It will offer a welcoming first point of contact with the church which meets young people on their own territory."

Sutherland: Assynt Christian Community Youth Project, Lochinver – continuation grant of £20,000 over two years towards the salary costs of youth worker

"ACCYP is able to bring together diverse groups in order to see the youth in Assynt have as many chances and opportunities that we can possibly provide. Through ACCYP, the churches can continue in unity and hopefully this will develop even more, spreading to other areas of church life within the local churches."

3.6 Family Support (£64,000/9% of total awarded)
Edinburgh: Liberton Kirk Family Support Worker (FSW) Project – grant of £17,000 over three years towards the salary costs of the Family Support Worker

"The Project aims to provide friendship and support to local families. KLM's church building is strategically located in a large housing estate. The church is surrounded by families, many of whom are newcomers, but its members have little direct contact with them. This project aims to offer support to these families, irrespective of faith or church connections."

Greenock and Paisley: The STAR Project – Building Better Futures – continuation grant of £12,000 over two years towards the salary costs of the Practice Development Co-ordinator

"One of the most significant contributions that the STAR project has made to the local church community is not only that it is a very effectively run project but that it is a clear example and model of what local congregations can achieve when they work together to address social need in the name of Christ."

Glasgow: 3D Drumchapel – continuation grant of £5000 for one year towards the costs of the Project Manager post

"We work with people who often have complex and inter-connected problems. These include addiction issues, poor physical and mental health, low educational achievements, low self-confidence and self-esteem. We seek to work with vulnerable parents, children and young people to encourage their personal development and participation in the wider community – to enable them to access community resources and be a force for change within their communities. Our faith is at the heart of what we do."

Stirling: Heart to Heart, Callander – continuation grant of £10,000 over two years towards the salary costs of staff

"Heart to Heart has grown steadily since its birth in 2003. It is a well-respected service providing unique support to people affected by divorce and separation. Working in the field of mental health it offers a group-based recovery programme. This has received excellent feedback from clients and referrers alike, with demand continuing to grow for services both locally and nationally. We wish to develop volunteer support courses and equip church communities across Scotland to provide Heart to Heart support in their own communities."

Dundee: St Andrews Church – Family Support Project – continuation grant of £20,000 over two years towards the salary costs of the Project Leader

"The project offers opportunities, facilities, and support for single parents (21 and under) and their children which may
not be available elsewhere. Some congregations both in the city centre and outwith are now much more aware of the project. The news is spreading. Dundee for Christ and our new quarterly newsletter keep people well informed. As members of the congregation hear about the problems the girls face and have faced there is a much greater understanding of their needs. As church members see girls progress the project is becoming much more 'real' in their eyes."

3.7 Older People (£24,000/ 3% of total awarded)
Hamilton: Utheo Befriend in Bellshill – grant of £24,000 over three years towards the salary costs of the Befriending Co-ordinator and core project costs

"BeFriend In Bellshill offers a befriending service for elderly and disabled people in Bellshill. Our project has identified elderly and disabled people in our area who have no social contact and suffer depression and loneliness. We work with other churches, support groups and referral agencies to reduce the social isolation and exclusion of elderly and disabled people."

3.8 Small Grants (£7,350) (£7,900)

3.8.1 Cranhill Community Project, Glasgow: training grant. £1,400

3.8.2 St Columba's Parish Church, Glenrothes: volunteers training. £1,500

3.8.3 K.A.R.T (Kirkcaldy Area Reachout Trust), Fife: feasibility study. £1,500

3.8.4 Rosyth Community and Heritage Development Project, Fife: community research. £1,500

3.8.5 The Steeple Church, Dundee – Parish Nursing Project: pilot project + conference costs. £1,450

In the name of the Committee

MARTIN FAIR, *Convener*
Vacant, *Vice-Convener*
GRAHAM LUMB, *Co-ordinator*

APPENDIX 1– ANALYSIS OF GRANTS 2003 – 2008

Funds awarded by type of work

Older People
£48,000
1%

Small Grant
£37,142
1%

Family Support
£196,000
5%

Community Outreach
and Development
£1,583,590
41%

Children and
Young People
£2,032,998
52%

Funds awarded by type of community

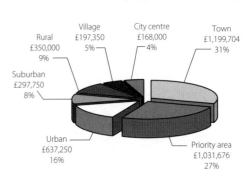

Rural
£350,000
9%

Village
£197,350
5%

City centre
£168,000
4%

Town
£1,199,704
31%

Suburban
£297,750
8%

Urban
£637,250
16%

Priority area
£1,031,676
27%

Funds awarded by Presbytery

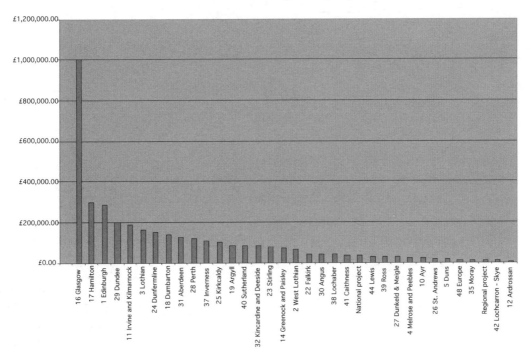

APPENDIX 2
EVALUATION OF THE PARISH DEVELOPMENT FUND OF THE CHURCH OF SCOTLAND

EXECUTIVE SUMMARY

&

FINAL CONCLUSIONS

Report of findings submitted by LPM Ltd.

supporting change   facilitating learning   enabling excellence

Submitted by:
Dr Eleanor M. Logan
LPM Ltd.
1 Cramond Place
Edinburgh, EH4 6LZ
0131 336 3773/07791749945
elogan@learningandchange.co.uk
Company Number: SC265291
www.learningandchange.co.uk

Summary of Findings and Conclusions

E1 This evaluation has been commissioned by the Parish Development Fund Committee in response to the General Assembly of the Church of Scotland who in 2008 instructed the Council of Assembly, in consultation with the Parish Development Fund Committee:

"to review the Parish Development Fund in the light of the expiry of the current funding arrangements in 2010, and bring proposals for its future to the General Assembly of 2009."

In taking forward this evaluation, the Parish Development Fund Committee wished to review the **success**, **impact** and **effectiveness** of the Parish Development Fund and use these as a foundation for recommendations on the future of the Fund. The Committee also wished to review the current context of the Parish Development Fund within the Church of Scotland.

This report presents the results of this in depth evaluation and gives much information on the impact of the Parish Development Fund. This section summarises the key findings and conclusions detailed within this report.

E2 The Parish Development Fund (PDF) was established by the General Assembly of the Church of Scotland in 2002 in response to the Church Without Walls Report to the General Assembly 2001. The Fund itself was conceived as being a mechanism to stimulate new ideas, facilitate the establishment of partnerships and be the catalyst for new responses to need within communities.

E3 The Parish Development Fund was established as an independent, stand alone body within the central Church of Scotland structure. This was done intentionally to ensure the following key aims highlighted in the Church Without Walls report were attained:
- To represent the interests of local congregations;
- To integrate and affirm the work of other Boards (Councils) of the Church through the grants made;
- To promote collaboration between the Boards (Councils) and parishes of the Church;
- To act as a broker between Boards (Councils) allowing them to channel their resources and expertise in a collaborative and interdependent way into the life of local congregations.

E4 The Parish Development Fund is governed by its own committee, which is appointed through the General Assembly and therefore represents congregations across Scotland. There are also co-opted members from across the Church of Scotland. The PDF Committee play an active role in ensuring the grant making is open, transparent and accountable and meeting the aims and criteria established for the PDF.

E5 The Parish Development Fund is therefore not just a grants fund but a funding body in its own right. In 2006, the Ministries Council of the Church of Scotland approached the PDF Committee to request that it take on the responsibility of developing and administering the Priority Areas Staffing Fund on behalf of Priority Areas Committee of the Ministries Council. The PDF Committee took on this responsibility and launched the fund in January 2007. To date 11 grants have been made and are being supported by PDF staff.

E6 Since its creation in 2002 the Parish Development Fund has had funding income of £4,323,840. It has funded 169 grants across 135 different congregations across Scotland. Over the last five years the fund has allocated **£3,415,879** of funding, with the remainder to be allocated over the next two years. Small grants of up to £5000 are available as well as larger multi-year grants of up to £45,000 over a three year period.

E7 Through promotion across the Church of Scotland, the PDF has attracted a spread of applications from across Scotland – working across rural and urban locations. In the recent funding round, applications were received from Lochinver through to Ayrshire – taking in the north east of

20

Scotland. Congregations credited the Church of Scotland for taking the approach of utilising central funds into which they contribute for work which potentially benefits all parishes and tackles un-met need across their communities.

E8 The evaluation showed that across the £521,350 awarded by the PDF in 2008, around **19,000** people are benefitting. As an indicative measure, the Church can therefore be seen to be investing an estimated **£27** per individual across the congregations benefitting from PDF funding. This is an incredibly cost effective investment given the levels of match funding the organisations attract and most importantly the significant benefit to individuals and impact across churches and communities generated.

E9 It is a requirement of funding that all funded projects obtain match funding. Whilst the funded projects can define the levels and sources of match funding they require, the current policy of the PDF requires that they obtain at least 50% match funding. This evaluation demonstrated that projects were obtaining an average of £32,279 match funding per project. With the average grant size being £19,309 they are being able to significantly attract match funding and hence generate a positive benefit to the local economy through not only the social support and community development being provided but through the generation of employment opportunities.

E10 PDF funding is generating **widespread** and **pervasive impact** – greater than anticipated given the modest investment provided. The **short term impact** reflects the immediate response to need but **longer term impact** across communities is also seen to be developing.

E11 PDF funding was seen to be **directly responding to social need in communities**. The predominant underlying social issue being tackled by the PDF projects is **social isolation**, closely followed by lack of local facilities within communities. **Dysfunctional family**

relationships and **alcohol/substance abuse** also feature and these were predominant themes across the projects working with **young people and families**.

E12 People are benefitting from having access to services which are designed to **meet their particular needs** and which are structured in such a way that will **build capacity in the community**. The funded projects are demonstrating grass roots community development based around the needs of quite vulnerable people.

E13 For many years the PDF was dominated by youth work projects and hence the demographic of beneficiaries was young. Whilst young people are still a key beneficiary of PDF funded projects other groups within the community are now benefitting. Within the current grants portfolio there are projects which directly target men, those providing specialist support to women, projects working across communities with families and projects providing a range of support to all community members in response to low income or poverty *etc*.

E14 In terms of longer term impact, the **Church based and/or driven solution** was often perceived to have a longer term and hence wider impact than other solutions. Projects which are set up in communities to work with vulnerable people need to **build up relationships** in order to be truly effective. Such work doesn't happen overnight – it takes time to build credibility and trust. Many agencies just cannot deliver this **long term approach** as they do not have a long term presence within communities.

E15 Another key evidence of impact was the **building of skills and capacity** within churches, across organisations and across communities. Through hosting these projects, the organisations running them (and hence the Churches) were developing their community development skills, learning about project and organisational development, building their ability to support vulnerable people *etc*. All of the projects encouraged volunteers from across the Church to get involved in supporting the funded project

– often providing a variety of volunteering opportunities. There was evidence that the spiritual life of the Church was also benefitting.

E16 The approach of the PDF **to encourage Churches to work in partnership** has been an area of success and has been integral in generating and sustaining impact. All of the funded projects pointed to this and all had a range of community partners depending on the client group they were working with. Other local churches and schools were popular partners cited by funded projects, but other sources included Social Work, the Police, the NHS, youth organisations, other local community organisations, Scripture Union, *etc.*

E17 However, one of the key challenges for funded projects was sustaining partnerships with other local churches and/or sustaining the interest of the host church. Often, this was dependent on one key champion which made the partnership quite vulnerable were they to move on. Local church politics and lack of support from presbyteries was also cited as an ongoing challenge for funded projects. Projects found it easier to sustain partnerships with external agencies and often this had more of an impact than the church partnerships.

E18 Other challenges included sustaining the staff and volunteer base and of course sustaining the funding packages and hence the funding base for the project. The current economic climate aligned to reduced public sector funding for voluntary sector projects is impacting heavily on PDF funded projects and will continue to compromise some of the ongoing sustainability of PDF funded work.

E19 Whilst projects were very successful in achieving match funding for their work, in doing so they are often using up all available sources of funding for their work in the first five years of funding. By the time the PDF involvement ceases, other charitable funders who are interested in this kind of work are also looking to move on

and fund other work. The requirement to obtain match funding also means that funded projects take time to get started as they cannot begin work until match funds are achieved and this can delay the delivery of benefits and impact to vulnerable people. It is recommended that the PDF continues its approach of encouraging projects to match fund, but consider this on a case by case basis. It may be that some projects and in particular those in priority areas, should receive 100% funding in year one to enable them to develop their project and capacity.

E20 The PDF do provide continuation funding to enable funded projects to receive support for a further two years, to enable them to develop their work and their sustainability. Whilst this is welcomed by funded organisations and it does enable a continued relationship between the funded organisation and the PDF, the amounts awarded can at times be quite small and will not in practical terms contribute greatly to building capacity. It is recommended that the PDF committee continue to award continuation funding but ensure the funds provided are not tokenstic but realistic.

E21 It is also recommended that, in order to continue to generate impact across Scotland, the PDF target the geographical areas which have not yet accessed PDF funding and are seen to be 'cold spots'.

E22 The PDF has been able to generate immediate and longer term impact not only through the provision of funding support but also through the direct support provided by the PDF staff.

E23 Across the interviews, the PDF was the **first funder** in 16 out of the 20 projects involved. In the others, the organisation had some other funding in place yet the projects were not viable until the PDF got involved. The organisations interviewed were clear that the PDF played a vital role in being **a catalyst** in taking their work forward through building capacity, providing grant aid and through giving them confidence that their project is worth supporting and that the Church believes in supporting their community.

E24 The PDF is unique amongst grant funders in that they make a contribution to the whole project and do not 'cherry pick' which parts of the budget they are willing to support. This is a mature approach as the PDF are contributing towards the outcomes of the project rather than choosing to fund any particular aspect of it. In addition, the PDF is perceived to be flexible in how these funds get applied across the project life.

E25 The Parish Development Fund provides a package of 'investment support' to applicants and funded projects. This includes support with developing an idea into a project, support for making an application, provision of advice and information to assist project development post grant, and provision of networking opportunities for funded projects. Funded projects are also able to access specialist employment advice through Glasgow Council for the Voluntary Sector Employers Advice Service. The PDF pay for this service to be available to all funded projects.

E26 The current support package is concentrated on the provision of pre-funding support for those preparing applications. Whilst all potential applicants receive advice on developing their concept into a viable project, only those who meet the criteria and have a credible idea are encouraged to make a full application to the PDF. This approach is structured to ensure that potential applicants are not wasting time developing applications which are unlikely to be successful. As such the success rate for those presenting an application to the Committee is high.

E27 This evaluation demonstrated that this support has been successful in the following areas:
- Building the capacity of local churches to develop their project and make a successful funding application
- Building the capacity of churches to attract other funding

- Building the capacity of churches to deliver their work
- Encouraging networking and learning across projects
- Promoting long term sustainability of funded work

The funded projects rated all aspects of the PDF support package highly but wished to see a little more support for sharing learning and networking post grant. Many are pushing boundaries in their communities and across their Churches and the opportunity to discuss these challenges with peers were seen as invaluable.

E28 This report recommends that the support to funded projects post grant receive more emphasis across the support package to enable capacity building post grant to be increased.

E29 It is also recommended that the PASF receive a dedicated support package which should include dedicated promotion of the fund. The PASF funded projects are working in particularly challenging communities and require enhanced support for capacity building and learning.

E30 Further recommendations around administration of the Funds included improving information capture and file management. The points raised here reflected that the funds had grown in size and the systems needed updating to reflect this growth. Whilst the PDF appears to some to have staff capacity, in reality there is only a staff complement of 2.5 full time equivalents providing over 550 hours of direct support to funded projects a year.

E31 The structure of the PDF as an independent committee now appears to be under review. It is not entirely clear how this has arisen but from the interviews there appears to be some concern that being an independent committee the current structure may not be compliant with the requirements of the Office of the Scottish Charity Regulator. This is surprising given that the PDF and PASF funded projects are quite clearly charitable in purpose and object and are in effect enhancing the ability of the Church of Scotland to meet their charitable objects.

E32 The concern possibly arises since the PDF Committee do not formally report through the Council of Assembly, but report directly to the General Assembly who continue to endorse their work through agreeing grant funding. This does need resolved and a pragmatic approach to building accountability would be for the PDF Committee to have a formal reporting relationship with the Council of Assembly where regular updates on progress across the Funds being administered by the PDF can be presented.

E33 It would not benefit the PDF nor the Church of Scotland to have the PDF 'mainstreamed' within the work of any one Council. If this was the taken forward then the above aims for the PDF of being a body which encourages Councils to collaborate, to work directly with local congregations through a central body which is independent, of being able to represent local congregations across the Church *etc.* would not be realised. It would also be counter to the wishes of congregations who contribute their income for this kind of work.

E34 The Church of Scotland should also consider carefully how it utilises the expertise available within the Parish Development Fund. Whilst this evaluation has highlighted areas for improvement in administration of the Fund, the Fund is demonstrating good practice in grant making and has developed a capacity for grant making which could be utilised across the Church of Scotland. This would build on the current role of PDF staff who actively works to generate links across the Church and sign post congregations to existing and new initiatives.

E35 This evaluation has highlighted how a small amount of income into a community based project is creating significant impact across individuals and communities. This would be compromised if current income levels into the PDF are not maintained and this would be a significant

loss felt across congregations and communities. This loss would impact on the profile and potential of the Church of Scotland.

E36 It is therefore an obvious conclusion that the funds made available for the Parish Development Fund be sustained if not increased. This would enable the PDF Committee to consider how it provides ongoing support to existing projects at the same time as extending the funding into some of the areas (geographical and thematic) that the PDF has not yet reached.

E37 Whilst the Church of Scotland like many institutions across Scotland is operating within tough economic circumstances, the value for money in delivering social change achieved through the Parish Development Fund should be recognised as a significant good news story for the Church of Scotland. As already highlighted it enables the Church to continue to evidence its charitable nature, but crucially the PDF is delivering the core mission and purposes of the Church of Scotland in the heart of congregations across Scotland.

1. Final Conclusions (extracted from the main Evaluation Report)

1.1 The Parish Development Fund is an intelligent funder, which invests in outcomes not actions. It takes a mature approach of supporting not just the funded project but also the organisation applying for funding. It is willing to listen and respond to need and take risks through funding new work.

1.2 The Parish Development Fund is an innovator of new work, through stimulating new ideas and putting funds to these. It builds the confidence in local congregations and communities and through this enables them to develop their own solutions. It also stimulates the development of the local economy through increasing employment and attracting other funds into communities. It builds social capital through stimulating people to volunteer and through communities being better connected.

1.3 As has been demonstrated, across 2008, for an investment of £521,350 the Church of Scotland was able to directly improve the quality of life for up to 19,000 people across Scotland. This represented an estimated investment of £27 per person. For this extremely modest investment the Church of Scotland has been instrumental in initiating far reaching, innovative work in communities across Scotland. This work is being driven by local churches that are building a wide range of local partnerships and embedding themselves in the life of local communities. These truly are churches without walls.

1.4 This report importantly demonstrates how the Church of Scotland has a stronger and deeper connection in communities than ever before. In addition to this, its profile in these communities has never been higher – from local people through to local and national decision makers. The Church of Scotland has gained respect for its role in supporting pressing need and stimulating new ideas and new approaches.

1.5 A further positive aspect of the Parish Development Fund is that it is providing funds to local congregations across Scotland. It enables the central Church to be putting funds into any Parish which has a good idea to tackle local need. This is a very positive counter argument for the Church of Scotland who regularly faces resistance from local congregations who are required to submit income to the central Church. If this funding is to be further reduced or withdrawn then it will clearly be challenged by local congregations who greatly welcome this type of funding being available.

1.6 What has been most surprising on carrying out this evaluation is how little recognition the PDF gets internally within the central Church of Scotland. This is in stark contrast to the recognition gained in the local communities. Any other funding body would be incredibly proud of the impact they were achieving in local communities and seek to showcase this as evidence of how they are meeting their mission.

1.7 One of the main conclusions that this evaluation has to come to is that the Parish Development Fund deserves better recognition from the Church of Scotland and that the responsibility for taking this forward does not just rest with the Parish Development Fund Committee and staff.

1.8 Hopefully this independent evaluation will provide the Council of Assembly with the confidence it needs to support a positive future for the Parish Development Fund. This evaluation has highlighted how a small amount of income is creating significant impact. It is a small amount and further impact and the sustaining of current impact will be compromised if funds are not maintained or indeed increased. The PDF is a small investment in comparison to the total income of the Church of Scotland and it is demonstrating how it can lever in the same amount of income again in match funding from a range of sources. The PDF building capacity of projects through the funding support package also contributes to excellent value for money.

1.9 It is therefore an obvious conclusion that the funds made available for the Parish Development Fund be increased. This would enable the Committee to consider how it provides ongoing support to existing projects at the same time as extending the funding into some of the areas (geographical and thematic) that the PDF has not yet reached.

1.10 The Church of Scotland should also consider carefully how it utilises the expertise available within the Parish Development Fund. Whilst this evaluation has highlighted areas for improvement, the Fund is demonstrating good practice in grant making and has developed a capacity for grant making which could be utilised across the Church of Scotland.

PROPOSED DELIVERANCE

The General Assembly
1.   Receive the Report and note the changes to the Trustees.
2.   Ratify the appointment of Hamish John Grundell Scott as a new Employer Nominated Trustee.

REPORT

1.   Scheme Statistics

As at 31 December 2008, the three Church of Scotland Pension Schemes had a total combined membership of 5674 with approximately £240m assets under management.

2.   Statutory & Discretionary Increases and Standard Annuity from January 2009.

2.1   Ministers' & Staff Schemes

After taking advice from the Schemes' Actuary, the Trustees regrettably decided not to award any discretionary increases to pensions in payment. The Trustees' discretion applies to pensions which accrued in respect of pensionable service prior to April 1997; increases to pensions in pensions in respect of service after that date attracted statutory increases at the rate of 5% for service accrued 1997-2005 and 2.5% for service accrued post 2005.

The Trustees decided to maintain the 2009 Standard Annuity, applicable to the Ministers' Scheme, at its 2008 level, *ie* £13,642.

2.2   National Mission Scheme

Pensions in respect of service accrued prior to 2005 were increased at the rate of 5% whilst pensions in respect of service accrued post 2005 were increased at 2.5%.

3.   Actuarial Valuations of the pension Schemes

The next Actuarial Valuations of the Pension Schemes are due as at 31 December 2009.

4.   Trustees

The Assembly is asked to note changes in the Board of Pension Trustees as follows:

4.1 David Drysdale Fotheringham FFA is retiring as Chairman of the Pension Trustees. He will remain a Trustee for the balance of his term.

Mr William John McCafferty ACII, ASFA, TEP has been appointed to serve as Chairman of the Pension Trustees for the next four years.

4.2 Arthur John Briggs has retired as a Trustee having given 17 years service to the Pension Trustees.

4.3 The Assembly is asked to ratify the appointment of Hamish John Grundell Scott as a new Employer Nominated Trustee for a six year term.

4.4 The Assembly is asked to note the following changes to the Member Nominated Trustees within the Church of Scotland Pension Schemes for Staff and National Mission.

Pauline Willder resigned from her position within the Church of Scotland and, consequently as a Member Nominated Trustee for the Staff Scheme, with effect from 31 December 2008.

The Rev John Chalmers and Mr Glenn Liddall both completed their terms as Member Nominated Trustees for the Staff Scheme on 9 February 2009; both are standing for re-election with the result unknown at time of going to print.

The Rev John Potter resigned as a Member Nominated Trustee for the National Mission Scheme in August 2008 having served for 12 years.

5. Pensions Manager

The Assembly is asked to note that Steven David Kaney was appointed as Church of Scotland Pensions Manager with effect from 1 October 2008.

In the name of the Trustees

DAVID D FOTHERINGHAM, *Chairman*
W JOHN McCAFFERTY, *Vice-Chairman*
STEVEN D KANEY, *Pensions Manager*

ADDENDUM

David Drysdale Fotheringham FFA first joined the Personnel Committee which dealt with the Staff Pension Scheme in 1987 and became a Pension Trustee in 1997. He has, therefore, given 22 years service in these roles. He became Chairman of the Trustees four years ago on the retiral of Bill Cameron and has provided a "steady hand on the tiller" giving sound leadership in recent volatile investment times.

As noted in the Report, he remains a Trustee, and so the Trustees and the Church will continue to benefit from his valuable experience.

W JOHN McCAFFERTY, *Vice-Chairman*
STEVEN D KANEY, *Pensions Manager*

PROPOSED DELIVERANCE

The General Assembly
1. Receive the Report.
2. Convert into a Standing Law of the Church the Overture amending Act IX 2002 anent Admission and Re-admission of Ministers (as amended), as revised and set out in Appendix II.

REPORT

1. Introduction

As will be seen from the return detailed in Appendix I, the Overture amending Act IX 2002 anent Admission and Re-admission of Ministers (as amended) sent to Presbyteries by last year's General Assembly, received sufficient support to be presented for enactment.

2. Presbyteries' Comments

The following comments were received, and will be taken into consideration by the Ministries Council in operating Act IX in its amended form.

2.1 Edinburgh

In the absence of a Presbytery interview, it is important to ensure that all the relevant documentary evidence is in the hands of the Ministries Council before they proceed to their interview of the applicant.

2.2 Dumbarton

(1) It would be helpful to have guidelines supplied by the Council to those Presbyteries who are still involved in the operation of the Act.

(2) The Presbytery was unsure which Presbytery was required to provide its opinion, in terms of section 7(a) as amended.

The Council is content that the provision refers to any Presbytery referred to earlier in the same paragraph, and recognises that this may involve more than one Presbytery.

2.3 Uist

The Presbytery was concerned that applicants from Reformed and non-Reformed churches would now be admitted on the same basis.

The Council re-assures the Assembly that it takes full account of the denomination of origin of each applicant, ensures his or her commitment to the polity and practice of the Church of Scotland, and sets training and familiarisation requirements that vary according to the level of knowledge and familiarity with the procedures of our Church. It is normal for successful applicants to be required to study Church Law to the same standard as candidates for the ministry do during their probationary period.

3. Perth

The Committee believes that only the comment from Perth is incompatible with the enactment of the measure (Perth having declined to approve the Overture). The Presbytery preferred to retain a system of Presbytery interview for all candidates coming routinely from WARC and non-WARC churches, both at the outset of the process and at the end of any familiarisation placement required by the Council. The Presbytery's concerns focussed mainly on the need to check applicants' familiarity with the polity and governance of the Church of Scotland.

The Council considers such familiarity an important aspect of its examination of each application, but does not agree that this could be investigated only by the re-institution of extensive Presbyterial involvement. Accordingly the Council believes that the General Assembly should proceed to enact the Overture as it stands.

4. Adjustment of Text

The Clerks have taken this opportunity to add a further section (section 10, as shown in Appendix II), which tidies up a phrase in Act III 2001 that was affected by a previous amendment of Act IX 2002. This does not represent any legislative change of effect, and had previously been indicated by marginal note in the annual updates materials.

In the name and by the authority of the Committee

FINLAY A J MACDONALD, *Convener*

APPENDIX I
OVERTURE AMENDING ACT IX 2002
ANENT ADMISSION AND RE-ADMISSION
OF MINISTERS (AS AMENDED)

No of Presbyteries		Members voting for	
Approving	Disapproving	Approval	Disapproval
44	1	2,194	83

APPENDIX II
OVERTURE AMENDING ACT IX 2002
ANENT ADMISSION AND RE-ADMISSION
OF MINISTERS (AS AMENDED)

The General Assembly, with the consent of a majority of Presbyteries, enact and ordain as follows:

Act IX 2002 anent Admission and Re-admission of Ministers, as already amended, is hereby further amended as follows:

1. Section 4 is amended to read as follows:
Ministers and Deacons – Standard Procedure
4. (1) Ministers and deacons referred to in section 4(2) shall have their application considered in terms of sections 6 and 7 below. Such determinations shall be subject to the right of appeal set out in section 12 below.

   (2) This section shall apply to any applicant who has been a minister or deacon of the Church of Scotland but who has been judicially deprived of status in terms of Acts VII 1935 or Act III 2001 (as amended), notwithstanding that he or she may also belong to one of the categories specified in section 5; and subject to the right of any Presbytery to require that the decision of the Committee be confirmed by the Commission of the General Assembly, at which the said Presbytery shall be required to appear and be heard.

2. Section 5 is amended to read as follows:
5. Applicants in the following categories shall have their applications considered in terms of section 6 below only:
   (a) All ministers and deacons of other churches, and former ministers and deacons of the Church of Scotland not referred to in sub-section 4(2) above.
   (b) All Graduate Candidates in respect of whom there is no current Graduate Candidate's certificate, except those referred to in paragraph 9(1)(d) below.
   (c) Licentiates of the Church of Scotland who have held the status of Licentiate for more than five years.

It shall be the responsibility of the Committee to determine whether the applicant's ordination is recognised by the Church of Scotland before referring his or her application to the Review Panel.

3. Section 6(a) is amended by addition, after the penultimate sentence, of a sentence reading:
"For the avoidance of doubt, the Committee shall have the right, always on its own initiative, to interview the Candidate after the recommendation of the Review Panel has been received."

4. Section 6(b) is amended by the removal of the phrase 'and appointments to office outwith the jurisdiction of the Church of Scotland (provided such office is one which, if held by a minister of this Church, entitles the holder to membership of Presbytery in terms of Act III 2000)'

5. Section 7 is amended to read as follows:
Consideration by Presbytery
7. (a) In respect of applications made in terms of section 4 above, the Secretary of the Committee shall forward to the Presbytery of residence, or, in the case of an applicant who has not resided in Scotland for three months prior to the date of the application, to the Presbytery of Edinburgh, and to any Presbytery within whose bounds the applicant may have been permitted to be appointed as a minister pending the outcome of the application (a) a copy of the application in full, (b) copies of any documents obtained by the Committee. The Presbytery shall, before the date of the meeting at which the application is to be first considered, provide the Committee with its opinion of the application.
    (b) The Committee shall make an interim decision in respect of the application, and the Secretary of the Committee shall inform the applicant of that decision and invite the applicant to determine whether or not he or she wishes to continue the application or appeal the decision.
    (c) When the Secretary of the Committee receives from the applicant an indication of his or her desire to proceed with the application, he or she shall intimate to all Presbyteries the applications that have been received, for their information and comment before the date of the meeting of the Committee at which the application is to be finally considered in terms of section 6(a) above.
    (d) In the event that the interim decision of the Committee is not to allow the applicant to proceed, it shall be open to the applicant to appeal, as set out in section 12 below.

6. Section 8 and paragraph 9(1)(b) are hereby repealed.

7. Section 12 is amended to read as follows:
For the purposes of appeals against decisions of the Committee in terms of this Act, Act VI 2007 anent the Ministries Appeals Panel shall apply, and the procedure shall be the ordinary appeals procedure set out in the Standing Orders of the General Assembly and referred to in section 3 of the said Act VI.

8. Schedule A (which is empty) is hereby removed.

9. Act VI 2007 shall be interpreted in conformity with this Act.

10. Act III 2001 (as amended) is hereby further amended by the removal, in section 1(1)(h)(iv) of the words 'section 8 of'.

At Dundee and within the Apex City Quay Hotel 5 – 8 September 2008

Debate One – Healthy Relationships

The National Youth Assembly took up consideration of "Healthy Relationships".

It was proposed that the National Youth Assembly:

1. Encourages the Church of Scotland to help combat stigma by raising awareness surrounding mental health problems in local congregations and encourage them to form informal support networks.
2. Urges the Church of Scotland to ensure that everyone, and in particular key figures in congregations, are aware of the issues surrounding and resources available to people with mental health difficulties and encourage these to be used.
3. Suggests that the Church of Scotland provide training and information on mental health issues for those who provide pastoral support, but recognise that there are boundaries and situations where reference to a medical professional is necessary.
4. Encourages pastoral support to be available to the families of those suffering from mental health problems, as well as the individuals themselves, while respecting the need for confidentiality.
5. Recognises that, although Ministers and others with a pastoral role should be trained and resourced in understanding mental health issues, it would be worthwhile to note that they are not mental health experts and should not be expected to be.
6. Encourages the churches in Scotland to work at being an inclusive community that celebrates the diversity of the gifts of its people and allows them to grow as individuals.

7. Encourages the churches in Scotland to support and develop the role of Street Pastors in their work with the homeless and other disadvantaged groups.
8. Recognises the quality of the Church of Scotland's work with the marginalised of society and encourages the extension of that work into the everyday life of congregations.
9. Loves the elderly.

Debate Two – The Media

The National Youth Assembly took up consideration of "The Media".

It was proposed that the National Youth Assembly:

1. Recommends that the Church of Scotland explores and utilises appropriate technology to further the Gospel to develop fellowship, locally, nationally and internationally.
2. Encourages the investigation of new avenues that technology opens to engage with people we may not have previously had contact with and provide training for key figures to utilise these technologies to the full.
3. Believes that people should relate with others online in an authentic way, mindful that Christ calls us to love one another as we are loved.
4. Encourages communities to use social media to continue and expand conversations, and to connect to the collective wisdom of the community.
5. Recognises the work needed to create resources and to acknowledge and value the ownership of work made available on line.
6. Encourages the implementation of a weekly Sabbath from unnecessary use of technology to ensure that personal relationships continue to have their proper

place at the heart of the Church of Scotland's ministry and witness.

7. Encourages education within churches concerning online safety, particularly with young people, including information on the dangers of disclosing personal information online.

8. Challenges all churches to have an online presence by 2010 and consider implementing a scheme such as that run by the United Reformed Church.

Debate Three – Sustainable Living

It was proposed that the National Youth Assembly:

1. Would like to develop ideas of eco-consciousness within the running of the NYA, for example reducing mailings, enhancing transport links, encouraging car sharing and providing buses.

2. Encourages:
   • the Church of Scotland to promote responsible use of the Earth's resources and support those who are vulnerable as a result of climate change
   • congregations to work with others to consider ways of becoming more ecologically sound.
   • members to be more eco-friendly in their day to day lives.

3. Encourages the UK and Scottish governments to devise legislation that promotes more efficient use of national grid and renewable technologies. Recognise that nuclear power has a role to play in the current energy climate.

4. Urges the Church and Society Council to lobby local authorities and central government to increase both the availability and convenience of public transport – especially outwith inner city areas. We would also encourage the development of greener transport initiatives such as hydrogen buses, urban tolls and free public transport. The Church of Scotland should actively encourage congregations to lead by example and make more use of these services.

5. Affirms that action needs to be multi-faceted. Even though there is no conclusive proof of anthropogenic climate change, we would regard the responsible attitude to be to continue current measures, using revenue raised by carbon taxation in humanitarian aid.

6. Encourages the UK and Scottish governments to address the issues of fuel poverty as a matter of urgency.

7. Believes that we should learn from the examples of other countries' complementary energy policies and that these schemes should be encouraged worldwide. We emphasise the need for our own country to be as energy efficient as possible before criticising other countries on their energy policies. As such, the NYA would encourage the UK government to advise other countries on their energy policies learning from our mistakes during the industrial revolution.

8. Calls upon the Church of Scotland to make all reasonable effort to reduce the consumption of paper and look to possible alternatives including electronic distribution and recycled paper.

9. Believes the Church's future is inextricably linked to the ideal of sustainable living not simply in forming centres for sustainable living on a local level, but also to use its influence in government to bring about change.

10. Encourages the Church of Scotland to use community buildings where possible for church meetings and vice-versa.

11. Suggests using the mission team model to send teams to join in sustainable church building projects.

12. Encourages the Church of Scotland to educate church members about sustainability projects like those in Bankfoot and Milton.

13. Would like the Church of Scotland to inform churches about grants that are offered by the government and other organisations for implementing green energy initiatives.

14. Encourages the Church of Scotland to consider employing further personnel to advise on issues of sustainable living, in recognition of its importance to the future of the church.

Debate Four – Future Church

The National Youth Assembly,

1. Believes that the future church should be a 24/7 church, as the wider world increasingly operates 24 hours a day, 7 days a week.
2. Believes that the church in Scotland should be identified as a community that discusses and studies, as well as a community that listens. This should involve times of reflection and discussion within worship.
3. Urges the church in Scotland to work towards bridging gaps between social groups, especially young and old, both within and outwith the church. We believe that we should celebrate the differences of each group as each has an equal role to play while recognising that different groups have different needs.
4. Believes that congregations are responsible for caring for each other and the community. All in the church should be encouraged and empowered to practically show Jesus to the community, without expectation of anything in return.
5. Recognises the value of small congregations working in the best interests of communities, and urges the church to support such congregations by the pooling of resources to avoid marginalisation and closure of these valuable congregations.
6. Encourages all churches, where possible, to develop ministry teams to fit the needs of their local communities.
7. Believes that the church of the future should be community focused, adopting an attitude of acceptance to those who are on the fringes of society. The concept of acceptance must be recognised to be far more than disabled access, but also include the use of car pooling and the provision of worship times, styles and spaces that are best suited to the local condition.
8. Believes that money should be shared between all churches so that the Gospel may be spread to the wider community.
9. Calls on the General Assembly to endorse the gifting to the Scottish people of the celebration of births, weddings and funerals as opportunities to start meaningful relationships and conversations. We ask that resources and training as how you do this be given to all ministers and elders.
10. Believes that Territorial Ministries as outlined in Article 3 have a complex impact on the mission of the church; it could be perceived as the focal point in relation to the calling and training of ministers without appropriate attention to the possibility of using lay ministers and particular callings. At the same time territorial ministry offers a precious universality in the support of the country's people.

23

PROPOSED DELIVERANCE

The General Assembly
1. Receive the Report.
2. Invite the Trustees to bring nominations of new Trustees to a future General Assembly.

REPORT

1. Chalmers Lectures 2004-08

The Rev Dr Marjory MacLean delivered her lectures entitled *The Crown Rights of the Redeemer* in the Universities of Aberdeen and Glasgow in the autumn of 2007. At the time of preparing this report these are in the process of being published by St Andrew Press, with subvention funding obtained from the Hope, Baird and Chalmers Trusts. It is intended that the lectures will be marketed to the legal as well as the theological community. The Trustees are grateful to Dr MacLean for her scholarly and practical contribution to current debate on the nature and constitution of the Church of Scotland.

2. Chalmers Lectures 2008-12

At the meeting of the Trust held in January 2009, the Trustees appointed Rev Dr Johnston Mackay as the next Chalmers Lecturer, with the request that his lectures address issues relating to the social engagement of the Church in the nineteenth and early twentieth centuries. Dr Mackay will deliver the lectures in the Universities of Edinburgh and St Andrews during the academic session 2011-12, and then will publish them in book form according to the normal conditions of the Trust.

3. Lectures marking the anniversary of the Scottish Reformation

The financial resources of the Trust being in a very healthy state, the Trustees decided to invite three experts in the fields of Scottish doctrine and worship to deliver one-off lectures over the next two years, as part of the celebration of the 450th anniversary of the Scottish Reformation. These lectures will each relate to the overall theme of all Chalmers Lectures (the headship of Christ over His Church), will be delivered in venues chosen by each lecturer, and will if possible be published as journal articles.

Rev Dr Doug Gay will deliver a lecture, probably before the end of 2009, relating to his recent work on the history of Scottish worship.

Rev Douglas Galbraith will deliver a lecture, probably around the time of the 2010 General Assembly, relating mainly to contemporary issues in worship.

Rev Dr Ian Hazlett will deliver a lecture, during 2010, discussing the Scots Confession, of which he has recently produced a new critical edition.

4. Trustees

At its January 2009 meeting, the Trust accepted the resignation of Rev David Beckett, and thanked him for his service to the Trust. They noted that vacancies now exist for up to three Trustees including two elders, and have resolved to provide suggestions to the Chairman for appointment by the General Assembly before the next scheduled meeting of the Trust in 2012 or 2013.

In the name of the Trust

FINLAY A J MACDONALD, *Chairman*

JOINT REPORT OF THE COUNCIL OF ASSEMBLY AND THE MISSION AND DISCIPLESHIP COUNCIL AND THE 'CHURCH WITHOUT WALLS' PLANNING GROUP
May 2009

PROPOSED DELIVERANCE

The General Assembly
1. Receive the Report.
2. Thank the *Church Without Walls* Planning Group for all that has been achieved since 2001.
3. Approve the integration of the *Church Without Walls* Planning Group with the Mission and Discipleship Council.

REPORT

1. The *Church Without Walls* Report was produced in response to the 1999 General Assembly seeking clarification on 'the purpose of the Church, the shape of the Church, and a process of continuing reform for the Church' as we entered a new millennium. At the 2001 General Assembly the Report was received with acclaim and the 'Church Without Walls' Celebration Group was set up as the 'Stakeholders Group, with a membership of seven people appointed by the General Assembly. Its remit was to continue the momentum of the *Church Without Walls* Report, and, in particular, to organise a national celebration in 2005. It received some administrative support from the former Board of National Mission and a special grant of £180,000 from the Mission and Renewal Fund.

2. At the 2006 General Assembly, the Council of Assembly, within the context of the re-structuring of the Church's central departments, brought a report to the General Assembly with proposals for taking forward the work of the Group. The Council noted the Group's desire to continue, and acknowledged the popularity of the various events which the Group had organised. At the same time the Council, mindful of its remit 'to keep under review the central administration of the Church with particular regard to resolving issues of duplication of resources', initiated discussions with the Mission and Discipleship Council, the General Assembly agency particularly charged with the work of congregational resourcing. In these discussions it was noted that the Mission and Discipleship Council had offered the Group from its own resources the sum of £60,000 over three years. Following receipt of the Report, the General Assembly resolved that the Group 'be continued for a further three years from the General Assembly of 2006'; and 'be located within the Mission and Discipleship Council', though with the continuing right, requested by the Group to report directly to the General Assembly.

3. Conscious that the extension of the Group's life for three years comes to an end at the 2009 General Assembly, the Council of Assembly has hosted discussions with the Mission and Discipleship Council and with the *Church Without Walls* Planning Group.

4. The two Councils and the *Church Without Walls* Planning Group are in agreement that the work of the

Planning Group should become an integral part of the Mission and Discipleship Council from the 2009 General Assembly. A welcome within the Council is assured for the Group's work, which will have a designated budget within the Council's budget for the first two years following integration. Beyond this it is anticipated that the *Church Without Walls* Task Group will be fully integrated within the Council's life and receive appropriate priority funding through the Council's budget. The Group would become one of the Council's Task Groups with the Group's Convener becoming a Vice-Convener of the Council, as with other Task Groups. Initially the *Church Without Walls* Task Group would be made up of five persons appointed by the Nominations Committee, and would have powers to co-opt appropriate additional members from time to time in order to operate with maximum flexibility.

5. It is hoped that an opportunity will be given for the Group to report on its work at a session of future General Assemblies designed to let Commissioners learn of exciting new developments in the Church's life.

6. The full integration of the Group into the work of the Council heralds the next phase of *Church Without Walls* thinking influencing the policy of the 'congregational resourcing' agency of the General Assembly, and through it, the whole life of the Church. As part of the Council, the *Church Without Walls* Task Group will continue its innovative work of supporting and encouraging new thinking in mission within the life of local congregations, Presbyteries, and the Councils of the Church through an on-going programme of conferences and events.

In the name of the Council of Assembly

ALAN GREIG, *Convener*
FINLAY MACDONALD. *Secretary*

In the name of the Mission and Discipleship Council

ANGUS MORRISON, *Convener*
DOUGLAS A O NICOL, *Secretary*

In the name of the Church Without Walls Planning Group

ALBERT O BOGLE, *Convener*

JOINT REPORT OF THE STEWARDSHIP AND FINANCE COMMITTEE AND THE COUNCIL OF ASSEMBLY
May 2009

PROPOSED DELIVERANCE

The General Assembly

1. Receive the Report.
2. Approve the proposal to establish an Audit Committee and the Remit detailed in the Appendix.
3. Approve the proposal to merge the work of the Stewardship and Finance Committee with that of the Budget Group of the Council of Assembly and reconstitute the Budget Group as a Finance Group of the Council of Assembly.
4. Approve the incorporation of the remit of the Stewardship and Finance Committee within the remit of the Council of Assembly.
5. Welcome the formation of a Stewardship and Finance Department.
6. Thank and discharge the Stewardship and Finance Committee.

REPORT

1. Review of changes made in 2004 and 2005

When the Council of Assembly was established on 1 June 2004, responsibility for preparation of the Co-ordinated Budget passed from the Board of Stewardship and Finance to the Council of Assembly. On 1 June 2005 the Board of Stewardship and Finance became the Stewardship and Finance Committee, one of six committees in the Support and Services Council. The Stewardship and Finance Committee continued to have responsibility for Christian Stewardship, Ministries and Mission Contributions, the Report and Accounts of the Unincorporated Councils and Committees, and matters relating to financial regulation.

Under these arrangements there has been a certain amount of duplication, with the same financial information being produced by the General Treasurer for both the Budget Group of the Council of Assembly and the Stewardship and Finance Committee. The continuing business of the Stewardship and Finance Committee has required very

few decisions to be made by the committee, with most of the work being operational and directed by the General Treasurer or the Head of Stewardship. Where decisions have been required, these have often been in relation to Regulations which subsequently required approval by the General Assembly. The main decision made by the Stewardship and Finance Committee each year has been the approval of the Report and Financial Statements of the Unincorporated Councils and Committees on the recommendation of its Audit Committee. The current structure, together with recent developments in Charity legislation and governance, suggests that the Council of Assembly would be a more appropriate body to approve the Report and Financial Statements, with the audit function moving to an independent Audit Committee.

In the light of experience the separation of the Co-ordinated Budget from Christian Stewardship and Ministries and Mission Contributions has not been beneficial to the Church. These three areas belong together. Christian Stewardship produces the income which enables congregations to make Ministries and Mission Contributions, which in turn provide the larger part of the Co-ordinated Budget.

The Budget Group of the Council of Assembly has developed an effective way of working, in fulfilling the Council's remit to monitor the income and expenditure of Councils and Committees. In recent years it has been able to reduce the total contributions required from congregations by ensuring that Councils and Committees make the fullest use of invested funds and other income. The Budget Group has been able to monitor the stewardship of financial resources by Councils and Committees by engaging directly with elected members and senior staff. This was beyond the remit of the former Board of Stewardship and Finance, but is an essential part of the promotion of Christian Stewardship within the Church.

2. Proposals

The Stewardship and Finance Committee and the Council of Assembly are jointly proposing that the way forward for the Church is to merge the remaining work of the Stewardship and Finance Committee with that of the Budget Group of the Council of Assembly and reconstitute the Budget Group as a Finance Group of the Council of Assembly. In making the proposals below it is noted that the practical arrangements for the working of Council of Assembly sub-groups may be reviewed from time to time by the Council in the light of experience.

It is proposed that:

(a) The Finance Group will consist of the Convener and Vice-Convener of the Council of Assembly plus four elected members of the Council and not more than two others, with relevant skills, co-opted by the Council of Assembly. The Secretary of the Council of Assembly and the General Treasurer will be the only members of staff who are present for, and have the right to participate in, all the business. This arrangement will allow for the continuing detailed discussion with representatives of Councils and Committees about their budgets, their income and their expenditure, which has proved to be an effective way of working for the present Budget Group. As with the Budget Group, the Finance Group will prepare recommendations for the Council of Assembly to consider.

(b) One elected member of the Council of Assembly will be a person with a particular interest in and passion for Christian Stewardship. This person will be a member of the Finance Group and will lead a Stewardship Support Group with two others co-opted by the Council of Assembly which will liaise with the Head of Stewardship and the Stewardship Consultants.

(c) The Head of Stewardship will have regular access to the Finance Group and be present for all business relating to Christian giving, the income of the Church, Ministries and Mission Contributions, and the overall size and shape of the Co-ordinated Budget. The Head of Stewardship will report annually to the Council of Assembly and will prepare a written report on Christian Stewardship for inclusion in the Council's Report to the General Assembly.

(d) The Finance Group will arrange an annual meeting with Presbytery Stewardship and Finance Representatives to which all members of the Council of Assembly will be invited. This meeting will provide a forum for discussion about the teaching and promotion of Christian Stewardship, Ministries and Mission Contributions from congregations, the Church's Co-ordinated Budget, and requirements for Presbytery and Congregational Finance.

(e) The Council of Assembly will be responsible for approving the audited annual Report and Financial Statements of the Unincorporated Councils and Committees.

(f) There will be an independent Audit Committee, responsible for External and Internal Audit. The composition of this Committee will be a Convener and two members appointed by the General Assembly through the Nomination Committee, together with one member of the Council of Assembly appointed by the Council on the recommendation of its Finance Group. The Convener of the Finance Group, the General Treasurer and the Secretary of the Council of Assembly will be non-voting ex-officio members. Representatives of the External and Internal Auditors will be in attendance. The remit of the Audit Committee is detailed in the Appendix. The Convener of the Audit Committee will have the right to report directly to the General Assembly when the Audit Committee deems this to be necessary.

(g) The present remit of the Stewardship and Finance Committee will be incorporated within the remit of the Council of Assembly.

For the avoidance of doubt, Regulations for Ministries and Mission Contributions, Congregational Finance and Presbytery Finance will continue to require the approval of the General Assembly.

With the approval of the Stewardship and Finance Committee, which is responsible for the Stewardship Department, and the Central Services Committee, which is responsible for the General Treasurer's Department, the Stewardship Department and the General Treasurer's Department will be merged to form a Stewardship and Finance Department from 1 June 2009. The General Treasurer will be the head of department, with the Head of Stewardship continuing to be responsible for the stewardship function and the General Treasurer and the Deputy Treasurer continuing to be responsible for the finance and accounting function.

The Stewardship and Finance Committee and the Council of Assembly commend this Joint Report to the General Assembly as a more effective and efficient way of fulfilling the stewardship and finance remit from the General Assembly.

In the name of the Stewardship and Finance Committee and the Council of Assembly

VIVIENNE A DICKSON, *Convener, Stewardship and Finance Committee*
ALAN GREIG, *Convener, Council of Assembly*

APPENDIX
REMIT OF THE AUDIT COMMITTEE

Financial Reporting

- To oversee the financial reporting processes implemented by management; and
- To review, and challenge where necessary, the actions and judgements of management, in relation to the annual Report and Financial Statements of the Unincorporated Councils and Committees and any other formal statement before submission to, and approval by, the Council of Assembly, and before clearance by the external auditors. Particular attention shall be paid to:
  - critical accounting policies and practices and any changes in them;
  - decisions requiring a significant element of judgement;
  - the extent to which the financial statements are affected by any unusual transactions in the year and how they are disclosed;
  - clarity of disclosures;
  - significant adjustments or issues arising from the audit;
  - compliance with relevant accounting and financial reporting standards.

Internal Control, Risk Management and Compliance

- To keep under review the effectiveness of the systems for internal financial control, financial reporting and

26

risk management, including compliance with the legal and regulatory environment within which the Unincorporated Councils and Committees operate; and

- To review procedures established by management for detecting fraud and whistle blowing and ensure that arrangements are in place by which staff may, in confidence, raise concerns about possible improprieties in matters of financial reporting or financial control.

Internal Audit

- To consider and make recommendations to the Council of Assembly on the appointment, re-appointment and removal of the internal auditors;
- To oversee the relationship with the internal auditors, including approval of their terms of engagement and remuneration and assessing their effectiveness and compliance with relevant professional and regulatory requirements;
- To monitor and assess the effectiveness of the internal audit function in the overall context of the risk management systems of the Unincorporated Councils and Committees;
- To consider and approve the remit of the internal audit function and programme of work, ensuring that it is adequately resourced and has appropriate access to information to enable it to perform its function effectively and in accordance with relevant professional standards;
- To receive reports on the internal auditors' work on a periodic basis;
- To review and monitor management's responsiveness to the internal auditors' findings and recommendations;
- To meet with the internal auditors at least annually without the presence of management to discuss their remit and findings.

External Audit

- To oversee the relationship with the external auditors, including approval of their terms of engagement and remuneration and assessing their effectiveness and compliance with relevant professional and regulatory requirements;
- To consider and make recommendations to the Council of Assembly on the appointment, re-appointment and removal of the external auditors;
- To discuss with the external auditors, before the audit commences, the nature and scope of the audit;
- To review with the external auditors, the findings of their work, including any major issues that arose during the course of the audit and have subsequently been resolved and those issues that have been left unresolved, key accounting and audit judgements, levels of errors identified during the audit, obtaining explanations from management and, where necessary, the external auditors as to why certain errors might remain unadjusted;
- To review the audit representation letter before consideration by the Council of Assembly, giving particular consideration to matters that relate to non-standard issues;
- To assess, at the end of the audit cycle, the effectiveness of the audit process;
- To review and monitor the content of the external auditors' management report in order to assess whether it is based on a good understanding of the business of the Unincorporated Councils and Committees and establish whether recommendations have been acted upon and, if not, the reasons they have not been acted upon; and
- To meet with the external auditors at least annually without the presence of management to discuss their remit and findings.

Reporting

The Audit Committee shall annually review its terms of reference and its own effectiveness and recommend any changes to the Council of Assembly.

The Audit Committee shall prepare a report to the Council of Assembly on its role and responsibilities and the actions taken to discharge those responsibilities, including, if appropriate, such information as may be required for inclusion in the annual Report of the Unincorporated Councils and Committees.

The Convener of the Audit Committee shall be entitled to report directly to the General Assembly on any matter which the committee believes to be of sufficient importance.

JOINT REPORT OF THE MISSION AND DISCIPLESHIP COUNCIL AND THE SAFEGUARDING COMMITTEE

FORGIVENESS AND PROPORTIONALITY WORKING GROUP

'FOR OF SUCH IS THE KINGDOM OF HEAVEN – CREATING A CHURCH WHERE ALL MAY SAFELY LIVE'

PROPOSED DELIVERANCE

General Assembly

1. The General Assembly receive the Report.
2. Adopt for immediate use the procedure and processes outlined in the report relating to how congregations should deal with the request of a sex offender to attend worship in a congregation, as detailed in the policy document attached to the report.
3. Instruct congregations when they identify the presence of a sex offender in their midst, to contact the Safeguarding Office and, with the assistance of the Safeguarding Office, commence the process of drawing up a 'Covenant of Responsibilities'. (Section 14.1)
4. Ensure that all perpetrators of sexual abuse who seek to worship in congregations of the Church of Scotland are advised that they must agree to be supported and monitored by the Safeguarding Panel within the Congregation. (Section 3.5)
5. Recognise that those who are members of the Safeguarding Panel of a congregation may require significant support from Safeguarding staff and/ or a Counselling Service. (Section 13.2.4)
6. Instruct congregations, especially in a vacancy, that they must seek the involvement of the appropriate Pastoral Adviser from the Ministries Council in the support of all who are involved in the local Safeguarding Panel charged with the support and monitoring of the sex offender.
7. Instruct the Church and Society Council to consult with the Scottish Government, Survivor Scotland and other appropriate agencies, to ensure that the voice of the Church is heard in the preparation of the responses made by the government to the issues of sexual assault on children and adults at risk.
8. Instruct the Working Group to prepare study materials, to assist congregations and presbyteries in the development of their understanding of the report and the complex issues involved, and commend the consideration of the materials for wide use throughout the Church.
9. Instruct the Safeguarding Committee to make appropriate arrangements for the development and support of the processes outlined in the report.
10. Instruct the Council of Assembly to ensure that appropriate financial resources are made available to the Safeguarding Office to ensure that the policies and processes of this report are operational as soon as possible.

CONTENTS

REPORT

Overview of the Report

The intention of this report is to discover and set out how the theological concept of forgiveness in Christianity may shape the policy and practice of the church in relation to the involvement of sex offenders in the life of congregations. The report develops its approach from the Interim Report approved by the General Assembly of 2008.

The report declares that forgiveness is a gift of God and is freely given, without reference to any prior conditions, or promises of alteration of behaviour. As a result of the acceptance of the gift of forgiveness, there are, however, serious implications for the life and behaviour of sex offenders. The forgiveness of God should lead to confession, repentance and a change of attitude. As a recipient of the grace of God, the sex offender should admit to responsibility for the serious consequences of his/her actions against children and/or adults at risk, and thereby release the power of forgiveness into his/her life.

This process of reformation and restoration will be supported and monitored through local safeguarding panels under the guidance of the Safeguarding Office of the Church. 'Covenants of Responsibilities' will be drawn up to ensure that the particular circumstances of each sex offender are recognised and that the appropriate oversight and support are offered in congregations.

These Covenants have two main and equally important aims. The first is to assure all victims of abuse and the families of children and adults at risk in a congregation that precautions and safeguards are in place to ensure 'safety from harm' in church premises. The second is to provide structure and support for the sex offender who seeks to make his/her life characterised by forgiveness and the opportunity to participate in the worshipping life of a congregation.

The report is based on a process of wide discussion with a number of experts who have brought varied perspectives on many of the issues. Attention was paid to theological works which consider aspects of this issue, and specific articles from a variety of sources were also consulted. A series of meetings with the representatives of over eighty congregations, from a variety of geographical locations also took place to ensure that the concerns and issues of those who will put the policy into practice have been heard.

All the recommendations of the report have been formed with the focus on the concern for safety of children and adults at risk, and in obedience to the command of Jesus that we remember that 'of such is the Kingdom of Heaven.' It has also been designed to assist the Church in its engagement with the challenge of appropriate welcome to those sex offenders who claim the forgiveness of God. A policy document has also been prepared for the consideration of the General Assembly.

The hymn 'Let us build a House where love can dwell and all can safely live'[1] has been used as a linking theme throughout the report.

'For of such is the Kingdom of Heaven – where all can safely live'

1. Introduction

1.1 Formation of Group

The Group was formed as a result of the deliverance agreed by the General Assembly in May 2007, attached to the report of the Safeguarding Committee. The text of the deliverance read as follows:

> Instruct the Committee to seek discussion with members of the Worship and Doctrine Task Group to discover a theology of forgiveness and proportionality related to sex offenders seeking to return to worship in congregations.

The Group began its work after the General Assembly of 2007, and produced an Interim Report for the General Assembly of 2008.

27

2. Interim Reports to the General Assembly of 2008

2.1 The Group, soon after it began its work, had to acknowledge the huge remit given by the General Assembly and the complexities of tackling a subject which was bound up with so many sensitive issues.

2.2 The Group, therefore, resolved to present to the General Assembly of 2008, a report which not only indicated the breadth and diversity of issues involved, but also some initial indications of the direction of the final report and the guidelines which might be produced for consideration by the General Assembly in 2009.

3. Statement of Deliverance of the General Assembly of 2008

3.1 Through its commitment to listen to a wide range of perspectives on the issue, the Group brought to the General Assembly of 2008 an Interim Report which generated positive discussion and reflection on the floor of the General Assembly. The Deliverances attached to the Interim Report were agreed without any objection, or contrary voice. These Deliverances read as follows, firstly:

Affirm the Church's commitment in partnership with Social Service organisations to ongoing pastoral care of survivors of sexual abuse and their families and reassert the commitment of the Church to create a safe environment for children and adults at risk in congregations.

3.2 The second part undertook to:

Reaffirm that the primary responsibility of the Church to children and young adults and vulnerable groups is their safety, which will mean the imposition of appropriate restrictions in congregations for those who have committed sexual offences.

The Working Group acknowledges that what is says about forgiveness is limited by the particular focus of this report. The Group is aware that much more might be said about

forgiveness in general, and how it might operate in other more public circumstances. There is no suggestion that we wish to alter a tradition of over 2000 years of interpretation of the concept of forgiveness. Instead, what we have set out here is a reflection on the particular and the unique nature of sexual abuse and assault as it affects the Christian community. It is therefore limited in its scope and does not touch upon issues of public aggression and violence. We make no apology for this as we were aware that the instruction of the General Assembly was clear and specific and could not wait for a full and comprehensive theology of forgiveness applicable to all situations to be formulated.

3.3 The third section of the deliverance gave approval to the process of wide consultation and research which had under-girded all the work of the group and wide consultation and research.

Commend the process of listening attentively to various perspectives on the complex issues facing the Group.

3.4 The final part of the deliverance gave a clear mandate to the Group to prepare this Report based on the principles set out in the Interim Report and developed in the light of the research and investigation undertaken by the Group. The Group was instructed to offer suggested processes for congregations to assist them in dealing with the challenge of appropriate inclusion and essential protection:

Instruct the Group to bring a report, including guidelines and outlines of processes, to the General Assembly of 2009.

3.5 The Group had made clear its direction, and this was affirmed by the General Assembly of 2008. While not wishing in any way to deny sex offenders who wish the opportunity to be involved in worship and church activities, this has to be managed and monitored to ensure the maintenance of appropriate safeguards for children and adults at risk, and support for the sex offender. This will require the sex offender to adhere to set guidelines and work within agreed structures, supported by an identified group within the congregation. This group will consist of the Safeguarding Panel as described in the legislation of the Church. The Group recognises the challenges and difficulties involved in this task. It is believed that it is essential for all such groups to collaborate closely with the Safeguarding Office of the Church to ensure that the work involved is managed effectively and appropriate expectations are set down for all parties. Sex Offenders must, as a matter of his/her discipleship journey, engage honestly and openly with the group in the congregation. This group will assist, guide, and help the individual explore his/her sense of membership in an environment which is still safe and secure for all who might be at risk.

3.6 The Group is aware that some sex offenders will not accept the need for such a structure in churches. Some will move on to other churches where there is no setting of appropriate boundaries. We can only work with those we know about. Of course some will not be known, but it is only right to expect that the Church will provide practical guidance and processes, structures and methodology, for dealing effectively with those who are known. There will be occasions where the perpetrator of sexual offences may exclude himself, or herself, from the life of the congregation. This will occur when he, or she, is not willing to work with the group appointed to oversee the Covenant, and continues to deny the lifelong consequences of their actions.

3.7 The Group also noted the comments made in the General Assembly of 2008 regarding the impact on the wider family of those accused of sex offences, and the families of those who have suffered abuse. These are recognised as part of the challenge in addressing the appropriate inclusion of all sex offenders within the life of congregations, and must be acknowledged. Some resources on this issue will be included in the study materials prepared by the Group for use in congregations following the reception of this report. However, the Group's prime focus has been the theological heritage of the Church and how it may create and shape a policy which, as far as will ever be possible, is supportive both of survivors of abuse and perpetrators of sexual offences, who wish to identify themselves with the lives of congregations within the Church of Scotland. There is, in the view of the Group, a tension and a challenge which cannot be ignored, and a primary responsibility to create and maintain, in the congregation, the recognition of the vulnerability of children and adults and their need for protection.

3.8 The Group is aware that all of its report will be subject to media interest and comment. This is only healthy and must be encouraged. However, it is vital that any report of its contents and conclusions reflects the powerful and persuasive arguments which the report has included and its whole tenor as one of ongoing pastoral concern, no matter from what particular perspective an individual may come.

4. Process
'Let us build a house where love may dwell and all can safely live'

4.1 Membership of Group
The Membership of the Committee is listed as an Appendix. As can be seen it includes professionals from the Safeguarding Office, members of the Safeguarding Committee, professionals with a deep appreciation of the practical aspects of the issues, and members of the Worship and Doctrine Task Group.

4.2 Consultation
'Let us build a house where prophets speak and words are strong and true'

4.2.1 The Group invited many people to share their experiences, knowledge and skills. The group listened and explored issues with those involved in the treatment of sex offenders, the teaching of practical theology and

27

Christian ethics, those who work with prisoners and others involved with the support of survivors of sex abuse. A general invitation was given to any in the Church to contact the Group through the website and offer their insight and experience.

4.2.2 A survey of ministers and others was undertaken to hear of their personal experiences of managing the tensions of working with sex offenders and protecting children. The contacts of the Safeguarding Office throughout the Church as a whole, including congregational safeguarding representatives, were all asked to offer questions and experiences, for the consideration of the Group.

4.2.3 Ecumenical contacts were made and materials from a number of churches were examined, and a presentation by the Church of England Safeguarding Officer, who is a Methodist Minister, was also received by the group. A visit to the staff involved in the care and treatment of sex offenders at Peterhead Prison also took place.

4.2.4 A number of road-shows in a variety of settings throughout the country were arranged to ensure that the Group brought to the Assembly the views, questions, and issues of Kirk Sessions and congregations who will have to implement any policy regarding the appropriate inclusion of sex offenders as agreed by this General Assembly. A workshop on this issue was also included in the Safeguarding Trainers Conference programme.

4.2.5 The Road-shows were attended by more than 200 people and representatives of Congregations in Presbyteries in the West, South West and Central Scotland were involved. (A full list of presbyteries involved appears in the Appendix). On the whole, the participants in the Road-shows were strongly in support of the approach of the Working Group to the issue presented. While they wish to record their pastoral concern and support of sex offenders who wished to become involved in the life of congregations, they also recognised the importance of

appropriate boundaries and safeguards to ensure that adults at risk and children were protected. Some would have liked the Working Group to extend their comments into other areas, including that of physical violence and abuse, but the Group was conscious of the directive of the General Assembly and the need to focus on this particular area of sexual abuse and assault.

4.2.6 Some interesting comments were recorded and have been used throughout this report as a means of reflecting the tenor and concern of the participants in the Road-shows. Some raised questions regarding the fact that women sexually abuse children and adults at risk, and that this is often forgotten. The Working Group acknowledges this as an issue which should not be neglected in any consideration of the complexities of protecting children and adults at risk.

4.2.7 The Working Group was challenged in the Road-shows by a very small number of negative reactions. In response, the Working Group would suggest to the General Assembly that what is presented in this report and proposed does not offer a 'politically correct' response or an easy and facile method of dealing with a thorny issue. Instead, we believe that the compassion and concern of Jesus for all sinful humanity is an essential characteristic of any of the proposals we have made.

4.2.8 What we are discussing is a process of 'costly grace' involving time and effort from the Safeguarding office working with volunteers in congregations, to ensure not just the safety and security of children and adults at risk, but the support and care of those sex offenders who wish to associate themselves with the life of a congregation in a journey of repentance and restoration. The monitoring and care of sex offenders in the wider community was not part of our remit, but we are keen to ensure that this issue is pursued by Church and Society Council in their discussions with the relevant groups within the Scottish Government.

4.2.9 The Group wishes to express its gratitude to all who gave their time and experience to enhance and expand the information and insights available to the Group. While the Group may not have followed any one individual's approach, it is happy to recognise that all views submitted have been valuable and creative. Views expressed have often challenged and disturbed the members as they struggled to formulate a clear and coherent, theologically sound and practical policy on this issue.

5. Evidence and Factual Basis

5.1 Some find the concept and implications of sexual abuse so disturbing that they avoid reflecting on the issues. Others may react to the statistics in such a way that they believe that discussion is not appropriate. We need to be clear about the extent of the occurrence of sexual assault. It is clear that 95% of sex abuse goes either unreported[2], or does not result in a prosecution. While we may be able to explain the reasons for the reticence and difficulty which some may face in engaging with this issue, it is also true that silence and inaction are quite inexcusable and may well allow abuse to continue in the Church. The Group appreciates the contributions of all who responded to the invitation to participate in the discussion and research by providing experiences and information.

5.2 It is clear that real efforts to provide an open and transparent policy must be made for the benefit of all concerned, regardless of their experience of abuse.

6. Particular Issues Raised

6.1 Central to the discussion is the matter of forgiveness. This will be discussed at some length further on in the report

6.2 The Group is clear that what is involved in trying to incorporate a sex offender in a congregation is a task of discipleship. The intention, according to the perspective of the Group, is for the sex offender to be given opportunities for growth and development without risking harm to children or adults at risk, in the congregation, or themselves. The inclusion of sex offenders must **never** be at the risk of harm to vulnerable groups within church settings.

6.3 The Group is all too aware that much of the discussion could enter the realms of esoteric debate and exploration of the ideal, rather than the practical application of guidance which creates a safe environment for all. While the theological issues are crucial, it must be recognised the issues of forgiveness and proportionality and the nature of grace must be discussed in relation to the facts of dealing with sex offenders, with their particular characteristics and problems. The reality is that many sex offenders are adept at disguising motives, confusing and covering up by the clever use of religious language and behaviour, and thereby, masking their actual intentions.

6.4 While it may be impossible to identify the genuine and the inauthentic, there is a strict requirement that whatever is allowed in the Church **must never** permit, collude, or approve the possibility of further sexual assault. The Group makes these statements in the light of the evidence presented by those involved in the care of victims and the prevention of abuse, alongside those who are working with sexual abusers. The contributions of the professionals in the field have been extremely valuable through the questions they have raised and the real life experiences they have brought to the attention of the Group throughout our deliberations.

6.5 Just as at the meetings of Alcoholics Anonymous, no alcohol is served, and at Narcotics Anonymous, no drugs are allowed, it is clear that with the patterns of compulsive, skilful and deceptive behaviour involved in sex offending, the sex offender should not be subject to situations of temptation, or everyday opportunistic situations. Therefore appropriate safeguards are necessary both for the potential victims, children and adults at risk **and** the sex offenders themselves. To neglect this responsibility would be both morally and ethically abhorrent and contrary to the Gospel principles of pastoral care which ought to characterise all Christian congregations. Any truly repentant sex offender will, we believe, recognise this and agree readily to the processes of protection.[3] The Church has a responsibility to create a safe environment for all.

6.6 It appears that, from all quarters in the Church, there is support for the principle that the Church must be made as safe a place as possible for everyone. There is agreement that the issue of 'trust' is separate from the concept of 'forgiveness', and therefore in relation to sexual abuse, the Church has a responsibility to expect the acceptance of limitations on the offender in order to protect children and adults at risk. The concept of some form of 'Covenant of Responsibilities' appears, in the opinion of the Group, to be an appropriate response to ensure that the Church environment may be secure and as free from danger as is humanly possible.

6.7 The Group is aware that there are those who would see the issues of dealing with sex offenders in congregations in a way similar to the action of the Truth and Reconciliation Commission in South Africa after the end of legalised discrimination on the grounds of colour and race. However, the Group is convinced that this is not applicable as, in the case of South Africa, the criminal acts were well known, publicly acknowledged and admitted, before they were then addressed. In the circumstances of sexual assault of vulnerable people there is secrecy and little public acknowledgement of its factual basis and its long term effects are often not recognised, or admitted. These crimes take place in private and are often denied, reduced in significance and 'explained away'. This Report in itself is one way of bringing the issue out into the open and letting the light of the Gospel enter the debate and discussion in the Church of Scotland.

7. The Incidence of Sexual Abuse
'Where all God's children dare to seek to dream God's dream'

7.1 Due to the enormous difficulties regarding securing a conviction when there are children or adults at risk, involved, only 5% of allegations of sexual assault actually lead to conviction. It must be noted that only a very tiny part of the 95% will be due to the fact that the allegation was false.[4] Against this background it should be noted that around 10% of prisoners in Scotland are sex offenders.[5]

7.2 The prevalence of child abuse appears to be, according to the World Health Organization, that about 20% of the population experience some form of sexual abuse in childhood.[6] While traditionally it was believed that more women than men suffer abuse in childhood, the group was informed that there is increasing awareness that the incidence among men is far greater than was once thought. Current research indicates that there is a far larger proportion of males abused than has been reported. Until recently very few males reported incidents for investigation, and therefore reporting is unlikely to reflect the full extent of the problem. Many are silenced by shame and family pressures and powerful dynamics within the structures of family life.

7.3 The Church, as a microcosm of society as a whole, cannot be exempt from the incidence rate. Therefore it is perhaps easier for the General Assembly to conceive of the extent of sexual abuse as meaning that there may be a victim, or survivor, of sexual abuse in every pew of the churches in Scotland. While the impact of child protection measures throughout the Church has, it is hoped, increased the awareness of significant dangers and prevented incidents of abuse within the Church, there is no doubt that there is a significant number of people in the congregations of the Church who have, endured some form of sexual abuse. While it may be true that there is no more physical or sexual abuse of children and adults at risk today than in days gone by, there is more openness about the problem. However, the Group is concerned regarding the alarming increase in computer and internet abuse. There are many new ways of reaching children and vulnerable people, and many of them are shrouded in secrecy and are perpetrated in an anonymous manner.

7.4 The Group believes that the issues in relation to the prevalence of sexual assault and the proliferation of internet sources of indecent images involving the abuse of children are of such importance that the Church and Society Council should be asked to consult with *Survivor Scotland,* the agency of the Scottish Government, concerned with the impact of abuse. This would ensure that the voice of the Church was heard in the processes whereby these major issues may be addressed by civil legislation and treatment programmes.

7.5 It is also clear that most abusers are known to the victims. In 4 cases out of 5 the sex offender is a familiar face to the child. Evidence suggests that 80% of sexual abuse takes place in the home, though not necessarily by family members.[7] This is a very important point which must be recognised in relation to the range of offenders. Government figures record that 30% of offenders against children and young people are adolescents and children themselves, 50% of offenders are adult males, and 5% to 20% are adult females. We should remember that there are female abusers and that they are not always coerced by men.[8] The Church by its nature offers a very open and accepting environment where links could be developed which could allow potential sexual predators to take advantage of, and groom, children and adults at risk.

7.6 The Group is also aware that the processes of protection suggested in this report are also to address the sex offenders who are guilty of the abuse of elderly women and other adults at risk. It was noted in our research that there is a proportion of younger prisoners who had been convicted of serious sexual assault of elderly women[9]. This may be of particular importance when the 'Covenant of Responsibilities' is drawn up to ensure that appropriate boundaries and safeguards are in place to protect elderly women in congregations.

8. Silencing of Survivors
'where hands will reach to heal and strengthen'

8.1 Survivors of abuse have often endured great suffering in trying to overcome the stigma and impact of the abuse on their lives. People may well have been harmed by abuse, but we do need to recognise that each individual experiences abuse differently and the impact on their lives is very varied. Some may be able to live positive and fulfilling lives. While that is true, some do not. There are statistics that indicate that people who have been abused have experienced a higher proportion of negative affects, including depression, relationship failures, alcoholism, mental health difficulties and attempted suicide.[10]

8.2 Any initiative taken by any group gives survivors hope. It provides them with the opportunity to be listened to with respect and dignity. When society openly recognises this abuse, there can be positive action. If, however, we stand back and are silent we collude with the abuse. The Church must ensure that it is positive and supportive of those who have endured sexual assault.

8.3 Abuse depends on silence, often forced by threat or presented as 'love'. This must be named and acknowledged as a complete distortion. Public acknowledgement of abuse gives hope. It implies that there are more of those who are not abusers than those who are.

8.4 If the Church does not take their pain, suffering and courage seriously, they suffer once again and are abused by the very institution, or group, which should, in its character and basis in the message of Jesus, support and protect them. We **all** know people who have been abused. It cuts across gender, class and all socio-economic grounds. More damage may be done by the Church covering up abuse than the actual abuse itself.

27

8.5 The Church, like all other groups, fears speaking out about this uncomfortable issue. The whole nature of sexual abuse is such that the powerlessness and disgust felt by most people hinders the discussion. By silence, the issue is denied and continues to damage and destroy lives. Abuse and sexual assault depend on silence to continue exercising power over individuals.

8.6 While the Group would not advocate the introduction of worship services that focus on the survivors of sexual abuse, it believes that the stories of the survivors of abuse may be acknowledged in worship, when appropriate. It has to be emphasised that abuse often silences victims. Therefore we must provide a safe environment and an appropriate place for survivors to be listened to, and know that they are heard. It is important for survivors to be able to tell their story, if they wish to, and for people from their congregation to listen with care. Many survivors feel that they do not want to prosecute, but may have a need for some accountability to be registered and an opportunity, or a forum, for them to 'bear witness' to the trauma of adults who have been abused as children.

8.7 Children are often frightened and because of the fear of not being believed, or of family breakdown, therefore do not speak about sexual assault.[11] Children often take responsibility for justice and often carry the burden of what they cannot talk about. A child wants love at all costs and often will be so desperate for love that they will endure any pain. Survivors need to be listened to respectfully and carefully. What all survivors need is pastoral care, which pays attention to their pain, while not attempting to solve it or take it away.

8.8 If we acknowledge that there is the possibility of a victim of some form of sexual abuse being in every pew of every church in the land, this must be recognised in the Church's life. Survivors will want to know: *'How safe is this place for me or my children?'*

8.9 It is also crucial to remember that due to the nature of sexual offenders and their defensive processes that they often 'minimise' the extent of their offences. The Church must not collude with this form of denial which endangers vulnerable groups. The Church must be alert to the complex nature of sex offending and prevent the Church being seen as a place where these offences are excused, or dismissed, as unimportant. While the risk can be minimised and reduced, it may not be eliminated entirely. The Group is advised that there is often a lack of insight in the perpetrator and they are unable to take personal responsibility. Perpetrators can suspend their behaviour, but do not make the necessary changes.

8.10 The church is a place where children attend in large numbers, and is also a place where survivors of abuse may also attend in significant numbers. Yet statistics also suggest that the church is a place where there is a higher percentage of sex offenders involved as compared with their presence in the general population. Research suggests that in Scotland alone 25% of the sex offender population attend worship.[12] In addition, we are aware from our discussions that there is also an issue of naivety in the Church, with church leaders being sometimes unaware of the compulsive nature of much sex offending, and the limitations of counselling.

8.11 Another important issue is the Church's use of the language of forgiveness. The confusion between forgiveness and trust is one reason why offenders have been allowed to continue in positions of pastoral responsibility even after it is known that they have abused children.

8.12 Our research has also suggested that there are other reasons for the Church's failure to protect children properly. These include denial, discomfort, Christian isolationism, misunderstanding the nature of confidentiality and a natural reticence to make judgments of another person's spiritual journey.[13]

8.13 Through our discussions with the Lucy Faithfull Foundation we were advised that the danger of further offending may be increased due to the paucity of treatment programmes for sex offenders. It is only in treatment that some real assessment of ongoing risk be undertaken.[14]

8.14 Of course the Church cannot know all who may pose a threat to children and adults at risk. Not all sex offenders will be known to the authorities and not all known offenders are reported to the congregations with which they are associated. Some will never have been convicted. Despite this, the Church has a real and important obligation to act responsibly when it **does** know of those who are sex offenders, so that appropriate safeguards may be instituted for all concerned.

9. The nature of sexual assault of children and adults at risk

9.1 It is clear from the literature and research that sexual assault is intimately related to the exercise of power. As one person we consulted has written:

(Sexual) abuse is an abuse of power. We may therefore understand significant vulnerability in those recovering from abuse, and that this is a recovery from that loss of childhood and of individual power. This is often very like a loss or bereavement. Healing, justice and restoration, therefore, need significant compassionate support and acceptance by those who listen and walk alongside them. Victims need choices and empowerment in a life long process of survival, and recovery for a sense of thriving.

Safeguarding challenges those in positions of authority (including those within families) who deny the issue, collude with it or cover it up. The Church needs to witness to this prophetic challenge, which affects all parts of society and all societies, to give priority to those who are vulnerable and hurting.

For the church to become a safer place, it needs to develop and nurture places of hospitable space or sanctuary. Church people need to develop a sense of hospitality which includes openness and careful listening. A sense of hospitable space and a careful welcome must also extend to the offender.[15]

In our research, we found our exploration and perspectives confirmed by one theological writer who summarised his research in the following way:

- The sexual abuse of children is fundamentally an abuse of trust and of power which exploits the age-related differentials between child and abuser, as well as enlisting, abusing, distorting and disorientating the child's needs for intimacy, affirmation, security, trust and guidance.
- Abuse is not adequately construed in terms of acts which might then have certain consequences; it is better thought of in terms of an expansive dynamic distorted relationality which may affect all of the child's relationships…and invade the relational ecology of other sets of relationships. (it is thus impossible clearly and cleanly to separate act from consequence.)
- Its core dynamic is that of entrapment and isolation, through which social and physiological transcendence may be blocked.
- That dynamic effects a form of traumatic confusion concerning the nature of reality in all its dimensions (social, moral, personal, material)
- A particular source of confusion is the incorporation of the child's active agency in psychologically 'accommodating' the abuse and keeping it secret.
- As a consequence, abuse easily leads to a radical distortion of the very core of self-identity.[16]

9.2 There is no doubt that sexual assault creates a legacy which may distort future relationships. We know that many abusers have been themselves abused. They have experienced many of the difficulties and obstacles of spiritual growth and discipleship which are common to the victims of sexual abuse. This does **not** excuse their abuse in any way and it does **not** acknowledge the fact that the majority who have been abused do not become abusers. What is important for the Church to recognise is that all are sinners in need of grace. We who claim to be the Church are, however, even more sinful if we allow the poor, the vulnerable and the powerless to become victims and neglect to provide the appropriate support systems for those who are penitent.

9.3 It is also important to be aware that the nature of sexual abuse is often, if not always, related to the exercise of power over victims. The sexual assault appears to be an expression of violence and victimisation, and a conflict in the abuser regarding his or her identity, and needs:

> ......*relatively few abusers appear to be possessed of an innate sexual attraction to children. Abuse is sometimes, though rarely, driven by straight forward (though distorted) sexual desire. More commonly, however, than the elevation of sexual appetites, abuse seems to be a means for resolving issues of personal identity that reflect distorted identity structures......For those abusers who are themselves survivors of sexual abuse, it is likely that they are modelling their own behaviour on that of their abusers......The association is particularly strong where the abuser and the victim are of the same sex; hence, the modelling of abusive behaviour is to be found more often among male than female survivors.*[17]

The Church is there to support those who have been abused.

9.4 The focus of the report must be upon the protection of the vulnerable and the abused. We must be unequivocal in our acceptance of the fact that children and adults at risk are **never** responsible or to blame for sexual assault:

> *The definition of sexual abuse implies that abuse is coincident with age-related disparities in power,*

status and knowledge. Those disparities mean that the child…cannot be operative as a cause of abuse. It also means…that he or she is unable effectively to resist the abuse.[18]

9.5 While that is acknowledged, those who have committed sexual assault still remain as the children of God. The Church has a duty to support them in their transformation and process of redemption. It is our responsibility and privilege to offer them a covenant to support them in the change required by God's grace. However, we are also clear that the responsibility is limited to the church premises, and we cannot in any way expect the monitoring and support to continue in all aspects of life.

9.6 In using the title *'Covenant of Responsibilities'* we are arguing that both parties, those responsible in the Church for its safety and security, and those penitent sexual offenders are engaging a process of articulation and expression of grace. Both parties are expected to accept their responsibilities and fulfill their obligations to God and the members of the Church.

9.7 The *'Covenant of Responsibilities'* proposed in this report is designed to achieve two purposes.
- The first is to create an environment of protection and security *'where all can safely live'.*
- The second is to support sex offenders by encouraging them to resist temptation, and therefore allow them to be safely and appropriately part of the worshipping Church community.

9.8 We need to declare clearly that the Bible has some very harsh things to say about those who would endanger the lives of children and the vulnerable. While society has created a system of secular protection, the Church needs to hear the warning that God expects much more of the Church. In vivid hyperbole, Jesus speaks of a millstone being attached to those who endanger the 'little ones',[19] and also in Luke's Gospel[20], and we must heed this warning to ensure that the Church is as free as possible from sexual assault.

10. Some Characteristics of a Sex Offender

10.1 While it is important that we do not caricature, or malign, all those who have been convicted of sexual assault on a child or adult at risk, there are several common features which may encourage the Church to take special precautions and care when dealing with them.

10.2 From the research undertaken by the Group, and from the contributions of those who are regularly involved in the care and have responsibility for sex offenders when they are released, it is clear that is naïve to ignore the nature of their offences as many have done unspeakably dreadful things. The professionals in the field are agreed that the sexual preference of a sex offender is extremely difficult to change. Often sex offenders are described as manipulative. They can be extremely clever in groups, and in individual contacts, seeking to gain control over those whom they perceive are weaker than they are. They often use the fact that they have 'changed' to hide their proclivity to continue to offend.

10.3 They are often solitary people without visitors when in prison, and often will seek the companionship of the Church, especially if they had church connections before conviction. Sex offenders may have other problems, including low self-esteem and problems with self harming. Many of those imprisoned for sexual assault have huge guilt issues and therefore seek forgiveness. Treatment programmes in prison can help them realise that forgiveness is a process which involves taking responsibility for their actions.

10.4 They also may use some very persuasive theological language to disguise their crimes, while at the same time claiming the forgiveness of God. It is real that they have no conception, or admission, of the impact of their criminal assault on their victims. This is often intimidating to people who have to deal with them in church situations who feel unable to counter their use of theological language, which often has no reality in their lives. It is therefore essential, that all who are expected to support and monitor sex offenders attending worship must be adequately supported and resourced to deal with this challenge. Resources for this important task will be prepared as part of the materials for congregations.

10.5 From the perspective of those involved in their care both in prison and on release, sex offenders are the most difficult to manage as they attempt to condition, undermine, and manipulate. On a visit to Peterhead Prison the group were advised that prisoners make good use of The Freedom of Information Act. For as much as it is the prisoners' right to view information about themselves it makes working with them time consuming and deflects attention from the main issue which is to address their criminal behaviour.

10.6 It is very easy to be so confused by them and their ability to manipulate that it is necessary for staff to remind themselves that they need to take the perspective of the abused rather than that of the abuser.

10.7 We cannot let naivety take over and allow the responsibility for the protection of children and adults at risk to be sacrificed in order to make sex offenders 'feel good about themselves'. Instead, while expecting, with the innocence of doves, the miraculous power of God's healing grace to be active, we need to be aware and alert to any attempt to open the boundaries beyond those of good sense. It is the hope of the Group that the Church may be equipped through the Safeguarding Office to support and ensure that all are encouraged on a journey of discipleship which includes a healthy sense and understanding of human frailty and responsibility for sin. The Group is persuaded that the liberation theologian is correct when he asserts:

27

Where are then the limits of tolerance? They are in suffering, in human rights and in the rights of nature. Tolerance ends whenever a person is dehumanized. No one has the right to impose unjust suffering on other.[21]

11. The Uniqueness of the Church
'Where all are named, their songs and visions heard'

11.1 The 21st Century Church is unique as a place where access is open to all men and women, their families, survivors of abuse, sexual abusers and their families. No other group or club, society or organisation, is so inclusive. This is the power of the Gospel and its nature of inclusiveness. However, in that process of inclusion, the Church must recognise the importance of providing structures, processes and systems where all may 'dwell in safety'.

11.2 Churches need to be prepared for situations where child sexual abuse is disclosed in church families, or in the life of the congregation. We all would hope that this would never occur in our Church. However, from all the evidence it is clear that sexual abuse does occur, even in devout Christian families, and that it also happens in church youth groups and other church activities. Sex offenders are found in **all** denominations and in people of many different theological persuasions. There are sex offenders who claim to be born again and to have been baptized in the Holy Spirit. No denomination is exempt. **No congregation can say 'It cannot happen here'**

12. Current Situation Surrounding Sexual Abuse and the Church
'Let us bring an end to fear and danger'

12.1 The incidence of sexual abuse has been discussed earlier. It is wrong to conclude that the 21st century is more dangerous than years ago. In fact, due to the heightened awareness of the issue, it is suggested by experts in the field, that there may be a significant reduction in the possibility of abuse. Only now, many years later, often generations later, have the facts of many crimes of abuse come to light. What the Church cannot allow to happen is the provision of an inclusive environment which is perceived by sex offenders as an 'easy' or 'soft' target for abuse.

12.2 The Church is a family of God's people and must try to ensure that a congregation operates within the boundaries that are appropriate to healthy family life. The Church must also work within the limits of the civil law, and this may mean that it has to exclude some people from working in the Church, or having access to vulnerable people.

12.3 At all times the Church must be vigilant and prepared to challenge those who might wish to 'groom' children, or 'take them on a journey of preparation for abuse which makes them vulnerable', and this necessitates the imposition of strict guidelines for appropriate access and boundaries to protect children and adults at risk. At no time, for any reason, must the desire to be inclusive or accepting, allow children and adults at risk to be placed at risk of harm. Their rights must **not** be neglected through attention to those of an abuser. Following the example of Jesus, we need always err on the side of protecting children and adults at risk

13. Safeguards
'Where all are named...loved and treasured'

13.1 The Group, having listened attentively to all perspectives presented, is convinced that Kirk Sessions, congregations and ministers, need the support of recognised processes to assist them in dealing with the inclusion of sex offenders in the life of a congregation. Too often in the past, some isolated individuals have been burdened by the knowledge of the presence of a convicted sex offender in a congregation, and this individual has believed, mistakenly, that no one else could, or should, be made aware of the situation. This must be rejected as both dangerous and destructive, and not at all helpful to all parties. Knowledge is power, and with the knowledge of the person's presence, shared appropriately, and a group designated, and supported, to work with the sex offender, the safety of all in the congregation may be more likely.

13.2 It is clear from the many reports and evidence presented to the group, that survivors of abuse in a congregation may be further abused, or children and adults at risk endangered, without appropriate agreements and boundaries being instituted and observed. Similarly, it is recognised that sex offenders may find their struggle to adjust and seek spiritual growth may be hindered by a lack of structure and significant individual support.

14. Biblical Background
'Live the Word they've known'

14.1 Old Testament
14.1.1 The Bible is a tension-filled book reflecting the faith journey of those who sought God's will as the Divine plan of Salvation unfolded. The Bible underpins this report and the Group has sought to discover a Theology of Forgiveness and Proportionality relating to sex offenders seeking to return to worship in Congregations which meets the scriptural imperatives and answers the contradictions. This has been no easy task.

14.1.2 What must be acknowledged is that there is a huge amount in the Old Testament which reflects the cultural milieu of the Ancient Near East where the idea of the protection of children and adults at risk would be a completely incomprehensible issue. Of course, as some of the feminist theologians have pointed out, there is a great deal of patriarchal domination and discrimination against women in the pages of several books of the Old Testament. Some very unsavoury incidents are recounted and there are some accounts where there is a grave absence of concern about the impact of the exercise of violence and sexual power.

14.1.3 However, alongside this undeniable content of terror and grave injustice, throughout the Old Testament, there is also a deep and abiding concern for the family. While the stories of the family life of the patriarchs, the descendants of Abraham, are often filled with unedifying accounts of intrigue, deception and malpractice, there is also a deep conviction about the importance of family life and the protection of those who will continue to be God's people, the inheritors of the covenant.

14.1.4 There is also a strong emphasis on the inclusion of the stranger and the meaning of hospitality. This is stressed in the work of the prophets and their denunciation of greed, corruption and perversions of God's gifts, and their need to hear the cries for justice for the poor, the fatherless, the widow, and those who struggle for existence. Yet all of these, according to the scripture, are also still chosen and loved by God.

14.1.5 While it may be an ideal, the vision of Zechariah[22] is one which is echoed throughout the annals of the Old Testament. The prophet challenges the people of God to bring to reality his vision of a safe and secure environment, a place where the old may live to enjoy the fruit of their labours, and children may play unmolested, free from fear, on the streets. It is a vision, sadly, which does not yet appear to be possible to achieve in this nation today, many centuries later.

14.1.6 The principles in the Old Testament narrative and accounts of the prophets' works, indicate that God is concerned with those who are defenceless and have no power, wealth or authority, and cannot claim this favour by right. The Old Testament, time and time again, emphasises the inclusive love of God which touches and raises up the forgotten, ignored and powerless. These features are vital in the view of the Group to any decisions regarding this issue:

> *'The Jewish prophets – and indeed the whole of the scriptures – are biased toward the powerless. Such a preferential option for the powerless*

implies a privileged hearing for those whose voices are excluded.' [23]

14.1.7 Forgiveness is challenging in the context of sexual offences against children. There is no doubt that a sex offender can experience God's forgiveness because the only unforgivable sin is blasphemy against the Holy Spirit.[24] In Genesis the story of Esau and Jacob is helpful.[25] Jacob cheated Esau of his birthright and of his father's blessing. The unfolding story describes, nevertheless, Jacob's growing faith: he dreamt of ladders to heaven; knew the assurance of God's continuing Covenant through him; wrestled with God (and lived). All the time, however, he lived with the fact that he was a cheat and a deceiver. We learn little of Esau's encounters with God. Not for him the dreams of the divine presence. Having been cheated twice, he had murder in mind. Forgiveness was far from his thoughts.

14.1.8 The unfolding story, however, tells two key things. Firstly, someone may walk with God; experiencing God's forgiveness, but the consequences of the sin of the past remains. The sin can be forgiven, but the past remains, both for the sinner and the one sinned against. The consequence of Jacob's behavior remained part of his life and anxiety in spite of his growing faith so much so that it was still a major worry as he returned home. It took years for Esau to forgive Jacob, but when he did it was emotional and whole-hearted.[26]

14.1.9 Secondly, living with consequences of the past is part and parcel of human life. Accepting the consequences of the past is altogether more difficult. David, the hero king of Israel, lived with his flawed behaviour. His adultery with Bathsheba led to the setting up of her husband, Uriah, so that he was certain to be killed. This is an appalling abuse of power.[27] In a very terse statement following Uriah's death the writer of 2 Samuel says 'But the thing David had done displeased the Lord.[28] That displeasure was, subsequently, articulated so well in the meeting between Nathan the Prophet and King David. Nathan makes two things very clear first that the Lord has forgiven him but the consequence of his adultery was that the child conceived with Bathsheba died. While we can acknowledge that David did indeed retain his position as King he did suffer the consequences of his actions. Our argument is that while we may include a sex offender in the life of the congregation, he, or she, is never free from the impact of the seriousness of their results of their actions just as David was. We do not intend excluding a sex offender who claims the forgiveness of God from the life of the Church. Instead, we intend that he, or she, should be supported in their ongoing journey of discipleship.

14.1.10 David's ambition was to build a temple for the Ark of the Covenant. This was an ambition unfulfilled because he had blood on his hands.[29] The consequences of his past cast a long shadow into the future.

14.1.11 This is also demonstrated in the story of the sexual assault on Tamar, sister of Absalom, son of King David.[30] It may be one example of the sexual assault of a child in the Bible, as Tamar is likely to have been very young when this attack took place. The impact of this attack on Tamar is not clearly recounted, though it is obvious that she suffered a great deal through the plotting and manipulation of Amnon, in the true style of a sexual predator. What is clear from the biblical account is the impact on a whole family and indeed a nation, of this act.

14.1.12 The action of Amnon remained unpunished by King David. According to some commentators, this inability and unwillingness to address a serious moral and ethical challenge proved to be a confirmation of David's unworthiness to exercise kingship. The inaction of David leads to Absalom's plotting to kill Amnon, which eventually brought about the full scale rebellion and conflict which rent David's family asunder. Absalom acts when David does not insist on responsibility and accountability. Absalom's action in killing Amnon is seen, in the text, as one in which justice is clearly enacted, and Amnon's public assassination declares that Absalom, rather than David, has defended the moral code appropriately. While it would be wrong to base all our safeguarding policy on this story, it has obvious lessons for us.

14.1.13 The first would be the condemnation of incest and sexual assault as contrary to the will of God and the moral code of his people. It also highlights the necessity for action to protect the innocent, and to institute legal process when they have been harmed. The issue here is the necessity of appropriate boundaries being upheld and, when they are broken down, the requirement of those who walk in the ways of God to ensure that moral chaos does not result.

14.2 The New Testament witness to the Teaching of Jesus
'Bear the image of God's face'

14.2.1 Jesus taught in a specific time and circumstance: he taught contradictions too. How many times must we forgive? Seventy times seven![31] 'Let the little children come to me, and do not hinder them, for the kingdom of heaven belongs to such as these'[32] 'And if anyone causes one of these little ones who believe in me to sin, it would be better for him to be thrown into the sea with a large millstone tied around his neck.[33] To the woman who had been caught in adultery Jesus said, 'Go now and leave your life of sin'[34]

14.2.2 The whole doctrine of the incarnation and the story of redemption from the account of the Garden of Eden through to the betrayal of Jesus by Judas, imply indeed that actions do have consequences. It is clear from the story of the woman taken in adultery, and the story of the Penitent Thief[35], that no conditions were attached to the forgiveness offered by Jesus. However, there was a clear expectation in his words that they would not continue in their life of sinfulness.

14.2.3 The question is, then, where do our priorities lie? Jesus was asked a question like that too. 'Is it right for us to pay taxes to Caesar or not?'[36] Jesus took a coin in answer to a question about where a citizen's priorities lay and asked 'Whose head is on the coin?' 'Caesar's', they replied. He said to them, 'Then give to Caesar what is Caesar's, and to God what is God's.'[37]

14.2.4 It is also the message of gracious concern for all who have no obvious political or economic power. This is demonstrated by the life of Jesus as portrayed in the Gospel narratives. Repeatedly his teaching goes against the cultural traditions and standards of Roman, Greek and Jewish cultures, by affirming the centrality, in the love of God, for the child, the women, the poor, the sick and the discriminated against. While, once again, the issue of sexual abuse is not directly discussed in the Gospels, it is impossible to escape the message of Jesus that respect for each person, no matter how small, or unimportant, in the world's eyes, is of crucial importance, to the love of God. Jesus is consistently portrayed in the Gospel narrative as having a deep and abiding concern and compassion, amounting to a preference almost for those who, like children and adults at risk, are considered powerless and voiceless:

> 'Prophetic language makes it possible to draw near to a God who has a predilection for the poor precisely because divine love refuses to be defined by the categories of human justice. God has a preferential love for the poor not because they are necessarily better than others, morally or religiously, but simply because they are poor and living in an inhuman situation which is contrary to God's will. The ultimate basis for the privilege of the poor is not in the poor themselves but in God, in the gratuitousness and universality of God's love…belief in God and God's gratuitous love leads to a preferential option for the poor and to solidarity to those who suffer wretched conditions, contempt and oppression, those whom the social order ignores and exploits.'[38]

27

14.2.5 In tackling the issue of how we might rightly extend God's grace to those who seek it in the Church, we must not forget how Jesus acted. Through the respect accorded to people as humans made in the image and likeness of God, he offered an opportunity for them to act according to the way of love, rather than the law. Each incident that we have conveys the principle that grace is radical, free and disturbing, shaking the foundations of our prejudices and safe structures. Equally, grace is such that it invites and enables, if he, or she, who receives it so desires, to adopt a new way of living and loving known as being in 'on the way with Jesus', or perhaps more accurately, 'accepting the discipline of discipleship':

> 'The poor merit preferential attention, whatever may be the moral or spiritual situation in which they find themselves. Made in the image and likeness of God to be his children, this image is dimmed and even defiled. That is why God takes on their defence and loves them. The ultimate basis of God's preference of the poor is to be found in God's own goodness and not in any analysis of society of or human compassion however pertinent these reasons may be.'[39]

14.2.6 There are several instances recorded where Jesus gives, in love and grace, a gift of a fresh start and a challenge to an individual: the woman at the well,[40] Nicodemus,[41] the rich young ruler[42] the man born blind[43] the ten lepers,[44] and asks them to accept the implications of this gift for their lifestyle. This is crucial, in the view of the Group, in any approach to the matter of proportionality and forgiveness. While grace is, by its very nature, free and unmerited, it confers on the individual responsibilities to be exercised in community. No one is able to escape the privilege and responsibility of being an adult, made in the image and likeness of God, and developing, through willing co-operation, a life of discipline and devotion, reflective of the principles of Jesus.

14.2.7 The Group has found support and clarification of its conclusions from the work of the contemporary theologian, Miroslav Volf. He argues that the issue of repentance in the preaching of Jesus as portrayed in the Gospels may have been a result of the Church's reflection on the implicit response required to the message of God's unconditional love. This is helpful in the view of the Group when we examine the need to insist on the nature and activity of repentance in the life of a sex offender who seeks to be part of the worshipping life of a congregation:

> 'To repent means to make a turnabout of a profound moral and religious import. Repentance implies not merely recognition that one has made a bad mistake, but that one has sinned. Jesus stated explicitly that he came "to call not the righteous but sinners" (Mark 2:17) and the evangelists report that he was engaged in the practice of "forgiving sins' (Mark 2:5)[45]

14.2.8 It is also vital to note that Jesus' last hours were marked by betrayal and denial and violence beyond imagination. Forgiveness does not seem to be a feature of the events of Gethsemane and Good Friday. Judas showed remorse and took his own life. Peter denied Jesus with oaths and curses in Pilate's Courtyard. A cock crowed. Jesus said nothing. All that is recorded is that 'The Lord turned and looked straight at Peter'[46] Peter recognised what he had done and he was filled with remorse. Jesus did not respond with a word of forgiveness. Forgiveness was delayed until resurrection morning.[47]

14.3 The New Testament Record of the Teaching of Paul

14.3.1 Similar tension exists through much of Paul's writings to the Church: in the Letter to Romans it is the tension between Law and Grace[48]; in the letter to the Galatians it is Flesh and Spirit.[49] Writing in the latter he has list of markers for the Spirit-filled life[50]– the fruit of the Spirit – and a list of markers for the flesh-orientated life – the works of the flesh – which include sexual immorality.[51]

Given the culture of the times, it is highly likely that sexual immorality would include the sexual abuse of children for, like women and slaves; children had no human rights worth mentioning.

14.3.2 Reflecting on the tension between 'flesh' and spirit' Professor John Barclay writes

'Christians are no longer 'under the law', that is under its restraining, disciplining and directing influence because the Spirit provides all the necessary guidance in the fight against the flesh. They do not need the law to marshal their behaviour: in the Spirit led battle against the flesh they have all the direction they need.'[52]

Also, he notes, quoting G S Duncan who 'rightly glosses this verse': 'If you know the life of the Spirit with its safeguards you neither require nor recognise the safeguards of the Law[53] In reality, those who are 'in Christ' are bound by ethical and moral standards that surpass those of the law, and in this case would not allow any involvement in the abuse of children and adults at risk.

14.3.3 Herein lies the problem relating to Safeguarding and a proportional response to those who have abused children. How do Safeguarders know that someone who has been involved with sexual abuse on a child in the past has experienced the saving grace of Christ and that the Spirit now directs their lives? How do Safeguarders know that there is no longer any intent to abuse a child? The short answer is that it is **not** possible to **know.** It is possible only to attempt to create an atmosphere of safety to minimize the risk. In a fallen world the only person who knows is the sex offender on the one hand, and God on the other.

14.3.4 While the ideal of the Spirit offers a high ethic dependent on the power of the Holy Spirit, Paul knows that the Spirit can be abused to become an excuse for all kinds of license. One need look no further than 1 Corinthians where Paul blasts sexual immorality 'so terrible that not even the heathen would be guilty of it' and he goes on 'the

man who has done such a thing should be expelled from your fellowship.'[54] The question this raises is Paul offering a proportionate response? Where is his forgiveness?

14.3.5 Here is the Safeguarders' dilemma which is the subject of this report.

14.3.6 While a huge amount has been written about Paul's attitude to the law, there is no evidence to suggest that he saw that the life of the convert to the way of Jesus was, in any way, without characteristic respect and honour of all parties. His work does not display contempt for the rules which allow society to operate creatively and lovingly. He questions, in the name of Jesus, any legalism which will constrict and damage, restrict and restrain, the love of God in Christian community. While this has been interpreted as a simplistic abandonment of all traditional legal structures, it is clear that Paul would expect the convert to abide by any community regulation which nourished his or her spirituality and supported their membership of that community known as the Church.

14.4 Biblical witness to the Church's Character *'Where peace and justice meet'*

14.4.1 The Church was born by the Holy Spirit on the Day of Pentecost[55] It is the body of Christ.[56] It is made up of people born into a fallen world redeemed by the Lamb of God. The Church is not the Church of perfection; rather it is the Church in which faults and failings are to be found side by side with love and virtue. Further, the Church operates in that tension which Jesus described as 'Caesar's' and 'God's: operating under authority of the civil legislature obedient to all kinds of laws, just as it operates under the authority of God and is obedient to the divine influence.

14.4.2 The Centurion who recognised authority in his conversation with Jesus first acknowledged that he was a man under authority; consequently he had authority placed on him.[57] The Church is under authority too – of

Christ the head of the Body[58] as are its individual members who, in the confession 'Jesus is Lord', acknowledge his authority.[59] While living in the life of the Spirit, members are under authority too: to obey the law of the land, of course, to accept the authority of the Church and example that goes back to the Apostle Paul himself who certainly exercised his authority when he wrote the Church at Corinth!

14.5 Impact of the Biblical Evidence for the Report

14.5.1 Given the context of the Report, then, and because we are under authority, we should recall that Jesus was the first person to express the paramount importance of children in relation to the Kingdom. It follows, then, that theologically, it is of paramount importance to protect children, young people and adults at risk.

14.5.2 Central to the Profession of Christian faith is that believers acknowledge that in Christ there is forgiveness of sin.[60] It is God's gift to humanity in Christ.[61]

14.5.3 Civil legislation has been created to minimise the risks to children, young people and adults at risk. Recognizing its responsibilities, the General Assembly has instructed that there must be a rigorous recruitment procedure for those who seek to work with such children, young people and adults at risk. For everyone that means interviews and references and Disclosure Checks. Further, on those known to have perpetrated sexual abuse, there are further demands because in the life of the Church (and State) the safety and protection of vulnerable people is the prime priority.

15. Church and Forgiveness
'Built of tears and cries and laughter'

15.1 In the early church, from biblical times, there was a development of Atonement Theory, or how the life and death of Jesus affected, or allowed, sinful humanity to be forgiven by God. While the Group recognise that all theories have their strengths and limitations, and may characterise, or dominate, some particular preaching traditions, all atonement theories make it plain that Christ's death was intended by God to enable men and women to become part of the redeemed community.

15.2 The biblical narrative asserts that Jesus came to bring individuals into community, where they are expected to exercise responsibility, while enjoying the privileges of membership. This important understanding of the process of atonement is persuasive, in the view of the Group. This supports its proposals which invite **all** parties in congregations where a sex offender seeks membership, to accept responsibilities for each other and the community as a whole.

15.3 The Group would affirm with Paul the perspective in that all of us are sinners and have fallen short of the intention of God for our lives[62], and are in need of forgiveness for some actions or inactions which have offended against God's will for the human lives which God has brought into being. There is no gradation of sin. All are in need of the redemptive love and capacity of God for new ways of living. It is from this approach that we are able to suggest to the Church that in the particular issues relating to sex offenders we may adopt the following understanding of forgiveness.

15.4 It appears that forgiveness is only activated when the person who is in receipt of forgiveness is able to admit that she or he requires the gift of forgiveness. Those who deny that they are guilty of any sinful act are not able to accept the fact of their wrongdoing and therefore make forgiveness itself irrelevant.

15.5 The Group believes that the forgiveness of God is a gift that is completely unmerited and cannot be earned, or based, on the fulfillment of conditions. It comes to the sinner as an act of grace, free and undeserved. However, it recognises in its core the fact that there has been an act that requires forgiveness. It is given despite the status, or character, of the person to whom it is offered. Yet, forgiveness cannot be active until the person engages with the reality of his or her need. Through this approach, the gift itself is not based upon any conditions – it is offered freely and fully, but it is only a potential for change that will come into existence in the lives of people once they are prepared to admit and perceive their actions as sinful and the destructive consequences of such actions. A person who rejects the idea that they have committed a sinful act is therefore rejecting the gift of God's forgiveness.

15.6   Perhaps there is merit in the metaphor, limited in scope as it is, of the gift of a cheque for a million pounds, given freely by a generous person to one of us. We are not however, millionaires until the gift is deposited in our account in the bank. While the gift itself is freely given and it does not depend on our action at all, the gift is still not transformative, or active, in changing our lives, until we act upon it. The generous activity of the giver is not in question, but the attitude and the response of the person to whom the gift is given. It is of crucial importance to recognise both the freedom of the giver, and admitting that the gift's impact is itself dependant on the recipient.

15.7   Another metaphor may be in the use of a parachute. While the parachute is packed after being carefully checked and examined to ensure that it will work effectively and save a life, it depends on the person using the cord appropriately to make a real and vital difference. The parachute may be intact and completely faultless, but if the person has not opened the parachute, he, or she, will be unable to reap the rewards, or the benefits. Similarly, God gives us the opportunity of forgiveness, but if there is no admission of guilt and sense of need, then the gift itself is not devalued, but is not able to accomplish God's best intentions for the individual who has been offered the gift.

15.8   Theological Issues relating to an understanding of forgiveness.

15.8.1   The Group wishes to reassert its view articulated in the Interim Report that the forgiveness of sex offenders is **not** in the gift of a congregation. The sex offender may be forgiven by God, and by those whom they have abused, but it is not the task of a congregation, or a minister, to perpetuate further – though different – abuse of a victim by demanding that the survivor forgives his or her abuser.

15.8.2   The Working Group believes that it can be helpful for some victims of abuse to forgive their abuser and by this process reduce its impact on their lives. While this may occur, the Group is convinced that it is **not** reasonable to expect this in all cases, and, in all circumstances of abuse, a scar of some description still exists. It is also clear that:

> Abuse can traumatize a self so terribly that it finds the very thought of forgiveness impossible.[63]

Recalling Thomas Aquinas the Group notes:

> 'accordingly, it is evident that the scars which Christ showed on His body after His Resurrection have never since been removed from His body'.[64]

The Group is, therefore, convinced that the following issues are both theologically and practically important for the Church in its consideration of any policy of responsible inclusion.

15.9   Forgiveness is not Forgetting

15.9.1   It was noted in the discussion that even God cannot change the past if we believe in a God who creates history and has created a causal universe. However, if the facts of events cannot be denied, it is possible for God, through the miracle of healing grace, to assist people in how they interpret these events in the present. As we have seen, it is possible for people to be the victims of terrible, damaging and destructive abuse and assault and for this not to restrict their present lives, or dictate their future. Perhaps in their triumph over the impact of sexual abuse, we see the grace of God as particularly active.

15.9.2   With this acknowledgement, we need to be clear that forgiveness can only be based on an acknowledgement of wrong, and **to deny** that any wrong or evil, took place is to make true forgiveness impossible. A wrong denied or treated as unimportant, means that transformative forgiveness cannot happen. Forgiveness and responsibility must walk hand in hand. In keeping with the biblical evidence, the Church must accept the principle that each person is accountable for his or her actions. There are times when forgiveness can be hiding from what you have done, so there is a need for honesty and openness. A member of staff at Peterhead Prison, who leads intensive treatment programmes stated: 'Finding God can be a way of hiding from their responsibilities. Faith should help them to accept responsibility for the hurt they have caused'[65]

15.9.3   It is rarely remarked upon, but Jesus does **not**, according to all the Gospel accounts, forgive those who tortured him and put him to death on the cross. Perhaps there is some real significance in the fact that what we do have is a record of Jesus imploring God to forgive, rather than Jesus offering a personal declaration of his forgiveness. This may suggest that the actual experience of forgiveness is dependent on prayer and it is something that the Church may encourage and support in those who have been perpetrators of sexual assault. In remembering the invitation central to the Lord's Prayer regarding forgiveness[66], perhaps all the victim can be expected to do is engage on a journey of spiritual development, knowing that God's forgiveness is crucial and that it is available to all who seek it truthfully.

15.9.4   While the Church may be a forgiving and forgiven community, it should not forget what **has happened. Acceptance is not forgiveness. Forgiveness is not excusing**. While we have a responsibility towards the offenders, that responsibility cannot be fulfilled at the expense of the survivors.

15.9.5   Forgiveness does not mean forgetting. There is an important issue here which is to remember that surviving abuse may be considered as living through a grieving process. It requires time. There are many reminders about it. God does not forget, but forgives. For example, Professor Shuster, in her commentary on St Matthew's Gospel writes:

We dare not ignore the fact that Scripture repeatedly makes clear that there are consequences for our behaviour. God is hardly depicted as a benevolent grandfather who overlooks his little darlings' foibles and misadventures as things they will outgrow as they get older[67]

15.9.6   It is clear that there is a need for clarity regarding what forgiveness means and it is necessary to stress that it is not excusing, and that there are always consequences of our actions. This understanding of what forgiveness means must be related to community, and therefore should have some bearing on how we, as the Church, might use the legislation creatively as a tool. The Church should not just act to protect ourselves, but to create an environment where survivors and their families may grow in safety. The concept of forgiveness must also be separated from a denial of the consequences of actions. Part of any recovery process must include the development of responsibility and acceptance of the consequences of what they have done. Forgiveness should make a sex offender responsible and aware of the impact of their crimes.

15.9.7   We do not have any real clear understanding about the forgiveness of God; save that is was out of love and grace. It was a gift Jesus, in his final agony, asked for those who had so cruelly abused him. Forgiveness is a mystery, and those who are forgiven by God through the exercise of grace are surely fortunate.

What does God do when forgiving? There is one thing that God does not do. God does not disregard the offence. God does not pretend it does not happen.[68]

15.9.8   This gift, we believe, should lead to following the paths of righteousness. While we may hope and trust that

God has forgiven people, including ourselves, we cannot act as if that forgiveness makes the present and the future clear of all consequences. We live in a universe, created by God, and need to teach by our structures and example, that we are responsible for our actions before God, even when we have assurance of forgiveness. Jesus' message was that forgiveness is given to allow the development of new possibilities of living in the way of God rather than the way of evil:

> "To forgive is to blame, not to punish. But those who forgive need not abandon all disciplinary measures against offenders. …A violent offender may need to be restrained if there is any danger he may harm others. Discipline for the sake of a wrong doers reform and the protection of the public is compatible for forgiveness. Discipline even for the sake of upholding the moral good assaulted by the offence is compatible for forgiveness. Those who forgive will have a system for discipline but retribution will not be part of it.[69]

When the abuser is not forgiven by those whom he, or she, has abused, the Church needs to accept this fact. However, the Church must not fall into the trap of allowing the abuser to scapegoat his, or her, victim and perpetrate further abuse by condemning them for a lack of forgiveness. The abuser must be willing to accept the truth about the actions he, or she, has perpetrated, and not evade the reality by inferring that the forgiveness of God means that this action has been forgotten. The biblical witness repeatedly reminds us that it is when God remembers that God acts in powerful love and grace. Forgetting is an approach which denies the reality of the activity which merits forgiveness. The greatest need is that of the survivors, and they this has to be the prime concern of the Church.

15.9.9 Forgiveness does not mean giving 'carte blanche' to everyone. The example of placing an alcoholic in charge of a bar may be relevant here. Forgiveness of sin is not a cancellation of debt, though much of the theological discussion appears to cloud this issue:

> We need to receive it (God's forgiveness) we receive the gift by trusting that God has indeed forgiven us and by accepting both accusation contained in forgiveness and the release from guilt and punishment. We believe and confess the wrong we have done. Without faith and repentance we are not forgiven God having done the forgiving not withstanding. God has given, but we have not received. Forgiveness is then stuck in the middle between the God who forgives and humans who do not receive.[70]

15.9.10 The narrative of this Report has drawn already on the teaching of Paul. In the context of this section of the Report it is helpful if we turn to the life of Paul. Our first introduction to Saul is that he was a witness who gave approval to Stephen's death.[71] Our second encounter with Saul is that he began to destroy the church.[72] Not content with this he sought authority to go and destroy the church in Damascus[73] Saul is an unsavoury character. However, change was on the way. Converted in his encounter with the risen Christ while he travelled to Damascus, a conversion witnessed by his travelling companions, Saul was not immediately welcomed into the Christian community. Ananias was very suspicious about Saul. Indeed when Saul returned to Jerusalem and tried to join the disciples they were afraid of him. Until Barnabas took him in hand.[74]

15.9.11 Reading Saul, now Paul's, testimony in Galatians[75] we discover that he underwent self imposed exile in Arabia, he went to Syria and Cilicia to prove his credentials. His conversion was not an instant step into congregational life. Clearly boundaries had been imposed on him. Trust had to be earned. Once that had been earned the welcome was assured.[76] The forgiveness begun on the Damascus Road continued throughout his life and ministry and was costly in terms of his emotional, spiritual and physical life. It is arguable that Paul spent three years in Arabia as a period of preparation, but it is not our understanding that this suggests that this was a period of punishment.

15.10   How might we understand forgiveness in this context?

15.10.1   The Group is convinced that forgiveness is **not:**
- Forgetting the crime committed
- Removing all mention of the impact of the action or acknowledgement of it is effects
- Destructive of those who have suffered wrong
- Silencing the Church in its condemnation of sexual assault
- A destination, a completed act that requires no further effort to make its results a reality in changed lives and behaviour
- A denial of the consequences of human sin on others
- An evasion of the consequences of our actions
- An excuse for continued destructive behaviour

15.10.2   The Group would assert that forgiveness in practice within the Church is:
- A journey, not a destination
- A process of discovery and recovery
- A continued recognition of our responsibility to create a just society
- An admission of our responsibility for the wrong we have done
- A clear understanding that some of our actions leave scars that may never heal fully
- A clear vision of forgiveness as a work of God's grace, seen supremely in the cross
- An awareness that the dynamics of forgiveness mean that we are never able to claim forgiveness as a permanent state
- A gift that is unconditional and cannot be earned, but which leads to admission of the sin and acceptance of the implications for a change of life
- An experience that many would like to have, but may be stopped by our inaction and attitudes
- Something that cannot be commanded by those outside, and can only come from the heart of an individual, depending on God's grace
- Desirable and admirable, but we cannot judge those who are incapable of it due to the trauma they have suffered at the hands of others

15.10.3   We also need to remember that there is a clear difference between the forgiveness of God and the forgiveness between human beings.

> *"We are not God, so it follows that when we give, we must give differently than God does…we give only because we have first received. God gives from what is originally, exclusively and properly God's own; we give from what is our own because God continually gives to us"*[77]

15.10.4   We cannot know what it is for God to forgive a sinful humanity. We can only glimpse that reality through our experience of human forgiveness that is free and undeserved, but cannot be commanded, or manipulated, but is given freely and simply out of the heart of another. There are links in the experience of forgiveness, but we must recall the mystical nature of God's act in Jesus Christ for a sinful humanity.

15.10.5   Forgiveness is a process that begins with some acknowledgment of the reality of the sin. This is clear from much of the literature and we would suggest that we are all on a journey towards an understanding of what forgiveness might mean. Forgiveness is perhaps the conclusion of an extensive process of confession, repentance and transformation. It involves the restoration of individuals within the Christian community where there is recognition of their needs and appropriate support and guidance offered. We, in the Church, may offer a reflection of God's grace to those guilty of sexual abuse and to their families. There needs to be sensitivity to the stages of this journey, with no evaluative or condemnatory statements made so that individuals cannot be alienated. However, the Church cannot do so without appropriate boundaries and structures to ensure that those who have suffered from sexual assault, or may suffer through carelessness or disregard of their rights, are protected:

> 'What does forgiveness do with the wrong doing? …first to forgive is to name the wrong doing and to condemn it…for Christians, forgiving always takes place in a triangle, involving the wrong doer, the wrong person and God. Take God away and the foundations of forgiveness become unsteady and may even crumble.'[78]

15.10.6 The Group is persuaded by the argument of Miroslav Volf when he reflects that:

> …what does it mean to receive forgiveness, then? It means to receive both the accusation and the release from the debt. How do we receive release from debt? We simply believe and rejoice in gratitude for the generous gift. But how de we receive the accusation? By confessing our offence and repenting of it. By confessing, I recognise myself as the one who needs forgiveness and who can appropriately receive it. By failing to confess, I declare that I am in no need of forgiveness…in that case, forgiveness is not a gift; it is an insult, a declaration that I have done the wrong that I have claimed not to have done.[79]

15.10.7 The Group also would strongly assert that confession and admission of sin are essential in the development of an understanding of this issue. As Professor Volf expresses it:

> 'Confession is hard. When I confess that I have committed an offence, I stand exposed, pointing an accusing finger at myself and the guilt of my offence…amazingly, God does not wait until we have confessed to offer or even enact forgiveness, God forgives before we even confess.'[80]

15.11 The Lord's Prayer

15.11.1 The petition in the Lord's Prayer relating to forgiveness was one which caused real concern and debate within the Group. The Church needs to recognise that the concepts in the Lord's Prayer about asking for forgiveness as we forgive others may be particularly difficult for a survivor of abuse. It is the conviction of the Group that survivors should not feel pressure by the Church to forgive abusers by the use of this prayer

15.11.2 The General Assembly is reminded of the fact that the General Assembly of 2008 affirmed the view of the Group that 'no one could force the victim of sexual abuse to forgive the person who had carried out the abuse.'

15.11.3 The Lord's Prayer does **not** have a conditional phrase. The Grace of God which is granted to us in prayer, and through the community of the Church is unconditional. God's forgiveness is not earned by our acts of recognisable forgiveness of others. Instead it is the hope that the Christian community will be secure in the knowledge of the Love and Compassion of God, and enabled to forgive others.

15.11.4 We are encouraged, rather than commanded to forgive. This is made clear in the in the response to question 'what do we pray for in the fifth petition?'[81]

> In the fifth petition,…we pray that God, for Christ's sake, would freely pardon all our sins; which we are the rather encouraged to ask, because by his Grace we are enabled from the heart to forgive others.

15.11.5 In any discussion of the Lord's Prayer we must be clear that the forgiveness of our own sin is not conditional on our willingness, or ability to forgive others. In the instruction of Jesus contained in this prayer, these are parallel processes each dependant upon God. When we pray in these words we acknowledge our need for God's power and grace to forgive others. It is also clear that being forgiven and extending forgiveness are processes rather than events with potentially variable timescales. In his recent book on the Lord's Prayer, Peter Lewis argues:

> *"Forgive our debts as we have forgiven our debtors"…*
> *Here we move in the Lord's Prayer from bread to forgiveness. Jesus takes us from what is essential for physical life to what is essential for eternal life. These words cannot be understood in a purely personal sense, much less in a merely therapeutic sense. They must first of all be understood against the biblical background of holiness and sin.*[82]

Later on in his discussion he points out:

> *'…people are often puzzled by the additional words "…as we also have forgiven our debtors" is this an attempt at a trade off, our forgiveness of others traded for God's forgiveness of us? Of course not… Jesus does not say, "forgive us on the grounds of the fact that we forgive our debts"'*[83]

15.11.6 The Group is clear that the Church cannot use this prayer as a means whereby it takes upon itself the role of victim and forgiver by proxy. Instead the Church is designed to be a safe environment for victims, where they may be accepted and supported in their journey towards a sense of wholeness, and find the healing that they rightly desire. The Church may also, within the bounds of safety, recognising the issues of the victims of sexual assault, offer acceptance and encouragement and the opportunity to worship to those who have committed sexual assault, who come in penitence and faith. However, the Church can only do this when it is safe and possible to do this without destructive consequences for victims.

15.11.7 The Group agrees with Miroslav Volf when he states

> *'(it is a misunderstanding to believe that) because you forgive your debtors God will forgive you……
> if that were the case, God's forgiveness would not be a gift but a payment…we would not receive forgiveness by faith but we would earn it or draw it out by our own forgiveness.'*[84]

15.11.8 The Group is of the view that the sense of the Lord's Prayer is given its direction from the wider Gospel narrative and would cite a miracle and a parable to illustrate. The healing of the paralytic man[85] is clearly unconditional. 'Take heart, son, your sins are forgiven'. There are no questions asked, or answered; no conditions or preconditions required. In this context the parable of the Prodigal Son[86] is as enlightening it seems that while the parable itself is multi-facetted, Leon Morris[87] says 'there can be no doubt that in the father's welcome of the younger son Jesus is teaching that the heavenly Father welcomes returning sinners'.

15.11.9 The Group affirms that forgiveness comes from God – recalling John Calvin who states

> *That the papacy had abrogated to itself certain powers – eg the authority to forgive sins, which by their nature belong to Christ himself.'*[88]

The consequence of that forgiveness is that Christians ought to forgive others. However, forgiveness is not an abstract cerebral process. The abuser has distinct responsibilities. The abuser cannot be forgiven unless he or she asks for forgiveness from God and repents of their actions. To do otherwise is to deny the enormity of the abuse and the lifelong consequences of it.

15.11.10 The implication of the Lord's Prayer, then, is that the Christian prays it first to be forgiven and secondly to discover the grace of the Lord Jesus Christ to be able to forgive when in a spirit of penitence the abuser seeks it: and that may take many years. We are also convinced that the victim of abuse may pray this prayer with integrity seeking God's grace clearly not dismissing the impact, or consequences, of a serious wrong. We would agree that it is vital to see the victim who prays this prayer as participating in a process which may involve stages on a journey:

> *'…forgiveness must never be a tyranny, nor must its necessary stages be treated lightly…*

there is also a need to separate out different kinds and levels of forgiveness and the stages of forgiveness. For example, not giving way to revenge would be the first, not deliberately feeding hatred and bitterness, and finding at the foot of the cross the strength to pray for the enemy and finally releasing them to God might be the final victory over darkness and despair. Most of us will never have to face the agony of the most extreme cases of hurt and wickedness and we might well reflect on that fact when we are called to forgive the lesser wrongs of lesser sinners' [89]

15.11.11   Many survivors within a Christian community are likely to struggle to forgive the person who has abused them. The Church must support the survivor through their struggle, rather than place unreasonable pressures on them to move to forgive.

15.11.12   While we might hope that the survivor can, depending on God's grace, reach a point where they may be able to forgive those who have committed sexual assault, we cannot expect this when there is no admission of the crime, and the person who has survived the assault is still in a place of powerlessness and fear. Only when the Church recognises the impact and scars of the crime on their lives can the individual reach an understanding of the fact that their experience of abuse does not diminish their worth in the eyes of God. Once the survivor has experienced a sense of restoration of power, it is possible, but not guaranteed, that he or she can embark on the challenging journey of recovery. The support of the community is vital here, and can only take place when the survivor is aware that proper safeguards and boundaries are being observed, which do not allow further opportunity for abuse and assault. Some survivors will find that it is only possible for them to grow and develop as God intended through the miracle of forgiveness, but this cannot be dictated, or expected, in all circumstances.

15.11.13   There will, however, be occasions when it is not possible for the survivor to forgive the abuser, and the community will have to accept this honestly, while continuing to support the prayer of all that they may receive forgiveness. The acknowledgment of the power of forgiveness and its necessity in our lives, cannot be used as a means of further abusing survivors.

15.11.14   While recognising the perspective of the survivor regarding forgiveness, we need also to attend to the issue of the perpetrator of sexual assault in relation to this concept. Forgiveness is not active unless the person who has committed a sin acknowledges its existence. It is like having a cheque, ready to deposit in the bank which will clear an overdraft, but refusing to place it in your account. The forgiveness of God is offered to the individual sex offender as a matter of grace, but it cannot be active, or transformative, unless he or she recognises their need of forgiveness. In the research of the group, it was clear that many sex offenders are not prepared to admit that they have done anything wrong, or committed any action which has caused harm to others. Therefore the whole concept of forgiveness in relation to them is null and void:

> *When God forgives, offenders need to respond in faith and repentance. But what if they do not repent? Like a package, forgiveness will then be stuck between the sender who dispatched it and the recipient who refuses to receive it. Offenders will remain unforgiven, the reality of God's forgiveness notwithstanding. The same is true when we forgive. We make God's sending of the 'forgiveness package' our own. That is all we can do. And that's what we have the power to do. Whether the package will be received depends on the recipients, on whether they admit to the wrongdoing and repent.* [90]

15.11.15   The Group is aware that some sex offenders who are involved in the life of the Church are extremely adept at using theological jargon and argument to dispute any requirements of the Church and covenants of responsibility. They often do not have any willingness to admit guilt, sinfulness and responsibility of actions which have harmed and continue to affect the lives of others. The group believes that all sex offenders who seek to be involved in the life of the church should be brought to an understanding of the nature of their crimes, that they are sinful and unjustifiable, and that part of their faith journey demands that they seek forgiveness. This may lead them to depart from the church or inability to adhere to the terms of the covenant, but it is a choice they make knowing the Church's desire to support them on the road to a clearer understanding of their responsibility and discipleship. All have fallen short and have need of grace. Only when this is admitted honestly and the consequences of actions are faced, can the individual be said to be able to claim the forgiveness and grace of God that is offered in Jesus Christ.

16. Reflections relating to Forgiveness and Proportionality

16.1   Silence is Not Golden

16.1.1   The Group shares the natural difficulty most people have of discussing such difficult issues as the sexual assault. While the Group has had to face unpleasant details regarding the behaviour of abusers in their devious attempts to exercise power over others and, damage people in a multitude of ways, it has come to one certain conclusion. The Church requires, if it is to be true to its nature, to face these issues honestly and openly. The Group recommends that the General Assembly acknowledges, once again, the facts of sexual assault in all its reality and its long lasting destructive consequences. The Church must be unequivocal in denouncing the sexual assault of children and adults as unacceptable and completely antithetical to the will of God.

16.1.2   In so doing, the Church must also be prepared, when circumstances and individual survivors of abuse demand, to listen and hear the stories of abuse, without excuse, condemnation and diminishing comment. Silence has too often been another form of abuse, ignoring and rejecting the valid claim for a hearing which these survivors have in the Church. Similarly, the Church must never demand that all speak about their experience of abuse in public, but must ensure that if they share their fears, concerns and questions, that they are faced honestly by Kirk Sessions, when the inclusion of sex offenders is being discussed.

16.2   Actions Speak Louder Than Words
'Let us bring an end to fear and danger'

16.2.1   The Church claims to be the body of Christ on earth. It has a heritage and responsibility of bringing the message of Jesus as reflected in the gospels, to the poor, the marginalised, the weak and the sick. It is **never** acceptable to pretend that there is no harm done. The Church must act, and speak so that the truth is heard and the sanctions necessary for the health of the Church and community are maintained. There is a duty incumbent in the Church to create an environment and culture in congregations where there is clarity of expectation and the courage and strength to administer the sanctions necessary for good discipline and discipleship.

16.2.2   The Second Book of Discipline drawn up by Andrew Melville distinguished between civil government and ecclesiastical government: the power of the sword and the power of the keys. The latter comes from God in Christ. Melville affirmed, as the *Scots' Confession* and the First Book of Discipline had that the true church on earth can be distinguished from the false by 'three indispensable notes'. The first is the true preaching of the word of God. Secondly, the right administration of the sacraments of Jesus Christ. Lastly, ecclesiastical discipline uprightly administered … whereby vice is repressed and virtue nourished. The government of the Church is by Assemblies – Courts – to which are entrusted the task of keeping 'religion and doctrine pure, to make rules to that effect and to discipline transgressors'[91] The latter is a means of cultivating biblical love among the Church's members.

16.2.3   While no one can claim that every action and spoken word uttered by the Church is an exact reflection of the will of God, the Church needs to subject its life to critical analysis in the light of Jesus, who is the Living Word. As Jesus exercised grace and truth in his ministry, so must the Church follow his example, without fear or favour. The Church has been given a mandate to demonstrate that the love of God calls us to a new humanity.[92] This inevitably means that the Church has to be vigilant in its protection of young people and adults at risk. The Church must never indulge in any permissive practice which allows giving free license to those who are known to be guilty of sexual assault.

16.2.4   In the experience of those working with sexual abusers, when some sex offenders claim that the Church has restricted 'their' rights, it is indicative that these individuals have failed to understand the basic truths of the gospel. While we may be forgiven by God, we are all sinners in need of grace and therefore need the support, care and structures of the Church to assist us in our journey. When sex offenders claim that the forgiveness of God has set them free from responsibility, they depart from the message of Jesus. This also addresses those in the church who wish to forgive and deny the danger of sex offenders because in their opinion the person has done no wrong.

16.3   Power and Privilege

16.3.1   We hear a huge amount today in popular debate about the rights, powers and privileges in society. The Group believes that all who are heirs of grace are given a new start by God. In that new beginning, we are **not** given power and privileges. Instead we are asked to accept responsibility for our actions and how they affect, shape and determine the lives of others with whom we live in community.

16.3.2   The Group wishes to note the Reformation principle that we are 'saved by grace not works', and that our merit, or activities of goodness, are quite irrelevant. John Calvin's teaching regarding election suggests that we are elected to participation in the Kingdom of God. The modern theological emphasis is on the fact of election for service rather than election for privilege. Therefore, we need to be reminded of the importance of the fulfilment of our duties, rather than claiming our powers and privileges, as the Children of God.

16.3.3   The pattern of sex offending is such that many are skilful in appearing penitent in order to have free access to those they plan to abuse. Many can be deceived by their pretences, and there is a clear need for 'informed vigilance' to prevent the offences being repeated. While the Church cannot know and understand the heart of an individual, it needs to operate within clear boundaries to ensure that the possibility of deception is reduced. Therefore strict operational boundaries and limits are necessary for sex offenders to participate in the life of a congregation.

16.4   Justice is Not Revenge

16.4.1   The Group believes that it is incompatible with its role to debate any question of what happens in the administration of justice and how it may develop into a process of legitimised vengeance. The Group proposes 'A Covenant of Responsibilities' in the belief that this is not a form of revenge. Rather, it is designed to offer structure, guidance and a means of adhering to a life of discipleship, while avoiding condemnation and exclusion.

16.4.2   What guides Christian forgiveness when an offender is not willing to repent, and where the victim has done nothing wrong? The Lord commands us to forgive, releasing the offence and the offender to Him. This is done in prayer to the Lord. God recognises these situations with this Scripture;

> 'Dear friends, never avenge yourselves. Leave that to God. For it is written, 'I will take vengeance; I will repay those who deserve it,' says the Lord'[93]

27

16.4.3   When we have been wronged, and know we did nothing to deserve harsh treatment from the offender, we normally begin to think of retaliation. Retaliation, or revenge, is not the right course of action for the Christian. Instead we no longer dwell on the offence when we relinquish a desire for vengeance, allowing God to take care of the vengeance in a fair, just and appropriate manner.

16.5   Actions have Consequences

16.5.1   The concept of a *'Covenant of Responsibilities'* takes seriously that all actions have consequences, and all choices made may lead to some form of sacrifice, limitation or restriction. As an example, the desire to be part of a visiting team of scientists to the Antarctic, on a long term mission, means that each person has to have an appendectomy before he or she can embark on this trip. This is a condition which must be accepted so that the group will not be endangered in order to provide medical help for someone who takes appendicitis in an isolated area. It is not designed to exclude anyone; instead, it enables people to be included, knowing that their own health will not, in this period, adversely affect the group.

16.5.2   This rather stark, secular example is presented to assist in understanding the proposed 'Covenant of Responsibilities' as a means whereby all might act appropriately. It acknowledges that consequences follow actions, but also that negative consequences do not automatically result, if the actions of the past are dealt with appropriately.

16.6   The Paramouncy Principle

16.6.1   In the context of the discussion, this paramouncy principle would extend to children, young people and adults at risk. This principle asserts that the rights of the vulnerable to be kept safe are of paramount importance and must come before all others. In practice this means that their protection, rather than the desires of others to abuse, exercise power over, or inflict damage on them is of prime importance and their rights have to be emphatically asserted.

16.6.2   Reference has been made earlier to the manner in which Jesus gave priority and conferred acceptance of the importance of the child. By setting such great value on children, Jesus was acting in a strongly counter –cultural way. Children, like women and slaves, had very few rights in the world of Jesus, meriting little respect, intrinsic worth, and were perceived as possessions, rather than as full human beings.

16.6.3   Jesus was clear that God judges the world through the eyes of the child and what is not acceptable to the child, is **not** acceptable to God. The gifts of the child and the honesty, openness and integrity of the child are praised by Jesus. For the Church, in any policy of inclusion, to ignore the value and appropriate respect to children would be to deny the place Jesus gave them. In his extreme warning, Jesus talks about the 'millstones' which will be attached to those who do not remember the vital concern of God for children, young people and adults at risk.

16.7   Justice for All

16.7.1   The Group is persuaded that no proposals for the inclusion of the sex offenders in congregations will be achieved without effort and acceptance of appropriate boundaries. Justice is not achieved without the protection of inalienable rights which include the freedom from fear, want, hunger and abuse.

16.7.2   Any proposed structure must seek to uphold the human dignity of both parties, the abused and the abusers; the abused families and the families of abusers. This must be attempted without endangering, or sacrificing, that which ensures the maintenance of their true humanity. Therefore, in order for congregations to include sex offenders, those who may be threatened or endangered by their inclusion must be given protection, reassurance and support.

16.7.3 The ability of survivors to be fully part of the life of the congregation cannot be sacrificed because of a genuine, but theologically misguided, commitment to the inclusion of all. Public protection should be the main aim of the Church in any of its proposals. Inclusion of sex offenders does not mean giving them freedom to act as they may wish to the damage of others. God is the judge, and we are not. However, without passing judgement on others, we have a serious responsibility. In the way of Jesus, it is our duty as followers to ensure that those who are convicted of sexual abuse are not given free rein in the Church, on the basis that they claim religious conversion and the forgiveness of God. Instead, the abused and all possible victims must be assured that the love of God in Christ demands that the congregation's physical building is as safe from threat as any place might be on earth.

16.7.4 This may mean that some areas or opportunities may be restricted for the protection of a child, or vulnerable adult. While we may wish to encourage initiative and freedom in a child, as responsible adults, we do not allow them to burn or scald themselves by giving them free access to a hot stove. They are "restricted" to an area that provides safety and security for them to grow and develop.

16.7.5 Similarly, the sex offender, while he or she may have served their sentence and completed the legal requirements of punishment, requires structures of care and affirmation of self discipline in their adaptation to life outside prison. The Group is advised that without the right structures in place, the sex offender is more likely to re offend and may not address the compulsive thinking and emotive patterns which have drawn them to the path of abusive behaviour. Although prisoners can undertake a treatment programme in prison the prison staff are clear that risk management is about supervision, **not** just treatment. Management is about risk as there is always a strong possibility of re-offending. If we wanted no risk at all we would keep sex offenders locked up forever. While the programmes offered within prisons may be successful

in the sense of producing evidence of a change in an individual, there is no evidence that their improvement will be sustainable when they are released without an adequate support system.

16.7.6 It is only when the sex offender is able to accept and appreciate the structure of a responsible and responsive congregation that he, or she, may be able to maintain and develop in a truly Christian manner. Without structures of respect and the creation of appropriate boundaries, the ends of justice, which surely coincide with those of God, are not able to be achieved. Justice requires punishment for wrong doing **and** the growth in an individual of an awareness of responsibility for his, or her, actions and the impact of such negative actions on the community. Through the operation of the *'Covenant of Responsibilities'* it is hoped that the sex offender will perceive this as an opportunity to move forward remembering that forgiveness itself is easy to talk about, while the more important thing is to be willing to engage and accept conditions which are there for their support and protection.

16.7.7 *Once this is acknowledged, the sex offender may accept the structures, limits and boundaries as a means of pastoral care and support. The fact that these exist, through the 'Covenant of Responsibilities' may be perceived as positive efforts of the Christian community to supply a means of grace for sex offenders who seek spiritual growth. As was commented at Peterhead Prison 'This is an opportunity to go forward in their life, and they will accept any condition if they are genuinely trying to get back to the straight and narrow.'*[94]

17. Practical Implications
'Let us build a house where hands will reach beyond the wood and stone'

17.1 Honesty and Openness
17.1.1 The Group cannot from any perspective hope to disguise, deny or diminish the consequences of sexual abuse. The reality of the impact of sexual assault upon all concerned, including the abuser and his/her

family must be acknowledged. All must know that what is required are a journey of change and transformation and a process of recovery which may be supported by the activities of the church.

17.1.2 The Group believes that it should be mandatory for any congregation which is facing the challenge of managing the integration of a sex offender into the life of the congregation to contact the Safeguarding Office and co-operate fully with the advice and guidance given by the safeguarding staff. This will allow the development of 'Covenants of Responsibilities' where the framework for safe and secure worship and witnessing communities is acknowledged. Past experiences of congregations who have been involved with such work should also be reported to ensure that information and guidance are given based upon experience.

17.1.3 Any denial of the facts of abuse and the repudiation of any possibility of future repetition of abuse cannot be accepted. When those who have been abused and those parents and families or supporters of the abused know that there are structures in place, they can more readily participate in the life of the congregation. Similarly, the sex offender and his/her family may also find comfort and grace through the provision of support and boundaries set out by a 'Covenant of Responsibilities'.

17.1.4 Prison staff stressed the importance of the offender being fully aware of the 'Covenant of Responsibilities' process before they were released so that they would know exactly what was involved when they wished to be involved in a congregation. Refusing to sign a covenant could be interpreted as an indication of failure to accept responsibility for their actions. The Covenant proposed is a support and protective mechanism which the professionals involved would see as worthwhile and important in process of preparing an offender for release.

17.1.5 It is clear that the Church and society as a whole would benefit from the Safeguarding Office of the Church of Scotland being able to participate fully in the process of cooperation which is facilitated by the Multi Agency Public Protection Arrangements (MAPPA) structures. It is the hope that the contacts and helpful links that have been established through the work of this group will facilitate the involvement of the Safeguarding Office in the future so that any pre-release plans which involve the church may be made with full awareness of the particular issues involved.

17.2 The Integration and Support of the Sex offender

17.2.1 This Group recognises the need for Safeguarding Panels in churches with members who are aware of the issues involved, so that they might be able to help people deal with the challenge of integration and safeguarding when a sex offender wishes to be associated with a congregation. The Group also recognises that there are potential difficulties in relation to a situation where a worshipper is or was a sexual offender but the offences are known only to the offender and his or her victim. The formation of a Safeguarding Panel may enable a victim to tell the Panel about an offence which has been committed. Should this happen then it is essential the Safeguarding Office is informed so that an appropriate response can be developed. The Safeguarding Panels are designed to offer pastoral care for all, and this means they have to be concerned about the possible victims and the survivors in a congregation, as well as the sex offender. The members of Safeguarding Panels require to be well supported, and resourced to meet this challenge. It has to be stressed that Safeguarding Panels in Churches only have responsibility for monitoring sex offenders in the church premises, and **cannot** be expected to take on extensive duties of care in society as a whole.

17.2.2 The Group is aware that the Church has a duty to be inclusive of sex offenders who desire to worship.

They must be supported in their good intentions and given the encouragement to adopt positive attitudes to the structures which the 'Covenants of Responsibilities' create. This will be an important part of the care offered to sex offenders, in the hope that they might aspire to do good things with their lives. There is a need for those who are supervising released prisoners to recognise potential warning signs.

17.2.3 Churches are, by their nature, places of trust. The Church is concerned to support reformation and responsibility in sex offenders and encourage their spiritual discipline and development, while minimising the possibility of further offences.

17.2.4 The stress on individuals involved in Safeguarding Panels is great. The burden is such that they often will need respite and further people to be included, while those who are supporting and monitoring the sex offenders require opportunities for development.

17.2.5 We need to be clear here that there are limits to what can be reasonably expected of a Safeguarding Panel in a congregation. There is no expectation that they will operate in a similar way to care professionals. They are there primarily to be supportive of a structure that maintains safety for children and adults at risk in a congregation. They may offer to give pastoral care to the sex offender, but this cannot be at the expense of the care of the vulnerable. The Safeguarding Panel should be encouraged to express concerns when any member believes there may be some signs of deviation from the expected behaviour. It is the task of the other members of the Panel along with any advisors to try to identify what the basis for the concern is and why the person may be feeling a level of anxiety.

17.2.6 The agreement is two-way. Something must be offered by the church to the sex offender in order to help and assist them not re-offend, and develop his or her discipleship. Those involved with the ongoing monitoring

of the sex offender must be aware of the effects of sex abuse in order to cope adequately with this issue. Congregations do face difficulties due to the fact that the offences are often minimized by a sex offender and reduced in importance. This needs to be recognised.

17.2.7 The Group would emphasise the frequent manipulation and abuse of a different kind perpetrated by sex offenders in congregations in their dealings with church leaders. They often use language which implies the Church is guilty of discrimination. They masquerade their desire to be given free access to children and adults at risk with talk of their 'rights' and civil liberties. The issue here is to focus clearly on the need for Christian discipleship and the effective acceptance of the limits they have brought upon themselves as a result of their actions. The 'limitations' they experience are limitations which they have created themselves as a consequence of their actions.

17.2.8 We are convinced that there must be no distortion of theological principles by sex offenders to excuse, or, justify and support his/her pleas to be allowed to operate without boundaries. While they may claim that the Church can only be 'loving' if it allows such freedom of access, the Group would contend that the love of God and the love which must characterise the Church, implies that boundaries are necessary for the safety and security of all, including sex offenders. The Church exists in the real world, out of the Garden of Eden where evil is real. The Church must be guided in all its operations in the way of Jesus. It cannot afford to sacrifice the innocence of doves, while neglecting to be as wise as the serpents.

17.2.9 The issue of sex offenders occupying positions of trust is one which troubles the Group. Obviously the Church must recognise the effective changes in the sex offender. However, any idea that the conferring of rights, or freedoms, as a 'reward' for their good behaviour would be extremely dangerous in practice. It is the contention of the Group that for the good of the Church community, any reference to the election or appointment of sex

27

offenders to positions of responsibility and trust, or to paid positions, in the Church must feature in the 'Covenant of Responsibilities'. The Covenant would outline clearly that such issues cannot be presumed as a right and may be subject to serious restriction in practice for the exercise of appropriate boundaries. The reasons for this caution are based on the fact that such may give a degree of prominence, and perhaps actually places an *'imprimatur'* on an individual. This obviously has to be recognised, and must be avoided, due to the adverse effects it may have on survivors of abuse in the congregation. The issues here are:

- the apparent condoning of criminal behaviour incongruent with the Gospel
- endangering the reputation of the Church
- allowing the survivor of sexual assault to perceive the Church as collusive with assault and destruction

17.2.10 Allowing a sex offender to be placed in a position of responsibility and trust could give a message that their behaviour has been accepted and that they have been given approval. This could be very difficult for anyone in the congregation, who is a survivor of abuse,

17.2.11 The Group recognise that there will be some people who have been convicted of a sexual offence which may not make them unsuitable for office at some stage. This is where the proportionality of any response must be considered. If we consider a young adult in his twenties who was charged with consensual under age sex at age 16 with a 15 year old girlfriend, it is unlikely that he will pose any threat to children. All this will be carefully reviewed in any process of consideration in collaboration with the Safeguarding Office to ensure that all covenants are drawn up appropriately.

17.3 Covenant of Responsibilities.
'Here the love of Christ shall end divisions'

17.3.1 In some denominations 'contracts' exist to help, when a congregation is aware of offenders entering its community. It teaches that consequences result from

actions, and contracts are based on risk assessment. Contracts are voluntary, and this is part of the issue.

17.3.2 The concept of 'Contracts' was also discussed as a term, and rejected as it is so associated with civil law, rather than the language of the Church. The Group also reflected on the concept of a "covenant of care", which implies that a two party participation must be undertaken to be acceptable. If sex offenders refuse to cooperate or sign, then they automatically become a higher risk, because they think they are forgiven, and are not subject to any restrictions. It is also recognised that there is a need for a concept of national and regional support structures for those who are willing to support sex offenders in congregations.

17.3.3 The principle of a 'Covenant of Care' was accepted as suggestive of the dynamic responsibility involved in the life of the Church, but it was agreed that a title particular to the Church of Scotland was necessary, which highlights the importance of both parties with Safeguarding Office, Congregation and sex offender being fully involved and committed to protection and care. The proposal for consideration of the General Assembly is that it should be a *'Covenant of Responsibilities'*. This infers that there needs to be consideration of a variety of components in order to prevent further abuse. These covenants will only reduce, but not eliminate, the possibility of abuse entirely.

17.3.4 The important thing is to remember that the Covenant of Responsibilities offers the possibility of growth, 'enabling discipleship', rather than just restricting an individual. There is a need to offer hope, while acknowledging the fact that there can be dangers in offering hope, without it being grounded in knowledge. Ignorance may lead to false opportunities of endangerment:

> *'Covenant…speaks both of autonomy and belonging, of individual commitments and ongoing social situatedness; covenant contains*

vital elements of voluntarism and consent and creates obligations which derive from the nature and history of relationship...Unlike contract, which defines a limited and reciprocal commitment, covenant structures an open-ended and morally ordered relationship' [95]

17.3.5 There are always problems in giving a person who is a sex offender 'perceived power', and this needs to be balanced with hearing the pain of the abused. It is also the Church's responsibility to put the vulnerable person **first** and give more priority to them than the offenders' wishes.

17.3.6 The sex offender who participates in a *'Covenant of Responsibilities'* must be aware of the need to acknowledge that all actions have consequences. They need to recognise this in all humility, and it may be that they will have to serve Christ in a very limited way in public. There are huge dangers in any 'endorsement,' by the church of a person who is known to be an abuser. Sex offenders' may operate by verbally acknowledging all the right things, but still may seek avenues to perpetrate abuse. This leads to the appropriate and the healthy questioning of the offender's motives by those charged with the maintenance of the safety of the Church community.

17.3.7 It is the view of the Group that **all** covenants must be drawn up under the guidance and direction of the Safeguarding Office to ensure that the congregation is given the benefit of professional support and input in the process. Congregations may, but not all will, have those who are familiar with the wide variety of issues involved. It is essential that the congregation informs the Safeguarding Office of the presence of the sex offender, and the fact the congregation is embarking on a process of covenantal relationship. This enables the design and structure of the covenant to take into account the types of issues and range of possibilities that are appropriate.

17.3.8 The review of a Covenant **must** involve consultation with the Safeguarding Office, and it is the recommendation that regular reviews of such covenants take place with the Safeguarding Office's knowledge and involvement. There are implications here for the budget of the Church so that adequate resources are supplied to assist congregations in meeting this challenge effectively.

17.3.9 The issue for the Church is the creation of a culture that is forgiving, yet not endangering, one in which good practices are upheld; one of 'informed vigilance.' It should be a place of care, support and monitoring around those who need some form of covenantal agreement.

17.3.10 The support system that the Church offers is two fold: it must not ignore the needs of the survivors, while trying to encourage and support perpetrators of sexual offences in new patterns of behaviour. The Church is extremely vulnerable and will often find itself in the midst of controversy no matter what action is taken. The fact that ministers, in particular, are often in the firing line was recognised, and this makes the implementation of the 'Covenant of Responsibilities', with its group dimensions, all the more important.

17.3.11 It was noted that some perpetrators of sexual offences are genuinely repentant and express remorse and guilt. Others, however, have very little acceptance of wrong doing and do not take any responsibility for their actions. They blame the child and are in deep denial. It appears that their internal inhibitions, or inhibitors, are overcome by a "mindset" which allows them to continue the abuse.

17.3.12 What happens if a person does not cooperate, or breaks such a Covenant? In the Methodist Church if it is not signed, or no cooperation is forthcoming, then the protection of the congregation is strengthened, and may lead, eventually, to exclusion of the individual, if necessary. It is the conviction of this working party that when an individual decides not to co-operate with the Covenant of Responsibilities, they choose, by their action, to exclude themselves from the life of the congregation.

17.3.13 It is important to consider whether an offender who refuses to co-operate with the agreed terms of the *'Covenant of Responsibilities'* (noting that it is constructed in the light of their particular criminal record), is serious about their faith, rehabilitation, or their forgiveness. While they are not be beyond the mercy and grace of God, or the ministry of the Church, they are, at least while refusing to co-operate, choosing to exclude themselves from the opportunity of participation in the life of the congregation in a particular location.

17.3.14 This would fulfill the third Article Declaratory of the Church of Scotland where the Church claims continuity with the Reformation in Scotland in 1560. The Church, through this Article, affirms its acceptance of "… its distinctive call to bring the ordinances of religion to the people in every parish of Scotland through a territorial ministry". Not withstanding the current debate on this Article, it is possible for congregations, in co-operation with others in a presbytery, to design opportunities for worship whereby the sexual abuser who did not wish to sign a 'Covenant of Responsibilities' would still not be denied the opportunity of Christian Worship.

17.3.15 The Church exists in the real world. While it may have a theological character and hope for the redemption of humanity, the Church cannot reject, or neglect, its protection of children and adults at risk through a misguided sense of having an over-riding duty to forgive and accept behaviour that is incongruent with the gospel. It also, following the instruction of Jesus, 'must render unto Caesar that which is Caesar's' and enjoin the obedience of the Church to the civil law which is devoted to the care and protection of children and adults at risk. It was asserted that a sex offender who was truly repentant and willing to

accept the implications of his criminal behaviour would readily accept the, sometimes life long, consequences of his actions.[96]

17.3.16 Once again it must be emphasised that the Church cannot exercise forgiveness on behalf of the survivors. Forgiveness lies in the person who was sinned against. It was noted that the ministers who were involved in these difficult situations often need the support of the Safeguarding Office. It appears that safeguarders cannot fulfill a function as pastors and, similarly, those who are pastors cannot be expected to exercise the role of safeguarders. Therefore, in practice, when a minister or other person in a pastoral role is called upon to exercise their function in relation to safeguarding, they must not operate from a perspective of the pastoral care of the sex offender. Instead, they require to engage with the issues from the perspective of the Church's position on the paramoucy of the rights of the child and adults at risk

17.3.17 When a Safeguarding Panel is drawing up a *'Covenant of Responsibilities'* it must recognise that what is being undertaken is an attempt to address the Church's pastoral responsibility towards children, adults at risk, survivors and offenders. It is about the behaviour required of the perpetrators of sexual offences and the appropriate support mechanisms in the church, which by its very nature is a forgiving community. What is being proposed here is a formal statement to assist the individual and congregation in the support of appropriate behaviour. Responsibility is often difficult and costly:

> 'The test of a person's reform and repentance is that any restrictions placed on him or her by the Covenant are accepted and recognised by the offender without argument'[97]

18. Proportionality.
'Let us build a house where all are named'

18.1 Not all congregations will be able to deal easily with the appropriate inclusion of sex offenders. Therefore the Group recommends that the General Assembly requires all congregations, through their Minister, or Interim Moderator, and Safeguarding Panel to contact the Safeguarding office when the presence of a sex offender in their congregation is known. This will enable the Safeguarding office to support, guide and assist the local Safeguarding Panel in undertaking the preparation of an appropriate 'Covenant of Responsibilities'.

18.2 The Sex Offenders Register was established in September 1997. The Register, which is managed by the police and is a tool used to monitor and track sex offenders in the community, is not retrospective, so does not include anyone convicted before 1997.

18.3 Given this background, then, it will be important to include guidance on the issues from the Safeguarding Office and these will be made available.

18.4 While local efforts are vital, the guidance of others, with professional expertise, outside the situation is essential to ensure objectivity and correct actions in what could develop into a divisive and destructive situation.

18.5 The Group also recommends that the Council of Ministries' Panel of Pastoral Advisors is made aware of the complexities of this issue and the importance of support for all those who are involved in providing the local arrangements. This would ensure that the Minister and his or her colleagues, in the local Safeguarding Panel have the important pastoral guidance that they may require in a role which may bring them into conflict with other members of the congregation.

19. Conclusion

While it is recognised that no possible guarantees can be offered regarding any system or process of safeguarding and inclusion, it is the hope of the Working Group that the methodology and theological reflections of this report may assist the Church of Scotland throughout its congregations *in 'building a house where love can dwell and all can safely live'.* The Group recall this contribution to the Report 'If a sex offender genuinely wants to worship he will accept any conditions that the Church lays down for his own protection as well as the protection of the public'.[98]

In the name and by the authority of the Working Group

JOHN C CHRISTIE, *Convener*
NIGEL J ROBB, *Secretary*

27

APPENDIX 1:
A DRAFT EXAMPLE OF A 'COVENANT OF RESPONSIBILITIES'

(The Terms included here may be developed to suit particular circumstances and individuals.)

1. *We will not allow (name) to be in a situation where they are alone with children or young people.
2. We will sit with (name) in a designated place in the church, stay with them and accompany them when they need to use other facilities; we will not allow them to place themselves in the vicinity of children and young people.
3. For the duration of this Covenant of Responsibilities it is agreed (name) will decline invitations of hospitality where there are children in the home.
4. *(Name) will accept that there are certain people who will need to be told of their circumstances due to the wider concerns of the Church, although these will be kept to a minimum and on a "need to know" basis.
5. *We accept that contact will be made between the Church of Scotland's Safeguarding Office staff and other statutory agencies as and when necessary.
6. *We understand that for the duration of this Covenant of Responsibilities, pastoral care will be provided by (name).
7. *We understand that if (name) chooses not to keep these conditions then they are choosing not to attend worship.
8. *We understand that any other concerns will be taken seriously and reported.
9. *We undertake to review this Covenant of Responsibilities on a regular basis (dependent on the individual's circumstances) with a named Safeguarding Office representative. The next review meeting will be held on ....

Signed

Witnesses

Date

*'we' in this Covenant refers to all parties including the Safeguarding Panel and the sex offender.

APPENDIX 2:
'INCLUDING THOSE WHO POSE A RISK'

A Church of Scotland policy for the safe inclusion of sex offenders in Congregations

Introduction

In the Church we are often so grateful to people who are prepared to volunteer for children's ministry that we find it difficult to refuse someone who would not, in reality, be a good children's worker. Equally, it is extremely difficult when someone expresses a desire to worship in your church, to contemplate that this may not be in the congregation's best interests.

We can forget that nobody has an automatic right to work with children and young people. Saying 'no' in a firm and kind way can be difficult but this should be the response when we believe that a person does not have the skills and personal qualities to work effectively with the young. It is even more difficult to suggest that someone's attendance at church should be limited to ensure the safety of all others in the congregation.

It is widely acknowledged by Safeguarding agencies that those who have committed acts of violence or sexual offences against children should not be allowed to work with children in either a paid or voluntary capacity. In many cases it would be illegal to allow them to do so. Some sex offenders may acknowledge their offences readily but have no depth of commitment to change. Commonly, imprisoned sex offenders have admitted several similar offences which they committed prior to the offence which led to their conviction, and with which they are never charged. Their behaviour is addictive and they require intensive therapy to assist them in their efforts to avoid harming children.

What is clearly now recognised is that although only a very small percentage of victims of childhood sexual abuse go on to harm others, a large percentage of abusers were actually abused themselves as children.

Where protection of the vulnerable in our congregations must remain our paramount objective it has to be recognised that the offender is very possibly a much damaged individual also in need of God's grace.

What we can do

Given all of the above, it is imperative that the Church does not allow people who have committed these types of offences free access to children. Not only is such a policy necessary for protecting children but it may also help to protect an offender from the temptation to abuse again, or risk malicious allegations.

Where a person is known to have harmed a child, the best guidance is that s/he can be welcomed into the church but within the framework of a 'covenant' which has been discussed and agreed by a small group of people ie offender, Minister, co-ordinator, offender's supervisor, and possibly the Session Clerk. This Panel will receive professional support and advice from the Safeguarding Office. We should remember that when such an individual is being integrated into a local community after a prison term s/he will usually be supervised and supported by a local criminal justice social worker. Even when an individual has been convicted of a serious offence, but does not serve a prison sentence, it is likely that they will also be supervised by a criminal justice social worker.

Depending on how the offender is perceived in terms of level of risk, there could be restrictions placed on her or him as to where they live, places they can visit, local groups they can join etc. These restrictions can be made as conditions of bail, prior to conviction or as part of a sentence after conviction or release from prison.

In many circumstances, the police or social work department will contact the Safeguarding Office or a local church directly, to inform them of their concerns about an individual in the congregation.

In either case the views of specialist professional workers should always be sought and it is strongly recommended that they are involved in all discussion relating to the safe integration of the person into the church. It is important that the Church's response to sex offenders is proportionate. Clearly, certain key individuals will need to be aware of the person's offence in order to ensure that children in the Church remain safe. However, offenders also have a right to privacy and advice should be sought as to what must be divulged and to whom.

The professional staff at the Church of Scotland's Safeguarding Office will advise and support you, should you find yourself dealing with a situation such as this.

What every Church must do

- It is important that every church establishes a Safeguarding Panel as per the Safeguarding Committee's deliverance to the General Assembly 2009. This Panel, with the knowledge and permission of the Kirk Session, manages confidential safeguarding matters that cannot, for legal reasons, be discussed in a bigger group.
- Every Church must be aware that the Church of Scotland has a Policy for the inclusion of sex offenders into congregations. When approached, that congregation can then respond in a confident and supportive manner. Wider knowledge of the policy and procedures in this area will also offer churches consistency in their approach and will encourage confidence from the statutory agencies in the community.
- It is important that the Safeguarding Office is always notified of when there is a sex offender in a congregation even when that individual chooses not to cooperate with a Covenant and leaves.

What to do when you discover a sex offender wants to worship in your Church (See flow chart opposite)

The fact that an offender wants to worship in your church may be brought to your attention by the police or social work department, by the Safeguarding Office or by the individual themselves.

- Once this information has been received a meeting of the Congregational Safeguarding Panel will be called. The panel should then familiarise themselves with relevant policy and procedures and make a minute of the decisions they make.
- Contact should be established with the Safeguarding Office, Advisory team. The Safeguarding Office will keep securely a confidential record of all relevant information and may, if appropriate liaise with the statutory services (police and social work) for further relevant information.
- There should be a discussion with the sex offender where it is made clear that their attendance is dependent on their cooperation with the Covenant. There should be **no** negotiation at this stage. If the offender does not want to cooperate then they have the option of reviewing their attendance at this stage.
- The congregational Safeguarding panel and the Safeguarding Office will liaise, and where practical meet, to draft a suitable Covenant of Responsibilities. The police/social work department may be consulted during this process.
- The Safeguarding Panel will meet with the offender, discuss the covenant and if all is agreed the covenant should be signed with a date set for a review.
- In consultation with the Safeguarding Office, and the statutory services where appropriate, regular reviews will be held.

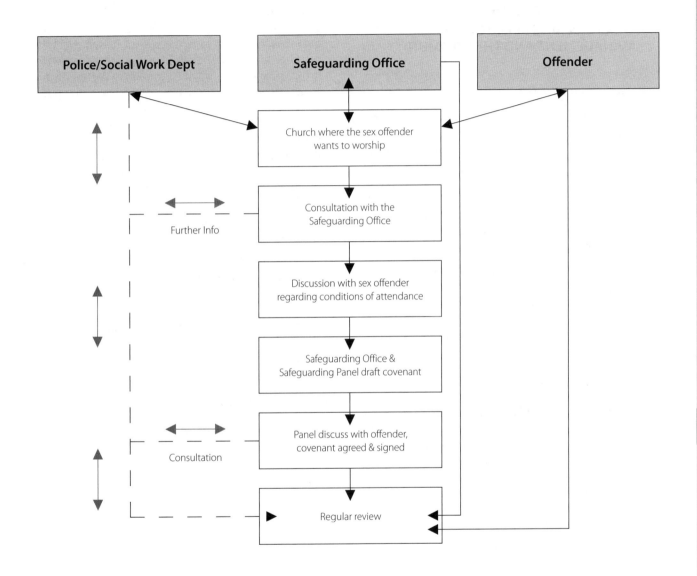

APPENDIX 3
CHAPLAINCY PROTOCOL: RISK MANAGEMENT AND THE COMMUNITY

Specified procedure in relation to prisoners whose offences have been of a violent or sexual nature.

Engaging with the wider community brings both opportunities and challenges for Chaplains in the Scottish Prison Service. Contact with a local faith community can be beneficial to a prisoner on release but there are obvious risks to the wellbeing of others who attend these places of worship. As part of the SPS, along with partner organisations, one of our primary objectives is to maintain the well-being of children and adults at risk in the community.

This protocol will clarify our policy regarding the following situations:
- Prisoners already in contact with a Church or faith community
- Prisoners seeking contact with a Church or faith community
- Contact with prisoners outside prison within a local church or faith community

Agreed Best Practice – 3 Key Components
- **Communication** – Communication within the Chaplaincy Team and with other colleagues is essential. Sharing relevant information is necessary for accurate risk assessment. With regard to risk management, the first point of contact is the Senior Social Worker in the Prison and the second responsibility is to alert fellow chaplains of any information given so as to avoid duplication or confusion.
- **Teamwork** – Chaplaincy is part of a wider group of statutory (Social Work & Police) and voluntary organisations within and outside of prison working together to facilitate rehabilitation of offenders while maintaining the safety of the community. We must work collaboratively and cooperate with fellow colleagues and professionals. In this important area, there is collective accountability; no one is solely responsible for managing an individual or assessing risk.
- **Participation** – Chaplains are to dovetail with existing procedures and protocols. As members of an interdisciplary team of professionals in the prison, Chaplains have a role in risk-managing individuals in contact with Chaplaincy and participating in pre-release case conferences. Chaplains will find an open door to their involvement.

To be avoided – 3 Potential Pitfalls
1. Making direct contact with an outside church or faith community.
2. Disclosing details of offences to an outside organisation or individual.
3. Operating in isolation from the prison's social work department or the wider Chaplaincy Team.

Summary of Protocol:
In all cases of contact between a prisoner and a church or faith community or where contact with an outside faith community is desired:
- Inform the Senior Social Worker by e-mail in the first instance
- Copy this e-mail to all Chaplaincy Team members for their information.

APPENDIX 4:
THE GLOSSARY OF TERMS USED THROUGHOUT THE REPORT

1. **Perpetrators of sexual abuse:** those who have been convicted and those who have been involved in sexual abuse of children and adults at risk, including involvement in internet crime.
2. **Grooming:** the calculated planned and plotted actions, often over a long period of time, whereby an abuser ensures that trust is built up to allow the perpetration of sexual assault on a victim.
3. **Survivors:** those children and adults who have experienced abuse.
4. **Recidivism:** the repeated criminal activity of a person whose actions are perceived as criminal
5. **Sexual assault:** the working group would suggest that this term covers the whole range of sexual abuse of children and adults at risk and conveys in a strong and vivid manner the actual harm and seriousness of the offences involved which are so often minimised by the offenders
6. **Scope of sexual abuse:** we believe that the victims of abuse are not just those who suffer horrific violent attacks, but all those whose well being is threatened and upset by inappropriate physical contact and also those who are forced to be involved in the production of material which is paraded on the internet.
7. **Sex abuse and sex:** we believe that the issue here is about sexualised behaviour. It is not about the gift of sex given by God. It is based on an abuse of power and trust which preys upon vulnerable individuals who are not powerful enough to resist or make their protests heard.
8. **Forgiveness:** Defining Christian forgiveness is done with words and actions. The word 'forgive' is a grace word in the English, as well as the Greek, meaning "to give or to grant." The meaning is 'to remit a debt, to give up resentment or claim for requital, or to pardon an offence'. Forgiveness is essentially a gift that is unconditional, but when it is conferred, there are changes in behaviour that are implied in the person forgiven. Christian forgiveness also encompasses action. Our confession with God involves us seeing our sins as He sees it, bringing God's forgiveness
9. **Sex Offender:** In the context of this report a sex offender is an individual who has committed a sexual crime whether convicted or not.

27

APPENDIX 5:
SOME SOURCES AND RESOURCES

Books:

Rebecca Andrews: *Policing Innocence*, Authentic Media, Milton Keynes, 2008

Leonardo Boff : *Limits of Tolerance*, website, July 8th 2005

Leonardo Boff : *Way of the Cross – Way of Justice,* Orbis Books 1992, Maryknoll, New York

Churches Together in Britain and Ireland: *Time for Action*, CTBI Publications, London 2002

Gustavo Gutierrez: *On Job: God Talk and the Suffering of the Innocent*, Orbis Books 1992, *Maryknoll, New York – 2008*

Peter Lewis: *The Lord's Prayer*, Paternoster 2008, Milton Keynes

Alastair McFadyen : *Bound to Sin*: *Abuse, Holocaust and the Christian Doctrine of Sin*, Cambridge University Press, 2000, Cambridge

Miroslav Volf : *Free of Charge,* Zondervan , Grand Rapids, Michigan, 2005

Miroslav Volf : *Exclusion and Embrace*, Abingdon, Nashville, 1996

Articles:

Child Molesters' Implicit Theories by T. Ward & T Keenan in *Journal of Interpersonal Violence*, Vol. 14, No 8, August,1999.

A Comparative Study of Demographic data relating to intra – and extra familial sexual abusers and professional perpetrators by J. Sullivan & A. Beech, published by the National Organisation for the Treatment of Abusers, 2004

Moral Repair with Offenders: Ethical Issues Arising from victimization Experiences by T. Ward & G. Moreton, in *School of Psychology Papers of Victoria University of Wellington, New Zealand*

On a clear day you can see forever: integrating values and skills in sex offender treatment by

T. Ward, published by the National Organisation for the Treatment of Abusers, 2007.

Study Leave Report by the Rev Andrew R. Black, Irvine Relief, Bourtreehill

Modus operandi of sexual offenders working or doing voluntary work with children and adolescents by B. Leclerc, J. Proulx, A. McKibben, published by the National Organisation for the Treatment of Abusers, 2005.

Sexual Abuse and Forgiveness by s. Tracy, in papers of Rosemead School of Psychology, Biola University, *Journal of Psychology and Theology*, 1999, Vol. 27

The Spiral of Sexual Abuse: A Conceptual framework for understanding and illustrating the evolution of sexually abusive behaviour, paper presented to The International Conference on Violence Towards Children in Lisbon, February 2000.

Sex offender Recidivism: A Simple Question 2004 – 03, by A. Harris & R.K. Hanson, published by Public Safety and Emergency Preparedness Canada. 2004

APPENDIX 6
GROUPS AND INDIVIDUALS CONSULTED

Very Rev Professor Iain R Torrance

Rev Donald McLeod

The Rt Hon The Lord Cullen of Whitekirk

Professor Duncan Forrester, Christian Ethics and Practical Theology, New College Edinburgh

Professor John Swinton, Practical Theology, Aberdeen University

Dr Brian Brock, Christian Ethics, Aberdeen University

Dr Andrew McLellan, H.M Inspector of Prisons (Scotland)

Rev Pearl Luxon, Safeguarding Adviser to the Methodist Church and the Church of England

Dr Donald Findlater, Lucy Faithfull Foundation

Rev W. Taylor, Scottish Prison Chaplaincy Service

Dr Jayne Scott, Safespace

Ms Anne McDonald, Survivor Scotland

Rev Dr David Ross and Staff of Peterhead Prison Sex Offenders Unit

A Session Clerk of a congregation which has had to face the challenge of engaging with a sex offender who wished to return to worship

Representatives from Congregations from the following Presbyteries:

Ardrossan, Angus, Argyll, Ayr, Falkirk, Glasgow, Hamilton, Lochaber, Stirling, Edinburgh, Dunfermline, Perth, Dundee, Irvine and Kilmarnock, Inverness, Lanark, Dumbarton, Greenock and Paisley, Dunkeld and Meigle, Skye

All those who contributed by telephone or email

APPENDIX 7:
MEMBERSHIP OF WORKING GROUP

Rev John Christie, Convener.
Ms Anne Black
Ms Dorothy Kinloch
Rev Karen Watson
Rev Alastair Cherry
Mrs Fionna Miskelly (Safeguarding)
Ms Jennifer McCreanor (Safeguarding)
Rev Nigel Robb (Secretary)

REFERENCES:

(Endnotes)
1 'All are Welcome' by Marty Huagen © 1994 by GIA Publications, Inc., 7404 S. Mason Ave., Chicago, IL, 60638. 1-800-442-1358. www.giamusic.com. All rights reserved. Used by permission. This is acknowledged with appreciation. (See eg Church Hymnary, Fourth Edition, Number 198, Canterbury Press, Norwich 2005)
2 The British Crime Survey 1994
3 A Professional Staff Member at Peterhead Prison
4 The British Crime Survey 1994
5 Reported at Peterhead Prison
6 Quoted by 'Survivor Scotland' in discussion with the Group
7 The Lucy Faithfull Foundation
8 Safeguarding (publication of the Methodist Church, November 2008, Pearl Luxon)
9 Reported at Peterhead Prison
10 'Time for Action, published 2002 by Churches together in Britain and Ireland',
11 Child Maltreatment in the UK NSPCC 2000
12 UK Christian Handbook 1996-97
13 Time for Action, CTBI, 2002
14 Confirmed by Professional Staff of Peterhead Prison responsible for sex-offenders' education
15 Safeguarding (publication of the Methodist Church, November 2008, Pearl Luxon)
16 Alistair McFadyen: Bound to Sin: Abuse, Holocaust and

27

the Christian Doctrine of Sin, Cambridge University Press, Cambridge, 2000, pages 78-79

[17] McFadyen: *op cit*, page 114

[18] McFadyen: *ibid* page 121

[19] St Matthew 18:6

[20] St Luke 17:2

[21] Leonardo Boff: website entry dated July 8th, 2005

[22] Zechariah 8:3

[23] Miroslav Volf: *Exclusion and Embrace*, Abingdon, Nashville, 1996. Page 219

[24] St Matthew 12:13

[25] Genesis 25:19 – 37:1

[26] Genesis 33:4

[27] 2 Samuel 11:12

[28] 2 Samuel 11:27b

[29] 2 Chronicles 28:2-3

[30] 2 Samuel 13:1-32

[31] St Matthew 18:22

[32] St Matthew 19:14; St Mark 10:14; St Luke 18:16

[33] St Matthew 18:6; St Mark 9:42; St Luke 17:2

[34] St John 8:3–11

[35] St Luke 23:40-42

[36] St Luke 20:22

[37] St Luke 20:25; St Mark 12:13-17; St Matthew 22:15

[38] Gustavo Gutierrez : *On Job: God Talk and the Suffering of the Innocent*, Orbis, Maryknoll, 2008, Page 94

[39] Gustavo Gutierrez : *ibid*, Page xiii

[40] St John 4

[41] St John 3

[42] St Mark 10: 17-22

[43] St John 9

[44] St Luke17:11-19

[45] Miroslav Volf : *Exclusion and Embrace* Page 113

[46] St Luke 22:61

[47] St John 21:15ff

[48] Romans 7:1-8:39

[49] Galatians 5: 13-26

[50] Galatians 5:22-23

[51] Galatians 5:17-21

[52] John Barclay: *Obeying the Truth*, T&T Clark Ltd, Edinburgh page 116

[53] G S Duncan: *The Epistle of Paul to the Galatians*, Moffatt New Testament Commentary, London 1934, page 169

[54] 1 Corinthians 5:1-2

[55] Acts 2

[56] Ephesians 5:23; Colossians 1:24

[57] St Matthew 8:9; St Luke 7 8

[58] Colossians 1:18

[59] 1 Corinthians 12: 13

[60] See, for example, 'The Apostles' Creed'

[61] St Matthew 26:28; St Mark 1:4; Acts 2:38

[62] Romans 3:9-21,

[63] Miroslav Volf: *Free of Charge*, Page 205

[64] Thomas Aquinas: *Summa Theologica see Question* 54 The quality of Christ rising again Article 4 'The scars which showed in His body'

[65] A Professional Prison Staff Member at Peterhead Prison

[66] "Forgive us our Debts as we Forgive our Debtors" or "Forgive us our Sins as we Forgive those Who Sin Against us"

[67] The Lectionary Commentary: Eerdmans, Grand Rapids, 2001, Page 110

[68] Miroslav Volf: *Free of Charge,* Page 170

[69] Miroslav Volf: *ibid,* pages 182-183

[70] Acts 7:54-8:1a

[71] Acts 8:3

[72] Acts 9:1

[73] Acts 9:10ff

[74] Galatians 1:11-24

[75] Galatians 1:24

[76] Miroslav Volf: *Free of Charge* Page 170

[77] Miroslav Volf: *ibid, page 61*

[78] Miroslav Volf : *ibid*, Page 153

[79] Miroslav Volf : *ibid*, Page 154

[80] Miroslav Volf: *ibid*, page 154

[81] Shorter Catechism question 105

[82] Peter Lewis: *The Lord's Prayer,* Paternoster, Milton Keynes 2008, Page 14

[83] Peter Lewis: *ibid*, page 151

[84] Miroslav Volf: Free of Charge Page 155

85 St Matthew 9:1-8

86 St Luke 15:11-31

87 Leon Morris: *Luke*, Tyndale New Testament Commentaries Intervarsity Press, Grand Rapids Michigan

88 John Calvin, Theological Treatises, trans. and introd. JKS Reid. Library of the Christian Classics, vol.22 (London: SCM, 1954) pp34-46

89 Peter Lewis : *op cit*, Page 171-172

90 Miroslav Volf: *Free of Charge* Page 197

91 Burleigh, J H S *A Church History of Scotland* Oxford University Press London 1960, pages 199-200

92 Romans 12:1-3

93 Romans 12:19

94 A Professional Prison Staff Member at Peterhead Prison

95 Miroslav Volf: *Exclusion and Embrace,* Page 150

96 A Professional Prison Staff Member at Peterhead Prison

97 A Participant at the Roadshow in Lochaber

98 A Professional Prison Staff Member at Peterhead Prison

At Edinburgh, and within the Church Offices, 121 George Street, the Third Day of October 2008, the Ministries Appeal Panel met and was duly constituted with prayer.

Sederunt: Mr Robert Brodie, Convener, the Rev Bruce McNicol, Vice-Convener, the Rev Grant Barclay and the Rev Jennifer Macrae.

In attendance: The Principal Clerk.

The Ministries Appeal Panel took up consideration of the Appeal of Dr Malcolm Kinnear against a decision of the Ministries Council and the Presbytery of Edinburgh of 24 April 2008 to terminate his candidature for the Ministry.

Dr Kinnear appeared for himself supported by Ms Alison Pearce, Solicitor and the Rev James Black.

There appeared for the Ministries Council and the Presbytery of Edinburgh the Rev Dr Martin Scott, the Rev Dr George Whyte, Mr Grant Gordon and Mrs Moira Whyte.

Parties were heard.

Questions were asked.

Parties were removed.

Following deliberation the Ministries Appeal Panel resolved unanimously to uphold the appeal of Dr Malcolm Kinnear on the basis that the Ministries Council and the Presbytery of Edinburgh acted ultra vires in terminating his candidature under Section 21(5) of Act X 2004, to recall said termination and to instruct the Ministries Council to make arrangements for a new final placement for Dr Kinnear.

Parties were recalled and judgement intimated.

The meeting was closed with prayer.

ROBERT BRODIE, *Convener*
FINLAY MACDONALD, *Clerk*

At Edinburgh, and within the Church Offices, 121 George Street, the Ninth Day of January 2009 the Ministries Appeal Panel met and was duly constituted with prayer.

Sederunt: Mr Robert Brodie, Convener, the Rev Bruce McNicol, Vice-Convener, the Rev Grant Barclay and Mrs Aileen Nimmo.

In attendance: The Principal Clerk.

The Ministries Appeal Panel took up consideration of the Appeal of Mr David S Todd in terms of Act X 2004 section 6(5) against the decision of the Committee Review by the Assessment Task Group of 27 August 2008 to uphold the decision of the National Assessment Conference of 15 June 2008 not to accept the Appellant as a Candidate in training for full time ministry. The Panel also took up consideration of Further Grounds of Appeal submitted the previous day by Mr Todd.

Mr Todd appeared for himself supported by Mrs Elizabeth King.

There appeared for the Ministries Council the Rev Dr Iain Greenshields, Mrs Helen McLeod, the Rev Dr Martin Scott and Mrs Moira Whyte.

Parties were heard initially on a motion by Mr Todd set out in the Further Grounds of Appeal to adjourn the diet to a later date.

Questions were asked.

Parties were removed.

The Ministries Panel resolved not to allow the adjournment on the grounds that that those matters raised in the Further Grounds which the appellant submitted required the adjournment were not within the competence of the Ministries Appeal Panel to determine.

Parties were recalled and this decision was intimated.

Parties were heard on the grounds of appeal.

Parties were removed.

Following deliberation the Ministries Appeal Panel resolved unanimously to dismiss the appeal of Mr David S Todd on the grounds:

(1)   that in the course of the National Assessment Conference and Committee Review by the Assessment Task Group there were no irregularities in process;
(2)   the final decision was not influenced by incorrect material fact;
(3)   the National Assessment Conference and Committee Review by the Assessment Task Group did not act contrary to the principles of natural justice.

Parties were recalled and judgement intimated.

The meeting was closed with prayer.

ROBERT BRODIE, *Convener*
FINLAY MACDONALD, *Clerk*

At Edinburgh, and within Palmerston Place Church, the twenty-first day of August 2008 years at 11 am, which day the Commission of Assembly appointed by the last General Assembly in terms of Act VI 1997, being met, was constituted with prayer.

Appeal of the Kirk Session of Dunnichen, Letham and Kirkden against a decision of the Presbytery of Angus.

The Commission of Assembly took up consideration of Appeal of the Kirk Session of Dunnichen, Letham and Kirkden against a decision of the Presbytery of Angus, dated 4 March 2008, relating to the planned closure of the Dunnichen church building.

The Principal Clerk read the relevant part of Standing Order 72.

Parties were called.

There appeared for the Kirk Session Mrs Ruth Miller, Mr Herbert McLeod and Mr Alisdair Dobie. There appeared for the Presbytery of Angus Rev Scott Rennie, Rev Matthew Bicket, Mrs Helen McLeod and Rev Michael Goss.

The Commission received the Report of the Investigating Committee appointed by the Legal Questions Committee in terms of Section 5(d)(iii) of Act VI, 1997, which was presented and slightly amended by the Convener, Rev Fraser Penny.

Parties were heard.

Questions were asked.

Parties were removed.

It was moved and seconded:

The Commission of Assembly grant the appeal, recall the decision of the Presbytery of Angus dated 4 March 2008, determine that the church building of Dunnichen should be categorised under paragraph (b) of section 5(2) of Act VII 2003 as amended, and further determine that the building shall be closed on whichever first occurs of (a) the completion of the refurbishment of the church building of Letham and (b) the expiry of three years from this date.

It was moved and seconded as a counter-motion:

The Commission of Assembly refuse the appeal by the Kirk Session of Dunnichen, Letham and Kirkden and sustain the decision of the Presbytery of Angus dated 4 March 2008 to categorise the Dunnichen church building under section 5(2)(c) of Act VII 2003 as amended.

The Principal Clerk read the relevant part of Standing Order 72.

On a vote being taken there vote for the motion 41 and for the counter-motion 28, and the Commission resolved accordingly.

Parties were recalled and judgement intimated.

This being all the business, the Sederunt was closed with prayer at 12.50 p.m.

Palmerston Place Church, Edinburgh, 21 August 2008

INDEX